The Cunning of Gender Violence

NEXT WAVE: NEW DIRECTIONS IN WOMEN'S STUDIES

A series edited by Inderpal Grewal, Caren Kaplan, and Robyn Wiegman

The Cunning *of* Gender Violence

....

GEOPOLITICS & FEMINISM

EDITED BY
Lila Abu-Lughod, Rema Hammami, and
Nadera Shalhoub-Kevorkian

DUKE UNIVERSITY PRESS   *Durham and London*   2023

© 2023 DUKE UNIVERSITY PRESS
All rights reserved
Printed in the United States of America on acid-free paper ∞
Project Editor: Bird Williams
Designed by Matt Tauch
Typeset in Arno Pro, SangBleu Kingdom, and SangBleu
Republic by Copperline Book Services

Library of Congress Cataloging-in-Publication Data
Names: Abu-Lughod, Lila, editor. | Hammami, Rema, editor. |
Shalhūb-Kīfūrkiyān, Nādirah, editor.
Title: The cunning of gender violence : geopolitics and
feminism / edited by Lila Abu-Lughod, Rema Hammami
and Nadera Shalhoub-Kevorkian.
Other titles: Next wave (Duke University Press)
Description: Durham : Duke University Press, 2023. | Series:
Next wave | Includes bibliographical references and index.
Identifiers: LCCN 2022045972 (print)
LCCN 2022045973 (ebook)
ISBN 9781478020431 (paperback)
ISBN 9781478019954 (hardcover)
ISBN 9781478024545 (ebook)
Subjects: LCSH: Women—Violence against. | Women—Violence
against—Religious aspects. | Women—Violence against—
Government policy. | Sexual minorities—Violence against. |
Sexual minorities—Violence against—Religious aspects. | BISAC:
SOCIAL SCIENCE / Gender Studies | SOCIAL SCIENCE /
Anthropology / Cultural & Social
Classification: LCC HV6250.4.W65 C88 2023 (print)
LCC HV6250.4. W65 (ebook)
DDC 362.88082—dc23/eng/20230310
LC record available at https://lccn.loc.gov/2022045972
LC ebook record available at https://lccn.loc.gov/2022045973

Cover art: Photo by JJ Mitchell.

This project was supported by a grant from the
Henry Luce Foundation.

CONTENTS

vii   *Acknowledgments*

1   Introduction: Circuits of Power in GBVAW Governance
       LILA ABU-LUGHOD, REMA HAMMAMI, AND NADERA
       SHALHOUB-KEVORKIAN

I   Securitization

55   ONE · Lawfare, CVE, and International Conflict Feminism
       VASUKI NESIAH

88   TWO · Securofeminism: Embracing a Phantom
       LILA ABU-LUGHOD

122   THREE · The Role of "Honor Killings" in the Muslim Ban
       LETI VOLPP

151   FOUR · Because Religion: Does Something Called "Religion" Cause Gender-Based Violence?
       JANET R. JAKOBSEN

II   States of Violence, Unruly Subjects

177   FIVE · GBV and Postcolonial India: Transnational Media, Hindutva, and Muslim Racializations
       INDERPAL GREWAL

209   SIX · The Politics of Legislating "Honor Crime" in Contemporary Pakistan
       SHENILA KHOJA-MOOLJI

233	SEVEN · State Criminality and Gender-Based Violence: Palestinian Schoolgirls between Books and Rifles
	NADERA SHALHOUB-KEVORKIAN
259	EIGHT · Power, Subjectivity, and Sexuality in Iranian Political Prisons
	SHAHLA TALEBI

III	Civilizing Interventions: Development and Humanitarianism
293	NINE · Child Marriage in the Feminist Imagination
	DINA M. SIDDIQI
324	TEN · Catastrophic Aid: GBV Humanitarianism in Gaza
	REMA HAMMAMI
361	ELEVEN · What Counts as Violence? Transgender Refugees, Torture, and Sanctions
	SIMA SHAKHSARI

IV	Media Frames
391	TWELVE · Weaponized Bodies: Female Genital Cutting and Immigrant Exclusion
	RAFIA ZAKARIA
405	THIRTEEN · Breaking the Frame: The Power of Media Narratives and the Question of Agency
	SAMIRA SHACKLE
422	FOURTEEN · Dressed Up, Stripped Down: Media Depictions of Conflict Rape
	NINA BERMAN

439	*Contributors*
445	*Index*

ACKNOWLEDGMENTS

It is humbling to finally acknowledge all those who have contributed to the collaborative conversations and hard work out of which this volume emerged. All political intellectual work is collective, building on the work of those who came before. We are indebted to the many extraordinary and committed feminist scholars from whom we have learned during our own journey to confront the conundrums presented by the geopolitics of feminist efforts to address the bewildering forms of gendered violence in our world. Many of their names can be found in the rich bibliographies we each have included in this book and we thank them all.

More directly, however, we want to acknowledge just how much we have learned from each other and every one of the scholars, students, practitioners, activists, and journalists who joined us in sessions that began with an early brainstorming meeting in New York, included public presentations at Columbia University, and culminated in intense workshops in Amman and New York. These were organized through the initiative that began in 2016 and that we first imagined as "Religion and the Global Framing of Gender Violence."

Pursued in the inspiring context of Columbia University's Center for the Study of Social Difference, a unique unit dedicated to supporting long-term scholarly working groups who wished to explore global social justice issues, we could not have done this without the visionary and constant encouragement of Dr. Toby Volkman. As director of the initiative on "Religion in International Affairs" at the Henry Luce Foundation, she saw the potential of our initial hunch about the importance of "the Muslim question" in relation to gender violence. She was convinced that we needed to follow through on our suspicions about the ways gender-based violence and its regulation had so successfully found their way into global geopolitics. Wise in her guidance, she was generous and patient in her support. Without the grant from the Luce Foundation we never could have devoted ourselves to this project. We could not have brought together such extraordinary colleagues for the "slow thought" and long-term exchanges that enabled the breakthroughs we are proud to offer in this book. We also thank Jonathan VanAntwerpen at Luce for extending the grant period until we could finish the book.

Our journey began with discussions among Lila Abu-Lughod, Rema Hammami, Janet Jakobsen, and Nadera Shalhoub-Kevorkian. Each of us came through different pathways to shared concerns about the politics of gender violence. We knew that complex questions required a collective effort and diverse disciplinary and regional expertises. The years we were able to spend together thinking, talking, learning, and eventually writing together were priceless gifts. We are honored to share here some of what we collectively discovered.

Our initial questions developed and deepened through exchanges with the other truly amazing critical feminist analysts whose contributions we were able to include in this book: Nina Berman, Inderpal Grewal, Shenila Khoja-Moolji, Vasuki Nesiah, Sima Shakhsari, Samira Shackle, Dina Siddiqi, Shahla Talebi, Leti Volpp, and Rafia Zakaria. Their work helped us articulate the central arguments, bringing into sharp focus the theme of the international visibility and forms of regulation of what we call GBVAW (gender-based violence/violence against women) and the circuits of power through which GBVAW travels.

Although their actual words could not be included in this volume under their names, the imprints of all those who participated in our international working group and the conferences and events we organized around these questions about feminism, violence, and geopolitics are everywhere in our final framing. The memories of their presence are indelible. What we all learned from each other's papers, presentations, and astute questions will last. The dispersed fellows who participated in our project "Religion and the Global Framing of Gender Violence" deserve special thanks, especially Sara Ababneh, Nadje Al-Ali, Nissreen Haram, Wafa Al-Khadra, Zahra Ali, Urooj Arshad, Hadeel Aziz, Qudsiya Contractor, Yasmin El-Rifae, Katherine Pratt Ewing, Amal Ghandour, Hala Ghosheh, Janet Halley, Sally Engle Merry, Rupal Oza, Maryam Saleh, Shagufta Shah, Kathryn Spellman Poots, Nafeesa Syeed, Miriam Ticktin, Aditi Surie von Czechowski, and Dubravka Žarkov.

The labor of talented and dedicated assistants is indispensable to carrying out any multiyear and multicountry project. Special thanks go to Joymala Hajra, who helped us launch the project and worked with us during its first years, expertly organizing conferences, writing up reports, advising us, managing our finances, and more. Beyond the call of duty, she also used her aesthetic talents to create stunning visuals for our academic work. For the last phase of the project, we are deeply indebted to Laura Marissa Charney, whose own intellectual journey brought her close to ours. Her passion for our project led her to offer us so much, not least of which included painstaking editing and fact-checking. Along the way, we appreciated so much what Laura Ciolkowski, Susanna Ferguson, Catherine LaSota, Paula Rozine Long, Liza McIntosh, Laura McTighe, Teresa Perosa, and Laela Shallal were able to contribute.

One of our goals was to internationalize scholarship; for this, we want to thank Safwan Masri, the head of Columbia University's network of Global Centers. His enthusiasm for this project and the strong collaboration he encouraged between us and Hanya Salah, the director of the Columbia Global Center | Middle East, Amman, provided us the chance to hold an incredible workshop in Amman that all the Center staff were excited to help with. We thank Aya Al Kabarity in particular for being attentive to every detail. The logistical and financial support were one thing; their hosting us in the beautiful and functional setting of the Amman Global Center was another. We were especially grateful for the ways they connected us with scholars and lawyers and practitioners from Jordan who enriched and grounded our discussions. We will never forget the dinner hosted by Nissreen Haram where we were introduced to the impressive members of the Amman activist scene. Although we had hoped to have our second international meeting in the other region on which our working group focused, the situation of visas and national politics in South Asia, followed by COVID-19, prevented us. We are grateful to Janet Jakobsen for having arranged instead for a wonderful second workshop at Barnard College.

We also want to thank Sharon Marcus, then Dean of the Humanities, for awarding the Center for the Study of Social Difference a small grant to help establish a wider initiative on "Reframing Gender Violence" at Columbia University that was linked to our own. The varied public events and groups we were able to bring together enriched the intellectual scene around feminism and contributed to our own thinking about the issues we cover in this book. We are grateful especially to Marianne Hirsch, Jean Howard, Dipali Mukherpadhyay, Anupama Rao, and Paige West for their input and to many graduate students and colleagues for joining us for these events and seminars. Those beyond Columbia and Barnard, including Jaskiran Dhillon, Nacira Guénif-Souilamas, and Sherene Razack were especially inspiring.

We also have to thank the patient team at Columbia University's Institute for Social and Economic Research and Policy (ISERP) who were responsible for administering our grant. They helped navigate us through Columbia's bureaucratic maze and exasperating procedures. Among the most constant in this saintly battalion were Adrianna Cedeno, Karen El Aguila, Jo-Ann Espaillat, Aileen Espinoza, Stacy Royster, and Elizabeth Torrez.

At Duke University Press we would like to thank the two anonymous readers whose great enthusiasm and encouragement for the book prospectus was as important for us as the very helpful critical comments on its various chapters. Their insights and profoundly productive questions and suggestions were pivotal in pushing us to articulate a more cohesive series of arguments. We cannot thank them enough. Along the way Ryan Kendall's support was essential in our getting all the details right as we prepared the manuscript for submission. Bird Williams expertly shepherded the manuscript into production. Diana Witt created a wonderful index for a complicated text and was generously responsive to our concerns and questions. We are especially grateful to Ken Wissoker, Duke University Press's senior executive editor, for his enthusiastic response to the manuscript and for guiding it through the process of approval and final publication.

We dedicate this book to our families and loved ones in hopes that it will contribute to making a better world for everyone.

INTRODUCTION · *Lila Abu-Lughod, Rema Hammami,
and Nadera Shalhoub-Kevorkian*

Circuits of Power in GBVAW Governance

Over the course of the last few decades, violence against women (VAW) and, subsequently, gender-based violence (GBV) have emerged as powerful agendas within international governance and law, increasingly folded into practices of state sovereignty and global security. What were once marginalized feminist concerns about the gravity of various forms of gendered violence and the silence that surrounded such harms now sit firmly at the nexus of powerful global networks of institutions and practices that have recast governmentality, human rights, development, and humanitarianism in line with post-9/11 global security rationales.

How did this happen? What are the politics, ideologies, and geographies of this feminist agenda? What are the modes and channels of operation of what we might call the master category of GBVAW (Gender-Based Violence/Violence Against Women) as both a technology and apparatus of rule? We use the awkward acronym GBVAW to denote the fusing of the normative agendas of "Violence against women" that rose to prominence in the 1990s and its later conjoining with the category "Gender-based violence" into one power-knowledge complex within contemporary global governance. We use the ordinary term "gender violence" (small g) to distinguish forms, formations, and lived experiences of violence as they intersect with other forms of oppression. These extend beyond or exceed the standard normative limits set by GBVAW and we are particularly interested in the contradictory effects these regulatory forms and norms have on those who are the subjects of violence as they experience gendered forms of violence inscribed on their bodies, lives, and social relationships. Has the conviction about the urgency of addressing violence against women and other forms of gender-based violence translated into better lives for the people it wanted to protect? These are key questions that lie at the heart of this book.

The Cunning of Gender Violence explores the dynamic political and institutional circuits that GBVAW inhabits, traverses, consolidates, and animates. It traces the silences and omissions of these categories and exposes, through carefully researched case studies, how prevailing assumptions that organize GBVAW may be affirming, enabling, or sustaining rationales and systems of power that are harmful, and at odds with the intentions of the feminists who pushed for them. The particular regions on which we focus, the Middle East and South Asia, are crucial analytical sites for developing this understanding because of the ways religion and racialized ethnicity, particularly "the Muslim question," appear so deeply embedded in the logics underpinning GBVAW in international governance. Activists who view the uptake of VAW and GBV into global governance as a feminist victory regularly express concern about these dynamics of racialization and Islamophobia, but tend to downplay them as uncomfortable baggage that burdens or hijacks the work of combating gendered violence. Yet the case studies presented in this book suggest that these dynamics may not be *external* to the ways the GBVAW agenda works but rather integral to whatever success this feminist agenda has had in previous decades. That is what we mean by the "cunning" of gender violence. In using this Hegelian term, we follow the leads of Elizabeth Povinelli (2002) whose *Cunning of Recognition* focused on the double-binds imposed on Indigenous Australians by the apparently benign liberal multicultural policies of recognition, and Nancy Fraser (2009) who puzzled over "the disturbing convergence" between some of second wave feminism's ideals and the demands of an emerging new logic of capitalism: post-Fordist, transnational, and neoliberal. The "cunning of history," Fraser argued, lay in the ways that the women's movement's economic and cultural visions were split such that their "utopian desires found a second life as feeling currents that legitimated the transition," a transition at odds with the movement's vision of a just society. Povinelli and Fraser's use of "cunning" highlights the way in which marginalized groups' demands for justice become entrapped and transformed through the politics of inclusion, but in ways that are Janus-faced. Systems of power appear responsive by taking up the language of injury and redress, while re-articulating their substance according to political rationales profoundly inimical to the original demands, as well as to the needs of those who made them.

Similarly, we find that, in practice, the GBVAW agenda often translates into exclusions and violences for those in whose name it claims to operate as protection or redress. The rhetoric of doing feminist good has become embedded in imperial and repressive state projects whose goals are antithetical to the basic principles of justice and dignity that feminism advances, often appearing as an active instrument in their logics. Through codification into legal norms and standardized frameworks and interventions, GBVAW has become a highly mobile technology almost immune to the specifics of the geopolitical and national contexts in which it operates. It shores up existing forms of structural and racialized violence and opens new pathways for militarized intervention. Even in the best of circumstances, the measures it offers for care or redress are incommensurate with what is actually needed. Too often, victims and those who seek to support them find themselves trapped in a coercive reiteration of the distorted truths demanded by the logics of power in order to access fragments for survival from the deeply flawed forms of care on offer.

At the time of the US invasion of Afghanistan in 2001, the harnessing of a feminist agenda to legitimize a project of imperial military intervention in the name of protecting Afghan women seemed like an exceptional and obvious instance of political instrumentalism (Abu-Lughod 2002; Hirschkind and Mahmood 2002; Kumar 2021). The ensuing decades have shown that GBVAW's entanglement with imperial projects has become the ongoing global order of things. In the case of the US invasion of Afghanistan, the instrumental use of VAW rallied a vital chorus of feminist criticism, whose foresight has been tragically borne out in the 2021 ending of the US occupation (and where echoes of the original debate about imperial intervention to "save women" continued to reverberate).[1] Over the subsequent two decades scholarship critically analyzing specific domains of GBVAW's ever-expanding reach has grown exponentially.[2] Yet many of the forms of state criminality and humanitarian rescue that we examine in this volume, and the novel ways in which GBVAW has been operating as an agent of global securitization in the conflicts in Iraq and Syria, remain less interrogated. When epistemic violence is embedded in what Engle (2020) calls the "common sense" of Sexual and Gender-Based Violence (SGBV), how do feminists resist co-optation?

There is perhaps no better evidence of the apparent success of what began as a radical feminist effort to produce a global consensus around the wrongs of gender-based violence than the awarding of the 2018 Nobel Peace Prize to Nadia Murad and Dr. Denis Mukwege. Both were commended for campaigning against rape and sexual assault as a weapon of war. The award seemed to represent a momentous shift in public consciousness and attitudes. Murad's lawyer, Amal Clooney, representing Yazidi survivors like Nadia Murad, later argued passionately in the Security Council that it had a chance to stand on the right side of history if it passed another resolution against rape and sexual violence in conflict: Clooney called it their Nuremberg moment (Ford 2019).

This Nobel Prize captures the paradoxes of the feminist achievement of making gender-based violence a serious matter of international concern, as well as its cunning. While the prize did recognize the personal and political courage of these two activists, the sleight of hand is in how the act of recognition works to confirm a regime of truth deeply at odds with what the award appears to validate. Here recognition implicitly pulls together and consolidates a series of deeper truth claims around race, gender, and violence: gender violence and its perpetrators are located in savage, racialized distant places and others; its victims suffer from the singular violence of bodily violation; and the liberal West (including its invading troops and peacekeepers) are the elect agents for their protection and rescue. The "international community"—including interested governments, corporations, arms dealers, or contractors—is rendered innocent of any role in producing the conditions for or sustaining these conflicts and the vast range of violence and destruction they incur, even while the most cursory historical analysis of the conflicts in Iraq and Syria, or in the Democratic Republic of Congo (where Dr. Mukwege treats rape survivors), would suggest otherwise.

The appeal to the Security Council itself is suggestive of another dimension of the cunning of recognition at work here. The feminist achievement of getting international governance institutions to finally acknowledge violence against women within their mandates has been attained at the price of singling out sexual violence in war as the sole focus of UN conventions, protocols, resources, and interventions. Feminist victories focused on making sexual violence in conflict a war crime (and a crime against humanity) at international tribunals over the 1990s set the stage for the achievement of the first Security Council Resolution, UN1325, that addressed gender violence.[3] Both in that original iteration as well as in the subsequent Security Council affirmations of the importance of addressing gender violence in war and conflict, sexual violence is the privileged and near-exclusive category of concern. The negative ramifications have been manifold for those seeking redress from violence (gendered or not) in the context of war and conflict, as well as for those who seek an end to war and armed conflict altogether. But sexual violence has been a very productive category, discursively subtending racial rationales for imperial intervention and materially through the economic flows that accompany these initiatives to protect or alleviate the suffering of those victimized by sexual brutality. One cannot ignore the ever-widening employment opportunities and career paths this category enables for lawyers, journalists, security contractors, politicians, and military personnel, along with psycho-social counselors and a growing cadre of global experts in everything from democracy promotion to gender mainstreaming in conflict. Around this grows a whole GBVAW knowledge industry of expert technical reports that recycle self-serving analyses and prescriptions.

The Cunning of Gender Violence focuses on the selective ways a visionary feminist project has folded itself into world affairs. For us as scholars and journalists who work within or on marginalized or violated communities, either in deadly conflict zones or sites of "ordinary" state violence, it has been important to foreground the experiences and voices of targeted groups and individuals even when analyzing the legal and bureaucratic apparatus that claims to address gendered forms of violence. How does GBVAW speak to the experience of Palestinian girls in Jerusalem trembling as they are threatened by police, dogs, and settlers on their way to school? How do women's organizations in Gaza confront the limits put on them by international aid organizations' definitions of how to respond to the layers of catastrophic violence women experience there at the hands of the Israeli state (whose violence must be bracketed)? Can it address the lynching of young Muslim men in India while the state insists on looking the other way, all the while fomenting divisions between Hindus and Muslims? Is it able to encompass the complex stories of Iranian women political prisoners anxious about potential sexual violence by guards because this threatens their sense of self as modern political subjects rather than as "women"? GBVAW traffics in honor crimes and female genital cutting as cultural violence; can it see the collusion of state and religious authorities in Pakistan in responding to a transgressive social media star whose biography challenges conventional scripts of feminist agency versus victimization? Or a US administration intent on racially securitizing its borders and immigration policies while fueling Islamophobia? How do the personal and political fuse and how can we disentangle gender from other aspects of being, experience, and location for those subjected to violence?

GBVAW is both strategic and selective, highlighting some perpetrators of violence while erasing others. Gender violence in weak or "failed" states is highly visible and individual perpetrators can be and are prosecuted at the International Criminal Court (ICC), as Nesiah shows in her chapter, while similar kinds of violence are invisible when in the hands of strong states that are usually allies of the West (Clarke 2019). Our concern is the way the GBVAW agenda may solidify rather than upset or challenge existing geopolitical logics of power and exclusion; we note the epistemologies of civilizational difference and racialized hierarchies that subtend these logics.

We pose three sorts of questions about the everyday geopolitics and political geographies of GBVAW. First, we ask how GBVAW travels. What are its channels, paths, and means—its political ecologies? Second, we ask what this category—as object, as knowledge producer, and as apparatus of social intervention—makes possible or impossible. What does it enable and disable? We consider political alliances and institutional structures; legal reforms and social movements; women's activism, NGOs (nongovernmental organizations) and social media; refugee asylum and human rights claims; discursive and media frames; as well as political economies. Third, we ask what narrative frames define and confine our fields of vision about violence, occluding, sidelining, or masking some powers and forces that inflict or enable violence. We track these frames not just in our ethnographic studies but in the analyses of policies and governmental practices and the seductions of hegemonic representations in the media.

We try to foreground the distinct ways violence is experienced by those subjected to its multiple forms, sensitive always to the ways it marks bodies, senses of worth, and connections to community. Because all of us work in and on regions where Muslims live or have been made into special objects of surveillance or intervention, we can never ignore the deadly ways that religion, race, and ethnicity have been implicated in GBVAW. How does this historic condition underwrite feminist engagements with geopolitical projects?

FEMINIST GENEALOGY: A PYRRHIC VICTORY?

The literature on how a well-meaning transnational activist feminist project (combatting violence against women globally) was able to ascend to become a set of norms in the UN system and legal instruments in international law focuses on the ways women's rights linked up with human rights to translate harms to women's bodily integrity into the existing international rights regime (Keck and Sikkink 2014; Merry 2006). The programmatic outcomes of that initial strand of the movement's strategy can be seen primarily in how GBVAW evolved into a global regulatory biopolitical project of instantiating women's rights and protections from bodily harm through the dual international frameworks of development and humanitarianism and their attendant flows of material aid and expertise. Within Development, the VAW agenda became translated into a plethora of national "best practice" technologies, where states of the Global South sign on to legal norms and adopt modular packages of governmental techniques designed to prevent, treat, and ultimately eradicate violence against women (Goldfarb and Goldscheid 2016; UN Women 2016; Johnson 2010; Merry 2006).

Within humanitarianism, the language changed to GBV and the rights strand of the original agenda evolved into norms and modular frameworks through which humanitarian assemblages became charged with treating victims of VAW within conflict zones and humanitarian spaces and preventing the recurrence of such violence under the auspices of their temporary sovereignty (IASC 2015; Dolan 2015).

Although the original feminist anti-VAW project attempted to universalize women's experience of violence and thus bridge both the racial/ethnic cleavages that marked second wave US feminism and the neocolonial hierarchies that ordered First and Third World subjects, the GBVAW regulatory/biopolitical project that has evolved over the past twenty years or so seems to reproduce these ontological divides. Now it is not only "white women saving brown women from brown men" that organizes the agenda but a vast apparatus that includes an army of UN bureaucrats, international NGOs, aid workers, private security companies, military specialists, UN peacekeeping missions, human rights lawyers, and high-level governance experts. GBVAW as global governance increasingly appears to be a mechanism through which certain masculine "others," particularly Muslim men, have been demonized and criminalized even as what is variously called dominance or carceral feminism has triumphed in the international sphere on the basis of an allegedly universalist critique of patriarchy (Bernstein 2019; Halley 2018; Halley et al. 2019).

The genealogy of the linkage of the original VAW agenda to the contemporary global politics of securitization, including ongoing iterations of the War on Terror such as in the most recent guise of Preventing Violent Extremism (PVE) lies in the specific feminist conceptualization put forth about the relationship between VAW, militarism, and armed conflict.[4] The 1990s were crucial for this, particularly in documents emanating from the 1995 Beijing UN Fourth World Conference on Women but then reiterated through feminist mobilizations around international courts and tribunals that succeeded in criminalizing sexual violence in war on the grounds that women's rights to bodily integrity were human rights. Those earlier iterations framed the relationship primarily in terms of women's greater vulnerability to specific types of violence in war due to their gender (and thus their need for protection), as well as their greater capacity for peace (Cohn 2008).

The current framing of gender violence against women as the normative issue of global security was then developed by activists within what became known as the "Women, Peace and Security agenda" (WPS). Feminists mobilized within the emerging UN "human security" discourse in the immediate aftermath of the Cold War and the result was the key UN resolution 1325, on Women, Peace and Security. An ensuing norm cascade put gender violence at the center of twenty-first-century global geopolitics (Engle 2020; Hudson 2012). That agenda was a conscious project to harness violations of women's rights to the new human security agenda emerging within global institutions by reframing VAW *as a cause* rather than simply a consequence of war and conflict. Securing women's rights (read primarily as bodily integrity) was no longer simply a human rights issue, as it was in Beijing, but a means to advance global security.[5] As Carol Harrington (2011) has pointed out, this reframing was enabled by the perfect geopolitical storm of the new world order that had emerged in the aftermath of the Cold War. This storm included the coming into being of a US-dominated unipolar world; the rise of the so-called new wars, epitomized by the conflict in the Democratic Republic of Congo (DRC); the emergence of the human security framework and the highly problematic Responsibility to Protect (R2P) doctrine that enabled imperial military intervention in the name of protecting populations; and the criminalization of rape as "a weapon of war" based on mobilizations around the hypervisibility of sexual violence in the armed conflicts of the Balkans, followed by Rwanda, Darfur, and the DRC (Zarkov 2020).

The timing of this particular linkage between women's human rights and the emerging security discourse was ill-fated: less than a year after passage of Security Council Resolution 1325, the world witnessed the events of 9/11. Along with the tragic loss of lives and the greater losses that would result from the responses to these events, hopes of a post–Cold War peace dividend and promise of the human security agenda were demolished under an ascendant global security regime called the "War on Terror."[6] Violence against women and global security were not decoupled but remained paired in the operations and iterations of this ongoing war machine. The instrumentalization of violence against women as a *casus belli* in the US war on Afghanistan was actually a harbinger of the post-9/11 new world order.

Apparatuses of Rule: Security, States, Humanity

If the critical feminist legal theorists who have brought into question the imbrication of the feminist agenda against gender violence with the juggernaut of securitization (e.g., Engle 2020; Engle, Nesiah, and Otto 2022; Ní Aoláin and Huckerby 2018) did so through following developments in international legal institutions, as anthropologists, sociologists, and those committed to regional study and ethnography as well as to close readings of cultural forms linked to the Middle East and South Asia, we take a different route in this book. We consider the specific political contexts of those subject to these agendas, the role of media in furthering the policies of national and international institutions as "common sense," and the experiences of those scarred by the everyday violence in peace and war that these GBVAW institutions and imperatives have sought to address.

Combatting gender violence no longer can be seen simply as a feminist project gone global. It is inextricable from the political projects that carry it forward. GBVAW put in the service of a variety of political and geopolitical projects can sequester from view many of the lived experiences of violence in the contemporary world. We are concerned about the ways it can operate to flatten, simplify, and narrow the perceptual fields through which gendered violences can rise to visibility, as well as how it may evict from the frame imperial complicity in the production of the very violences feminist activists are seeking to prevent, mitigate, or eradicate.

The Cunning of Gender Violence interrogates these framings, practices, networks, and shifting dynamics of power. Tracking mobilizations of the GBVAW apparatus and the networks along which it travels enables us to examine key features of the intersecting political orders and uneven force fields of our current world. Our sense is that GBVAW has been recomposed according to the logics of the larger security or governance projects of which it seeks to be a part. Its "uptake," modest as disappointed practitioners claim it is, has involved a process of recalibration that risks making feminist concerns about gender violence active instruments in hegemonic political projects. Just how this occurs, and with what profound effects, are subjects taken up in various ways by the grounded case studies brought together here.

To better understand the way violence works in the global governance of the intimate and the ways it sustains global and local inequalities, conferring hierarchies of civilizational status, we follow the multiple circuits of power in which it is entangled. We interrogate the global and local operations of GBVAW in the wider matrices of violence that mark everyday lives. These are hidden and apparent, fluid and shifting, and they work through plural modes and operations. Since gender violence and its treatment through GBVAW lie at the center of multiple global political arrangements and dynamics of governance—imperial, colonial, settler colonial, and authoritarian—the book is divided into four parts, each of which interrogates the relationship of gender violence to the codified GBVAW agenda in a major political formation of governance and rule. The chapters in part I examine the co-implication of gender, violence, and religious difference in the dominant political formation of the global security world order. Part II shifts the focus to the modalities through which states and political institutions perpetrate or enable forms of gendered violence and asks why these remain largely invisible, or are only selectively made visible, by GBVAW in international governance. Part III traces the contemporary itineraries and evolutions of the GBVAW apparatus in the context of two key arms of global governance: the civilizational industries that intervene in other parts of the world in the name of "development" or "humanitarianism." Codified GBVAW works in tandem with both the epistemologies and rationales of these three circuits or modalities of governance in the new world order—securitization, state criminality, and the projects to uplift victims for the sake of capitalist development, or save them from the ravages of armed conflict and mass displacement. Part IV consists of reflections by journalists about the complicity of Western media in legitimizing these dynamics of power through the ways they structure reporting on gender violence.

PART I: SECURITIZATION

Launched as part of the War on Terror after 9/11, the grip and reach of the ideological and militarized governance and surveillance formation that goes under the banner of securitization have expanded dramatically over the last two decades. Security has cemented global alliances among powerful and pliant nations from the United States and France to Pakistan and Kenya, escalating fear of terror, proliferating measures and institutions of counterterrorism, and converging in the past decade on a consensus that violent extremism is the threat.

The first four chapters examine some of the ways feminist GBVAW projects are imbricated in these politics of security and counterterrorism. They provide context for the way Nadia Murad was singled out for care and acclaim, balancing appreciation of the feminist achievements this Nobel Prize affirms with the dangers inherent in the way it has consolidated a tight rhetorical nexus between gender and religion, with sexualized violence having come to practically define religious "extremism." We are witnessing a thickening of the circuits of globalized securitization and the growing legitimation of criminalizing Muslim men, as an earlier Nobel Prize awarded to a schoolgirl victim of Muslim men's violence signaled. Malala Yousafzai, shot by some Taliban in Pakistan allegedly for promoting Muslim girls' education at a time when empowering girls was being pushed as the neoliberal solution to global poverty (Khoja-Moolji 2015, 2018; Murphy 2013; Hengeveld 2017; Siddiqi, this volume) captivated world attention. Between that incident and the deplorable sexual violence perpetrated by a newer militant Islamist group that emerged in response to the US invasion and occupation of Iraq, not Afghanistan, the enemy shifted. Girls are now to be saved from "violent extremists" in the widening global War on Terror (Abu-Lughod, this volume; Al-Bulushi 2018).

Vasuki Nesiah fills in the genealogy of feminist engagement with security and counterterrorism and the troubling entailments of the long efforts through the Women, Peace and Security agenda to criminalize sexual violence in conflict. The title of her chapter, "Lawfare, CVE, and International Conflict Feminism," is a provocation to attend to the ways gender is being weaponized on global terrain and a reminder of Audre Lorde's (1984) warning that the master's tools can never dismantle the master's house. Suspicious of the way key international feminist legal organizations were so quick to celebrate the arrest in 2018 of Al-Hassan Mahmoud, the Malian former chief of the Islamic police and member of Ansar Dine, an Islamist paramilitary group, on charges of war crimes and crimes against humanity to be adjudicated in the International Criminal Court, Nesiah considers the novelty of the charges of war crimes and crimes against humanity in light of the developments since 2000 of International Conflict Feminism: he is accused of the persecution of the Timbuktu civilian population "on the grounds of religion and on the grounds of gender."

Lila Abu-Lughod introduces the term "securofeminism" to name this phenomenon of the engagement of feminists with security in the wider arena in the United States and Europe in which religious culture has come to be blamed for gender violence. "Securofeminism" examines the process by which a range of women's rights advocates have maneuvered to participate in the fast-growing initiatives of the last decade or so to Counter Violent Extremism (CVE) or Prevent it (PVE). This enterprise is often called soft counterterrorism. Many feminist advocates caution about the human rights risks of securitization. Despite ambivalence within the global international feminist community, including those working within the Women, Peace, and Security framework, about this, she notes that a surprising number of feminist practitioners have promoted themselves as uniquely positioned to combat "extremism" on the basis of their experience and expertise in addressing gender violence, thus engaging with the logics outlined by Volpp and Jakobsen in the next two chapters of attributing gender violence largely to Muslims. Critical of the mainstream security discourses and sensationalized media reports about Muslim women who began traveling to Iraq and Syria to join the Islamic State (challenging the formula that had exempted women from the extremist category) even cautious organizations like UN Women and International Crisis Group produced reports that cited flawed policy papers with attention-seeking titles like "The Sultanate of Women" (Patel 2017) or "Caliphettes" (Rafiq and Malik 2015). The cadre of diverse professional gender experts and governance feminists (Halley, 2018, 16) find themselves caught in troubling contradictions as they seek inclusion in the entwined spheres of GBVAW and security whose outlines Nesiah has traced.[7]

Leti Volpp's dissection of the Trump administration's attempts to limit immigration through successive versions of the Executive Order on "Protecting the Nation from Foreign Terrorist Entry into the United States" in 2017 reveals exactly how this logic of linking gender violence to security has worked to devastating effect for so many. An apparently "feminist" concern with "honor killing" as an element of GBVAW was inserted into a project that blocked people from entry and vilified Muslims by collapsing differences among them and presenting them, on the basis of misleading and unsubstantiated data, as potential security threats. Volpp considers the curious inclusion in the first two versions of the Executive Orders of clauses identifying "honor killing" as a problematic practice by "foreign nationals" that warranted their exclusion, revealing one way that GBVAW becomes "a proxy for xenophobic exclusion."

The project of protecting women from violence is in this case clearly wedded to Islamophobia, as all the legal challenges to the "Muslim Ban" have argued. But in the same way religion and gender were conjoined in the publicity around Nadia Murad and the case of the Yazidis, a key element of the Executive Order was the way it smuggled in a special dimension of "extremism." Once refugee admissions were to be resumed, priority was to go to refugees from "minority religions." This was intended, as Trump announced on the Christian Broadcasting Network, to assist persecuted Christians.[8] Muslim immigrants, in other words, were to be banned not only for their potential for terrorism but because they endanger liberal values of tolerance and Christianity itself, an example of what Jakobsen argues in her chapter is characteristic of the way the secular and religious are bridged in the political management of sexual violence. Volpp's conclusion is significant for appreciating the ways GBVAW and security have become conjoined: the specter of violence against women playing a key role in the Trump administration's exclusion of Muslims with the rhetoric and illusion of (concocted) data working together to fuel a phantasm locking "foreign terrorist entry" to a culturally specific form of harm in the GBVAW arsenal.

There is a larger context in the United States for this particular and extreme moment of mobilization against "the Muslim threat" through gender. In "Because Religion," Janet Jakobsen unpicks the epistemological process by which disparate threads in American public discourse about gender, sex, and religion have been woven together to produce the common sense that "religion" (particularly excessive religion) causes "gender violence." This alchemy has been used to make the policies of US administrations successive to George W. Bush's that use violence to confront those deemed patriarchal and labeled terrorists seem sensible. If the general view in the United States is that religion is a source of conservatism regarding gender and sexuality, she shows that it is more crucial to this common sense that the world is divided into secular liberal versus religious conservative but that religions themselves split into good (moderate) and bad (fundamentalist), and that Christianity is more aligned with secular moderation than Islam. These beliefs come together to produce a coherent truth claim: that religiously based violence can be attributed to Islamic extremists.

PART II: STATES OF VIOLENCE, UNRULY SUBJECTS

Part II shifts the focus to the modalities through which states and political institutions perpetrate, manipulate, or enable forms of gendered violence. State political violence targets individual bodies and populations through various technologies. These are violences often hidden by the dominant focus on states' security "necessities" and international GBVAW discourse and legislation that target nonstate actors whether in war or peace, or that concentrate on what are presented as localized forms of patriarchy. Some scholars have developed the concept of state crime to capture these forms of violence, referring to the overlapping area between human rights violations and state organizational deviance mediated by the degree of the perceived legitimacy of the actions involved (Green and Ward 2000).[9] Yet it is rare for this literature to recognize how deeply gendered state political violence is.

Feminist scholars of state crime and militarization have shown that gendered violence is central to state-making and sustaining state power (Ali et al. 2019; Visweswaran 2013). We have to look beyond the most apparent violent tactics of control by states to see how violence reorganizes social structures, alters everyday relations, and impacts affect (Grewal 2005). State violence can even work through humanitarian registers of sympathy, "stealing the pains of others" (Razack 2007), creating new "grammars of rights, or producing colonized populations in need of saving." Here the state emerges as a benevolent patriarch reaching into every aspect of life (Bhan 2014; Varma 2016).

When analysts of Governance Feminism note the way feminists began to "walk the halls of power" they risk reproducing Euro-America as the site of feminist theory and activism, rendering the Global South a site of mere application of theory and policy imitation. Decolonial and postcolonial critiques and Third World International Law reject analyses that close their eyes to state repression and the actual experiences of violence. As such they raise broader questions about state crime (Nesiah 2021). Censure or prosecution of such violence has involved international institutions, tribunals, and resolutions from the International Criminal Court to the UN Security Council. However, Engle, Nesiah, and Otto (2022, 175) warn that the successful projects of what they call International Conflict Feminism "have reinforced many dangerous aspects of both feminism and international law, as they have used a focus on harm to women—particularly sexual harm—to aid in the legitimization and extension of coercive state power, often against marginalized individuals and communities, and less powerful states." In other words, in the ways international human rights law appeals to states and their apparatuses to "investigate, prosecute, and punish non-state actors for serious human rights violations against women," it often "remove[s] direct responsibility from states, pinning sexual violence on individual actors on all sides of a given conflict or on non-state actors who the state is simply responsible for punishing." Kamari Clarke's (2019) analysis of the racial overrepresentation of individual African perpetrators in the emotive cases brought before the ICC reveals the patterning of blame and the affective dynamics of accountability. Addressing both gender violence and the apparatus of GBVAW from a state crime perspective assists in detecting the ways state violence works through gender and allows feminists to engage with the violence of state institutions and law, draws from indigenous conceptualizations of justice, examines everyday life and politics, and goes beyond the state and its local and global capitalist economy.

Based on rich ethnographic and textual analyses of diverse situations in Iran, Israel/Palestine, India, and Pakistan, the chapters in part II reveal the fluid but deadly dynamics of gender violence for which state regimes should be held accountable. While acknowledging the ways nation-states are inevitably shaped by international power politics, these chapters concentrate on forms of gendered violence that are inflicted by or in the service of state power and ruling elites. This violence can be direct, administered by punitive state institutions and agents, or it can be indirect, connected to states through their promotion of patriarchal or nationalist ideologies that incite or condone violence or through creating the conditions that constitute or enable violence.

If the persistent efforts of feminists over the past two decades have resulted in global attention to gender violence that is visible in the frames of GBVAW, there has been less political interest in exposing the violence of state ideologies and practices such as the intimate violence of house invasions by armed men, solitary confinement and physical torture under arrest, or the frightening interrogations that reveal the level of surveillance one is under such that even a woman's shampoo brand is known. This has made feminism a silent bystander for many everyday forms of state criminality. There are many reasons why state actors, institutions, and structures are not held accountable. There are the fictions of state sovereignty in the current world order. There is the faith in the inherent legitimacy of states' monopoly on violence. On a practical level, the difficulties of documenting state violence, particularly in states with high levels of political surveillance and securitization and with weak independent infrastructures of monitoring and free media, compound the problem. Governments can and do manipulate or suppress information and mask and reframe what might otherwise be recognized or classified as state criminality.

So while GBVAW has been criminalized in the global arena through a range of international legal instruments and institutions of varying efficacy, the culpability of states for forms of gendered violence—whether in cases such as those analyzed in these chapters including the policing of schoolgirls in Israel/Palestine (Shalhoub-Kevorkian), the deeply gendered "communal" violence that plagues postcolonial India (Grewal), the rape and threats of sexual violence in political prisons in Iran (Talebi), or even the layered enforcement of gendered norms of sexual propriety that Khoja-Moolji tracks in the Qandeel Balochi "honor killing" in Pakistan—is less apparent, despite the devastating consequences for vulnerable citizens and subjects.

The cunning of gendered violence can be integral to the workings of state power, whether wielded in biopolitical governance or subtending authoritarian or necropolitical colonial political projects of exclusion and expulsion. The ways gendered violence undermines communities, is used to withhold rights and citizenship or suppresses dissent, and reinforces social hierarchies and discriminatory norms should all be counted as state crimes of GBVAW. State perpetration of gender violence can be direct and visible, as in militarized checkpoints or prison torture cells. More often, though, it is indirect—unacknowledged, operating through forms of incitement, silence, or tacit encouragement of groups and individuals to use violence with impunity. In the case of structural and psychological violence, it is gendered in the ways it weakens and dismembers communities, invades the most intimate aspects of life, assaults the senses, and orchestrates affects. Although practices such as rape as a weapon of war and political torture are recognized as state crimes, we need to attend also to the ways that states enforce discriminatory social hierarchies that constrain the behavior and damage the lives of their citizens or subjects. State violence can govern, as the Palestinian prisoner Walid Duqqah (2010) put it eloquently, without "making noise."

The literature on state crime has not always considered gender violence. Yet when "state crime" occurs in patriarchal social orders, women and girls are particularly vulnerable. Denying equal access to social, political, educational, and economic power, or subjecting women and girls to institutional neglect, could be considered gender-based state crimes (Shalhoub-Kevorkian and Ihmoud 2016). Where women are excluded or subordinated, gender-based violence also tends to be treated as natural. Gendered violence extends to men and boys of minoritized groups, as well as to sexual minorities. Some of the most egregious instances of gendered state crime are the violences that target women from marginalized social groups, because, as scholars like Smith (2003) and Thobani (2015) have shown, race and class always intersect with patriarchal structures. The dynamic is intensified in colonial conditions, wars, or after natural disasters.

States govern through biopolitics—controlling and managing bodies and livelihoods. In imperial, colonial, and postcolonial states, the bodies of devalued "others" are terrains of political, social, legal, religious, and cultural struggle. Feminist scholars have brought out links between control over women's bodies and control over nature and the occupation of land (Merchant 1980; Caputi 1993; Ruether 1975). The symbolic connection between women and "mother earth" as well as women's responsibilities for reproduction tends to give them a special place in ideologies of the national collective (Yuval-Davis 1980). When women are made to carry the burden of reproducing the social order, the power of "other" women to ensure their community's continuity in colonial conditions is threatening.

That states' violence can be driven by racist, nationalist, and religious beliefs and agendas is an important aspect of the biopolitical. These routinized forms of violence are legitimized by arguments about the need to counter threats and protect citizens. If, as earlier chapters showed, Muslim groups are increasingly criminalized in a securitized global sphere—framed as perpetrators of religiously motivated and "extremist" gender violence—in the chapters in this part we glimpse the ways states govern through religious divisions, identities, and ideologies that they use to subject their citizens to gendered forms of violence. In these states in the Middle East and South Asia, we can see how violence works through demonizing internal groups through ethno-religious ideologies, whether Islamization, Hinduization, or Judaization, not to mention political differences and class.

Some feminist scholars have refused to normalize state atrocities whether in prison cells or in occupied, militarized, or colonized spaces such as refugee camps, reserves in Canada, or at the US border with Mexico. These scholars have also highlighted the ways gendered state violence works through cultural, ethnic, racial, or religious logics. Turning a blind eye to the criminality of states by accepting their framings of the violence they inflict as necessary for security or for humanitarian ends makes it easier to recognize and condemn GBVAW in the savage acts of racialized others. The violence hidden by the rhetoric so pervasive in the global security discourses analyzed in the chapters in part I—of saving minority women from their bad cultures or of defending peace, democracy, and liberal ideals—characterize state discourses in many situations.

States escape censure because, as a number of scholars of state crime have noted, they often deflect blame as part of a strategy of denial, outsourcing violence to nonstate groups they can disavow (Chambliss 1989; Green and Ward 2009; Ward and Green 2016; Jamieson and McEvoy 2005; Cohen 2001). Among the methods Jamieson & McEvoy (2005) describe, for example, are nonformal collusions with "indigenous terror groups" to operate counterinsurgency actions against a common "enemy" that the state itself has already abjected.[10] Inderpal Grewal's analysis of the "random" violence against Muslim men under the current Hindu nationalist regime in India shows that the outsourcing can be more subtle and indirect. Khoja-Moolji's analysis of how the naming of murders as "honor crimes" similarly distracts from alternative explanations that would implicate the wider political conditions and the responsibilities of the state and religious institutions for the individual violent crime. When there are material or political benefits to other states, allies, or the international system from the forms of state violence, there is little motivation from outside the state to intervene in national affairs. The international arms trade illustrates this dynamic perfectly as it abets the gendered violence of militarized policing as well as the ready availability of lethal weapons to be used by individuals.[11]

The forms of state violence that GBVAW feminists have succeeded in uncovering tend to be those in failed or unstable states where the violence appears lawless and there is little international stake in protecting state regimes. In stable or powerful states, such violence tends not to trigger international interference, especially when directed against internally "otherized" groups. Yet critical feminist scholars, as noted above, have been skeptical about the efficacy of criminal law to address gender-based violence and the totality of the penal apparatus, whether within states or through the international system (Ní Aoláin 2014; Razack 2004; Shalhoub-Kevorkian 2015). Scholars who take Third World approaches to international law (TWAIL) warn that the focus on sexual and gender-based violence as the ultimate crime has displaced other feminist and human rights concerns including social and economic inequalities (Nesiah 2006; Nesiah 2011, 43). The carceral and legal turn in this zeal to prosecute SGBVAW internationally has also hardened conservative gender and sexual norms (Bernstein 2019; Engle 2019, 2020; Halley et al. 2019), resulting in the creation of what Kapur (2018) called a "liberal fishbowl."

Doing gender through law, then, problematic enough in the international sphere, is no less problematic in the case of trying to regulate state crimes of gender violence. If we are to keep at our moral center the concern with human harm, we should use the experiences and voices of those who are subjected to this violence to grasp the intertwined and accumulating consequences of state criminality. This is precisely what the chapters in part II do. As Hartman (1997) writes in *Scenes of Subjection*, the bruised body of Frederick Douglass speaks to us about the violence he suffered as a slave but even more about the slave-master relation. The hurt bodies of the victims of state crime tell us as much about the suffering and pain the victims experience as the kinds of violence their oppressors inflict.

Each of the chapters in part II centers the experiences of the subjects of state violence to expose its intertwined and accumulating force. But to return to Hartman (1997; 2019), we are reminded that in addition to exposing and acknowledging the forms of direct and indirect gender violence that states wield, we must listen and look for refusals, resistances, and expressions of power of violated subjects if we do not want to redouble this violence. The voices shared in these chapters are replete with such stories, even as they uncover and dissect the gendered violence of what should be recognized as state crime. We read about the street protests by Muslim women and their allies in Shaheen Bagh, Delhi. We hear the defiance of Palestinian school girls "talking back" against their "daily torture" on the way to school. We follow the incisive words of a provocative social media star who dared to scandalize a prominent religious cleric, calling out the moral hypocrisy of the patriarchal Islamized Pakistani state. The survival and refusal to give up or give in of the imprisoned women dissidents Talebi introduces us to from the Islamic Republic's political prisons cannot fail to move.

Inderpal Grewal's chapter, "GBV and Postcolonial India," analyzes visual, print, and social media representations of terrible forms of violence in the recent history of India to show that what have been made to appear as communal mob violence or random cases of individual violence must not be exempted from the projects of state governance. Examining the representations of gendered violence against Muslim men and women that have blighted the nation under the Hindu Right government, from the Gujarat "pogrom" in 2002 to the recent spate of "lynchings" of Muslim men as the BJP came to power, she suggests that these should be understood instead as the gendered technologies of power through which the government seeks to render Muslims a subordinated minority group along with Dalits and Adivasis. That these spectacularized violences, mostly by Hindu cadres or individuals and directed at non-Hindu minorities, should be recognized as indirect forms of state violence is evident in the relative impunity for the perpetrators and the way the population is incited to violence by the government's nationalist ideologies.

Shenila Khoja-Moolji provides a different example of the indirect ways states can be responsible for gendered violence. In "The Politics of Legislating 'Honor Crime' in Contemporary Pakistan" she takes the spectacularized case of Qandeel Baloch, a young Pakistani social media star who was strangled to death by her brother in what was immediately characterized as an "honor killing." The murder was used by women's rights advocates to push through a stalled legal bill, coercing the state into appearing to step up as a defender of women and their rights. The problem Khoja-Moolji raises in the Pakistani case is analogous to that which Engle, Nesiah, and Otto (2022) raise about the limits of the law in the turn to the state in international feminist efforts to criminalize gender violence. State institutions are strengthened and state regimes are absolved of complicity.

Nadera Shalhoub-Kevorkian's "State Criminality and Gender-Based Violence" documents one of the modalities of direct violence in the settler colonial state of Israel. Listening to Palestinian school girls in Occupied East Jerusalem talk about the effects of the harassment and intimidation they experience on their daily walks to and from school, violence coming from Israeli soldiers and police, as well as settlers and bystanders, Shalhoub-Kevorkian concludes that these acts should be treated as state crimes of gender violence and even sexual violence.

Talebi's "Power, Subjectivity, and Sexuality in Iranian Political Prisons" offers a haunting analysis of a case of direct state violence and shows how its gendering works as much through the body as the psyche. Writing about the stories of three Iranian political prisoners, Talebi shows both how the violence inflicted by the state to crush political dissidents was gendered and how women prisoners experienced the violent practices of prison guards, emboldened as agents of the state, when these included threats of sexual violence and actual rape. The specific ways that religious ideology and moral language justified systematic violence toward prisoners under Khomeini's regime is a sobering reminder of the ways state power disempowers threatening groups and individuals by demonizing and dehumanizing them.

PART III: CIVILIZING INTERVENTIONS:
DEVELOPMENT AND HUMANITARIANISM

The chapters in part III focus on GBVAW within three main circuits of contemporary global governance: development aid, humanitarian intervention, and the refugee asylum regime. Superficially, these apparatuses of bio/geopolitical governance might appear as more legitimate channels through which feminist aspirations to do good "out there" in the world might be achieved since they are tasked with civilizational uplift and rescue rather than militarized containment and suppression. But as the studies in this part show, much of the same "baggage" that GBVAW carries through its inclusion in global security regimes is present when operating through humanitarianism and development.

The particular circuits through which this master category and its allied technologies travel are diverse bureaucratized fields of action, producing ever-evolving reigning objects of intervention, linked to the particular governing rationale to which GBVAW has attached itself. Here it appears in a variety of guises: as global norms against child marriage carried by development agendas in Bangladesh (Siddiqi); as a dense humanitarian infrastructure charged with delivering pedagogies against domestic violence to Gazans immiserated by war and international sanctions (Hammami); and as frameworks of acceptable queerness to validate Iranian LGBTI asylum claims in the refugee regime's Turkish borderland (Shakhsari). In each case, we see how a particular and singular form of injury is drawn out of its complex history and social life, made legible through being flattened and repackaged into a matrix of abstract universal rights, girded with norms of evidence, and put to work through rules of bureaucratic procedure that activate specific technologies of intervention. This process of making the particular social ill legible as GBVAW always involves scripting it across the dualism of backwardness (cause) and civilization (solution) that is a foundational metonym of this master sign. In all three chapters, Islam is a salient part of the context; thus, the scripting relies on ready-made Orientalist assumptions that render local culture (represented as Islamic patriarchy) as the cause of the particular "violation" in need of the particular global intervention.

The authors all center the voices and experiences of those made subject to the salient category of injury and its allied technologies that are operating in their context. Through close ethnographic readings, they uncover the mechanisms through which GBVAW translates into a powerful force in everyday lives of individuals and communities in contexts marked by modes of global dispossession. In particular the chapters highlight the entanglements of local activists, NGOs, or frontline workers. We find them trapped between the rigid frames and racialized representations of the global interventions and the urgent need to find context-specific solutions for individuals and communities whose forms and source of injury always exceed the normative limits of GBVAW. As such, the chapters offer a critical counter to one of the longstanding arguments for continued feminist inclusion in global institutions; that despite their limitations, GBVAW frameworks and their allied resources are empowering to women's rights activists on the ground. Rather than empowerment and changed consciousness, what the cases show is frustration, resignation, or just making do with the deeply flawed resources and the coercive relationship of dependency in the absence of any alternatives.

Dina Siddiqi's contribution traces the history of GBVAW's enmeshment with development imperatives in Bangladesh and its most recent ruling category, "child marriage," now posited as a critical obstacle to achieving the country's economic development goals. Globally, development institutions and their reigning agendas were some of the first circuits (along with international human rights law) where GBVAW's antecedent (VAW) gained traction in global governance. Sally Engle Merry's foundational 2006 book charted this particular story of feminist negotiation at the centers of power while providing some early hints of how it unfurled within development agendas of post-colonial states on the ground. Indeed, early on, the dominant narrative of GBVAW as feminist success story was dogged by counteranalyses that emerged from situated ethnographic readings of its operations in the developmental contexts of Latin America (Alcade 2011; Parson 2010), Southeast Asia (Kwiatkowski 2011a, 2011b), Africa (Archambault 2011; Hodžić 2009; Abramowitz and Moran 2012), the South Pacific (Jolly, Stewart, and Brewer 2012; Biersack, Jolly, and Macintyre 2016) and Turkey (Shively 2011). Much of this work relied on Merry's concept of vernacularization of women's human rights, but also exceeded it. These studies testified to the problematic gulf in the concept of "local translations" between normative rights frames and context-specific understandings of gender violence, as well as showing how "best practice technologies" of intervention were at odds with the needs of victims and the situated knowledge of antiviolence frontline workers and activists. These early studies, however, tended to assume that GBVAW circuits of knowledge and resources, though problematic, were largely geopolitically benign.

In contrast and in parallel were works that focused on national contexts where GBVAW's entry was obviously tethered to an epochal geopolitical project of the time: the post-Soviet "democratic-transitions" of former east bloc countries (Hemment 2004; Fábián 2010; Johnson 2009; Johnson and Robinson 2006). These highlighted its embeddedness within flows of aid and expertise accompanying neoliberal shock doctrine policies and the differential power between this highly resourced Western feminist agenda and emergent local women's organizations seeking independence from repressive state feminisms while grappling with the violent outcomes of Western-led structural adjustment. GBVAW was revealed as a powerful, well-resourced agenda capable of eclipsing local feminist meanings and reshaping organizations and activisms in ways that foreshadow arguments in this part of *The Cunning of Gender Violence*.

These works were written more than a decade ago, and there has been little subsequent research on GBVAW's new power constellations and evolving frames of intervention as it circulates through development agendas into postcolonial nation-state governance.[12] Dina Siddiqi's contribution does just that by focusing on the sudden appearance of the category of "child marriage" as an object of developmental concern in contemporary Bangladesh. She interrogates how this novel and unanticipated category propounded by international organizations pulls in and rallies state agencies, local activists, and NGOs to produce a common sense that eradicating child marriage is an urgent imperative for attaining Bangladesh's economic development. Originally listed as one among many "harmful cultural practices" in GBVAW normative definitions, Siddiqi locates this category's rise to prominence in the evolving rationales of corporatized neoliberal development at the turn of the millennium. While earlier neoliberalized development agendas centered the laboring body of the Third World woman as a "good investment," she is now displaced by the powerful economic potential of girls. Hence the shift in GBVAW priorities of concern; domestic violence against women is now eclipsed by the "intractable cultural norm" of child marriage. In contrast to the earlier literature, Siddiqi's analysis highlights new players within the global constellation through which GBVAW circulates within development imperatives; corporate-sponsored foundations fronted by celebrities now round out the list of UN institutions, bilateral aid agencies, and international NGOs. To unravel these larger operations of power, Siddiqi centers the history of women's issues and activisms in Bangladesh; the gendered social worlds that shape young women's desires; and the ways in which local NGOs and activists negotiate between need and skepticism in relation to global agendas.

The chapters by Hammami and Shakhsari focus on GBVAW's integration in two interlinked circuits of humanitarian governance: the interventionary assemblages tasked with managing "humanitarian emergencies" and the bureaucratic apparatus of the global refugee asylum regime. Again, through centering their analyses on those made subject to its operations, they are able to expose the real-world effects of the limiting frames and technologies and the context-specific dynamics of power and dependence they produce for activists, victims of violence, or their wider communities.

Scholarship on GBVAWs, humanitarian variants has exploded over the past two decades, reflecting the ascendance of humanitarianism to its current dominant status in global governance (Barnett 2005; Duffield 2001). In comparison to the literature on its Developmental variant, the analyses of GBVAW's integration into various arms of post-Cold-War humanitarianism is highly critical, but dominated by feminist legal and IR scholars who highlight the dangers of the sexualized and racialized assumptions subtending the discursive frames and legal instruments of the main humanitarian agendas such as sexual violence in war, refugee asylum, and sex/human trafficking. Ethnographically informed scholarship that interrogates GBVAW's Humanitarian variants from the perspective of those targeted by its operations is more limited and overwhelmingly focuses on the category of sexual violence in war (SGBV) given that this category remains the supreme ruling object having a monopoly in humanitarian discourse and representation, programming, and scholarly literature.[13] The consistently damaging findings of these latter ethnographic studies raise acute questions for any narrative of "feminist achievement."

The contributions by Hammami and Shakhsari find much in common with the critical analyses offered by these ethnographic studies of SGBV, but join a few others (Grabska 2011; Lokot 2019; Olivius 2016a, 2016b; Mai 2018; Luibhéid 2018; Giametta 2016) that defy its hegemony by focusing on alternative categories and formations of humanitarian GBVAW that have been marginalized. How does humanitarian GBVAW operate in contexts such as Gaza's "humanitarian emergency" or as "sexual humanitarianism" in the refugee regime bureaucracy tasked with managing LGBTI+-based asylum claims? In both cases, although sexual violence is missing, many of the critical insights from the ethnographic literature on SGBV still apply. This suggests that the rationales and logics that initially formed around "sexual violence in war" continue into humanitarian GBVAW's other forms and sites of intervention.

Critical ethnographies of SGBV interventions highlight how the affective power of combatting sexual violence is indivisible from its material productivity: it is a very lucrative category of human suffering across global publics. On the ground, this results in large and selective resource flows to treat this particular harm, creating reinforcing loops of what Heaton (2014) has called "perverse incentive structures." Humanitarians, local communities, and victims are incentivized to keep reproducing the singular SGBV narrative in order to capture the aid to which it is linked.[14] Victims and communities constantly express frustration with the way humanitarian resources are channeled into this singular category of harm. They consistently voice needs that are at odds with its frames: housing, financial support, work, and education for their children. Similar to the findings on Yazidi refugees cited in Shackle's chapter, interventions are also at odds with the context-specific needs and socially embedded forms of care prioritized by actual victims of sexual violence. Veit and Tschörner (2019) link this lack of a context-specific response back to the political economy of SGBV; local "problem contexts" must be framed within reigning global mandates, technical frames, and networks in order to capture their allied funding streams.

The dynamics exposed by ethnographic studies of SGBVAW reflect the political and economic inequality that underpins humanitarianism more generally. Didier Fassin (2007, 2011) has called this a politics of life marked by hierarchies of humanity. The massive imbalance in resources and power between humanitarian caregiving and precarious aid recipients creates a relationship of dependency that forecloses much of the latter's agency. With most access to care channeled into the limited frames of interventions, the outcome is a coercive form of care that forces individuals, local activists, and sometimes whole communities to engage in what Utas (2005) has called "victimcy," presenting themselves as victims within the well-known scripts in order to survive (Meger 2016). This form of "humanitarian paternalism" (Barnett 2010) often appears indistinguishable from control.

In Hammami's analysis of GBVAW operating within humanitarianism in Gaza, we see how the category of "sexual violence" continues to be salient through its absence. For the humanitarian assemblage operating there, it is the desired, relentlessly searched-for but mostly elusive, normative object of their longing. This open-air prison, saturated with multiple forms of Israeli colonial violence and buttressed by a layer of devastating international sanctions is guilefully categorized as a "protracted humanitarian crisis" which activates a subset of humanitarian GBVAW interventions that are reserved for postconflict transitions or intractable refugee situations. In the absence of SGBV, these take the form of "norm changing pedagogies" that target the "backward culture" at the root of Gazans' already predetermined gender violence problem. Hammami centers her analysis on local mediators, Palestinian women activists, and NGO frontline workers caught between the coercive logics of GBVAW "best practice frameworks" and the need to find relevant solutions for victims and women more generally in a context where funding for humanitarian interventions circulates within a political economy of mass immiseration. Like elsewhere, this creates its own coercive dependency and perverse incentive structures. Humanitarian GB-

VAW in Gaza emerges in her analysis as a self-referential operation of power: a closed circle of recurrently fabricated expert "evidence" of Gaza's epidemic level of domestic violence, justifying the need for ever more "awareness raising" workshops and public antiviolence campaigns that dispense with the messy and expensive work of providing practical solutions to the problems voiced by Gazan women or by the local frontline women's organizations that attempt to meet them. The chapter brings back into the frame what GBVAW in Gaza evicts: the collusion of the humanitarian apparatus with the geopolitical rationales of Israeli violence, as well as a counterworld of more relevant home-grown Gazan responses to gender violence, including those offered by women activists of the Hamas governing authority.

Shakhsari focuses on GBVAW within "sexual humanitarianism" (Mai 2014): the recent and uneven recognition of nonnormative sexuality and gender identity as criteria for asylum within the global refugee regime. Centering the experiences of Iranian queer and trans asylum seekers trapped in the refugee borderland of Turkey, Shakhsari shows how they attempt to navigate through the trap laid by the rigid norms and procedures that adjudicate both refugee and LGBTI+ recognition and eligibility for rights of asylum or citizenship. As much of the literature on asylum for LGBTI+ individuals within the logics of sexual humanitarianism makes clear, discursive humanitarian technologies impose a rigid script of nonconforming gender and sexual identity based on hegemonic Eurocentric models to which the asylum seeker is forced to conform (Fassin and Salcedo 2015; Giametta 2016; Miller 2004; Sabsay 2013). These homonormative (Duggan 2002) and homonationalist (Puar 2007) scripts not only serve to reproduce the sanctification of the Western sexual rights regime, including its "sexual democracy" (Fassin 2010), but as Shakhsari's chapter shows, are usually in conflict with the lived realities and lifeworlds of asylum seekers made subject to its logics.

In the case of Iranian trans and queer asylum seekers, GBVAW operating through sexual humanitarianism identifies vulnerability to gender confirming surgeries by the Iranian state as the singular category of violence through which they might be recognized as worthy of asylum. Shakhsari underlines how this exclusive focus on what is designated "state-perpetrated torture" obscures more immediate forms of violence, as well as the complicity of the international refugee regime in sustaining them. In the case of Iranian asylum seekers this includes the devastating effects of Western sanctions on Iran that generated the need to seek asylum in the first place. It also erases messy, counterfactual understandings: reducing the complex history of Iranian state policies toward LGBTI+ identities to the geopolitically convenient Orientalist trope of violent homophobia.

Shakhsari also underlines the much greater coercive power exacted by the frames of care offered by GBVAW as sexual humanitarianism. As per Ticktin's (2016) argument, the contemporary asylum regime is predicated on exclusion and suspicion; it must separate out the exceptional, innocent, deserving "real refugee" from the mass of undeserving migrants. Thus, overcoming suspicion of LGBTI+ asylum seekers and proving oneself deserving of care go far beyond a performance of innocence and "victimcy"; it includes proving the "truth" of one's gender or sexual identity when queer and trans bodies are already assumed to harbor deception.

As an activist on behalf of Iranian LGBTI+ asylum seekers, Shakhsari confronts the acute dilemmas that normative inclusion into the refugee asylum regime creates. What can activists do when the only mechanism to save precarious lives involves actively mobilizing civilizational tropes around race, culture, and sexuality that the system demands? Does accepting the logic of saving individual "exemplary victims" make activists complicit in the asylum regime's fundamental work of evicting the mass of refugees from humanity?

Variations on these dilemmas are voiced across the critical ethnographies of GBVAW in humanitarianism already touched upon earlier. What is striking is that despite laying bare the glaring gaps, erasures, and forms of bodily, social, and political harm produced by these ruling frames and their technologies, those who present these critiques regularly offer a caveat. They insist that their intention is not to bring about the end of donor interventions or activisms, no matter how compromised, mismatched, or irrelevant to needs, because without them actual victims would be left with nothing. This represents a tragic recognition by critical feminist and queer scholars and activists that within the contemporary landscape of global geopolitics and its civilizational rhetorics, it is only these flawed and sometimes injurious forms of humanitarian care that are on offer. We address these dilemmas and search for alternatives to this tragic stance in the conclusion.

PART IV: MEDIA FRAMES

Deepa Kumar's *Islamophobia and the Politics of Empire: 20 Years after 9/11* considers the media as a key node in what she analyzes as the matrix of anti-Muslim racism. The dominant spheres in the matrix are the security apparatus, politicians, think tanks, and academia, and she notes the flows between them, in ways that our work on the circuits of power to which GBVAW attaches notes. However, the media are crucial in shaping public understandings. If Grewal's chapter on India reveals the power of media to name, hide, expose, and incite, Kumar is sensitive to the internal differentiations within the institutionalized fields of media, roughly characterizing the media's role and connections to the other spheres of power, at least for the US and Britain in terms of mainstream, progressive, and right-wing media.

The media are indeed crucial to the framing of problems and solutions in relation to gender violence as well, and the chapters in this final part are all by practicing journalists who alert us to the way coverage of gender violence, at least in the US and Britain, are tied to the logics of securitization, state power, and the rescue industries of development and humanitarianism we examine in this book. The silencing of critical questions about the deployment of the GBVAW common sense is evident in Rafia Zakaria's attempt to investigate a legal case in Michigan that coincided with the introduction of national programs directed at women immigrants that involved surveillance and profiling at national airports in the name of protecting them from female genital cutting. This is an iconic form of GBV that links culture and religion and that, like the "honor crime" that Volpp analyzes in her chapter on the "Muslim Ban," has been made a prominent cause by the Ayaan Hirsi Ali Foundation in particular, as a good example of the matrix of think tanks, politicians, and right-wing media that Kumar exposed as producing the racialization of Muslims that stokes Islamophobia. She shows how certain questions about the political mobilization for anti-immigrant discourse and policies of exclusion in the United States and Europe are untouchable. No scrutiny is allowed of the policing and surveillance of Black and brown women's bodies through "public health" measures like Operation Limelight at British (see Khoja-Moolji 2020) and American airports.

Writing against the limited framing devices imposed on reporters working for Western media who cover gender violence in "other" places like Pakistan or Iraq, or even in racial minority communities in the UK, British journalist Samira Shackle reveals the ways stereotyping and homogenization in coverage of violence against Muslim women remove women's agency and blame culture and religion. Reflecting on her experiences as a journalist running up against editors who reframe her stories or working with colleagues in the field as they try to research stories such as those of the Yazidi women and girl survivors of ISIS with troubling ethical practices, Shackle suggests guidelines for the important work of reporting on gender violence that might help break the narrative frames and lessen the complicity of media in those matrices of power that reinforce Islamophobia, xenophobia, and securitization. Responsible reporters should not shy away from reporting on gendered violence, even when it risks racializing communities, as so much reporting in Europe and the United States does. Besides listening to the women and foregrounding their agency, they should place incidents within their wider political contexts and histories, including the ways that states fail their citizens. These are precisely what our scholarly essays in this volume do.

Humanitarian emergencies and the sexual violence of conflict situations are key topics of news reporting, as they are the sites of feminist GBVAW interventions, whether legal as Engle (2020) documents or humanitarian, as in the case of Gaza analyzed by Hammami in this book. Nina Berman, a photojournalist who has long worked in the context of the Balkans that catalyzed the establishment of the International Criminal Tribunal for the Former Yugoslavia in 1993 that prosecuted wartime sexual violence, writes about the ethics of journalistic practices and representations of sexual violence. She reveals the marked differences between what is allowed and encouraged in the American and European media in depicting dark-skinned "victims" in Africa—Congo, Sudan, Rwanda—and what is conventional for the US context, whether in reports on campus rape or coverage of American soldiers' acts during the Vietnam War.

Feminism has succeeded in recent decades in making sexual violence a serious subject for reporters, not just a women's side issue. But the question is *how* this subject is treated, especially through photographic essays. Using examples such as the celebrated *New York Times* photo feature on the released Chibok girls from Boko Haram in Nigeria, the *Time* magazine cover with an anonymous naked pregnant rape victim now living in Uganda, who, like many of the Chibok girls, had become the subject of Christian humanitarian care, and the invasive and prize-winning *Newsweek* photography project on the children of rape in Rwanda, Berman shows how the impulse to bestow dignity and humanity is undermined by the ethical failures to protect identities, the systematic racial stereotyping, and the depoliticization of these dressed-up or dressed-down victims. Instead of instigating investigations of accountability and justice, they are rendered objects of benevolent humanitarian saving. In this, the mainstream media becomes another circuit in which

GBVAW operates, undermining its resistance to the dominant political forces that contribute to the vilification of Muslim and dark men that continues to justify military interventions and the "War on Terror."

FEMINIST CONUNDRUMS: HOBSON'S CHOICE OR FAUST'S BARGAIN?

The reasons for the "success," productivity, visibility, and wide public embrace in popular culture and international policy of the GBVAW agenda are complex and, as this book argues, troubling. There is plenty of criticism from within about the agenda's failure to deliver an end to gender violence, despite high-profile global rituals such as UN Women's annual "16 Days of Activism Against Gender-Based Violence" and not insignificant funding for feminist forums, policy initiatives, and organizations, all the way from local grassroots women's organizations in Kenya and Pakistan up to the Global Counter-Terrorism Forum and UN Security Council. There is no question that a diverse set of feminist activists have worked hard over decades and in good faith for the goals of addressing and condemning gendered violence.

Much of the praxis-focused feminist literature bemoans the fact that these efforts have not had the intended or desired impacts, noting how alliances with the law, security, and international institutions have neither created the infrastructures to adequately protect or support victims nor to bring perpetrators to justice. The mainstreaming of GBVAW has been especially disappointing to those who lament the watering down of feminist aspirations and emancipatory visions as compromises that had to be made to gain traction for their struggle to confront the scourge of gendered violence, from domestic abuse to sexual violence in war. In her ambivalent analysis of the emergence of Governance Feminism (defined as the varieties of feminism and feminists who have entered into or worked with institutions of power— national or international) Halley has identified what she calls the "five c's" that alignments with power risk or entail: collaboration, compromise, collusion, complicity, and cooptation (Halley 2018, xiii). Some who charge that the feminist agenda was hijacked or puzzle over the existence of strange bedfellows prefer Nancy Fraser's (2009) observation that feminism's "uncanny doubles" have come to roam the halls of institutional power (e.g., Engle, Nesiah, and Otto 2022). Given this disappointing record, continuing arguments for engaging with GBVAWs' institutional circuits tend to render them as a feminist Hobson's choice. Take for instance, Fionnuala Ní Aoláin, currently the first feminist appointed Special Rapporteur on the Promotion and Protection of Human Rights and Freedoms While Countering Terrorism.[15] She outlines the conundrum that she, like others, faces because of this engagement with security regimes and the WPS agenda:

> While accepting the real harm caused by terrorism and counterterrorism for women in many parts of the world, it is important nevertheless to give serious consideration to the potential negative effect on the WPS agenda of its becoming harnessed to the pursuit of broader military and ideological goals. I accept that the decision whether to be within or without the terrorism and counterterrorism sphere is a form of Hobson's choice for feminist activists. The "exile of inclusion" [Otto 2009] forces compromise, requires concessions and entails forgoing the option of objection to many of the basic premises of the collective security system. To remain outside is to forfeit the possibility of exercising any influence on the decisions and actions that affect the lives of millions of women and girls across the globe living through situations of extremity and violence. (2016, 278)

Posing it as a mutually exclusive choice between influencing or forfeiting the possibility of influencing "decisions and actions" with ramifications for women and girls globally is a longstanding argument used by feminists who have gone for inclusion.[16] *The Cunning of Gender Violence* regards the conundrum as more of a Faustian bargain than Hobson's choice. As the studies in this volume suggest, another dimension of the cunning of GBVAW lies precisely in presenting feminists with a false choice between inclusion for influence or exclusion as an "inability to act." This framing legitimates the simplified categories and institutional embedding of GBVAW as the only way to address gender violence. In turn, this begs the question: What type of feminist influence and feminist action does inclusion produce?

A dispiriting assessment by intelligent and engaged activists in a report by the International Crisis Group marking the twentieth anniversary of the WPS resolution exemplifies the problem. The report, entitled "A Course Correction for the UN Women, Peace and Security Agenda," highlights the agenda's "too few and too modest gains" as well as the real harms it creates for women through aligning their needs with state security priorities such as countering terrorism. Yet instead of presenting a robust challenge to the logics of securitization, militarization, and humanitarian rescue, the report concludes with the ongoing common sense; it recommends even more inclusion of "civil society units within both the UN Counter-Terrorism Executive Directorate and the UN Office of Counter Terrorism" to give "women activists a platform to relay concerns" and assure that gender considerations run through evolving security policies (International Crisis Group 2020, 18).

These pleas for inclusion and the promotion of feminist advocacy for more substantial mainstreaming of gender into the workings of hegemonic power politics are part of the problem, likely doing "more harm than good," as David Kennedy (2002) earlier charged human rights work. Inadequate attention to gender or the absence of women from what these groups characterize as the masculine world of security and state power is a minor problem compared to what our chapters reveal about the effects of GBVAW's imbrication with major circuits of power in undermining feminists' capacity to identify and call out the specific modes and causes of so many forms of violence that poison lives and suppress possibilities.

Missing from the calculations of "engagement versus forfeiting influence" is a reading of the nature of power in the rationales wielded by these hegemonic institutions as well as a critical accounting of the politics of feminist representation on which "inclusion" is based. As Dianne Otto points out in relation to the WPS agenda, "[I]t is puzzling that there has been so little feminist debate about the wisdom of engagement with the patently undemocratic and secretive Security Council, the seat of power of the world's superpower(s), whose permanent members are also the world's largest arms dealers" (2014, 160). She adds: "Abandoned are feminist commitments to democratic and transparent decision-making, to bottom-up rather than top-down politics, to cooperation rather than power politics, to justice as well as order, and to critiques of imperial, military and unaccountable power" (2014, 163).

But perhaps another dimension of the cunning of GBVAW is that not all of the institutional circuits of global governance that carry it forward appear to be such patent sites of militarized superpower interest as the Security Council. This certainly applies to the variegated governmental assemblage we call the United Nations with its myriad global conferences and forums, infinite number of expert meetings, and proliferating agencies covering everything from Indigenous rights and arms control to human rights and climate change. The hard power of security, militarism, and economic neoliberalism are all enmeshed with these openings for "civil society" to participate in building a better world. Arguably, at a founding moment of GBVAW's entrance into global governance—the 1995 Beijing World Conference on Women—these "soft" openings were accessed productively by a diverse range of women's movements answerable to their organized constituencies across the global south and north.[17] At the very least, transnational feminist activists of that era such as Peggy Antrobus recognized that changing the status quo inside these institutions depended on the pressure of activists and social movements from outside of them (Antrobus 2005).

But in the subsequent post–Cold War era, as many of the chapters here reveal, the nature of hard (and soft) power that the United Nations wields across the globe dramatically changed. So did the nature of "civil society" forums and the representational politics of those who attend them. In a recent review of the impact of Beijing twenty-five years on, the authors note the loss of the enabling role that UN global forums had played in the 1980s and 1990s for women activists and movements from the south and north (Sandler and Goetz 2020). They argue, however, that this is compensated for by the emergence of independent initiatives, citing the largest contemporary global women's rights conferences that are convened by the US-based NGO called "Women Deliver." Described as the world's highest profile women's rights organization, it is led by a CEO; has myriad corporate sponsors; and provides consultation to the G-7, international agencies, and even the private sector as it advances "the investment case for gender equality."[18] In the contemporary institutional circuits of GBVAW, this narrowly framed corporatized platform is what now stands in for any notion of deliberative politics exercised by transnational women's activists. This should at the very least raise the critical question of who is included in the institutional processes of "inclusion" and what, if any, constituencies they represent.

Moreover, driven by the urgency to address the horrors of sexual violence in war and conflict, feminists may have seized on the power of international institutions to bring public attention to human rights violations around gender. But in the process, as Engle (2020, 78) notes, feminists "backgrounded or suppressed commitments to more nuanced conceptions of ethnicity, culture, sexuality, and women's agency." Nicola Pratt put it more bluntly. Pratt argues that the WPS agenda "re-sexed race," reproducing "the racialized–sexualized and gendered hierarchies of colonialism" (2013, 776–77). The racial-sexual hierarchies are even more apparent in security discourses and the "War on Terror," which leads Pratt (2013, 780) to characterize the WPS 1325 resolution as an "imperialist feminist project (Orford 2003) rather than a transnational feminist project from below (Al-Ali and Pratt 2009, 4–8)." Indeed, through our case studies, we can see the consistent ways that the GBVAW discourse, supported by social and mass media, appears to have made its gains on the backs of racialized others, whether as individuals, groups, or nation-states. This cannot be disavowed as "unfortunate baggage" that has hijacked a good project: rather we see GBVAW carried forward on the global politics of Islamophobia and racialization.

Here the cunning lies in how it confers generic identities on women and sexual minorities or other vulnerable groups to which a set of abstract rights and values can be attached, values that consolidate a colonial feminist imaginary and politics of uniting around these generic categories of victims in need of being freed from the prison houses of their cultures, religions, and patriarchal communities. As Inderpal Grewal (1999) suggested early on, these universalisms and the imputed solidarities to which they gave rise masked and misrecognized the differential power among feminists presumably "united in global sisterhood" as well as the structure of geopolitical power in which their efforts gained traction.

What has this narrow definition and selective visibilization of what constitutes gender violence—as object of knowledge and intervention—kept out of the frame? Who is benefiting from the GBVAW apparatus and who is being harmed? Engle's astute observation of the grip that sexual violence has gained over the WPS agenda led her to conclude that "when human rights became the primary avenue for feminist interventions in the new conflicts, their focus on ending the abuse of women *in* war, rather than on ending war itself, side-lined or transformed the women's peace advocates and their aims" (2020, 124). Across the spectrum of critical studies of GBVAW projects, we see the same imperative to refrain from talking about structural factors and to focus only on the personal stories of gender violence.[19] This is one of the costs of "inclusion." When Iraqi women activists, following the US invasion of their country, spoke at a UN WPS-sponsored forum and openly voiced their concerns and priorities in terms of the destructive impacts of US imperialism and militarism as well UN sanctions, instead of sticking to the script about women as victims and peacemakers, the reaction of their feminist hosts was to figure out how to prevent such an embarrassing and destructive form of messaging from happening again (Gibbings 2011).

We also share with Halley and colleagues a concern with the distributional effects and practices of these narrow frames. Can a careful distributional analysis of the differential workings of the GBVAW apparatus in different places reveal more about who is benefiting and who pays the price for its success and uptake? Over more than two decades, it has produced ever-expanding opportunities for scholarly experts, professional consultants, development and humanitarian bureaucrats, and practitioners. It has established feminist think tanks and academic centers that offer a range of

WPS and other related university degrees enabling career paths of future GBVAW professionals. It has also produced a plethora of NGOs and networks and provided women employment in male-dominated UN peace-keeping missions. And as we show here, it also creates frames of possibility and limitation for scholars, journalists, international activists, and perhaps most significantly, for local activists. The chapters on Gaza, Bangladesh, and Iranian LGBTI+ refugees show that rather than offering "empowerment," local activists and frontline antiviolence workers often find themselves desperately trying to negotiate through the deeply constrained and irrelevant frames in order to extract some way of getting the resources to do the real work of addressing gender violence. And even this access to the deeply compromised aid GBVAW provides is premised on disguising what they are doing and obscuring what they know intimately about the complex causes of gender violence in their context. When instead they try to call out the agents of global power, neoliberal destitution, and militarized destruction as the fundamental forces of violence in their lives, their benefactors erase their voices. *The Cunning of Gender Violence* suggests that only the vicissitudes of experiences with gender violence and analysis of the workings of the GBWAW apparatus at different scales can give us answers.

In short, the cunning of GBVAW is that in its efforts to foreground forms of gender violence, it forecloses a radical questioning of the very systems that are producing the conditions for so many forms of gendered violence and harm, many of which are not even named as such. It has become a form of capital in the rise of the security state and world order, in the execution of state violence and criminal behavior toward abject or vilified "others," and in the growth of a global regime of humanitarian mitigation that serves to bandage the wounds of victims the geopolitical system itself has produced.[20] How much can the GBVAW apparatus treat other forms of slow, structural violence, including "legitimate" state violence, when its efficacy depends on its attachment to existing forms of power that are responsible for these violences?

Our sensitivity to these issues has emerged both from our theoretical orientations and our locations and commitments to the everyday lives of the subjects of violence who are the objects of these hegemonic strands of feminist antiviolence intervention. Though often lapsing into a feminist singular in our critique of GBVAW, we see feminisms as always a diverse and evolving plurality of epistemologies, locations, projects, and possibilities—and yes, sometimes dominations and enclosures. As such, we do not call for a "time out" from feminism, because this would grant the form of feminism that is at the center of our critique here the singular status that it attempts to assume. We have pointed out the danger, erasures, and colonizing moves of the versions of feminism that have a singular focus on women (whether or not in the language of gender). Though driven by concerns for those inscribed by gender, we do not presume it can be disentangled from race, class, indigeneity, and other historical and contemporary forces and markers of difference and inequality. We understand governance as both biopolitical and necropolitical (Mbembe 2019), rather than just a matter of law and policy, and thus share fundamental ground with the long traditions of feminist activism and thinking centered in the Third World/Global South that assume feminism is indivisible from broader struggles for social and economic justice, and view geopolitical inequality and power as fundamental feminist concerns. And as is obvious, given the regions where we are located or attached, we share with postcolonial, indigenous, anticolonial, and decolonial feminists elsewhere a profound awareness of the continuing power of ongoing material and discursive legacies of colonialism on the lives of women and men in our contexts.[21]

Our primary locations in scholarly rather than policy worlds, perhaps, along with our alignments with world regions that have been targeted for intense militarization, securitization, policing, surveillance, and violent management, means that "inclusion" is not part of our political sensibilities and lifeworlds. At the same time, the location of some of us within militarized "conflict zones"—contexts targeted by GBVAW and where the lines between local activists and scholars are more blurred—has meant that we have firsthand experience grappling with these interventions as they unfurl on the ground. This makes us highly attentive to the dilemmas they produce. Our contributors have listened closely to those in harm's way, looking with them at the range of violences that frame their lives. Rather than offering a singular answer to the dilemmas raised by GBVAW, we instead start by asking: How might a different politics emerge if we centered the narrative of GBVAW on the voices, experiences, and readings of gender violence from its so-called global margins? Perhaps we might be able to see that these silenced "margins" are really at the center of how feminism(s) might actually be returned to its place as a radical, expansive, and truly inclusive transformative project.

Acknowledging the genuine concerns and critical internal debates within feminist communities, the question that an intervention like ours provokes is: What alternatives could there be? How can we take gender violence seriously as real and disturbing—and abhorrent—while challenging the

GBVAW apparatus that has been developed over the past decades to address it, marked by its exclusivist foci and specific channels of operation? Can the dense networks of power be disrupted and undone as we hold firm to the ethical responsibility to respond to violence? The careful, detailed, and close studies of policies, representations, and the everyday stories of those subjected to violence in *The Cunning of Gender Violence* offer clues about how to rethink feminist projects to address gender violence so as to escape the Faustian bargain that embeddedness requires.

There are many ways we might subvert the cunning of GBVAW. A first step is to map this cunning. If securitization, state violence, corporate developmentalism, and humanitarianism are all recognized as in themselves violent, then we must attend to how they are gendered and what GBVAW does and does not do when it attaches itself to them. We do this by tracking GBVAW in the work of Executive Orders to International Criminal Court rulings to UNHCR offices to programs for Combating Extremist Ideologies. We do this by looking to the everyday experiences of the subject(s) of violence, whether lynched, searched, or threatened alongside the cultural representations and the vocabularies deployed to justify such violence. The best clues in the studies in this book come from close listening to people in specific situations, whether Pakistani social media stars like Qandeel Baluch or Iranian trans asylum seekers in Turkey, political activists imprisoned in Iran or Palestinian activists struggling to meet the needs of women in their Gazan community under siege. Their everyday stories and their analyses offer alternatives to the ossified categories and definitions of GBVAW that circulate through and across policy domains, reports, and funding proposals. Can the faces, the names, and the narrations of these individuals, in their specific locations and within the contexts of their histories and memories, form the backbone of such alternative understandings of violence?

By privileging the insights and resistances of survivors we come to appreciate their multiplex identities as women, men, youth, heterosexual and homosexual, trans and cis, refugees, migrants, lower class or ethnicized minority, Pakistani, Indian, Palestinian, Nigerian, Iranian, and immigrants. Their political histories, their current contexts, and their places in society are as crucial to their stories as their gender. Legal work, like many other kinds of interventions, risks codifying and emptying the categories of content. Vocabularies of suffering and languages from the daily lives of those involved push against this standardization. Establishing bonds with the subjects of violence does not privatize individual ordeals or subsume them under wider stories of political economy or geopolitical power; it keeps the search open for feminist language and praxis against gender violence based in the ethics of what bell hooks and Amalia Mesa-Bains (2018) call "the homegrown."

Untangling the multiple entwined and layered forms of violence that devastate the lives—physical, social, and psychic—of so many around the world is a first step to resisting the selectivity of the violences that are made visible, the willed blindness to "collateral" harms, and the suspension of judgment about the complex political interests at stake in the worlds we inhabit. We fail the subjects we care most about if we let antiviolence feminist projects get caught up in and then inadvertently shore up apparatuses of rule that are inimical to the political convictions and wider visions of justice that feminisms, at their best, seek to embody.

NOTES

1 Calls for US troops to stay in order to protect gains made for Afghan women were now pitted against the stark history of twenty years of unending violence and insecurity and an impending future looking similar to what all Afghans faced at the outset of the US invasion.

2 The analysis offered here draws on the diverse range of critical feminist work that continues to grow on specific domains of GBVAW's operations, be it from international law and feminist legal theory (Halley 2006; Halley 2018; Halley et al. 2019; Engle 2020; Otto 2010, 2014; Nesiah 1996, 2006, 2011, 2012; Razack 2004); feminist international relations (Jabri 2004; Zalewski and Runyon 2013; Eriksson Baaz and Stern 2013) and security studies (Carpenter 2006; Meger 2016; Pratt and Richter-Devoe 2013; Shepherd 2008; Zarkov 2018, 2020); postcolonial feminism (Grewal 2005; Chowdhury 2011); critical humanitarian studies (Ticktin 2011); the emerging school of Queer IR (Puar 2007; Luibhéid 2018); as well as studies in anthropology (Merry 2006; Hemment 2004).

3 This was achieved at the International Criminal Court and the International Criminal Tribunals for the Former Yugoslavia and subsequently for Rwanda.

4 It comes as no surprise that fifteen years on from the original achievement of UNSC 1325, marking the UN Security Council's initial recognition of women's vulnerability to violence in war, UNSC 2242 explicitly includes the language of "preventing violent extremism" (PVE) within the purview of its ongoing Women Peace and Security mandate.

5 A relationship subsequently consecrated in 2010 by then US Secretary of State, Hillary Clinton, and colloquially known as the "Hillary Doctrine." See Hudson and Leidl 2017.

6 For more on the costs of the post-9/11 wars in Afghanistan and Iraq, see Brown University's "Costs of War project" (https://watson.brown.edu/costsofwar/).

7   Note the similarity to the language of DDR (disarmament, demobilization, and reintegration of ex-combatants) well known in postconflict state and peacebuilding operations.
8   Katie Reilly noted this in a *Time* magazine article from January 27, 2017: "President Trump Says He Will Prioritize Persecuted Christians in Refugee Policy."
9   Critical legal scholars and criminologists have struggled to define the concept of "state crime" and to draw its boundaries. The difficulty of defining state crime is related to the way its practices appear normal and may even be legal. Most now accept this delineation: "[G]overnmental or state crimes are illegal, socially injurious, or unjust acts which are committed for the benefit of a state or its agencies, and not for the personal gain of some individual agent of the state" (Kauzlarich, Matthews, and Miller 2001, 175). State crimes thus can include human rights violations such as genocide, war crimes and torture, police violence, and corruption in the control by elite groups of national natural resources. Green and Ward (2000) go further to include any state actions that violate citizens' human rights, whether they are deliberate or through failure to protect individuals and groups. Others emphasize the structural foundations of liberty and rights that provide humans with basic opportunities and conditions for well-being; they would brand as criminal the failures of states to provide food, shelter, or medical services.
10 For an example in Israel, see Shalhoub-Kevorkian and David (2015).
11 For the Israeli context, see Mazali (2016).
12 For exceptions, see Siddiqi (2015), Roy (2017), and Kowalski (2018).
13 The scholarship on SGBV has been criticized for fetishizing sexual violence (Boesten and Henry 2018; Meger 2016) and producing a "sexual violence industry" (Douma and Hillhorst 2017). Sexual violence in conflict emerges as a particularly potent category of human suffering put to use in the affective politics of mobilizing compassion for distant others—what Didier Fassin (2011) has termed *humanitarian reason*. The power to rally humanitarian sentiment is inseparable from representations of sexual violence that rest on and reproduce colonial tropes around race, sexuality, and gender. Sexual violence becomes a marker of racialized "other" masculinities rather than a general marker of militarized masculinities in war (Boesten 2015; Eriksson Baaz and Stern 2013; Hilhorst and Jansen 2012; Mertens and Myrttinen 2019; Mertens and Pardy 2016). Wars are de-historicized and de-contextualized so that they can be reduced to savage conflicts carried out by backward cultures (Abramowitz and Moran 2012; Autesserre 2012; Eriksson Baaz and Stern 2013; Zarkov 2018, 2020). Particularly through the discourse of "rape as a weapon of war," sexual violence marks a line between just civilized wars and unjust savage conflicts, inviting humanitarian intervention in the latter where all local men are figured as armed perpetrators and all local women civilian victims (Engle 2020; Hilhorst, Porter and Gordon 2017; Mertens and Pardy 2016). This powerknowledge formation evicts all other types and structures of violence (and their

14. genealogies and histories) as well as other victims (e.g., men) from humanitarian concern.
14. SGBV interventions hold a near monopoly on aid: in one case, it garnered twice the amount of funding available to cover the basic needs of 1.4 million Congolese IDPs (Heaton 2014). In many contexts, the only medical care available to entire populations is devoted to sexual violence (D'Errico et al. 2013; Autesserre 2012), a situation reflected in the Nobel Prize award to Dr. Mukwege.
15. She reports to UN Human Rights Council on the effects of counterterrorism regulations on the rights of women, girls, and family. See Ní Aoláin's 2020 report: https://www.ohchr.org/EN/Issues/Terrorism/Pages/Annual.aspx.
16. Back in 2003, Jacqui True, a leading academic in WPS circles, framed the dilemma in similar terms saying that it was "not how feminist scholars and activists can avoid cooptation by powerful institutions, but whether we can afford not to engage with such institutions, when the application of gender analysis in their policymaking is clearly having political effects beyond academic and feminist communities" (True 2003, 368).
17. For a counter view, see Spivak (1996).
18. In 2020 former and current staff publicly challenged the organization for its toxic environment of structural racism and discrimination against Black, Indigenous, and people of color, and LGBTQA+ people, as reported by Talha Burki in her 2020 report published in *The Lancet*, "Report Released on Women Deliver Allegations," available at https://www.thelancet.com/journals/lancet/article/PIIS0140-6736(20)32330-8/fulltext.
19. In the Sangtin Writers Collective and Richa Nagar's *Playing with Fire* (2006) a collective autobiographical project about experiences with gender violence of a group of grassroots activists in India, the consequences of challenging the social hierarchies within a large national NGO and refusing the demands for public personal confession that are the bread and butter of donor support were astonishingly punitive. In a settler colonial situation such as that of Palestinian Bedouin women in the Naqab, the cunning of gender violence lies in turning the source of their dispossession and displacement into the primary and benevolent referent for saving them from pain. Using VAW discourses and Resolution 1325 forced women to both individualize and ahistoricize their pain. Only stories of divorces, imposed marriages, and other family problems could be told, ignoring what the women all saw as other dimensions of their suffering (Shalhoub-Kevorkian et al. 2014.)
20. This is similar to what Meister (2010) argues for the perpetrators who now promote themselves as the champions of human rights.
21. We do not invoke the concept of transnational feminism readily because despite agreeing with much of Chandra Mohanty's initial definition, the term has become vexed by its politically polyvalent use. For a critique on transnational feminism, see Conway (2017).

REFERENCES

Abramowitz, Sharon, and Mary H. Moran. 2012. "International Human Rights, Gender-Based Violence, and Local Discourses of Abuse in Postconflict Liberia: A Problem of 'Culture'?" *African Studies Review* 55, no. 2: 119–46. https://doi.org/10.1353/arw.2012.0037.

Abu-Lughod, Lila. 2002. "Do Muslim Women Really Need Saving? Reflections on Cultural Relativism and Its Others." *American Anthropologist* 104, no. 3: 783–90. https://www.jstor.org/stable/3567256.

Al-Ali, Nadje, and Nicola Pratt. 2009. *What Kind of Liberation? Women and the Occupation of Iraq*. Berkeley: University of California Press.

Al-Bulushi, Samar. 2018. "Twenty Years On: The War on Terror in East Africa." *Items: Insights from the Social Sciences*, August 7. https://items.ssrc.org/from-our-fellows/twenty-years-on-the-war-on-terror-in-east-africa/.

Alcade, Cristina. 2011. "Institutional Resources (Un)Available: The Effects of Police Attitudes and Actions on Battered Women in Peru." In *Anthropology at the Front Lines of Gender-Based Violence*, edited by Jennifer Wies and Hilary Haldane, 91–106. Nashville: Vanderbilt University Press.

Ali, Nosheen, Mona Bhan, Sahana Ghosh, Hafsa Kanjwal, Zunaira Komal, Deepti Misri, Shruti Mukherjee, Nishant Upadhyay, Saiba Varma, and Ather Zia. 2019. "Geographies of Occupation in South Asia." *Feminist Studies* 45, nos. 2–3: 574–80.

Antrobus, Peggy. 2005. "Critiquing the MDGs from a Caribbean Perspective." *Gender and Development* 13, no. 1: 94–104. https://doi.org/10.1080/13552070512331332280.

Archambault, Caroline. 2011. "Ethnographic Empathy and the Social Context of Rights: 'Rescuing' Maasai Girls from Early Marriage." *American Anthropologist* 113, no. 4: 632–43. https://doi.org/10.1111/j.1548-1433.2011.01375.x.

Autesserre, Séverine. 2012. "Dangerous Tales: Dominant Narratives on the Congo and their Unintended Consequences." *African Affairs* 111, no. 443: 202–22. https://doi.org/10.1093/afraf/adr080.

Barnett, Michael. 2005. "Humanitarianism Transformed." *Perspectives on Politics* 3, no. 4: 723–40. https://doi.org/10.1017/S1537592705050401.

Barnett, Michael. 2010."Humanitarianism, Paternalism, and the UNHCR." In *Refugees in International Relations*, edited by Alexander Betts and Gill Loescher, 105–32. Oxford: Oxford University Press.

Bernstein, Elizabeth. 2019. *Brokered Subjects: Sex, Trafficking, and the Politics of Freedom*. Chicago: University of Chicago Press.

Bhan, Mona. 2014. *Counterinsurgency, Democracy, and the Politics of Identity in India: From Warfare to Welfare?* New York: Routledge.

Biersack, Aletta, Margaret Jolly, and Martha Macintyre, eds. 2016. *Gender Violence & Human Rights: Seeking Justice in Fiji, Papua New Guinea & Vanuatu*. Canberra: The Australian National University Press.

Boesten, Jelke. 2015. On Ending Sexual Violence, or Civilising War. *International Development Institute Working Paper* 2015, no. 2: 1–18. https://doi.org/10.13140/RG.2.1.3544.6645.

Boesten, Jelke, and Marsha Henry. 2018. "Between Fatigue and Silence: The Challenges of Conducting Research on Sexual Violence in Conflict." *Social Politics: International Studies in Gender, State & Society* 25, no. 4: 568–88. https://doi.org/10.1093/sp/jxy027.

Brown University. 2022. "Costs of War Project." Accessed October 9, 2021. https://watson.brown.edu/costsofwar/.

Caputi, Jane. 1993. *Gossips, Gorgons and Crones: The Fates of the Earth*. Santa Fe, NM: Bear Publishing.

Carpenter, R. Charli. 2006. *"Innocent Women and Children": Gender, Norms, and the Protection of Civilians*. Farnham, UK: Ashgate Publishing.

Chambliss, William J. 1989. "State-Organized Crime." *Criminology* 27, no. 2: 183–208. https://doi.org/10.1111/j.1745-9125.1989.tb01028.x.

Chowdhury, Elora H. 2011. *Transnationalism Reversed: Women Organizing against Gendered Violence in Bangladesh*. Albany: State University of New York Press.

Clarke, Kamari Maxine. 2019. *Affective Justice: The International Criminal Court and the Pan-Africanist Pushback*. Durham, NC: Duke University Press.

Cohen, Stanley. 2001. *States of Denial: Knowing about Atrocities and Suffering*. Cambridge: Polity Press.

Cohn, Carol. 2008. "Mainstreaming Gender in UN Security Policy: A Path to Political Transformation? In *Global Governance: Feminist Perspectives*, edited by Shirin M. Rai and Georgina Waylen, 185–206. New York: Palgrave Macmillan.

Conway, Janet M. 2017. "Troubling Transnational Feminism(s): Theorising Activist Praxis." *Feminist Theory* 18, no. 2: 205–27. https://doi.org/10.1177/1464700117700536.

D'Errico, Nicole, Tshibangu Kalala, Louise Nzigire, Felicien Maisha, and Luc Kalisya. 2013. "'You Say Rape, I Say Hospitals. But Whose Voice Is Louder?' Health, Aid and Decision-Making in the Democratic Republic of Congo." *Review of African Political Economy* 40, no. 135: 51–66. https://doi.org/10.1080/03056244.2012.761962.

Dolan, Chris. 2015. "Letting Go of the Gender Binary: Charting New Pathways for Humanitarian Interventions on Gender-based Violence." *International Review of the Red Cross* 96, no. 894: 485–501.

Douma, Nynke, and Dorothea Hilhorst. 2017. "Beyond the Hype? The Response to Sexual Violence in the Democratic Republic of the Congo in 2011 and 2014." *Disasters* 42, no. S1: 79–98. https://doi.org/10.1111/disa.12270.

Duffield, Mark. 2001. *Global Governance and the New Wars: The Merging of Development and Security*. New York: Zed Press.

Duggan, Lisa. 2002. "The New Homonormativity: The Sexual Politics of Neoliberalism." In *Materializing Democracy: Toward a Revitalized Cultural Politics*, edited by Russ Castronovo and Dana D. Nelson, 175–94. Durham, NC: Duke University Press.

Duqqah, Walid. 2010. *"Searing the Consciousness." Sahr al-wa'y: aw fi jadat ta'rif al-ta'dhib* [Searing the Consciousness: Towards Defining Torture]. Beirut: al-Dar al-'Arabiya li al-'Ulum, Nashirun.

Engle, Karen. 2019. "Feminist Governance and International Law: From Liberal to Carceral Feminism." In *Governance Feminism: Notes from the Field*, edited by Janet Halley, Prabha Kotiswaran, Rachel Rebouché, and Hila Shamir, 3–30. Minneapolis: University of Minnesota Press.

Engle, Karen. 2020. *In the Grip of Sexual Violence in Conflict: Feminist Interventions in International Law*. Stanford, CA: Stanford University Press.

Engle, Karen, Vasuki Nesiah, and Dianne L. Otto. 2022. "Feminist Approaches to International Law." In *International Legal Theory: Foundations and Frontiers*, edited by Jeffrey Dunoff and Mark Pollack, 174–96. Cambridge: Cambridge University Press. https://doi.org/10.1017/9781108551878.008.

Eriksson Baaz, Maria, and Maria Stern. 2013. *Sexual Violence as a Weapon of War? Perceptions, Prescriptions, Problems in the Congo and Beyond*. London: Zed Books.

Fábián, Katalin. 2010. *Domestic Violence in Postcommunist States: Local Activism, National Policies, and Global Forces*. Bloomington: Indiana University Press.

Fassin, Didier. 2007. "Humanitarianism as a Politics of Life." *Public Culture* 19, no. 3: 499–520. https://doi.org/10.1215/08992363-2007-007.

Fassin, Didier. 2011. *Humanitarian Reason: A Moral History of the Present*. Berkeley: University of California Press.

Fassin, Eric. 2010. "National Identities and Transnational Intimacies: Sexual Democracy and the Politics of Immigration in Europe." *Public Culture* 22, no. 3: 507–29. https://doi.org/10.1215/08992363-2010-007.

Fassin, Eric, and Manuela Salcedo. 2015. "Becoming Gay? Immigration Policies and the Truth of Sexual Identity." *Archives of Sexual Behavior* 44: 1117–25. https://doi.org/10.1007/s10508-015-0551-z.

Ford, Liz. 2019. "UN waters down rape resolution to appease US's hardline abortion stance." *The Guardian*, April 23, 2019. https://www.theguardian.com/global-development/2019/apr/23/un-resolution-passes-trump-us-veto-threat-abortion-language-removed.

Fraser, Nancy. 2009. "Feminism, Capitalism and the Cunning of History." *New Left Review* 56 (March/April): 97–117. https://newleftreview.org/issues/ii56/articles/nancy-fraser-feminism-capitalism-and-the-cunning-of-history.

Giametta, Calogero. 2016. "Narrativizing One's Sexuality/Gender: Neoliberal Humanitarianism and the Right of Asylum." In *Sexuality, Citizenship, and Belonging: Transnational, and Intersectional Perspectives*, edited by Francesca Stella, Yvette Taylor, Tracey Reynolds, and Antoine Rogers, 55–72. New York: Routledge.

Gibbings, Sheri Lynn. 2011. "No Angry Women at the United Nations: Political Dreams and the Cultural Politics of United Nations Security Council Resolution 1325." *International Feminist Journal of Politics* 13, no. 4: 522–38. https://doi.org/10.1080/14616742.2011.611660.

Goldfarb, Sally, and Julie Goldscheid. 2016. "International Human Rights Law on Violence Against Women and Children and Its Impact on Domestic Law and Action." In *Women and Children as Victims and Offenders: Background, Prevention, Reintegration. Suggestions for Succeeding Generations* (Vol. 1), edited by Helmut Kury, Sławomir Redo, and Evelyn Shea, 3–46. Switzerland: Springer International.

Grabska, Katarzyna. 2011. "Constructing 'Modern Gendered Civilised' Women and Men: Gender-Mainstreaming in Refugee Camps." *Gender and Development* 19, no. 1: 81–93. https://doi.org/10.1080/13552074.2011.554026.

Green, Penny, and Tony Ward. 2000. "State Crime, Human Rights, and the Limits of Criminology." *Social Justice* 27, no. 1: 101–15. https://www.jstor.org/stable/29767193.

Green, Penny, and Tony Ward. 2009. "The Transformation of Violence in Iraq." *British Journal of Criminology* 49, no. 5: 609–27. https://doi.org/10.1093/bjc/azp022.

Grewal, Inderpal. 1999. "Women's Rights as Human Rights: Feminist Practices, Global Feminist, and Human Rights Regimes in Transnationality." *Citizenship Studies* 3, no. 3: 337–54. https://doi.org/10.1080/13621029908420719.

Grewal, Inderpal. 2005. *Transnational America: Feminisms, Diasporas, Neoliberalisms.* Durham, NC: Duke University Press.

Halley, Janet. 2006. *Split Decisions: How and Why to Take a Break from Feminism.* Princeton, NJ: Princeton University Press.

Halley, Janet. 2018. "Preface: Introducing Governance Feminism." In *Governance Feminism: An Introduction,* by Janet Halley, Prahbha Kotiswaran, Rachel Rebouché, and Hila Shamir, ix–xx. Minneapolis: University of Minnesota Press.

Halley, Janet, Prahbha Kotiswaran, Rachel Rebouché, and Hila Shamir, eds. 2018. *Governance Feminism: An Introduction.* Minneapolis: University of Minnesota Press.

Halley, Janet, Prahbha Kotiswaran, Rachel Rebouché, and Hila Shamir, eds. 2019. *Governance Feminism: Notes from the Field.* Minneapolis: University of Minnesota Press.

Harrington, Carol. 2011. "Resolution 1325 and Post–Cold War Feminist Politics." *International Feminist Journal of Politics* 13, no. 4: 557–75. https://doi.org/10.1080/14616742.2011.611662.

Hartman, Saidiya V. 1997. *Scenes of Subjection: Terror, Slavery, and Self-Making in Nineteenth-Century America.* Oxford: Oxford University Press.

Hartman, Saidiya V. 2019. *Wayward Lives, Beautiful Experiments: Intimate Histories of Riotous Black Girls, Troublesome Women, and Queer Radicals.* New York: Norton and Company.

Heaton, Laura. 2014. "The Risks of Instrumentalizing the Narrative on Sexual Violence in the DRC: Neglected Needs and Unintended Consequences. *International Review of the Red Cross* 96, no. 894: 625–39. https://doi.org/10.1017/S1816383115000132.

Hemment, Julie. 2004. "Global Civil Society and the Local Costs of Belonging: Defining Violence against Women in Russia." *Signs: Journal of Women in Culture and Society* 29, no. 3: 816–40. https://doi.org/10.1086/381104.

Hengeveld, Maria. 2016. "Girl Branded: Nike, the UN and the Construction of the Entrepreneurial Adolescent Girl Subject." *Rapoport Center Human Rights Working Paper Series* 3. Austin: The Bernard and Audre Rapoport Center for Human Rights and Justice at the University of Texas School of Law.

Hilhorst, Dorothea, and Bram J. Jansen. 2012. "Constructing Rights and Wrongs in Humanitarian Action: Contributions from a Sociology of Praxis." *Sociology* 46, no. 5: 891–905. https://doi.org/10.1177/0038038512452357.

Hilhorst, Dorothea, Holly Porter, and Rachel Gordon. 2017. "Gender, Sexuality, and Violence in Humanitarian Crises." *Disasters* 42, no. S1: S3–S16. https://doi.org/10.1111/disa.12276.

Hirschkind, Charles, and Saba Mahmood. 2002. "Feminism, the Taliban, and Politics of Counter-Insurgency." *Anthropological Quarterly* 75, no. 2: 338–54. https://www.jstor.org/stable/3318265.

Hodžić, Saida. 2009. "Unsettling Power: Domestic Violence, Gender Politics, and Struggles over Sovereignty in Ghana," *Ethnos* 74, no. 3, 331–60. https://doi.org/10.1080/00141840903053113.

hooks, bell, and Amalia Mesa-Bains. 2018. *Homegrown: Engaged Cultural Criticism*. New York: Routledge.

Hudson, Natalie Florea. 2012. *Gender, Human Security and the United Nations: Security Language as a Political Framework for Women*. London: Routledge.

Hudson, Valerie, and Patricia Leidl. 2017. *The Hillary Doctrine Sex and American Foreign Policy*. New York: Columbia University Press.

Inter-Agency Standing Committee (IASC). 2015. "Guidelines for Integrating Gender-Based Violence Interventions in Humanitarian Action." https://gbvguidelines.org/en/.

International Crisis Group. 2020. "A Course Correction for the Women, Peace and Security Agenda." *Crisis Group Special Briefing No. 5*, December 9, 2020. https://d2071andvipowj.cloudfront.net/b005-women-peace-and-security-agenda.pdf.

Jabri, Vivienne. 2004. "Feminist Ethics and Hegemonic Global Politics." *Alternatives: Global, Local, Political* 29, no. 3: 265–84. https://doi.org/10.1177/030437540402900302.

Jamieson, Ruth, and Kieran McEvoy. 2005. "State Crime by Proxy and Juridical Othering." *British Journal of Criminology* 45, no. 4: 504–27. https://ssrn.com/abstract=905661.

Johnson, Janet E. 2009. *Gender Violence in Russia: The Politics of Feminist Intervention*. Bloomington: Indiana University Press.

Johnson, Janet E. 2010. "Foreign Intervention and Violence Against Women." In *The International Studies Encyclopedia*, edited by Robert A. Denemark, 2366–83. Chichester: Wiley-Blackwell.

Johnson, Janet E., and Jean Robinson. 2006. *Living Gender after Communism*. Bloomington: Indiana University Press.

Jolly, Margaret, Christine Stewart, and Carolyn Brewer, eds. 2012. *Engendering Violence in Papua New Guinea*. Acton: The Australian National University Press.

Kapur, Ratna. 2018. *Gender, Alterity and Human Rights: Freedom in a Fishbowl*. Cheltenham, UK: Edward Elgar Publishing.

Kauzlarich, David, Rick A. Matthews, and William J. Miller. 2001. "Toward a Victimology of State Crime." *Critical Criminology* 10, no. 3: 173–94. https://doi.org/10.1023/A:1015744304749.

Keck, Margaret E., and Kathryn Sikkink. 2014. *Activists beyond Borders: Advocacy Networks in International Politics*. Ithaca, NY: Cornell University Press.

Kennedy, David. 2002. "The International Human Rights Movement: Part of the Problem?" *Harvard Human Rights Journal* 15: 101–25.

Khoja-Moolji, Shenila. 2015. "Reading Malala: (De)(Re)Territorialization of Muslim Collectivities." *Comparative Studies of South Asia, Africa and the Middle East* 35, no. 3: 539–56. https://doi.org/10.1215/1089201X-3426397.

Khoja-Moolji, Shenila. 2018. *Forging the Ideal Educated Muslim Girl*. Berkeley: University of California Press.

Khoja-Moolji, Shenila. 2020. Death by Benevolence: Third World Girls and the Contemporary Politics of Humanitarianism. *Feminist Theory* 21, no. 1: 65–90. https://doi.org/10.1177/1464700119850026.

Kowalski, Julia. 2018. "Bureaucratizing Sensitivity: Documents and Expertise in North Indian Antiviolence Counseling." POLAR 41, no. 1: 108–23. https://doi.org/10.1111/plar.12243.

Kumar, Deepa. 2021. *Islamophobia and the Politics of Empire: 20 Years after 9/11*. New York: Verso.

Kwiatkowski, Lynn. 2011a. "Cultural Politics of a Global/Local Health Program for Battered Women in Vietnam." In *Anthropology at the Front Lines of Gender-Based Violence*, edited by Jennifer R. Wies and Hillary J. Haldane, 139–64. Nashville: Vanderbilt University Press. https://doi.org/10.2307/j.ctv16b78b5.

Kwiatkowski, Lynn. 2011b. "Domestic Violence and the 'Happy Family' in Northern Vietnam." *Anthropology Now* 3, no. 3: 20–28. https://doi.org/10.1080/19492901.2011.11728331.

Lokot, Michelle. 2019. "The Space between Us: Feminist Values and Humanitarian Power Dynamics in Research with Refugees." *Gender and Development* 27, no. 3: 467–84. https://doi.org/10.1080/13552074.2019.1664046.

Lorde, Audre. 2007 [1984]. "The Master's Tools Will Never Dismantle the Master's House," 110–13. *Sister Outsider: Essays and Speeches*. Berkeley, CA: Crossing Press.

Luibhéid, Eithne. 2018. "Same-sex Marriage and the Pinkwashing of State Migration

Controls." *International Feminist Journal of Politics* 20, no. 3: 405–24. https://doi.org/10.1080/14616742.2018.1442735.

Mai, Nicola. 2014. "Between Embodied Cosmopolitism and Sexual Humanitarianism: The Fractal Mobilities and Subjectivities of Migrants Working in the Sex Industry." In *Borders, Mobilities and Migrations, Perspectives from the Mediterranean, 19–21st Century*, edited by Lisa Anteby-Yemini, Virginie Baby-Collin, and Sylvie Mazzella, 175–92. Brussels: Peter Lang.

Mai, Nicola. 2018. *Mobile Orientations: An Intimate Autoethnography of Migration, Sex Work, and Humanitarian Borders*. Chicago: University of Chicago Press.

Mazali, Rela. 2016. "Speaking of Guns: Launching Gun Control Discourse and Disarming Security Guards in a Militarized Society." *International Feminist Journal of Politics* 18, no. 2: 292–304. https://doi.org/10.1080/14616742.2016.1147874.

Mbembe, Achille. 2019. *Necropolitics*. Durham, NC: Duke University Press.

Meger, Sara. 2016. "The Fetishization of Sexual Violence in International Security." *International Studies Quarterly* 60, no. 1: 149–59. https://doi.org/10.1093/isq/sqw003.

Meister, Robert. 2010. *After Evil: A Politics of Human Rights*. New York: Columbia University Press.

Merchant, Carolyn. 1980. *The Death of Nature: Women, Ecology and the Scientific Revolution*. San Francisco: Harper and Row.

Merry, Sally Engle. 2006. *Human Rights and Gender Violence: Translating International Law into Local Justice*. Chicago: University of Chicago Press.

Mertens, Charlotte, and Maree Pardy. 2016. "'Sexurity' and Its Effects in Eastern Democratic Republic of Congo." *Third World Quarterly* 38, no. 4: 956–79. https://doi.org/10.1080/01436597.2016.1191341.

Mertens, Charlotte, and Henri Myrttinen. 2019. "'A Real Woman Waits'—Heteronormative Respectability, Neo-Liberal Betterment and Echoes of Coloniality in SGBV Programming in Eastern DR Congo." *Journal of Intervention and Statebuilding* 13, no. 4: 459–97. https://doi.org/10.1080/17502977.2019.1610992.

Miller, Alice M. 2004. "Sexuality, Violence against Women, and Human Rights: Women Make Demands and Ladies Get Protection." *Health and Human Rights* 7, no. 2: 17–47.

Murphy, Michelle. 2013. "The Girl: Mergers of Feminism and Finance in Neoliberal Times." In *Gender, Justice and Neoliberal Transformation*, edited by Elizabeth Bernstein and Janet R Jakobsen. *The Scholar and Feminist Online* 11.1–11.2. https://sfonline.barnard.edu/gender-justice-and-neoliberal-transformations/the-girl-mergers-of-feminism-and-finance-in-neoliberal-times/.

Nesiah, Vasuki. 1996. "Towards a Feminist Internationality: A Critique of US Feminist Legal Scholarship." In *Feminist Terrains in Legal Domains: Interdisciplinary Essays on Women and Law in India*, edited by Ratna Kapur, 11–35. New Delhi: Kali for Women.

Nesiah, Vasuki. 2006. Truth Commissions and Gender: Principles, Policies, and Procedures. *International Center for Transitional Justice* 18: 7–8.

Nesiah, Vasuki. 2011. Humanitarian Aid and the Politics of Crisis. *WSQ: Women's Studies Quarterly* 39, nos. 3–4: 297–303. https://www.jstor.org/stable/41308367.

Nesiah, Vasuki. 2012. "Uncomfortable Alliances: Women, Peace and Security in Sri Lanka." In *South Asian Feminisms: Contemporary Interventions*, edited by Ania Loomba and Ritty Lukose, 139–61. Durham, NC: Duke University Press.

Nesiah, Vasuki. 2021. "'A Mad and Melancholy Record': The Crisis of International Law Histories." *Notre Dame Journal of International & Comparative Law* 11, no. 2, Article 5: 232–55. https://scholarship.law.nd.edu/ndjicl/vol11/iss2/5.

Ní Aoláin, Fionnuala. 2014. "Gendered Harms and Their Interface with International Criminal Law: Norms, Challenges and Domestication." *International Feminist Journal of Politics* 16, no. 4: 622–46. https://doi.org/10.1080/14616742.2014.952126.

Ní Aoláin, Fionnuala. 2016. "The 'War on Terror' and Extremism: Assessing the Relevance of the Women, Peace, and Security Agenda." *International Affairs* 92, no. 2: 27591. https://doi.org/10.1111/1468-2346.12552.

Ní Aoláin, Fionnuala, and Jayne Huckerby. 2018. "Gendering Counterterrorism: How to, and How Not to—Part I." *Just Security*, May 1, 2018. https://www.justsecurity.org/55522/gendering-counterterrorism-to/.

Olivius, Elisabeth. 2016a. "Refugee Men as Perpetrators, Allies or Troublemakers? Emerging Discourses on Men and Masculinities in Humanitarian Aid." *Women's Studies International Forum* 56, no. 2: 56–65. https://doi.org/10.1016/J.WSIF.2015.12.004.

Olivius, Elisabeth. 2016b. "Constructing Humanitarian Selves and Refugee Others: Gender Equality and the Global Governance of Refugees." *International Feminist Journal of Politics* 18, no. 2: 270–90. https://doi.org/10.1080/14616742.2015.1094245.

Orford, Anne. 2003. *Reading Humanitarian Intervention: Human Rights and the Use of Force in International Law*. Cambridge: Cambridge University Press.

Otto, Dianne. 2009. "The Exile of Inclusion: Reflections on Gender Issues in International Law Over the Last Decade." *Melbourne Journal of International Law* 10, no. 1: Legal Studies Research Paper No. 431: 1126. https://ssrn.com/abstract=1508067.

Otto, Dianne. 2010. "Power and Danger: Feminist Engagement with International Law through the UN Security Council." *Australian Feminist Law Journal* 23, no. 1: 97–121.

Otto, Dianne. 2014. "Beyond Stories of Victory and Danger: Resisting Feminism's Amenability to Serving Security Council Politics." In *Rethinking Peacekeeping, Gender Equality and Collective Security*, edited by Gina Heathcoate and Dianne Otto, 157–72. London: Palgrave Macmillan.

Parson, Nila. 2010. "Transformative Ties: Gendered Violence, Forms of Recovery, and Shifting Subjectivities in Chile." *Medical Anthropology Quarterly* 24, no. 1: 64–84. https://doi.org/10.1111/j.1548-1387.2010.01085.x

Patel, Sofia. 2017. "The Sultanate of Women: Exploring Female Roles in Perpetuating and Preventing Violent Extremism." *Australian Strategic Policy Institute.* https://s3-ap-southeast-2.amazonaws.com/ad-aspi/import/SR100_Sultanate-of-women_v2.pdf.

Povinelli, Elizabeth. 2002. *The Cunning of Recognition.* Durham, NC: Duke University Press.

Pratt, Nicola. 2013. "Reconceptualizing Gender, Reinscribing Racial-Sexual Boundaries in International Security: The Case of UN Security Council Resolution 1325 on 'Women, Peace and Security.'" *International Studies Quarterly* 57, no. 4: 772–83. https://doi.org/10.1111/isqu.12032.

Pratt, Nicola, and Sophie Richter-Devoe. 2013. "Women, peace, and security: new conceptual challenges and opportunities." NOREF Norwegian *Peacebuilding Resource Center.* Policy Brief—February 2013.

Puar, Jasbir. 2007. *Terrorist Assemblages: Homonationalism in Queer Times.* Durham, NC: Duke University Press.

Rafiq, Haras, and Nikita Malik. 2015. "Caliphettes: Women and the Appeal of the Islamic State." *Quilliam Foundation,* https://issuu.com/m.r.mohamed/docs/caliphettes-women-and-the-appeal-of.

Razack, Sherene. 2004. "Imperilled Muslim Women, Dangerous Muslim Men, and Civilised Europeans: Legal and Social Responses to Forced Marriages." *Journal of Feminist Legal Studies* 12, no. 2: 129–74. https://doi.org/10.1023/B:FEST.0000043305.66172.92.

Razack, Sherene. 2007. "Stealing the Pain of Others: Reflections of Canadian Humanitarian Responses." *Review of Education, Pedagogy, and Cultural Studies* 29, no. 4: 375–94. https://doi.org/10.1080/10714410701454198.

Roy, Srila. 2017. "Enacting/Disrupting the Will to Empower: Feminist Governance of "Child Marriage" in Eastern India." *Signs: Journal of Women in Culture and Society* 42, no. 4: 867–91. https://doi.org/10.1086/690954.

Ruether, Rosemary Radford. 1975. *New Woman, New Earth: Sexist Ideologies and Human Liberation.* New York: Seabury Press.

Sabsay, Leticia. 2013. "Queering the Politics of Global Sexual Rights?" *Studies in Ethnicity and Nationalism* 13, no. 1: 80–90. https://doi.org/10.1111/sena.12019.

Sandler, Joanne, and Anne Marie Goetz. 2020. "Can the United Nations Deliver a Feminist Future?" *Gender and Development* 28, no. 2: 239–63. https://doi.org/10.1080/13552074.2020.1753432.

Sangtin Writers Collective and Richa Nagar. 2006. *Playing with Fire: Feminist Thought and Activism through Seven Lives in India.* Minneapolis: University of Minnesota Press.

Shalhoub-Kevorkian, Nadera. 2015. *Security Theology, Surveillance and the Politics of Fear.* Cambridge: Cambridge University Press.

Shalhoub-Kevorkian, Nadera, and Yossi David. 2015. "Is the Violence of Tag Mehir a State Crime?" *The British Journal of Criminology* 56, no. 5: 835–56. https://doi.org/10.1093/bjc/azv101.

Shalhoub-Kevorkian, Nadera, Antonia Griecci Woodsum, Himmat Zu'bi, and Rachel Busbridge. 2014. "Funding Pain: Bedouin Women and Political Economy in the Naqab/Negev." *Feminist Economics* 20, no. 4: 164–86. https://doi.org/10.1080/13545701.2014.946941.

Shalhoub-Kevorkian, Nadera, and Sarah Ihmoud. 2016. *In the Absence of Justice: Embodiment and the Politics of Militarized Dismemberment in Occupied East Jerusalem.* UN Women, Palestine Country Office.

Shepherd, Laura. 2008. *Gender, Violence and Security: Discourse as Practice.* New York: Zed Books.

Shively, Kim. 2011. "'We Couldn't Just Throw Her in the Street': Gendered Violence and Women's Shelters in Turkey." In *Anthropology at the Front Lines of Gender-Based Violence*, edited by Jennifer Wies and Hilary Haldane, 71–90. Nashville: Vanderbilt University Press.

Siddiqi, Dina M. 2015. "Scandals of Seduction and the Seductions of Scandal." *Comparative Studies of South Asia, Africa and the Middle East* 35, no. 3: 508–24. https://doi.org/10.1215/1089201X-3426373.

Smith, Andrea. 2003. "Not an Indian Tradition: The Sexual Colonization of Native Peoples." *Hypatia* 18, no. 2: 70–85. https://doi.org/10.1111/j.1527-2001.2003.tb00802.x.

Spivak, Gayatri. 1996. "'Woman' as Theatre: United Nations Conference on Women, Beijing 1995." *Radical Philosophy* 75 (January/February 1996): 24.

Thobani, Sunera. 2015. "Sovereignty, Culture, Rights: The Racial Politics of Gendered Violence in Canada." *Borderlands* 14, no. 1: 1–27.

Ticktin, Miriam. 2011. "The Gendered Human of Humanitarianism: Medicalising and Politicising Sexual Violence." *Gender and History* 23, no. 2: 250–65. https://doi.org/10.1111/j.1468-0424.2011.01637.x.

Ticktin, Miriam. 2016. "Thinking Beyond Humanitarian Borders." *Social Research* 83, no. 2: 255–71. https://muse.jhu.edu/article/631162.

True, Jacqui. 2003. "Mainstreaming Gender in Global Public Policy." *International Feminist Journal of Politics* 5, no. 3: 368–96. https://doi.org/10.1080/1461674032000122740.

UN Women. 2016. "Ending Violence Against Women: Key Reference Documents." https://www.unwomen.org/media/headquarters/attachments/sections/library/publications/2016/essentials-for-addressing-vaw-key-references-en.pdf?la=en&vs=3524.

Utas, Mats. 2005. "Victimcy, Girlfriending, Soldiering: Tactic Agency in a Young Woman's Social Navigation of the Liberian War Zone." *Anthropological Quarterly* 78, no. 2: 403–30. https://doi.org/10.1353/anq.2005.0032.

Varma, Saiba. 2016. "Love in the Time of the Occupation: Reveries, Longing, and Intoxication in Kashmir." *American Ethnologist* 43, no. 1: 50–62. https://doi.org/10.1111/amet.12262.

Veit, Alex, and Lisa Tschörner. 2019. "Creative Appropriation: Academic Knowledge and Interventions against Sexual Violence in the Democratic Republic of

Congo." *Journal of Intervention and Statebuilding* 13, no. 4: 459–79. https://doi.org/10.1080/17502977.2019.1627041.

Visweswaran, Kamala, ed. 2013. *Everyday Occupation: Experiencing Militarism in South Asia and the Middle East*. Philadelphia: University of Pennsylvania Press.

Ward, Tony, and Penny Green. 2016. "Law, the State, and the Dialectics of State Crime." *Critical Criminology* 24: 217–30. https://doi.org/10.1007/s10612-015-9304-5.

Yuval-Davis, Nira. 1980. "The Bearers of the Collective: Women and Religious Legislation in Israel." *Feminist Review* 4, no. 1: 15–27. https://doi.org/10.1057/fr.1980.4.

Zalewski, Marysia, and Anne Sisson Runyan. 2013. "Taking Feminist Violence Seriously in International Relations." *International Feminist Journal of Politics* 15, no. 3: 293–313. https://doi.org/10.1080/14616742.2013.766102.

Zarkov, Dubravka. 2018. "From Women and War to Gender and Conflict? Feminist Trajectories." In *The Oxford Handbook of Gender and Conflict*, edited by Fionnala Ní Aoláin, Naomi Cahn, Dina Francesca Hayes, and Nahla Valji, 17–34. Oxford: Oxford University Press.

Zarkov, Dubravka. 2020. "Conceptualizing Sexual Violence in Post–Cold War Global Conflicts." In *The Oxford Handbook of Gender, War, and the Western World since 1600*, edited by Karen Hagemann, Stefan Dudink, and Sonya O. Rose. Oxford: Oxford University Press. https://doi.org/10.1093/oxfordhb/9780199948710.013.32.

I SECURITIZATION

ONE · *Vasuki Nesiah*

Lawfare, CVE, and International Conflict Feminism

INTRODUCTION

In early 2018 the International Criminal Court issued a warrant for the arrest of Al Hassan Mahmoud[1] of Timbuktu, Mali. The arrest warrant charged that Al Hassan was responsible for persecuting the Timbuktu population on the grounds of both religion and gender as well as other actions undertaken in his role as chief of the Islamic police and member of Ansar Dine, an insurgent paramilitary group in Northern Mali.[2] Al Hassan surrendered to the ICC in March 2018 and is facing charges of war crimes and crimes against humanity.[3] Hearings to confirm the charges were convened in July 2019, and on September 30, 2019, the Pre-Trial Chamber I decided that there were substantial grounds to believe that Al Hassan was responsible for those crimes; the charges were confirmed. Throughout the legal process the court has grappled with various procedural issues such as the submission of evidence and amendment of the charge sheet by the prosecution to include additional charges of torture, cruel treatment, and other crimes.[4] The case is ongoing and Al Hassan remains in custody in the Hague.

Al Hassan is charged with multiple crimes, but this case has drawn particular interest because the crimes against humanity charges include the parallel and intersecting charges of persecution on the grounds of gender and persecution on the grounds of religion. In the prosecutor's submissions, Ansar Dine is described as advocating for certain practices that persecute women and religious minorities in the name of an ideological commitment to Islam: "There was religious persecution in Timbuktu: all the rules and prohibitions imposed on the residents stemmed from the ideological and religious vision of Ansar Dine and AQIM [Al-Qaeda in the Islamic Maghreb]" (Bensouda 2019). She goes on to say that this religious persecution was characterized and compounded by "gender-based persecution" and that "it was the women and girls of Timbuktu and the region who suffered the most." This chapter does not delve into Ansar Dine and its political and religious agendas, or its interpretation and implementation of Islamic law. Instead, our focus is on structures of global governance, with particular attention on the International Criminal Court.

The Rome Statute inaugurated the codification of gender-based persecution as a crime in Article 7(1)(h), and this case may prove the first substantive interpretation and application of these provisions. The legendary feminist human rights lawyer Rhonda Copelon is credited by many for inaugurating the discussion of gender-based persecution in international criminal law. Widney Brown and Laura Grenfell (2003) see the Rome Statute's recognition of gender-based persecution in positive law as an affirmation of a customary law recognition of gender-based persecution as a violation of international law.[5] Another legal scholar, Valerie Oosterveld, links the Rome Statute provisions to developments in International Refugee Law, where there has been recognition of gender-based persecution (2006).[6] Article 7(2)(g) of the Rome Statute defines persecution as "the intentional and severe deprivation of fundamental rights contrary to international law by reason of the identity of the group or collectivity," and Ansar Dine's establishment of Sharia law is seen to have deprived women of many fundamental rights recognized in international law. Alexandrah Bakker of the Public International Law and Policy Group describes these rights violations following the imposition of the Sharia law regime in Timbuktu as including: "For example, women were made to follow a strict dress code, they were not allowed to go outside without being accompanied by a man, and they were not allowed to be alone with men other than their husbands. In schools, boys and girls were separated. Many women were forced into marriage with members of the militia. Those found to be in violation of the rules were beaten and imprisoned, and sometimes even raped while in detention" (2020). Another commentator on the case, Georgina Epure, a fellow at the Open Society Justice Institute, speaks to how these crimes were linked to the charges against Al Hassan: "Al Hassan was in charge of enforcing the new rules by taking part in police patrols, arresting and detaining civilians, participating in the policy of forced marriages, and implementing sanctions imposed by the Islamic court" (2020).

As soon as the charges were made public, feminist groups immediately voiced support for the ICC's case against Al Hassan and applauded the "potentially groundbreaking new prosecution for the crime of persecution on the grounds of gender" (Burke 2018). The preeminent feminist group focused on international criminal law, The Women's Initiative for Gender Justice, promptly released a statement conveying support for the case, stating that they were heartened by this development and were encouraged by the ICC's actions. Similarly, the Global Justice Center applauded "Prosecutor Bensouda's commitment to securing justice for sexual and gender-based crimes," noting that "this potentially groundbreaking case could be the first time that the Court will consider the crime of gender-based persecution and has the potential to define the Court's jurisprudence around gender" (2018). Marie Forestier of International Law Girls asserted that "Al-Hassan's trial should be a stepping stone for that the gender perspective naturally becomes an integral part of any proceeding" (2018). Feminists also celebrated the implications of the gender-based persecution charge in the Al Hassan case on the International Law Commission (ILC)'s work on the draft articles on Crimes Against Humanity (Grey et al. 2019).

This is not the only ICC case where the alleged perpetrator belongs to a group whose self-definition includes religion. For instance, Joseph Kony, among the most famous targets of an ICC prosecution, heads the Ugandan Christian militant group, the Lord's Resistance Army. However, in Kony's case the charge sheet did not include persecution on either the grounds of religion or the grounds of gender.[7] With the important exception of the genocide against the Rohingya in Myanmar, in all cases where such charges are part of the conversation the religion concerned is Islam. Charges have not been brought in the Myanmar case as of yet but investigations are ongoing.[8] The other prominent contexts where the ICC is considering pursuing gender-based persecution charges are those against the Boko Haram in Nigeria and the Taliban in Afghanistan.[9] Similarly, it has been urged to pursue such charges in places such as Iraq, where ISIS is in operation. Thus, the Global Justice Center emphasized that not only was the Al Hassan case important for the prosecution of gender-based crimes but that it was "an important first step in prosecuting the gender-based crimes that are a central tactic of extremist groups in conflicts around the world" (2018). Indeed, the pursuit of gender persecution cases in relation to religious extremism was highlighted by some feminist commentators as an advance for intersectional feminism. Thus, in eager anticipation of the Al Hassan case, one commentator notes that in the past, "the ICC and international tribunals have tended to speak of persecution on isolated grounds: race or religion for example. In the Al Hassan case, the Prosecution has challenged this trend by alleging *'persécution religieuse, laquelle s'est doublée d'une persécution sexiste,'* in other words, persecution on the grounds of religion and gender coupled together" (Grey 2018). It is striking that gender-based persecution charges have traveled only as companions to contexts where religion-based persecution charges are co-travelers, and thus far, only where that religion is Islam. This becomes increasingly important in situating the slippage between Islam and violent extremism in much of the related feminist commentary on persecution charges.

The ICC's overwhelming focus on Africa has been a recurrent subject of debate and critique. In 2016, three African countries (Burundi, Gambia, and South Africa) announced intentions to withdraw from the ICC; a year later Burundi followed through on its threat. There are official and unofficial claims that others might follow (including Chad, the DRC, Kenya, Namibia, and Uganda) with the African Union also raising the possibility of a continent-wide withdrawal. Oumar Ba reflects the criticism of the international criminal justice system when he says that it has rendered Africans "subjects of the law without being protected by it" (2017, 46).[10] That said, in contrast to discussions of the ICC's role in Sudan, Kenya, Uganda, and elsewhere, the ICC's role in Mali does not have significant play in debates about the ICC's role in Africa.[11] In fact, with the foregrounding of CVE, the Mali case is much more likely to be discussed in relation to the ICC's potential role in Afghanistan or even Iraq and Syria. Thus, in the same period when the ICC's role in the rest of Africa was being understood in terms of global North-South politics, its role in Mali was more likely to be framed in terms of terrorism/counterterrorism—or, even more likely, in the new nomenclature of CVE. If neocolonial intervention became repackaged over several decades as humanitarian intervention (i.e., military intervention in the name of humanitarian goals), humanitarian intervention then morphed into the war on terror, and we now have these interventions that have advanced under the banner of "countering violent extremism" (CVE).

This nexus of international criminal law, violent extremism, Islam, and gender is the focus of this chapter. The still-ongoing Al Hassan case is not the direct focus and this chapter does not address the guilt or innocence of Al Hassan, or the evidentiary and procedural issues at stake in the case. Rather, I am interested in how this nexus came about in creating the space for the Al Hassan case and in seeding the ground for similar cases in relation to Boko Haram, ISIS, or the Taliban. To this end, I adopt a wide-angle perspective of the case by describing and analyzing the background global governance projects that have contributed to the emergence of this case and defined the terms through which various atrocities in Northern Mali are understood and engaged with. In particular, I argue that there are three important and interrelated projects that map the coordinates of this wide-angle perspective—namely, Countering Violent Extremism (CVE), Lawfare, and International Conflict Feminism (ICF).[12] By describing them as "global governance projects" I seek to capture how each of these entails an amalgam of ideologies and institutional arrangements with transnational currency in the current moment. That currency feeds off dominant structures of global governance and makes their driving logics the thinkable default option, rendering their legitimacy a matter of common sense for diverse groups, from feminist lawyers to military strategists. Each of these projects is the primary focus of one of the three sections that follow.

The Al Hassan case is the prism through which we examine the universe of actors, structures, and institutional practices that have been strengthened—and those that have been defeated—by this case coming forward. By foregrounding the complex architecture of these three governance agendas, I seek in this chapter to better understand how notions of "Islamic extremism" get mobilized in conjunction with gender-based persecution and the work of this convergence in the terrain of international criminal law.

COUNTERING VIOLENT (ISLAMIC) EXTREMISM:
THE NEW FACE OF INTERVENTION

In January 2013, citizens of Konna and Diabaly in central Mali found themselves being bombarded by French air strikes in the name of counterterrorism.[13] With the hubris borne of representing an ex-colonial power, François Hollande described the military operation, known as Operation Serval, as support for Malian troops on the ground in confronting "terrorist aggression [whose] brutality and fanaticism" was known to "the whole world" (Chrisafis, Hirsch, and Hopkins 2013). Operation Serval has both a regional backstory, linking military escalation of CVE activities in Libya and other parts of the Sahel, and a global backstory of ongoing escalation of military, cultural, and legal interventions linking Islam to "violent extremism" in Mali, France and elsewhere in Europe, and the United States.

CVE was promoted as a "hearts and minds complement" to military antiterrorism activities—or as the Center for Security Studies (CSS) describes it, "both hard and soft measures" (Frazer and Nünlist 2015, 2). If Obama's famous Cairo speech was one performance of a reboot of the relationship between security talk and Islamophobia, then the shift from counterterrorism to CVE was another.[14] The CVE framework arose partly from disappointment with a narrowly militarized approach that was both thought to be ineffective in some contexts and charged with having exacerbated the underlying causes of terrorism in others. CVE was presented as encompassing not only the combating of militants deemed terrorists but as incorporating a preventive focus on deradicalization and integration. As part of a shift in approach the Obama administration convened meetings "to discuss concrete steps the United States and its partners can take to develop community-oriented approaches to counter hateful extremist ideologies that radicalize, recruit or incite to violence" (The White House Office of the Press Secretary 2015). A focus on prevention and addressing root causes was one approach. In this vein RUSI, a European defense- and security-focused think tank, describes CVE as a "field of theory and practice that seeks to complement counterterrorism with non-coercive measures, particularly using preventative approaches which seek to address the drivers of terrorism and violent extremism."[15] It's a theory that includes both more explicit and more subtle invocations of the clash of civilizations and globalized Islam as the reference points for CVE. When originally introduced in the United States it was perceived as an Obama-era corrective to the hard militarism of the Bush-Cheney era of counterterrorism, demonstrated, for example, by the Obama administration's investment in not appearing to be at war with the Islamic world.[16] Indeed the Obama administration was criticized for framing policy goals as addressing "violent extremism of all sorts" and refusing to foreground Islam (Roberts 2015). One Obama administration official put the refusal to make Islamic the permanent prefix to the word *terrorism* as follows: "You can call them what you want; we are calling them terrorists. . . . We are not treating these people (as) part of a religion" (Roberts 2015). This reticence may have been primarily a question of surface optics (exemplified by Obama's Cairo speech), but it also conveys a not-insignificant acknowledgment that counterterrorism had taken an Islamophobic cast in both national and geopolitical registers. Subsequently when Obama officials did speak of Islam in the context of CVE, they took pains to describe it as a perversion of the religion: "we do not believe that they represent Islam. There is definitely no justification for [terror] in any religion, and that's the view of the vast majority of Muslims" (Roberts 2015).

As the Obama era unfolded there were more continuities than discontinuities with the security policies of the Bush and Obama eras, and between counterterrorism and CVE, but the performance of the reboot was a de facto acknowledgment of the underlying civilizational discourse and conveyed an embarrassment about its Orientalist, imperial, and Islamophobic character. In contrast, in Europe, even this embarrassment seems absent; CVE is often explicitly described as focusing on Islamic extremism, or as CSS describes it, the "fear of home grown Islamic terrorisms" (Frazer and Nünlist 2015). Indeed there was talk that the Obama administration was trying to remove the explicit references to Islam in the public statements of European officials such as President François Hollande (Perez 2016). However, by the time of Operation Serval, there was more convergence than divergence between the American and European approaches. For defense ministries on both sides of the Atlantic, the targets of CVE-aligned military intervention have of course been Muslim-majority countries regardless of whether that targeting is implicit or explicit. As Glenn Greenwald (2013) noted in the wake of Operation Serval in Mali, "there is one simple statistic that provides the key context: this west African nation of 15 million people is the eighth country in which western powers—over the last four years alone—have bombed and killed Muslims—after Iraq, Afghanistan, Pakistan, Yemen, Libya, Somalia and the Philippines (that does not count the numerous lethal tyrannies propped up by the west in that region). For obvious reasons, the rhetoric that the west is not at war with the Islamic world grows increasingly hollow with each new expansion of this militarism."[17]

In the context of Mali, Operation Serval represented both contemporary forms of war with the Islamic world as well as longer patterns of French colonial history in the nation.[18] Moreover, in important ways CVE constituted an expansion of the ambit of security measures by focusing on civil society and the recruitment of Muslims to report on other Muslims (Kazi 2017). In cultivating a sense of vulnerability in subjugated communities, the state employs panoptical pressure to prove your antiterrorism bona fides so that CVE becomes an insidious self-disciplining and self-surveilling presence internal to Muslim communities.[19] Thus CVE is an important register of different scales of discipline and surveillance auditing and shaping "leadership" within minority Muslim communities. This dynamic is operative not only within minority Muslim communities in the West and elsewhere but also in the leadership of Muslim-majority states in small countries like Mali (and in contrast to powerful Muslim-majority countries like Saudi Arabia or Turkey). Thus, it is no surprise that Mali requested French support and "invited" their own compromised sovereignty. As with self-referrals to the ICC, this "invitation" from the government of Mali to the government of its former colonizer can also be seen as yet another instance of how "technologies of governmentality and government have fused local ownership to global governance" so that the Malian sovereignty that is vested in and represented by the Malian government is not a bulwark against imperial governance but its instrument (Nesiah 2016).

The focus by CVE on "soft measures" has meant that the military strategy manuals have been accompanied by a new industry of cultural, legal, and policy expertise regarding indicators of extremism and strategies for de-radicalization that are focused on a theory of Islamicization. For instance, wearing the niqab gets listed as an indicator of radicalization (De Leede et al. 2017). When women evince "a [new] interest in politics" that is another. "Disengaging from contact with the opposite sex" is yet another (De Leede et al. 2017, 25). As these few examples indicate, embedded within the theory of Islamicization are particular notions of normative gender identity and behavior that it mobilizes as its reference point. Moreover, such indicators of radicalization in security policy and CVE initiatives get assimilated into the discourse of saving Malian women (Abu-Lughod 2013). This assimilation is enacted not only under the rubric of military strategy but also within the broader rubric of international conflict feminism.

Consider for instance the following depiction of Malian women's political subjectivity within an ICF framing. The Women, Peace and Security (WPS) Index on women's well-being and empowerment lays out criteria ranking Mali among the "10 worst countries in the world for women."[20] The report of this finding is accompanied by a photograph of an older woman smiling and clapping her hands in the wake of French military–assisted Malian troop movements with the caption "A Malian woman cheers Malian soldiers arriving in a convoy at the military base in Timbuktu, Mali." International intervention, the caption suggests, is good for women in Mali. The invocation of women beneficiaries, especially Islamic women beneficiaries, is now a familiar part of the package of Western military interventions undertaken in the name of CVE. Ever since the Laura Bush's infamous defense of bombing Afghanistan post-9/11 ("the fight against terrorism is a fight for the rights and dignity of women"), the coupling of counterterrorism and saving Muslim women has become the standard two-part strategy of the military playbook. These converging dynamics have both domestic and international dimensions. Thus, in July 2014, the same month that Operation

Serval was completed and a new military campaign, Operation Barkhane, was being prepared, the European Court of Human Rights upheld the 2011 French ban against face covering (the "Burka ban") in the name of women's rights, French culture, and public security.[21] From the French government's perspectives, the streets of Paris and the streets of Timbuktu were two intertwined fronts in the war on terror.

In addition to its longer prehistory in colonization, French military intervention in the region also has a more proximate history in the bombing of Libya by the United States and its allies in the name of humanitarian goals, including "the responsibility to protect" (R2P).[22] R2P is a soft-law policy framework that creates an obligation for international intervention to protect civilians under certain conditions, namely conditions of genocide, war crimes, ethnic cleansing, and crimes against humanity. Thus, rather than intervention being an incursion on sovereignty, this post–Cold War policy framework rendered intervention an obligation of international political ethics. It serves as a backdrop to a spate of Security Council resolutions that speak directly and indirectly to trigger conditions for international action such as SCR 1820 (dealing with the international obligations to address sexual violence), SCR 2242 (dealing with the international obligations to address gender dimensions of violent extremism), and SCR 1373 (dealing with an obligation to take action on countering terrorism).

Moreover, just as CVE evolved in the direction of what the Department of Homeland Security (2019) describes as a "whole-of-society" oriented counterterrorism, humanitarianism became more explicitly political. As Michael Barnett has noted, "humanitarianism was now part of military strategy, integral to winning 'hearts and minds' and thus instrumental for furthering American goals"—or indeed the goals of France and any of the other NATO powers (2013, 192–93). These strategies had both intended and unintended consequences—that exceeded, and in some cases defeated, their expectations. In this case, Tuaregs, a nomadic community with a strong presence in Northern Mali and Libya (among other countries, including Niger, Burkina Faso, and Algeria) were displaced or forcibly pushed out of the Libyan military and paramilitary groups in Libya with the fall of Gaddafi. Ansar Dine, the organization that Al Hassan was a part of, is perhaps the most significant of such organizations. Ansar Dine was, along with other groups in Mali, armed and trained by the Americans in the name of counterterrorism yet soon played a central role in the 2012 coup that overthrew the elected Malian government. Thus even if we bracket the longer dynamics of colonial governance and Tuareg resistance to focus on the last decade, we can situate the 2013 French bombing of Mali, as itself a consequence of the America and French led 2011 bombing of Libya, of American counterterrorism operations arming and training militants in the region (which can themselves be seen to have engendered a new target for the next phase of counterterrorism operations), and "the west is once again at war with the very forces that it trained, funded and armed" (Greenwald 2013). Thus the citizens of Mali were already prefigured as disposable lives in a necropolitical military strategy directed at Libya.

In the context of the "soft measures," what is particularly resonant between developments in Libya and developments in Mali is the link between military bombing campaigns and the work of the ICC. The Security Council passed twinned resolutions regarding legal and military intervention in Libya in the spring of 2011—the Libyan situation was referred to the ICC by the Security Council on February 26; three weeks later, on March 19, it passed Resolution 1973 authorizing military intervention. Promptly responsive, the ICC issued indictments against Muammar Gaddafi, his son Seif Gaddafi, and Libyan intelligence chief Abdulla Senussi the very next month. The knock-on effects of the Libyan intervention were felt in Mali almost immediately and by the next spring groups like Amnesty International (2012) were reporting that the human rights situation in Mali was the worst it had been for fifty years. Moreover completing the cultivation of supplicant abject leadership in subjugated states (or what we referred to as "local ownership of global governance"), the Malian government referred the situation to the ICC in July 2012 (Nesiah 2016). While key humanitarian groups have pushed against the blurring of lines between humanitarian intervention and CVE, the international criminal law community does not shy away from that connection (O'Leary 2018). Thus the French began bombing Mali in March 2013 (almost two years to the date of the bombing of Libya), and the ICC initiated a full investigation of the situation in Mali in January of that same year and had begun to issue warrants by 2015. Al Hassan was the second man indicted. Thus, even bracketing the specifics of the charges it has pursued, the ICC's presence in Libya and Mali is deeply entangled with Western military presence in the region; this entanglement of legal and military terrains is the focus of the following section.[23]

INTERNATIONAL CRIMINAL COURT: A NEW PHASE OF LAWFARE

Law has always played a significant role in both advancing and contesting militarism and its rationales. The most familiar notion of lawfare entails the mobilization of specific laws or particular arguments regarding legality and illegality so that they are invoked or interpreted in ways that empower particular military actions. This instrumentalist notion of the term "lawfare" has a longer history, but its increased usage in the context of the post-9/11 world is often attributed to an American colonel, Charles Dunlap, who wrote about "a method of warfare where law is used as a means of realizing a military objective." [24] For instance, in recent years, as Neve Gordon and Nicola Perugini have recounted, military campaigns by powerful countries in Afghanistan, Iraq, Syria, Gaza, and elsewhere have invoked international humanitarian law provisions condemning the use of human shields to treat civilian spaces such as hospitals as military targets. In response to this kind of use—or some might say misuse—of law for military aims, the term "lawfare" has often been invoked as a pejorative term indicating the cynical manipulation "of law for war." Moreover, it was this type of usage that provoked critical commentary regarding the defense of the invasion of Iraq at the United Nations through self-serving interpretations of Security Council resolutions and the law of war, as well as the subsequent Bush administration use of black sites and various approaches to "counterterrorism" through legal maneuvers escaping the protections of constitutional jurisdiction and civilian courts for prisoners, or the restraints of IHL and IHR laws and norms regulating the conduct of war.

Lawfare signals the law-war nexus, while also suggesting that there is some normative, legitimacy-producing work attributable to legal terrains that does work on the battlefield. In fact the US government's Counterinsurgency (COIN) Guide underscores that victory and defeat on the battlefield does not depend on military prowess alone ("the decisive effort is rarely military"); instead, the guide defines COIN as a "blend of comprehensive civilian and military efforts designed to simultaneously contain insurgency and address its root causes" with initiatives "strengthening the rule of law" playing a critical role (United States Government Interagency Counterinsurgency Initiative 2009, i, 2, 14).

Concomitantly, while the employment of law as a narrowly instrumental military tool could corrode the legitimacy of the rule of law itself, those who foreground this "whole-of-society" strategy for rule of law projects situate CVE initiatives not as military interventions but as a law and justice intervention. Thus, in this latest phase of international intervention, lawfare is invoked not only in reference to the narrowly instrumental usage just described but also in reference to a more broadly ideological claim about the relationship between particular systems of law and the CVE or COIN goals more generally. Indeed, law is often presented as having an especially distinctive significance for the "soft measures" CVE approach. Consider this statement from the American Bar Association's (ABA) Rule of Law Initiative report on *Rule of Law Approaches to Countering Violent Extremism*: pressing for a more holistic rather than narrowly militaristic approach the ABA argues that "it should now be clear that militarized counterterror approaches by the United States and others are insufficient to address the threat" (Robinson and Kelly 2017). In contrast, CVE is advocated for as an alternative or supplemental "whole-of-society" strategy that is rooted in soft power and "encompasses the preventative aspects of counterterrorism as well as intervention to undermine the attraction of extremist movements and ideologies that seek to promote violence." It is significant that the ABA report draws attention to the stakes of CVE lawfare in its arguments for putting the rule of law on the front stage and military maneuvers on the backstage in CVE. The rule of law is presented here as central to such a "whole-of-society" strategy—one that promises stability, the nonviolent resolution of conflict, and a restraint on those in power:

> Frequently the most successful way to address drivers of violent extremism will be to frame CVE interventions through a rule of law rubric, encompassing goals such as promoting justice, respect for rights, and inclusiveness. . . . Rule of law donors, implementers, and local partners will all have to make strategic choices about whether to conceive of their work as CVE-relevant programming, whether to publicly brand it as such, and how much to focus research, measurement, and evaluation on specific CVE-related goals. Implementers should seriously consider framing CVE-related goals as one subset of a broader rule of law strategy that motivates their work. In other words, CVE-relevant rule of law programming should situate attempts to counter violent extremism within broader efforts to further justice in society, rather than attempting to frame efforts to improve the rule of law through a narrower CVE prism. (22)

The authors of the report warn that a narrowly military strategy—and certainly a narrowly military branding—can be counterproductive. In this they represent a strand of liberal internationalism that Michael Ignatieff (2003) has described as "Empire Lite"—determinedly interventionist, but with rule of law programs and "nation building" initiatives as their first calling card.

This dimension of lawfare is part of the policy package associated with "rule of law" promotion in dominant development and governance discourse. It has been associated over the years with a range of related policy families such as the Washington consensus governance agendas of austerity and structural adjustment policies where deregulation was a dimension of rule of law programs. This also includes the work of NGOs doing community-oriented democracy promotion work alongside de facto support of military intervention; Colin Powell (a Bush-era actor with an Obama-era sensibility) described civilian NGOs as "force multipliers" that should be considered "an important part of our combat team" (2001). In addition to this more generalized "whole-of-society" approach, the rule of law is presented as having a special CVE function in contexts of conflict where it also functions as companion to military operations by legitimating military operations as a clearing ground for CVE. For instance, the Rule of Law Field Force (ROLFF) in Afghanistan is framed as a CVE intervention that performs a role within a broader COIN operation. The description advanced by Jack Goldsmith, one of lawfare's most noted advocates, captures this approach to the rule of law as part of a comprehensive COIN policy: "The basic idea of ROLFF is to revive governance and rule of law functions in the Pashtun south where the insurgency is strongest during the 'hold' phase of COIN operations (i.e., just after an area has been cleared of insurgents)." He then connects these rule of law goals to boots on the ground: "General Martins, his soldiers, and their Afghan partners are literally fighting to bring ordinary Afghans criminal justice capacity, dispute resolution services, and anti-corruption institutions, all with the aim of promoting the legitimacy of the Afghan government and defeating the insurgency. If that's not 'using law as a weapon of war,' I don't know what is.'" In this view, these areas of the Pashtun are by definition lawless; any local or customary law that is operative there does not rise to his notion of legality. In Afghanistan and elsewhere alternative legal systems, even when used by the local community to resolve disputes, are declared criminal rather than legal, and those terrains are described as lawless and needing interventions like that of the NATO's Rule of Law Field Support Mission (NROLFSM). NROLFSM makes clear that from NATO's perspective the "rule of law" can be the only legal regime endorsed and setup by NATO; it dismisses the justice apparatus that the Taliban have set up even though the Afghan people use the Taliban courts to obtain redress: "While Afghans disagree with the harsh punishments of the Taliban, they often find this 'extreme justice' their sole recourse for injustice. The redress of grievances is one of the few areas where the insurgency continues to compete with legitimate governance" (Goldsmith 2011). The framing of such regions as devoid of law reactivates the colonial legal concept of *terra nullius* that allowed outsiders to take indigenous land that was declared to be a bare, unpeopled land, a land without law and political society, a lawless land without law and political society. NATO's rule of law mission declares all competing legal authority criminal so that it alone can introduce a law and political society that meets Western approval. This gives new meaning to the "whole-of-society" strategy: if the military counterinsurgency operations were hard power counterterrorism, this reintroduction of a NATO-approved legal and political system is soft power CVE, and all aligned with larger COIN goals.

In a similar vein, in making her case for Al Hassan's guilt under international criminal law, the prosecutor foregrounds her role within the system of law introduced by Ansar Dine and AQIM, to argue in effect that this is not a system of law but a system of criminality: "As soon as the members of Ansar Dine and AQIM seized the city, they set up their own agencies of control and repressive law enforcement. In particular, they set up the Islamic Police, of which Al Hassan Ag Mahmoud, the suspect appearing before this Court today, was the zealous, key *de facto* commissioner. By setting up these bodies, the members of these groups held the helpless civilian population of the city and region of Timbuktu in their merciless grip. They subjected the men and women of Timbuktu to their power, invoking and, above all, imposing their religious vision with considerable brutality and abuses constituting crimes against humanity and war crimes under the Rome Statute" (Bensouda 2019). Here the description of military moves melds into the description of Islamic law with Islamic law zoned into the realm of abusive criminality and of law enforcement in such a society as indicative of a society bereft of law. In making her case to the trial chamber for the confirmation of charges, Prosecutor Bensouda is calling for ICC intervention, for non-Islamic law, to guarantee that the principle of legality will be upheld.

It is worth calling attention to the ways in which the "Empire Lite" internationalists are not pulling away from the imperialist military interventions associated with hard power counterterrorism. Rather, they offer an alternative vision and defense of an imperial global governance agenda that foregrounds the rule of law. For instance, prominent international lawyers from the Obama state department (such as Anne-Marie Slaughter) supported the bombing of Libya, just as Harold Koh prepared legal briefs in defense of drone use in Afghanistan (Rogin 2011; Slaughter 2011).[25] Both these military policies had and continue to have brutal and far-reaching impacts in Mali, Libya, Afghanistan, Pakistan, and beyond. Both of these military policies echoed and replicated colonial relationships of invading and occupying powers and the local population. Indeed, both these military policies have further defeated local sovereignty in already troubled contexts, encouraged violent extremism, and supported policies that were deeply unjust and antithetical to the best one would hope for in the human rights regime. However, what is especially striking about these actors is that they were much more invested than the Cheney-Rumsfeld team, in advancing military intervention in the name of justice and human rights.

During the period of the bombings in Libya and Mali, international criminal law scholars and practitioners were advocating that the ICC have a particularly significant role in counterterrorism campaigns, and they were analyzing provisions of the Rome Statute that could be interpreted in ways that could serve such efforts. For instance, Aviv Cohen argued that the ICC was an unused tool in counterterrorism in his 2012 article "Prosecuting Terrorists at the International Criminal Court: Reevaluating an Unused Legal Tool to Combat Terrorism." In a complementary vein, Cóman Kenny's article, "Prosecuting Crimes of International Concern: Islamic State at the ICC?" argues that the ICC should seek to assert jurisdiction over what he describes as the "innately criminal modus operandi" of ISIS and lays out the legal arguments that could pave the way for the court to do just that (Kenny 2017, 122). A member of the Office of the Co-Prosecutors of the Extraordinary Chambers in the Courts of Cambodia, Kenny saw the ICC "as uniquely positioned to take on ISIS as ISIS represents a *sui generis* non-State group and a particularly grave and novel threat to international law" and by taking on such a challenge the Court will be able to demonstrate that it is "capable of dealing with matters of immediate and pressing international concern and ensure that perpetrators of the most egregious violations of international law do not go unpunished" (2017, 122). The ICC's own legitimacy as an institution of global governance becomes symbiotic with its ability to be victoriously weaponized in CVE. These interventions represent a distinct turn toward rule-of-law approaches, and criminal prosecutions in particular, in countering violent extremism. For instance, Parliamentarians for Global Action (PGA) welcome the ICC's involvement in Mali as demonstrating that "serious human rights violations committed by violent extremist groups across the world should foremost be considered as international crimes and be investigated and prosecuted under the Rule of Law."[26] They argue that targeted killings and other militarized counterterrorism initiatives are ineffective and offer bad optics in the long run. In framing CVE interventions to "improve the rule of law" and "further justice in society" the ABA draws attention to the kind of work they have done in Libya in the aftermath of the intervention on issues that range from constitutionalism to women's rights as examples of how the rule-of-law–CVE nexus can be productively employed (Robinson and Kelly 2017). The ICC's actions in Libya as well as Mali can be understood as problematic adjuncts to imperial military intervention that have been advanced through the nexus with CVE.

Extrapolating from the ABA's framing then, the stakes of the ICC's pursuit of the Al Hassan case includes, crucially, a performance of accountability; it is a performance directed at furthering justice in the society being bombed. It is significant that the charge sheet against Al Hassan alleges that he had particular responsibilities in implementing Sharia law. The charge sheet narrates a list of crimes he prosecuted and the punishments he meted out in implicit contrast to the liberal legalism invoked by the international criminal law regime that was holding him to account. The first decade of the ICC's reign was faulted as a neocolonial project focused on protagonists in civil wars in African states—states often depicted as lawless and failed. In this second decade, as the ICC has turned its attention more and more to Muslim majority countries, the "other" that emerges is not lawlessness but contexts that are home to a toxic illiberal legality. Furthermore, if gender-based crimes were primarily focused on rape and sexual violence in that first decade, in this second decade, the Al Hassan case may be signaling a turn to attention on sexism and patriarchy under the charge of "gender-based persecution." Widney Brown and Laura Grenfell (2003) develop the potential of the "gender-based persecution" charge in going beyond sexual violence alone to address discrimination against women by the Taliban that is severe, widespread, and systematic enough to be analogous to the crime of apartheid and crimes against humanity more generally. Others also link the gender-based persecution charge to a broader ambit of international human rights law, including CEDAW and the Maputo Protocol on the Rights of Women in Africa (Epure 2020). The focus on gender and the foregrounding of feminism oils the wheels of both military and legal interventions within the CVE rubric.

INTERNATIONAL CONFLICT FEMINISM:
A NEW FACE OF THE CULTURE WARS

It is against the backdrop of the CVE-ICC conjuncture that we can appreciate ICF's role in shaping prosecutorial action at the ICC. In particular, Al Hassan's case offers a window into the ICC as an important terrain for lawfare in the converging agendas of ICF and CVE. Typically the ICF discussion describes the significance of gender mainstreaming CVE through a two-pronged argument that emphasizes women's heightened vulnerability to VE and women's potential power in combating VE.[27] As noted above, ICF refers to feminist agendas for law and policy in contexts of conflict that contributed to and gained particular momentum with the passage of Security Council Resolution 1325 (SCR 1325) in October 2000; SCR 1325 calls for special attention to the interests and vulnerabilities of women and girls in contexts of conflict, including their participation in processes of conflict resolution and peace making. To the approval of the ICF community, ICC Prosecutor Fatou Bensouda launched her tenure as chief prosecutor in 2012 by highlighting sexual and gender-based violence as a central priority for her prosecutorial agenda.

The Women's International League for Peace and Freedom (WILPF), one of the ICF groups that advocated for SCR 1325 and monitors its progress, has argued that the current climate requires a pivot to a women's peace and security (WPS) approach to CVE as a new arena of security (Khan 2018). The reference to WPS in a range of resolutions passed by the Security Council regarding CVE and counterterrorism (SCR 2122, SCR 3178, SCR 2195) culminated in SCR 2242 where the Security Council elaborated more specifically on what was entailed in increased "attention to women, peace and security as a cross-cutting subject in all relevant thematic areas of work on its agenda, including threats to international peace and security caused by terrorist acts" (2015). This resolution included commitments regarding financing and other measures of institutional support for integration of WPS approaches to protection, participation, and accountability in CVE efforts and the incorporation of gender expertise in specific organizations such as the Counter-Terrorism Committee (CTC), the Counter-Terrorism Committee Executive Directorate (CTED), and the Counter-Terrorism Implementation Task Force (CTITF).[28] Accordingly, Sarah Sewall, former Under Secretary for Civilian Security, Democracy, and Human Rights, describes

"CVE as a vital new dimension of the Women, Peace and Security Agenda" and makes a strong statement about CVE and WPS as symbiotic agendas:

> Violent extremists are among the greatest threats to the empowerment of women and girls across the globe, not only in the crimes they commit, but in how they can fuel misogyny by exploiting local resistance to gender equality. Violent extremists repress women in both their ideology and their methods of violence. By contrast, empowered women provide powerful antidotes to violent extremism. They are able to refute extremist narratives and nihilistic visions with independence and authenticity. Societies that respect the rights of all and fully engage the participation of all have no room for violent extremism. So women's empowerment is not only essential for defeating violent extremism; defeating violent extremism is essential for women's empowerment. The two go hand-in-hand. (2016)

One of the most important expressions of the integration of WPS agendas and CVE agendas is in the arena of international criminal law. Some feminist court watchers had voiced discontent that no charges of gendered persecution had come before the ICC in the almost two decades of its existence. In fact, in the DRC-focused case of Callixte Mbarushimana (2011), the only other case where gendered persecution was potentially on the table, proceedings ran aground at the confirmation stage for insufficient evidence, and Callixte Mbarushimana was released. In their annual report card regarding the ICC's work, Brigid Inder, then Director of the Women's Initiative for Gender Justice, commented that "While gender-based crimes are regularly charged by the ICC, they continue to be the most vulnerable category of crimes addressed by the Court," because "a high proportion of these charges are dismissed before the trial phase due to quirky judicial decisions, insufficient evidence or incorrect characterization of the facts regarding sexual violence." With a vigilant coterie of ICF court watchers scrutinizing their record, pressure has been mounting on the court to improve their record regarding ICF priorities.

Significantly, a few months prior to the Al Hassan indictment, some of the organizations that had been in the forefront of ICF for several decades, petitioned the court to turn to the ICF-CVE conjuncture. The Human Rights and Gender Justice Clinic (HRGJ Clinic, or HRGJ) of the City University of New York (CUNY) School of Law, MADRE, and the Organization of Women's Freedom in Iraq (OWFI) filed a ninety-page report with the ICC pursuant to Article 15 of the Rome Statute, which empowers the prosecutor to "initiate investigations *proprio motu* on the basis of information on crimes within the jurisdiction of the Court" (2017). The report offers evidence and legal analysis regarding gender-based crimes committed by foreign fighters in the Islamic State of Iraq and al-Sham/Greater Syria (ISIS, also known as "ISIL," "Daesh," or "IS"), and on that basis, urges the Office of the Prosecutor (OTP) to launch an investigation and calls "on the international community to confront violations of women's rights by ISIS and other extremists" (CUNY HTGJ Clinic, MADRE, and OWFI 2017, 6). This report asserts an agenda at the CVE-ICF-ICC nexus and offers a model for what the prosecutor's case against Al Hassan might look like if the charges proceed beyond the confirmation stage.

As noted earlier, Al Hassan's role as an upholder and enforcer of Islamic law is central to the prosecutor's case against him. This is of course a historical moment where Sharia panic stalks the halls of the Council of Europe and American state legislatures, and Islamic law is often presented as inimical to women's rights (ACLU 2011).[29] Groups like the European Center for Law and Justice advocated for the discussion at the Parliamentary Assembly of the Council of Europe (PACE) on the incompatibility of the Sharia law with human rights.[30] Against this backdrop, the Al Hassan case plays a particularly significant role in burnishing the court's feminist credentials while underscoring its value to dominant CVE agendas. The case information sheet released by the ICC highlights what it describes as Al Hassan's role as "de facto chief of the Islamic police" and says "Mr. Al Hassan was involved in the work of the Islamic court in Timbuktu and participated in executing its decisions." The purported "criminality" and "lawlessness" of the Islamic court is said to render women particularly vulnerable and renders these charges of religious persecution and gender-based persecution intertwined: as ICC Prosecutor Fatou Bensouda noted, "there was religious persecution in Timbuktu: all the rules and prohibitions imposed on the residents stemmed from the ideological and religious vision of Ansar Dine and AQIM. There was also gender-based persecution. Indeed, it was the women and girls of Timbuktu and the region who suffered the most. One witness reported that women had become the primary targets" (2019). Significantly, this shapes the way particular crimes are constructed and the gendered political subjectivity that gets shaped in this prosecutor's approach. For instance, in the Al Hassan case, forced marriage is one of the charges advanced against him as a crime committed in his role as a member of Ansar Dine and as the chief of police enforcing Islamic law. In bringing the forced marriage charges to the fore with only female victims, the court creates a notion of gendered persecution where women are always already victims, and men are always already perpetrators. Like with the niqab, here too there is resonance between actions taken in Mali and in Europe. Thus in 2018 even while Al Hassan was taken into custody and charged with responsibility for forced marriages, the parliamentary assembly of the Council of Europe (2018) passed a resolution condemning forced marriage, marking that the practice imposed costs on women and girls and asking member states to take action locally and globally in fighting the practice. The court's condemnation of Ansar Dine's approach to Islamic law became a way to position itself in the foreground of the fight against violent extremism, and with ICF informing the stakes of that fight enabling CVE interventions to appeal, as the ABA advocated, to broader questions of rights and justice.

The Al Hassan case is not the first in which marriage is a subject of international criminal law. In 2009, the Sierra Leone Special Court was adjudicating *Prosecutor v. Issa Sesay, Morris Kallon and Augustine Gbao* (known as the Revolutionary United Front or RUF cases) and ruled on forced marriage as a crime against humanity for the first time in international criminal law. The case was the subject of much debate because it not only focused attention on particular acts of rape or sexual violence but because the term "forced marriage" potentially included arranged marriage practices that may have long local roots.[31] There were concerns that the case was criminalizing "culture" by framing forced marriage as necessarily entailing rape and sexual violence. In the Al Hassan case, the court is also making a claim about its ability to adjudicate Islamic law and declare in effect that the way marriage is recognized and legalized in the school of Islamic law upheld by Ansar Dine is indicative of a criminal code. One expression of "Sharia panic" emerges in claims of a fundamental incompatibility between Islam and ICL in ways that position ICL as an Archimedean point, speaking for humanity and representing universal interests, against a regressive system, riddled with normalized cruelties and entrenched biases.[32]

The move from the Sierra Leone case to the Mali case reflects the ICC's new emphasis not just on African societies, but also on Islamic societies (including some that are African). This marks an important new phase in the vexed trajectory of "culture" arguments in international criminal law through the regulation of the normative marriage contract and the normative family structure. For some ICF commentators, this opportunity to socially situate and condemn "cultural practices" is precisely the yield of the Al Hassan case. Rosemary Grey emphasizes in her blog *International Law Girls* that a social constructivist understanding of gender allows the court to make judgements on Northern Mali society: "A definition can be found in Article 7(3) of the Statute, which states: 'For the purposes of this Statute, it is understood that the term "gender" refers to the two sexes, male and female, within the context of society.... For the Al-Hassan case, this means that the Court need not box itself into a corner where it ends up arguing that women in Timbuktu were oppressed, barred from public life and subjugated to sexual violence simply because they have two x-chromosomes instead of one. Rather, the court can examine what it meant to be female, in social terms, for women living under the rule of Ansar Dine and AQIM" (Grey 2018). Thus the Al Hassan case's defining and adjudicating of categories such as gender and gendered persecution in relation to forced marriage will mean that the ICC process becomes imbricated in the creation of new meanings, knowledges, and legal practices regarding institutions of sex, gender, and marriage within processes of global governance as they present in Mali—and in other contexts where Islamic jurisprudence is being invoked, and social practices dubbed Islamic can be criminalized with the weight of international criminal law precedent. The forced marriage case draws attention to the extraordinary reach of the ICC's intervention in extending lawfare regarding the public sphere at the intersection of CVE-ICC-ICF, to lawfare regarding the private sphere. As the court exerts its authority in navigating the distinction between law and crime, between legitimate traditions and illegitimate ones, what gets defined is not just gender but also Islam. There is a slippage between ideas, practices, policies, and rules regarding gender, sexuality, and family law outside of a Western register, and the claim that we are already in the terrain of VE—in other words, one might say there is a slippage between Islam and VE.

I have sought in the preceding paragraphs to recount how the dual persecution charges come together to channel a notion of transgression and individual political subjectivity that carries with it a hierarchy of societies on the basis of its dominant social codes. In the context of contemporary Islamophobia the employment of criminal charges in forced marriage cases even in domestic contexts has drawn criticism for how family structures and marital practices of minority and racial others have been framed as "cultural," and specifically as culturally retrograde—functioning often as a proxy for hierarchical racial categorization (Volpp 2000). For critics, "radicalization" indicators targeting minority women and so-called cultural practices require intersectional analysis of dominant religious and gender biases within the CVE framework. Significantly however, within the ICF framework, commentators supporting the ICC's charges against Al Hassan have flipped the intersectionality analysis to celebrate the simultaneous pursuit of religious and gender persecution charges as a new dawn for intersectional analysis in the domain of international criminal law. For instance, Grey (2018) declares that the Al Hassan case is a pioneering and welcome prosecution "on the grounds of religion and gender *coupled together*." She argues further that "this formulation puts the Court in a strong position to find that persecution on intersecting grounds is possible, as a matter of law. Such a finding would be a positive development in the jurisprudence, not just for gender-based persecution but for persecution on all grounds." Others also see future potential of intersectionality analysis informing prosecution policy within an ICF framework against groups like ISIS. For instance writing in the *Yale Law Journal*, Emily Chertoff advocates for advancing persecution charges against ISIS for the treatment of Yazidi women in ways that are motivated by the victims' intersecting identities: "we must firmly declare our disapproval of those who doubly persecute other human beings and offer our support for those who are doubly victimized" (2017, 1117). She argues a case against ISIS should be just the beginning of these intersectional prosecutions; she recommends the court then look at parallel cases in Afghanistan, DRC, and beyond and indeed that "a series of prosecutions" might be just what is needed in "restoring the legitimacy of the ailing ICC" (Chertoff 2017, 1116). Thus as ICF reaches forward, an intertwined focus on Islam appears a likely set of next steps for the court's work on gender and religion-based persecution charges.

It is worth observing this is a striking turn for intersectionality analysis. In the history of critical race theory intersectionality was an important vantage point for vulnerable groups to hold powerful actors accountable; accordingly, the vantage point was a bottom-up heterodox feminist perspective aimed at better illuminating the nature of oppression. However, with intersectionality being employed by the ICC in ways that ally its prosecutorial vantage point with NATO's CVE campaign, we are left with questions about what gets illuminated, and what gets obscured from this top-down perspective.

CONCLUSION

This chapter has bracketed the legal and evidentiary analysis of the war crimes and crimes against humanity (including persecution on gender and religious grounds) that Al Hassan is charged with. Instead, I have sought to situate the very fact of Al Hassan in the ICC's docket within a broader frame. It has sought to lay the groundwork for analysis of how gender gets defined, fixed, and troubled by the court proceedings at various moments and how this in turn channels the ways Islam and Islamic societies get coded and interpolated. If CVE, lawfare, and ICF represent force fields of law, policy, and human rights activism that created mutually reinforcing dynamics, this synergy was itself a "force multiplier," to use Colin Powell's telling phrase.

These dynamics made the Al Hassan case the logical next step for the ICC and a cause célèbre for the most influential strands of ICF. This convergence of religion and gender-based persecution charges does raise important questions about the work of feminism in this nexus. How have women's rights discourse and feminist projects become conscripted into colonial/racialized/Islamophobic tropes and legacies regarding rights in and against culture that connect the dots between battlefields and court rooms, judges and generals? For instance, does ICF's employment of (and synergy with) CVE and lawfare agendas in highlighting Al Hassan's abuse help obscure the abuses committed in the pursuit of the CVE and lawfare agendas? What is the vision of political subjectivity and emancipation that will shape how the ICF understands what counts as persecution? How do alternative, heterodox feminist agendas fare in this process? In the coming together of these forces, dominant strands of ICF get propelled to a new role in governance, from determining the contours of the normative marriage contract to shaping which interpretations of Islamic law should be criminalized. In bringing together how ICF is situated in relation to the intertwined developments of CVE and lawfare, we throw into relief the profoundly troubling drivers that have birthed cases like Al Hassan's and raise questions about ICF entanglements. Neither leader nor follower, ICF operates in a political, legal, and normative ecosystem, and we need to study that ecosystem to understand how certain kinds of codependencies and convergences between different global governance projects become thinkable, sustainable, and from some vantage points, inevitable. Law and policy agendas coupling discourse about women's ever-present vulnerability, alongside the ever-present threat of VE, shape and legitimize a sexual/terrorism panic inflected role for the ICC. Concomitantly, it concedes or even supports hegemonic approaches to international law as a champion of secularism and liberal "freedoms" against a global Islamic jihad persecuting women and minorities. The Al Hassan case may be specimen A in this project.

NOTES

My thanks to Lila Abu-Lughod, Nadera Shalhoub-Kevorkian, Rema Hammami, Janet R. Jakobsen, and other participants for close engagement with this chapter at the Barnard conference Global Governance of the Intimate as well as Gina Heathcote and Vanja Hamzic for very valuable engagement and feedback on this chapter as the inaugural Gender and Law Lecture at SOAS in October 2019. Finally my thanks to the anonymous reviewers of the book from Duke for their very helpful input as well.

1   His full name is Al-Hassan Ag Abdoul Aziz Ag Mohamed Ag Mahmoud. For the charge sheet, see the ICC's Summary of Judgment and Sentence: https://www.icc-cpi.int/mali/al-hassan/Documents/al-hassanEng.pdf. This paper follows the prosecutor in referring to the group as "Ansar Dine"; the ICC also uses "Ansar Eddine."

2   The ICC's Mali files first gained global attention in relation to its prosecution of Ahmad Al Faqi Al Mahdi for the destruction of the Sufi mausoleums in Timbuktu as a war crime; see https://www.icc-cpi.int/itemsDocuments/160926 Al-MahdiSummary.pdf.

3   For the 2018 press release and the warrant of arrest, see the International Criminal Court website: https://www.icc-cpi.int/Pages/item.aspx?name=pr1376.

   In her application for the warrant for Al-Hassan's arrest, the prosecutor alleged that there were reasonable grounds to believe that he was criminally responsible for the following crimes within the terms of the Rome Statute: (a) crimes against humanity, viz. torture, rape, sexual slavery, persecution on religious and gender grounds, and other inhumane acts perpetrated in Timbuktu, Mali, between April 2012 and January 2013; and (b) war crimes, viz. violence to person, outrages upon personal dignity, the passing of sentences without previous judgment pronounced by a regularly constituted court affording all judicial guarantees which are generally recognized as indispensable, rape and sexual slavery, perpetrated in Timbuktu, Mali, between April 2012 and January 2013; and the war crime of intentionally directing attacks against buildings dedicated to religion and historic monuments, perpetrated in Timbuktu, Mali, between late June and mid-July 2012.

4   For instance, see the International Criminal Court's 2021 press release on the recharacterization of the charges at https://www.icc-cpi.int/Pages/item.aspx?name=pr1600.

5   Brown and Grenfell trace this to Copelon's response to widespread rape in the war in the former Yugoslavia in Copelon's (1994) influential article "Surfacing Gender: Reconceptualizing Crimes against Women in Time of War."

6   Gender-based persecution counts as grounds for asylum in some jurisdictions.

7   Kony was charged with twelve counts of crimes against humanity and twenty-one counts of war crimes committed during the LRA's insurgency in northern Uganda between 2002 and 2004. The crimes against humanity charges cover

murder, enslavement, sexual enslavement, rape, and inhumane acts—but not persecution based on gender or religion.

8   While charges have not yet been brought in the Myanmar case, the trial chamber has approved investigations, concluding that "widespread and/or systematic acts of violence may have been committed that could qualify as the crimes against humanity of deportation across the Myanmar-Bangladesh border and persecution on grounds of ethnicity and/or religion against the Rohingya population," as Ewalina U. Ochab (2019)notes.

9   In its 2016 Preliminary Examinations Report, the International Criminal Court discusses the potential charges against Afghanistan, and discusses the potential charges against Boko Haram in its 2018 report (International Criminal Court Preliminary Examinations, 2018).

10 Ba believes however that the current debate about the ICC's Africa bias is reductionist and misses other dimensions of the ICC-Africa relationship, including the agendas of African states as discussed further in relation to the "cultural heritage" case in Mali.

11 In an important intervention, Oumar Ba makes the argument that African states are themselves using the terrain of international criminal justice to wage their own battles, sometimes against internal enemies. He doesn't engage with the Al-Hassan case, but in speaking of the first ICC case involving Mali, the case against Al Mahdi for the destruction of Sufi mosques and mausoleums, he argues that this case did not address the gravest issues in the war and it was not a priority for the citizens of Timbuktu—indeed, that they saw it as a "distraction." However, both the Mali government and the ICC prioritized that case because of their own interests in legitimizing themselves with the international community; this case aided the ICC in doing that by demonstrating both unprecedented efficiency in the administration of justice, and it aided the Mali government in affirming the global "world heritage" significance of Timbuktu and Mali more generally (Ba 2020). Ba lays out his broader argument about Africa and the ICC in "International Justice and the Postcolonial Condition" (2017).

12 I use ICF to describe the advocacy of agendas that contributed to and gained momentum from the passage of SCR 1325 on Women, Peace and Security. As I outline in *Governance Feminism* (2019), these include "a complex of policies that take as their starting point the notion that women are victimized by conflict and excluded or marginalized in peace and security decision-making and postconflict recovery. Against this backdrop, ICF seeks remedies for that victimization and law and policy interventions directed at the inclusion and empowerment of women in conflict and postconflict contexts. ICF encourages a particular focus on women as victims of sexual violence and, concomitantly, a focus on prosecution of sexual violence crimes as an especially high priority. In addition to SCR 1325 and the Security Council resolutions that have followed, ICF also manifests in the gender jurisprudence of international courts and tribunals. In postcon-

flict institution-building/nation-building initiatives; and in development and reconstruction policies and projects. As indicated in the 2015 UN Global Study, in each of these arenas ICF emerges from and in turn organizes a global women's rights network. For instance, ICF jurisprudence in international courts and tribunals was shaped by lawyers and judges within these institutions, as well as an active engaged community of feminist activists, scholars, and organizations that tracked, reviewed, and pressured the gender jurisprudence of these bodies."

13 There has of course been widespread analysis of the French bombing as an imperial intervention, motivated by military interests in regional power and economic interests in uranium and other resources. For instance, note the work of University of Lausanne professor Jean Batou's (2013) analysis of the intervention. In addition, there was speculation on the Pan African News Wire that the bombing was motivated by French efforts to demonstrate its new bombers and clinch a military trade deal with India regarding those bombers.

14 Titled "A New Beginning," Obama's (2009) speech was aimed at conveying a hopeful universalism against the clash of civilizations approach identified with his predecessor's regime in Washington: "I've come here to Cairo to seek a new beginning between the United States and Muslims around the world, one based on mutual interest and mutual respect, and one based upon the truth that America and Islam are not exclusive and need not be in competition. Instead, they overlap, and share common principles—principles of justice and progress; tolerance and the dignity of all human beings."

15 Established by the Duke of Wellington in 1840, RUSI was an institution of the British Empire that has transitioned into its postcolonial role as a champion of empire as such, with celebrants like Henry Kissinger. https://rusi.org/CVE.

16 For instance, a USAID (2018) brochure on its CVE work in Mali makes no explicit reference to Islam. It speaks instead through euphemisms such as radicalization, violent conflict, vulnerable communities, etc.

17 France's role in the bombing of Libya has come under similar scrutiny with reports that Sarkozy was seeking to paint himself as an opponent of Gaddafi in the context of fending off a corruption case linking him to Gaddafi. For more on France's role in the bombing of Libya, see Joe Penney's (2018) investigation in *The Intercept*.

18 Batou's (2013) article describes the "neo-colonial character" of the bombing, as well as history of French colonialism in Mali and local resistance.

19 For instance, Nazia Kazi (2017) describes the emergence of a Muslim misleadership class: "A Muslim misleadership class would, by definition, comply with the very structures of law enforcement that demonize and devastate their constituencies. It would accept CVE grant funding, effectively introducing mechanisms of surveillance and policing into Muslim spaces. It would comply with border patrol or local law enforcement, perhaps arguing that each of these institutions ought to be made more 'culturally competent' and 'inclusive.'"

20 The Georgetown Institute for Women, Peace and Security and the Peace Re-

search Institute of Oslo have collaborated on what they term a WPS Index on women's well being and empowerment. They describe the index as follows: "The WPS Index offers a more comprehensive measure of women's wellbeing and their empowerment in homes, communities, and societies more broadly ... we draw on recognized international data sources to rank 153 countries on both peace and security—and women's inclusion and justice. The associated tools and analysis highlight key achievements and deficits from each country." https://giwps.georgetown.edu/about-the-index/.

21 This decision was given even wider scope when the European Court of Justice ruled in 2017 that European companies can outlaw the headscarf, and reaffirmed it with even greater detail in 2021 (Rankin 2021).

22 While R2P is not itself a treaty, it reformulates the basic legal architecture of the international system, including the Security Council's exercise of its Chapter VII powers for intervention. Developed post-Kosovo (where NATO intervened in the name of humanitarian crisis) and post-Rwanda (where the international community retreated), R2P was developed in the 1990s by an international commission, was endorsed by the UN member states in the 2005 Global Summit, and invoked by the Security Council in over eighty resolutions, typically in relation to contexts deemed conflict zones such as Syria, Burundi, Yemen, the Central African Republic, and of course most consequentially, for its 2011 military intervention in Libya. The Security Council has a responsibility to determine that an R2P obligation has been triggered, but as the intervention in Libya indicates, this authorization does not insulate an intervention from debate and questions regarding the legitimacy of intervention.

23 Itself linked to economic and geopolitical interests in Libyan oil fields and other resources.

24 John Carlson and Neville Yoemans (1975) claim first usage of the term in a 1975 article advocating approaches to conflict mediation within an IHL framework that speaks positively of how "lawfare replaces warfare and the duel is with words rather than swords."

25 A critical summary of the various justifications for the Libyan invasion by Slaughter and others can be found in Micah Zenko's (2011) article "Libya: 'Justifications' for Intervention"; and of Slaughter in particular in Steve Breyman's (2014) article, "The Aptly Named Anne-Marie Slaughter."

26 They released a statement supporting the launch of ICC action in Mali where the first indictment was against Al Hassan's Anise Dine colleague, Almed Al Faqi Al Mahdi, http://www.pgaction.org/news/mahdis-trial-by-icc-rule-of-law.html. A fuller statement of their approach to CVE with a focus on law rather than military action—although not ruling out the latter—is available at the Parliamentarians for Global Action website: http://www.pgaction.org/campaigns/violent-extremism.html.

27 For instance, in her speech "The Role of Women and Girls in Countering Violent Extremism," Pamela Hamamoto, the former US Permanent Represen-

tative to the UN in Geneva, describes this approach: "Facts tell us that women are the targets of violence perpetrated by ISIL and ISIS; facts tell us that at the same time, many women flock to the ranks of ISIS—according to the *New York Times*, roughly 10 percent of its Western recruits are female; but, most crucially, common sense and past experience tells us that women wield significant influence in their families and can counter violent extremism. If we can reach women—wives and mothers and daughters—we can support them in creating a new narrative, a narrative where empowered women can focus on the concerns of their families and neighbors—of their communities." See also Abu-Lughod (this volume).

28 The resolution has been followed by renewed advocacy for ICF approaches in CVE. For instance, Lana Baydas, Lauren Mooney, and Paul Nguyen-Cong-Doc of the DC-based policy think tank, Center for Strategic and International Studies (CSIS), argue that: "It is in the US national security interests to design and implement the most effective counterterrorism strategy possible—and undeniably, a gender approach that recognizes the various roles of women and girls to countering terrorism and resolving conflict will lead to the most success" (2018).

29 See the Council of Europe Parliamentary Assembly's 2016 report, *Compatibility of Sharia Law with the European Convention on Human Rights: Can State Parties to the Convention Be Signatories of the "Cairo Declaration"?*

30 See Nicolas Bauer, "Showdown: Sharia and Human Rights," *European Centre for Law and Justice* (2018). https://eclj.org/religious-freedom/coe/confrontation-de-la-charia-islamique-et-des-droits-de-lhomme-au-conseil-de-leurope/.

31 Concern expressed by Rhonda Copelon at the Bellagio conference on Gender and Transitional Justice, 2005. Copelon preferred the use of "sexual slavery" to distinguish the crime from alternative marriage practices.

32 For instance, see Kelly (2008).

REFERENCES

Abu-Lughod, Lila. 2013. *Do Muslim Women Need Saving?* Cambridge, MA: Harvard University Press.

ACLU. 2011. "Nothing to Fear: Debunking the Mythical 'Sharia Threat' to our Judicial System." *American Civil Liberties Union*, May 2011. https://www.aclu.org/report/nothing-fear-debunking-mythical-sharia-threat-our-judicial-system.

Amnesty International. 2012. "Mali's Worst Human Rights Situation in 50 Years." *Amnesty International*, May 16, 2012. https://www.amnesty.org/en/latest/news/2012/05/mali-s-worst-human-rights-situation-50-years/.

Ba, Oumar. 2017. "International Justice and the Postcolonial Condition." *Africa Today* 63, no. 4: 45–62. https://www.jstor.org/stable/10.2979/africatoday.63.issue-4.

Ba, Oumar. 2020. "Contested Meanings: Timbuktu and the Prosecution of the Destruction of Cultural Heritage as War Crimes." *African Studies Review* 63, no. 4: 743–62. https://doi.org/10.1017/asr.2020.16.

Bakker, Alexandrah. 2020. "Gender Based Persecution at the International Criminal Court." *Public International Law and Policy Group*, November 25. https://www.publicinternationallawandpolicygroup.org/lawyering-justice-blog/2020/11/25/gender-based-persecution-at-the-international-criminal-court-questions-and-implications.

Barnett, Michael. 2013. *Empire of Humanity: A History of Humanitarianism*. Ithaca, NY: Cornell University Press.

Batou, Jean. 2013. "Mali: A Neo-Colonial Operation Disguised as an Anti-Terrorist Intervention." *New Politics* 14, no. 3: 2937. https://newpol.org/issue_post/mali-neo-colonial-operation-disguised-anti-terrorist-intervention/.

Baydas, Lana, Lauren Mooney, and Paul Nguyen-Cong-Duc. 2018. "A Panoramic Gender Lens to Fight Terrorism and Counter Violent Extremism." *Center for Strategic and International Studies*. https://www.csis.org/analysis/panoramic-gender-lens-fight-terrorism-and-counter-violent-extremism.

Bensouda, Fatou. 2019. *Statement of the Prosecutor of the International Criminal Court, Fatou Bensouda, at the opening of the Confirmation of Charges Hearing against Al Hassan*. https://www.icc-cpi.int/Pages/item.aspx?name=180708-otp-statement-al-hassan.

Breyman, Steve. 2014. "The Aptly Named Anne-Marie Slaughter." *Truthout*, May 24. https://truthout.org/articles/the-aptly-named-anne-marie-slaughter/.

Brown, Widney, and Laura Grenfell. 2003. "The International Crime of Gender-Based-Persecution and the Taliban." *Melbourne Journal of International Law* 5: 347–75. https://ssrn.com/abstract=3396224.

Burke, Jason. 2018. "ICC prosecutes Islamist militant on groundbreaking gender-based charges." *The Guardian*, April 12. https://www.theguardian.com/law/2018/apr/12/icc-prosecutes-islamist-militant-al-hassan-ag-abdoul-aziz-ag-mohamed-ag-mahmoud-gender-persecution.

Carlson, John, and Neville Yeomans. 1975. "Whither Goeth the Law—Humanity of Barbarity." In *The Way Out—Radical Alternatives in Australia*, edited by M. Smith and D. Crossley. Melbourne: Lansdowne Press.

Chertoff, Emily. 2017. "Prosecuting Gender-Based Persecution: The Islamic State at the ICC." *The Yale Law Journal* 126, no. 4: 908–1241. https://www.yalelawjournal.org/note/prosecuting-gender-based-persecution-the-islamic-state-at-the-icc.

Chrisafis, Angelique, Afua Hirsch, and Nick Hopkins. 2013. "France launches air strikes on Mali." *The Guardian*, January 11. https://www.theguardian.com/world/2013/jan/11/france-launches-airstrikes-on-mali.

Cohen, Aviv. 2012. "Prosecuting Terrorists at the International Criminal Court: Reevaluating an Unused Legal Tool to Combat Terrorism." *Michigan State International Law Review* 20: 219–57. https://digitalcommons.law.msu.edu/cgi/viewcontent.cgi?referer=https://search.yahoo.com/&httpsredir=1&article=1080&context=ilr.

Copelon, Rhonda. 1994. "Surfacing Gender: Reconceptualizing Crimes against Women in Time of War." In *Mass Rape: The War against Women in Bosnia-Herzegovina*, edited by Alexandra Stiglmayer, 197–208. Lincoln: University of Nebraska Press.

Council of Europe Parliamentary Assembly. 2016. *Compatibility of Sharia Law with the European Convention on Human Rights: Can States Parties to the Convention Be Signatories of the "Cairo Declaration?"* Doc. 13965. http://assembly.coe.int/nw/xml/XRef/Xref-XML2HTML-EN.asp?fileid=22447&lang=en.

Council of Europe Parliamentary Assembly. 2018. *Forced Marriage in Europe*, Resolution 2233. http://assembly.coe.int/nw/xml/XRef/Xref-XML2HTML-EN.asp?fileid=25016&lang=en.

De Leede, Seran, Renate Haupfleisch, Katja Korolkova, and Monika Natter. 2017. "Radicalisation and Violent Extremism—Focus on Women: How Women Become Radicalised and How to Empower Them to Prevent Radicalisation." *Policy Department for Citizens' Rights and Constitutional Affairs, European Union*. http://www.europarl.europa.eu/RegData/etudes/STUD/2017/596838/IPOL_STU(2017)596838_EN.pdf.

Department of Homeland Security. 2019. "Counterterrorism Futures: A Whole-of-Society Approach." 2019. Public-Private Analytic Exchange. https://www.dhs.gov/sites/default/files/publications/ia/ia_counterterrorism-futures.pdf.

Epure, Georgiana. 2020. "Writing the Jurisprudence on Gender-based Persecution: Al Hassan on Trial at the ICC." *International Justice Monitor*, July 16. https://www.ijmonitor.org/2020/07/writing-the-jurisprudence-on-gender-based-persecution-al-hassan-on-trial-at-the-icc/.

Forestier, Marie. 2018. "Malian Suspect at ICC: New Opportunity for Accountability for Sexual Crimes." *IntLawGrrls*, June 19. https://ilg2.org/2018/06/19/malian-suspect-at-icc-new-opportunity-for-accountability-for-sexual-crimes/.

Frazer, Owen, and Christian Nünlist. 2015. "The Concept of Countering Violent Extremism." *CSS Analyses in Security Policy* 183. https://css.ethz.ch/content/dam/ethz/special-interest/gess/cis/center-for-securities-studies/pdfs/CSSAnalyse183-EN.pdf.

Global Justice Center. 2018. "The Global Justice Center Applauds ICC for Issuing Warrant for Gender-Based Persecution." Global Justice Center Press Release, April 13. http://globaljusticecenter.net/press-center/press-releases/907-gjc-applauds-icc-warrant-gender-based-persecution.

Goldsmith, Jack. 2011. "ROLFF-A Gets a Boost From NATO," *Lawfare*, June 9. https://www.lawfareblog.com/rolff-gets-boost-nato.

Greenwald, Glenn. 2013. "The Bombing of Mali Highlights All the Lessons of Western Intervention." *The Guardian*, January 14. https://www.theguardian.com/commentisfree/2013/jan/14/mali-france-bombing-intervention-libya.

Grey, Rosemary. 2018. "International Criminal Court Poised to Interpret the Crime of 'Gender-Based Persecution' For the First Time." *IntLawGrrls*, April 12. https://ilg2.org/2018/04/12/international-criminal-court-poised-to-interpret-the-crime-of-gender-based-persecution-for-the-first-time/.

Grey, Rosemary, Jonathan O'Donohue, Indira Rosenthal, Lisa Davis, and Dorine Llanta. 2019. "Gender-based Persecution as a Crime Against Humanity: The Road Ahead." *Journal of International Criminal Justice* 17, no. 5: 957–79. https://doi.org/10.1093/jicj/mqz048.

The Human Rights and Gender Justice (HRGJ) Clinic of the City University of New York (CUNY) School of Law, MADRE, and The Organization of Women's Freedom in Iraq (OWFI). 2017. "Communication to the ICC Prosecutor Pursuant to Article 15 of the Rome Statute Requesting a Preliminary Examination into the Situation of: Gender-Based Persecution and Torture as Crimes against Humanity and War Crimes Committed by the Islamic State of Iraq and the Levant (ISIL) in Iraq." https://www.madre.org/sites/default/files/PDFs/CUNY%20MADRE%20OWFI%20Article%2015%20Communication%20Submission%20Gender%20Crimes%20in%20Iraq%20PDF.pdf.

Ignatieff, Michael. 2003. *Empire Lite: Nation Building in Bosnia, Kosovo, Afghanistan*. Toronto: Penguin Canada.

International Criminal Court. 2016. "Report on Preliminary Examination Activities (2016)." *The Office of the Prosecutor*, November 14. https://www.icc-cpi.int/itemsDocuments/181205-rep-otp-PE-ENG.pdf.

International Criminal Court. 2018. "Report on Preliminary Examination Activities (2018)." *The Office of the Prosecutor*, December 5. https://www.icc-cpi.int/itemsDocuments/181205-rep-otp-PE-ENG.pdf.

Kazi, Nazia. 2017. "Against a Muslim Misleadership Class." *Jacobin*, February 6. https://www.jacobinmag.com/2017/06/islamophobia-countering-violent-extremism-muslim-leaders.

Kelly, Michael J. 2008. "Islam & International Criminal Law: A Brief (In)compatibility Study." *Yearbook of Islamic and Middle Eastern Law Online* 14, no. 1: 3–25. https://doi.org/10.1163/22112987-91000205.

Kenny, Cóman. 2017. "Prosecuting Crimes of International Concern: Islamic State at the ICC?" *Utrecht Journal of International and European Law* 33, no. 84: 120–45. http://doi.org/10.5334/ujiel.364.

Khan, Scheherazade. 2018. "An Approach to Prevention and Countering Terrorism and Violent Extremism?" *Women's International League for Peace & Freedom*, July 19. https://wilpf.org/a-women-peace-and-security-approach-to-prevention-and-countering-terrorism-and-violent-extremism/.

Nesiah, Vasuki. 2016. "Local Ownership of Global Governance." *Journal of International Criminal Justice* 14, no. 4: 985–1009. https://doi.org/10.1093/jicj/mqw046.

Nesiah, Vasuki. 2019. "Indebted: The Cruel Optimism of Leaning into Empowerment." In *Governance Feminism: Notes from the Field*, edited by Janet Halley, Prabha Kotiswaran, Rachel Rebouché, and Hila Shamir, 505–54. Minneapolis: University of Minnesota Press.

Obama, Barack. 2009. "The President's Speech in Cairo: A New Beginning." *The White House of President Barack Obama*, June 4. https://obamawhitehouse

.archives.gov/issues/foreign-policy/presidents-speech-cairo-a-new-beginning.

Ochab, Ewalina U. 2019. "The ICC Is Taking a Pro-Active Approach to Myanmar." *Impakter*, May 13.

O'Leary, Emma. 2018. "Principles under Pressure: The Impact of Counterterrorism Measures and Preventing/Countering Violent Extremism on Humanitarian Action." *Norwegian Refugee Council*. https://www.nrc.no/resources/reports/principles-under-pressure/.

Oosterveld, Valerie. 2006. "Gender, Persecution, and the International Criminal Court: Refugee Law's Relevance to the Crime Against Humanity of Gender Based Persecution." *Duke Journal of Comparative and International Law* 17: 49–90. https://scholarship.law.duke.edu/djcil/vol17/iss1/2.

Penney, Joe. 2018. "Why Did the US and Its Allies Bomb Libya? Corruption Case against Sarkozy Sheds New Light on Ousting of Gaddafi." *The Intercept*, April 28. https://theintercept.com/2018/04/28/sarkozy-gaddafi-libya-bombing/.

Perez, Chris. 2016. "White House Censors French President for Saying 'Islamist Terrorism.'" *New York Post*, April 2. https://nypost.com/2016/04/02/white-house-doctors-video-to-remove-islamic-terrorism-quote/.

Powell, Colin L. 2001. "Remarks to the National Foreign Policy Conference for Leaders of Nongovernmental Organizations." *The Avalon Project: Documents in Law, History, and Diplomacy*, October 26. https://avalon.law.yale.edu/sept11/powell_brief31.asp.

Prosecutor v. Callixte Mbarushimana, Case no. ICC-01/04–01/10. International Criminal Court. December 16, 2011. https://www.icc-cpi.int/CourtRecords/CR2011_22538.PDF.

Rankin, Jennifer. 2021. "EU Companies Can Ban Employees Wearing Headscarves, Court Rules." *The Guardian*, July 15. https://www.theguardian.com/world/2021/jul/15/eu-companies-can-ban-employees-wearing-headscarves-religious-symbols.

Roberts, Dan. 2015. "White House Resists Calls to Focus on Islamist Terrorism at Three-Day Extremism Summit." *The Guardian*, February 17. https://www.theguardian.com/us-news/2015/feb/17/white-house-islamic-terror-extremism-summit.

Robinson, Nicholas, and Catherine Lena Kelly. 2017. *Rule of Law Approaches to Countering Violent Extremism*. American Bar Association's Rule of Law Initiative. https://www.americanbar.org/content/dam/aba/directories/roli/misc/rule-of-law-approaches-to-countering-violent-extremism-2017.authcheckdam.pdf.

Rogin, Josh. 2011. "Anne-Marie Slaughter Tweets Call for Intervention in Libya." *Foreign Policy*, February 24. https://foreignpolicy.com/2011/02/24/anne-marie-slaughter-tweets-call-for-intervention-in-libya/.

Sewall, Sarah. 2016. "Women and Countering Violent Extremism." US Department of State Archived Content. March 17, 2016. https://2009-2017.state.gov/j/remarks/254868.htm.

Slaughter, Anne-Marie. 2011. "Fiddling While Libya Burns." *New York Times*, March 13. https://www.nytimes.com/2011/03/14/opinion/14slaughter.html.

United Nations Security Council Resolution 2242. 2015. *To Improve Implementation of Landmark Text on Women, Peace, Security Agenda*, S/Res/2242. https://undocs.org/S/RES/2242(2015).

United States Government Interagency Counterinsurgency Initiative. 2009. "U.S. Government Counterinsurgency Guide." *Bureau of Political-Military Affairs*. https://fas.org/man/eprint/ciguide.pdf.

USAID. 2018. "Countering Violent Extremism (CVE) Activity." *USAID/Mali Countering Violent Extremism Overview*, February 2018. https://www.usaid.gov/sites/default/files/documents/1860/ USAID _ PDG _-_ CVE_Program_Overview _-_Feb_18_Final.pdf.

Volpp, Leti. 2000. "Blaming Culture for Bad Behavior." *Yale Journal of Law and the Humanities* 12, nos. 2–3: 89–116. https://digitalcommons.law.yale.edu/yjlh/vol12/iss1/3.

The White House Office of the Press Secretary. 2015. "FACT SHEET: The White House Summit on Countering Violent Extremism." *The White House of President Barack Obama*, February 18. https://obamawhitehouse.archives.gov/the-press-office/2015/02/18/fact-sheet-white-house-summit-countering-violent-extremism.

Zenko, Micah. 2011. "Libya: 'Justifications' for Intervention." *Council on Foreign Relations*, June 24. https://www.cfr.org/blog/libya-justifications-intervention.

TWO · *Lila Abu-Lughod*

Securofeminism

Embracing a Phantom

In May 2017, the leaders of Saudi Arabia, Egypt, and the United States, placed their hands on a glowing globe to signal their united resolve to combat the global threat of violent extremism (Hunt 2017). This moment during the visit to Saudi Arabia by the then-new US president Donald Trump unveiled for the world a high-tech node in the international apparatus of security and counterterrorism. The Global Center for Countering Violent Extremist Ideologies, whose launch was being celebrated, marked the maturation of the strategy of supplementing militarization and policing with ideological warfare, ideology having been construed as fundamental to extremists in the way that propaganda was presumed fundamental to communists during the Cold War (Kundnani 2014; Kundnani and Hayes 2018). In a twenty-first century obsessed with social media and the power of the internet, the center's mission was to monitor the internet and deploy artificial intelligence to intercept messages that, in security-speak, lured vulnerable subjects to extremism.

A slick brochure gives the center's Arabic name as *E'tidal*, meaning moderation. Moderation is an antonym of extremism. The center's mission was to disseminate counternarratives about Islam over the internet, a tactic it shared with a host of other initiatives that have brought internet giants like Google and Facebook together with national and international organizations from the UN, EU, and USAID to grassroot nongovernmental and civil society organizations (NGOs and CSOs). Countering extremist ideologies is providing jobs for security personnel, psychologists, religious scholars, advertising and public relations firms, and, perhaps surprisingly, feminists.

Since 2010 or so, gender experts and women's rights advocates have been clamoring for inclusion in this "soft" branch of the global security enterprise that goes under the name CVE (countering violent extremism) or PVE (preventing violent extremism). In their practical projects, these initiatives have become increasingly gendered as they target women and "youth" to enhance "community resilience" and undermine "radicalization" (Fadil and de Koning 2019). This chapter analyzes the advocacy by feminists and women's rights groups for "mainstreaming" gender into CVE and installing women in leadership positions in this rapidly expanding field. I call this heterogeneous group "securofeminists"; I worry that their engagements with the new face and phase of global counterterrorism implicate them in problematic projects of suspicion and surveillance. In seeking to bring gender awareness to counterterrorism they have, wittingly or unwittingly, embraced a phantom: the undefined and undefinable category of violent extremism. In accepting this term they contribute to Islamophobic public discourse in ways they would disavow. In accepting the ground rules of securitization, they also endanger men and women around the world.

Securofeminism has emerged as a strand of what Halley et. al. (2018, 2019) call governance feminism, by which they mean "every form in which feminists and feminist ideas exert a governing will within human affairs" whether through incorporation into state, statelike, and state-affiliated power or well beyond and into other public and private governance networks (2019, xii). Securofeminists work outside of official military and security sectors and align themselves with women's rights, human rights, and the UN Women, Peace, and Security agendas that seek to engage women in conflict resolution and recognize their needs in conflicts and their aftermaths in ways that Karen Engle (2020) has recently documented thoroughly.[1]

In the spirit of feminist internal critique, and grounded in my own perspective on the politics of gender violence from research in and on the Muslim world, I want to challenge the twin premises of securofeminism: its acceptance of the validity of the category "violent extremism" and its self-justifying deployment of the charge that extremists are perpetrators of extreme forms of gender-based violence. Securofeminists downplay the extremity of other forms of violence, including those perpetrated by states and condoned in the international system and accept a category that has little explanatory value for political understanding. I also examine the securofeminists' responses to the unraveling of their strategy of promoting the gendering of CVE as they had to confront in the mid-2010s the flow of women migrants to Syria and Iraq seeking to live under the Islamic State.

Grassroots human rights advocates and some gender policy experts who work closely with the institutions of international and state power have cautioned about the risks of this engagement with the security apparatus. Critical scholars of international human rights law, as well as sociologists and anthropologists attuned to the dangers of the traffic between policy worlds and academia, have been especially wary and vocal in their concerns (e.g., Fadil, de Koning, and Ragazzi 2019a; Modirzadeh 2016). Yet, whether because of the extraordinary opportunities CVE opens up to feminists for influencing policy, attracting funding, or bolstering careers; the longstanding hostility many feminists have toward religion, with a special animus toward Islam; the current dominance of both liberal and carceral politics in feminism that aligns easily with the "War on Terror"; or simply because activists have been worn down by the numbing repetition of terms and frameworks that have accompanied the global security agenda's growing hegemony, these critiques have not had much traction.

In an article published just before CVE emerged fully onto the international scene, Nesiah (2013, 127–28) observed that 2000 marked the arrival of International Conflict Feminism (ICF) as a player in global power politics. With the UN Security Council's passage of Resolution 1325 on Women, Peace and Security—a victory for women at the UN who fought hard to highlight the gendered impact of war and to urge the incorporation of women into peacekeeping processes and postconflict reconstruction—the way was opened for feminist inclusion in the field of global security. Nesiah concluded her analysis of the earlier feminist controversies over the WPS agenda by warning that feminists should "unpack the background assumptions and assess the distributive consequences of security, the rule of law, and a range of attendant political vocabularies and policy agendas that have shaped the normative common sense that brokered the marriage of ICF and counter-terrorism" (Nesiah 2013, 151). With the shift to CVE, we need now to assess the implications of securofeminist appeals for and engagement with what some call "inclusive security"—security inclusive of women and with attention to gender violence.

CLAMORING FOR INCLUSION

Femocrats like Sarah Sewall, US Under Secretary for Civilian Security, Democracy, and Human Rights, have presented the CVE agenda as a new opportunity for those who care about women's rights and empowerment. She hailed CVE as "a vital new dimension of the Women, Peace and Security agenda" that would offer women "an opportunity to reframe their rights and roles as part of the most salient international security effort of the 21st century." Brushing aside concerns voiced by some feminist critics within the UN and NGO worlds—cautions I explore below—this government official urged women to "get in on the ground floor of this nascent architecture and shape the agenda to ensure that women are involved, and their perspectives incorporated" into the security agendas of the UN (Sewall 2016).

Scores of policy papers drafted around that same period for think tanks, NGOs, governmental agencies, and international governance institutions deplored the fact that counterterrorism had previously been a man's world. They extoll the values of gender inclusion in volumes like *A Man's World: Exploring the Roles of Women in Countering Terrorism and Violent Extremism* (Fink, Zeiger, and Bhulai 2016) produced by Hedayah, a "center for excellence" in counterterrorism funded by the United Arab Emirates. In the dialect of international governance, calls for including women in PVE or CVE are framed in terms of their concern as "stakeholders." To clarify what these stakes are, every document invokes the special dangers violent extremists pose to women.[2]

Compiling the already fast-growing quantity of material being produced about women and CVE, the Global Counter Terrorism Forum in 2015 published a prescriptive document called "Good Practices on Women and Countering Violent Extremism." It urged both the mainstreaming of gender into CVE and the protection of women's human rights. Good Practice number 5 (of 22), for example, is: "Prevent and address the direct and indirect impacts of violent extremism and terrorism on women and girls." With no supporting documentation, it then made the assertion that has become a truism: "Violent extremists and terrorist groups often target women and girls for gender-based violence, including abductions, forced marriages, sexual violence, forced pregnancies, attacks on women human rights defenders and leaders, attacks on girls' access to education, and restrictions on their freedom of movement" (GCTF 2015, 4). As Sewall (2016) put it hyperbolically, "Violent extremists are among the greatest threats to the empowerment of women and girls across the globe, not only in the crimes they commit, but in how they can fuel misogyny. Violent extremists repress women in both their ideology and their methods of violence."

A growing number of securofeminists, feminists not directly tied to governmental or global counterterror agencies, began to echo these statements. The International Civil Society Action Network for Women's Rights, Peace and Security (ICAN), for example, notes that "the gender lens is a very effective 'early warning' indicator of rising extremism—because the violence it condones against women and sexual minorities is often either invisible or deemed to be 'cultural,' yet it is the same phenomenon that metastasizes and spreads into society and becomes 'terrorism' or 'violent extremism.'"[3] (Note the ominous cancer metaphor.)

One of the most intriguing groups to have emerged was the Women's Alliance for Security Leadership (WASL), led by women's rights advocates from the Global South. They make the case for inclusion in CVE on related but slightly different grounds, pointing instead to women's histories of pioneering work against extremism. Their brochure asserts, "Across the Americas, Asia, Africa and the Middle East world, women's rights groups have been warning against the rise of extremism for nearly three decades." I should note that in previous decades the term was not used; the villain was fundamentalism. WASL credits these women's rights groups with being the "first to notice, and often bear the brunt of, these regressive forces that represent the antithesis of basic principles of human rights, democracy and pluralism" (Anderlini 2016, 2).

In offering their services and promoting themselves for leadership in CVE efforts, WASL reports that "local women-led NGOs and community-based organizations in Iraq, Syria, Pakistan, and elsewhere have developed innovative approaches to tackle the spread of extreme ideologies and violent practices of both state and non-state actors in their communities. . . . Working at the grassroots, nationally and transnationally, they have a unique credibility and authenticity to provide insights into the problems and guidance on the solutions" (Anderlini 2016, 2).[4]

A policy brief in 2017 by the US Civil Society Working Group on Women, Peace and Security, produced in the first week of the Trump administration, repeated the standard reasons for including women, but added one. This document praised the principles of the WPS agenda, noted the pioneering work of women's organizations, and made strong political criticisms of several US allies. It urged the new US president to hold states accountable if they suppressed or endangered women's rights activists, especially in the name of counterterrorism. In condemning extremist groups, however, the document recycled the tropes, highlighting the role of religious ideologies: "Extremist groups, particularly religious and ethno-nationalist ones, commonly espouse the marginalization or oppression of minorities and inequality between men and women. . . . Women's rights are perceived as 'Western immorality' and feminism as an extension of colonialist politics. Extremist groups often create legal and physical boundaries between women and men to keep them segregated, including by curtailing women's access to public spaces. These groups promulgate rigid understandings of religious texts that define what it means to be a good wife, daughter, or woman" (Anderlini, de Jonge Oudraat, and Milani 2017, 1–2).

This description of religious rigidity and conservative gender ideologies could, of course, apply equally to Hindu nationalist groups and Christian evangelicals (see Grewal and Jakobsen, this volume), but the cues—gender segregation, accusations that feminism is "Western," and references to colonialist politics—line up more closely with standard Western representations of Muslim societies. What goes without saying, and remains unsaid in all these documents that followed the Obama administration position that violent extremism is not confined to any one religious or ethnic group, is that Muslims are the ones who pose special threats to women. All the Trump administration did was to name this extremism Islamic.

Even if many securofeminists disagree with Sewall's enthusiastic promotion of "getting in on the ground floor"—either because they have qualms about the way that gender equality and human rights goals can be compromised by security concerns or because they are alert to the conservative gender ideologies that undergird most CVE projects—they nevertheless contribute to the legitimacy of CVE by linking something called violent extremism to gender-based violence.

THE ARCHITECTURE OF FEAR

There has been an exponential growth of the number and type of feminist groups engaging CVE since 2010. At the national level, the US Institute of Peace, US Department of State, and US Agency for International Development, for example, collaborated on a panel, "Women and Countering Violent Extremism: Strengthening Policy Responses and Ensuring Inclusivity" in Washington, DC, on July 21, 2015. The US State Department and USAID Joint Strategy for CVE in 2016 pledged to work with the UN on the topic, mentioning the need to collaborate with UNDP and UNESCO, as well as GCTF (Global Counterterrorism Forum), GGERF (Global Community Engagement and Resilience Fund), Hedayah, the Sawab Center in UAE, the Strong Cities Network, the RESOLVE network, the World Bank, and the European Union (US Department of State 2016). In 2016, the UN Commission on Human Rights supported global student research on gender and CVE. UN Women sponsored a report on the impact of Security Council Resolution (UNSCR) 1325 (Women, Peace and Security) that included a chapter on CVE. Conferences and summits, reports and policy briefs, tool kits and exercises proliferated. The reports are replete with buzzwords like "gender sensitivity," "gender mainstreaming," "gender inclusivity," "empowerment," "resilience," and the "human rights" of women and girls. The shared vocabularies reveal the participation of sophisticated gender experts.

The rush to work on women and CVE is also clear from a 2017 contract research report on "Women and Countering Violent Extremism" prepared for the Australian government (Idris with Abdelaziz 2017). It compiled a list of fifty-eight initiatives or networks working on women and CVE. The acronyms of these organizations are suggestive: AWARE, ICAN, SAVE, RESOLVE, WARN, COVER, FATE, and BRAVE. The more descriptive names are ungainly: MyHack, Extremely Together, Extreme Dialogue, Women and Extremism Network, Inclusive Security, and Mothers for Life.

These groups promote their own work in competition for attention and funding. The Georgetown Institute for Women, Peace and Security has partnered with the United Arab Emirates, a major funder of forums on CVE and counterterrorism. Even though many Muslim community groups have been wary about taking funds from the Department of Homeland Security and USAID, government investments indicate the wide acceptance of women's involvement in CVE. Congress allocated $10 million for grants to organizations working on CVE in the last year of the Obama administration. Various European governments from Norway to Austria have similarly put money into CVE work by women.

On the one hand, securofeminists involved in CVE work bemoan the relative lack of funding for gender-sensitive work compared to other forms of counterterrorism security initiatives. On the other, they urge caution in the ways CVE is funded at the local and grassroots levels in different parts of the world. They tend to criticize cumbersome reporting requirements, strict oversight, lack of trust by big organizations in local initiatives, antiterrorist financial restrictions, and the risks to the women activists who receive these funds if they are directly associated with counterterrorism initiatives.

Despite these reservations, however, securofeminists continue to promote women's inclusion in CVE. The scale of the demand can be gauged by a letter sent to UN Secretary General Antonió Guterres on April 21, 2017. A group of forty-eight women's civil society organizations signed a letter to him in response to his report on the efforts the UN system would be making "to assist Member States in implementing the United Nations Global Counter-Terrorism Strategy." After politely commending him for taking terrorism and PVE seriously, they used standard UN language to remind him that civil society is crucial to these efforts. They urged him to champion the "whole-of-society" approach outlined in the 2016 Secretary-General's PVE Plan of Action. They invoked Security Council resolutions that affirmed the role of women and civil society organizations (CSO) in peace and security. They urged him to involve independent CSOs like themselves as stakeholders with expertise in women and PVE. Three years later, a 2020 report by the International Crisis Group reiterated this recommendation but with a new twist: "Involving women in crafting and reforming security policies, ensuring that laws and strategies meet women's specific needs and protecting them during war and its aftermath are essential, both to *stabilizing volatile societies* and advancing gender equality" (2020, 19; my emphasis).

It is not only governmental, intergovernmental, and civil society organizations that contribute to CVE and benefit from its funding. The private sector has also capitalized on this new enterprise that offers business opportunities for experts from psychologists to computer programmers. Ross Frenett, one of the contributors to *A Man's World* (Saltman and Frenett 2016) and coauthor of one of the reports on female radicalization discussed below, parlayed his work on gender and extremism into a startup called Moonshot CVE. According to the company's website in 2019, the firm would "place the exponential power of emerging technology at the heart of efforts to counter violent extremism." His promotional video asserts that extremists, though admittedly small in numbers, "succeed because they are willing to take risks and innovate at a fast rate." Likewise, Moonshot CVE introduces "start up thinking to the field of CVE" (2019).[5]

Women-led consulting firms have not wanted to be left out. Creative Associates International, which began in 1977 as an education and human development firm founded by four idealistic women of diverse backgrounds who (according to their website) wanted to have a social impact, recently branched out into CVE, hiring a female West Point graduate with thirty years of experience in the US military and the State Department to lead the initiative across all their "practice areas." Rewriting the company's history and goals, it claims on its website: "For almost 40 years, Creative Associates International has addressed root causes of violent extremism" (n.d.).

Smaller-scale initiatives subsist on donations and small grants, including those from local government. Women without Borders/SAVE, with help from the Austrian government, set up MotherSchools with the goal of sensitizing mothers to recognize the signs of radicalization and empowering them "for security as an 'ally' in the home." Piloted in Tajikistan, Kashmir, Nigeria, Pakistan, Indonesia, and Zanzibar (note that these are all Muslim-majority countries), the project intends to work closer to home and introduce the schools in Europe, presumably for immigrant Muslim mothers. The curriculum is based on mothers' potential for preventing extremism. The implication is that Muslim mothers are inadequate at parenting since the curriculum includes not just de-radicalization techniques but "applied parenting skills" (Women Without Borders 2019).

Another effort to counter "extremist ideologies" through mothers' agency can be seen in an unusual NGO, Mothers for Life, sponsored by the German Institute on Radicalization and De-radicalization Studies. It is described as a support network for women who have lost their children to ISIS or "jihadi radicalization." These mothers published two open letters on successive Mother's Days in 2016 and 2017, hoping to persuade their sons that they had fallen for twisted interpretations of Islam. Like other initiatives to mobilize "moderate" Muslims and religious authorities for countermessaging, they attempt to counter ISIS propaganda by quoting from the Qur'an and Hadith (sayings of the prophet). In one letter they plead with their sons to recognize their gendered responsibilities to protect and care for women in their families: "We know that some of you went to become the 'true Muslims' and seek out justice and to protect the helpless. But is this justice that you leave your mothers and sisters unprotected?" In another, they try to dissuade them by quoting from well-known Islamic hadith texts: "Even if you think death will give you that 'better' life, remember that even the Prophet Muhammad (peace and blessings be upon him) said: 'Paradise lies at the feet of your mother' [Musnad Ahmad, Sunan An-Nasâ'i, Sunan Ibn Mâjah]. . . . " (German Institute on Radicalization and De-Radicalization Studies 2015).

Complex political issues get trivialized in the promotion of all this work. A good example is the pop logo used by the United States Mission to the UN in Geneva when it sponsored an initiative called "The Future She Deserves." Following the trend of shifting feminist activism from concerns about the victims of gender-based violence (GBV) to promoting women as agents in CVE, it announced a US tour for women from Europe, the Middle East, North Africa, South Asia, and Central Asia who had participated in their project called "Women Preventing Extremism." The logo was a stylized cartoon on a pink background of a woman/girl holding up a stop sign.[6]

Does CVE offer a positive, less violent alternative than militarized counterterrorism? Many feminists and progressives have deplored the effects on Muslim communities of CVE programs like PREVENT in Britain and the other antiradicalization programs that have sprung up all over Europe.

There is strong evidence that such programs have serious side effects, from profiling and stigmatizing Muslims to facilitating state surveillance of the private worlds of ordinary Muslim citizens in homes, schools, and hospitals. Targeting children for removal from their families, a practice with a colonial pedigree for which settler-states like Australia and Canada have been forced to apologize, and enlisting mothers to report "tell-tale signs" of radicalization enforce norms on families and restrict gender roles. They open women up to suspicion and danger in their own communities.

For both pragmatic and principled reasons, therefore, some feminists have insisted on strictly enforcing a separation between security and work for women's rights and for development. In contrast to some security specialists who push for an integrated approach to women and CVE, they even praise the existing "silos" that separate policymaking on human or women's rights from that on CVE and security more broadly (Bhulai, Peters, and Nemr 2016). The comprehensive UN Women report by Coomaraswamy (2015, 225), quoted above on the implementation of the UNSCR on Women, Peace and Security, opposes the embrace of CVE. Even if women's rights and empowerment are "key bulwarks against extremism," argues the report, efforts to support these goals must be kept separate from security because "not only does any association with security endanger women's groups working for these goals, but human rights and the promotion of gender equality should be ends in and of themselves." Nevertheless, the misogyny of "extremists" is invoked to justify concern: "Across religions and regions, a common thread shared by extremist groups is that in each and every instance, their advance has been coupled with attacks on the rights of women and girls—rights to education, to public life and to decision-making over their own bodies" (Coomaraswamy 2015, 223). As the title of the chapter on CVE—"Countering Violent Extremism While Respecting the Rights and Autonomy of Women and their Communities"—indicates, the report chooses to operate *within* the CVE paradigm, not outside of it.

THE PUZZLE OF WOMEN RECRUITS

Questions of women and CVE have come together most directly in a puzzle that at first confounded all those, including the securofeminists, who had taken pains to represent "extremists" as the enemies of women and serious dangers to their safety. They presented women as targets of extremists to justify their work and assert their credentials as allies in countering extremism, even as the most critical of them insist, rightly, that women must not be treated as a homogenous group and that privileging security carries grave risks to human rights.[7]

A story on the website of the Organization for Security and Co-operation in Europe (OSCE) introduced a new wrinkle in 2017 as it asked: "Why is it so crucial that we apply a gender analysis when shaping our response to violent extremism?" The ominous answer given by Chantal de Jonge Oudraat, president of Women in International Security (WIIS), is that "the pool of potential terrorists is no longer just angry young men" (OSCE 2017). A new specter had emerged on the scene that confused the picture painted by securofeminists to justify their inclusion. This is the non-innocent woman. The occasional reports that had begun to be published a few years earlier on women as "perpetrators" rarely mentioned historical precedents, such as women's roles in anticolonial or liberation struggles. Contemporaneous involvements, such as Palestinian women's opposition to Israeli occupation, receive occasional attention, though usually in reference to the suicide bombings of women associated with Islamist groups. The focus began to shift to the women who supported IS, and especially those who began to travel to Syria and Iraq from Europe. Some reports use the term that the women themselves prefer, because of its historico-religious connotations—they call them *muhajirat*, or migrants. Most feminists and scholars eschew the sensational terms preferred by the right-wing media—"female jihadists" or "jihadi brides."

How the gender experts in the security world portrayed these women reveals a good deal about the ways their broader politics intersect with feminism. Female migrants mostly were represented as vulnerable individuals who had been *lured* by extremist propaganda. A summary of a workshop held at the US Institute of Peace in March 2017 marked the expulsion of such women from the safe space of sympathy: "From the Nazi regime of the 1940s through the Islamic State of today's Middle East . . . an obscured element of history runs though the phenomenon of violent extremism: the participation of women. Contrary to the classic image of women as victims or, at least more recently, peacemakers, new research shows how women can stoke, support and sometimes directly join in violent action" (Strasser 2017).

Most reports on such perpetrators are not based on interviews or ethnographic fieldwork. They rely on press reports, a database built from monitoring migrant women's tweets and social media posts, or interviews with returnees via the deradicalization mentors assigned to them in custody. The sample sizes are tiny. The information is thin. In a study of "female jihadists in America" produced for the Program in Extremism at George Washington University, the dramatic cover page trades shamelessly on ISIS graphics by using a handwritten script, white on black, that looks a bit like Arabic, with the symbol for female drawn in the middle. Its title, *Cruel Intentions*, is judgmental. Based on media reports of twenty-five US cases (the sum total the author could manage to find), the female subjects are grouped into three categories: plotters, supporters, and travelers. Only three individuals were classified as plotters (the most "extreme" category). And of these only one carried out a violent attack (in San Bernardino, California). Even though the study concludes that there is no single profile or demographic pattern to the sample, it nevertheless ends with a dark warning: "A diffused, non-localized interpretation of violent jihad means that anyone, including women, can heed the call to action if they so desire" (Alexander 2016, 8).

Since it would appear that not many have "heeded the call" it makes sense that the security experts have focused more on the women from Europe who have traveled or attempted to travel to Syria to live in what they call the Caliphate. These women are violent extremists only by association. The expert recommendations circle around ways to counter the seductive ideologies and manipulative media campaigns of extremists who lure vulnerable women through the internet.

Most reports try to explain why these women migrated by reducing the drivers to "push and pull factors," always three of each. Two reports, both published by the Women and Extremism program of the Institute for Strategic Dialogue, epitomize this genre of work on women and CVE. Both analyze the social media posts of a small number of Western female migrants to Syria to live under ISIS and rely on interviews with UK deradicalization mentors who work with the government programs CHANNEL and PREVENT. The reports carry trite titles: *Becoming Mulan? Female Western Migrants to ISIS* (Hoyle, Bradford, and Frenett 2015) and *"Till Martyrdom Do Us Part': Gender and the ISIS Phenomenon* (Saltman and Smith 2015). The latter report neatly lays out the so-called push and pull factors: "[*f*]*eeling* isolated socially and/or culturally, including questioning one's identity and uncertainty of belonging within a Western culture . . . *Feeling* that the international Muslim community as a whole is being violently persecuted . . . and [*a*]*nger, sadness* and/or frustration over a *perceived* lack of international action in response to this persecution" (2015, 9; my emphasis).

Even when the reports include, in passing, evidence for why the women might "feel" this way or "perceive" the world this way—like mentioning that women who wear a headscarf or veil in Europe "have been shown to experience discriminatory comments in public more frequently than Muslim men due to their appearance"—the racism and discrimination are interpreted in psychological, emotional, and cultural terms. The report qualifies the effects of this treatment: "While the *experience* of persecution alone does not turn someone into a jihadist or a supporter of violent extremism, it does serve to fuel *feelings* of isolation within a larger community and a sense of distance from the culture or society one lives in (Saltman and Smith 2015, 10; my emphasis).

The second "push factor" is also translated into a problem of feelings or perception. The women's posts, according to the reports, show them to be deeply concerned about "the oppression of Muslims internationally. These women point to a range of international conflicts that have become *perceived* attacks on the ummah." The women share imagery that shows "violence towards women and children or the deadly aftermath of bombings" (Saltman and Smith 2015, 11). This too is set aside. "As explained by one mentor . . . throughout the process of radicalization a *cognitive behavioural pathway* starts to build itself around the extremist propaganda that manifests itself as an alternative reality. The *belief* solidifies that Muslims, as an international community, have been persecuted violently by 'non-believers' throughout history" (2015, 11).

The third push factor identified—anger and frustration at the inaction of the international community to respond to this "perceived" violence—is also dismissed by Saltman and Smith (2015, 13) through emotion and beliefs: "The empathy that women undergoing a process of radicalization *feel* for the Muslim victims of violence, combined with the complicity they *believe* Western powers are showing, ultimately perpetuating the conflict, is a highly influential factor in their decision to leave the West and seek an alternative society" (my emphasis).

The agency, the political analyses, and the empathy these women feel for victims of imperial violence are dismissed through psychologizing or showing how romantic their views are while the pull factors are described with wonder. The women "embrace positive incentives and motivational reasonings" including "idealistic goals of religious duty and building a utopian 'Caliphate state' [nation-building and work]; the lure of belonging and sisterhood; and a romanticization that 'plays heavily on romantic notions of adventure and finding romance in the form of a husband or wife'" (2015, 16).

Push and pull factors never include women's political motivations or analyses, and only sometimes their religious aspirations. Rather than taking seriously their grievances about wars, injuries, invasions, and superpower intervention in the Middle East and South Asia or referring to the well-documented discrimination and racism they experience as Muslims in Europe, the United States, Australia, and other places where they are minorities, the reports dismiss these women as serious actors and present them as driven by emotions, perceptions, and "various layers of reasoning" that make them susceptible to "extremist propaganda" (Hoyle, Bradford, and Frenett 2015).

The reports on the potential for these women to become violent extremists prescribe developing counternarratives and strengthening community resilience, often through public-private partnerships. They praise programs like One2One, in which mentors engage online or meet in person with those being "lured," trying to challenge these women who, according to one mentor, "live in this fantasy world where they think 'we're going take over, put a stop to American invasion of Muslim lands, stop them taking our oil, exploiting us, we're going to stand up for ourselves, we are the army of Allah, the army of Islam'" (Saltman and Smith 2015, 56). The emotional and intellectual vulnerabilities of individual women (and youth) are understood to make them susceptible to online messaging. Intercepting media and disseminating counternarratives that spin such "fantasies" are key to CVE work. Several studies recommend exposing the negative "elements of the reality for females upon arrival in ISIS-controlled territory."

One of the more active groups in women and CVE, the US Institute for Peace in Washington, DC, has organized numerous panel discussions on women and gender in CVE. Their Thought for Action Kit for *Women Preventing Violent Extremism* has bold attractive illustrations, short essays, and exercises for activists and practitioners to use in their work "dealing with violent extremist ideologies." As with other documents in the genre, the authors use terrorism and violent extremism interchangeably. They justify this by noting, as do others, that "internationally speaking, there are no agreed upon definitions of terrorism or violent extremism" (USIP 2015, 4).[8]

Despite token nods to women in other extremist/terror groups like the Tamil Tigers, which Nimmi Gowrinathan calls female fighters (USIP 2015; Gowrinathan 2015, 2021), this document concentrates on Muslim groups like Al-Qaeda, Boko Haram, and ISIL. It subliminally invokes Muslims through mentions of "conservative" families. The essay by Edit Schlaffer (2015, 30), founder of Women without Borders, Sisters Against Violent Extremism (SAVE), and the MotherSchools, repeats her refrain: "Mothers, are strategically located at the heart of the family. . . . Mothers can reach the young before they become entangled in such highly emotional appeals of ideas and ideologies and *lose their grip on reality*" (my emphasis).

Like most others, this document analyzes women extremists under the rubric of push and pull factors—all individual, psychological, or social factors. The only pull factors listed are the "messages, relationships, and recruitment campaigns that *lure* individuals into participation in extremist activities" (USIP 2015, 27). Yet even the more critical report for UN Women on Women Peace and Security by Radhika Coomaraswamy (2015, 233) cited above underplays women's agency, noting that ISIS "*lures* fighters and supporters, including women, from around the world with sophisticated social media campaigns and promises of meaningful employment."

GENERALIZING THE MUSLIM THREAT

When securofeminists do not directly challenge the frameworks by which so-called women's radicalization is understood and the very category of "extremism" into which some women are being absorbed, they contribute to a homogenizing of Muslims that risks placing them all under the sign of extremism. Appeals to security justify domestic crackdowns and hysteria across Europe and Australia about Muslim women's attire, from burkinis to niqabs. Vigilante actions in the United States have been fueled by such representations. The problem with CVE is that it is almost impossible to separate efforts to counter violence against women from these wider Islamophobic frameworks that extend suspicion to all Muslims. If there are "jihadi brides" or mothers who encourage their sons' violence—never mind "Caliphettes" (Rafiq and Malik 2015) or denizens of the "Sultanate of Women" (Patel 2017), then the need to guard human rights from the risks of securitization may not seem as urgent when it comes to Muslim women. The equivocation found in the conclusion of a much-cited report by Mercy Corps in Jordan (based on interviews with families with male members who left for Syria to fight) had already begun to shake the claims of securofeminists like those of WASL that women were uniquely qualified to lead the CVE effort: "Given the exalted position of the mother in Islam, women's peace groups offer a serious potential counter to VE propaganda," notes the report. It adds a caution, however: "Admittedly, women's roles within these communities is ambivalent: they are variously the encouragers and discouragers of violence" (Mercy Corps 2015, 10).

There is little academic research on these female "extremists" although a good investigative journalist finally published in 2019 a contextualized and sensitive reconstruction of different motivations for traveling to live in the Caliphate and varied experiences with ISIS from interviews with a dozen women and some of their family members. *Guest House for Young Widows* (Moaveni 2019) avoids the term "extremism" and shows how the women and their circumstances differed, and even changed over a short period of time. None of the studies take into account the extensive ethnographic work on pious women in the wider Islamic revival that might have also challenged their simplistic arguments about push and pull factors. Anthropologists have analyzed how many Muslim women interpret their faith and responsibilities in ways that challenge liberal and Western feminists' gender ideologies or understandings of empowerment. Those who have written about converts and Salafi women in Europe, women in the mosque movement in Egypt, Pakistan, Indonesia, and elsewhere, and even women in Islamist political parties like Hizballah, Hamas, the Muslim Brotherhood, or Morocco's Justice and Spirituality Party, uncover values that are not necessarily shared by secular and human rights feminists (see for example Ababneh 2014; Deeb 2006; Hafez 2011; Hammer 2019; Jad 2005; Inge 2017; Mahmood 2005; McLarney 2015; Moors 2017; Özyürek 2014; Rinaldo 2013; Salime 2011; Yafout 2015). Although women who join more militant Islamic groups might aspire to leadership and insist on their rights as fellow Muslims, few prioritize the elements of gender equality that CEDAW enshrines and that most securofeminists promote. And thus it is perhaps hard for securofeminists to recognize their agency. Even Islamic feminist groups like Musawah that seek to reform Muslim family law from within and are attentive to which of its elements align with principles of international covenants begin with the importance of faith and Muslim belonging (Musawah 2011).

A few mainstream political science articles on the *muhajirat* have taken seriously the arguments that women recruits voice. Loken and Zelenz (2017) evaluate the four dominant social scientific theories about why women migrated to live under the Caliphate. On the basis of their analysis of over five hundred Tumblr and Twitter posts by these women, they conclude that one must take religious women's agency seriously. They argue that women joined Daesh for the same reason as men—as part of an ideological commitment to create and maintain the Caliphate motivated by a belief in God (Loken and Zelenz 2017, 63–66). The only difference is that the women refer more often than men do to religious discrimination against them as a reason to leave Europe. The conclusion of this article then comes as a surprise. Loken and Zelenz write, "We contend that the *muhajirat* [migrants] are extremists actively engaged in political action" (2017, 67). They grant these women political agency (if driven by "religion" or ideology rather than political or economic critiques of the world order) but do not question the basic identification of these women as extremists. They also do not go so far as to recommend engaging in critical self-reflection about the political and historical dynamics that have led to the formations of such groups or the resort by these "non-state actors" to violence.

One can ask what the effect is of this fascination with the small number of Muslim women—many of them converts, in the case of European migrants—who for a few years between 2013 and 2016 went to Syria and Iraq as affiliates of the Islamic State. The disproportionality of attention is clear from a report published in July 2018 by the International Centre for the Study of Radicalisation, one of the many think tanks whose bread and butter is the multimillion dollar security and CVE business. On the basis of "mining public data sources" on the women and minors who traveled to join Daesh or IS, Cook and Vale present a total of 4,761 such women in those five key years. That would be an average of about a dozen female returnees per country, such as the ones in the United Kingdom who served as the subjects of the two reports discussed above. They admit there is no evidence that these women were involved in any violent activities, noting that Daesh policy specifically excluded women from combat roles, a situation that changed only in the final months before defeat according to Winter and Margolin (2017).

Nevertheless, the final chapter of the report warns of the potential security threat the returning women and children pose and recommends that they receive special treatment and attention, including scholarly attention (more grants for "experts" like themselves?), as part of a gender-sensitive inquiry. Since studies of these women based on online chats and posts and the rich stories presented by Moaveni (2019) suggest that most are widows with children who are coming out of extremely difficult conditions, one might wonder what sort of threat they pose. They might rather want to rebuild their lives (Dadu and Forestier 2019; Moors 2019).[9]

The hypervisibilization of these women has the effect of invisibilizing the majority of Muslim women and their diversity. Like the representations of Muslim migrant women that psychologize and dismiss their political critiques, reports like these reconfirm the association of Muslims with fearful and irrational violence. Remnants of earlier representations of Muslim women as in need of saving by a benevolent West, the international community, or by concerned securofeminists do persist; but the innocence of such women that had justified feminist leadership in CVE to save them from violent extremists has been compromised by the Daesh women.

The obsession with women as perpetrators or as allied with violent extremism seems to be fading as ISIS was defeated in Syria and Iraq and most of the women and men associated with it are dead, disappeared, or in prison awaiting trial, especially in Iraq.[10] But this is not the end. The focus is shifting to a new project for women. On February 19, 2019, the US State Department issued the "U.S. Strategy to Support Women and Girls at Risk from Violent Extremism and Conflict" (Pompeo 2019). Besides agreeing to do what securofeminists had long lobbied for, such as looking to women as leaders in CVE, protecting and including women in all efforts, and integrating them into a more inclusive CVE, this strategy added a new goal of countering women's roles in terrorism: "Addressing the specific role of women as radicalizers, facilitators, or perpetrators of violence must play a role in any CVE strategy. Reintegrating former female members or supporters of terrorist organizations also requires tailored approaches to disengagement and reintegration."

What seems to be emerging alongside earlier concerns to protect women from violent extremists and some language coming out of UN Women on "the symbiosis between misogyny and extremism" (Castillo Diaz and Valji 2019) is less of a gender exception for the global securitizing of Muslims (see Amar 2011). Yet securofeminists are alert to the latest gender blindness found in the international response to "the issues facing women and children who are associated with VE groups." They are exploring new "lines of work" in the agenda that calls for DRR—disengagement, rehabilitation, and reintegration. *Invisible Women*, a report jointly prepared by the United Nations Development Programme and ICAN in 2019 attempts to reconcile genuine feminist concerns about violence against women that had infused earlier arguments for inclusion in CVE with cautious capitulation to the terms set by the global counterterrorism industry, admitting that "As with the concept of violent extremism itself, the United Nations uses the terms 'disengagement,' 'rehabilitation,' and 'reintegration' in the context of terrorism and violent extremism without offering a specific definition" (Anderlini and Holmes 2019, 28).[11] So why accept these new terms and ask to lead DRR?

COUNTERING A DEMONIC PHANTOM

Securofeminists who demanded inclusion in P/CVE have found themselves in a world of undefined terms, trite advertising campaigns, and shoddy studies based on small numbers that play on fear of Muslims. Their acceptance of stock terms, equivocal or ambivalent as it often has been, makes it impossible for them to challenge the hegemony of security discourse and to explore more seriously the roots and character of the widespread violence that marks everyday lives around the world. If gender experts in national security and international governance effuse about "getting in on the ground floor" of CVE, grassroots women's advocates working within the frameworks of human rights and approaches to gender equality, as well as governance feminists working at the critical peace-building edges of the WPS agenda, have tried to be more cautious.

Many have warned about the dangers of allying with the global security industry, whether because of the instrumentalization of women or the demotion of the fight for gender equality to an ancillary piece of CVE. An early comprehensive article in *Foreign Policy* by Mlambo-Ngcuka and Coomaraswamy (2015) for example advocated for broadening the frame, describing the collateral damage of counterterrorism for the well-being of women and those who advocate for them. But even this article rationalized, perhaps for instrumental reasons, the critique of counterterrorism by warning about radicalization. Noting that militarized counterterrorism operations disrupt economic and social activity and civilian infrastructures on which women depend, divert government resources from health, family, and educational services, and displace civilians, leaving "women and girls vulnerable to sexual and gender-based violence, including, with grim regularity, crimes committed by the security forces supposed to be protecting them" it nevertheless conjured the same phantom. The authors warned that these dire effects of militarized counterterrorism "result in women's re-victimization, and ultimately in more poverty, more desperation, and more *radicalization*" (my emphasis).

Based on consultation only with standard secular women's and human rights groups, the report Coomeraswamy had just authored for UN Women sidelined the agency of women like those who had begun by then to migrate to Syria and Iraq to live under the Caliphate. It also ignored the aspirations of many on whose behalf feminists and women's advocates see themselves working—women who are pious. While one can commend the efforts of legal activist-scholars like Fionnuala Ní Aoláin, the first UN Special Rapporteur on the Promotion and Protection of Human Rights and Fundamental Freedoms While Countering Terrorism, to insist that her mandate include analysis of the "gendered security harms" (Huckerby 2020) of CVE and counterterrorism measures, studying the ways these measures affect the human rights of women, girls, and families, the problem is whether there is any way to reconcile security and human rights law. Does accepting the parameters of respecting the rights of women *"while* countering terrorism or violent extremism" reinforce the legitimacy of securitization as policy?

The securofeminist CVE literature is not only committed to the basic agenda of international human rights and gender equality enshrined in CEDAW, with the secular modern values Merry (2006) noted, but generally accepts the compromised series of Women, Peace and Security resolutions that critics like Cohn (2008) and Otto (2018, 2019) have faulted for not challenging the international world order, militarism, or traditional gender binaries. In Cohn's ethnographic study of the processes and politicking that led to the successful passage in 2000 of UNSCR 1325 after it was initiated by feminist NGOs but taken forward by women's advocates within the UN, she focused on "the impact on the activists of re-shaping their activities and political agenda into a form that would make them acceptable, even attractive and valuable participants in UN policy-shaping processes" (Cohn 2008, 192). Issues central to the antiwar feminists who initiated the work were pushed aside as "too political." The working group ended up seeking only to install women at the peace-making table, leaving "dominant political and epistemological frameworks untouched" (Cohn 2008, 202).

Otto, a legal scholar of the history of the Women's International League for Peace and Freedom (WILPF) founded in 1919, is even more critical of the compromises imposed by trying to pass resolutions through the Security Council (Otto 2018, 2019). She charges that feminist arguments have been manipulated to support the expanding exercise of unaccountable power by the Security Council since the end of the Cold War and to legitimize its militaristic and carceral approach in the name of protecting women, mostly from sexual violence, and promoting their rights.

Imbricated in a security paradigm that has produced policies and programs that have done serious damage to multiple communities around the world, my critique builds on these by suggesting that a key problem is the resort to the undefined and undefinable concept of violent extremism. This is a phantom with real effects: it justifies the security industry that demonizes Muslims internationally even while securofeminists bend over backward not to name or blame Muslims. Specific country studies by critical feminist observers like Sahla Aroussi (2021), who writes about Kenya, show the dangerous consequences for women of the folding in of the WPS agenda to CVE in the everyday dynamics of racialization and militarization.

The contortions produced by trying to define violent extremism without mentioning Muslims were apparent early on in the otherwise strong statements about women's experiences put forth by the Women's Alliance for Security Leadership (WASL). Grounded in specific knowledge of various situations in which their global network of feminist activists worked, WASL stumbled when it got to the section where they try to define extremism in their brochure, *Uncomfortable Truths; Unconventional Wisdom*. First, they define extremism as "when a person's beliefs move from being relatively conventional to being radical, and they want a drastic change in society." In many progressive circles, this would be considered positive, given the scale of injustices in the world. But then we learn that extremism is tied to religion:

> Increasing religious devoutness or commitment to unconventional beliefs is not the same as radicalization towards violent extremism. Religious Extremism is defined as rigid interpretations of religion that are forced upon others using social or economic coercion, laws, intolerance, or violence. It is accompanied by non-fluid definitions of culture, religion, nationalism, ethnicity or sect, which move citizens into exclusionary, patriarchal and intolerant communities. Only a small percentage of religious conservatives are extremist in this sense. The use of violence justified for religious ends is a characteristic of some extremist movements, but not all. (Anderlini 2016)

The equivocation is symptomatic. The obvious question is how could the referent for extremism *not* be confusing? *Extreme*, after all, is a relative term. Is its antonym *moderate*, as we saw with the Arabic name of the Saudi Center for Countering Violent Extremist Ideologies and the US State Department investments in supporting "moderate Islam" (Mahmood 2006) or tolerance (Brown 2008)? Is violent extremism only that violence carried out in the name of a particular religious ideology or group?

Many consider any resort to violence extreme. Pacifists, feminist critics of war, and those working against the patriarchal norms of masculinity and male dominance in politics have long organized against violence, in the home, the prison, and the international spheres. "State terror" or "state criminality" are terms that do not appear in the securofeminist literature even though some feminists such as Shalhoub-Kevorkian (this volume) have found the concept of state criminality a powerful analytic. One might ask whether the extreme violence of "shock and awe" carried out by powerful armies, bombers, drones, and proxy militias should be excluded. Their effects on people and communities are catastrophic. So then, is it only the violence perpetrated by groups on the ever-growing US terror list that is extremist?

The point is that violent extremism is as much of an "empty signifier" as is its partner term "radicalization" (Fadil, de Koning, and Ragazzi, 2019b, 3). Its deployment reduces complex political and historical dynamics to simple problems with pat solutions, depoliticizing and decontextualizing violence while dehumanizing certain groups or communities. Recall ICAN's warning that gender-based violence, like a disease, can metastasize and spread into violent extremism.

Discussions of violent extremism lean toward the psychological, explaining through individual emotion and perception, or the cultural/religious, rather than looking at political injustice, or history. Just as Nikolas Kosmatopoulos (2020) has shown how complex long-standing conflicts in Lebanon have been reduced—or "micro-sized," as he puts it—by the conflict management techniques, crisis reports, and flying workshops of professional "Peace Experts" to more manageable and universal concepts like "ethnic conflict" and hollowed terms like "sectarianism," so it seems that CVE experts, including the securofeminists who have ambivalently joined their ranks, are trying to contain terrible events and specific social and political problems or forms of political dissidence by using tool kits that simplify and mobilize empty signifiers like radicalization.[12]

It is hard to find in the securofeminist discussions of CVE reflexive analyses of US and European policies toward the parts of the world and the communities where "violent extremists" are said to "breed." In the proliferation of forums and digital products we rarely see considerations of whether such policies might be drivers of "grievances." Domestic policies of austerity, racial discrimination, and criminalization of certain populations seem off limits (Guénif-Souilamas 2017).

Proposals for protecting women from extremist violence through CVE rarely recommend that security states change course and pursue political rather than military solutions; ban global arms production and sales; halt support for violent allies or proxies; or seek radical ways to limit massive destruction, injury, deprivation, and death. Questioning the capitalist imperative that entrenches gross global inequality is outside the frame. Securofeminist engagements with CVE rarely challenge priorities in the allocation of global resources since all is outside the purview of security-speak, even when the costs of the twenty-year "War on Terror" are astronomical.[13] And the "Costs of War" project at the Watson Institute at Brown University calculates the costs of the wars in Afghanistan and Iraq—not just in weapons and death tolls, but in alternative ways such funds could have been spent—on education, health, and welfare. These are all core feminist issues.[14]

The extensive scholarship documenting and analyzing the historical and political dynamics of what, in CVE-talk, is reduced to the cultural, ideological, psychological, or religious problem of violent extremism, does not appear often enough in securofeminist pleas for gender inclusion in CVE or for preserving human rights while countering terrorism. Scholarship on the modern history of Iraq, for example, from the documentation of the effects of US sanctions, overthrow of the regime, installation of sectarian governance, and militarization that produced the flight of millions of refugees seeking safety, as well as the humiliation of political prisoners, has shown these conditions to have been integral to the formation of ISIL. The devastating effects on women's security, safety, freedom of movement, access to education and employment, and women's activist movements in Iraq have been well studied by feminist scholars (Ali 2018; Al-Ali and Pratt 2009), even if the media has preferred to cover the gruesome news of Yazidi "sexual slavery" under ISIS.[15]

International power politics exacerbate conflicts in the region by backing and arming different groups, as in Syria (Mukhopadhyay and Howe 2023). The human and material costs, whether in monuments destroyed or people massively displaced to Jordan, Turkey, and Europe, are incalculable. Countering violent extremist ideologies through intercepting messages or improving parenting skills of Muslim mothers makes a mockery of these devastating situations of violence and fear and precludes taking them into account as structural roots of some abhorred forms of political violence. Colonial partitions, political machinations, power politics, competing interests, resource exploitation, and the irreversible trains of action/reaction, once set in motion, are all erased by CVE talk about monstrous extremists with their women casualties.

Securofeminists are complicit in the simplification of complex problems and the micro-sizing and universalizing of the phantom category of violent extremism when they adopt the standard vocabulary of radicalization, drivers, push and pull factors, and lures. Arguments for inclusion contribute to these erasures and simplifications because mainstreaming gender into security entails accepting its truth terms—that there is a menace and crisis called "violent extremism" that we can counter with best practices and professional expertise, including women's. There is research to be done, preferably "evidence based"; advising and briefings to be commissioned; security apparatuses to beef up; and counternarratives or proper forms of moderate religious education to be created.

When even the most thoughtful securofeminists justify their involvement in CVE by charging violent extremists with engaging in extreme gender-based violence, they enter a field furrowed by right-wing Islamophobes. I have argued in *Do Muslim Women Need Saving?* (2013) and tracked in the responses to my book (2016) that honor crimes have been a lynchpin in pernicious anti-Muslim campaigns by right-wing Islamophobic groups. Others have shown how such forms of gender violence often labeled "traditional" and the revived crime of "sexual slavery" have been abused politically. Feminists should be wary when they see how the successful international feminist campaigns over the past two decades to treat gender-based violence as a serious violation of human rights—a success that some scholars of international law have regarded with suspicion for the ways it has narrowed analyses of gender and power, strengthened legal instruments, and made criminalization the solution, with little evidence of its efficacy as a deterrent (Engle 2020)—is set alongside the forms of selective condemnation of stigmatizing violences against women that are associated with dark others, including Muslims.

The gendered lens of feminism is crucial. But it needs to be wide-angled, not trained only on subjects predefined by others and rife with obfuscating terms. Gender-based violence and misogyny are not, sadly, the monopoly of any particular group. We have seen the fallout when they are used as alibis for war, as in Afghanistan. The same could be said for deadly forms of violence that go under the name of counterterrorism. Violent extremism too is an alibi.

It would be better if feminists exposed "violent extremism" for what it is and concentrated on specific ways to address particular political, social, and economic problems in the world. Rather than dismissing out of hand what political dissidents say (by labeling them grievances or the results of brainwashing) or blaming religion, we can ask what might have led them to see the world as they do and to use their insights to challenge the security imperative. Rather than seeking inclusion in the latest iteration of CVE—in the work of deradicalization and rehabilitation of women and girls—feminists interested in human security might stick to their demands that we take stock of the conditions that are producing violence, as well as the power and interests, state and nonstate, that perpetuate such violations of human and women's rights and safety.

Feminist politics have always been contentious. Securofeminists argue about how best to address gender violence and how closely to align themselves with global and national efforts at securitization. Recalling Nesiah's arguments about International Conflict Feminism establishing itself on the cusp of the emergence of CVE in international affairs, feminists and progressives could distance themselves from the global security discourse of CVE, resisting the "lure" of "pull factors" like a chance to provide gender-sensitive influence. Refusing the incitement to discourse, taking the lead in sharpening sober analyses of all forms of political and economic violence, and undermining the reproduction and circulation of the phantom of "violent extremism" might be better strategies. The effects of spreading securitization across a gendered global social field and framing Muslims as violent perpetrators, in the name of combatting gender-based violence and violence against women, seem more likely to undermine than to advance feminist dreams for secure, peaceful, and equitable futures.

NOTES

A version of this paper was first presented at the workshop on Religion and the Global Framing of Gender Violence on September 11, 2017, at the Columbia Global Center | Middle East, Amman, through the project at the Center for the Study of Social Difference funded by the Henry Luce Foundation. I owe thanks to many. Saidiya Khan asked me questions about women's NGOs and CVE that set me on this trail; Joymala Hajra and Laela Shallal provided invaluable research assistance; many encouraged and challenged me, including audiences at Amherst College, Columbia's School of International and Public Affairs, Jawaharlal Nehru University, the University of Alberta, Vassar College, Wesleyan University, and Yale University. Karen Engle, Nadia Fadil, Aryana Elizabeth Ghazi Hessami, Shenila Khoja-Moolji, Catherine Lutz, Timothy Mitchell, Dipali Mukhopadhyay, Mayssoun Sukkarieh, Anu Sharma, Leti Volpp, and the anonymous reviewers of this volume deserve special thanks.

1 Their next campaign played on the double meaning of wise, the acronym of their organization, and resulted in a book called WISE UP: *Knowledge Ends Extremism* (WISE 2018). The link to the book is at https://www.wisemuslimwomen.org/programs/wise-up-knowledge-ends-extremism/wise-up-campaign/.

2 As early as April 2013 a policy brief for the Center for Global Counterterrorism

Cooperation called "The Roles of Women in Terrorism, Conflict, and Violent Extremism" advocated incorporating a gender perspective into all conflict and counterterrorism policy and programming (Fink, Barakat, and Shehtret 2013). CVE was just on the horizon but "violent extremism" was already part of the standard vocabulary.

3   See Global Solutions Exchange (GSX) for core principles informing ICAN's (International Civil Society Action Network for women's rights, peace and security) approach to extremism (ICAN 2017). http://www.icanpeacework.org/our-work/global-solutions-exchange/. Accessed September 5, 2021.

4   There is good evidence for this in the pioneering work of several important Muslim feminist organizations even if we must challenge the very category of extremism. The WISE (Women's Initiative for Spirituality and Equality) Shura Council initiated a Jihad against Violence in 2010 (Abu-Lughod 2013, 182–84) in which they linked domestic violence with violent extremism and called for women's "good leadership" on the model of the Queen of Sheba in the struggle against both. Their next campaign was WISE UP to Extremism. They are playing on the double meaning of wise, which is an acronym. The campaign is related to a book that the same organization published, called *WISE UP: Knowledge Ends Extremism*. https://www.wisemuslimwomen.org/programs/wise-up-knowledge-ends-extremism/wise-up-campaign/ (WISE 2018). Since the 1990s, Women Living Under Muslim Laws, a more secular feminist group, had been documenting violations of women's rights by what they called Muslim fundamentalists, defined as those wielding conservative and misogynistic readings of Islamic texts and law.

5   Frenett's enmeshment in the corporate world is reflected in his previous work with AVE (Against Violent Extremism), "a unique private sector partnership between ISD, Google Ideas, the Gen Next Foundation and rehabstudio" that "uses technology to connect, exchange, disseminate and influence all forms of violent extremism." See the AVE Network website at http://www.againstviolentextremism.org/about.

6   Although the logo and news item are no longer available on the website, a description of the program is included in a 2015 speech delivered by Pamela Hamamoto, the Permanent Representative of the United States to the UN, found at: https://geneva.usmission.gov/2015/02/13/the-role-of-women-and-girls-in-countering-violent-extremism/?_ga=2.130396367.1398802369.1630433366-1635555577.1630433366.

7   The annual report to the 46th session of the UN Human Rights Council by Fionnuala Ní Aoláin, the Special Rapporteur on the promotion of human rights and fundamental freedoms while countering terrorism, summarizes these arguments eloquently focusing on the "human rights impact of counterterrorism and countering (violent) extremism policies and practices on the rights of women, girls and the family" (2021).

8   See also Ní Aoláin's sharp assessment of the mission creep of security as in

9   UNSCR 2242, which "suffers from the same generic defect as UNSCR 1373: violent extremism, terrorism and terrorist acts are all condemned but their scope remains undefined. If nothing else, one would hope that a feminist response to the ambiguity of the terms 'terrorist' and 'terrorism' would underscore the potential exploitation that can follow from indiscriminate and unmediated application of the label in the service of political expediency" (2016, 283).

9   To their credit, Cook and Vale advocate in their sequel *From Daesh to Diaspora II* that European states treat their citizens better and create a "transparent and rights-based process" to "provide justice for both Islamic State members and their victims." This is staged, however, as a backhand insult to "extremists," since they argue that this would "demonstrate the values of the international community in contrast with the Islamic State" (2019, 17).

10   See the details in the *Human Rights Watch Submission to the Committee on the Elimination of All Forms of Discrimination Against Women on Iraq* (Human Rights Watch 2019).

11   They introduce the problem this way: "As 2019 dawns, the spectre of violent extremism remains at the forefront of the global peace and security discourse and practice. *As the number of deaths due to terrorism continues to fall* . . . a new set of challenges emerges: that of the disengagement, rehabilitation, and reintegration of men, women, boys and girls associated with violent extremist (VE) GROUPS. . . . Current policies and programming tend to either ignore women and girls associated with VE groups or oversimplify the issues. They frame women and girls in binary terms, either as victims or perpetrators of violence. . . . In order to design effective responses for this cohort, we must understand and address the initial drivers, conditions and motivations of their association with VE groups" (Anderlini and Holmes 2019, 12, my emphasis).

12   With the cottage industry around the returnees (Brown 2019; Cook and Vale 2018; Cook and Vale 2019), we even get practical manuals such as the Institute for Strategic Dialogue's 2019 "Women, Girls and Islamic Extremism: A Toolkit for Intervention Practitioners."

13   Ghosh et al. (2016) have early figures for the War on Terror. Kundnani and Hayes (2018) set figures for US State Department spending on CVE programs at $188 million, spending that Sahar Aziz argued in congressional testimony was a waste of government resources (Aziz 2017).

14   See the Costs of War project website at https://watson.brown.edu/costsofwar/.

15   Could this panic over sexual slavery be responsible for the insertion of a new item into the 2019 "United States Strategy on Women, Peace, and Security" published by the Executive Office of the President? Repeating the adage that "women are often the first targets of terrorism and violent extremist ideologies, which restrict their rights and can lead to increases in violence against them." The report goes on to say, "Terrorists often advocate for, and carry out, the enslavement of women and girls" (United States Executive Office of the President 2019, 9).

REFERENCES

Ababneh, Sara. 2014. "The Palestinian Women's Movement versus Hamas: Attempting to Understand Women's Empowerment outside a Feminist Framework." *Journal of International Women's Studies* 15, no. 1: 35–53. http://vc.bridgew.edu/jiws/vol15/iss1/3.

Abu-Lughod, Lila. 2013. *Do Muslim Women Need Saving?* Cambridge, MA: Harvard University Press.

Abu-Lughod, Lila. 2016. "The Cross-Publics of Ethnography: The Case of 'the Muslimwoman.'" *American Ethnologist* 43, no. 4: 595–608.

Alexander, Audrey. 2016. *Cruel Intentions: Female Jihadists in America*. Washington, DC: George Washington University Program on Extremism. https://cchs.gwu.edu/sites/cchs.gwu.edu/files/downloads/Female%20Jihadists%20in%20America.pdf.

Al-Ali, Nadje, and Nicola Pratt. 2009. *What Kind of Liberation?: Women and the Occupation of Iraq*. Berkeley: University of California Press.

Ali, Zahra. 2018. *Women and Gender in Iraq*. Cambridge: Cambridge University Press.

Amar, Paul. 2011. "Turning the Gendered Politics of the Security State Inside Out? Charging the Police with Sexual Harassment in Egypt." *International Feminist Journal of Politics* 13, no. 3: 299–328. https://doi.org/10.1080/14616742.2011.587364.

Anderlini, Sanam Naraghi. 2016. "Uncomfortable Truths, Unconventional Wisdoms: Women's Perspectives on Violent Extremism and Security Interventions." Women's Alliance for Security Leadership: A Brief on Policy and Practice for Mitigating Extremism and Advancing Sustainable Development. http://www.icanpeacework.org/wp-content/uploads/2017/03/WASL-Security-Brief-2016.pdf.

Anderlini, Sanam Naraghi, Chantal de Jonge Oudraat, and Leila Milani. 2017. "Violent Extremism and the Women, Peace and Security Agenda: Recommendations for the Trump Administration." US Civil Society Working Group on Women, Peace and Security Policy Brief, Thursday, January 5, 2017. https://www.futureswithoutviolence.org/wp-content/uploads/Violent-Extremism-and-the-WPS-agenda.pdf.

Anderlini, Sanam Naraghi, and Melinda Holmes. 2019. "Invisible Women: Gendered Dimensions of Return, Rehabilitation and Reintegration from Violent Extremism." United Nations Development Programme (UNDP) and the International Civil Society Action Network (ICAN). https://www.icanpeacework.org/2019/01/11/invisible-women/.

Aroussi, Sahla. 2021. "Strange Bedfellows: Interrogating the Unintended Consequences of Integrating Countering Violent Extremism with the UN's Women, Peace, and Security Agenda in Kenya." *Politics and Gender* 17, no. 4: 665–95. https://doi.org/10.1017/S1743923X20000124.

Aziz, Sahar. 2017. "Losing the 'War of Ideas': A Critique of Countering Violent Extremism Programs." *Texas International Law Journal* 52, no. 2: 255–79. https://doi.org/10.7282/T38S4TG7.

Bhulai, Rafia, Allison Peters, and Christina Nemr. 2016. "From Policy to Action: Advancing an Integrated Approach to Women and Countering Violent Extremism." Global Center on Cooperative Security, June 2016. https://www.globalcenter.org/wp-content/uploads/2016/06/From-Policy-to-Action_Women-and-PCVE_Policy-Brief_Global-Center_Inclusive-Security.pdf.

Brown, Katherine. 2019. "Gender Dimensions of the Response to Returning Foreign Terrorist Fighters: Research Perspectives." UN Security Council Counter-Terrorism Committee Executive Directorate. CTED Trends Report.

Brown, Wendy. 2008. *Regulating Aversion: Tolerance in the Age of Identity and Empire*. Princeton, NJ: Princeton University Press.

Castillo Diaz, Pablo, and Nahla Valji. 2019. "Symbiosis of Misogyny and Violent Extremism: New Understandings and Policy Implications." *Journal of International Affairs* 72, no. 2: 37–57. https://www.jstor.org/stable/26760831.

Cohn, Carol. 2008. "Mainstreaming Gender in UN Security Policy: A Path to Political Transformation?" In *Global Governance: Feminist Perspectives*, edited by Shirin M. Rai and Georgina Waylen, 185–206. New York: Palgrave Macmillan.

Cook, Joana, and Gina Vale. 2018. "From Daesh to 'Diaspora': Tracing the Women and Minors of Islamic State." International Centre for the Study of Radicalisation, King's College London. Updated July 2019. https://icsr.info/2018/07/23/from-daesh-to-diaspora-tracing-the-women-and-minors-of-islamic-state/.

Cook, Joana, and Gina Vale. 2019. "From Daesh to 'Diaspora' II: The Challenges Posed by Women and Minors after the Fall of the Caliphate." *Combatting Terrorism Center Sentinel* 12, no. 6: 3-45. https://ctc.usma.edu/wp-content/uploads/2019/07/CTC-SENTINEL-062019.pdf.

Coomaraswamy, Radhika. 2015. *Preventing Conflict, Transforming Justice, Securing the Peace. A Global Study on the Implementation of United Nations Security Council Resolution 1325*. New York: UN Women. http://wps.unwomen.org/index.html.

Creative Associates International. n.d. "The Beginning: Four Women, One Vision." Accessed April 24, 2019. https://www.creativeassociatesinternational.com/history/.

Creative Associates International. n.d. "Building Resilient Communities to Prevent Violent Extremism." Accessed January 2, 2022. https://www.creativeassociatesinternational.com/cve-and-pve/.

Dadu, Saagarika, and Maire Forestier. 2019. "The Gendered Impact of the Conflict in Iraq on IS-Affiliated Women." *London School of Economics Centre for Women Peace and Security* (blog), March 28, 2019. https://blogs.lse.ac.uk/wps/2019/03/28/gendered-impact-of-the-conflict-in-iraq/.

Deeb, Lara. 2006. *An Enchanted Modern: Gender and Public Piety in Shi'i Lebanon*. Princeton, NJ: Princeton University Press.

Engle, Karen. 2020. *In the Grip of Sexual Violence in Conflict: Feminist Interventions in International Law*. Stanford, CA: Stanford University Press.

Fadil, Nadia, and Martijn de Koning. 2019. "Turning 'Radicalization' in to Science: Ambivalent Translations into the Dutch (Speaking) Academic Field." In *Radicalization in Belgium and the Netherlands: Critical Perspectives on Violence and Security*, edited by Nadia Fadil, Martijn de Koning, and Francesco Ragazzi, 53–80. London: Bloomsbury.

Fadil, Nadia, Martijn de Koning, and Francesco Ragazzi, eds. 2019a. *Radicalization in Belgium and the Netherlands: Critical Perspectives on Violence and Security*. London: Bloomsbury.

Fadil, Nadia, Martijn de Koning, and Francesco Ragazzi. 2019b. "Radicalization: Tracing the Trajectory of an 'Empty Signifier' in the Low Lands." In *Radicalization in Belgium and the Netherlands: Critical Perspectives on Violence and Security*, edited by Nadia Fadil, Martijn de Koning, and Francesco Ragazzi, 3–28. London: Bloomsbury.

Fink, Naureen Chowdhury, Rafia Barakat, and Liat Shetret. 2013. "The Roles of Women in Terrorism, Conflict, and Violent Extremism: Lessons for the United Nations and International Actors." Center on Global Counterterrorism Cooperation, April 2013. https://www.globalcenter.org/wp-content/uploads/2013/04/NCF_RB_LS_policybrief_1320.pdf.

Fink, Naureen Chowdhury, Sara Zeiger, and Rafia Bhulai, eds. 2016. *A Man's World? Exploring the Roles of Women in Countering Terrorism and Violent Extremism*. Abu Dhabi: Hedayah and the Global Center on Cooperative Security. https://wiisglobal.org/wp-content/uploads/2016/07/AMansWorld_FULL.pdf.

German Institute on Radicalization and De-Radicalization Studies. 2015. "Open Letter to Our Sons and Daughters From Mothers For Life." Accessed April 24, 2019. http://www.girds.org/files/openletter.pdf.

Ghosh, Ratna, Ashley Manuel, W. Y. Alice Chan, Maihemuti Dilimulati, and Mehdi Babei. 2016. "Education and Security: A Global Literature Review on the Role of Education in Countering Violent Religious Extremism." Tony Blair Institute for Global Change. https://institute.global/sites/default/files/inline-files/IGC_Education%20and%20Security.pdf.

Global Counter-Terrorism Forum (GCTF). 2015. "Good Practices on Women and Countering Violent Extremism." https://www.thegctf.org/Portals/1/Documents/Framework%20Documents/2016%20and%20before/GCTF-Good-Practices-on-Women-and-CVE.pdf?ver=2016-09-09-112914-837.

Gowrinathan, Nimmi. 2015. "Motivations of Female Fighters." In *Women Preventing Extremism: Charting a New Course*, 22–24. U.S. Institute for Peace. https://www.usip.org/sites/default/files/files/Women-Preventing-Violent-Extremism-Charting-New-Course.pdf.

Gowrinathan, Nimmi. 2021. *Radicalizing Her: Why Women Choose Violence*. Boston: Beacon Press.

Grewal, Inderpal. 2017. *Saving the Security State: Exceptional Citizens in Twenty-First-Century America*. Durham, NC: Duke University Press.

Guénif-Souilamas, Nacira. 2017. "Restrained Equality: A Sexualized and Gendered

Colour Line." In *Austere Histories in European Societies: Social Exclusion and the Contest of Colonial Memories*, edited by Stefan Jonsson and Julia Willén, 161–81. London: Routledge.

Hafez, Sherine. 2011. *An Islam of Her Own*. New York: New York University Press.

Halley, Janet, Prahbha Kotiswaran, Rachel Rebouché, and Hila Shamir. 2018. *Governance Feminism: An Introduction*. Minneapolis: University of Minnesota Press.

Halley, Janet, Prahbha Kotiswaran, Rachel Rebouché, and Hila Shamir, eds. 2019. *Governance Feminism: Notes from the Field*. Minneapolis: University of Minnesota Press.

Hammer, Juliane. 2019. *Peaceful Families: American Muslim Efforts against Domestic Violence*. Princeton, NJ: Princeton University Press.

Hoyle, Carolyn, Alexandra Bradford, and Ross Frenett. 2015. "Becoming Mulan? Female Western Migrants to ISIS." Institute for Strategic Dialogue. https://www.isdglobal.org/isd-publications/becoming-mulan-female-western-migrants-to-isis/.

Huckerby, Jayne C. 2020. "In Harm's Way: Gender and Human Rights in National Security." *Duke Journal of Law and Policy* 27: 179–202. https://scholarship.law.duke.edu/djglp/vol27/iss1/11.

Human Rights Watch. 2019. "Human Rights Watch Submission to the Committee on the Elimination of All Forms of Discrimination Against Women on Iraq." 74th Pre-Sessional Working Group, March 5. https://www.hrw.org/news/2019/03/05/human-rights-watch-submission-committee-elimination-all-forms-discrimination-4.

Hunt, Elle. 2017. "'One Orb to Rule Them All': Image of Donald Trump and Glowing Globe Perplexes Internet." *The Guardian*, May 22. https://www.theguardian.com/us-news/2017/may/22/one-orb-to-rule-them-all-image-of-trump-and-glowing-globe-perplexes-internet.

Idris, Iffat, with Ayat Abdelaziz. 2017. *Women and Countering Violent Extremism* (GSDRC Helpdesk Research Report 1408). Birmingham, UK: GSDRC, University of Birmingham. https://gsdrc.org/publications/women-and-countering-violent-extremism/.

Inge, Anabel. 2017. *The Making of a Salafi Muslim Woman*. Oxford: Oxford University Press.

International Civil Society Action Network (ICAN). 2017. "Global Solutions Exchange: Civil Society Leadership on Preventing Violent Extremism." Accessed April 24, 2019. http://www.icanpeacework.org/our-work/global-solutions-exchange/.

International Crisis Group. 2020. "A Course Correction for the Women, Peace and Security Agenda." Briefing No. 5: Gender and Conflict. https://www.crisisgroup.org/global/b05-course-correction-women-peace-and-security-agenda.

Jad, Islah. 2005. "Islamist Women of Hamas: A New Women's Movement?" In *On Shifting Ground; Muslim Women in a Global Era*, edited by Fereshteh Nouraie-Simone. New York: The Feminist Press.

Kosmatopoulos, Nikolas. 2020. "Master Peace: Techno-Moral Cosmopolitanisms and the Crisis of Critique." *Institute for Advanced Study Working Paper Number 66*. https://doi.org/10.13140/RG.2.2.33232.33287.

Kundnani, Arun. 2014. *The Muslims Are Coming! Islamophobia, Extremism, and the Domestic War on Terror*. Brooklyn, NY: Verso.

Kundnani, Arun, and Ben Hayes. 2018. *The Globalisation of Countering Violent Extremism Policies: Undermining Human Rights, Instrumentalising Civil Society*. Amsterdam: Transnational Institute.

Loken, Meredith, and Anna Zelenz. 2017. "Explaining Extremism: Western Women in Daesh." *European Journal of International Security* 3, no. 1: 45–68. https://doi.org/10.1017/eis.2017.13.

Mahmood, Saba. 2005. *Politics of Piety*. Princeton, NJ: Princeton University Press.

Mahmood, Saba. 2006. "Secularism, Hermeneutics, and Empire: The Politics of Islamic Reformation." *Public Culture* 18, no. 2: 323–47. https://doi.org/10.1215/08992363-2006-006.

McLarney, Ellen Anne. 2015. *Soft Force: Women in Egypt's Islamic Awakening*. Princeton, NJ: Princeton University Press.

Mercy Corps. 2015. "From Jordan to Jihad: The Lure of Syria's Violent Extremist Groups." *Mercy Corps Policy Brief*, September 28. https://www.mercycorps.org.uk/research-resources/jordan-jihad-lure-syrias-violent-extremist-groups.

Merry, Sally Engle. 2006. *Human Rights and Gender Violence: Translating International Law into Local Justice*. Chicago: University of Chicago Press.

Mlambo-Ngcuka, Phumzile, and Radhika Coomaraswamy. 2015. "Women Are the Best Weapons in the War Against Terrorism." *Foreign Policy*, February 10. https://foreignpolicy.com/2015/02/10/women-are-the-best-weapon-in-the-war-against-terrorism/.

Moaveni, Azadeh. 2019. *Guest House for Young Widows: Among the Women of ISIS*. New York: Random House.

Modirzadeh, Naz. 2016. "If It's Broke, Don't Make It Worse: A Critique of the UN Secretary-General's Plan of Action of Preventing Violent Extremism." *Lawfare*, January 23. https://www.lawfareblog.com/if-its-broke-dont-make-it-worse-critique-un-secretary-generals-plan-action-prevent-violent-extremism.

Moonshot CVE. 2019. Accessed April 24, 2019. http://moonshotcve.com/#g-extensionmain.

Moors, Annelies. 2017. "Adopting a Face-Veil, Concluding an Islamic Marriage: Autonomy, Agency, and Liberal-Secular Rule." In *Personal Autonomy in Plural Societies: A Principle and its Paradoxes*, edited by Marie-Claire Foblets, Michele Graziadei, and Alison Renteln, 127–39. London: Routledge.

Moors, Annelies. 2019. "The Trouble with Transparency: Reconnecting Ethics, Integrity, Epistemology and Power." *Ethnography* 20, no. 2: 149–69. https://doi.org/10.1177/1466138119844279.

Mukhopadhyay, Dipali, and Kimberly Howe. 2023. *Good Rebel Governance: Revolu-*

tionary Politics and Western Intervention in Syria. New York: Cambridge University Press.

Musawah. 2011. CEDAW *and Muslim Family Laws: In Search of Common Ground.* Malaysia: Musawah. https://www.musawah.org/resources/cedaw-and-muslim-family-laws-in-search-of-common-ground/.

Nesiah, Vasuki. 2013. "Feminism as Counter-terrorism: The Seduction of Power." In *Gender, National Security, and Counter-Terrorism: Human Rights Perspectives,* edited by Margaret L. Satterhwaite and Jayne Huckerby, 127–51. London: Routledge.

Ní Aoláin, Fionnuala. 2016. "The 'War on Terror' and Extremism: Assessing the Relevance of the Women, Peace and Security Agenda." *International Affairs* 92, no. 2: 275–91. https://doi.org/10.1111/1468-2346.12552.

Ní Aoláin, Fionnuala. 2021. "Human Rights Impact of Counter-terrorism and Countering (Violent) Extremism Policies and Practices on the Rights of Women, Girls and the Family: Report of the Special Rapporteur on the Promotion and Protection of Human Rights and Fundamental Freedoms While Countering Terrorism." *Human Rights Council, 46th session.* A/HRC/46/36. https://documents-dds-ny.un.org/doc/UNDOC/GEN/G21/015/08/PDF/G2101508.pdf?OpenElement.

Organization for Security and Co-Operation in Europe (OSCE). 2017. "Women in Security: Countering Violent Extremism." OSCE Secretariat. Last modified January 16, 2017. https://www.osce.org/secretariat/293631.

Otto, Dianne. 2018. "Women, Peace, and Security: A Critical Analysis of the Security Council's Vision." In *Oxford Handbook of Gender and Conflict,* edited by Fionnuala Ní Aoláin, Naomi Cahn, Dina Francesca Hayes, and Nahla Valiji, 105–18. Oxford: Oxford University Press.

Otto, Dianne. 2019. "Contesting Feminism's Institutional Doubles: Troubling the Security Council's Women, Peace and Security Agenda." In *Governance Feminism: Notes from the Field,* edited by Janet Halley, Prahbha Kotiswaran, Rachel Rebouché, and Hila Shamir, 200–29. Minneapolis: University of Minnesota Press.

Özyürek, Esra. 2014. *Being German, Becoming Muslim: Race, Religion, and Conversion in the New Europe.* Princeton, NJ: Princeton University Press.

Patel, Sofia. 2017. "'The Sultanate of Women': Exploring Female Roles in Perpetuating and Preventing Violent Extremism." Australian Strategic Policy Institute Special Report, February 2017.

Pompeo, Michael. 2019. "Release of the United States Strategy on Women, Peace, and Security." Last modified June 11, 2019. https://www.state.gov/release-of-the-united-states-strategy-on-women-peace-and-security/.

Rafiq, Haras, and Nikita Malik. 2015. "Caliphettes: Women and the Appeal of Islamic State." *Quilliam.* https://issuu.com/m.r.mohamed/docs/caliphettes-women-and-the-appeal-of.

Rinaldo, Rachel. 2013. *Mobilizing Piety: Islam and Feminism in Indonesia.* Oxford: Oxford University Press.

Salime, Zakia. 2011. *Between Feminism and Islam: Human Rights and Sharia Law in Morocco*. Minneapolis: University of Minnesota Press.

Saltman, Erin Marie, and Melanie Smith. 2015. "'Till Martyrdom Do Us Part': Gender and the ISIS Phenomenon." *Institute for Strategic Dialogue*. https://www.isdglobal.org/wp-content/uploads/2016/02/Till_Martyrdom_Do_Us_Part_Gender_and_the_ISIS_Phenomenon.pdf.

Saltman, Erin Marie, and Ross Frenett. 2016. "Female Radicalization to ISIS and the Role of Women in CVE." In *A Man's World? Exploring the Roles of Women in Counter Terrorism and Violent Extremism*, edited by Naureen Chowdhury Fink, Sara Zeiger, and Rafia Bhulai, 142–63. Hedayah and The Global Center on Cooperative Security.

Schlaffer, Edit. 2015. "Charting New Ways with New Partners." In *Women Preventing Violent Extremism: Charting a New Course*. Washington: U.S. Institute for Peace. https://www.usip.org/sites/default/files/files/Women-Preventing-Violent-Extremism-Charting-New-Course.pdf.

Sewall, Sarah. 2016. "Women and Countering Violent Extremism." US Department of State. New York City: Commission on the Status of Women. https://2009-2017.state.gov/j/remarks/254868.htm.

Strasser, Fred. 2017. "From Nazis to ISIS: Women's Roles in Violence: History Can Aid Understanding of Gender in Conflict." United States Institute of Peace, March 2, 2017. https://www.usip.org/publications/2017/03/nazis-isis-womens-roles-violence.

U.S. Department of State. 2016. "Department of State & USAID Joint Strategy on Countering Violent Extremism." Last modified May 25, 2016. https://2009-2017.state.gov/j/ct/rls/other/257725.htm.

United States Executive Office of the President. 2019. United States Strategy on Women, Peace, and Security. June 2019. https://www.hsdl.org/?abstract&did=826079.

United States Institute of Peace (USIP). 2015. *Women Preventing Violent Extremism: Charting a New Course*. Accessed April 24, 2019. https://www.usip.org/sites/default/files/files/Women-Preventing-Violent-Extremism-Charting-New-Course.pdf.

Winter, Charlie, and Devorah Margolin. 2017. "The Mujahidat Dilemma: Female Combatants and the Islamic State." *Combating Terrorism Center Sentinel* 10, no. 7: 23–28.

Women's Islamic Initiative in Spirituality and Equality (WISE). 2018. WISEUP. Accessed July 2, 2019. https://www.wisemuslimwomen.org/projects/wise-up/.

Women without Borders. 2019. "MotherSchools Explained." Accessed April 24. https://www.women-without-borders.org/.

Yafout, Merieme. 2015. "Islamist Women and the Arab Spring: Discourse, Projects, and Conceptions. *Comparative Studies of South Asia, Africa, and the Middle East* 25, no. 3: 588–604. https://muse.jhu.edu/article/605750/pdf.

THREE · *Leti Volpp*

The Role of "Honor Killings" in the Muslim Ban

Seven days after his presidency began on January 20, 2017, Donald Trump issued an executive order (No. 13769) titled "Protecting the Nation from Foreign Terrorist Entry into the United States" (hereinafter, EO-1). The order invoked the terrorist attacks of September 11, 2001, and indicated that the United States sought to "prevent the admission of foreign nationals who intend to exploit United States' immigration laws for malevolent purposes." In order to accomplish that goal, EO-1 temporarily suspended the entry of noncitizens from seven countries, temporarily suspended the US refugee program, and indefinitely suspended the entry of any Syrian refugees.

Mass chaos ensued, as travelers were turned away from flights to the United States, stranded overseas while in transit, and detained upon arrival at US airports. Amid the outcry about EO-1, observers missed a curious fact. Overlooked by most was the fact that the text of EO-1 invoked, twice, the idea of "honor killings"—first, identifying "honor killings" as a problematic practice by "foreign nationals" condemned in the Purpose section of the Order, and, second, mandating data collection and reporting about "honor killings" (Volpp 2017).

In March, 2017, facing a losing battle to defend EO-1 in the courts, the Trump administration replaced EO-1 with Executive Order No. 13780, bearing EO-1's identical title of "Protecting the Nation from Foreign Terrorist Entry into the United States" (hereinafter, EO-2). The Purpose section of EO-2 was stripped of any reference to "honor killings," but EO-2 retained the mandate for data collection and reporting about "honor killings." On September 24, 2017, the Trump administration once again revised its approach in the face of legal challenges and issued a Presidential Proclamation (hereinafter, EO-3), which replaced most, but not all of EO-2. While EO-3 made no reference to "honor killings" in its text, it left the mandate for data collection and reporting on "honor killings" of EO-2 intact.[1] On June 26, 2018 the Supreme Court upheld EO-3 in a split 5–4 decision (*Trump v. Hawaii* 2018).

Why did "honor killings" appear in these executive orders? What is accomplished by invoking "honor killings"? And how have "honor killings" been constituted as a problem for US governance? An initial answer to these questions can be gleaned from the social, political, and legal uses of the phrase "honor killings," a term taken to refer to "the killing of a woman by her relatives for violation of a sexual code in the name of restoring family honor" (Abu-Lughod 2011, 17).

The use of the term to isolate one form of gender-based violence as distinct from other forms is hotly contested and assists in the portrayal of only certain communities as sites of aberrant violence.[2] As Lila Abu-Lughod explains, "honor killings" are marked as "culturally specific," as "distinct from other widespread forms of domestic violence" and are "constantly associated" with reports from the Middle East and South Asia or immigrant communities originating from those regions (Abu-Lughod 2011, 17–18).[3] This division of "honor killings" from other forms of gendered violence reflects the way motivation for acts of gender-based violation is selectively narrated through the media and public discourse so that different explanations are proffered, depending upon the identity of the perpetrator.

Bad acts by immigrant communities tend to be attributed to culture or religion, as opposed to bad acts by white Americans, which are usually described as either the product of individual deviancy or psychological factors (Volpp 2000, 96; Razack 2004, 152).[4] These explanatory choices mask the entrenchment of gendered violence in US culture. Even in the era of #MeToo and long-delayed attention to sexual abuse and harassment, the term "honor killings" divides the universe into societies believed to be motivated by a primitive premodern religion from those conceptualized as modern, rational, and secular. The term "honor killing" circulates as what Inderpal Grewal (2013) calls a "media-ted" concept, which diagnoses both the nature of a crime and its solution as confined to certain communities, following a racial logic. Discursively, "'honor killings' work as a 'comforting phantasm,'" juxtaposing an "assumed gender inequality and oppression of women by Islam" with a "quintessentially American gender-egalitarianism and respect for women's rights." (Abu Lughod 2013, 127; Hammer 2013, 33). They help create an illusion that only some communities engage in violence against women, since "modern" societies are thought to be sites where such violence only occurs when perpetrated by immigrants (Grewal 2013).

On these readings, the use of the phrase "honor killings" in the executive orders can be understood as evincing a professed concern for violence against women, while actually serving to reinforce a perception of Muslim barbarity and inferiority. The invocation of "honor killings" thus functions as the kind of coded signal called a "dog whistle," purporting to convey one message while in fact communicating another to those who are aware of the speaker's true intent (Haney Lopez 2013; Toosi 2017).[5] This cynical deployment of feminist concerns as a proxy for xenophobic exclusion is troubling enough. But what is equally disturbing is that the notion that "honor killings" are a problem in the United States has been constructed through false and misleading claims about data. As explained further below, the idea that there are "23–27 honor killings" occurring annually in the United States was circulated by former Attorney General Jeff Sessions when he was a senator, and is expressed in the report produced by the Departments of Justice and Homeland Security in response to the transparency and data collection mandate of EO-2. This figure emerged from a concerted campaign led by Ayaan Hirsi Ali's AHA Foundation, which has worked vigorously to generate concern among academic and political circuits about "honor killings" as a phenomenon.[6]

In what follows, I first briefly explain the legal backdrop of EO-1, EO-2, and EO-3. I then focus on the role of "honor killings" in EO-1 and EO-2, as well as on legal strategy, and judicial decisions. Next, I examine how "honor killings" functioned in the context of Trump's speeches, which constitute a kind of legislative history of the executive orders. I then sketch a genealogy of how "honor killings" became a focus of US governance, to explain how this as an issue managed to appear in these key public articulations of the Trump administration, as concretized through an annual rate of death that is in fact imagined.

While we do not know who specifically inserted the "honor killing" provisions into the executive orders, White House advisors Stephen Miller and Steve Bannon were described as primarily involved in EO-1's development (Bennett 2017). Regardless of who authored EO-1 and EO-2, the idea that Muslim women are particularly oppressed now appears in US discourse as a kind of common sense. The project of "saving women" is knitted into Islamophobia in the United States, with the literal barring of Muslim bodies from entering the United States in the name of purportedly protecting Muslim women from violence.

LEGAL BACKGROUND

EO-1 sought to suspend the entry of immigrants and nonimmigrants (temporary visitors) from seven countries—Iran, Iraq, Libya, Somalia, Sudan, Syria, and Yemen—for a period of ninety days. Syrian refugees were to be indefinitely barred from the United States, while refugee admissions in general were to be suspended for 120 days. Once refugee admissions resumed, refugees from "minority religions" were to be given priority, which, Trump announced on the Christian Broadcasting Network, was intended to assist persecuted Christians (Reilly 2017). Critics quickly labeled EO-1 a Muslim ban, as the manifestation of Trump's campaign promise to create such.

After several lawsuits challenging the constitutionality of EO-1 were filed, leading to multiple provisions of EO-1 being barred from implementation, the Trump administration issued EO-2. While EO-2 deleted several of EO-1's provisions in an attempt to immunize the administration from legal challenge, including the language prioritizing refugee claimants from "minority religions," as well as the indefinite bar preventing entry by Syrian refugees, critics quickly labeled EO-2 "Muslim Ban 2.0," signifying that it continued EO-1's project.[7] EO-2 was attacked in the courts as violating both the US Constitution and the federal Immigration and Nationality Act, culminating in a brief and unsigned decision issued on June 26, 2017, by the Supreme Court (*Trump v. Int'l Refugee Assistance Project* (2017)). This decision promised to review the rulings by lower courts once the Supreme Court's October 2017 term commenced and also allowed the ban to be implemented against those without a "bona fide relationship" to a person or entity in the United States.

On September 24, 2017, the Trump administration once again attempted to rewrite its ban in order to withstand legal challenges. This appeared in the form of a Presidential Proclamation ("EO-3"). Critics called this Proclamation "Muslim Ban 3.0," as it indefinitely suspended the entry of particular groups of individuals from several countries—continuing the ban on Iran, Libya, Somalia, Syria, and Yemen, while also newly adding Chad, North Korea, and Venezuela to the list. This action led the Supreme Court to strike the challenges to EO-2 from the docket. Challenges to EO-3 were immediately filed, leading district court judges in Hawai'i and Maryland to partially block EO-3's enforcement bars on Iran, Libya, Somalia, Syria, Yemen, and Chad.[8] On December 4, 2017, those injunctions were lifted by the Supreme Court, and EO-3 was put into effect. On June 26, 2018 the Supreme Court upheld EO-3. In a 5-to-4 vote, a majority of the justices held that Trump's statutory authority to suspend the entry of aliens into the United States had been lawfully exercised, without violating either the Immigration and Nationality Act or the Establishment Clause of the Constitution.[9] In a vehement dissent, Justice Sonia Sotomayor highlighted the history lost in translation as litigation jumped from EO-1 to EO-2 to EO-3, writing that "[t]he full record paints a far more harrowing picture, from which a reasonable observer would readily conclude that [EO-3] was motivated by hostility and animus toward the Muslim faith" (*Trump v. Hawaii* 2018, 2435). While EO-3 did not mention the term "honor killings," it nonetheless left EO-2's mandate to collect and publish data on "honor killings" still in force, a requirement that the Department of Homeland Security and Department of Justice followed until President Joe Biden revoked EO-2 along with EO-3 in one of the first acts of his administration, on January 20, 2021.[10]

"PROTECTING THE NATION"

Let us now turn to the specific text of the executive orders. "Honor killings" first appear in the Purpose section of EO-1. After stating that the visa-issuance process plays a "crucial role in detecting individuals with terrorist ties and stopping them from entering the United States," invoking the terrorist attacks of September 11, 2001, and "numerous foreign-born individuals" who were "convicted or implicated in terrorism-related crimes" since that date, and asserting that "[d]eteriorating conditions in certain countries ... increase the likelihood that terrorists will use any means possible to enter the United States," the EO-1 goes on to state:

> In order to protect Americans, the United States must ensure that those admitted to this country do not bear hostile attitudes toward it and its founding principles. The United States cannot, and should not, admit those who do not support the Constitution, or those who would place violent ideologies over American law. In addition, the United States should not admit those who engage in acts of bigotry or hatred (including "honor" killings, other forms of violence against women, or the persecution of those who practice religions different from their own) or those who would oppress Americans of any race, gender, or sexual orientation. (US Presidential Exec. Order No. 13769 2017, 1)

First, we should note the prominence of what the government labels "honor killings" in EO-1. The Purpose section of an executive order, like the preamble or purpose section of an act of legislation, is used to help the reader discern the intent behind an order or legislative act. Here, the Purpose section of EO-1 is composed of only three paragraphs: the first singling out the government's issuing of visas as linked to the detection and exclusion of terrorists; the second raising the specter of September 11, 2001, and the possibility of "foreign-born nationals" seeking to harm Americans being admitted as visitors, students, employees, or refugees; and the third asserting that some persons who would enter the United States as "foreign nationals" bear animus toward the nation, its Constitution, or its founding principles.

The reference to those with "hostile attitudes," who "would place violent ideologies over American law," appears intended to evoke both the concept of what Trump has repeatedly called "Islamic terror" as well as the image of a growing group of individuals supplanting American law with Sharia law; both evocations suggest that Muslim individuals are dangerous to the American republic (Beauchamp 2017; Ali 2012; Quraishi-Landes 2013; Razack 2007). Immediately folded into this vision is the statement that the United States should exclude those who engage in "acts of bigotry or hatred" with two parenthetical iterations of such acts provided: violence against women and the persecution of those who practice religions different from their own. "'Honor' killings"—which appears immediately after "acts of bigotry or hatred"—is ostensibly provided as an example of violence against women, yet the term precedes the general category of violence against women, suggesting a greater emphasis on the example than on the general category.

What is signaled here, then, is that the generic concern is not so much "violence against women" as it is "honor killings"—a point borne out by Trump's attacks on women and their rights, both personally and through his administration. As Nora Caplan-Bricker writes, by making it clear that sexual violence is emphasized only as a priority for Homeland Security, and not for other government agencies, Trump is "communicating that sexual violence isn't wrong unless it's perpetrated by a foreigner. Otherwise, as our president has said, 'You can do anything.... Grab them by the pussy'" (Caplan-Bricker 2017). If the Trump administration truly cared about protecting women, it would be "strengthening domestic violence programs and allowing women refugees in . . . [rather than] using women as political pawns" (Attiah 2017). This is "repackaging xenophobia as feminism" (Ryan 2017).

We should also note the coupling of "'honor' killings" and the "persecution of those who practice religions different from their own." Recall that

EO-1 provided a preference for refugee admissions for those refugees who were members of minority religions, which was explicitly intended to benefit Christian refugees fleeing persecution. As such, the "persecution of those who practice religions different from their own" should be understood to invoke the vision of Muslim persecution of Christians; its placement in EO-1 in proximity to "honor killings" helps cement the understanding of which "foreign nationals" are to be banned from the United States.

Next, note that EO-1 follows the statement that the United States should not admit those who engage in "acts of bigotry or hatred" with the assertion that the United States should also not admit "those who would oppress Americans of any race, gender, or sexual orientation." This may seem a curious addition to EO-1, particularly given the administration's stance on issues of racial, gender, or LGBTQ equality. But the inclusion of this phrasing should be understood to reflect and reiterate a potent narrative that positions Muslim immigrants as direct threats to sexual freedom and gender equality in the United States. In addition to the "common sense" that women must be saved from Islam, gay rights discourses have been incorporated in US and Western imperial projects through what Jasbir Puar (2007) has articulated as "homonationalism."

The suggestion in EO-1, made through the proximity of the text of "honor killing" to "violence against women," and "persecution of those with religions different from their own," is that Muslims are the oppressors who would harm Americans on the basis of race, gender, or sexual orientation. Thus, EO-1 informs its readers that Muslim immigrants are to be banned not only for their terroristic threat; they are also to be banned because they are dangerous to purported Western liberal values. This idea, one also propagated in Europe by politicians such as Pim Fortuyn and Geert Wilders and nationalist political parties, was already circulated during the campaign by Trump (Bayoumi 2017; Tait 2017; Kolbert 2002).

While on the surface the text of EO-1's Purpose section suggests the administration is concerned about gendered violence, discrimination, and inequality, we can understand the rationale of these passages as reinforcing the presumption that Muslims, as particularly engaged in these forms of abhorrent behavior, must be kept out of the United States.

TRANSPARENCY AND DATA COLLECTION

"Honor killings" also appear in the section of EO-1 titled "Transparency and Data Collection." This section mandates the Secretary of Homeland Security, in consultation with the Attorney General, to "collect and make publicly available within 180 days, and every 180 days thereafter" information regarding particular acts in order to "be more transparent with the American people, and to more effectively implement policies and practices that serve the national interest" (US Presidential Exec. Order No. 13769 2017, 10). These include the number of foreign nationals charged with terrorism-related offenses, as well as "the number and types of acts of gender-based violence against women, including honor killings, in the United States by foreign nationals."

The language from the Purpose section in EO-1 was replaced in EO-2 with a more sober and detailed accounting of why nationals from the six designated countries present "heightened risks" to the security of the United States. Yet the data-gathering requirement about "honor killings" remains in section 11 of EO-2, mandating "information regarding the number and types of acts of gender-based violence against women, including so-called 'honor killings,' in the United States by foreign nationals" to be collected and made publicly available.

In considering the transition from EO-1 to EO-2, we could note the slippage in punctuation and choice of language, from "'honor' killings" in EO-1's Purpose section, to "honor killings" in EO-1's reporting section, to "so-called 'honor killings'" in EO-2's reporting section. This inconsistency betrays an uncertainty about how to label "honor killings" as a phenomenon, which arguably exposes an underlying uncertainty about whether these are, in fact, a phenomenon.

Why did "honor killings" disappear from the Purpose section of EO-2 but remain as a mandated category for data collection? To understand this shift requires parsing how the purpose of EO-1 and EO-2 became perceived as potentially unconstitutional, while the transparency and data collection section received less scrutiny.

A panel of the Ninth Circuit had noted that there were serious allegations raised that EO-1 violated the Establishment and Equal Protection Clauses because it was intended to disfavor Muslims (*Washington v. Trump* 2017). In response, the administration stripped EO-2 of any explicit reference to religion and devoted a lengthy paragraph to explicitly denying that religious animus motivated EO-1 (US Presidential Exec. Order No. 13780, 2017). Nonetheless, Federal District Court Judge Derrick Watson's analysis in *Hawai'i v. Trump* (D. Haw. 2017) found that, despite the absence of any explicit reference to religion in the text of the order, evidence of past public statements of Trump and of his associates and statements contemporaneous with the issuance of EO-2 suggested that "[a]ny reasonable, objective observer would conclude . . . that the stated secular purpose of the Executive Order is . . . secondary to a religious objective of temporarily suspending the entry of Muslims." Judge Watson did not point to EO-2's reporting mandate in ascertaining anti-Muslim animus.[11]

In *IRAP v. Trump*, Federal District Court Judge Theodore Chuang of Maryland also ordered a temporary halt to implementing the provisions of EO-2 affecting visa issuance for nationals of six majority-Muslim countries. In addition to analyzing the constitutional claims concerning religious discrimination that the plaintiffs claimed infected EO-2, Judge Chuang focused on provisions of the immigration statute that forbid nationality discrimination in the issuance of immigrant visas and concluded that the plaintiffs' challenge to the ninety-day ban was likely to succeed on both grounds. There was no mention by Judge Chuang of the reporting mandate.[12]

With the administration challenging both district court decisions, litigation continued. Numerous amicus briefs were filed in both the Ninth and Fourth Circuits, most on behalf of the parties challenging the ban. Forty-eight amicus briefs were filed in the *Hawai'i* case. Of these, six pointed to EO-2's requirement of reporting and data collection about "honor killings." Seven of the forty-eight amicus briefs filed in *IRAP v. Trump* pointed to the provision. All of these amicus briefs singled out the provision as another source of evidence as to the constitutionally impermissible motive underlying the executive orders.

By far the most developed argument about the appearance of this provision is found in amicus briefs filed in both courts on behalf of Muslim Rights, Professional and Public Health Organizations, which rely upon a declaration filed by the anthropologist Lila Abu-Lughod. As articulated in the amicus brief filed in the Ninth Circuit, the "invocation of private violence against women in the context of national security policy" may seem, "[a]t first blush . . . puzzling and out of place."[13] Yet it in fact constitutes "evidence of the invidious stereotypes about Muslims that underpin the Muslim ban policy." Quoting Abu-Lughod, the brief states "the term 'honor killing,' or 'honor crime,' has become a means of signaling a class of violence purportedly linked to Islam and committed by Muslim men," and is therefore "a way of stigmatizing and demeaning Islam as a faith and Muslim men as a group as uncivilized and dangerous." The brief goes on to quote Abu-Lughod: "Neither Islamic law nor its religious authorities, however, uniformly or consistently condone honor crimes . . . the term 'honor crime' is commonly invoked by individuals and groups with an anti-Muslim agenda because it reinforces the [false] stigmatization of Muslims as violent and backward." The brief concludes this discussion by asserting that the term in both executive orders, which are "instruments that are purportedly about national security rather than domestic violence," is "evidence of the invidious stereotypes about Muslims that underpin the Muslim ban policy" (Brief of Muslim Rights 2017, 16).

The Ninth Circuit decision, which largely upheld the district court's order, did so on statutory grounds, finding both that EO-2 ran afoul of anti-discriminatory provisions in the immigration statute and that the president had exceeded his authority, stating "immigration, even for the President, is not a one-person show" (*Hawai'i v. Trump*, 9th. Cir., 2017). The decision made no mention of the "honor killings" provision, a corollary of the court's decision not to base its ruling on any constitutional grounds that would have required discerning the question of religious discrimination and Trump's intent. In contrast, the Fourth Circuit gave the "honor killings" provision some attention. First, in a footnote, the court pointed to the provision as a basis on which to rebut the administration's claim that the order was "facially neutral," calling it "yet another marker" that "its national security purpose is secondary to its religious purpose":

> Plaintiffs suggest that EO-2 is not facially neutral, because by directing the Secretary of Homeland Security to collect data on "honor killings" committed in the United States by foreign nationals, EO-2 incorporates "a stereotype about Muslims that the President had invoked in the months preceding the Order." Numerous amici explain that invoking the specter of "honor killings" is a well-worn tactic for stigmatizing and demeaning Islam and painting the religion, and its men, as violent and barbaric. The Amici Constitutional Law Scholars go so far as to call the reference to honor killings "anti-Islamic dog-whistling." We find this text in EO-2 to be yet another marker that its national security purpose is secondary to its religious purpose. (*Int'l Refugee Assistance Project v. Trump* 2017, 596 n.17)

In addition, in a concurring opinion, Judge Stephanie Thacker wrote that "the record in this case amply demonstrates the primary purpose of EO-2 was to ban Muslims from entering the United States in violation of the Establishment Clause." She stated: "Last, but by no means least, EO-2 identifies and discriminates against Muslims on its face. It identifies only Muslim majority nations, thus banning approximately 10% of the world's Muslim population from entering the United States. It discusses only Islamic terrorism. And, it seeks information on honor killings—a stereotype affiliated with Muslims—even though honor killings have no connection whatsoever to the stated purpose of the Order" (*Int'l Refugee Assistance Project v. Trump* 2017, 635).

The data collection and reporting requirement as to "honor killings" that remained in EO-2 would thus have been important in helping the Supreme Court discern whether that provision violated the Constitution, had EO-2 ever reached the Court. As put by Gerald Neuman (2017), the "tangential footnote" was possibly "the most important passage" in the Fourth Circuit decision. The data collection and reporting requirement "has no conceivable relation to the alleged national security purpose of the travel ban, and it continues to reveal the true underlying purpose of both orders," as "facial evidence of illegitimate purpose."[14]

We can also understand the data collection and reporting requirement as part of a generalized approach by the Trump administration. Two days before issuing EO-1, Trump had issued another executive order, "Enhancing Public Safety in the Interior of the United States" (US Presidential Exec. Order No. 13768), which mostly received media attention because of its provisions threatening so-called sanctuary jurisdictions. As with EO-1 and EO-2, there is a "Transparency" section, which mandates the collection of data and production of reports on the immigration status of noncitizens who are incarcerated in federal and state prisons. There is also a requirement that so-called sanctuary jurisdictions, which engage in various forms of noncollaboration with ICE, be penalized through publicity about "criminal actions committed by aliens" in their jurisdictions. And the order also announces the creation of "VOICE," a new office for victims of "immigrant crime," to provide services to "victims of crimes committed by removable aliens" and to generate quarterly public reports.

An amicus brief filed by history professors and scholars in *IRAP v. Trump* clearly elucidates how we might understand these reporting requirements as similarly motivated and designed (Shams 2017; Drum 2017). As the brief states, "Throughout modern history, criminal reporting targeting particular groups have been used to demonize those groups and incite bigotry" (Brief for History Professors 2017, 2). Pointing to and discussing an array of examples, from the association of Jews with criminality in Nazi Germany, to the use of criminal association to exclude Italian immigrants and Chinese immigrants from the United States, to the portrayal of immigrants as sexual threats to US citizens, and to the stereotyping of African American men as rapists, the brief asserts: "Historical studies have shown that crime reporting that disproportionately focuses on members of a social or political minority has routinely been used as a tool of mass stigmatization and criminalization, anchoring disparate human outcomes including nation-based exclusion from the United States. In some instances, the association of a particular community with criminality, and the reinforcement of that association in the public mind through official government action and rhetoric, have led to widespread state and vigilante violence against members of the identified group."

Recall the importance of "immigrant crime" to the 2016 Republican National Convention, which featured a parade of family members whose loved ones had been killed or injured by undocumented immigrants. In a speech on July 28, 2017, to law enforcement personnel on Long Island, describing members of MS-13, a gang which originated in Los Angeles in the 1980s, Trump alleged gang members have "transformed peaceful parks and beautiful, quiet neighborhoods into blood-stained killing fields. They're animals" (Woody 2017). Recall as well his campaign invocation of Mexicans as "rapists" and "criminals." Trump governed through invoking the specter of immigrant crime, including through an ad he tweeted suggesting refugees in migrant caravans posed a criminal threat, an ad pulled off multiple television networks because of its racism. Although foreign-born residents are less likely to commit crimes than native-born citizens, the depiction of "foreign nationals" as dangerously criminal functioned as a key element of Trump's campaign and governance strategies, which mobilized support through fear (Landgrave and Nowrasteh 2017; Ghandnoosh and Rovner 2017).

We can now return to the question why "honor killings" disappeared from the Purpose section of EO-2 but remained in the Transparency and Data Collection section. In fact, an answer is offered in the one amicus brief, filed with the Supreme Court when EO-2 was still pending there, that focuses entirely on the invocation of "honor killings."[15] The Brief of Social Science Scholars—signed by Lila Abu-Lughod, John Bowen, Inderpal Grewal, Charles Kurzman, Sherene Razack, and Joan Scott—argues that the reference to "honor killings" is a "veiled reference intended to invoke association with a particular religious minority. It is what is colloquially known as a 'dog whistle.'"[16] The brief describes cases where violence by men is retroactively classified as "honor killings" without regard to the evidence of actual motives.[17] As the brief notes, "The term 'honor killing' is a way of misleadingly categorizing violence against women as a Muslim problem" (2017, 13). Forcefully arguing the impetus behind the retention of the term in EO-2, it states: "But the term was not included in the text by accident—and certainly not preserved from EO-1 and carried into EO-2 by chance. The only plausible rationale for invoking 'honor killings' in the text of both executive orders was to trigger a negative association with Muslims" (2017, 16–17).

TRUMP'S SPEECHES

Just as the litigation against the Muslim ban traced the prehistory of the executive orders through examining Trump's campaign statements in order to determine whether the orders constituted constitutionally impermissible religious discrimination, we can examine Trump's articulations during his campaign connecting "Muslims," "honor killings," violence against women, and acts of violence against lesbians and gays, to better understand what lies beneath the surface of the words of EO-1, EO-2, and EO-3. There are three relevant speeches to examine.

On June 13, 2016, after the massacre by Omar Mateen of 49 persons at Pulse, a gay nightclub in Orlando, Trump delivered a speech in New Hampshire, stating:

> Our nation stands together in solidarity with the members of Orlando's LGBT community. . . . A radical Islamic terrorist targeted the nightclub not only because he wanted to kill Americans, but in order to execute gay and lesbian citizens because of their sexual orientation. It is a strike at the heart and soul of who we are as a nation. It is an assault on the ability of free people to live their lives, love who they want and express their identity.
> Radical Islam is anti-woman, anti-gay and anti-American.
> The bottom line is that the only reason the killer was in America in the first place was because we allowed his family to come here. We have a dysfunctional immigration system which does not permit us to know who we let into our country, and it does not permit us to protect our citizens. . . .
> We cannot continue to allow thousands upon thousands of people to pour into our country, many of whom have the same thought process as this savage killer. Hillary Clinton said "Muslims are peaceful and tolerant people, and have nothing whatsoever to do with terrorism.". . . Hillary

Clinton can never claim to be a friend of the gay community as long as she continues to support immigration policies that bring Islamic extremists to our country who suppress women, gays, and anyone who doesn't share their views.

Ask yourself, who is really the friend of women and the LGBT community, Donald Trump with his actions, or Hillary Clinton with her words? Clinton wants to allow Radical Islamic terrorists to pour into our country—they enslave women and murder gays. (Beckwith 2016)

Trump's speech facilitates an opposition between the Muslim immigrant and the concepts of sexual freedom and gender equality through a number of tactics. First is the conflation of individual terrorists with Muslims in general, and the transmutation of a homegrown problem into a foreign threat. Omar Mateen, a US-born citizen, stands in for "thousands upon thousands" of "[r]adical Islamic terrorists" who have been "pouring into our country." Second, the identity markers of race, religion, and immigration status disappear for victims of terrorist attacks, even while they become hypervisible for the perpetrator. The Latinx victims of the Pulse massacre appear in Donald Trump's speech as "gay and lesbian citizens" and as "gay and lesbian" victims of radical Islamic terror.

Several of the victims in the Pulse massacre were undocumented—reporting indicates one Salvadoran man and one Mexican man were injured, and one Mexican man, his identity not revealed because of the potential consequences to his family, was murdered (Burnett 2016). In Trump's invective, they are not worthy of mention as Latinx, or as immigrants, but instead, as "gay and lesbian citizens" who register as presumptively white (Robinson 2014). As Maya Mikdashi writes, "US political discourse on the war on terror has starkly divided the world into victims (Europeans and Americans) and perpetrators (Muslims and Arabs)" (2016). The victims of the Pulse massacre are thus mourned as Americans, or mourned as gay and lesbian victims of Islamic terrorism. What violence they may have faced as Latinx, as Puerto Rican, as Mexican, as Salvadoran, is not worthy of mention.

The patriotism demanded by the war on terror makes race—other than the race of the Muslim terrorist—disappear. Queerness is folded into what Jasbir Puar and Amit Rai (2002, 117) called the "project of docile patriotism." They describe how after 9/11 the United States was depicted as a feminist and gay safe haven—even while the American state, after being "castrated and penetrated," promised to violently emasculate others. Witness, for example, the reports of the poster circulating after 9/11 in New York of Osama

Bin Laden being sodomized by the Empire State Building titled "The Empire Strikes Back"—or the US Navy bomb aboard the USS Enterprise with "Hijack this, fags" scrawled upon it (Puar and Rai 2002; Ahmad 2002, 101 and 109).

Despite the erasure of terrorist victims' racial or ethnic markers, race and immigration status become hypervisible for perpetrators of terrorist attacks. Indeed, the hyperracialization of the killer matches the deracination of the victims (Mikdashi 2016). This hyperracialization is also meant to signal sexual deviation. As Puar and Rai write, the construct of the terrorist relies on the idea of the monster, who has always been a sexual deviant and who has a kind of failed heterosexuality. This is evident in the whirlwind of media focus on Omar Mateen's supposed queer desires. The idea is of pent up sexual desires repressed by Islam so that the cultural backwardness of immigrant and nonwhite families leads their children to psychological compulsion (Shakhsari 2016). As Sima Shakhsari writes, one is supposed to "Come out, get married and be normal!" (2016); the repression of homophobic cultures of color is what supposedly leads to violence. Normal is white gay visibility.

Trump's speech attributes Omar Mateen's homophobia, transphobia, misogyny, and racism to Islam, an Islam which in turn engenders perverse subjects. Mateen was not understood to perform a homophobic and misogynistic American masculinity enabled by everyday militarism, attributable not to his parent's birthplace or religion but to a North American culture of violence and toxic masculinity (Shakhsari 2016; Chamseddine 2016). Omar Mateen worked for nine years—despite being outed by coworkers as racist, homophobic, sexist, and possibly violent—for the world's largest private security firm, G4S, which is the world's third largest private employer; it runs several Israeli checkpoints and prisons as well as many US prisons. Thus, we might understand Mateen as a hypermasculine and homophobic male in a culture that prizes masculinity in a Trumpian world of beauty contests, women as fat slobs, and penis size (Shakhsari 2016).

In a subsequent speech, on "fighting terrorism" on August 15, 2016, Trump explicitly used the term "honor killings," suggesting that terrorism and "honor killings" shared the same "breeding ground," stating:

> Just as we won the Cold War, in part, by exposing the evils of communism and the virtues of free markets, so too must we take on the ideology of Radical Islam.
>
> While my opponent accepted millions of dollars in Foundation donations from countries where being gay is an offense punishable by prison

or death, my Administration will speak out against the oppression of women, gays and people of different faith.

Our Administration will be a friend to all moderate Muslim reformers in the Middle East, and will amplify their voices.

This includes speaking out against the horrible practice of honor killings, where women are murdered by their relatives for dressing, marrying or acting in a way that violates fundamentalist teachings. . . . Shockingly, this is a practice that has reached our own shores.

One such case involves an Iraqi immigrant who was sentenced to 34 years in jail for running over his own daughter claiming she had become "too Westernized." To defeat Islamic terrorism, we must also speak out forcefully against a hateful ideology that provides the breeding ground for violence and terrorism to grow. (Trump 2016a)

The case Trump is describing here is the 2009 murder of Noor Almaleki in Arizona; what he fails to note is that the jury found her father guilty of second-degree murder, meaning it did not find the act either premeditated or an "honor killing" (CBS News 2012). Instead, what we find in this speech is, as with his speech following the Pulse massacre, a linking of repression of women, gays, and "people of different faith" with "Radical Islam," articulated as a problem not just in the "Middle East" but as reaching "our own shores."

Lastly, Trump gave a speech on August 31, 2016, in Phoenix on immigration, where he outlined several reforms he hoped to implement. They included the following:

> Another reform involves new screening tests for all applicants that include, and this is so important, especially if you get the right people. And we will get the right people. An ideological certification to make sure that those we are admitting to our country share our values and love our people.
>
> (APPLAUSE)
>
> Thank you. We're very proud of our country. Aren't we? Really? With all it's going through, we're very proud of our country. For instance, in the last five years, we've admitted nearly 100,000 immigrants from Iraq and Afghanistan. And these two countries according to Pew Research, a majority of residents say that the barbaric practice of honor killings against women are often or sometimes justified. That's what they say.
>
> (APPLAUSE)

That's what they say. They're justified. Right? And we're admitting them to our country. Applicants will be asked their views about honor killings, about respect for women and gays and minorities. Attitudes on radical Islam, which our president refuses to say and many other topics as part of this vetting procedure. And if we have the right people doing it, believe me, very, very few will slip through the cracks. Hopefully, none. (Trump 2016b)

In addition to the visible use of gender and sexual equality as a proxy for xenophobia and Islamophobia, we also see in these speeches the crime victim as what Jonathan Simon has called the "idealized political subject" whose only request of the state is punishment (Simon 2007, 136–140). It is as if the victim of crime that the gay immigrant murdered in the Pulse nightclub or the Muslim woman subject to an "honor killing" may be folded into a national object of concern—when alive, they face exclusion from the borders of the United States; through their deaths they are incorporated into fellow citizenship.

THE DATA

In September 2016, then-Senator Jeff Sessions had an exchange with Simon Henshaw, the State Department official in charge of its refugee program, who was testifying about the Obama administration's approach to the issue of Syrian refugees. Sessions asked Henshaw about "honor killings":

SESSIONS: We had 27 honor killings last year in the United States according to DOJ, do you ask if you adhere to the practice of honor killings for people who violate certain religious codes before admitting into the United States?" [sic]

HENSHAW: I'm not sure those honor killings took place among the resettled refugee community in the United States. I see they're becoming good American citizens, members of the military, members of our police, member—people with US American values, that's what I see when I visit refugee populations in the US.

SESSIONS: Well if they're illiterate in their home country they're not likely to be a police officer the next week in the United States, are they? And with regard to honor killings, you have evidence that 27 people were killed in the United States for honor killings according to a DOJ report.

HENSHAW: I have no evidence that there were any honor killings among the refugee population resettled in the US, sir.

SESSIONS: Well, it's from the same cultural background I would say. (Serwer 2017)

Referred to by Jeff Sessions, what is this report's source of the claim that there were "27 honor killings last year in the United States"? There are multiple assertions, in addition to that of Jeff Sessions, that this was a study conducted by the Department of Justice. Typical reporting states that this DOJ report found that there are between twenty-three and twenty-seven victims of "honor killings" annually in the United States (Zoroya 2016; Schilling 2017; Winston 2017).

In fact, there is no such data. The report Sessions referred to was not produced by the Department of Justice but was commissioned by the Department of Justice and conducted by the research firm Westat, which carries out research for US government agencies, as well as other sectors (Helba et al. 2014). The twenty-three-to-twenty-seven "honor killings" per year is not a figure produced by Westat, but rather emerged from an unpublished study mentioned in the Westat report, as first reported by Jesse Singal in *New York Magazine* (Singal 2017; Helba et al. 2014). And the purported statistic of twenty-three-to-twenty-seven "honor killings" per year is not based on any actual cases in the United States.

The story of the birth and continued life of this "data" is a story of the mobilization of a "broad array of technologies of governance," thanks to the traction of this issue (Grewal 2013, 8). It is also attributable to the efforts of former Dutch MP and Hoover Institute and American Enterprise Institute fellow Ayaan Hirsi Ali and the organization she founded, the AHA Foundation, which describes itself as "the leading organization working to end honor violence that shames, hurts or kills thousands of women and girls in the US each year, and puts millions more at risk." Hirsi Ali is a well-known critic of Islam. In February 2012, the AHA Foundation provided draft language and a letter of support to Republican Representative Frank Wolf of Virginia, for an Appropriations Bill that would mandate the US government to begin tracking "honor violence" and to determine if extant federal data collection mechanisms could be used to estimate the prevalence of such violence in the United States. This mandate was issued by Congress in 2014

(COSSA 2014).[18] The AHA Foundation reports that it was "frequently consulted during the drafting" of the report commissioned from Westat for the Bureau of Justice Statistics and that AHA Foundation staff "provided significant background information about honor violence and our programs," and "shared our studies on honor killing and forced marriage carried out by the John Jay College of Criminal Justice" (AHA Foundation 2015, 5–6).

The Westat report begins by noting that there are no reliable summary data available for the United States regarding the prevalence of "honor violence" and that such cases appear to be rare compared to other types of crime in the United States (Helba et al. 2014, 1). The report attempts to study four types of "honor violence": forced marriage, "honor-based domestic violence," "honor killing," and "female genital mutilation" (1–3).

The report then notes the frequently quoted estimate of 5,000 "honor killings worldwide"—a statistic that is repeatedly cited but never explained—and mentions the twenty-three-to-twenty-seven figure from an unpublished study (Helba et al. 2014, 1–5).[19] Acknowledging that there is little strong empirical research and that information is "not always of rigorous scientific origin," the researchers outline their methodology: they reviewed research literature, reviewed materials directed at law enforcement created by the AHA Foundation, reviewed websites focusing on "honor violence," watched three movies about "honor violence," including (the heavily criticized) *Honor Diaries*, tried to interview US law enforcement, who either did not respond or said they had no cases to discuss or were not familiar with the topic, and then interviewed, with the help of the AHA Foundation, individuals in the Netherlands and the UK, as well as the detectives who worked on the Noor Almaleki case.[20]

The report authors also spoke with five academic researchers, held several conversations with a representative of the AHA Foundation, and reviewed existing victimization surveys. Finally, the authors reviewed online sources about cases that either occurred in the United States, were planned in the United States, and/or were somehow connected to people or events in the United States, searching the web for "keywords such as 'honor violence,' 'honor killings,' 'honor crime,' 'forced marriage,' and 'female genital mutilation.'" Searching over a twenty-four-year period, from 1990 to 2014, the authors found fourteen "honor killings," one suspected "honor killing," one threatened "honor killing," and two cases of "honor violence." The study notes that this "does not appear to be consistent with the estimate" of twenty-three-to-twenty-seven killings per year in the unpublished study—the rate of "honor killing" would instead be fewer than one per year in the United States (Helba et al. 2014, 5–2).

Examining the particulars of the eighteen cases that are identified in the Westat study, several involve sexual abuse and histories of family violence, histories of domestic violence, and cases of what might seem "routine" domestic violence murders were it not for the "cultural" background of the parties involved and the invocation by the media of "honor." We know that "honor killings" are often post-hoc generalizations (Abu-Lughod 2011). The most prominently publicized of the eighteen cases—that of Tina Isa, and the case of Sarah and Amina Said—feature complex webs of causal factors that are erased by the invocation of "honor killing," as I have previously argued.[21]

We turn now to the unpublished study responsible for the assertion of twenty-three-to-twenty-seven "honor killings" per year in the United States. Titled "A Comparative Approach to Estimating the Annual Number of Honor Killings in the United States Among People from North African, Middle Eastern, and Southeast Asian (MENASA) Countries," and with nine authors led by Ric Curtis of John Jay College, the study acknowledges support from the AHA Foundation (Curtis et al. 2014).

The call of the introduction is to "ask if honor violence of the type that the international community has recently addressed is a problem among migrants in the United States that merits greater scrutiny and action by policy makers, professionals and researchers." The study explains its decision to focus on what it calls people from "MENASA" countries (the authors mistake Southeast Asia for South Asia), labeling these countries as placed within what Curtis et al. call "the patriarchal belt" (Curtis et al. 2014, 5).[22] Given the paucity of official statistics about "honor killings" in the United States, the authors decided to use primary data sources from Germany, the UK, and Holland, to establish an annual expected "rate" of "honor killings" in other countries, which is then used to project expected numbers of "honor killings" in the United States.

The statistical validity of this kind of comparison is limited. As the study reports, Germany, with a population about one quarter the size of the United States had 690 homicides in 2010; in the United States that year there were 12,996 (Curtis et al. 2014, 8). Obviously, there are enormous differences between the United States and Germany that are not being controlled for.[23] There are also no official data collected about "honor killings" in either country. But there are "more than 4 million people from MENASA countries" in Germany, so Curtis et al. decided this would be an apt comparison. While there is no reported data, Curtis et al. found a study by German researchers who estimated the prevalence of "honor killings" in Germany by looking at known cases of homicide and by searching a news agency database for homicide articles that focused on "cultural explanations" that happened in "ethnic minority groups" that portrayed "family relations" as a cause (Oberwittler and Kasselt 2011). Since cases of gendered subordination are often selectively blamed on culture, not on the basis of any empirical evidence but on the identity of the actor, any homicide case involving people of color (or what in German is called a *Migrationshintergrund*, or migration background) may be attributed in this study as an "honor killing" (Volpp 2000). Over the nine-year period covered by the study, the German researchers found what they believed to be seventy-eight cases and attempts through this kind of post-hoc assumption (Curtis et al. 2014, 8).

The United Kingdom, with three million people from MENASA countries, is the next target of comparison. Perhaps most breathtaking, official police estimates in the United Kingdom turn out to be "based simply on a casual remark made by a police official in a 2003 speech" of "10–12 honor killings" each year (Curtis et al. 2014, 12). This number becomes the UK statistic of annual "honor killings" in that country. Holland reports "on average 13 cases" every year, according to researchers at the National Centre of Expertise on Honour Violence. This number includes "cases that the others do not: manslaughter cases, suicides and men" (14–15).

To develop a "per capita" "killing rate," Curtis et al. took the number of MENASA people in each country, divided by the number of annual "honor killing" cases in each country, and then calculated the rate per 100,000 people. Germany, with nine "honor killings" per year, has a .22 "per capita rate"; the UK with twelve, has a .26 "per capita rate," and Holland, with thirteen, has a 2.06 "per capita rate."

To estimate the annual rate of "honor killings" in the United States, Curtis et al. take the "per capita killing rate" for these three countries, and adjust the rate downward for the Netherlands, which has the highest rate, and adjust the rate upward for missing cases in the United Kingdom and Germany, in an attempt to reach parity among these three countries. To align the numbers, they try subtracting eight deaths from the Dutch total and adding three to the figures for Germany and the UK; alternatively they subtract seven deaths from the Dutch total and add four to the figures for Germany and the UK. These calculations yield two alternatives for an "EU killing rate": a ".467 EU Honor killing rate" or a ".533 EU Honor killing rate." Curtis et al. then multiply these two possible rates with the MENASA population in the United States, yielding the range of 23.45 to 26.76, or "23–27" "honor killings" per year (Curtis et al. 2014, 23).

The authors admit in the study that estimating "the annual number of honor killings in the US by proxy is far from ideal." Ric Curtis, in an interview with reporter Jesse Singal, described their study's methodology thus: "It's not terribly scientific" (Singal 2017). That the Curtis et al. report, with this methodology, has transmuted into the widespread perception that the US government has documented an average of twenty-three-to-twenty-seven "honor killings" per year in the country is deeply disturbing.

Would this kind of unsubstantiated claim work in any other realm? Of course, the idea of data works its own magic, carrying the notions of objectivity, science, and truth. Yet there is also a willing belief in the prevalence of "honor killings" among Muslims that aligns with long-standing narratives of the dangerous Muslim man and imperiled Muslim woman.[24] The relationship of stereotype, threat, evidence, and consequence is reminiscent of the forced relocation of Japanese American citizens and noncitizens into concentration camps, based not upon real dangers but, quoting Justice Murphy dissenting in *Korematsu*, on "an accumulation of . . . misinformation, half-truths and insinuations" directed against Japanese Americans.[25]

CONCLUSION

In January 2018, the reporting requirements of Section 11 of EO-2 materialized in the form of an "Initial Section 11 Report" issued jointly by the Department of Justice and the Department of Homeland Security (US Presidential Exec. Order No. 13780). In responding to EO-2's requirement to present data "regarding the number and types of acts of gender-based violence against women, including so-called honor killings, in the United States by foreign nationals," the report states: "There is no federal statute specifically prohibiting 'honor killings' and the federal government lacks comprehensive data regarding incidents of such offenses at the state and local levels. Although the federal government lacks independent data regarding incidents of honor killings, a study commissioned and provided to the DOJ's Bureau of Justice Statistics in 2014 estimated that an average of 23–27 honor killings occur every year in the United States."

In other words, the perception of "23–27 honor killings" per year in the United States lives on, now bolstered through its rearticulation in the executive order's official DOJ and DHS Report.

Rhetoric and the illusion of data have worked together in fueling a phantasm that links "foreign terrorist entry" with "honor killings." The specter of violence against women played an important role in the Trump administration's executive orders seeking to bar Muslims from entry, and continues to rationalize the notion that the nation must be protected through their exclusion. Yet the role of "honor killings" in the Muslim ban was largely overlooked, presumably because the "common sense" beliefs that link Muslim immigrants with security threats, attacks on sexual liberty, and gender-based violence are so pervasive today as to be unremarkable.

NOTES

This chapter is a revised version of Leti Volpp, "Protecting the Nation from 'Honor Killings': The Construction of a Problem." *Constitutional Commentary* 34 (2019): 133–69.

1. Presidential Proclamation No. 9645, from September 24, 2017, was titled "Enhancing Vetting Capabilities and Processes for Detecting Attempted Entry into the United States by Terrorists or Other Public-Safety Threats."
2. For a discussion of the effects of portraying only certain communities as sites of aberrant gendered violence, see Volpp (2001).
3. As Nadera Shalhoub-Kevorkian and Suhad Daher-Nashif (2013) write, it is critical to "counter dominant culturalized depictions of such crimes" [explaining the choice of the term "femicide" instead of "honor killings" or "crimes of passion"].
4. Razack (2004) describes "honor killings" as purportedly about culture, and involving the body, as opposed to "crimes of passion" which are thought to originate in gender, to involve the mind, and to be the product of individual practices born of deviancy or criminality and not culture. We see this kind of dichotomy operating with mass killings in the United States as well, divided between "terrorists" and "shooters," with the former motivated by a racialized religion and the latter motivated by mental illness.
5. A "dog whistle" refers to coded signals that only certain constituencies understand (dogs can hear whistles at frequencies that humans cannot).
6. The AHA Foundation, founded in 2007, works to end honor violence, and is named after its founder Ayaan Hirsi Ali.
7. EO-2 also removed Iraq from the list of seven countries due to concern about the impact on US military operations and no longer denied entry to lawful permanent residents, travelers who already had a visa, and dual nationals with citizenship in a country that is not banned.
8. See *State of Hawai'i v. Trump*, 265 F. Supp. 3d 1140 (D. Haw. 2017) (order granting temporary restraining order) and *Int'l Refugee Assistance Project v. Trump*, 265 F. Supp. 3d 570 (D. Md. 2017) (memorandum opinion).
9. See *Trump v. Hawaii*, 138 S. Ct. 2392 (2018). Section 212(f) of the Immigration and Nationality Act vests the president with authority to restrict the entry of aliens when their entry "would be detrimental to the interests of the United States."

10 See President Biden's "Proclamation on Ending Discriminatory Bans on Entry to the United States," Proclamation No. 10141, 86 Fed. Reg. 7005 (Jan. 20, 2021).
11 In his issuance of a temporary restraining order against EO-3, Judge Watson similarly did not mention "honor killings."
12 In his issuance of a temporary restraining order against EO-3, Judge Chuang also did not mention "honor killings," although this had been singled out for discussion by the Fourth Circuit.
13 See "Brief of Muslim Rights, Professional and Public Health Organizations as Amici Curiae, in Support of Appellees, and in Opposition to Appellant's Motion for a Stay and on the Merits" at 16. *Hawai'i v. Trump*, 864 F.3d 994 (9th Cir. 2017).
14 As Neuman (2017) explains, this facial illegitimacy is important as the key Supreme Court precedent in the immigration context requires the government to show that a restriction is based on a "facially legitimate and bona fide reason." For more see *Kleindienst v. Mandel*, 408 U.S. 753 (1972). This means both that the reason of the government is legitimate on its face and that the government must be acting in good faith. Additionally see *Kerry v. Din*, 135 S. Ct. 2128 (2015).
15 Seventy-seven amicus briefs were filed. Ten of the briefs mention or discuss "honor killings."
16 See the "Brief for Social Science Scholars as Amici Curiae Supporting Respondents," *Trump v. Int'l Refugee Assistance Project* (2017) at 9. I assisted with identifying scholars to sign this brief but was not responsible for its content.
17 The brief mentions the case of Sarah and Amina Said, murdered by their father, who had a long history of family violence, as described in Volpp (2011), and the case of a woman murdered by her husband in Buffalo just after she obtained a restraining order against him, which was quickly labeled an "honor killing."
18 This resulted in the Consolidated and Further Continuing Appropriations Act of 2015, PUB. L. NO. 113–235, 128 Stat. 2191.
19 For a criticism of the "5,000 honor killings per year, worldwide" figure, see Abu-Lughod (2013, 136).
20 This is the case described above, invoked by Trump as an "honor killing" case, where the jury refused to find premeditation for an "honor killing" (CBS News 2012).
21 The federal government accused Tina Isa's father and two other men of murdering her because of fears she would disclose their Abu Nidal cell, not of committing an "honor killing" (Volpp 2006, 1631 and 1633–1634). Sarah and Amina Said's mother and brother both described a history of family and domestic violence and refuted the idea that this was an "honor killing" (Volpp 2011, 90–91).
22 The MENASA countries listed by Curtis et al. are as follows: Algeria, Bahrain, Djibouti, Egypt, Iraq, Palestine/Israel, Jordan, Kuwait, Lebanon, Libya, Mauritania, Morocco, Oman, Qatar, Saudi Arabia, Sudan, Syria, Tunisia, United Arab Emirates, Yemen, Iran, Afghanistan, Pakistan, India, Bangladesh, Sri Lanka, and

Nepal. The authors write: "We have also included Turkey, despite its position between Europe and Western Asia" (Curtis et al. 2014, 6).

23 There are also large differences between the MENASA populations in these countries.

24 It is important to also note a recent shift in the perception of Muslim women as not just subordinated victims of Islam but also as terrorist threats. Aziz (2012) and Hussein (2019) elucidate this.

25 See *Korematsu v. United States*, 323 U.S. 214, 239 (Murphy, J. dissenting). For a discussion of how the War Department concealed evidence from the courts as to the nondangerousness of Japanese Americans, see Izumi et al. (2001). In fact, *Korematsu* had been analogized to the Muslim ban in amicus briefs, including many filed by Japanese American organizations and individuals. Justice Roberts, writing for the majority in *Trump v. Hawai'i*, called *Korematsu* morally repugnant and a wholly inapt comparison to the "facially neutral policy" of EO-3 and took the opportunity to state that *Korematsu* had been overruled "in the court of history" (2018, 2423). In her dissent, Justice Sonia Sotomayor saw the relationship of *Korematsu* to EO-3 very differently, pointing instead to the stark parallels between both cases and the same dangerous logic employed, sanctioning discriminatory policy motivated by animus toward a disfavored group, all in the name of a superficial claim of national security.

REFERENCES

Abu-Lughod, Lila. 2011. "Seductions of the 'Honor Crime.'" *Differences* 22, no. 1: 17–63. https://doi.org/10.1215/10407391-1218238.

Abu-Lughod, Lila. 2013. *Do Muslim Women Need Saving*? Cambridge, MA: Harvard University Press.

Ahmad, Muneer. 2002. "Homeland Insecurities: Racial Profiling the Day After September 11th." *Social Text* 72, no. 20: 101–15. https://doi.org/10.2979/racethmulglocon.4.3.337.

Ali, Yaser. 2012. "Shariah and Citizenship—How Islamophobia is Creating a Second-Class Citizenry in America." *California Law Review* 100, no. 4: 1027. https://doi.org/10.15779/Z38481V.

AHA Foundation. 2015. *Annual Report*. https://www.theahafoundation.org/wp-content/uploads/2016/09/AHA%20Annual%20Report2015.pdf.

Attiah, Karen. 2017. "How Trump's Travel Ban Uses Muslim Women as Pawns." *Washington Post*, March 16. https://www.washingtonpost.com/news/global-opinions/wp/2017/03/16/how-trumps-travel-ban-uses-muslim-women-as-pawns/.

Aziz, Sahar. 2012. "From the Oppressed to the Terrorist: Muslim American Women Caught in the Crosshairs of Intersectionality." *Hastings Race and Poverty Law Journal* 9, no. 2: 191–263. https://ssrn.com/abstract=1981777.

Bayoumi, Moustafa. 2017. "How the 'Homophobic Muslim' Became a Populist Bogeyman." *The Guardian*, August 7. https://www.theguardian.com/commentisfree/2017/aug/07/homophobic-muslim-populist-bogeyman-trump-le-pen/.

Beauchamp, Zack. 2017. "Trump's Counter-Jihad." *Vox*, February 13. https://www.vox.com/world/2017/2/13/14559822/trump-islam-muslims-islamophobia-sharia.

Beckwith, Ryan Teague. 2016. "Read Donald Trump's Speech on the Orlando Shooting." *Time*, June 13. http://time.com/4367120/orlando-shooting-donald-trump-transcript/.

Bennett, Brian. 2017. "Travel Ban Is the Clearest Sign Yet of Trump Advisors' Intent to Reshape the Country." *Los Angeles Times*, January 29. https://www.latimes.com/politics/la-na-pol-trump-immigration-20170129-story.html.

Brief for History Professors and Scholars as Amici Curiae Supporting Plaintiffs-Appellees, *Int'l Refugee Assistance Project v. Trump*, 857 F. 3d 554 (4th Cir. 2017).

Brief for Social Science Scholars as Amici Curiae Supporting Respondents, *Trump v. Int'l Refugee Assistance Project*, 137 S. Ct. 2080 (2017).

Brief of Muslim Rights, Professional and Public Health Organizations as Amici Curiae in Support of Appellees, *Hawai'i v. Trump*, 864 F. 3d 994 (9th Cir. 2017).

Burnett, John. 2016. "Families of Undocumented Victims of Orlando Face Unique Challenges." NPR, June 19. http://www.npr.org/2016/06/19/482668952/families-of-undocumented-victims-of-orlando-face-unique-challenges.

Caplan-Bricker, Nora. 2017. "Donald Trump Plans to Track 'Honor Killings' Even as He Slashes Violence Against Women Grants." *Slate*, January 25. https://slate.com/human-interest/2017/01/donald-trumps-immigration-order-will-track-violence-against-women-by-foreign-born-men.html.

CBS News. 2012. "Was Noor Al-Maleki the Victim of an Honor Killing?" September 1. Accessed April 26, 2021. http://www.cbsnews.com/news/was-noor-almaleki-the-victim-of-an-honor-killing/5/.

Chamseddine, Roqayah. 2016. "After Orlando." *Middle East Research and Information Project*, June 17. http://www.merip.org/after-orlando.

Consortium of Social Science Associations (COSSA). 2014. "Analysis of the FY 2014 Omnibus & Implications for Social and Behavioral Science," January 27. http://www.cossa.org/volume33/FY14approps.pdf.

Curtis, Ric, Sheyla Delgado, Evan Misshula, Alana Henninger, Laila Alsabahi, Engy Hanna, Lisa Robbins-Stathas, Popy Begum, and Anthony Marcus. 2014. *A Comparative Approach to Estimating the Annual Number of Honor Killings in the United States among People from North African, Middle Eastern and Southeast Asian (MENASA) Countries*. January 2014. (Unpublished paper on file with author.)

Drum, Kevin. 2017. "Trump Amps Up the Racial Demagoguery Yet Again." *Mother Jones*, March 6. https://www.motherjones.com/kevin-drum/2017/03/trump-amps-racial-demagoguery-yet-again/.

Ghandnoosh, Nazgol, and Josh Rovner. 2017. "Immigration and Public Safety." *The Sentencing Project*. http://www.sentencingproject.org/wp-content/uploads/2017/03/Immigration-and-Public-Safety.pdf.

Grewal, Inderpal. 2013. "Outsourcing Patriarchy: Feminist Encounters, Transnational Mediations, and the Crime of 'Honour Killings.'" *International Feminist Journal of Politics* 15, no. 1: 1–19. https://doi.org/10.1080/14616742.2012.755352.

Hammer, Juliane. 2013. "Gendering Islamophobia: (Muslim) Women's Bodies, Islamophobia, and American Politics." *Bulletin for the Study of Religion* 41, no. 1: 29–36. https://doi.org/1558/bsor.v42i1.29.

Haney López, Ian. 2013. *Dog Whistle Politics: How Coded Racial Appeals Have Reinvented Racism and Wrecked the Middle Class.* Oxford: Oxford University Press.

Hawai'i v. Trump, 241 F. Supp. 3d 1119 (D. Haw. 2017).

Hawai'i v. Trump, 859 F. 3d 741 (9th Cir. 2017).

Hawai'i v. Trump, 864 F. 3d 994 (9th Cir. 2017).

Helba, Cynthia, Matthew Bernstein, Mariel Leonard, and Erin Bauer. 2014. "Report on Exploratory Study into Honor Violence Measurement Methods." WESTAT, November 26. https://www.ojp.gov/pdffiles1/bjs/grants/248879.pdf.

Hussein, Shakira, 2019. *From Victims to Suspects: Muslim Women Since 9/11*. New Haven, CT: Yale University Press.

Int'l Refugee Assistance Project [IRAP] v. Trump, 265 F. Supp. 3d 570 (D. Md. 2017).

Int'l Refugee Assistance Project [IRAP] v. Trump, 857 F.3d 554 (4th Cir. 2017).

Izumi, Carol L., Eric K. Yamamoto, Margaret Chon, Jerry Kang, and Frank H. Wu. 2001. *Race, Rights, and Reparation: Law and the Japanese American Internment.* New York: Wolters Kluwer.

Kerry v. Din, 135 S. Ct. 2128 (2015).

Kleindienst v. Mandel, 408 U.S. 753 (1972).

Kolbert, Elizabeth. 2002. "Beyond Tolerance." *The New Yorker*, September 9. https://www.newyorker.com/magazine/2002/09/09/beyond-tolerance.

Korematsu v. United States, 323 U.S. 214, 239 (Murphy, J, dissenting).

Landgrave, Michelangelo, and Alex Nowrasteh. 2017. "Criminal Immigrants: Their Numbers, Demographics, and Countries of Origin." *Cato Institute* (1). March 15. https://object.cato.org/sites/cato.org/files/pubs/pdf/immigration_brief-1.pdf.

Mikdashi, Maya. 2016. "After Orlando." *Middle East Research and Information Project.* June 17. http://www.merip.org/after-orlando.

Neuman, Gerald. 2017. "Neither Facially Legitimate Nor Bona Fide—Why the Very Text of the Travel Ban Shows It's Unconstitutional." *Just Security*, June 9. https://www.justsecurity.org/41953/facially-legitimate-bona-fide-why-unconstitutional-travel-ban/.

Oberwittler, Dietrich, and Julia Kasselt. 2011. *Ehrenmorde in Deutschland 1996–2005: Eine Untersuchung auf der Basis von Prozessakten*. Köln: Wolters Kluwer Deutschland GmbH.

Puar, Jasbir. 2007. *Terrorist Assemblages: Homonationalism in Queer Times.* Durham, NC: Duke University Press.

Puar, Jasbir, and Amit Rai. 2002. "Monster, Terrorist, Fag: The War on Terrorism and the Production of Docile Patriots." *Social Text* 20, no. 3: 117–48. https://doi.org/10.1215/01642472-20-3_72-117.

Quraishi-Landes, Asifa. 2013. "Rumors of the Sharia Threat Are Greatly Exaggerated: What American Judges Really Do with Islamic Family Law in Their Courtrooms." *New York Law School Law Review* 57, no. 245: 24557. https://ssrn.com/abstract=2409154.

Razack, Sherene H. 2004. "Imperilled Muslim Women, Dangerous Muslim Men and Civilised Europeans: Legal and Social Responses to Forced Marriages." *Feminist Legal Studies* 12, no. 2: 129–74. https://doi.org/10.1023/B:FEST.0000043305.66172.92.

Razack, Sherene H. 2007. "The 'Sharia Law Debate' in Ontario: The Modernity/Premodernity Distinction in Legal Efforts to Protect Women from Culture." *Feminist Legal Studies* 15, no. 3: 3–32. https://doi-org.ezproxy.cul.columbia.edu/10.1007/s10691-006-9050-x.

Reilly, Katie. 2017. "President Trump Says He Will Prioritize Persecuted Christians in Refugee Policy." *Time*, January 27. http://time.com/4652367/donald-trump-refugee-policy-christians/.

Robinson, Russell. 2014. "Marriage Equality and Postracialism." *UCLA Law Review* 61: 1012–80.

Ryan, Erin Gloria. 2017. "The Right Wing's Xenophobic Feminism." *The Daily Beast*, March 6. https://www.thedailybeast.com/the-right-wings-xenophobic-feminism.

Schilling, Chelsea. 2017. "Trump Orders Reports on US Honor Killings, DOJ Estimates 23–37 Victims Each Year in America." *WND*, March 6. http://mobile.wnd.com/%E2%80%8C2017/03/trump-orders-reports-on-u-s-honor-killings/.

Serwer, Adam. 2017. "Jeff Sessions's Fear of Muslims Immigrants. *The Atlantic*, February 8. https://www.theatlantic.com/politics/archive/2017/02/jeff-sessions-has-long-feared-muslim-immigrants/516069/.

Shakhsari, Sima. 2016. "After Orlando." *Middle East Research and Information Project*. June 17. http://www.merip.org/after-orlando.

Shalhoub-Kevorkian, Nadera, and Suhad Daher-Nashif. 2013. "Femicide and Colonization: Between the Politics of Exclusion and the Culture of Control." *Violence Against Women* 19, no. 3: 295–315. https://doi.org/10.1177/1077801213485548.

Shams, Alex. 2017. "Trump's 'Honour Crimes' Order Is a Racist Distraction." *Al Jazeera*, March 11. https://www.aljazeera.com/indepth/opinion/2017/03/trump-honour-crimes-order-racist-distraction-170309080923757.html.

Simon, Jonathan. 2007. *Governing through Crime: How the War on Crime Transformed American Democracy and Created a Culture of Fear*. Oxford: Oxford University Press.

Singal, Jesse. 2017. "Here's What the Research Says about Honor Killings in the U.S." *New York Times Magazine*, March 6. http://nymag.com/intelligencer/2017/03/heres-what-the-research-says-about-american-honor-killings.html.

State of Hawai'i v. Trump, 265 F. Supp. 3d 1140 (D. Haw. 2017).

Tait, Robert. 2017. "Geert Wilders Calls for Trump-style Muslim Travel Ban in Europe." *The Guardian*, December 17. https://www.theguardian.com/world/2017/dec/17/geert-wilders-calls-for-trump-style-muslim-travel-ban-in-europe.

Toosi, Nahal. 2017. "'Honour Killings' Highlighted under Trump's New Travel Ban." *Politico*, March 6. https://www.politico.com/story/2017/03/trump-travel-ban-killings-235731.

Trump, Donald. 2016a. "Full Text: Donald Trump's Speech on Fighting Terrorism." *Politico*, August 15. https://www.politico.com/story/2016/08/donald-trump-terrorism-speech-227025.

Trump, Donald. 2016b. "Transcript of Donald Trump's Immigration Speech." *New York Times*, September 1. https://www.nytimes.com/2016/09/02/us/politics/transcript-trump-immigration-speech.html.

Trump v. Int'l Refugee Assistance Project, 137 S. Ct. 2080 (2017).

Trump v. Hawaii, 138 S. Ct. 2392 (2018).

U.S. Presidential Executive Order No. 13768 (Jan. 25, 2017).

U.S. Presidential Executive Order No. 13769 (Jan. 27, 2017).

U.S. Presidential Executive Order No. 13780 (March 6, 2017).

U.S. Presidential Proclamation No. 9645 (Sept. 24, 2017).

U.S. Presidential Proclamation No. 10141 (Jan. 20, 2021).

Volpp, Leti. 2000. "Blaming Culture for Bad Behavior." *Yale Journal of Law and the Humanities* 12, no. 89: 89–116. https://digitalcommons.law.yale.edu/yjlh/vol12/iss1/3.

Volpp, Leti. 2001. "Feminism Versus Multiculturalism." *Columbia Law Review* 101, no. 5: 1181–1218. https://doi.org/10.2307/1123774.

Volpp, Leti. 2006. "Disappearing Acts: On Gendered Violence, Pathological Cultures, and Civil Society." PMLA 121, no. 5: 1631–38. http://www.jstor.org/stable/25501636.

Volpp, Leti. 2011. "Framing Cultural Difference: Immigrant Women and Discourses of Tradition." *Differences* 22, no. 90: 90–110. https://ssrn.com/abstract=2127473.

Volpp, Leti. 2017. "Trump's Mentions of 'Honor Killings' Betrays the Truth of His 'Muslim Ban.'" *The Hill*, February 22. https://thehill.com/blogs/pundits-blog/immigration/320632-trumps-mention-of-honor-killings-betray-the-truth-of-his.

Washington v. Trump, 847 F.3d 1151, 1168 (2017).

Winston, Kimberly. 2017. "Trump Travel Ban Orders a Report on Honor Killings." *Religion News Service*, March 6. https://religionnews.com/2017/03/06/trump-travel-ban-orders-a-report-on-honor-killings/.

Woody, Christopher. 2017. "Trump: The MS-13 Gang Has Turned 'Peaceful Parks' and 'Quiet Neighborhoods' in the US into 'Blood-Stained Killing Fields.'" *Business Insider*, July 28. https://www.businessinsider.com/trump-ms-13-has-turned-us-into-blood-stained-killing-fields-2017-7.

Zoroya, Greg. 2016. "'Honor Killings': 5 Things to Know." *USA Today*, June 9. https://www.usatoday.com/story/news/world/2016/06/09/honor-killings-united-nations-pakistan/85642786/.

FOUR · *Janet R. Jakobsen*

Because Religion

Does Something Called "Religion" Cause Gender-Based Violence?

"Does religion cause violence?" This question is posed in an essay by William T. Cavanaugh (2007), who argues that it is reflective of the contemporary US common sense. This common sense contributes to the legitimation for public policy about responding to violence in various forms, from policing in response to intimate violence to militaristic responses to global "terrorism." In both cases, connections between religion and its presumed interest in gender and sexuality form a key part of the commonsensical framework. Yet as Cavanaugh points out, this common "sense" is actually a "morass of unclear thinking," raising a series of questions regarding how this set of ideas about and connections among religion, gender, and violence should have become common sense in the first place. In this chapter, I focus on how "religion" is conceptualized in ways that contribute to the morass and keep the idea of gender-based violence operative in circuits of power.[1] I explore the intertwined role the invocation of "religion" and, specifically of Islam, has in state responses to "gender-based violence" and in the post-9/11 "war on terror" with its correlative expansion of the US security state. The intertwining of frameworks for discourse about gender-based violence, terrorism, and Islam is more than politically pragmatic legitimation (although it is that); it is also the historical product of how religion is conceptualized.

Religion as an object of knowledge is intimately bound up with both the European colonial project and the modern production of secularism as a space separate from religion. The invocation of religion as a comparative category by colonial administrators supported the differentiation of colonial civilization from its other(s). The imbrication of religion within the colonial project ensured that the dominant European religion of Christianity was instituted as the normative model for the category as a whole.[2] This differentiation was reinforced by the creation in Enlightenment thought of a category of reason separated from religious "tradition."[3] When religion is defined in opposition to secularism, religion is set into mutually reinforcing circuits of attribution that connect religion to both gender and violence while secularism is positioned as the site of universal (and, therefore, supposedly not gender-specific) freedom, peace, and reason.

The normative model of religion as based on predominant versions of Christianity establishes the key elements of the category: belief in the divine, the centrality of sacred texts, and a hierarchical authority structure. One basis for the current critique, then, is that, as religious studies scholars point out, these elements are not all found in all social formations widely understood as religious. So, for example, faith in a divine being or central sacred texts may or may not be part of religions that make practice primary to belief (such that one can be an atheist and still practice religion) or those that emphasize the centrality of relations with the land. Similarly, the organization of authority structures varies across religions, including those that emphasize horizontal or communal authority structures.

The critique is not just about particular applications; it goes to the status of the category itself. It is not just that this or that idea of what religion might be is inadequate, but rather that the category is mutually constituted by the relations of Enlightenment, secularization, Christian hegemony, and colonialism. Whatever the content of the category, its effects are materialized within the context of these relations. Even when invoked in virtually opposite ways, the discursive effects of the category reiterate its constitutive relations. For example, David Chidester's (1996) exposition of scholars who documented religion in southern Africa during the colonial period shows how the scholarly narrative of "religion" in the region shifts with the changing needs of colonial rule. Sometimes Southern Africans are supposed to have a religion comparable to that of the colonists, and sometimes they are supposed to have no religion at all. Because these relations are dynamic, they create ambivalent processes by which indigenous practices and traditions both do and do not become integrated into the category of religion (Wenger 2009).

These contradictions in the deployment of the category have materialized religion in paradoxical ways, such that religion is both an artifact of colonial epistemology and a site for counterhegemonic action.[4] The challenge for analysis is how to maintain a focus on both the dominant Christian assumptions of religion as a category and enactments that dislodge claims to religion from determination by hegemonic social relations.

The contemporary invocation of religion in US public discourse with regard to Islam reiterates many of these effects. As with Chidester's analysis of Southern Africa, Islam is sometimes treated as just like Christianity and sometimes as utterly different. Islam is often treated as a religion like Christianity with regard to the idea that Muslims must share the gender and sexual ethics of conservative Christians. In 2019, for example, Secretary of State Mike Pompeo (himself a conservative Christian) put together a high-level panel to review the meaning of "human rights," so as to separate "unalienable" rights, such as religious freedom, from "ad hoc rights," such as equal rights for women and LGBTQ people. In this instance, the panel included an Islamic scholar and a rabbi implying a unified religious opposition to equal rights on gender and sexuality (Wong and Sullivan 2019).[5] Although Pompeo and the Trump administration that he represented staged this agreement among conservative Islam, Judaism, and Christianity, the administration also initiated actions that took the idea that Islam is "different" to an extreme. As Leti Volpp discusses in this volume, invocation of "honor crimes" in President Trump's executive order limiting travel from some Muslim-majority countries connected security-state concerns about "terrorist" violence to concerns about gender-based violence. And in these same early days of the Trump administration, then-National Security Advisor Michael Flynn also claimed that Islam was "not a religion," but "only" a political ideology (Zurcher 2017).

This back-and-forth in relations among US state policy, religious commitments, and gender and sexuality, like the back-and-forth charted by Chidester, indicates the invocation of religion remains contradictory and is based on the state's pursuit of colonial and postcolonial power relations. The dynamic persists with both the normative comparison to Christianity invoked by appeals to religion and with the ways in which such appeals also invoke the distinction between religion and secularism. Positioning religion as a special motivator of gender-based violence implies that there is an alternative, nonreligious or secular, realm free from, or at least with less propensity for, gender hierarchy and the direct violence of gendered domination. This idea is part of a larger narrative, often called the "secularization thesis," which Ann Pellegrini and I describe in *Secularisms* as follows: "The secularization thesis makes for a narrative that connects a number of elements—most notably, modernity, reason, and universalism—into a network that has strong moral as well as descriptive implications. The broad historical narrative generally associated with secularization develops these moral implications by describing change over time. . . . Implicit within the narrative is the idea that each step forward in time also marks a moral advance: a move away from religious authority and toward greater intellectual freedom and more knowledge, leading eventually to governance by reasoned debate and ultimately to democracy and peace" (2008, 4).

The presumptions underlying this narrative mean that those who resist the moral claims of secularization can also be read as resisting freedom, progress, modernity, and even reason itself. Moreover, the traditional secularization narrative creates not just a boundary between religion and secularism but a three-way division between good, reasonable religion and secularism on one side and bad, unreasonable religion that is intolerant and unenlightened on the other (Mandair and Dressler 2011). As Mandair and Dressler argue in *Secularism and Religion-Making*, in the three-way division, bad religion is often defined by being "too" religious, particularly with regard to those religious formations that have been marked as "fundamentalist."[6] To understand the relations among religion, gender, sex and violence thus requires outlining a complex network of relations while also tracing particular strands in relation to each other.

INTERTWINED NARRATIVES ABOUT VIOLENCE

As with the category of religion itself, the connections among religion, gender, and violence can either unite all instances of religion as "the same" or be the defining site of "difference." Religious studies scholar Heather Shipley (2015) argues, for instance, that an assumed consonance between religiosity and sexual conservatism is understood to cross boundaries among religions. Sexual conservatism is not only presumed to unite different religions; it also divides the religious, and supposedly sexually conservative, from the secular, and supposedly sexually liberal. The idea of religion as a front for gender and sexual conservatism is promoted by both religious conservatives, who hope to naturalize this connection (and thereby make opposition to sexual regulation the same as opposition to religion itself) and by progressive advocates who hope to resist sexual regulation.[7]

Importantly, though, a second narrative runs in a contrary direction with regard to religion and gender. Examples abound of the invocation of gender and sexuality as proof of religious difference. For example, the political theorist Samuel Huntington's (2005) critique of US immigration policy, *Who*

Are We?, made Catholic reproductive practices a critical part of his argument for the inability of immigrants he named as "Hispanic" to assimilate."[8] This argument then became central to Huntington's call for a radical defense of Anglo-Protestant culture in the United States.

The movement to "ban Sharia law" in the United States has similarly focused on practice with regard to gender and sexuality as a primary symbol of religious difference. State legislation to prevent US courts from referencing Islamic law has little practical effect but is part of a broader movement to institutionalize Islamophobia. This movement is largely sponsored by the Center for Security Policy (Gardiner and Olalde 2019), which has published a report that cites gender and sexuality as one of three main areas of Sharia's influence (Center for Security Policy 2016, 12).

How are we to understand this type of complicated relationship in which sexual politics both unites religion as a category distinct from secularism and also marks the dividing lines among different religions? This question is particularly important because the two seemingly opposing stories about religion, gender, and sexuality—that all religions agree on gender and sex and that gender and sex reveal where religious difference is embodied—can be interrelated in powerful ways, particularly when it comes to discourse about gender-based violence and terrorism.

The narrative of religion as a cause of gender-based violence is based squarely on the idea of an overarching category called "religion," with the presumption that all particular instances of this category include a commitment to sexual conservatism. This presumption of gender and sexual conservatism creates a common sense understanding about religion. Claims about religion and gender-based violence are often used to distinguish between religious and secular actors, particularly between religious actors and the secular state. If gender is primarily the purview of religion and religion is always conservative on gendered issues and if gendered violence is a problem, then gender as a religious motivation for violence becomes a common sense explanation, taken up by both proponents and critics of traditionalism, including many antiviolence activists.

And in the intertwining of differing narratives about religion, the three-way division among secularism, good religion, and bad religion creates a discourse in which such claims can both draw upon the supposed gendered conservatism of "all religions" and distinguish among some religions. When it comes to narratives about gender-based violence, all religions can be presumed to be conservative with respect to gender relations, even as distinctions can be made to separate out those religions that take this conservatism "too far." And this sense—that some religions take gender conservativism to ends that are often named as fundamentalist—can then be tied to the idea that some religions also support terrorism.

This complex discourse of religion and gender-based violence is part of the scaffolding that undergirds public understandings of terrorism in the United Sates and is particularly active in US public discourse with respect to Islam. As we have seen, the propensity for violence among all religions (both gender-based violence and violence in general) can simultaneously be used to distinguish good religions from bad. The general story of religion and violence can lend credence to the more specific story of some religions promoting terrorism such that the story of religion and terrorism makes certain religions seem particularly threatening. And this attribution of a particular threat then makes action, including violent action, against such threatening religionists seem both necessary and honorable. When the presumed gender-conservatism of religion simply provides the background for public discourse about both gender-based violence and terrorism, a complex story about religion, gender, and violence appears straightforward and obvious.

Or, in another example, geared more toward alliance than antagonism between the United States and Muslim political projects, the US government has used the sense that Islam and Christianity are similar, particularly with regard to religious leadership and hierarchical authority in their attempts to find and/or create religious partners for both military and political initiatives. Although Islam does not have the formal hierarchical structure of Christianity (imams are not formal congregational leaders in the same way that ministers and priests are in Christian congregations), the United States has invested in empowering imams as "religious leaders" who could serve as partners for US actions. As both Saba Mahmood (2006) and Rosemary Corbett (2016) have documented, in the project of "reforming" Islam, these efforts often created new religious formations by, for example, promoting religious leaders during US military operations in Iraq who were more conservative on gender and sexuality than most of Iraqi society had been prior to the war. In this case, the idea that Islam must have religious leaders "like" Christianity contributed to forms of gender and sexual conservatism. At the same time, the US government also undertook military policy with regard to Afghanistan, Iraq, and Iran based on the idea that Islam was fundamentally "different" than Christianity, a difference supposedly made manifest through gender and sexual conservatism.

NARRATIVES ENACTED

And, thus, we find ourselves returned to the complex narrative of religion, gender, and violence. Here's how it works in practice: the common belief that religious commitment is conservative provides the background for claims that gender-based violence is a specific instance of this overarching religious conservatism. And gender-based violence is then linked up to other forms of violence, like terrorism, that are also supposed to be religiously motivated. The narrative produced by these links can then be deployed to demonstrate the need for the state to employ its own violence to stop gender-based violence and terrorism.

This common sense is produced in part by arguing that all religions, or religiosity itself, contribute to gender and sexual conservatism. But when this form of reasoning is invoked as a common sense data point in narratives of violence, it is often focused on one specific religion—Islam. The potential contradiction between all religions and a focus on only one is mitigated by the commonsense nature of the data. If all religions are sites of gender conservatism and violence, then Islam must surely be such a site. It's obvious on the face of it.

And the obviousness of the obvious is here produced in the context of the three-way divide that is the relation between religion and secularism—a specific religion can be a specifically dangerous cause of gender-based violence even though all religions are sexually conservative as long as the specifically dangerous religion can be positioned as "bad religion." Because Christianity provides the model for the category of religion, particularly in the US public sphere, then it fits with common sense to assume that Christian conservatism represents good religion—the kind of religion that does not undermine freedom or hold back progress. In contrast, when a non-Christian religion is discussed, it is much easier to make the slide from sexual conservatism to gender-based violence to terrorism. Thus, George W. Bush could present himself as both a deeply sexually conservative Christian by, on the one hand, reinstating the "global gag rule" to restrict reproductive health services worldwide, and on the other hand, saving women from Islam in Afghanistan through the military violence of the secular state.[9]

It can be particularly helpful to attend to public discourse about religion, gender, and violence across different presidential administrations, so as to show that it is the discourse, rather than a particular politician or political party that drives the narrative. As a result, this discourse produced surprisingly consistent policy with regard to the "war on terror" across three different presidential administrations representing both major US political parties. So, for example, while the Obama administration claimed to end the war on terror, started by George W. Bush, Obama continued many of its elements, sustaining the US war in Afghanistan throughout his administration and expanding drone warfare.[10] Donald Trump made similar claims about opposing the war while also sustaining it and expanding drone warfare.

President Biden has, in contrast, moved to end the "forever wars" and shift the focus of the security state away from its twenty-year spotlight on Islam, turning that spotlight instead toward domestic terrorism. There is much contention over the referent of the name "domestic terrorism," but rarely is it suggested that right-wing violence in the United States should be called "Christian terrorism," even though commitment to the idea of the United States as a "Christian nation," including among people who might not otherwise identify as Christian or as religious, is one of the major predictors of right-wing activity in the United States (Whitehead and Perry 2020). Thus, the naming of "domestic" terrorism as a new threat leaves Christianity unnamed as a source of violence, maintaining a sense that Islam is the only religious source of violence.[11]

This commitment to Christian nationalism, even for otherwise secular actors, extends the history (dating to the Colonial period) of dynamic intertwining between religion and race in the United States.[12] The contemporary manifestation of this dynamic in the frequent conflation between Islam and Arab Americans after 9/11 intensified the racialized opposition between Islam and Euro-American whiteness (Puar 2007).[13] Given this discursive context, although the Biden administration's move away from the direct Islamophobia of the Trump administration is undoubtedly important, it also leaves in place the discursive apparatus that associates Christianity with whiteness, security and the US nation-state and Islam with racial otherness and violence.

Gender and religion are interwoven at various points of public discourse throughout the history of the war on terror (even as it extended beyond its official ending).[14] At the very beginning of the post-9/11 wave of US war, the administration of George W. Bush deployed the trope of concern for women in the face of gender-based violence to support the invasion of Afghanistan. Laura Bush, who had been distinctly reticent to make public statements in her role as First Lady, nonetheless notably expressed her great support for women's well-being in Afghanistan in November 2001 by speaking on this topic in the weekly radio address usually given by the president.[15]

The major media in the United States also articulated the narrative that, the US state was simultaneously secular and Christian as the necessary rhetoric to subtend the invasion. This narrative was explicitly drawn upon by Andrew Sullivan in a cover story entitled "This *Is* a Religious War," for the *New York Times Magazine* on October 7, 2001. Sullivan's article engages in the types of claims about the connections between Islam and violence that were ubiquitous at the time and have continued to be so in the nearly two decades since the war commenced. In contrast to Islam, Christian violence, including gender-based violence and acts of terrorism like the killing of doctors who perform abortions, rather than representing a strain of "Christian civilization," is an exception to a broader Christian history that leads to religious tolerance.[16] Sullivan makes the claim that the United States is the land of religious freedom because it is the descendant of this specifically Christian history. Thus, the United States is presented as simultaneously secular and Christian and as a result as both tolerant and superior. In Sullivan's argument Christianity and secularism are intertwined: secularism and, perhaps even more importantly, religious freedom are not simply secular and separate from religious identity but are specifically tied to Christianity and distanced from Islam. Good religion and secularism are tied together and distinguished from bad religion. Sullivan makes this distinction between Christianity and Islam again in a 2009 essay supporting Obama's troop surge in Afghanistan: "These are desperately dangerous times. They are dangerous primarily because religion has been abused by those seeking power and control over others—both in the mild version of Christianism at home and the much, much more pernicious and evil Islamism abroad" (Sullivan 2009). The war on terror becomes a simultaneously secular and religious war—a war in defense of freedom that is tolerant of Islam and a war against Islam.[17]

The doubling between claims of tolerance toward Islam and a focus on Islam as the cause of violence continued throughout the Bush administration. President Bush addressed warlike rhetoric toward Islam at some points, including calling the war a "crusade" in remarks at the White House on September 16, 2001 as he announced a turn from a period of mourning over the loss of life in the September 11 attacks to a period of war: "We need to go back to work tomorrow and we will. But we need to be alert to the fact that these evil-doers still exist.... This is a new kind of—a new kind of evil. And we understand. And the American people are beginning to understand. This crusade, this war on terror is going to take a while." Bush tried to walk back this language the next day by visiting the Islamic Center of Washington and speaking briefly on the distinction between war against Islam and war on terror.[18]

The framework Sullivan articulates so directly has reappeared repeatedly and not just during the administration of George W. Bush.[19] In the Obama administration's justification for its own expansive military endeavors, Obama framed his understanding of Islam through a reaffirmation of calls for the "reform of Islam." In a 2016 interview in *The Atlantic* magazine, entitled "The Obama Doctrine," that he clearly sees as articulating the legacy of his foreign policy, Obama rhetorically creates ties among "reformation," "modernity," and "progress": "I was hoping that my speech [in Cairo] could trigger a discussion, could create space for Muslims to address the real problems they are confronting—problems of governance, and the fact that some currents of Islam have not gone through a reformation that would help people adapt their religious doctrines to modernity" (Goldberg 2016). For Obama (as for Bush and Sullivan), movement along the path attributed to Christianity and toward secular modernity is necessary to the creation of good religion.[20]

Over the course of his administration, Obama wove this "doctrine" of reform through interrelated threads that were not always visible but that sometimes showed up in unexpected places. At its start, the administration reiterated ties among religion, gender norms, and national security in its vision for the Office of Faith-Based and Neighborhood Partnerships, showing the ways in which good religion was understood not just to encompass gender and sexual relations but also to be central to the security state. According to the administration's original vision, published in 2009:

> The Office's top priority will be making community groups an integral part of our economic recovery and poverty a burden fewer have to bear when recovery is complete.
>
> It will be one voice among several in the administration that will look at how we support women and children, address teenage pregnancy, and reduce the need for abortion.
>
> The Office will strive to support fathers who stand by their families, which involves working to get young men off the streets and into well-paying jobs, encouraging responsible fatherhood.
>
> Finally, beyond American shores this Office will work with the National Security Council to foster interfaith dialogue with leaders and scholars around the world. (The White House 2009)

Although Obama is not a sexual conservative in Bush's mold, when it comes to faith-based initiatives, we find ourselves in the land of relatively traditional Christian family values. The overall effect of the two policies dedicated to gender and sexuality is to create a vision of binary gender roles, family structures, and their implications for policy. We have an explicit gendering in that different policy initiatives are directed toward women and men, and in its explicitness the policy is also traditional: women are tied to children, and while they need to be supported, unlike the fathers they apparently don't need well-paying jobs. Trans, lesbian, gay, or queer people are nowhere named. In this initial charge to the office, the move is relatively swift from a recognition of the importance of community-based activists—"no matter their political or religious beliefs"—to Christian family values: a two-parent family of complementary genders, with the father working and the mother caring for children (although she may work, there is no mention of government support for mothers working anywhere other than at home). In putting together these specific values with a claim to openness no matter one's "beliefs," the Obama administration is here enacting the same combination of Christian values and secular norms—the same Christian secularism—offered by Sullivan.

We also move very rapidly from economic recovery through the Christian family to the somewhat startling naming of the National Security Council in the charge for an office focused on "neighborhood" partnerships. Why did the Obama administration presume that "faith" and national security are related? And how is it that the domestic (in every sense of the word) gender normativity of the office was tied to what the administration here calls the world "beyond American shores"?

The Obama administration's approach was undoubtedly different from that of the Bush administration, but as Obama's own description of his speech in Cairo shows, it was also tied to the colonial and postcolonial idea that moderate Christianity provides the model for all religions that might be good religions and thus that might be placed effectively in dialogue with the needs of the secular security state. In broad strokes, what Obama offered to the "Muslim world" in his view of the relation between religion and security in Cairo and among religion, gender, and security in the Office of Faith-Based and Neighborhood Partnerships is American religious freedom. Winnifred Sullivan (2005) argues that the proffered freedom is "impossible," because it slips so easily into a hierarchical religious tolerance in which the norms and values of institutionalized Christianity form the framework for secular law and democracy.[21] In short, the overall framework upon which Obama drew maintains the Christian hegemony of the neoliberal world order offering a religious freedom, in which the opportunity to be religiously "free" is the opportunity to be like a mainstream Christianity that fits with modern secularism.

If Obama's Christian secularism was an earnest moral framework that nonetheless subtended war, the Trump administration's appeal to the rhetoric of defending women from religion-based violence was much more cynical. It is nonetheless important to consider the Trump administration's offers of protection from violence against women. That the Trump administration made such appeals in an administration that sought very little moral legitimation for its actions demonstrates the persistence and power of the rhetoric. Early in Trump's presidency (when perhaps there was more concern with ethical appearances), the administration included in its second version of the anti-Muslim "travel ban" (The White House 2017a) a reference to "acts of gender-based violence against women, including so-called honor killings," as part of a section describing "terrorism-related" crimes that the United States would now publicize when committed by immigrants. Many commentators (Toosi 2017) pointed out that threatening to connect violence against women to a published list of crimes committed by immigrants intensified the traditional Islamophobic rhetoric that had marked many of Trump's pronouncements about the travel ban.[22] Justice Sonia Sotomayor included in her dissent from the US Supreme Court's decision to uphold a later third version of the ban (The White House 2017b), what she called a "harrowing" list of these pronouncements against Muslims.[23] In 2018 the Trump administration returned to the well-worn connection between militarism and concern for women's rights when it started to support Iranian feminists—as part of a strategy to build support for "regime change" in Iran (Moaveni 2018). Despite Trump's claims to be different from previous administrations, his administration seamlessly adopted the dual assertion of sexual conservatism and concerns for women's "freedom" used throughout the twenty-year history of the war on terror.

CHANGING THE USUAL STORY

The usual story—so ubiquitous it was drawn upon by three different presidents despite their three different political perspectives—is created, in part, by a series of habitual ways of thinking that make religious sexual conservatism utterly obvious. In this thought pattern religion is separated from other social relations that help to constitute both religion and sexual politics—those of nationalism, race, and economics, among others. Disembedding religion allows it to be located as the "cause" of sexual conservatism, so that politicians from both major political parties can attribute their more or less conservative stances on gender and sex (their own or that of the voters) to religiosity. Both religious conservatives and sexual progressives then tend to focus on religion as the appropriate framework for discussing sex, even as complex and historically variable religious traditions come to represent a single thing—sexual conservatism.

And, in turn, this presumption narrows the field of conceivable reality—this version of reality does not, for example, encompass religious people whose values are not conservative, nor does it account for the sexual conservatism of secular actors—particularly the secular state (Alpert 2000). If religion is taken to be the driving force in sexual politics then those politics are not just about gender and sex but also about the status of religion in society, creating an incentive for people to commit to sexual conservatism as part of their religious identities. The very narrative that religious identity and gender conservatism correlate can lead to the idea that one should articulate one's religious identity through gender conservatism.

Any stance more open to sexual diversity can then come to seem like a threat to religion itself, rather than a different possible incarnation of religiosity.[24] Conversely, progressives come to see religion as a threat to their sexual politics, making it more difficult for them—or anyone—to be open to any relation between religion and sex that does not fit the usual story. Instead, progressives can actually come to agree with conservatives that when thinking about gender and sex, social analysts should be focused on religion and, concomitantly, when thinking about religion, social analysts should be focused on sexual politics. Religion may be part of the story driving sexual conservatism, and it may be an element in some acts of violence, but if it is invoked as part of the common sense analysis, the story becomes misleadingly simplistic—even as it is exceedingly powerful.

The problematic effects of invoking religion as an analytic category have led some scholars to suggest that we should not use it at all (Fitzgerald 2000), but other critics of the category suggest that the analytic problems cannot be solved with a single renunciation. For example, in an essay in an anthology analyzing secularism and gender, Ann Braude (2013) argues that we should look to unexpected sites and sources to understand religion as sites for multiple possibilities. Too often, for instance, we focus on progressive activism as if it is only secular, when in fact religious actors play key roles.[25]

Braude's approach to recognizing religion in unexpected places could extend well beyond the question of religious progressivism. Moving away from the expected also opens possibilities for analyzing phenomena that are generally seen as elements of the larger category of religion without simply placing these elements within the confines of the usual story. For example, Nadine Naber (2012) has documented how some Arab American campus activists in the 1990s adopted a "Muslim first, Arab second" framework that enabled acting on their feminist commitments. For the young women with whom Naber worked pursuing their activities within a religious framework grounded their feminism in ways that allowed them to articulate their positions powerfully to family members, fellow activists, and the broader public.

Breaking out of the usual story not only allows us to understand instances when religion may support feminism, it may also allow for shifts in understandings of violence. David Chidester takes up the question of religion and violence in *Wild Religion* (2012). He argues that it is ultimately impossible to separate political and religious violence either analytically or in practice. Part of Chidester's argument depends on a recognition of the persistence of violence in history. Most analyses of violence start from a presumption that peace prevails until violence interrupts peaceful existence. An analysis of religion and violence based on this assumption would lead to questions about how violence came to start—was it religiously motivated? Chidester argues that in South Africa, at least, violence has been endemic through the colonial period and in a particularly intense form during the era of the apartheid government beginning in 1948. Even since the change in government and the first democratic elections in 1994, the legacy of violence in South Africa has been enacted through everyday violence that may now be "ordinary" rather than the "extraordinary violence of apartheid." But this violence is still often organized through myth and ritual that can't let go of the legacy of "armed religion" in South Africa's history. Thus, all actors were—and are—working in a context that is already suffused with a violence that is both political and religious. Religion and violence inhabit each other, shifting the usual narrative: religion may be involved in violence but then so is secular "political reason."

The story of the war on terror is one in which a war waged by the secular state is a morally good and obviously viable response to violence by non-state actors. This narrative is stabilized by making connections across several sets of assumptions, many of which are empirically dubious and may well be contradictory. The integuments that provide these connections include the connections George W. Bush makes (supported by political commentators, like Andrew Sullivan) between a good Christian morality of gender conservatism and religious tolerance and the militarism of the secular state. The integuments also include the secularization narrative which connects progress, modernity, and freedom with modern secularism and modern gender norms, connections that Barack Obama drew upon to promote the "reform" of Islam. And these integuments also include the type of direct Islamophobia that Donald Trump repeatedly and in Justice Sotomayor's words, "harrowingly," invoked. But, this Islamophobia can't make sense in US public discourse without destabilizing the sense that the United States is a religiously open, tolerant, or even free society. In the loosely coordinated reasoning of US common sense, it simply makes sense that "religion" is both patriarchal and terrifyingly violent, so surely the way out of "desperately dangerous times," as Sullivan says, is to go to war on religion and on one religion specifically. One could, of course, argue conversely that such a war is a way of instituting and maintaining "desperate danger."

CONCLUSION

In conclusion, I will focus on one suggestion for change, which is that feminist activists support recent moves to reconsider the secular state as a viable site for responding to gender-based violence, at the international scale of military action or at the scale of police responses to domestic violence. Community-based organizations and social movements are working to challenge the narrative that religion is the cause of gendered violence, so as to create new possibilities for responding to violence. For example, the Barnard Center for Research on Women (BCRW) worked with activist fellow Tiloma Jayasinghe, former Executive Director of Sakhi for South Asian Women in New York City, on a project called "Responding to Violence, Restoring Justice" (Jayasinghe and Ward 2018).

Sakhi is an important site for such efforts because it takes up organizing in the midst of narratives that presume the predominance of religious conservatives among immigrant communities. The presumption is that religious traditionalism will hide and even promote violence while the state will protect women and prevent violence. In recognizing that this story is not true, Jayasinghe's project shows that the religion-secularism binary creates an oscillation between religious and secular authority, in which South Asian women disappear into a choice between the secular state or the presumed masculine authorities of religious community. Instead, Sakhi takes up an activist approach in which religion is not automatically considered a source of violence, and feminists may well draw upon religious resources for responding to violence. Perhaps most importantly, restoring justice does not require separating the religious from the secular or vice versa. Making such a distinction is no longer the key to ending violence. When one takes Braude's advice in looking at putatively secular organizing, one can often find religious acts that are often not counted as such, including in feminist acts that refuse secularism as their framework and that may also refuse traditional religious and community authority but nonetheless take religion seriously.

Reframing gendered violence involves taking seriously both the pragmatic and local work done by organizations like Sakhi to respond to violence and the expansive work of envisioning a world beyond the framework of secular modernity. Another world is possible. But building another world requires both new analyses of this world and creative imagination about possibilities that summon social justice.

NOTES

1 Both of the categories often associated with religion and violence, that of being "gender-based" and of "terrorism," can also be helpfully subject to critique, as they are in this volume (e.g., Abu-Lughod, Nesiah, Volpp). Thus, the critique of the category of religion, which is the focus of this essay, is part of a larger project for analyzing social relations.
2 See, for example, Hume (1992) as an Enlightenment text central to this project.
3 Kant's (1960) configuration of religion as "within the limits of reason alone" illustrates both the separation of religion from reason and the sense that Enlightenment religion could be sustained as reasonable.
4 On the import of an analysis of paradoxes, see Scott (2004) and Kauanui (2018).
5 Similarly, in a speech to the UN General Assembly, Secretary of Health and Human Services Alex Azar presented a statement signed by nineteen countries, including the United States and several Muslim-majority countries, which argued that UN documents should not include reference to "sexual and reproductive health and rights," because not all UN member states supported such rights (McCammon 2019).
6 On the history of the category "fundamentalism" and the political effects of its deployment in the US context, see Watt's (2017) book, *Antifundamentalism in Modern America*.
7 For just a few examples of this presumption, see UN Women (2014) or a version published in the liberal magazine the *New Yorker* (Ross 2012).
8 Huntington previewed this argument in a 2004 article in *Foreign Policy* called "The Hispanic Challenge."

9   The "global gag rule," officially known as the "Mexico City Policy," was instituted by President Reagan to refuse US funding to any organization that promoted or even mentioned abortion. The policy has been repeatedly rescinded by Democratic presidents (Clinton and Obama) and reinstated by Republican presidents (Bush and Trump) (Wong 2019).

10 The Obama administration officially brought the "war on terrorism" to an end, initially renaming related military activity as "overseas contingency operations," but continued to prosecute the war in Afghanistan, including a troop surge in 2009 and expanded the use of drone warfare in a number of countries, such as Pakistan, Yemen, and Libya. Given this continuation of the actions initiated as a "war on terrorism," I join many other scholars in continuing to use the phrase despite the official renaming. For examples, see Maher (2009) and McCrisken (2011).

11 For a description of Biden's focus on domestic terrorism that also advocates a continuing focus on Islamism as a source of violence, see Baumann (2021).

12 For histories of the ways in which racial differences were constituted in and through religious differences with regard to both the colonization of indigenous lands and enslavement, see Goldschmidt and McAlister (2004) and Sweet (2003).

13 For a helpful analysis of how a combination of conflations and displacements among race, religion, and culture work in British law, see Samantrai (2002).

14 For an earlier reading of this history of US policy across presidential administrations, see Jakobsen (2021).

15 For the full text of her address, see the transcript in the *Washington Post* (L. Bush 2001).

16 For more on the contrast between hierarchical religious tolerance and religious freedom, see Jakobsen and Pellegrini (2008).

17 After promoting this position from 2001 through the duration of the Obama administration, Sullivan (2018) eventually changed his views on the US wars in Afghanistan and Iraq, arguing that they had been "useless" and admitting that he had been pro-war in the run-up to Iraq, but not acknowledging either his leading voice for the invasion of Afghanistan nor his approval of President Obama's decision to extend the US mission in Afghanistan in 2009.

18 Bush stated, "These acts of violence against innocents violate the fundamental tenets of the Islamic faith. And it's important for my fellow Americans to understand that. The English translation is not as eloquent as the original Arabic, but let me quote from the Koran, itself: 'In the long run, evil in the extreme will be the end of those who do evil. For that they rejected the signs of Allah and held them up to ridicule.' The face of terror is not the true faith of Islam. That's not what Islam is all about. Islam is peace. These terrorists don't represent peace. They represent evil and war. When we think of Islam we think of a faith that brings comfort to a billion people around the world. Billions of people find comfort and solace and peace. And that's made brothers and sisters out of

every race—out of every race." For critiques of Bush's rhetoric in the aftermath of 9/11, see Bouie (2015) and Blest (2015).

19 Controversy over the extent of Bush's tolerance toward Islam was revived in the 2016 presidential election campaign when commentators began to point to the contrast with the 2016 Republican candidates, particularly Donald Trump, who directly called for registration of Muslims. Former Florida Governor Jeb Bush (brother to George) was perhaps the most interesting in his responses to this particular controversy in that at different points in the campaign he, too, expressed a willingness to treat Islam as somehow separate from any claim to religious freedom, suggesting for example that the US should accept Christian, but not Muslim, refugees from Syria. Before making this suggestion, Mr. Bush had spoken passionately about the importance of protecting religious freedom in the United States at a speech in May 2015 at Liberty University, but in this speech he referred only to issues related to Christianity (Holland 2015). Jeb Bush's praise for his brother's tolerance was in contrast to Marco Rubio who criticized President Obama for visiting a mosque and delivering a speech on tolerance. See also Brooks and Collins (2016); on Obama's visit to the mosque, see Harris (2016).

20 Following the Obama interview, philosopher Gary Gutting (2016) reiterated this Christian secular narrative as the philosophical background to Obama's call for the reform of Islam in an article titled, "How Religion Can Lead to Violence": "Christians eventually embraced tolerance through a long and complex historical process.... To put it bluntly, Islam as a whole has not made the concessions to secular values that Christianity has. As President Obama recently said, 'Some currents of Islam have not gone through a reformation that would help people adapt their religious doctrines to modernity.'" Critics of Gutting's position (and ones like his, e.g., Rumi [2015]) highlight the ways in which the early modern reformation and counterreformation were not the modern, liberal Protestantism that seems to fit well with contemporary secularism but were radical, iconoclastic, and sometimes violent movements; see, for example, Simon (2015). See also Zubaida (2016) for a somewhat more complex discussion.

21 In particular, the dialogue model for interrelation across religious difference claims to be based on equality and openness but is actually framed by a Christian understanding. The model of interfaith dialogue offers negotiation among different "faiths," a view of religion that mirrors the Christian emphasis on belief as definitive of religion. If, however, practice or land is the basis for one's religion, then dialogue might not be the way to approach conflict. For interfaith dialogues, the issue is talking through beliefs, rather than, say, negotiating about land rights. As with the secular calendar, which is at once used across cultures and specifically Christian, these assumptions make the Office of Faith-Based and Neighborhood Partnerships' claim to be open to working with community activists "no matter [their] political or religious beliefs" into a claim that is simultaneously universalist and Christian.

22 Commentators also pointed out that this list of crimes committed by a particular group—in this case immigrants—represented a similar tactic to the list of "crimes by Jews" published by the National Socialist government in the 1930s (Erickson 2017).

23 Sotomayor (2018) writes: "The full record paints a far more harrowing picture, from which a reasonable observer would readily conclude that the Proclamation was motivated by hostility and animus toward the Muslim faith" (4). And she goes on to list instances in which the president expressly stated that the "travel ban" was directed toward Muslims (4–10).

24 On a feedback loop between political discourse and religious identity, see Kruse (2015) and Margolis (2018).

25 "While scholars need to subject to critique both secular and religious claims to advance women's interests, we also need to be able to acknowledge both religious and secular successes in fighting discrimination, whether on the basis of gender or religion" (Braude 2013, 75).

REFERENCES

Alpert, Rebecca. 2000. *Voices of the Religious Left: A Contemporary Sourcebook*. Philadelphia: Temple University Press.

Baumann, Zsofia. 2021. "Biden's National Security Strategy: Domestic Terror Threats Take Centre Stage." International Center for Counter-Terrorism, The Hague Publications, April 8. https://icct.nl/publication/bidens-national-security-strategy-domestic-threats/.

Blest, Paul. 2015. "The False Resurrection of George W. Bush: Don't Be Fooled by Calls to Reassess His Loathsome Legacy." *Salon*, November 25. http://www.salon.com/2015/11/25/the_false_resurrection_of_george_w_bush_dont_be_fooled_by_calls_to_reassess_his_loathsome_legacy/.

Bouie, Jamelle. 2015. "George W. Bush Needs to Speak to His Party." *Salon*, November 20. http://www.slate.com/articles/news_and_politics/politics/2015/11/george_w_bush_needs_to_speak_to_republicans_the_former_president_should.html.

Braude, Ann. 2013. "Religion and Women's Political Mobilization." In *Religion, the Secular, and the Politics of Sexual Difference*, edited by Linell E. Cady and Tracy Fessenden, 69–76. New York: Columbia University Press.

Brooks, Arthur C., and Gail Collins. 2016. "What's God Got to Do with It?" *New York Times*, February 9. https://www.nytimes.com/2016/02/09/opinion/campaign-stops/whats-god-got-to-do-with-it.html.

Bush, George W. 2001. "On Islam and Terrorism." Resources on Faith, Ethics & Public Life, Berkley Center for Religion, Peace and World Affairs. September 17, http://berkleycenter.georgetown.edu/quotes/george-w-bush-on-islam-and-terrorism—3.

Bush, Laura. 2001. "Laura Bush on Taliban Oppression of Women." *Washington Post*, November 17. https://www.washingtonpost.com/wp-srv/nation/specials/attacked/transcripts/laurabushtext_111701.html.

Cavanaugh, William T. 2007. "Does Religion Cause Violence?" *Harvard Divinity Bulletin* (Spring/Summer 2007). https://bulletin.hds.harvard.edu/does-religion-cause-violence/.

Center for Security Policy. 2016. "Sharia: The Threat to America." Center for Security Policy Press. https://www.centerforsecuritypolicy.org/wp-content/uploads/2018/03/Team_B_Abridged.pdf.

Chidester, David. 1996. *Savage Systems: Colonialism and Comparative Religion in Southern Africa*. Charlottesville: University Press of Virginia.

Chidester, David. 2012. *Wild Religion: Tracking the Sacred in South Africa*. Berkeley: University of California Press.

Corbett, Rosemary R. 2016. *Making Moderate Islam: Sufism, Service and "The Ground Zero Mosque" Controversy*. Stanford, CA: Stanford University Press.

Erickson, Amanda. 2017. "Adolf Hitler Also Published a List of Crimes Committed by Groups He Didn't Like." *Washington Post*, March 2. https://www.washingtonpost.com/news/worldviews/wp/2017/03/02/adolf-hitler-also-published-a-list-of-crimes-committed-by-groups-he-didnt-like/?utm_term=.6734d7d5501c.

Fitzgerald, Timothy. 2000. *The Ideology of Religious Studies*. New York: Oxford University Press.

Gardiner, Dustin, and Mark Olalde. 2019. "Islam, Sharia Law: How Far-Right Group Gets Model Bills Passed." *USA Today*, July 21. https://www.usatoday.com/in-depth/news/investigations/2019/07/17/islam-sharia-law-how-far-right-group-gets-model-bills-passed/1636199001/

Goldberg, Jeffrey. 2016. "The Obama Doctrine." *The Atlantic,* April 2016. http://www.theatlantic.com/magazine/archive/2016/04/the-obama-doctrine/471525/.

Goldschmidt, Henry, and Elizabeth McAlister. 2004. *Race, Nation, and Religion*. New York: Oxford University Press.

Gutting, Gary. 2016. "How Religion Can Lead to Violence." *New York Times*, August 1. http://www.nytimes.com/2016/08/01/opinion/how-religion-can-lead-to-violence.html?action=click&pgtype=Homepage&clickSource=story-heading&module=opinion-c-col-right-region&region=opinion-c-col-right-region&WT.nav=opinion-c-col-right-region.

Harris, Gardiner. 2016. "Obama, in Mosque Visit Denounces Anti-Muslim Bias." *New York Times*, February 3. http://www.nytimes.com/2016/02/04/us/politics/obama-muslims-baltimore-mosque.html.

Holland, Steve. 2015. "At Christian University, Jeb Bush Seeks Support from Evangelicals." *Reuters*, May 9. http://www.reuters.com/article/us-usa-election-bush-idUSKBN0NU0L820150509.

Hume, David. 1757. *The Natural History of Religion* (1992), edited by James Fleser. New York: Macmillan.

Huntington, Samuel P. 2004. "The Hispanic Challenge." *Foreign Policy*, March/April 2004.

Huntington, Samuel P. 2005. *Who Are We? Challenges to America's National Identity*. New York: Simon & Schuster.

Jakobsen, Janet R. 2021. *The Sex Obsession: Perversity and Possibility in American Politics*. New York: New York University Press.

Jakobsen, Janet R., and Ann Pellegrini, eds. 2008. *Secularisms*. Durham, NC: Duke University Press.

Jayasinghe, Tiloma, and Erin Ward. 2018. "Responding to Violence, Restoring Justice." *New Feminist Solutions* 10. New York: Barnard Center for Research on Women. http://bcrw.barnard.edu/publications/responding-to-violence-restoring-justice/.

Kant, Immanuel. 1960. *Religion within the Limits of Reason Alone*. Translated by Theodore M. Greene and Hoyt H. Hudson. La Salle, IL: Open Court Publication.

Kauanui, J. Kehaulani. 2018. *Paradoxes of Hawaiian Sovereignty: Land, Sex, and the Colonial Politics of State Nationalism*. Durham, NC: Duke University Press.

Kruse, Kevin. 2015. *One Nation Under God: How Corporate America Invented Christian America*. New York: Basic Books.

Maher, Heather. 2009. "The End of the US War on Terror." *Radio Free Europe/Radio Liberty*, April 16. https://www.rferl.org/a/The_End_Of_The_US_War_On_Terror/1609936.html.

Mahmood, Saba. 2006. "Secularism, Hermeneutics, and Empire: The Politics of Islamic Reformation." *Public Culture* 18, no. 2: 323–47. https://doi.org/10.1215/08992363-2006-006.

Mandair, Arvind-Pal S., and Markus Dressler, eds. 2011. *Secularism and Religion-Making*. New York: Oxford University Press.

Margolis, Michele. 2018. *From Politics to the Pews: How Partisanship and the Political Environment Shape Religious Identity*. Chicago: University of Chicago Press.

McCammon, Sarah. 2019. "At UN Trump Administration Professes 'No International Right to an Abortion.'" *NPR*, September 23.

McCrisken, Trevor. 2011. "Ten Years On: Obama's War on Terrorism in Rhetoric and Practice." *International Affairs* 87, no. 4: 781–801. https://www.jstor.org/stable/20869759.

Moaveni, Azadeh, 2018, "How the Trump Administration Is Exploiting Iran's Burgeoning Feminist Movement." *New Yorker*, July 9. https://www.newyorker.com/news/news-desk/how-the-trump-administration-is-exploiting-irans-burgeoning-feminist-movement.

Naber, Nadine. 2012. *Arab America: Gender, Cultural Politics, and Activism*. New York: New York University Press.

Puar, Jasbir. 2007. *Terrorist Assemblages: Homonationalism in Queer Times*. Durham, NC: Duke University Press.

Ross, Alex. 2012. "Love on the March." *The New Yorker*, November 12, https://www.newyorker.com/magazine/2012/11/12/love-on-the-march?mbid=nl_Daily%20

062418&CNDID=22005605&spMailingID=13750639&spUserID=MTMzMTc5ODA5NzM3S0&spJobID=1422200749&spReportId=MTQyMjIwMD c0OQS2.

Rumi, Raza. 2015. "Islam Needs Reformation from Within." *Huffpost*, March 18. https://www.huffpost.com/entry/islam-needs-reformation-f_b_6484118.

Samantrai, Ranu. 2002. *AlterNatives: Black Feminism in the Postimperial Nation*. Stanford, CA: Stanford University Press.

Scott, David. 2004. *Conscripts of Modernity: The Tragedy of Colonial Enlightenment*. Durham, NC: Duke University Press.

Shipley, Heather. 2015. "Challenging Identity Constructs: The Debate over the Sex Education Curriculum in Ontario." In *Religion and Sexuality: Diversity and the Limits of Tolerance*, edited by Heather Shipley, Pamela Dickey Young, and Tracy J. Trothen, 97–118. Vancouver: University of British Columbia Press.

Simon, Ed. 2015. "ISIS Is the Islamic 'Reformation.'" *Religion Dispatches*, March 3. http://religiondispatches.org/isis-is-the-islamic-reformation/.

Sotomayor, Justice Sandra, with Justice Ruth Bader Ginsburg. 2018. Dissent in *Donald J. Trump, President of the United States, et al., Petitioners v. Hawaii, et al. On Writ of Certiorari to the United States Court of Appeals for the Ninth Circuit*. June 26. https://www.supremecourt.gov/opinions/17pdf/17-965_h315.pdf.

Sullivan, Andrew. 2001. "This *Is* a Religious War." *New York Times Magazine*, October 7.

Sullivan, Andrew. 2009. "The Tragedy of Hope." *The Atlantic*, December 11. https://www.theatlantic.com/daily-dish/archive/2009/12/the-tragedy-of-hope/193096/.

Sullivan, Andrew. 2018. "The Establishment Will Never Say No to a War." *New York Times Magazine*, December 21. https://nymag.com/intelligencer/2018/12/andrew-sullivan-establishment-will-never-say-no-to-a-war.html.

Sullivan, Winnifred. 2005. *The Impossibility of Religious Freedom*. Princeton, NJ: Princeton University Press.

Sweet, John W. 2003. *Bodies Politic: Negotiating Race in the American North, 1730–1830*. Baltimore, MD: Johns Hopkins University Press.

Whitehead, Andrew L., and Samuel L. Perry. 2020. *Taking America Back for God: Christian Nationalism in the United States*. New York: Oxford University Press.

The White House. 2001. "George W. Bush Remarks upon Arrival." September 16. http://georgewbush-whitehouse.archives.gov/news/releases/2001/09/20010916-2.html.

The White House. 2009. "Obama Announces Office of Faith-Based and Neighborhood Partnerships." February 5. www.whitehouse.gov.

The White House. 2017a. Executive Order Protecting the Nation from Foreign Terrorist Entry into the United States. March 6, https://www.whitehouse.gov/presidential-actions/executive-order-protecting-nation-foreign-terrorist-entry-united-states-2/.

The White House. 2017b. Presidential Proclamation Enhancing Vetting Capabilities and Processes for Detecting Attempted Entry into the United States by Terrorists or Other Public Safety Threats. September 24, https://www.whitehouse.gov/presidential-actions/presidential-proclamation-enhancing-vetting-capabilities-processes-detecting-attempted-entry-united-states-terrorists-public-safety-threats/. Accessed August 10, 2018.

Toosi, Nahal. 2017. "'Honor Killings' Highlighted under Trump's New Travel Ban." *Politico*, March 6. https://www.politico.com/story/2017/03/trump-travel-ban-killings-235731.

UN Women. 2014. "Expert Group Meeting: Envisioning Women's Rights in the post-2015 Context." New York: November 3–5.

Watt, David Harrington. 2017. *Antifundamentalism in Modern America*. Ithaca, NY: Cornell University Press.

Wenger, Tisa. 2009. *We Have a Religion: The 1920s Pueblo Indian Dance Controversy and American Religious Freedom*. Chapel Hill: University of North Carolina Press.

Wong, Edward. 2019. "US Expands Anti-Abortion Policies with New Overseas Funding Rules." *New York Times*, March 26. https://www.nytimes.com/2019/03/26/us/politics/state-department-abortion-funding.html.

Wong, Edward, and Eileen Sullivan. 2019. "New Human Rights Panel Raises Fears of a Narrowing of US Advocacy." *New York Times*, July 8. https://www.nytimes.com/2019/07/08/us/politics/state-human-rights.html.

Zubaida, Sami. 2016. "Islamic Reformation?" *The Global Dispatches*, January 6. http://www.theglobaldispatches.com/articles/islamic-reformation.

Zurcher, Anthony. 2017. "What Trump Team Has Said about Islam." *BBC News*, February 7. https://www.bbc.com/news/world-us-canada-38886496.

II STATES OF VIOLENCE, UNRULY SUBJECTS

FIVE · *Inderpal Grewal*

GBV and Postcolonial India

Transnational Media, Hindutva, and Muslim Racializations

When the Citizenship Amendment Act (CAA) was passed by the Indian Parliament and the BJP (Bharatiya Janata Party) government in December 2019, Muslim women began to protest in Shaheen Bagh in Delhi, in a predominantly Muslim area of the metropolis. The BJP, with Narendra Modi at the helm, had come to power in 2014, determined to create a Hindu state based on the right-wing nationalism (known as Hindutva) of the organization called the Rashtriya Swayamsevak Sangh (RSS). The RSS was founded almost a century ago and emerged as an anti-Gandhian and anti-Muslim movement to produce a militant and muscular Hinduism based on hierarchies of caste and religion (Jaffrelot 2010). The protesters at Shaheen Bagh brought their children families, and friends; they were joined by other young women and men, feminist activists, college and university students and professors, Dalit and Adivasi activists, and farmers groups and leaders; the protests also spread to other regions and cities of India. The BJP government sent its supporters to create disruptions to paint the protestors as antinational or violent, but they were unsuccessful, and in February 2020, Hindu activists carried out a pogrom in another Muslim neighborhood of Delhi, clearly as a warning to the protesters about what might happen to them. The pogrom killed sixty people and injured, displaced, and traumatized—and terrorized—many more. However, the protests at Shaheen Bagh continued until the pandemic rules and lockdown enabled the police to clear out the protest site.

The protests became memorable for the participation of older women from the community, the *nanis* and *dadis* (grandmothers on the maternal and paternal sides). They drew on slogans such as "Azadi," which translates as "freedom," and resonates powerfully because of its longer history during India's anticolonial movements, in the struggles against militarism in Kashmir, and for Dalit movements against casteism (Hussain 2018; Mehta 2006). Women chanted, "we will not show our papers" and "we are Indians," while singing the national anthem. In doing so, protestors claimed Indian nationalism and patriotism as belonging to them and asserted that citizenship documents were implicitly designed to denationalize and render people illegal, undercutting the claim of the BJP government and supporters that documents were meant simply to provide welfare or other benefits and that, according to colonial law, protests were seditious. Those gathered in Shaheen Bagh claimed their patriotism and rights to Indian citizenship by expanding the notion of freedom that referenced the military occupation of Kashmir, discrimination against Muslims in border zones, women's rights (led by Pinjra Tod—a movement to end curfews in women's hostels), youth rights, and Dalit rights to be free from violence by upper-caste Hindus. These protests raised questions about how people are being sorted into citizens and subjects and what and how citizenship is constructed through the exclusion of Muslims, new regimes of surveillance, and biometric identity cards (Sengupta 2020). The protests incorporated political speeches, lawyers explaining the new laws and what these might do to poor communities, and music, art, and poetry. The protests also centered on women's activism, despite the presence and voices of many male activists. The protests became hugely popular, with crowds of over one hundred thousand gathering for speeches, poetry, and songs.

Images and videos from the protest in Shaheen Bagh became visible on numerous online and print newspapers and on television all over the world, as well as on social media, including Twitter and Facebook pages run by protest organizers and supporters. These photographs and media representations offered a different image of Indian Muslim women than has been standard in Indian visual culture, showing their ability to speak and organize and revealing the support for their efforts, not just in India, but around the world (Kazim 2020). Protestors emphasized their opposition to the government's stance on gender, an opposition captured by poet Nabiya Khan reciting her poem about freedom for the protestors: that freedom would come "wearing a *bindi* (the dot on the forehead), *churiyan* (bangles and bracelets), *burqa*, and *hijab*" (Khan 2020). This was a movement in which women claimed national citizenship as a cause for women, but not just on behalf of women.

For many of the young women who participated, these protests were a forum in which they could reveal their rage about sexual assault and sexual violence in India alongside continued discrimination in education and employment. In this particular context of Shaheen Bagh, their presence, and those of many others, suggested solidarities across difference based on caste, religion, and gender that pushed back at the new citizenship laws. The protests targeted a new form of state-sponsored precarity, since the renewed implementation of a National Register of Citizens and National Population Register would have the power to question the citizenship of many and to render stateless not just Muslims but also poor women and men across India; the laws would subject them to intensified modes of governmental and bureaucratic power (Bhowmick 2020). The demand for people to produce new forms of documentation, biometric and otherwise, disproportionately affects the poor, especially migrants from rural areas and those low-income groups who do not have the wherewithal to verify births or residence (Lahiri 2021). These laws were blatantly Islamophobic in that they offered asylum in India to refugees from religious communities other than Muslims. The goal of the CAA implied that India's Muslims were aliens, although they have been part of the Indian subcontinent since shortly after Islam was founded, and comprise both the second largest religious group in the country and the second largest population of Muslims in any country (after Indonesia). What is happening in India is, however, not anomalous: denationalization has become a weapon that many governments around the world use to designate certain populations as noncitizens and to refuse their demands for rights or welfare (Pepi 2018).

These international and nonofficial media images of protest were different from the images produced by the Indian government that represented Muslim women as needing to be rescued from their (Muslim) men by Hindu men. The central government had recently made this argument by passing a law entitled, "The Muslim Women (Protection of Rights on Marriage) Bill" that criminalized "triple talaq" (instant divorce), contravening the Muslim Personal Laws that allowed the practice. The new law was ostensibly enacted to specifically help Muslim women, though there had been women's rights groups which had been seeking this goal for some time, because the practice has been outlawed in most Muslim-majority countries. However, given the publicized events showing Muslim women thanking the prime minister for saving them (Press Trust of India 2019b), it became clear that the strategy of the government was to show Modi and his government as saviors of Muslim women while dividing the Muslim community by gender (Sur 2018). Many civil society organizations also came to oppose the bill arguing that it was a sham in many ways, especially since there was nothing in it ensuring women's financial support and well-being (Bhowmick 2020; Scroll Staff 2019). The claims by Modi and his government that they were working for women's "empowerment" were used to bolster his credentials by claiming that he had Indian women's interests in mind: projects such as building toilets for women and providing gas cylinders for cooking had previously been publicized, with numerous posters featuring Modi's image displaying this support for women. However, as the Shaheen Bagh protest revealed, for many Muslim women, those changes in Muslim family law, or the provision of cooking gas cylinders and toilets, however useful, could not make up for other laws designed to deprive their entire communities of any rights—especially rights of citizenship and sovereignty.

The visibility of the Shaheen Bagh protests, because they were undertaken by nonelite and predominantly low-income women in alliance with other groups and because they continued for months, brought international scrutiny. They later led to the harassment and incarceration of activists by the Modi government on the pretext that they were worsening the COVID-19 pandemic (Venugopal 2020; Bhatnagar 2021). Given that slogans raised by Hindu Right activists exhorting violence and a pogrom against Muslims went unpunished, the charge of incitement was designed to harass and intimidate. The protests added to the international attention created earlier, when after a landslide reelection in 2019 that continued BJP rule at the center in New Delhi, Modi intensified the Hindutva agenda through the lockdown of Kashmir (curfews, no internet or other external communication, and military everywhere) before taking away its self-governing status (Mehta 2019; Ganguly 2019). The BJP government embarked on a neoliberal privatization of public goods; for instance, new laws allowing corporations to control food grain markets led to the farmers' protests, which began in October 2020 and continued into 2021. These protests brought further global scrutiny, with many diasporic activists and groups opposing the new policies.

The national and transnational media visibility that resulted from the Kashmir lockdown, the Shaheen Bagh protest, the pogrom in Delhi in February, and the farmers' protests became a public relations problem for the BJP government. The circulation of images of violence both within India and around the world, uploaded by national and global supporters of

Hindutva as evidence of their power, and a disparate opposition made up of people in India and its diaspora, as well as international media, led the government to actively work to counter the disastrous press coverage (Kumar and Lacy 2020). For a government deeply desiring both global recognition and diasporic support, such images of Shaheen Bagh and the pogrom were detrimental to the recognition of India as a powerful Hindutva state, since in the 2019 election campaign, Modi had promised to make India a global superpower. Even Gulf states that had close connections with the Indian government through the presence of migrant workers and trade began speaking up about the Islamophobia exhibited by BJP politicians and their supporters on social media, speculating that any remarks the prime minister made about national harmony were emerging only in response to international criticism (Pasha 2020).

One important consequence of this media coverage is that Hindutva violence as state violence has become part of a global narrative, countering to some extent the national media control by the BJP government, with its IT cells that trolled and harassed any opposition. BJP and Hindutva groups, while extremely powerful within India and across its diasporas, were not wholly able to control the narrative, especially when media organizations such as *Time*, the BBC, and Radio Deutchevelle lauded one of the grandmothers of Shaheen Bagh, Bilquis, as an important activist; *Time* called her one of the one hundred most influential people in 2020. The art and music and the crowds at Shaheen Bagh were widely covered by international media interested in attracting readers, a heterogenous online public sphere made up of Indians, Muslims around the world, and India's diasporas, international observers and press, and researchers and journalists including feminist activists. The advent of such a burgeoning media ecosystem, one that every protest also actively used (through Facebook pages and Twitter handles), meant that images of protest and of violence circulated widely, revealing both the heavy hand of the state and the resistance to it. Such images resonate both with the globalized Hindutva movement that draws supporters transnationally and with detractors within India and outside it. All of these groups vie with each other to make sense of the many images of violence and protest coming out of India—images that constitute the ongoing process of producing subjects and citizens. This is the struggle over meaning, one that, as Stuart Hall famously theorized, constitutes a key modality of power within culture; it is this "battlefield," as Hall called it, in which right-wing Hindutva power, the media industries that hope to reach transnational audiences, and the multiple and contending desires of heterogenous audiences all struggle to narrate and define images and events (Hall 1989). Visuality is critical for such a struggle.

In the remainder of this chapter, I focus on two key moments when the struggle over visual representation of Muslims in postcolonial India became part of this "battlefield" within popular and media culture: first, in the 2002 pogrom in Gujarat, and second, in the many instances of violence against Muslim men and boys since the BJP came to power and which have circulated in transnational print and digital news media. In analyzing the latter images that accompany accounts of "pogroms" and "lynchings" as these events are termed by researchers and journalists, I suggest that what becomes visible is a transnational racialization of Muslims; such a racialization is used by Hindutva supporters as well as by its opponents. Scholars such as Muneer Ahmad and Sherene Razack have suggested that after 9/11 and the advent of the Global War on Terror (GWOT), Muslims became a racial group in the United States (Ahmad 2002); Razack argues that the GWOT has racialized Muslims globally (Razack 2022). I argue that a longer historical framework can shed light on the particularity of this racialization in the Indian context. This means that such a racialization began much earlier with the British colonial state's construction of religious identities and "communal" divisions, and the postcolonial state continued this process by its communal identity and caste projects, with the US-sponsored GWOT adding a new layer of racialized "security" logics in the new century. I end the chapter by returning to why the Shaheen Bagh women mobilized for their community and not just for women, suggesting both where the politics of gender-based violence (GBV), another term in transnational circulation, helped to highlight the violence of the state and the powerful nationalisms that it engenders, and where it is limited in its ability to address the longer history of discrimination and inequality of Muslims in India.

THE VIOLENCE OF THE POSTCOLONIAL STATE AND GUJARAT 2002

State violence is not a new phenomenon in modern India. It would be difficult to argue that the violence we see today is wholly caused by the BJP or by Hindutva nationalism, since that would not account for other major events of violence of the postcolonial nation, nor for the caste-based violence against Dalits or for the dominant anti-Muslimness of many Indians. Under the Congress Party, to which the first prime minister of India,

Jawaharlal Nehru, as well as his daughter, Indira Gandhi, belonged, there were other events of horrific violence committed on particular communities such as the Nellie massacre in Assam in 1983, in which over two thousand Muslims were killed by Assamese groups; the Sikh pogrom of 1984 carried out by Hindu supporters of the Congress Party; and the violence around the Babri Masjid demolition in Ayodhya. The 2002 pogrom against Muslims took place in Gujarat when Narendra Modi, a BJP politician, was the chief minister of that state during the BJP's second time in power from 1998 to 2004. All of these "events" (Badiou 2006) that ruptured the façade of postcolonial secularism and modernity included what have been called "atrocities," a term used in a 1989 law defining violence against those called Scheduled Castes and Tribes and the "communal" violence often termed "riots" in the Indian press. However, each has included horrendous acts of sexual violence against women, as well as the displacement, traumatizing, and terrorizing of thousands of people. It is telling that for many Dalits and Indigenous communities, the Indian independence did not offer freedom from servitude or from dispossession of lands or livelihoods.

In recent decades, the term "pogrom" has come to be used by researchers as well as by transnational media for events such as the killings of Sikhs in Delhi and other parts of India in 1984 and for the killings of Muslims in Gujarat (Ahmad 2020). The political scientist Paul Brass argues that what took place in 2002 in Gujarat was not, as the common phrase had it, a "riot"—which has been the most frequent term used in the Indian media—but more properly a "pogrom," because it fit the definition of the term: a pogrom could be defined as an attack on a community that has the implicit sanction of authorities and in which the attackers have impunity. The notion of "riot," he argues, does not account for the political calculations that produce and move the violence and the way that attackers are supported and enabled by the party in power (Brass 2003). Though Brass proposes that the Delhi killings of Sikhs in 1984 was not a pogrom, because it was not state-sanctioned and the perpetrators did not have impunity, it was well known that Congress Party cadres had committed the horrendous violence and the Congress Party tried to cover up its responsibility.[1] There have been many incidents which have been called "communal riots," "atrocities," or "mob violence" in the past that might also be termed "pogroms." The problem is that Brass's definition of pogrom, based on who can or cannot be held responsible, does not get at the broader contexts of intolerance and racialization (such as the ideology of Hindutva that underlies the BJP, or the intransigent casteism in India, or the representations of Sikhs and Muslims as "terrorists" threatening the state) that pervades social life or how the violence is instrumentalized for political gain by the different regimes in power. Scholars such as Ahmad (2020) and Ghassem-Fachandi (2012) have suggested that the term references the anti-Muslim political and ideological conditions that pervade communities. The role of the state in producing such conditions is inescapable.

In India, the visual culture of what has been called "communal violence" has a colonial history that constructed violence as caused by religious animosities *between* Muslims, Hindus, and Sikhs (often erasing the violence of caste Hindus on Dalit and Adivasi communities), enabling what Ahmad (2020) calls a "ditto" theory that two communities, Muslim and Hindu, were and remain equally responsible for the violence. This notion of "communalism" has come to explain, quite reductively, the violence that carried over to Partition and its history, exculpating the colonial state's responsibility (Pandey 2006). As scholars have shown, religious reform movements in colonial India constructed communities as bounded religious identities, replacing the plural, shifting and multiple practices of a heterogenous realm of activity loosely defined as religion (Mandair 2009), with a textualist and bounded identity of ritual and practice (Doniger 2010; Malhotra and Mir 2012; Chatterjee 2013; Oberoi 1994).

Photographs of the violence of Partition by Margaret Bourke-White for *Life* magazine and Sunil Janah for the Communist party newspaper, *Indian Age* were important for this visual history of what was called "communalism," and these photographs continue to be used as dominant representations of the Partition. The postcolonial state's control over television and radio continued the language of "riots" and "communal violence" while presenting itself, especially under Nehru, as aligned with the state ideology of the secular-modern. State ownership of television and radio allowed print media to remain somewhat free of state control, albeit still in the hands of upper castes, though media coverage could be controlled by the government through control of paper and its heavy advertisement that supported newspapers.

That representational practice of the secular-modern postcolonial in visual culture changed with television and digital media, cable channels, corporate and transnational ownership, and above all, the changing politics of the Indian state. The advent of neoliberalism in the 1980s, seen as "liberalization" from a socialist Nehruvian past, opened up television and radio to private companies and individuals, including some international ones; CNN entered the Indian television market in 1991, inaugurating national and transnational corporate media (Rajagopal 2001). The first live television coverage of what came to be called a pogrom was broadcast in 2002, with the attack on a Muslim community in Gujarat. If, before the advent of corporate and multiple television channels, images of the 1984 pogrom on Sikhs in New Delhi (and elsewhere in the country) were sparse as the horrific events unfolded, covered only by those few journalists, photographers, and activists who were able to rush to the scene and blocked out by the government control of television, the 2002 pogrom of Muslims in Gujarat played out on television sets around the nation and the world.

Saifuddin Ahmed (2010) points out that the difference in media coverage was due to the advent of multiple television channels, owned by a variety of corporations, both national and transnational. The absence of state control enabled extensive coverage of the event and enraged the Modi-led BJP government in Gujarat as well as the central government, both of which were controlled by the BJP. The live cable television news on private channels such as Star TV, Aaj Tak, and Zee News carried extensive coverage, often naming the religious identities of both attackers and victims, despite guidelines formulated by the government entity, the Press Trust of India, not to do so. Government officials in Gujarat, with Modi as leader, asked cable operators not to carry these channels, and some obeyed, showing blank screens in the areas where the violence was the worst (Ahmed 2010). Because some media outlets refused this demand, the Gujarat government accused them of exaggerating and adding to what was being called "mob violence" or "riots" or "communal passions"; some were termed a "Marxist-Mullah combine" for criticizing the BJP and Hindutva attackers. While local Gujarati-language media supporting the Hindutva cadres and justifying the killings led every segment of news by claims that Muslims had been behind an earlier attack on Hindus on a train in Godhra, national television stations sensationalized the violence, and national and English-language dailies condemned the violence (Ahmed 2010). The demand for the blank screen, then, reveals the blindness that the state wishes for its population; we should not be able to look or witness—indeed, we should be denied the right to look (Mirzoeff 2011).[2]

Nalin Mehta argues that though the coverage was sympathetic to the victims, the BJP was able to turn the narrative into one sympathetic to them by claiming that national media was against a Hindu Gujarati identity and community (Mehta 2006). But it was also the ideological context that the anthropologist, Parvis Ghassem-Fachandi, found most disturbing in his ethnography of the pogrom (2012). He calls this context "the psychological

Gleichschaltung (coordination) of 'ordinary' Gujaratis," many of whom he knew well as his informants. Ghassem-Fachandi understood the violence as a sacrifice, enabled also by the context of global antiterrorism that became available for right-wing Hindutva forces to use after 9/11, and subtended by middle-class refusals to address the hierarchies and inequalities that comprise Indian society and that are easily mobilized by political actors. In his documentary on the pogrom, *Final Solution* (2004), Rakesh Sharma captures this easy and ordinary context of hatred and bigotry as he documents the sentiments of perpetrators and victims, and identifies the state as the instigator of the pogrom (Sharma 2004).[3]

Analysis of the pogrom revealed the role of the state, which used disinformation and rumor to encourage violence. The police and bureaucrats shared the state ideology so that there was an anti-Muslim consensus across institutions, fragmenting cohabitation and collectivity. Ghassem-Fachandi points out that those disagreeing with the consensus were attacked and lost their positions or even their lives (2012, 278). A national consensus of othering also underlay the pogrom against the Sikhs in 1984, as large sectors of the Indian public came to see Sikhs as essentially terroristic and threatening to the Indian/Hindu nation. Yet what Ghassem-Fachandi points out is that these practices of othering also include gender, accounting for the horrific sexual and brutal violence done by "ordinary" Gujaratis to Muslim women and that emerged in evidence and testimonies of survivors. The violence on Muslim men and women was a project meant to render the entire community as subservient and disempowered, and it has led to Muslim communities living segregated in poorer enclaves. Attacks on pregnant women and on children, including the gang rapes of women, underlined the racialization implicit in the pogrom, evidenced in the almost genocidal fury evinced by the attackers.

There are some videos of the Gujarat pogrom available on YouTube, uploaded by NGOs working for justice for the victims. The pogrom, including the gruesome murder of Ehsan Jafri, a Muslim politician from the Congress Party, has remained in the public memory because legal cases continue, years and decades later; obtaining justice is extremely difficult because the state protects the perpetrators. However, a photograph taken by a photojournalist that became the iconic image of the pogrom was of Qutubuddin Ansari, taken by the photographer Arko Dutta, who worked for Reuters (figure 5.1). Showing Ansari, tearful and terrified, with his hands folded, begging the police to protect him, the image revealed Ansari as a helpless victim begging to be saved, revealing desperation, fear, and abjection. Dutta had taken a ride with the Rapid Action Force, belatedly deployed to stop the violence (though Hindutva groups had already killed more than 1,000 Muslims by that time), and he found Ansari in his camera lens as the police positioned themselves around him.

Arvind Rajagopal (2001) argues that images of violence reveal the visual culture of humiliation on the other. Such a humiliation does describe the image, since the photograph of Ansari is, as Soutik Biswas, the Delhi correspondent of the BBC, points out, a "disturbing study of fear and helplessness" (2012). It is this very combination of affect that made this image so iconic and so mobile. The image circulated across political divides representing the power of Hindutva politics and the Gujarati state over Muslims as well as allowing transnational media such as the BBC to show the disempowerment and subordination of the Muslim victims (and the violence of the Indian postcolonial state). Images of humiliation are also ubiquitous in India, central to the affective politics of caste in India, as upper castes, according to Gopal Guru (2009), have imposed on Dalits the racial humiliations that they themselves experienced at the hands of the British. Yet it was not just humiliation that came about for Ansari but also accompanying material and emerging economic and social impacts of targeting Muslims as "terrorists," a state project that combined Indian politics and American imperial geopolitics. In the context of India, while it was previously Assamese groups, Maoist guerillas, Tamil groups in Sri Lanka, Sikhs, and Kashmiri Muslims who had been seen as national threat, all Muslims were emerging as the threat to the Hindu nation. Ansari remained a threat rather than a victim.

The history of the photograph and its global dissemination as iconic reveal the power of this image to hurt rather than help Ansari and show that such images may not benefit the victims of violence or even provide any form of testimony or belonging. Being a witness can result in being targeted, and in this case, the image of Ansari's humiliation replaced and removed his ability to be a witness to the violence from which he fled or to be a threat as Hindutva representations would assert. Ansari left Gujarat after the pogrom in order to find a job and restart his life, but everywhere he went, he would be identified and fired from his job because of the photograph. He was blamed for bomb attacks and used by politicians for getting votes from Muslims. Though he also received some positive attention, his fame had negative effects since the photograph that captures the moment of his abjection was of little help in providing him with a job or a future (Khan 2019).[4]

The photograph of Ansari as the abject Muslim male, with its circulation in the media, was not an image that allowed him to become a victim. Rather it put him under suspicion of being a terrorist. Ansari's helplessness and position as victim could not ensure he would not be seen as a threat, even as his very Indianness was considered suspect.[5] While Arko Dutta, the photographer, came to believe the image evoked empathy, his subject lived in fear of being recognized. Consequently, in what has become the hallmark of the Indian state's Hindu nationalist violence, it is the victims who live in fear of being recognized while the perpetrators consider themselves sovereign subjects of the Hindu security state.

In the aftermath of the pogrom, activists and victims have been harassed in order to undermine both their credibility and their ability to act as witnesses, despite the number of images of the horrific events. The state protected the perpetrators of the violence; as sovereign Hindu subjects, they had impunity. In the Best Bakery case, in which fourteen people were killed during the pogrom, all of the accused were first acquitted by the Gujarat High court, though later the Indian Supreme Court sentenced four of the accused to life in prison. The complexities of the case and witness tampering became legendary, with immense pressure and coercion on one witness, a nineteen-year-old young woman named Zaheera Sheikh, who saw some of her family murdered in the pogrom (Kumar 2016). Amnesty International reported that police did shoddy work collecting evidence, provided garbled testimony in the courts, and threatened witnesses so that the case had to be transferred out of Gujarat (Amnesty International 2005).

The image of Zaheera Sheikh (figure 5.2) in a burqa heading to the court, protected by a bodyguard with a powerful weapon, serves as a witness—not to the event of the pogrom or even the spectacle of violence but to the difficulty of witnessing and to state violence; governments and politicians exert power on the bodies of activists and witnesses to provide impunity to perpetrators. Sheikh, who was nineteen years old, was threatened, intimidated, bribed, and turned into a hostile witness. She became associated with problems of witness intimidation and the plight of a poor, young woman who had to testify to the crimes of powerful politicians. Rather than being a witness, she came to be associated with the difficulty of being a witness, as this photograph reveals. Bilquis Yakub Rasool, raped by multiple men and left for dead, was another victim of the pogrom, whose search for justice ended only in 2017, fifteen years after the event, when life sentences were given to eleven of the men involved in the attack. That case was also marked by police both refusing to investigate and tampering with evidence

FIGURE 5.1 Qutubuddin Ansari, photo by Arko Dutta.

(*Deccan Chronicle* 2017). The tenacity of women such as Rasool and that of numerous activists who worked on both the Best Bakery and Rasool cases is remarkable, especially given that they were opposing the power of BJP, which is now the ruling party in India.

"LYNCHINGS" AND THE VISUAL CULTURE OF HINDUTVA SOVEREIGNTY

In contemporary India, the emergence of a terminology of "lynchings" of Muslim men has most often been seen in the context of "cow-protection," where a Muslim is believed to have killed a cow, an illegal act in many states

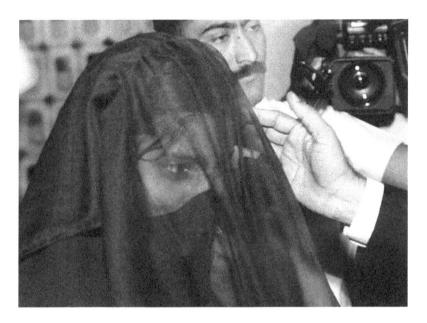

FIGURE 5.2 Zaheera Sheikh heading to the court to testify, July 9, 2012. As Zia (2019) notes, Hindutva violence—and also a longer history of state violence in Kashmir, for instance—has long included gendered violence in imposing state power.

of the country.[6] The veneration of the cow as sacred and the taboo against eating beef came about during the Hindu and Sikh religious reform movements of the late nineteenth century. "Cow-protection societies" and sporadic violence associated with them have existed throughout the twentieth century (Van der Veer 1994), but under the BJP, trading in beef or leather became criminalized in some states. It is not just Muslims who have been killed because they were accused of cow slaughter, but also Dalits—and these are groups who work in the leather industry because that is the occupation that discriminations based on caste have permitted to them. Because Dalits are also targeted, these discussions of so-called communal violence also have to include the intransigent history of caste violence in India; Anand Teltumbde (2018) points out that atrocities are carried out with impunity against Dalits and Adivasis every day, and only become news when they are particularly spectacular or when by chance they come to the notice of activists or NGOs. Furthermore, "communal violence" leaves out the fact that in recent decades, much of the violence has been committed by Hindu cadres against Muslims, Sikhs, and Christians (Ahmad 2020). Both the Congress Party (when it held power) and BJP have encouraged religious conflict against religious minority communities for electoral gain.

Under the Modi government, the notion of cow protection was taken up as a platform for Hindutva nationalism. Along with laws forbidding cow slaughter in most Indian states, there emerged vigilante violence, often state-sanctioned, in the name of cow protection. Since Muslims and Dalits are involved in the beef and leather industries, they are most impacted by these new laws and the impunity given by the Hindutva state to violence in its name. The BJP coined the term "love jihad" to vilify any romantic relationship with Muslims; as with Jim Crow America, Muslim men have been lynched for being with non-Muslim women. Lynchings are a demonstration of the power of the state not only on matters of life or death but also on the economic life of the community—a community that has suffered discrimination and inequality for decades. In 2006, the Sachar Committee, appointed by a Sikh prime minister, Manmohan Singh, belonging to the Congress Party, reported on the extent of deprivations and discriminations suffered by Muslims in India, revealing their reduced rights of mobility, employment, education, and habitation (Sachar Committee Report 2006), which made them even more impoverished and disenfranchised than Dalits. There has been little improvement since then (Kim 2019; Hasan 2010).

Lynchings became daily news once Modi came to power as prime minister. Junaid Khan, Mohammad Akhlaq, Zafar Hussein, Mohammed Ayub Pandith, Pehlu Khan, Mohammad Mjloom, Inayatulla Khan, Alwar Khan, Azmat Khan: this is but a partial list of the Muslim men and boys who have been lynched by so-called mobs, since Prime Minister Modi and his party, the right-wing Hindu BJP, came to power in 2014 (StoriesAsia 2018). There might also be other killings not covered by the news media. As Aijaz Ahmad reports, the Indian parliament heard that almost a hundred Muslims had been killed in 751 attacks in 2016, and over a hundred killed in 822 attacks in 2017 (Ahmad 2020). As these are official numbers, no doubt the actual number of such incidents is much larger. What are being called "lynchings" in the national and transnational media reveal the complex politics of Hindutva violence that relies on new laws built on religion and caste, but they also signal a transnational recognition that this state violence is a deliberate and racialized targeting of the Muslim community (Citizens Against Hate 2017). The national and transnational media enable circulation of these images because there are multiple audiences for such violence, from those supportive of it to those opposed to it.

Unlike a pogrom, lynching is associated, particularly in the history of Jim Crow violence in the United States, with violence against an individual or a few individuals rather than an entire community, even as the acts are designed to terrorize a group. A lynching disaggregates violence by intensifying its impact on one person who comes to represent the community, as a lone person going about their daily activities becomes the target of a powerful group who feel themselves empowered by the state to use violence. Lynchings have taken place, for the most part, in those states in India where the BJP is the ruling government and where there are no consequences for the violence. The images of lynchings are circulated across cell phones via WhatsApp, Youtube, Instagram, and Twitter, and these recorded images further enact traumatic violence on viewers. Such images circulate a threat against the Muslim community and serve as records of the violence of the Hindu right. The narratives and visual coverage of lynchings enable terror by the Hindutva security state and circulate the visual spectacle of violence across the population, while producing the victims either as nonsovereign citizens or as threats to the citizenry. Banerjee (2012) argues that in drawing on the "muscular" male tradition of Hindu nationalism, Hindu nationalism attacks Muslim men using spectacular violence to provide evidence of its power.

The visual culture of this violence is quite different from the communal-liberal vision of the early decades of independent India because it places Muslims not within a notion of "communal" violence between two Indian communities but also by racializing them as aliens and threats to the Indian state (Anand 2005). For instance, Amit Shah, BJP's home minister, has called Muslims "termites" and "illegal immigrants"—the latter a term also being used globally in Europe and the United States for immigrants from both Asia and Africa (Press Trust of India 2019a). Muslims have been referred to as Pakistanis and are often told to leave their country. This is the project that the Citizenship Amendment Law sanctifies in law, and which created the protests in Shaheen Bagh. The lynchings reveal that it is not simply a matter of a religious difference, but a racial distinction that is enabled by new laws that target Muslims when violence against all Muslims goes unpunished (Sagar 2018).

That the young are as much in danger of lynching as adults also indicates a broader project of racialization that is targeting the future of the community. This is evidenced in the killing of Junaid Khan. On June 23, 2017, sixteen-year-old Junaid Khan was murdered, as numerous media stories reported, in a train in the state of Haryana as he was returning home from Delhi with his brothers after going shopping for Eid (*Deccan Chronicle* 2017). A national newspaper, *The Hindu*, reported that he was called a "beef eater" and "anti-national," following an argument over seats on the train (Faridabad 2017). A group of men pulled out knives and stabbed him. His brothers desperately pulled on the emergency chain to stop the train and called for help, but to no avail. The crowd threw Junaid's body and his brothers out of the train at the next station.

The photograph of Junaid's lynched body on the NDTV online website (NDTV is one media company that resisted the BJP for several years) and the *Deccan Herald* website (figure 5.3) was circulated widely, picked up by numerous media outlets online and in print. In this image, Junaid and one of his brothers are at the station where they were thrown off the train; again, they had called repeatedly for the police, but no one came to help. One of Junaid's arms is swathed in clothes or bandages, suggesting that perhaps his brother had tried to staunch the wound. We see the feet and legs of watchers—mostly men, in worn-out sandals—surrounding them. There is one pair of legs in jeans, while another man seems to be dressed in what might be a police uniform. Junaid's body is on the floor of the station, and there is no doctor, no ambulance, no medical assistance visible. Other feet and legs visible in the image seem to belong to young men. These are not wealthy people on the platform. Junaid and his brother appear destitute in the way that they remain on the bloody floor of the platform. The photograph shows the loneliness of Junaid and his brother, one dead, the other holding him, his arm flung out in despair, hunched over. The photograph makes visible their abjection.

The photograph is cropped on the sides as if to blur the faces of others who might have been there and as if the photographer has chosen not to show any others surrounding the two victims. It is possible the image came from a bystander, as so many media images seem to be, since there is no attribution to any named staff photographer or news agency. One pair of legs seems to belong to a policeman, though we do not see his face and he cannot be identified via the photograph. The crowd responsible for the lynching has disappeared; the train has departed from the station, taking the crowd away. Police, news reports relate days later, apprehended five men, some in their twenties and one in his fifties. No doubt there are video cameras in the train or cell phones that recorded the lynching, but this scene seems quiet and still, and it is a photograph rather than a video. The image, from the NDTV website, is in black and white, hiding the blood that is visible in the color version of this photograph that I found on other websites. Perhaps it was culled from a black-and-white newsprint version.

Unlike in so many historic and contemporary photographs of lynchings, the victim is not alone. He is held by his brother, whose arms are spread out

FIGURE 5.3 From the website of NDTV, July 8, 2017 (Biswas 2017).

in a gesture of helplessness, as if there is nothing he can do, but they are together. They are surrounded by people who may not have been indifferent to the violence, and the photograph is thus testimony to the complex meanings that reveal the struggles in India against Hindutva populism. On the one hand, the photograph does reveal Junaid's youth—his face is childlike, and his brother's gesture manifests a stark togetherness that captures pain. On the other hand, this is also an image of abjection—not humiliation as was Ansari's image, but of loss of both life and the power of a state that does little to help. Some bystanders and witnesses might have been Muslims unable to stop the violence, but the image does not mention the names of the others in the image—it is not unusual that bystanders hesitate to be identified lest they become witnesses.

Despite the large number of images and videos of violence against Muslims in India that are being uploaded and sent to the media outlets that solicit them, it is difficult to argue that these have changed the anti-Muslim ideology that enabled Modi to come to power. This may be because photographs of lynching can also hide as much as they reveal, and they can misdirect and prevent witnessing. This next image, from 2015 (figure 5.4), reveals a crowd—what we see is the media script of the nameless, faceless "mob" represented as responsible for the violence; here blame is deflected away from the state that enables the violence. Syed Sarifuddin Khan was in jail, accused of rape, but a crowd took him out of jail and lynched him, accus-

FIGURE 5.4 Hundreds of people dragged a Bengali man, Syed Sarifuddin Khan, through the streets of Dimapur, Nahaland, in 2015 before killing him. Photo: Reuters.

ing him also of being an illegal immigrant from Bangladesh (Faleiro 2015). He was later confirmed to be an Indian citizen from the neighboring state of Assam and in a consensual relationship, and the accusation of assault was later determined to be unfounded. The violence occurred in the northeastern region of India, which has a long history of insurgency of Indigenous groups against the Indian state; some of the groups seek an independent ethnic state. More recently, these groups, only some of which are allied to the BJP, have begun to accuse Muslims of being migrants from neighboring Bangladesh. The central BJP government uses biometric identification and citizenship laws to generate suspicion that all Muslims in the region are migrants and thus to be expelled from citizenship unless they can provide evidence that they have lived in the region since 1971, when Bangladesh was founded (Raj and Gettleman 2019).

The crowd is the focus of the image, their arms held high as they take photographs of the lynching with their cell phones. The news agency Reuters is credited with the photograph, though there seems no attribution to any photojournalist. The photograph does not show the lynched body. The image suggests the victim could not escape; there are so many people in the frame that even they could not move. The photograph is a souvenir, not of the violence, but rather of the spectacle and the spectators who are in the foreground with cellphones recording and circulating the images of the lynching. The photograph suggests that the lynching is the work of a faceless, nameless "mob," a designation that has long been used to remove culpability from particular individuals or groups for the crime, but which also signals the ideological context that enables the violence even as it hides the enabling structures of state criminality that provide impunity.

I bring these two contrasting photographs of "lynchings" together to direct attention to both the audiences and the perpetrators of the lynching as well as to the circulation of the lynching images, which were captured digitally and thus easily transmitted by the same reputable media outlets that recorded the killings. Despite supporting the dominant cultural script, the images reveal a struggle over meaning, referencing the visual history of lynching in the United States in which Jim Crow racism was evident both from what was in the photographic frame and what was absent from it (Goldsby 2006). In the photograph of the killing of Junaid Khan, we do not see the train that has departed, but we see the station floor, the police, and the watchers—young men in jeans or in worn sandals. The train and the station are not visible but are important as property of the government, and it was in one of the spaces of the state that the lynching of this young Muslim took place. Postcolonial Indian history is full of incidents of violence on trains; the Partition violence involved the killing of people on trains as they tried to move across a border that had suddenly come into existence (Sarna 2015). Violence on the train suggests both this Partition violence and the struggle over mobility and sovereignty. The victimization of the Muslim male body is on display, as is the presence of audiences consuming and condoning the murder that takes place, and also the state that provides the space and the place of violence and thus its complicity.

The racial logics of the violence of a patriarchal state are also gendered, and the violence of the state continues to construct gender; in the case of Syed Sarifuddin Khan, the male Muslim body is lynched under the guise of "protection" of Hindu women from what is represented as a rapacious and oversexed Muslim man. The Modi government has enabled a context of political violence against Muslims and impunity for the perpetrators so that violent actions and events can be viewed and circulated by people struggling over who can be a citizen and who is a threat (Das 1998). In those cases where rumors are believed to have incited these lynchings, the government tries to blame technology for the violence rather than the political and social context of Hindu right-wing nationalism in which violence is incited (Das 1998) and the ways that Muslims have become racialized both within India and transnationally.

What enables the violence and what the use of the term "lynching" references is the presence of the state and its racial project, where police and other security forces repress dissent and protest and witnessing. Often the state constructs itself as a bystander, a belated but hidden presence, but one which allows vigilante groups to assault communities. In the Delhi assault on Sikhs in 1984 by Congress Party cadres, police were absent from the scene; in Gujarat in 2002, the police became bystanders who only intervened when the television coverage created outrage. One Human Rights Watch (HRW) report mentions that calls to police in Gujarat were ignored and callers said that the police had no orders to save them (HRW 2002). Police may arrive late to the scene of violence or even stand by while it happens. An environment of impunity is thus created by direct repression and violence by this evasion of responsibility, by harassment of witnesses and dissenters through threats of violence, by foot-dragging related investigations and court cases, or by mismanaged or destroyed evidence.

Yet police in both the colonial and postcolonial state have been more than bystanders. In 2019, Human Rights Watch reported that in the eleven attacks on Muslims it examined that year, "the police initially stalled investigations, ignored procedures, or even played a complicit role in the killings and cover-up of crimes" (HRW 2019). Attacks on and killings of Sikhs and Sikh human rights activists from the 1980s, 1990s, and 2002 are yet unresolved, and the perpetrators have not brought to justice. As with so many legal quagmires created to prevent those responsible from being brought to justice, perpetrators know that they are protected. For instance, a sting operation by the NDTV channel found one of the suspects of the lynching of Qasim Qureshi in Rajasthan when he boasted of the killing in an undercover interview (Shukla 2018).

Prime Minister Modi spoke out against the lynching of Junaid Khan on June 29, 2017, a week after the teenager was killed (Doshi 2017). In his statement, Modi asked people not to take the law into their own hands and to practice nonviolence, while relating a sentimental story from his childhood about watching a cow crying after trampling a child. He tacitly showed his sympathy with the cow-protection groups and with the right-wing Hindu nationalists, while calling for an end to vigilantism. Given this mixed message, it was not surprising when a day later another lynching took place in the BJP-controlled state of Jharkhand, and another Muslim man, Mohammed Alliumuddin, was killed by a mob on suspicion that he was carrying beef in his van.

GBV: ITS USES AND LIMITS

Gendered violence under the BJP erupted into visibility during the Gujarat pogrom in 2002, with its horrifying violence against male and female Muslim bodies. It has continued with the lynchings of Muslim men that have taken place since BJP came to national power. Attention to gender has been critical in generating global attention toward India, building upon the work done by Indian feminists and human rights and civil rights activists to address the many sexual assaults that take place, especially by upper-caste men on Dalit women and girls. Sexual violence is part of the history of India, from the hysterical rhetoric of protection of white Englishwomen from Indian men during the 1857 revolution against colonial rule (Sharpe 1993), to the violence during Partition which colonial rule did very little to prevent (Butalia 2000). As with other nationalisms, Hindu nationalist violence under Modi uses the rape and protection of women to recruit followers by representing the Muslim as a threat to Hindu women, and for attacking other men. It also uses economic and physical violence, and it does so by providing laws that give impunity to the perpetrators of the violence.

Amrita Basu (2000) has argued that sexual violence appears to get more attention than other issues within feminist movements globally. One consequence is that economic or political violence seems not to receive the same attention by feminists. There is no doubt that sexual violence against women by the state has been an important focus for activists seeking accountability, especially that committed by the Indian military in border areas or in Indigenous communities (Bora 2010). Kashmiri feminist activists have publicized sexual violence by the Indian military to highlight their oppression by the Indian state (Misri 2014; Zia 2019). The horrendous gang rape and murder in 2018 of eight-year-old Asifa Bano, a member of the nomadic Muslim Bakarwal community, showed the immunity of Hindu men, especially the four men, comprising three police officers and a government official who were responsible. Subsequently two BJP politicians attended a rally in support of the perpetrators. Reports about sexual assaults and sexual violence have now become commonplace in the news, especially in India, though many such crimes may still go unmentioned. Their complex commodification takes place because of corporate control of media, which will air such news in the most sensational way possible, even as there is often little accountability for the perpetrators, given the militant and patriarchal nationalism that has emerged in the Hindu right. Yet sexual violence remains a cultural battlefield; feminist movements in India continue to bring attention to its ubiquity, especially as it is used against Dalit and poor women. In the 2012 rape case in Delhi that created national protests and international attention, these events of spectacular violence on women came to include what Srila Roy (2021) calls "multiscalar transnational and divergent publics that expanded notions of gendered subjectivity to include caste and religion."

Such transnational publics are also the consumers of the violence of right-wing Hindu nationalism on the Muslim community in India. I have argued in this essay that the use of terminologies such as pogroms and lynchings to refer to violence against Indian Muslims makes visible transnationally the racialization that targets men and women in particular ways. The visual culture of India reveals the ideology of the patriarchal Indian state and its racialization of Muslims as gendered perpetrators or victims, as national or international security threats, and as aliens in the very land they have lived in for centuries. Patriarchal violence, one that feminists have long analyzed and protested, also inflicts violence on men.

Though much of the research on GBV has since moved away from a single-minded focus on violence against women, women continue to be perceived as its main victims, even as resistance to this limited use has emerged. R. Charli Carpenter (2006), for example, advocates for a new term, "gender-based violence against men," that would include "sexual violence, forced conscription, and sex-selective massacre" as GBV. The emergence of the expanded terminology of sexual and gender-based violence as documented by Davies and True (2015) tries to account for structural inequalities as the source of violence and to expand the victims of violence to sexual minorities. There is some attention to rape of men, especially in conflict and war contexts. Despite these interventions, the term "gender-based violence" has, over the last couple of decades, been deployed mostly to bring attention to violence on women, especially in the contexts of war, reveals a history of imperial logics and policy-making (Engle 2020; introduction, this volume). Humanitarian empire mobilizes affect and sentiment around GBV to create consent to war and militarism (Grewal 2017).

Any use of terms such as GBV must also refer to the particular ways that states construct gender through patriarchy and its masculinities. Patriarchal states use economic violence to target men in their traditional roles as wage earners within the family, while also disallowing any other forms of masculinity. In the context of India, attention to colonial and postcolonial constructions of gender through religion, caste, and class remain important. The existence of religious personal laws in India means that religious patriarchy governs gendered identity and gendering practices. The importance of personal laws governed by religion also implies that Indians do not identify solely as women or men; they identify as Hindu women, or Muslim women, or Sikh women. Marriage, divorce, inheritance, maintenance, custody of children—all these are governed by laws through which people's lives are gendered through religion, and their lives governed by religious patriarchies that interpret religious laws. Personal laws in postcolonial India produce gender in ongoing, shifting ways.

For Muslim women, this question of personal laws has long been a flashpoint, as Muslim women are caught between a state that does not have community interests at heart and thus would like to dissolve personal laws for a uniform civil code and a community patriarchy that is interested in upholding its power and protecting its religious identity (Hasan 2010). Thus, the government's show of concern for Muslim women through laws forbidding "triple Talaq," for example, is intended to contest the community's control over "its" women. The Indian state supports Muslim women by suggesting that Muslim patriarchy was unable to reform its laws and thus did not have Muslim women's interests at heart. The ongoing project of producing what is called "communal violence" by the BJP reveals how all masculinities come to be created through heteronormative violence and control over women and men. Violence on all bodies, gendered differently, continues to be productive in all sorts of ways, especially for nationalisms.

Hortense Spillers (1987) identified "ungendering" as the "grammar" of racial violence against African Americans, suggesting the complexity of gender as it pertains to race in the United States. Muslim men are not "ungendered," since the law also gives Muslim patriarchy the power over their communities because of the existence of religious personal laws. Yet what is clear is that under BJP rule, Muslim men are constructed as threats to the state and to Hindu and Muslim women. They are made unequal by reducing their powers of patriarchy, rendering them unable to support their communities and families, especially by laws around cow protection or accusations of beef eating as well as by vigilantism that confines them to crowded neighborhoods; discriminations and inequalities limit their life chances. Though other communities, such as Dalits, Indigenous groups, and other minorities, have suffered discrimination and violence in particular ways in colonial and postcolonial India, a patriarchal Hindu nationalism targets Muslim patriarchy in racial ways—rendering Muslim men aliens, for one—while generating patriarchal masculinity within its own ranks. Right-wing nationalism is active in constructing gender and race through the modes and instrument of state power, a legacy of colonial, imperial, and postcolonial state-making, in which violence, rather than welfare, binds the nation, as evidenced in visual histories of the Indian nation. This kind of nationalism aims to eliminate any type of masculinity that does not align with the hierarchies of heteropatriarchy, making different groups of men compete to be more patriarchal than each other—all with huge violent impacts on Muslim women, and indeed, all women: right-wing nationalism presents women as requiring protection against strangers while rendering them subject to violence within their own community.

The protests in Shaheen Bagh deliberately did not focus on violence against women but instead addressed the condition of the entire community that was made vulnerable in India by the new laws governing citizenship. Muslim women protested and showed they could be heard around the world. The point here is that gender-based violence (GBV), which has focused mostly on violence against women (Basu 2000; Engle 2020), cannot capture adequately the many kinds of violence through which the state constructs gender, nor can it address the clear intent and practice of this government to render all Muslims as a racialized and subordinated minority group who do not belong in an India where they have lived for centuries.[7] Though the terminology of the "pogrom" leaves out gendered violence (Astashkevich 2018), references to "lynching" do bring attention to gendered violence on male bodies.

Terminologies such as "lynching" and "pogrom" and their national and transnational circulation reveal the failure of popular democracy because of a Hindu and Hindutva upper-caste sovereignty that began with Indira Gandhi in the early 1970s (Prakash 2019). More recently, colonial and postcolonial laws combined with the imperial "security" focus of the Global War on Terror produced a multilayered racialization of Muslims in India. Muslims became visible as subject to multiple temporalities of racialization: by the colonial British state, by the postcolonial state as it enforces a Hindu nationalism on a heterogenous country, and finally by the power of an imperial US state in collaboration with Hindu nationalism as it deploys and circulates narratives of an American-sponsored Global War on Terror.

Media and popular culture and their visibility are part of the struggle against BJP domination, one that is made even more difficult because the platform of the struggle—the media—remains firmly controlled by national and transnational patriarchies. State and nationalist violence produces gender and patriarchy in a global context in which authoritarian patriarchies have captured many states, and where capital—and transnational media corporations—also remains within patriarchal control and often, as in India, subject to the state. Yet as Stuart Hall argued, though the culture industries do reproduce the ideologies of the dominant, there is no "once-for-all victories... but always... strategic positions to be won or lost" (Hall 1989). That means that attention to the racialization of Muslims through the images and narratives of "pogrom" and "lynching" that circulate across Indian, diasporic, and transnational audiences *can* bring publicity to the violence of the state. As the protests in Shaheen Bagh and the farmers, protests in 2020 reveal, there are new solidarities being forged, and the battle is not won on either side.

NOTES

My thanks to the editors of this volume for their support and editorial help, particularly Nadera Shalhoub-Kevorkian, Lila Abu-Lughod, Rema Hammani, and Laura Charney. My thanks also to Goldie Asuri, and audiences at Columbia University, Queen Mary University, and to Sherene Razack and the UCLA Racial Violence Hub, for helpful responses to my essay.

1. The difficulty here is that the question of how "authorities" or the state give sanction to violence may be not obvious in some instances, and may need the state—and by that we mean the government in charge—to take measures to hide its culpability. It is also important to note that the attack on Sikhs was carried out by the supposedly secular Congress Party, unlike the unabashedly right-wing anti-Muslim BJP who were responsible for the Gujarat violence in 2002.
2. My thanks to Jenny Tang for pointing out the significance of the blank screen.
3. Documentarians such as Sharma, Anand Patwardhan, Teena Kaur Pasricha, and many others have added to this visual history.
4. This article is deeply problematic in suggesting a "friendship" between victim and killer, since the story of the latter reveals the impunity given to Hindutva cadres.
5. The BJP depicts Muslims as aliens to India and to a "Hindu nation," and through creating new modes of enumerating and digitalizing citizenship, the BJP government is now denationalizing Muslims living in the northeast by suggesting that they are citizens of Bangladesh.
6. For a short sample of the use of the term in Indian and international media, see Mukesh Rawat, 2019. "With 43% Share in Hate Crimes, UP Still Most Unsafe for Minorities, Dalits." *India Today*, July 19. https://www.indiatoday.in/india/story/dalits-minorities-harassment-attack-cases-uttar-pradesh-india-1570980-2019-07-19; Sonia Faleiro. 2015. "The Lynching of Syed Sarifuddin Khan." *Foreign Policy*, March 20. https://foreignpolicy.com/2015/03/20/the-lynching-of-syed-sarifuddin-khan/; IndiaTV. 2017. "Man Lynched by Mob for Allegedly

Carrying Beef in Jharkhand." YouTube Video, 5:59. Posted June 29, 2017. https://www.youtube.com/watch?v=iTezQT5LcGY; Arun Janardhanan. 2018. "A WhatsApp Message, a Rumour, a Mob and a Lynching." *The Indian Express*, May 20. http://indianexpress.com/article/india/kerala-a-whatsapp-message-a-rumour-a-mob-and-a-lynching-5183681/; Harsh Mander. 2019. "Lynching, the Scourge of New India." *The Hindu*, October 16. https://www.thehindu.com/opinion/lead/lynching-the-scourge-of-new-india/article29693818.ece; Supriya Nair. 2017. "The Meaning of India's 'Beef Lynchings.'" *The Atlantic*, July 24. https://www.theatlantic.com/international/archive/2017/07/india-modi-beef-lynching-muslim-partition/533739/; Lauren Frayer. 2019. "'This Is It. I'm Going To Die': India's Minorities Are Targeted In Lynchings." NPR, August 21. https://www.npr.org/2019/08/21/751541321/this-is-it-im-going-to-die-indias-minorities-are-targeted-in-lynchings.

7   Implicit in this subordination is a Brahmanical idea of caste that considers Muslims and Christians as untouchable groups, and as Dalits, because they converted to Islam and Christianity to escape the caste system.

REFERENCES

Ahmad, Aijaz. 2020. "Strictly Technical." *London Review of Books*, March 7. https://www.lrb.co.uk/the-paper/v42/n06/aijaz-ahmad/strictly-technical.

Ahmad, Muneer. 2002. "Homeland Insecurities: Racial Violence the Day after September 11." *Social Text* 20, no. 3: 101–15. https://muse.jhu.edu/article/31937.

Ahmed, Saifuddin. 2010. "The Role of the Media during Communal Riots in India: A Study of the 1984 Sikh Riots and the 2002 Gujarat Riots. *Media Asia* 37, no. 2: 103–11. https://doi.org/10.1080/01296612.2010.11771982.

Amnesty International. 2005. "Justice, the Victim—Gujarat State Fails to Protect Women from Violence (Summary report)." *Amnesty International Secretariat*. London: Amnesty International.

Anand, Dibyesh. 2005. "The Violence of Security: Hindu Nationalism and the Politics of Representing 'the Muslim' as a Danger." *The Round Table: The Commonwealth Journal of International Affairs* 94, no. 379: 203–15. https://doi.org/10.1080/00358530500099076.

Astashkevich, Irina. 2018. *Gendered Violence: Jewish Women in the Pogroms of 1917 to 1921*. Boston: Academic Studies Press.

Badiou, Alain. 2006. *Being and Event*. Translated by Oliver Feltham. London: Continuum International Publishing Group.

Banerjee, Sikata. 2012. *Make Me a Man! Masculinity, Hinduism, and Nationalism in India*. Albany: State University of New York Press.

Basu, Amrita. 2000. "Globalization of the Local/Localization of the Global: Mapping Transnational Women's Movements." *Meridians* 1, no. 1: 68–84. https://www.jstor.org/stable/40338428.

Bhatnagar, Gaurav Vivek. 2021. "Delhi Arrested 34 Under UAPA in 2020. Here's Why the Home Ministry Won't List Them Out." *The Wire*, August 16. https://thewire.in/government/details-of-the-9-uapa-firs-that-the-union-govt-refused-to-share-in-parliament.

Bhowmick, Nilanjana. 2020. "India's New Laws Hurt Women Most of All." *Foreign Policy*, February 4, 2020. https://foreignpolicy.com/2020/02/04/india-citizenship-law-women/.

Biswas, Soutik. 2012. "The Face of the Gujarat Riots Meets His 'Saviour.'" *BBC News*, February 27, 2012, sec. India. https://www.bbc.co.uk/news/world-asia-india-17150859.

Bora, Papori. 2010. "Between the Human, the Citizen, and the Tribal." *International Feminist Journal of Politics* 12, nos. 3–4: 341–60. https://doi.org/10.1080/14616742.2010.513100.

Brass, Paul R. 2003. *The Production of Hindu-Muslim Violence in Contemporary India*. Seattle: University of Washington Press.

Butalia, Urvashi. 2000. *The Other Side of Silence*. Durham, NC: Duke University Press.

Carpenter, R. Charli. 2006. "Recognizing Gender-Based Violence against Civilian Men and Boys in Conflict Situations." *Security Dialogue* 37, no. 1: 83–103. https://doi.org/10.1177/0967010606064139.

Chatterjee, Indrani. 2013. *Forgotten Friends: Monks, Marriages, and Memories of Northeast India*. Oxford: Oxford University Press.

Citizens against Hate. 2017. "Lynching without End: Report of Fact Finding into Religiously Motivated Vigilante Violence in India." New Delhi: Citizens against Hate. http://www.misaal.ngo/wp-content/uploads/2017/09/FINAL-report-Lynching-without-End.pdf.

Das, Veena. 1998. "Specificities: Official Narratives, Rumour, and the Social Production of Hate." *Social Identities* 4, no. 1: 109–30. https://doi.org/10.1080/13504639851915.

Davies, Sara E, and Jacqui True. 2015. "Reframing Conflict-Related Sexual and Gender-Based Violence: Bringing Gender Analysis Back In." *Security Dialogue* 46, no. 6: 495–512. https://doi.org/10.1177/0967010615601389.

Deccan Chronicle. 2017. "Junaid Lynching Case: Family Says 'Living in Fear,' Wants Death Penalty for Accused," July 9. https://www.deccanchronicle.com/nation/current-affairs/090717/ballabhgarh-lynching-junaids-family-demands-death-penalty-for-accused.html.

Doniger, Wendy. 2010. *The Hindus: An Alternative History*. New York: Penguin.

Doshi, Vidhi. 2017. "Modi Finally Speaks out against Lynchings of 'Beef Eaters.'" *Washington Post*, June 29. https://www.washingtonpost.com/world/modi-finally-speaks-out-against-lynchings-of-beef-eaters/2017/06/29/f171e042-5ccf-11e7-aa69-3964a7d55207_story.html.

Engle, Karen. 2020. *In the Grip of Sexual Violence in Conflict: Feminist Interventions in International Law*. Stanford, CA: Stanford University Press.

Faleiro, Sonia. 2015. "The Lynching of Syed Sarifuddin Khan." *Foreign Policy*, March 20. https://foreignpolicy.com/2015/03/20/the-lynching-of-syed-sarifuddin-khan/.

Faridabad, Haryana. 2017. "Junaid Lynching: Main Accused 'Confessed' to Crime, Say Police." *The Hindu*, July 9. https://www.thehindu.com/news/national/other-states/junaid-lynchingmain-accused-confessed-to-crime-say-police/article19245913.ece.

Frayer, Lauren. 2019. "'This Is It. I'm Going to Die': India's Minorities Are Targeted in Lynchings." NPR, August 21. https://www.npr.org/2019/08/21/751541321/this-is-it-im going-to-die-indias-minorities-are-targeted-in-lynchings.

Ganguly, Sumit. 2019. "Modi Crosses the Rubicon in Kashmir: New Delhi Upends the Status Quo in the Disputed Territory." *Foreign Affairs*, April 16, 2020. https://www.foreignaffairs.com/articles/india/2019-08-08/modi-crosses-rubicon-kashmir.

Ghassem-Fachandi, Parvis. 2012. *Pogrom in Gujarat: Hindu Nationalism and Anti-Muslim Violence in India*. Princeton, NJ: Princeton University Press.

Goldsby, Jacqueline. 2006. *A Spectacular Secret: Lynching in American Life and Literature*. Chicago: University of Chicago Press.

Grewal, Inderpal. 2017. *Saving the Security State: Exceptional Citizens in Twenty-First-Century America*. Durham, NC: Duke University Press.

Guru, Gopal, ed. 2009. *Humiliation: Claims and Context*. New Delhi: Oxford University Press.

Hall, Stuart. 1989. "Notes on Deconstructing the Popular." In *People's History and Socialist Theory*, edited by Raphael Samuel, 227–40. London: Routledge.

Hasan, Zoya. 2010. "Gender, Religion and Democratic Politics in India." *Third World Quarterly* 31, no. 6: 939–54. https://doi.org/10.1080/01436597.2010.502726.

Human Rights Watch (HRW). 2002. "'We Have No Orders to Save You': State Participation and Complicity in Communal Violence in Gujarat." *Human Rights Watch*, April 30. https://www.hrw.org/report/2002/04/30/we-have-no-orders-save-you/state-participation-and-complicity-communal-violence.

Human Rights Watch (HRW). 2019. "Violent Cow Protection in India: Vigilante Groups Attack Minorities." *Human Rights Watch*, February 18. https://www.hrw.org/report/2019/02/18/violent-cow-protection-india/vigilante-groups-attack-minorities.

Hussain, Shahla. 2018. "Kashmiri Visions of Freedom: The Past and the Present." In *Kashmir: History, Politics, Representation*, edited by Chitralekha Zutshi, 89–112. Cambridge: Cambridge University Press.

IndiaTV. 2017. "Man Lynched by Mob for Allegedly Carrying Beef in Jharkhand." YouTube Video, 5:59. Posted June 29, 2017. https://www.youtube.com/watch?v=iTezQT5LcGY.

Jaffrelot, Christophe. 2010. *Religion, Caste, and Politics in India*. Delhi: Primus Books.

Janardhanan, Arun. 2018. "A WhatsApp Message, a Rumour, a Mob and a Lynching." *The Indian Express*, May 20. http://indianexpress.com/article/india/kerala-a-whatsappmessage-a-rumour-a-mob-and-a-lynching-5183681/.

Kazim, Rafia. 2020. "At Shaheen Bagh, Muslim Women Take Their Place as Heroes of the Movement." *The Wire*, January 30. https://thewire.in/women/shaheen-bagh-muslimwomen.

Khan, Nabiya. 2020. "*Aayega Inquilab Pehenke Bindi Chudiyan Burqa Hijab*- An Inspiring Poem by Nabiya Khan." *The Companion*, February 12. https://thecompanion.in/aayega-inquilab-pehenke-bindi-chudiyan-burqa-hijab-an-inspiring-poem-by-nabiya-khan/.

Khan, Saeed. 2019. "In an Unlikely Friendship, Face of 2002 Riots Fear Inaugurates 'Ekta' Shop of 'Aggressor.'" *The Times of India*, September 6. https://timesofindia.indiatimes.com/india/in-an-unlikely-friendship-face-of-2002-riots-fear-inaugurates-ekta-shop-of-aggressor/articleshow/71018530.cms.

Kim, Heewon. 2019. *The Struggle for Equality: India's Muslims and Rethinking the UPA Experience*. New Delhi: Cambridge University Press.

Kumar, Megha. 2016. *Communalism and Sexual Violence in India: The Politics of Gender, Ethnicity and Conflict*. London: Bloomsbury.

Kumar, Rashmee, and Akela Lacy. 2020. "India Lobbies to Stifle Criticism, Control Messaging in US Congress Amid Rising Anti-Muslim Violence." *The Intercept*, March 16. https://theintercept.com/2020/03/16/india-lobbying-us-congress/.

Lahiri, Shoma Choudhury. 2021. "Women's Struggles over Religion and Citizenship in Contemporary India." *Contemporary South Asia* 29, no. 2: 281–87. https://doi.org/10.1080/09584935.2021.1915245.

Malhotra, Anshu, and Farina Mir. 2012. *Punjab Reconsidered History, Culture, and Practice*. New Delhi: Oxford University Press.

Mandair, Arvind. 2009. *Religion and the Specter of the West—Sikhism, India, Postcoloniality, and the Politics of Translation*. New York: Columbia University Press.

Mander, Harsh. 2019. "Lynching, the Scourge of New India." *The Hindu*, October 16. https://www.thehindu.com/opinion/lead/lynching-the-scourge-of-new-india/article29693818.ece.

Mehta, Nalin. 2006. "Modi and the Camera: The Politics of Television in the 2002 Gujarat Riots." *South Asia: Journal of South Asian Studies* 29, no. 3: 395–414.

Mehta, Pratap Bhanu. 2019. "Winning Kashmir and Losing India." *Foreign Affairs*, October 3. https://www.foreignaffairs.com/articles/asia/2019-09-20/winning-kashmir-and-losing-india.

Mirzoeff, Nicholas. 2011. *The Right to Look*. Durham, NC: Duke University Press.

Misri, Deepti. 2014. *Beyond Partition: Gender, Violence and Representation in Postcolonial India*. Champaign: University of Illinois Press.

Nair, Supriya. 2017. "The Meaning of India's 'Beef Lynchings.'" *The Atlantic*, July 24. https://www.theatlantic.com/international/archive/2017/07/india-modi-beef-lynching-muslim-partition/533739/.

Oberoi, Harjot. 1994. *The Construction of Religious Boundaries: Culture, Identity, and Diversity in the Sikh Tradition*. Chicago: University of Chicago Press.

Pandey, Gyanendra. 2006. *The Construction of Communalism in Colonial North India*. Delhi: Oxford University Press.

Pasha, Seemi. 2020. "India's Coronavirus-Related Islamophobia Has the Arab World Up in Arms." *The Wire*, April 19. https://thewire.in/communalism/indias-coronavirus-related-islamophobia-has-the-arab-world-up-in-arms.

Pepi, Eda. 2018. *Marital States: Kinship, Ethnicity, and Gendered Citizenship in Jordan*. PhD diss., Stanford University.

Prakash, Gyan. 2019. *Emergency Chronicles: Indira Gandhi and Democracy's Turning Point Department of History*. Princeton, NJ: Princeton University Press.

Press Trust of India. 2019a. "Illegal Immigrants Are Like Termites, Will Throw Them out If BJP Comes Back to Power: Amit Shah." *India Today*, April 12. https://www.indiatoday.in/elections/lok-sabha-2019/story/bjp-amit-shah-hindu-refugees-mamata-bannerjee-1499691-2019-04-11.

Press Trust of India. 2019b. "Muslim Women Thank PM Modi on Passage of Triple Talaq Bill." *The Economic Times*, July 31. https://economictimes.indiatimes.com/news/politics-and-nation/muslim-women-thank-pm-modi-on-passage-of-triple-talaq-bill/articleshow/70465902.cms.

Raj, Suhasini, and Jeffrey Gettleman. 2019. "A Mass Citizenship Check in India Leaves 2 Million People in Limbo." *New York Times*, August 31. https://www.nytimes.com/2019/08/31/world/asia/india-muslim-citizen-list.html.

Rajagopal, Arvind. 2001. *Politics after Television: Hindu Nationalism and the Reshaping of the Public in India*. Cambridge: Cambridge University Press.

Rawat, Mukesh. 2019. "With 43% Share in Hate Crimes, UP Still Most Unsafe for Minorities, Dalits." *India Today*, July 19. https://www.indiatoday.in/india/story/dalits-minorities-harassment-attack-cases-uttar-pradesh-india-1570980-2019-07-19.

Razack, Sherene. 2022. *Nothing Has to Make Sense: Upholding White Supremacy through Anti-Muslim Racism*. Minneapolis: University of Minnesota Press.

Roy, Srila. 2021. "Transnational Feminism and the Politics of Scale: The 2012 Antirape Protests in Delhi." In *Transnational Feminist Itineraries: Situating Theory and Activist Practice*, edited by Ashwini Tambe and Millie Thayer, 71–85. Durham, NC: Duke University Press.

Sachar Committee Report. 2006. "Social, Economic and Educational Status of the Muslim Community of India." Prime Minister's High Level Committee, Cabinet Secretariat, Government of India. New Delhi: Government of India.

Sagar. 2018. "Hapur Lynching: Police Attempt a Cover-Up Even as Families Of Assailants Admit to Mob Attack on Suspicion of Cow Slaughter." *Caravan*, June 23. https://caravanmagazine.in/crime/hapur-lynching-police-attempts-a-cover-up-even-as-families-of-assailants-admit-to-mob-attack-on-suspicion-of-cow-slaughter.

Sarna, Ira. 2015. "Khushwant Singh's Train to Pakistan and Margaret Bourke White's Partition Photographs: Clash of Narratives or Postmemory Project?" In *Cracow Indological Studies vol. 17*, edited by Tatiana Dubyanskaya, 270–92. Krakow: Institute of Oriental Studies, Jagiellonian University.

Scroll Staff. 2019. "Triple Talaq Bill Is a 'Complete Charade' and Against Minorities, Say Civil Society Members." *Scroll.in*, July 31. https://scroll.in/latest/932325

/triple-talaq-bill-is-a-complete-charade-and-against-minorities-say-civil-society-members.

Sengupta, Shuddhabrata. 2020. "Lessons That Shaheen Bagh Teaches Us about Citizenship. *The Caravan*, February 2. https://caravanmagazine.in/politics/lessons-that-shaheen-bagh-teaches-us-about-citizenship.

Shalhoub-Kevorkian, Nadera. 2019. *Incarcerated Childhood and the Politics of Unchilding*. Cambridge: Cambridge University Press.

Sharma, Rakesh, dir. 2004. *Final Solution*. https://vimeo.com/329340055.

Sharpe, Jenny. 1993. *Allegories of Empire*. Minneapolis: University of Minnesota Press. https://www.upress.umn.edu/book-division/books/allegories-of-empire.

Shukla, Saurabh. 2018. "'They Killed Cows, I Killed Them,' Lynching Accused Brags: NDTV Expose." NDTV, August 7. https://www.ndtv.com/india-news/ndtv-expose-when-key-accused-in-lynching-cases-admit-to-their-crimes-1896161.

Spillers, Hortense J. 1987. "Mama's Baby, Papa's Maybe: An American Grammar Book." *Diacritics* 17, no. 2: 65–81. https://doi.org/10.2307/464747.

StoriesAsia. 2018. "The Caravan Features StoriesAsia: Surviving a Lynching." *Caravan*, July 11. https://caravanmagazine.in/crime/storiesasia-surviving-a-lynching.

Sur, Esita. 2018. "Triple Talaq Bill in India: Muslim Women as Political Subjects or Victims?" *Space and Culture, India* 5, no. 3: 5–12. https://doi.org/10.20896/saci.v5i3.299.

Teltumbde, Anand. 2018. *Republic of Caste: Thinking Equality in the Time of Neoliberal Hindutva*. New Delhi: Navayana.

Van der Veer, Peter. 1994. *Religious Nationalism: Hindus and Muslims in India*. Berkeley: University of California Press.

Venugopal, Vasudha. 2020. "Shaheen Bagh Vacated | Delhi Lockdown: Anti-CAA Protesters Removed from Shaheen Bagh, Other Places." *Economic Times*, March 25. https://economictimes.indiatimes.com/news/politics-and-nation/coronavirus-lockdown-delhi-police-vacate-protesters-at-shaheen-bagh/articleshow/74785253.cms.

Zia, Ather. 2019. *Resisting Disappearance: Military Occupation and Women's Activism in Kashmir*. Seattle: University of Washington Press.

SIX · *Shenila Khoja-Moolji*

The Politics of Legislating "Honor Crime" in Contemporary Pakistan

On July 15, 2016, Qandeel Baloch, a social media celebrity in Pakistan known for her sexually provocative videos, was strangled to death by her brother, Waseem. He gave her a sleeping pill and then choked her to death with the help of two accomplices. Speaking later at a press conference, Waseem explained that he killed her because she was bringing dishonor to his family (Perry 2016). The news of this incident spread like wildfire in Pakistan, making Qandeel a household name. In life Qandeel had been at best a minor celebrity; the reason for her murder, however, catapulted her to global fame. She was instantly framed as yet another victim of an "honor killing," a "scourge in most Muslim countries and . . . carried out with impunity in Pakistan," as Lubna Khalid claimed on the *News*, a Pakistani news site (2016). Her murder became a rallying cry for women's rights activists and within a few months enough pressure was put on the state that it passed an amendment to the Pakistan penal code that had been stalled for years. The amendment included harsher punishments for those who committed "honor crimes," and also partially closed a loophole whereby family members of victims could forgive the perpetrator of the crime. The successful mobilization of civil society in the aftermath of Qandeel's killing signaled not only the widespread disapproval of honor-based crimes in Pakistan, at least among the political and social elite, but also an ever-increasing deployment of, and affinity with, the language of rights as the key vocabulary of human dignity, freedom, and equality. Activists expressed disdain toward local norms that condone honor killings and called for the recognition of women's rights.

In this chapter, I undertake the difficult task of both acknowledging how the frame of honor killing and the language of rights have created space for activists in Pakistan to coerce the state into instituting important measures to protect women *and* arguing that these frames reiterate the state as a purveyor of women's rights, effectively masking the complicity of the state and religious elites in creating the conditions for women's subordination. The seductive frame of honor killing emerges as a hegemonic interpretive category for a wide range of diverse cases of violence against women (Abu-Lughod 2011). The phrase is invoked to describe different practices, including *karo kari* in Sindh, *siyahkari* in Baluchistan, *kala kali* in Southern Punjab, and *tor tora* in the Khyber-Pakhtunkhwa (Shah 2002). As such, it truncates critical analysis of specific crimes and fails to reveal the multiple social, political, and economic specificities that may provide alternate explanations or frameworks for the violence. I take the example of Qandeel to illustrate how the category of honor crime hides the different forces, actors, and institutions that were at play. In framing her murder as an honor crime, and seeking redress from the state, activists may end up bolstering statist sovereignty, which is ultimately tied to gendered practices of violence and rebuke (Khoja-Moolji 2021). Activist mobilization in the Pakistani context therefore produces ambiguous effects.

I begin by first providing an overview of the role of Pakistani and Anglophone media in articulating Qandeel's murder as an honor killing. This articulation of Qandeel's murder is not a given; it was socially produced and did crucial political and cultural work. As Stuart Hall (1985) reminds us, articulations are connections or links which require "particular conditions of existence to appear at all," and they have to be "positively sustained by specific processes" that are to be constantly reiterated and renewed (Hall 1985, 113–14). Otherwise, the connections or linkages would dissolve, and new connections—re-articulations—would be forged. The conditions that enabled the articulation of Qandeel's murder as an honor killing include the recent history of Pakistani activists' efforts to pass anti–honor killings laws. However, the frame of the honor killing precludes other story lines. A close examination of Qandeel's self-representations tells a very different story about her murder. This story turns out to be less about her family and their honor and more about her politicized contestation of the state and religious elites, and her naming of male lust as an organizing principle in Pakistani society. Her critiques threatened specific national elites and were inflamed by the local media. Paying attention to these logics undermines any easy reduction of her murder to the seductive category of honor killing and instead shows the complex and intertwined local hegemonies, besides those of the family, that also were at play in this murder.

In unpacking Qandeel's story this way, I am following Inderpal Grewal's (2013) call to push back against the framing of honor killings by naming and giving voice to the many forms of violence that get subsumed under this hegemonic category. In this case, for instance, we observe how a confluence of forces interact—from historical association of women with honor, state, and religious sanctioning of this equivalence to the hegemony of liberal categories to name violence against Muslim women. Indeed, Qandeel's example shows that even though activists appealed to the state for redress, the conditions of her murder were determined by the close imbrication of state and religious authorities in the first place. The case thus shows that feminist mobilizations around the seductive and loaded cultural category of the "honor crime" to push through a stalled legal bill may occlude the ways in which the state is implicated.

THE MAKING OF AN HONOR CRIME VICTIM

Born into a working-class family in the rural village of Shah Sadarddin, Fauzia Azeem, who later took on the screen name of Qandeel Baloch, became a social media sensation between 2013 and 2016. Although she had been working in television before, she had experienced harassment and was not able to get the kind of break she desired. She decided to curate her own platform, and social media turned out to be a fortuitous space for her. Over time she boasted over 700 thousand followers on Facebook and over 40 thousand followers on Twitter (Zubair 2016). Qandeel's posts were sexually provocative. She showed more skin than is the norm in Pakistan. She appeared in tank tops with her cleavage visible, in tight form-fitting clothes, in short dresses that revealed her legs, and in swimwear. She sang, danced, and shared everyday details of her personal life, such as when she had a fever or was getting bored. She would twerk, gyrate, twirl, pout, roll on her bed, caress her breasts, trace the outline of her waist, and moan. She cursed and yelled. Qandeel established a sense of familiarity with her audience through her use of colloquial language addressing her audience in second person pronouns. She chose her words carefully and modified her body—through clothes, makeup, and cardio exercises—to appeal to her imagined audience. She would unabashedly call herself sexy and hot. She often asked her viewers: "How I'm looking? [sic]" She stoked male desire and actively invited their gaze, coyly asking: "Am I looking cute?" She pushed the limits of how much of a woman's body could be seen and consumed by a viewing audience. She worked at her craft and presented herself as providing entertainment; as she herself once announced, "I am a superstar. I am an international entertainment [sic]" (Baloch 2016a).

In reality, however, Qandeel remained only a minor celebrity, and her antics elicited scorn from upper-class celebrities. Unlike other Pakistani celebrities who came from middle- or upper-class backgrounds, Qandeel's accent and broken English betrayed her lower-class origins. She was thus easily dismissed. Indeed, the few occasions on which she entered mainstream television or news media were when other celebrities expressed disdain for her performances, or when television anchors invited her on to engage her in a yelling match with other invited guests. Actresses from middle-class and elite backgrounds described her as lazy and untalented. Upon Qandeel's death, Momina Mustehsan, a popular singer, tweeted: "#QandeelBaloch was not an epitome of women empowerment. If anything, she was portraying the opposite: the only asset a woman has is her body" (Naveed 2016). Likewise, in an interview on One News where Qandeel was invited alongside another actress, Maria Zahid, the latter exclaimed, "people like you create difficulties for girls . . . girls of *sharif* (respectable) families" (Zahid 2016). On another occasion, a male anchor, Raja Matlub, insulted her by charging: "you have exposed yourself a lot [on Instagram and Facebook], no *gharayloo* (domestic, implying someone with shame) girl does this, no Muslim girl does this" (Matlub 2016). However, the manner of her death and the events just preceding it catapulted Qandeel to international fame. She transformed from a minor celebrity not worthy of attention to a feminist icon who became a victim of honor crime.

Qandeel's death was widely articulated as yet another example of the scourge of honor killing in Pakistan, where men kill their womenfolk to salvage their familial reputation. Presumed to be a characteristic of specific societies—predominantly Muslim, Middle Eastern, and South Asian—honor killings have been a prominent cultural frame in and through which women's murders in these societies are interpreted globally. Qandeel's murder was quickly articulated through this familiar frame that spotlights the apparently unique propensity of Muslims to engage in violence. Consider the headlines in Anglophone online and print media: the *Wall Street Journal* reported, "Qandeel Baloch, a Pakistani Internet Celebrity, Is Killed in 'Honor Killing'" (Nauman 2016); the *New York Times* informed us, "Qandeel Baloch, Pakistani Social Media Celebrity, Dead in Apparent Honor Killing"

(Masood 2016); *Al Jazeera* observed, "Pakistan: Anger after Honour Killing of Qandeel Baloch" (Chughtai 2016); NBC *news* quoted the police as saying, "Outspoken Pakistani Model Qandeel Baloch Strangled in 'Honor Killing'" (W. Khan 2016); the *New Yorker* expressed its righteous anger as: "The Outrageous 'Honor Killing' of a Pakistani Social-Media Star" (S. Khan 2016); and the *Diplomat* inquired, "Pakistan and Honor Killings: Will the Recent Murder of a Celebrity Finally Prompt the Government of Pakistan to Act?" (Notezai 2016).

The frame of honor killing was also one of the primary ways in which Qandeel's death was decoded within Pakistan. Sultan Azam, a senior police officer with the Multan police, for instance, quickly interpreted the murder as an honor killing: "Qandeel Baloch has been killed, she was strangled to death by her brother, apparently it was an incident of honour killing" (Gabol and Subhani 2016). Women's rights activists in the country, such as prominent documentary film maker Sharmeen Obaid-Chinoy, tweeted: "#QandeelBaloch killed in an #honorkilling—how many women have to die before we pass the Anti Honor Killing Bill?" (as cited in Nauman 2016). A couple of months later Obaid-Chinoy released a short video on Qandeel's life which received praised from American actress Madonna who invoked the same frame: "Proud to narrate my friend #SharmeenObaidChinoy's latest film about Qandeel Baloch, the Pakistani social media star who was murdered by her brother in an 'honor killing'" (as cited in Entertainment Desk 2016).

HONOR CRIMES AND WOMEN'S RIGHTS ADVOCACY IN PAKISTAN

While women in Pakistan have been agitating against gender-based violence for decades, in recent years mobilization around honor killings has gained momentum. Activism around this issue often draws on the language of rights, which itself has become in recent decades the hegemonic idiom for imaging human dignity and seeking justice (Khoja-Moolji 2017; Shah 2016). For instance, honor killing is viewed primarily as a violation of the assaulted woman's rights. In its informational booklet, the prominent women's rights organization in Pakistan, *Shirkat Gah*, describes honor killings as,

> a term used to denote the murder of women (and also sometimes men) under the pretext of restoring and/or reviving the "lost honour" of the

family. Mostly, victims of "honour" killings and/or crimes of violence are accused of inappropriate sexual behaviour that, it is claimed by those committing the murder, led to the loss of family "honour." In Pakistan, the "inappropriate behaviour" for which hundreds of women have lost their lives includes exercising their right to marry or divorce without the specific approval of family members and challenging oppressive traditions such as supporting the right of a daughter to marry someone she chooses. (Shah 2002)

Even though this definition is quite broad, advocates as well as police and lawyers argue that it not too hard to determine if a murder took place in the name of honor. Asad Jamal, a lawyer who fought on behalf of a rare survivor of such an attempted murder said, "If a brother murders his sister, or a father murders his daughter, the first possible reason would be honor" (U. Ali 2016). Qandeel's murder thus fit these frames neatly and was instantly termed as an honor killing and interpreted as a violation of Qandeel's rights to live as she pleased.

Furthermore, what troubles activists such as Maliha Zia, who represents another major women's rights organization in Pakistan, *Aurat Foundation*, is that such cases are often tried under the *Qisas and Diyat Ordinance* (as cited in U. Ali 2016), which permits the assaulted person or his or her family to either punish the perpetrator in a like manner (*qisas*) or demand monetary compensation (*diyat*) instead. Oftentimes perpetrators of "honor killings," who are almost by definition family members, are forgiven by the family of the victim. Activists have thus been calling for addressing this legal loophole for decades. Introduced in September 1990 by the then president Ghulam Ishaq Khan, the *Qisas and Diyat Ordinance* redefined certain crimes and punishments under the Pakistan Penal Code (PPC, Act XLV of 1860) and the Code of Criminal Procedure (CCP, Act of 1898) to bring them into conformity with the injunctions of Islam. Since both the PPC and CCP are legacies of the British colonial period and are based on common law, during the 1980s the former president Zia-ul-Haq set out to "Islamize" these laws (Burki 2016; Brightman 2015). He established a Federal Shariat Court, which was empowered to review any law and decide whether or not it was in line with Islam. If this court deemed a law to be repugnant to Islam, then the government was compelled to amend it. The *Qisas and Diyat Ordinance* of 1990 was linked to other laws relating to murder and bodily harm which the Federal Shariat Court had found to be contrary to Islam (for more see Amnesty International 1991). While the ordinance was introduced in 1990, it was under Prime Minister Nawaz Sharif's government that it passed in the Parliament in 1997. This ordinance transformed women's murder, when linked to honor, from a crime against the state to a crime against the person (as cited in U. Ali 2016). Instead of prosecuting the perpetrator, the family could engage in a compromise; thus the law created a loophole for families to forgive the perpetrators. Since in most honor-related crimes the perpetrator is a member of the family, this loophole in the law has been used to exonerate family members. The loophole thus can be interpreted as the state's sanction of women's murders in the name of honor. At times families have also hired assassins and then used this loophole to ensure they avoid prosecution. The public killing of Samia Sarwar in 1999 in her lawyer's office is a case in point.

At seventeen years old, Samia was married to her cousin by her family. She endured her husband's abuse for several years and then decided to leave him. Her parents allowed her to come back to their home but said that a divorce was out of question as it was against prevailing Pashtun norms and would hinder the marriage of her young sister. Samia eventually fell in love with another man and filed a petition for divorce without the knowledge of her parents. She fled to Lahore and sought legal advice from the prominent human rights lawyer Hina Jilani. Over the next few weeks, Samia's parents persuaded Samia and her lawyer that they were willing to accept the divorce and arranged a meeting in Jilani's office. Samia's mother and uncle brought along a man, Habibur Rehman, who they said was their driver. Rehman was actually a hit man hired by the family. He shot and killed Samia in the lawyer's office. While Jilani filed a complaint against Samia's parents, the police delayed the investigation. The mother and uncle were not even tried because the *Qisas and Diyat Ordinance* calls on the heirs of the victim, instead of the state, to file charges. As Hina Jilani explained:

> Killings are private offences, against the individual, not the state, so who will bring and pursue the charges of murder? If the father or brother kills a woman, the family of the girl will not pursue the case, as in their eyes no wrong has been done.... The prosecution case collapses in almost all the scenarios of an honour killing: In *karo-kari* cases there is no aggrieved party to pursue the case, society as a whole approves of the killing.... If a brother kills his sister on the ground of honour, her guardian, her father[,] can forgive his son. (as cited in Palo 2008, 93–94)

The case rose to prominence because Samia belonged to an elite, upper-class family, and her father was a prominent politician in the NWFP province. Even so, when Iqbal Haider, a senator, put forward a resolution condemning the killing, only nineteen of his colleagues supported it (Fisk 2010). A prominent senator from NWFP, Ajmal Khattak even argued that when it is a question of "honour," there is no room for discussion (Cowasjee 2003). While there was some public uproar, no one was convicted in the case. Instead, Samia's lawyers were maligned by a number of religious organizations and the Chamber of Commerce in the NWFP (Samia's father was the president of this organization) for "misleading women in Pakistan and contributing to the country's bad image abroad" (Ali 2001). The case illustrated the alliance between the family and the state as they shared control over women's bodies—in life and death.

Since this episode, women's rights activists have been seeking to introduce several amendments to the Pakistan Penal Code, in particular to address the loophole that allows families to forgive the murderer. Introduction of amendments is a popular activist strategy for dealing with liberal bureaucracies; it allows activists to build on the infrastructure that is already available. While opportunistic, such strategies are often the most immediate ways to provide relief. Yet, since activists work within the framework of liberal bureaucracies, substantial redress remains elusive. In 2004 Senator Syeda Sughra Imam introduced the Anti-Honor Killings Laws (Criminal Laws Amendment), which called for increasing the penalty for offenses committed in the name or on the pretext of "honour." It also gave the courts authority to reject compromises made by the victim's family. Specifically, it stipulated that the family could not pardon the perpetrator. This bill passed through the Senate in 2015 but stalled in Parliament later that year.

Momentum for the bill increased in 2016 when Obaid-Chinoy's documentary, *A Girl in the River: The Price of Forgiveness*, was nominated for, and later won, an Oscar. The documentary follows nineteen-year-old Saba Qaiser, who was beaten up and shot in the head by her father and uncle, then stuffed in a bag and thrown in a river. They said that she had shamed her family by marrying someone of her own choice. Miraculously, Saba survived. She filed a case against her kin but was coerced by extended family to forgive them. Obaid-Chinoy told Saba's story with the express purpose of launching a national conversation about honor killings. In an interview with *Newsweek* she said, "I wanted to tell the story of a victim of honor killing because I wanted to start a national discourse about this issue and build momentum to garner support for key legislation" (M. Khan 2016). In another interview, this time with *Al Arabiya*, Obaid-Chinoy said, "with the world watching, the film has elevated the issue of honor killings to the national sphere. We have launched a nationwide campaign to push all stakeholders to pass the Anti-Honor Killings Laws Bill 2014 in the Parliament" (Naar 2016). Obaid-Chinoy's Oscar win was widely deemed a win for "women's rights" (Rehman 2016) in Pakistan and launched honor killings as a topic of national conversation.

Obaid-Chinoy also started to gather signatures on a petition meant to show the then prime minister Nawaz Sharif the will of the public. She circulated her message through newspapers, television, radio, and social media. Sharif eventually invited her to meet him and publicly announced his support for her activism against honor killing. He said:

> Customs and practices such as honor killings have nothing to do with the divine principles and theories of Islam. The revolution brought by Islam in the world manifested through the life of Prophet Muhammad (PBUH) was the most successful movement for change of social reforms which has altered the course of history for all times to come. It was Islam which first recognized the rights of women.... Women are the most essential part of our society and I believe in their empowerment, protection and emancipation of achieving the shared goal of a prosperous and vibrant Pakistan. (as cited in *Newsdesk* 2016)

In these remarks, Sharif skillfully erases the state's long-standing culpability in sanctioning violence against women through legal loopholes, which also are interpretative moves made by the judges to bring the law into alignment with the scripture. In fact, it was during Sharif's tenure in 1997 that the *Qisas and Diyat Ordinance* passed in Parliament. Instead, he imagines an Islam that can never inspire such laws and aligns the state with that imagined Islam. In doing so, Sharif continues to grant the state moral authority over women's lives and deaths. It is precisely this authority that Qandeel undermined as we will see below. Commenting on the film and Saba's story, Sharif again removes the state's culpability in instituting laws and blames it instead on societal regressive attitudes: "This film and its message are incredibly important to me, to Pakistan. It is clear in the film that Pakistan's social services, including our rescue services and police worked for Saba and came to her aid in a timely manner. What was evident is that it was the societal pressure combined with the way the law is framed, which left Saba pressurized to forgive the perpetrators of the attempted honor killing" (*Newsdesk* 2016).

Sharif ultimately committed to closing the legal loophole (Refworld 2016). Just as these negotiations were taking place, Qandeel Baloch was murdered, and her murder gave further momentum to the activists' struggles. So much so that within a few months the stalled amendment, Criminal Law Amendment 2016, passed in Parliament. The legislation closed the loophole that had permitted family members to forgive the killers through *diyat* (financial compensation paid to heirs of the victim) and instituted a mandatory prison sentence of twenty-five years. While the family members would still be allowed to forgive the murderer in the event of a death penalty verdict, the culprit would not be able to avoid jail time. While the activism around honor killing was useful in closing the loophole, this frame fails to account for the long-standing alliance between the state and religious authorities in regulating women. Sharif, for instance, was able to emerge from this episode as a benevolent patriarch and an advocate for women's rights. Blame, instead, was shifted onto backward Others who engage in inappropriate interpretations of Islam.

To avoid making honor crimes a simple villain for feminists it is important to pay attention to the specificities of the violence under consideration, as well as the political and social conditions in which violence against women is occurring (Abu-Lughod 2013, 115). Dicle Koğacıoğlu in her analysis of so-called honor crimes in Turkey observes that "even the most superficial examination of such crimes . . . reveals that factors such as one's ethnic identity as a minority, one's activism, or one's position in relation to state structures and contestations are integral to the perpetuation of honor crimes. In other words, honor crimes stand at the intersection of multiple political and social dynamics" (Koğacıoğlu 2004, 119). Other scholars, such as Gill and Brah (2014), argue that honor codes differ even within a particular context, let alone transnationally. They note that the specific acts that bolster or erode honor are subject to contestation and appear differently as they also depend on socioeconomic status, geographic location, or regional culture (Gill and Brah 2014). Relatedly, Abu-Lughod argues that prevailing assumptions about moral codes, including honor codes, often cast them as necessarily detrimental to a society, when in fact such codes are complex systems that help social groups organize themselves. Moral systems, Abu-Lughod (2005) argues, based on her ethnographic work with Awlad 'Ali Bedouin in Egypt, set ideals for not only men but also women, and both men and women are often invested in upholding these codes as they provide protection and respect. Therefore, a reduction of moral codes to men's oppression of women does not to allow us to understand how men and women who engage in these systems actually experience them, live by them, and also critique them.

With this in mind, alongside Koğacıoğlu's insistence that we attend to the imbrication of honor killings in various institutions of the modern state, below I tell a different story about Qandeel Baloch. I examine her own media performances as well media narratives about her during her lifetime and after her death, to provide a thick description of the circumstances that led to her killing. In doing so, I hope to orient our frames away from the seductive category of "honor crime" and toward other story lines, namely, her exposure of the alliance between the state and religious elite in regulating Pakistani women, as well as her naming of male desire as an organizing principle in society.

ENTANGLED STORY LINES

If writings about Qandeel proliferated in the aftermath of her killing, she herself had produced many narratives and performed a specific persona in her videos and interviews in life. Most of what we know about Qandeel Baloch is through these mediated texts—writings about her as well as her own performances. For the purpose of this analysis of the politics of legislating the "honor crime" in contemporary Pakistan, I reviewed her interviews with Pakistani and international media, specifically *Neo News, One News, 24 News, Images Dawn,* and BBC; her posts on Facebook and Twitter; and her press conference from June 2016. Most of these materials are from 2015 and 2016 as that is when she rose to national prominence. In addition, I reviewed documentaries produced about her after her death, specifically those produced by the *Guardian,* BBC *Urdu,* and *NewsAsia,* as well as numerous YouTube clips featuring her mother, sister, and father, and leaked phone conversations. I reviewed these materials with an eye to how she exposed the forces that enforce women's subjection, highlighting in particular the role of the political elite, media, and religio-moral authorities in violence against women.

Qandeel skillfully created a persona through social and televisual media that exploited her audiences' desires. She commodified her body and played with societal anxieties around women's sexuality. She courted controversy for the purpose of entertainment, often speaking directly to or about politicians, media, and sports personalities. When reprimanded and sanctioned for it, she defended herself by questioning the prevailing customs and mores around women's bodies and sexuality. Over time, she was invited to television talk shows that sought to create on-screen drama. It was during these talk shows that she offered incisive critiques of social and gender norms in Pakistan as she pushed back against her critics. However, she pushed the most sensitive boundaries and became perceived as a real threat when she pointed to the hypocrisy of the religious establishment. Even though she may not have intended to, she ended up exposing the multiple ways in which women are policed in Pakistan. I highlight two assertions by Qandeel—in relation to religious authority, and to the male gaze and desire—that crystalize the ways in which she disturbed ongoing power/knowledge regimes. This alternate story line directs attention away from the simplistic frame of honor killings and toward her critique of local patriarchal formations—from the state to religious elites—that transformed her into a threat.

"No One Here Should Issue Fatwas about Me"

In March 2016, Qandeel posted a video in which she addressed the Pakistani cricket team and its captain, Shahid Afridi, regarding an upcoming match against India. Qandeel offered to strip dance for Afridi if he led the team to a win. In the video, we see Qandeel lying on her bed, wearing a pink tank top that shows off her bosom, including a tattoo on the right upper breast. Seductively, in a low voice, she says: "Just win the match once . . . just once. Then see how Qandeel strip dances for you, seriously. I will do such a strip dance for you, such a strip dance for you . . . I will take your name over and over again . . . Afridi . . . Afridi . . . I will say and strip. Boom Boom [Afridi's nickname] . . . I will say and strip. Afridi, just win the match. Please, my love (*mere jaan*). Win . . . the . . . match . . . " (Baloch 2016c).

She ends the video with a soft smile. Later, she extended the offer to the entire country: "I will strip dance for the entire country" (Baloch 2016d). She then went on to publish a trailer of what this strip dance might look like. Wearing a lime green bikini under a loosely tied bathrobe, Qandeel looks down at the camera, slowly jerking her hips and caressing her breasts.

These videos were deemed to be controversial and thrust Qandeel into the limelight. She was invited to appear on national television talk shows, and though in the past she had shied away from such interviews, this time she accepted some requests. A close reading of these interviews provides insight into how Qandeel drew on the language of rights to make her claims for autonomy but more so to expose how women's bodies are policed. These interviews, therefore, reveal the kinds of discourses that she was pushing back against and the idioms that she used to do so. Consider the following conversation between Qandeel and Farid Raees, the host of a talk show entitled *Jamhur*:

FARID RAEES: [This is] Pakistan, Islamic Republic of Pakistan, an Islamic country. The types of trailers you post . . . and pictures you post . . .

QANDEEL BALOCH (cutting him off): Pakistan is a free (*azad*) country. As a free country, every citizen has the right to live as they please in this country . . . there is no vulgarity in the trailer. I think it is hot.

FARID RAEES: What do you mean by *azadi*? What is the limit of freedom?

QANDEEL BALOCH: As far as Islam is concerned, I respect Islam . . . I am answerable to God. I have to go to my grave. No one can disagree with that. (Baloch 2016e)

While Raees seeks to discipline her through references to Islam and the nation, Qandeel draws on the same discourse of nation and religion, as well as the discourse of rights, to argue that as a citizen of a free country she has the right to do as she pleases. She further proposes an engagement with Islam that is personal, and not subject to the interpretive frames of the elite. She acknowledges that while she is accountable for her actions, the accountability and its related punishment or reward is not for society to dole out; instead, it is God who will be her judge.

Consider another conversation, this time with a religious cleric, Mufti Naeem, during a talk show on *One News*:

MUFTI NAEEM: I wanted to let you know that this is the Islamic Republic of Pakistan. Muslims live here. The culture here is different than the West and other places.

QANDEEL BALOCH: Certainly. Agreed.

MUFTI NAEEM: That is why there should be restrictions on these things.

QANDEEL BALOCH [scoffs]: Restrictions . . .

MUFTI NAEEM: And government departments should keep an eye on such things. This way our young children and girls, who belong to Islam, they will not turn away from religion. And there will be a time when our leaders will want to, I will want to, and you will want to but we will not be able to control this [phenomenon]. We have to see Allah, Allah's messenger, and Quran and the Day of Judgment . . .

QANDEEL BALOCH [raising her voice to talk over the mufti]: The accountability on the day of judgment ... I have my own conscience ... I have to go to my grave (*qabr*) ... I am answerable to God. Okay? No one here should issue religious injunctions (*fatwas*) about me. There is no need. I have to die. I will answer to Allah. (Baloch 2016f)

Whereas Mufti Naeem draws on the well-established alliance between religious bodies and state institutions to further the moral regulation of women when he says, "government departments should keep an eye on such things," Qandeel continues to evade capture. She argues that while one is accountable for one's actions, judgment rests with Allah and not the elite religious establishment that issues *fatwas* (religious rulings). She resists the imposition on her of a cleric-sanctioned version of Islam that constrains public expression of sexual desire. Instead, she positions herself as an autonomous Muslim subject who can decide as to how and when to please God, if at all.

In taking this stance, however, she challenges the authority that clerics (*ulema*) have enjoyed in Pakistan, particularly in relation to clarifying for the population that which is permissible in Islam and that which is not (see Zaman 2002 and 2018). In fact, another incident later in 2016 shows how she actively sought to unmask religious patriarchy. She exposed a high-ranking and renowned cleric, Mufti Abdul Qavi, by highlighting his duplicitous stances. Qandeel first met Qavi during an interview at *Neo News*, where he was likely invited to pronounce a moral judgment against her strip dance offer to Afridi. Qavi playfully mentioned that he would like to meet her the next time he was in Karachi, and she, respectfully, welcomed the meeting. They indeed met later, in his hotel room, where Qandeel, wearing a close-fitted shirt and tight pants—not typically worn by respectable Pakistani women and especially when meeting a religious cleric—filmed the meeting. She subsequently posted a few selfies with Qavi in which we see her wearing his signature cap, with her mouth wide open, in mocking horror at this blasphemous act. That these images and videos were read as threatening, not only by Qavi but also by the state and religious establishment, is apparent in the backlash that followed. Qandeel had exposed a state-endorsed cleric for being in the proximity of a woman not related to him by blood or marriage, and for expressing interest in her. In doing so, she not only humiliated him but also the state because Qavi was a member of the elite Eid moon-sighting government committee, *Ruhat-e-hillal*, from which he was immediately suspended. He was also suspended from the political party, *Pakistan Tehrik-e-Insaaf*, for which he acted as a "religious advisor." It is also reported that the Federal Ministry for Religious Affairs revoked his membership from the National Ulema and Mushaikh Council, another elite state body composed of religious scholars. On June 22, 2016, in a session of the Punjab provincial assembly, Pakistan Muslim League-Nawaz's members Hina Pervez Butt and Sheikh Ejaz publicly condemned Qavi and called for a formal investigation (*The News* 2016). Pakistan Peoples Party's Sardar Shahabuddin also staged a symbolic walkout from the Punjab Assembly to signal his disappointment at Qavi's behavior (*The News* 2016.).

Qandeel's casual and frank encounters with the mufti had thus not only exposed this particular individual's duplicity—condemning her for breaching religious morals on public television while then lusting after her in private—but also the duplicity of the entire establishment, religious and political, that claims authority through religious idioms. The *institutional* responses—from suspension and investigations to reprimand—thus were attempts to preserve the mandate and authority of the *ulema* and the state. In light of this provocation, Qandeel quickly became an object of intense backlash from all quarters. She started receiving death threats from the mufti's followers. During a press conference on June 28, 2016 she clarified her position:

> Not all *muftis* are bad, not all *ulema* are bad. I am not saying that all of them are bad. "Being a Muslim girl" [she uses this phrase in English] I respect all religious scholars, I respect all *maulvis*, because they have kept Islam alive. . . . People like Mufti Qavi are those who behind closed doors give a bad name to Islam . . . his entire life he has sinned, he has made a fool of people. Today he has come in the grip of God, and I am only the medium (*zariya*). He got caught due to me. (Baloch 2016g)

In another interview Qandeel directly questioned his authority: "He is a blot on the name of Islam. Who is he to claim to be a guardian of the faith?" (as cited in Ahmed 2016). Death threats continued, and while she repeatedly asked the local government for protection, it never arrived (R. Ali 2016; Baloch 2016b).

In raising these questions about one influential cleric, Qandeel was by implication interrogating the control that the ulema exercise in family and religious affairs. Since the 1980s, due to General Zia's Islamization policies, the realm of the family and the female body have increasingly come under the control of religious functionaries, as they were given the responsibility of bringing cultural norms as well as laws in line with Islam. This has resulted in, as Amina Jamal observes, a steady restriction on "women's access to the public sphere and . . . regulat[ion] of morality through strict prescriptions for women's dress and deportment" (2006, 300). In addition, Jamal notes that there has been a reconfiguration of the private and public spheres. Areas such as sexuality, personal relationships, and modes of dress that are typically private are brought under the purview of the public, and public matters such as murder are pushed into the domain of the family and community. Women's autonomy has been pathologized (Toor 2007; Standish 2014). It is this legal and social context that provides muftis and other religious clerics the authorizing environment to discipline and reform women publicly. This is precisely what Qandeel was rejecting. She was doing so by discrediting Qavi's, and through him the state's, claims to religious authority, as well as by seizing back control over her body and sexuality from both the family and state. She left a forced marriage against the wishes of her family and used social media to bring sexuality from the bedrooms into the dining rooms. Now, with her critique of Qavi, she was exposing the falsity of the moral superiority claimed by the state and religious elites.

"Har Banda Tharki Hai"

Qandeel was regularly humiliated and shamed on national television for her choices. Television anchors would repeatedly ask if she would feel comfortable showing her videos and photographs to members of her family, particularly her father and brothers. She would sometimes decline to respond to such questions, but at other times retort back with: "har banda tharki hai" (everyone is tharki) (Baloch 2016i). The Urdu term "tharki" can be translated to "pervert," someone who lusts or is lascivious. Qandeel was adamant that the judgmental gaze on her actions had to be refocused onto male lust and desire. She did not even spare her father. Raja Matlub of *Neo News* asked her, "Does your father come in this category too?" She responded: "No, no, no not my father, but yeah when he shares his stories of youth then he too was *mashallah* [what God has willed] quite a big . . . but he's too old now" (Baloch 2016h). Matlub continued, "Does he share stories of his youth with you? [He must be a] very liberal father." Qandeel responded, looking away, "Yes, many. Many stories from youth. *Baba* used to have many girlfriends. Eessshh just don't ask." (Baloch 2016h)

Qandeel thus raised a topic that is widely understood but rarely named and discussed: male desire, gaze, and lust. This made her simultaneously a beloved and a hated figure. In one of her videos she pointed out this two-faced, present-absent, character of male desire. Addressing her supposedly male audience, she said: "You are such nasty people by the way... double standard people. You like to watch me and then you say, 'Why don't you die?' 'Just die.' If I die, another Qandeel Baloch won't come here. Another Qandeel Baloch will not be born for another 100 years. And you guys will miss me. *Muwah. Acha chalo* [ok let's go] I am going. Ok. Byee" (Baloch 2016j).

Qandeel inverted the line of questioning that sought to humiliate her by calling attention to how her media products, and their consumption and circulation, were bound up with male hypocrisy. The culprit to her, then, was male desire. In making such claims, Qandeel was broaching a topic that remains underdiscussed in Pakistan. Indeed, as Joan Cocks (1989) observes: "desire expresses itself most fully where only those absorbed in its delights and torments are present" and "that it triumphs most completely over other human preoccupations in places sheltered from view. Thus it is paradoxically in hiding that the secrets of desire come to light" (as cited in hooks 1992, 115). Qandeel called out how society permitted men to fulfill their desires through polygamy, sexual violence, flirtation, and harassment, but then looked down on her when she exploited that same desire to make a living or to expose a religious charlatan. On one occasion, we even find Qandeel mocking the hypocrisy of those who criticize her for showing too much skin by donning a veil and a Baloch *shalwar kameez* which covered her entire body, but then dancing erotically: "Happy?" she asked her audience.

Qandeel's views about male desire and privilege were no doubt shaped by her experiences of forced marriage and sexual harassment in the workplace. She left her husband because he was abusive but then suffered abuse in the media industry as well: "You know what kinds of offers they make to girls here. You know how they try to misuse girls who are new to the industry. Nothing is good in this society. This *mardon ki society* (men's society) is bad" (as cited in Chaudhry 2016). Elsewhere she said, "Nothing is good in this society. This patriarchal society is bad" (Images staff 2016).

BEYOND "HONOR CRIMES"

My effort at exploring Qandeel's self-articulation is not aimed at discovering Qandeel's truth: instead, what I have tried to present are some of the ways in which her performances disturbed prevailing societal hierarchies. In doing so, she crossed borders and pushed many boundaries—she moved from working class to middle class; she dabbled in television but quickly learned that the industry was not hospitable for her and moved into social media, and then she pushed the boundaries of what constituted a respectable woman by flaunting her sexuality. She commoditized her body, wresting it away from the realm of the private—where it is too often exploited in ways sanctioned through legal, cultural, and often religious codes—to the public, where it is not even supposed to be except in circumscribed ways, and definitely not in relation to experiencing pleasure. Once established, she became more critical of authority figures that sought to restrain women at large while nevertheless seeking to derive pleasure by consuming women like her. She pointed out the double standards of media for shaming her while allowing sexual harassment to prevail within the industry. She criticized politicians for being corrupt. And most scandalously, she revealed the duplicitous behavior of a leading religious cleric.

Given these multiple and entangled story lines, to reduce her death to an honor crime—explaining that her brother killed her because her actions shamed him as a family member—would entail turning a blind eye to these broader social and political worlds within which the crime against her occurred. In tracing how she moved about in the social world, I have tried to present the different contestations and politics that are occluded by the category of honor killing. Indeed, if Qandeel's murder continues to be articulated as an honor crime, then provocations by other state-sanctioned actors such as Mufti Qavi, Nawaz Sharif's effective erasure of the state's culpability, the failure of the state to provide her protection when she asked for it, and the violence of those who denigrated her for her social class positioning can be imagined to stand outside of it. The framing of honor crimes confines our analysis to the operation of honor and shame in the context of the family, and precludes an analysis of the role of other societal institutions and actors, political, legal, and religious that too are complicit in the gendered violence that shaped both her life and death. Abu-Lughod (2013, 140–50) has therefore called on feminist activists to be more attentive to specifics of the crimes, including the political and social institutions that are at play in the scenes as conditions. Qandeel's case shows that her murder was made possible due to a longer history of state and religious hegemony over religio-morality that Qandeel had challenged publicly. In naming male desire as a structuring force in women's lives and then playing with the same desire, she laid bare its operation in society. She thus emerged as a threat and was silenced.

The discussion in this chapter does not imply that Pakistani activists' efforts are not laudable; these activists have been able to push an amendment to a prevailing legislation that allowed for the killing of women with impunity. However, according to some political analysts, the reformed law has not had the desired effect (Zakaria 2019). It is reported that some murderers do not mind jail time as it is viewed as an acceptable outcome of protecting their own or their family's honor (as cited in Zia 2019). Crucially, there exists a diversity of activist tactics. While some have appealed to the state, others have more recently taken to the streets to reject surveillance and control of women in intimate as well as public spaces. In particular, since 2019, multiple self-proclaimed feminist groups in Pakistan have mobilized Qandeel as a feminist icon during annual Women's Marches (Aurat March Karachi 2020). The following excerpt from the organizers of the Karachi arm of the march signals how Qandeel is reanimated to destabilize statist, religious, and familial control:

> Q is for Qandeel. No one shook the patriarchy using digital media more than Qandeel Baloch. A renegade, a rebel, a firecracker, she smiled, giggled and batted her lashes in the ultimate display of fearless femininity. Qandeel is why we march. Forced in a marriage she didn't want, she left Multan to seek stardom and fought her way to Pakistan Idol, where she was ridiculed and humiliated. But the underdog with unheard of social media savvy soon built an audience on Facebook, where she was admired and vilified in equal measure. And for that she was murdered by her own brother. Or was it just him? Who truly killed Qandeel? Honor killing is a crime that shares bloody hands: from individual participants who watched Qandeel's provocative videos on one screen and spewed venom against her on the other, even after her death. To the media that is unheeding of the danger they place women in when they leaked her information on national TV, to the family member whose hands did the deed—all the way to the legal systems that delayed and denied her justice. The patriarchy works to silence those who do not comply with the system. And so, when Qandeel took a step too far and exposed the morals of a man considered a religious gatekeeper, she was brutally murdered. Qandeel Baloch will live on as a symbol of what we fight for—to live life on our terms, to occupy digital spaces and not be moral policed for it. For paving the way, we thank you, Qandeel." (@AuratMarchKHI, February 28, 2020)

I conclude with this tweet in order to signal the diversity of feminist activism in Pakistan (see Khoja-Moolji 2022). Such groups draw on the category of honor crime but move beyond it to name the multiple intersecting forces that shape women's lives in Pakistan. These activists assert their right to assembly through staging protests, and in doing so, become the very bodies in public that make state and religious elites nervous in the first place. They point to what a feminist politics of abolition, rather than inclusion within statist apparatuses, might look like in Pakistan.

REFERENCES

Abu-Lughod, Lila. 2005. *Dramas of Nationhood: The Politics of Television in Egypt*. Chicago: University of Chicago Press.

Abu-Lughod, Lila. 2011. Seductions of the "Honor Crime." *differences: A Journal of Feminist Cultural Studies*. 22, no. 1: 17–63. https://doi.org/10.1215/10407391-1218238.

Abu-Lughod, Lila. 2013. *Do Muslim Women Need Saving?* Cambridge, MA: Harvard University Press.

Ahmed, Issam. 2016. "I Wish I'd Sent That Message." *Correspondent AFP*, July 20. https://correspondent.afp.com/i-wish-id-sent-message. Accessed August 9, 2018.

Ali, Rabia. 2001. The Dark Side of 'Honour': Women Victims in Pakistan. *Shirkat Gah*. https://cdn.atria.nl/ezines/IAV_606755/IAV_606755_2001.pdf.

Ali, Rozina. 2016. The Death of Qandeel Baloch. *The Cairo Review*, July 21. https://www.thecairoreview.com/global-forum/the-death-of-qandeel-baloch/.

Ali, Umer. 2016. "Law and Honour." *Friday Times*, March 18. https://www.thefridaytimes.com/law-and-honour/.

Amnesty International. 1991. "Pakistan: New Forms of Cruel and Degrading Punishment." *Amnesty International*, March 1. https://www.amnesty.org/en/documents/asa33/004/1991/en/.

Aurat March Karachi (@AuratMarchKHI). Twitter post. February 28, 2020. https://twitter.com/AuratMarchKHI/status/1233301929654194176.

Baloch, Qandeel. 2016a. "Qandeel Baloch Funny Interview—Ajeeb Sa 17 April 2016." YouTube video, 29:44. From televised interview with *Ajeeb Sa*. *Neo TV Network*. Posted April 17, 2016. https://www.youtube.com/watch?v=7c20z8BvgLs.

Baloch, Qandeel. 2016b. "Qandeel Baloch Married Three Men, Not Two, Claims Ex-Husband." *Dunya News*, July 14. http://dunyanews.tv/en/Entertainment/345051-Qandeel-Baloch-married-three-men-not-two-claims-.

Baloch, Qandeel. 2016c. "Qandeel Baloch Strip Dance Offer 2 Shahid Afridi If Win." YouTube video, 1:58. From *RRP Newspage*. Posted March 19, 2016. https://www.youtube.com/watch?v=9Q84et_rXfg.

Baloch, Qandeel. 2016d. "Qandeel Baloch Will Do a Strip Dance for Shahid Afridi." YouTube video, 1:17. Posted March 14, 2016. https://www.youtube.com/watch?v=CjDGnnE23dM.

Baloch, Qandeel. 2016e. "Jamhoor Fareed Rais K Sath: Qandeel Baloch Model Exclusive Interview—Wednesday, March 30, 2016." *Pakistan Herald*, March 30. http://www.pakistanherald.com/program/38230/30-march-2016/special-transmission-jamhoor-fareed-rais-k-sath(col)-qandeel-baloch-model-exclusive-interview/.

Baloch, Qandeel. 2016f. "Qandeel Baloch Exclusive Interview in Nadia Mirza Live Show." DailyMotion video, 30:34. From *One News*. https://www.dailymotion.com/video/x4ojaio.

Baloch, Qandeel. 2016g. "Qandeel Baloch Press Conference." YouTube video, 11:37. From *Dawn News*. Posted June 28, 2016. https://www.youtube.com/watch?v=TuyTR4oOBvs.

Baloch, Qandeel. 2016h. "Interview on *Ajeeb Sa*." YouTube video. From *Neo News*. Posted April 10, 2016 (removed online). https://www.youtube.com/watch?v=yFBlYlPPug8. Accessed August 9, 2018.

Baloch, Qandeel. 2016i. "Interview on *Ajeeb Sa*." YouTube video. From *Neo News*. Posted April 17, 2016 (removed online). https://www.youtube.com/watch?v=yFBlYlPPug8. Accessed August 9, 2018.

Baloch, Qandeel. 2016j. "Qandeel Baloch Sick." YouTube video (removed online). https://www.youtube.com/watch?v=94tlvYtTnPE. Accessed August 9, 2018.

BBC. 2016. "Qandeel Baloch: She 'Supported All of Us, Including My Son Who Killed Her,' Father Says." BBC, July 18. https://www.bbc.com/news/world-asia-36823098.

Brightman, Sara. 2015. "Rights, Women, and the State of Pakistan." *Contemporary Justice Review* 18, no. 3: 334–51. https://doi.org/10.1080/10282580.2015.1057706.

Burki, Shireen. 2016. "The Politics of Misogyny: General Zia-ul-Haq's Islamization of Pakistan's Legal System." *Contemporary Justice Review* 19, no. 1: 103–19. https://doi.org/10.1080/10282580.2015.1101683.

Chaudhry, Hufsa. 2016. "No One Gives Me Any Credit for Speaking about Girl Power: Qandeel Baloch." IMAGES, updated July 15, 2020. https://images.dawn.com/news/1175807.

Chughtai, Alia. 2016. "Pakistan: Anger after Honour Killing of Qandeel Baloch." *Al-Jazeera*, July 17. https://www.aljazeera.com/news/2016/07/pakistan-anger-honour-killing-qandeel-baloch-160716140502239.html.

Cowasjee, Ardeshir. 2003. "Are We Inhuman?" *Dawn Newspaper*, February 23. https://www.dawn.com/news/1072697/are-we-inhuman.

Entertainment Desk. 2016. "Madonna Lauds Sharmeen Obaid Chinoy's Documentary on Qandeel Baloch." *The Express Tribune*, October 12. https://tribune.com.pk/story/1197770/madonna-lauds-sharmeen-obaid-chinoy-upcoming-documentary-qandeel-baloch/.

Fisk, Robert. 2010. "Relatives with Blood on Their Hands." *Independent*, September 8. https://www.independent.co.uk/voices/commentators/fisk/robert-fisk-relatives-with-blood-on-their-hands-2073142.html.

Gabol, Imran, and Taseer Subhani. 2016. "Qandeel Bloch Murdered by Brother in Multan: Police." *Dawn News*, July 16. https://www.dawn.com/news/1271213.

Gill, Aisha, and Avtar Brah. 2014. "Interrogating Cultural Narratives about 'Honour'-Based Violence." *European Journal of Women's Studies* 21, no. 1: 72–86. https://doi.org/10.1177/1350506813510424.

Grewal, Inderpal. 2013. "Outsourcing Patriarchy: Feminist Encounters, Transnational Mediations, and the Crime of 'Honor Killings.'" *International Feminist Journal of Politics* 15, no. 1: 1–19. https://doi.org/10.1080/14616742.2012.755352.

Hall, Stuart. 1985. Signification, Representation, Ideology: Althusser and the Post-Structuralist Debate. *Critical Studies in Mass Communication* 2, no. 2: 91–114. https://doi.org/10.1080/15295038509360070.

hooks, bell. 1992. *Black Looks: Race and Representation*. Boston: South End Press.

Images staff. 2016. "Pakistan Reacts to Qandeel Baloch's Shocking Murder." *Dawn Newspaper*, July 16. https://images.dawn.com/news/1175823/pakistan-reacts-to-qandeel-balochs-shocking-murder.

Jamal, Amina. 2006. "Gender, Citizenship, and the Nation-State in Pakistan: Willful Daughters of Free Citizens." *Signs: Journal of Women in Culture and Society* 31, no. 2: 283–304. https://doi.org/10.1086/491676.

Khalid, Lubna. 2016. "When Honor Is Shame." *The News*, August 8. https://www.thenews.com.pk/magazine/you/144378-When-honour-is-shame.

Khan, Mishaal. 2016. "Pakistan: The Shame of It All." *Newsweek*, February 24. http://newsweekme.com/pakistan-the-shame-of-it-all/.

Khan, Saira. 2016. "The Outrageous 'Honor Killing' of a Pakistani Social-Media Star." *The New Yorker*, July 19. https://www.newyorker.com/news/news-desk/the-outrageous-honor-killing-of-a-pakistani-social-media-star.

Khan, Wajahat. 2016. "Outspoken Pakistani Model Qandeel Baloch Strangled in 'Honor Killing': Police." *NBC News*, July 16. https://www.nbcnews.com/news/world/outspoken-pakistani-model-qandeel-baloch-strangled-honor-killing-police-n610791.

Khoja-Moolji, Shenila. 2017. "The Making of Humans and Their Others in and through Transnational Human Rights Advocacy: Exploring the Cases of Mukhtar Mai and Malala Yousafzai." *Signs: Journal of Women in Culture and Society*, 42, no. 2: 377–402. https://doi.org/10.1086/688184.

Khoja-Moolji, Shenila. 2021. *Sovereign Attachments: Masculinity, Muslimness, and Affective Politics in Pakistan*. Berkeley: University of California Press.

Khoja-Moolji, Shenila. 2022. "Patriarchy as an Assemblage: Qandeel Baloch, and the Expansion and Narrowing of Patriarchy." *Journal of South Asian Studies* 45, no. 1: 1–18. https://doi.org/10.1080/00856401.2021.1969138.

Koğacıoğlu, Dicle. 2004. "The Tradition Effect: Framing Honor Crimes in Turkey." *Differences: A Journal of Feminist Cultural Studies* 15, no. 2: 118–51. https://muse.jhu.edu/article/170546.

Masood, Salman. 2016. "Qandeel Baloch, Pakistani Social Media Celebrity, Dead in Apparent Honor Killing." *New York Times*, July 16. https://www.nytimes.com/2016/07/17/world/asia/qandeel-baloch-pakistan-internet-celebrity-killed.html.

Matlub, Raja. 2016. "Interview on *Ajeeb Sa*." YouTube Video. From *Neo News*. Uploaded April 10, 2016. https://www.youtube.com/watch?v=yFBlYlPPug8. Accessed August 9, 2018.

Naar, Ismaeel. 2016. "Q&A: Pakistani Oscar-Nominated Film Sheds Light on Honor Killings." *Al-Arabiy*a, February 24. http://english.alarabiya.net/en/life-style/entertainment/2016/02/24/Q-A-Pakistani-Oscar-nominated-film-sheds-light-on-honor-killings.html.

Nauman, Qasim. 2016. "Qandeel Baloch, a Pakistani Internet Celebrity, Is Killed in 'Honor Killing.'" *Wall Street Journal*, July 16. https://www.wsj.com/articles/pakistani-internet-celebrity-qandeel-baloch-killed-in-honor-killing-1468675455.

Naveed, Soha. 2016. "Resurfacing of Momina Mustehson's Old Tweet on Qandeel Baloch Is Raising a Lot of Questions." *Parhlo*, October 14. https://www.parhlo.com/resurfacing-of-momina-mustehsans-old-tweet-on-qandeel-balooch-is-raising-a-lot-of-questions/.

Newsdesk. 2016. "PM Nawaz Sharif Meets Sharmeen Obaid Chinoy." *The News*, February 16. https://www.thenews.com.pk/magazine/instep-today/98757-PM-Nawaz-Sharif-meets-Sharmeen-Obaid-Chinoy.

Notezai, Muhammad. 2016. "Pakistan and Honor Killings: Will the Recent Murder of a Celebrity Finally Prompt the Government of Pakistan to Act?" *The Diplomat*, September 4. https://thediplomat.com/2016/09/pakistan-and-honor-killings/.

Palo, Stephanie. 2008. "A Charade of Change: Qisas and Diyat Ordinance Allows Honor Killings to Go Unpunished in Pakistan." *University of California Davis Journal of International Law and Policy* 15, no. 1: 93–110.

Perry, Juliet. 2016. "Brother of Pakistan's Qandeel Baloch: I'm 'Proud' of Strangling My Sister." CNN, July 19. https://edition.cnn.com/2016/07/18/asia/pakistan-qandeel-baloch-brother-confession/index.html.

Refworld. 2016. "Pakistani PM Vows to Eradicate Honor Killings after Oscar Nomination." *Refworld*, January 15. https://www.refworld.org/docid/56c429028.html.

Rehman, I. A. 2016. "Sharmeen's Win and Women's Rights." *Dawn News*, March 3. https://www.dawn.com/news/1243155.

Shah, Hassam Qadir. 2002. "Don't Let Them Get Away with Murder. Booklet on Criminal Procedures." *Shirkat Gah Women's Resource Centre*. https://beenasarwar.files.wordpress.com/2014/05/honour-killing-criminal-procedures-hassam-qadir-shah-shirkat-gah.pdf.

Shah, Nafisa. 2016. *Honour and Violence: Gender, Power and Law in Southern Pakistan*. New York: Berghan Books.

Standish, Katerina. 2014. "Understanding Cultural Violence and Gender: Honour Killings; Dowry Murder; the Zina Ordinance and Blood-Feuds." *Journal of Gender Studies* 23, no. 2: 111–24. https://doi.org/10.1080/09589236.2012.739082.

The News. 2016. "Qandeel Baloch Discussion Dominates Punjab Assembly." June 22. https://www.thenews.com.pk/latest/129857-Qandeel-Baloch-discussion-dominates-Punjab-Assembly.

Toor, Saadia. 2007. "Moral Regulation in a Postcolonial Nation-State." *Interventions* 9, no. 2: 255–75. https://doi.org/10.1080/13698010701409186.

Zahid, Maria. 2016. "Qandeel Baloch Exclusive Interview in Nadia Mirza Live Show." DailyMotion video, 30:34. From *One News*, posted March 26, 2016. https://www.dailymotion.com/video/x40jaio.

Zakaria, Rafia. 2019. "The Crime of 'Shame Washing'" *Dawn News*, May 22. https://www.dawn.com/news/1483803/the-crime-of-shame-washing.

Zaman, Muhammad Qasim. 2002. *The Ulama in Contemporary Islam: Custodians of Change*. Princeton, NJ: Princeton University Press.

Zaman, Muhammad Qasim. 2018. *Islam in Pakistan: A History*. Princeton, NJ: Princeton University Press.

Zia, Afiya. 2019. "Can Rescue Narratives Save Lives? Honor Killing in Pakistan." *Signs: Journal of Women in Culture and Society* 44, no. 2: 355–78. https://doi.org/10.1086/699342.

Zubair, Hamna. 2016. "The Tragedy of Qandeel Baloch." *Slate*, July 19. http://www.slate.com/articles/news_and_politics/foreigners/2016/07/pakistani_social_media_star_qandeel_baloch_was_a_revolutionary.html.

SEVEN · *Nadera Shalhoub-Kevorkian*

State Criminality and Gender-Based Violence

Palestinian Schoolgirls between Books and Rifles

INTRODUCTION

Maha, a Palestinian girl from Occupied East Jerusalem (OEJ) whom I often met on her morning walk to school near Jerusalem's Damascus Gate, was walking quickly. She usually greeted me on these morning walks with a big smile and by sharing her news, worries, and recent adventures. This day was different. I sensed her fear; she was walking fast and breathing hard. She grabbed my hand and asked, "Aren't you walking with me to school?" "Of course," I said.

As we walked, I asked her, "Where is your school bag? No books today?" She kept walking, eyes forward, without looking to either side or responding to my question. We climbed the steep stairs of her school and went into her classroom. Still, she held my hand tight. After she sat in her seat she said, "They took my school bag yesterday. They took my books." With tears in her eyes, she continued, "But I do not need schoolbooks. I am a pupil who does not need any schoolbooks. I look around me and read it all . . . I read my life when they stop me and scare me on my way to school. I read their theft. I read their violence. I read their crimes . . . I do not need books. I know what crime is . . . I live it day and night."

The experiences and voice of the girl-child are rarely considered when discussing gender-based violence in colonized zones or militarized states, especially those that enjoy international legitimacy, like Israel. Schoolgirls like Maha, whose experiences and words I present in this essay, give us insight into the intimate and commonplace forms of state violence they endure at the hands of their colonial occupiers. They force us to reconsider the dominant frameworks of gender-based violence and to consider the utility of a nonnormative conceptualization of "state crime" that legal theorists and criminologists have been developing over the last couple of decades (Chambliss 1989; Kauzlarich 1995; Ward and Green 2000, 2016). States resort to regimes of violence to control, discriminate against, and govern subjugated populations while producing a spiral machinery of violence that locks the subjugated community within a maze of injustice. State crime is commonly defined as "illegal, socially injurious, or unjust acts which are committed for the benefit of a state or its agencies, and not for the personal gain of some individual agent of the state" (Kauzlarich, Matthews, and Miller 2001, 175). When political violence is integrated into a gendered state power and its structures, its legitimacy constitutes an important component, for it intertwines systems of power with "beliefs" and "values" that guarantee the validity of governance (Green and Ward 2000). These acts include a range of human rights violations of the rights to safety, to education, and to a childhood. Sexual violence as well as the fear and horror imposed through imagined sexual threats become a tool of the state to penetrate and violate bodies that are already perceived as impure and desecrated (Green, MacManus, and de la Cour Venning 2015; Shalhoub-Kevorkian 2020; Smith 2003).

In the context of the settler-colony, the different modalities of everyday violence perpetrated against schoolchildren—violence that works to extend and solidify Israeli colonial control over the territory it has occupied—can be characterized as state-imposed gender-based violence. According to the Fourth Geneva Convention, Israel, as an occupying power, is legally obliged to secure the human rights of Palestinians. Both boys and girls in OEJ are subjected to dehumanizing psychological and physical threats on their way to school. Witnessing overt state violence against schoolboys contributes to the terror and insecurity the girls experience, as we will see, but the testimonies of Palestinian schoolgirls allow us to identify specific forms of violence that the Israeli state uses against them and to appreciate the ways this violence, both direct and indirect, is deeply gendered and even experienced as sexualized.

Following the footsteps of Maha and her peers allows us to trace an obscured form of violence against Palestinian children, one that has grave social and cultural consequences for them and is a direct product of the militarization of educational spaces and the policing of bodies in the service of the Israeli state's larger political goals. Maha's experience of having her books confiscated and her body touched by Israeli soldiers is just one example of the daily violence children in OEJ encounter on their paths to school. These are routine violations whose impact is minimized by those who carry them out using arguments about "security necessities" (Shalhoub-Kevorkian 2015a). The trauma experienced by Palestinian children in OEJ as they walk to school is dismissed by the authorities and by Israeli media, but Maha's emotional response to the violence reveals the way the occupying power positions Palestinian schoolchildren as gendered and racialized subjects. Their abuse and degradation must be understood as integral to the extension of the Israeli state's territorial control.

This chapter examines the nexus of state crime, settler colonialism, and dominant frameworks of gender-based violence (GBV). It aims to uncover invisible and sexualized state GBV to expand our understanding of the geopolitics of gender violence. It introduces the violence against Maha's body and the everyday spaces she and her peers inhabit to open up questions about the international invisibility and impunity of state violence. To counter the dehumanization of these Palestinian schoolgirls, I center their voices and listen to their narratives. Based on the schoolgirls' descriptions of what they experience on their way to school in OEJ, I argue for the expansion of the standard definitions of gender-based violence in two ways. First, the policing of schoolchildren en route to school is a form of criminal gender-based state terror. The ideological justifications for these practices in the "othering" of Palestinians should be included in charges that these acts are gender-based state crimes. Second, I argue that in this context of militarization, the regular and intimate invasions of schoolchildren's bodily safety by armed soldiers and police are experienced as forms of sexual violence.

The girls' experiences on their way to school allow us to focus on how the spiraling violence in OEJ operates through the most mundane acts and yet is part of a broader racialized demographic project. The girls' testimonies invite us to inspect the multifaceted forms of Israeli state violence. Palestinian schoolgirls wrote letters and discussed their experiences with me as part of my long-term investigation as an activist feminist scholar of children's experiences (see Shalhoub-Kevorkian 2019).[1] The hypersurveillance of children's lives and spaces that is part of the settler-colonial regime of dispossession, with its biopolitical and geopolitical forms of control, stamps Palestinians for what Wolfe (2006) calls "elimination" from these invaded spaces. Violence, enacted through the reordering of space and daily life, evicts Palestinians from their homes and homeland, and marks them as "others" whose bodies and lives are penetrable and unwanted. The schoolgirls' narratives reveal something more specific however: the gendered nature of the violations of military occupation and state-sanctioned aggression.

To give context to the girls' words, I offer a brief history of Israel's colonial dispossession of Palestinians, show the complicity of so-called law enforcement personnel, and outline the biopolitical regime of control through which the state manages and regulates Jerusalemite residents in its push to create a fully Judaized space. Human rights reporting and formal statistics about educational inequality fill out the picture of the dynamics of gendered violence in the context of occupation. As in other settler-colonial situations, we see how the state seeks to increase its power by diminishing the native's political status, rendering the native always ready for eviction and invading the most intimate spaces to injure families and individual bodies and minds from birth to death (Shalhoub-Kevorkian 2014, 2015a). This violence creates a climate of constant anxiety and fear. The schoolgirls' frank descriptions allow us to understand exactly how this works, laying out the operational dynamics and giving us glimpses of its visceral effects.

STATE MANAGEMENT OF SUSPECT OTHERS

Investigations of gendered violence must historicize and specify context. In this case, the question is how abuses suffered by schoolgirls are intertwined with land theft, evictions, incarceration, and political domination. Israel occupied the Palestinian Territories, including East Jerusalem, in 1967 (Benvenisti 1996; Jabareen 2010). Since then, the state has constructed a complex web of legal and bureaucratic systems that control the lives of Palestinians living in the occupied territory (Jabareen 2017). The Israeli state applies multiple technologies, including the spatial, social, political, economic, and legal, to assert its power as a militarized occupying force. It infiltrates each aspect of Palestinian life, disrupting continuity, cutting off spaces, and dismembering the community. Israel applies discriminatory laws and bureaucracies that evict residents and demolish homes, hinder mobility, and restrict space. The state has set up military checkpoints and constructed the separation wall. The surveillance regime utilizes visible and invisible modes of control, penetrating both home life and psychic realms and driving cycles of violence.

Legalized differentiation of Palestinians through individual or group identification assists surveillance strategies and creates racialized hierarchies of domination. Israeli authorities justify these systems as emergency security measures (Shalhoub-Kevorkian 2015a). This justifies the inhumane treatment and injustices Palestinians face daily, including what Maha and her friends experience on their way to school. Also justified are the policies toward East Jerusalem—legal, spatial, and socioeconomic—that give the advantage to the Israeli Jewish population over the Palestinian population (Nitzan-Shiftan 2006; Nasrallah 2008). Infrastructure and services are unequally distributed; the Jerusalem municipality disproportionately invests in Jewish Israeli areas as it dispossesses Palestinians of their homes and land while building new settlements for Jews. On the Palestinian side of the Old City, infrastructure is neglected, and public space is packed with police, soldiers, and settlers (Chiodelli 2018; Pullan 2013).

In OEJ, the Israeli state demonstrates its political power not only through control of space and land but also by reordering intimate familial relations. Racialized discrimination within the identification system is a key way in which Israel manages families (Tawil-Souri 2011a). There are laws against family unification as well as residency laws and regulations in OEJ. Schoolgirls explained both in writings and in interviews how much they feared being stopped and asked for a *kushan* (a kind of birth certificate similar to an ID card). They described how such a racialized system can divide family members, as some may be considered resident while others are marked as invaders who risk eviction.

Among the strongest indicators of the ongoing colonization of Jerusalem are the direct and indirect forms of Israeli violence to rearrange space (Usher 2006). Evictions, the policing of movement, and the frequent incarceration of native Palestinians are strategic. Arrests and imprisonment of family members and the broader policing and militarization of spaces are complemented by the aesthetics of gun culture, with pistols and rifles dominating public space. These are meant to be witnessed as Palestinians go about their daily lives, on their way to work, clinics, home, and school, where they can always be stopped or threatened. The schoolgirls testify to the effects of this policing.

EDUCATION UNDER OCCUPATION

In OEJ, despite international recognition of children's access to education as a fundamental right and its provision as a duty of states, education is systematically obstructed. Denial of access to education begins in early childhood: there are approximately 15,000 children between the ages of three and four years old who are entitled to free education under Israeli law, yet approximately 90 percent are not enrolled in preschool (ACRI 2008). Only two municipal preschools operate in East Jerusalem, compared with fifty-six in West Jerusalem (OHCHR 2011).

East Jerusalem has eighty-eight public schools that are managed by the Jerusalem municipality, ninety-seven recognized but unofficial schools that receive partial funding from Israel's Ministry of Education, and seventy-nine private schools (ACRI 2017). Palestinian students comprise 40 percent of all students in Jerusalem (ACRI 2015), yet only 41 percent of Palestinian children are enrolled in public municipally managed schools due to classroom shortages (ACRI 2017, 2). Another 41 percent attend unrecognized schools, while 18 percent are forced to attend private schools that their families struggle to afford (ACRI 2017, 2). This situation is due in part to a shortage of 2,000 classrooms in the official municipal education system and the fact that a great number of the existing classrooms are defined as "substandard" (ACRI 2017, 2).

The gap between education budgets allocated in East and West Jerusalem over the years reveals a stark situation for Palestinian education. According to the Israeli newspaper *Haaretz*, in 2008, 577 NIS (New Israel Shekel; approximately US$150) were spent on each primary school student in East Jerusalem, compared to 2,372 NIS (approximately US$656) for a student in the mainly Jewish western part of the city. The gap was the same eight years later, in 2016; the Ministry of Education budget for the 12,864 high school pupils in East Jerusalem's municipal high schools was 106 million NIS, while the government budget totaled 136 million NIS for the 7,009 high school pupils in West Jerusalem (Hasson 2016).

Hence, it is not surprising that the school dropout rate for Palestinian students is four times higher than that of the Jewish population in Israel, reaching 33 percent of twelfth graders (Hasson 2016). Instances of increased political violence, such as occurred after the Second Intifada, further restrict children's access to schools (Shalhoub-Kevorkian 2006). Security measures result in delays at checkpoints, forcing children to take long detours to reach school. The total number of Palestinian children in Jerusalem who do not attend school is not known; however, there are reportedly 17,717 students about whom the Israeli education system has no information (ACRI 2017).

Spatial violence—the way in which space and architecture are designed, constructed, and socially and economically regulated to violate safety at home and in the public sphere—has affected Palestinian children's physical access to education on what should be a mundane daily walk to and from school. As a result of the separations made by Israeli authorities between different zones of Palestinian residency in OEJ, many students who live in Jerusalem study in Palestinian schools located on the other side of the separation wall—within the municipal boundaries of Jerusalem, in Kafr Aqab, or in cities in the occupied West Bank such as Ramallah and Bethlehem. Unfortunately, there are no official figures tracking either the movement or the number of Palestinian students who must cross checkpoints on the way to school and back home to access education. Yet many Palestinian children do cross fixed checkpoints every day. Crossing these checkpoints is often accompanied by rigorous security checks, including body and strip searches, vehicle inspections, and bag searches, resulting in long delays. Wait times to cross at checkpoints such as Qalandiya can be as much as ninety minutes during peak hours. Long wait times, unpredictable interactions at the checkpoints, and frequent clashes disrupt many aspects of these pupils' daily lives (Hammami 2004, 2019; Tawil-Souri 2011b).

Physical access to education in OEJ can be dangerous as well, as Palestinian pupils are in constant contact with Israeli border police, especially at mobile checkpoints placed along roads leading to schools. Indeed, Israeli closures of Palestinian neighborhoods include roadblocks where motorists and pedestrians are searched; these are often strategically placed near schools and hospitals. In times of intensified political conflict, such as the 2014 military invasion of the Occupied Palestinian Territories (OPT), or during the waves of violence in 2015, these spaces become militarized. In October 2015, for example, Israeli border police set up twenty-nine roadblocks and internal checkpoints in OEJ. Given the fact that most Palestinian Jerusalemites do not hold Israeli citizenship but rather are considered only "residents" of Jerusalem, they are especially vulnerable since their residency is constantly in question and at risk of revocation.

The general focus on the systemic structural inequalities and the collective experience of occupation, however, obscures the specific difficulties Palestinian children face in their attempts to attend school. Indeed, the educational system is used to normalize violence against children

(Shalhoub-Kevorkian and Ihmoud 2016). The occupation severs Palestinian children from access to education by making the act of going to school a risk to bodily safety and security. Palestinian children's compromised access to education affects both boys and girls, but in different ways. There is an increased incidence of early marriage among Palestinian girls in OEJ today. Early marriage is a survival mechanism for girls experiencing violence such as the militarization of the route to school, spatial policing, poverty, homelessness, and constant displacement. This phenomenon was demonstrated in a recent report that showed that OEJ has the highest rate of marriage of underage girls in Israel (Israeli National Council for the Child 2016). A recent study by the Women Studies Center (Shalhoub-Kevorkian and Ihmoud 2016), moreover, revealed a particular increase in girls' marriage rates in areas of OEJ such as Silwan, Issawiyyeh, the Old City, Ras el Amoud, and Al-tour—all areas with an increase in newly established Jewish settlements where Palestinian residents suffer from high rates of settler violence, evictions, and home demolitions as well as a strong militarized presence.

MILITARISM AND THE GENDERED WEAPONIZATION OF LIFE, BODY, AND SPACE

The day-to-day contact with police and military personnel induces fear. The separation wall, daily stops, and bodily searches hinder pupils' journeys to school. Children are terrorized by the actual and theatrical use of guns and rifles, in addition to the use of dogs and horses, and the violent presence of mobile checkpoints. In Israel, there are between 6,700 and 20,000 assault rifles in the public sphere, all owned by the military (Hever 2015; Mazali et al. 2017).[2] Most of these weapons are located near military bases and conflict areas, such as Jerusalem. The bearing of arms in the civilian public space divides people into two categories: (1) those who feel safe around these guns, primarily Jewish-Israelis, and (2) those who perceive these guns as threats, mainly Palestinians, including Palestinians living in OEJ.

The girls' narratives reveal the terrorizing effects of the use of pistols, guns, and dogs by police and soldiers. Their descriptions of dog attacks against young children make vivid the sense of helplessness they feel during such assaults. One fourteen-year-old wrote:

> We are at risk of being shot every day, being bitten and attacked by police and military dogs. All of us, all those walking in the street were horri-

fied ... just look around you ... you know that all those weapons can be emptied in our bodies ... fast.... But last Tuesday, I felt fear that I never felt before. The dog's mouth was so big. I saw [the soldiers] planning an attack on us schoolgirls. We started crying and begging them not to harm us. I stopped talking, and my legs could not walk. I hate them.

This girl's fear, while unable to physically protect herself even by walking away, is echoed in a peer's story shared during a group interview:

We all saw the three dogs ... they were huge ... scary ... and hungry ... they do not feed them when they bring them to our area.... The sixth graders were terrified. We had no other choice, as we were on our way back from school. We held each other's hands and stuck our bodies to the wall, but the soldiers screamed at us and asked us to walk faster. Some of us tried, but I could not move. I was so scared. I held the hand of my friend and cried, begging her not to leave me ... but she walked and they [her friends] all dragged me down the street ... look at my hands, my legs, and face ... all bruised from that day.

The schoolgirls repeatedly described how pleased the police and soldiers looked as they watched the girls, terrified, confused, or tripping and falling. Indeed, the younger schoolgirls spoke in greater detail about the voyeurism of the soldiers watching their bodies being searched. One thirteen-year-old described the way soldiers used iron bars to trap the schoolgirls and touch them. The girls were both terrorized and angry. The girl who helped drag away her friend who was terrified of the dogs said, "I was dragging her while feeling I wanted to kill those soldiers ... but you know what, they were enjoying seeing our fear ... gratified by seeing our bodies being pulled and dragged."

Another girl confided:

Soldiers not only used bad, really bad words [whispering to me the word *sharmouta*, or whore] when ordering the female soldier to search our bodies.... They even asked questions with sexual meanings.... One soldier told my classmate that if he touched her ... she might like it.... I feel they take pleasure in watching us scream, cry, shiver from fear, or call for help. My friend challenged them, screamed back at them, and two soldiers hit her, one with his rifle, the other with his stick.... I am telling you ... they take pleasure in searching schoolgirls ... and if we were not strong girls who fight back ... they would not stop ... and will do more ... much more.

In over half of the letters I gathered from schoolgirls, they discussed not just police but also settler violence against them.[3] They describe harassment and attacks on their way to school, such as settlers pulling at their headscarves, using weapons to frighten them or their own security guards to assist soldiers in catching boys and girls, or loudly accusing children of stabbing and stone throwing. One schoolgirl wrote, "I hate feeling scared while on my way to school . . . most of all, I hate the way settlers pull our head scarves. . . . I can't do anything to them because the police and the soldiers are their friends, and they all hate us."

Yet another girl shared a story typical of the experiences of her peers:

Last week, I was running from them [the settlers], after they shoved me and my sister twice. I ran from one place to the other . . . like a mouse hiding from a big cat . . . and they were speaking Hebrew, saying things, plotting to catch us from different spaces . . . exactly like a little mouse . . . and they jumped in front of my face . . . I felt all my body shivering . . . and by the time I reached home, I had a red rash all over my face and skin.

As these shared experiences reveal, it is not only soldiers and formal security personnel that keep children in a constant state of fear as they shoot, arrest, and kill children. Abusive language and violence also come from private citizens, including settlers, shoppers, and casual passersby. Stories of settlers harassing and attacking families and schoolchildren came up in each focus group, in every participatory observation, and in each discussion with me. This was true while I was collecting data and conducting my participatory observations between 7:00 and 8:00 a.m. in the Old City of Jerusalem, and when I was running focus groups or having school meetings with students and teachers to share and learn about their modes of resisting these daily attacks. Schoolgirls talked about abusive language spray-painted in black on their home walls and episodes involving shoving, pushing, stealing belongings, invading schools and homes, breaking shop windows, destroying personal possessions, tearing and damaging books, and pulling at veils. The problem is that no one punishes the perpetrators. As Maha explained, "They [settlers] always, always bother us. They hit, push, break, write on our walls, walk with their big flags while hitting us with their sticks . . . and we post it on YouTube and Facebook, but no one takes note of these crimes against us . . . I told you I know what crime is, but crimes against us are not considered crimes."

THE GENDER OF STATE VIOLENCE

Maha's comment on how settlers' violence against her body, life, family, friends, and land is not considered important led immediately to a discussion of the case of Muhammad Abu-Khdeir.[4] Abu-Khdeir was a boy kidnapped while standing in front of his house and burned alive in July 2014 (Ihmoud 2015; Silver 2020). Maha said, "Did they punish the settlers that burned him alive? Did they even pay attention to his death?" In focus group discussions and letters, the girls often referred to the burning alive of Abu-Khdeir and a baby in Duma who burned to death in a settler attack (*Al Jazeera* 2015).

The horrific nature of the violence against these boys and young men terrified the girls and affected their daily routine and academic achievement. The daily arrest of young children, mainly boys, and these immolations of innocent boys' bodies, carried out with impunity by settlers, are forms of gendered violence that affect boys and girls in different ways. The girls worried about their loved ones, knowing that the murders of these boys who were set on fire went unpunished, their bodies not allowed dignified burials. Further, settler violence and its associated impunity are what theorists of state criminality have identified as a form of outsourcing, which Grewal's analysis (in this volume) of pogroms and lynchings in India unpacks.

While boys and girls are subjected to some of the same forms of violence, other forms are different, driving a wedge between them. Boys are subjected to more extreme searches than girls. They are forced to open their trousers and take off their belts, shirts, and socks in public settings in front of armed soldiers. While schoolgirls' honor and dignity may be attacked through pushing, shoving, and unveiling them, schoolboys are emasculated by being forced to expose their bodies in close proximity to armed soldiers and by being kept standing in public, barefooted, awaiting approval from soldiers or police to release them.

State violence can reinforce rigid gender roles through psychological and physical harm that strips both genders of their humanity. One girl described an incident where a fellow pupil tried to protect her from being harassed by a soldier. The soldier punished the boy and hit him, forcing him to crudely denounce the State of Palestine in front of his peers. The theatricality of the boy's humiliation was intended to subjugate both girls and boys, reminding them of the degree to which they are unprotected. The helplessness forced upon them undermined their capacity to rely on one another, breaking their camaraderie and weakening the resources of their community.

A letter from a sixteen-year-old girl shows how differentiated violence against boys and girls contributes to the way she experiences violence:

> Here in Jerusalem, we girls are persecuted. From the moment I leave home, the settlers start my morning with their harassment. Today, one of them blocked my way out of our home and I stood there, waiting for him to move to the side so I could pass. I called my mother and we were both pushed inside the house by three of them. Finally, I walked to school, looking around me, checking if they were pulling at my veil like they did yesterday, or using a string to trip me and make me fall. They intimidate, harass, and scare women and young girls. They humiliate and kill boys and men—those settlers and soldiers with their guns and rifles, those security men and women with their big rifles, and that stick. They invade our breathing.

Masculinized military violence feminizes both girls' and boys' bodies and minds while marking them as distinctly male and female subjects through the unique forms of violence to which they are subjected. Girls are robbed not only of the camaraderie of their male peers, as noted above, but also of the closeness to their adult male relatives. In addition to witnessing and absorbing the trauma that boys and men experience, the girls insisted that their interventions to save some boys or men from abuses could result in furthering the indignities and suffering. In a letter entitled "These Streets Are All Packed with Pain," Arwa, a tenth grader, shared her experience:

> I reach home devastated . . . after those soldiers and police, holding their guns and rifles pained me . . . really caused me pain . . . physical and psychological . . . and I didn't know how to explain it to my family. See, my father walks on the same path, and he feels the same . . . but he is not a young girl, he is not a woman, no one pushes a rifle between his legs. . . . They can shoot him without hesitating . . . so, when he passes, he does it fast, and tries to not think about his humiliation. . . . Do you think he would think about what his little girl feels? It is too bad. . . . He can barely raise his head when walking . . . He can't see my pain . . . too hard . . . I prefer to leave him with his pain . . . and keep in mind that he works in one of their shops . . . yes, an Israeli shop, he cleans it, to feed us.

The girls were afraid not just because their path to school was unsafe but also because this taught them that their own bodies and the bodies of their siblings and even their fathers are at risk. They bear witness to each other's struggles, compounding the experience of the violence to which they are each subjected, when sometimes they support and stand by each other, and at other times fail to do so. Among other things, schoolgirls expressed severe distress when failing to stand by Palestinians facing humiliation, oppression, or physical violence; content when taking an obvious stand and intervening to save a child in need during his or her arrest or a shop owner from a settler's attack; and rage at themselves and others when witnessing mundane atrocities and then normalizing the experience, just to reach school on time. Bearing witness to each other's struggle, as the schoolgirls pointed out, carried heavy psychological burdens and accumulated every day. Their pain and power, rage and refusal, and resistance and denial of suffering affected their well-being, social relations, and ability to disclose abuse to parents and teachers. These burdens created major walls of disbelief and mistrust between them and Palestinian adults and, at other times, motivated them to connect with other networks for solidarity and to share, act against, and participate in various activities, such as Dabkah dancing, community activism, music, and art.

ARMED OCCUPATION AS SEXUAL VIOLENCE

Bodily violence is not just gendered but also sexualized in spaces of education and military occupation in East Jerusalem. Understanding sexualized violence against schoolchildren requires an inquiry into both the historical and present treatment of Palestinians. Israeli ideology treats the colonized Palestinians as a demographic threat to be eliminated. Andrea Smith (2003) writes in her work on the sexual colonization of native peoples that the native Other is rendered "sexually violable and 'rapeable'" within the framework of colonialism. The treatment of schoolgirls within the Israeli biopolitical colonial regime similarly can be read as constructing them not just as disposable but also penetrable "Others," especially through the use of guns.

The displays of the power of the killing machine in the settler colony create uncertainty and insecurity in the native population, and activate the intensity of the power of gendered violence. Firearms are machines that shoot, kill, and as many feminists have argued, construct the masculinity of "men seeking to arm their desires" (King 2007, 89). Indeed, some argue that the penis is "championed as a love pistol, meat pistol, sex pistol, pocket pistol, or even a piece, or moreover, the phallus and the firearm become interchangeable" (Springwood 2014, 464). Guns, in the Palestinian context, animate and symbolize penetrating dominance, carrying a sexual connotation for children when they have guns pointed at them. This affect, combined with the bodily violation of searches and unwanted touching, sexualizes the violence experienced by children. These elements manifest power, fear, in/security and violence, history, and presence (Springwood 2014; Mazali et al. 2017).

During walks to school, the girls reported that they are required to submit to body searches by Israeli police and military. The forced removal of girls' veils is a form of gendered violence. The colonial state administration orders and reorders space, regulating the Palestinians through law enforcement personnel who are heavily armed and carry phallic rifles. The sexualization of this violence is not lost on the schoolgirls. As one girl noted in a group discussion:

> The walk to school is tricky. . . . I wish I could fly to school rather than walking between them [the soldiers]. . . . They harass us. . . . They gaze at us . . . and all of us here [the group of eight girls participating in the group discussion] can tell you stories of feeling the rifle on our behind, heads, faces, even between our legs. . . . Only yesterday Hanan tripped because one of them pushed his rifle between her legs.
>
> On hearing this, another girl reacted in an irritated voice, "Just watch how they carry their rifles, just watch how they stand facing us. . . . I sincerely feel someone is penetrating [me]."

Maha's voice of resistance, alongside her deep sense of pain, suggests that she and her peers experience multiple forms of violent domination. In the four interviews I had with Maha, I heard stories of rifles and guns being pointed at her small body as she walked to school, loud voices screaming at her in a language that she does not understand, and public humiliation in the theatricality of a public body search on the stairs of Damascus Gate and the confiscation of her school bag and books. Strip searches, as Aretxaga (2001) argues in the case of Ireland, constitute a gendered form of political domination driven by scenarios of state sexual violence. While Maha did not ever undergo a strip search, as defined by Aretxaga, the body search and unveiling of this female twelve-year-old child on her way to school at 7:15 a.m. is not a sexually neutral act. The politically sexualized and gendered performance taking place along the educational path, in the physical spaces used by children on their way to school, is a specific form of violence against the female child. Jacqui Alexander (1994) has noted in another context: "not just (any) body can be a citizen."

Maha's case shows that not just (any) girl child can be a child. Maha is not being treated as a child but as a suspect—a dangerous entity that must undergo a body search. The techniques of control constitute a form of gendered state sexual abuse that violates her childhood along with her right to education. She talked about her experience being searched: " They made me take off my veil. . . . They made me untie my hair, yes . . . they took the hair tie . . . and everyone around saw them searching my body. The female soldier was so nasty when checking my body. . . . She is the one that insisted that I untie my hair, and remove totally the veil."

Despite the guard's female gender, Maha experienced her body search as having a sexual charge. The racialized violation of girls' bodies is turned into a public spectacle. The logic of the schoolgirl's personal and communal belief system is desecrated with the act of unveiling: she is sexually violated by her unveiling while also being stripped of her national and religious/Muslim identity and marked as a criminal suspect.

The political violence these girls experience on the way to school has psychological as well physical effects; the visuality and enactment of the cruelty of routinized militarized violence undermines layers of social respectability. As Maha lamented:

> I was born in September 2005 and have lived all my life . . . I mean, all of it, scared of the big rifles the settlers and soldiers carry, the looks and nastiness of the Israeli police and Border Patrol. My mother and father always worried about us, mainly my eldest brother, and told us to always be safe. I always feared them . . . my body starts shivering when I see their weapons and rifles. They fear my shivering and starry eyes. . . . They fear me when I run home fast . . . and I run because I fear them, and fear their horses, cars, guns and rifles. . . . But, to remove my veil . . . means they stripped me naked. . . . They are after us . . . all the time . . . because we are Palestinians.

The brutality of soldiers standing nearby with weapons and pointing them at children, as the schoolgirls described, is felt to be sexual. Sexual violence comprises an integral part of colonial and settler-colonial technologies of domination and control, but the gendered nature of the violence is expressed differently for boys and girls in the Palestinian context. Arwa's letter drew our attention to the sexualized violence apparent in soldiers' and settlers' use of rifles. Her letter and a group discussion with four of her classmates, reveals that guns are not only read as phallic, but also used in multiple ways. As Nora explained, "One time they will point at our faces. Another time they point them at our homes, or schools, or they try to shoot our backpacks, or the groceries we carry... Most of the time, they direct the guns at our bodies, or push them between our legs to suggest they can rape us.... Of course they can't because we are everywhere.... We protect each other.... We stay, walk, and safeguard each other as much as we can."

Schoolgirls' descriptions of the weapons used to terrorize them on their paths to school, as well as the gendered invasion of their space and bodies, make clear the ways in which schoolchildren's bodies are viewed as penetrable territories of dispossession. The inscription of power through the ability to rape both the body and the land was often raised by the girls when they talked about the ways the security guards body-searched them in public, violating all social and traditional mores, not to mention children's human rights. The creation of small corridors for children to walk to school and the zoning of some areas as accessible only to Jews both serve to highlight who is respected in the space and who is viewed as endangering the "peacefulness" of the city. The violent expulsions that mark OEJ's geography also remind schoolchildren of the long history of such evictions. As one girl wrote in her letter, referring to the mass expulsion at the founding of the Israeli state in 1948, "Aren't we still living the Nakba?" Other letters reveal how schoolgirls feel trapped in the violence and are aware of the colonizer's goal to displace them, "as they displaced us in the past" and to "keep them [Palestinians] away from al Quds, away from the Haram, away from our land."

ACCOUNTABILITY FOR STATE TERROR

Maha's voice urges us to consider a new analytical space of children's rights, education, and racialized gendered and sexualized violence. In theory, the need to protect children's education comprises a nonnegotiable value upon which both global and local players should agree. However, in the colonial reality of OEJ, we can see the psychosocial harm the Israeli state works through the dispossession of land and resources and the displacement or massacre of entire villages and communities. It is also conducted, operationalized, and maintained through violations of children's rights to education.

Acts of racial profiling and sexualized gendered violence are directed against Maha and other Palestinian children daily. Time, space, land, and schoolchildren's bodies are entangled. Even schoolbooks, as Maha explained, can be confiscated and "neutralized." "Neutralization" is the term used by the Israeli Defense Forces when they shoot or kill a Palestinian. Maha described to me the way Palestinian schoolgirls and boys are shot and killed: "with no mercy. . . . and they are children." Yet despite the anxieties all these schoolgirls described, their desire to resist occupation and their refusal to accept the everyday policing of their bodies, spaces, and paths were apparent in our discussions and their letters. One has to admire their perseverance, courage, and ability to articulate their traumas.

Scholarly work on other settler-colonial contexts has exposed how children were and are regularly subjected to physical, sexual, and emotional abuse. In Australia, for example, the government forcibly removed Indigenous children from their communities from the early twentieth century up to the 1970s, creating an entire "stolen generation" (Jacobs 2005, 2009; Moses 2004). In the United States and Canada, native children were subjected to mass abductions, forced removal to boarding schools, and loss of their languages and religious traditions in the name of assimilation, integration, and modernization (Battell Lowman and Barker 2016; De Leeuw 2009; Hinton, Woolford, and Benvenuto 2014; Razack 2015). If, as in these examples, children are vital political targets for settler-colonial regimes, how does this settler tactic translate into the context of Palestine and the schoolgirls of Jerusalem? Do settlers want to "kill the Indian in the child" and "save" the child, as in those other historical contexts (Churchill 2004)? Or does the evidence point instead to their intent to just "kill the child"?

An examination of the Israeli "shoot-to-kill" (Human Rights Watch 2017) policy reveals that the majority of shootings and extrajudicial killings of schoolchildren happen on the way to and from school.[5] The usual justification is that the accused Palestinian child tried to stab an Israeli state agent (police, soldier, or other security personnel), as was the case with Fatmeh Hajij, the fifteen-year-old girl who was killed in 2017 by five Israeli soldiers using live ammunition (Wilson 2017). Maha insisted on reminding us that Fatmeh was a schoolgirl, one who had been previously arrested and tortured while in custody. Her dead body was turned into a spectacle after the rifles penetrated her body with more bullets than the number of years she had been alive. Her dead body was left bleeding on the ground while the soldiers postured with their guns erect over her motionless body. We do not have reliable data on the number of schoolchildren targeted, and in some ways it does not matter because each child's death is a loss.[6]

Imagine a situation in which soldiers, heavily armed, are stationed to "protect" space in an occupied land and thus feel surrounded by "dangerous" Others. Imagine a landscape in which settlers construct walls and checkpoints that dismember and oppress native individuals, families, and communities. The settlers use tear gas bombs and military and police vans and jeeps to police stolen land, and bulldozers to demolish schools and homes. The settlers' heavily armored bodies express their racial power and supremacy. In their daily lives, traveling to school, girls pass through the various gates in the Old City of Jerusalem, including Damascus Gate. At these sites, settlers, soldiers, and police posture with guns to "maintain" order, sending a message to the children about who holds the power. Because Israeli society casts the Palestinian subject as inherently dangerous, police and soldiers stationed around the city seek to create order through their location, presence, and stance. They carry their rifles as an extension of phallic power, controlling the space and transit of schoolchildren, teachers, and family members. It is the entanglement of this militarized space, the use of Hebrew to speak to non-Hebrew-speaking young girls and boys, the racially arranged bodies moving through the city (the disposable and nondisposable), and the soldiers' assertive body language that create these spaces of abuse.

Israelis see the settlers, and soldiers' masculinized violence, as contributing to an admirable goal: making possible ongoing structural accumulation. The posturing and rhetoric of "preserving order" and "neutralizing" the native schoolgirl's body justify the colonial project. The soldiers and police act as members of a Jewish-only family that is working for the Israeli nation. The gendered affirmations of a racialized nationhood operate in a global context in which the Israeli Jewish state presents itself as the younger brother of white nations. Israel's gendered colonial violence—subjugating the "dangerous" racial population—lends credibility to its claims to be civilizing and civilized. Because any act of resistance to this rule confirms to the colonizer that Palestinians "irrationally hate us, and want to kill us," the normalization of state terror in practices such as the "neutralization" of "threatening" schoolgirls reaffirms the aspirations of the national project.

The declaration that "Israel is fighting a savage war for peace" draws from biblical claims of a sacred nation fighting against the profane Other, promising racial unity for the national family. The racial supremacy of the Jewish citizen is integral to the grand narrative of moral superiority that resonates beyond the nation's borders. The bodies, weapons, language, and acts of the state's agents at checkpoints and walls, in streets and neighborhoods, and on the routes that Palestinian children have to take to school are part of the ruling apparatus. Political leaders rely on and reinforce this apparatus as part of a regime of control.

Bodily violence in spaces of education under military occupation must be recognized as sexualized gender violence enacted by or in the service of the state. The voices of the schoolgirls shared above reveal much about the nature of the encounters between Palestinian children and Israeli security personnel. Soldiers, police, and settlers are committed to the Zionist colonial ideology that is focused on maintaining safety for Jews only. The biopolitics of this state-sanctioned sexualized and gendered abuse through techno-machineries and weapons reinforce the conviction that the presence of the native is dangerous, even if it is just Palestinian schoolgirls.

This biopolitical understanding and the dominant ideology of the state that seeks to eliminate the Palestinians as alien spills over into treating schoolchildren as dangerous Others (Shalhoub-Kevorkian 2019). These girls' voices suggest to us that there is no occupation without a gendered politics of dispossession. Engaging with girls' writings and insights as oppositional politics can assist in dismantling the ideologies that enable this structural oppression. Privileging the girls' analysis of the violence directed against Palestinian children compels us to recognize Israel's state terror as sexualized GBV and a form of state criminality, and highlights the urgent need to trace the silences and omissions of invisible categories of GBV and its systems of power.

Critical legal scholars and criminologists have struggled to define the concept of "state crime" and to draw its boundaries.[7] The difficulty of defining state crime is related to the way in which its practices appear to be normal and even legal, as demonstrated in the schoolgirls' narrations. State crimes can include human rights violations such as genocide, war crimes and torture; police violence; and corruption in elite control of national natural resources. Ward and Green (2000) go further to include any state actions that violate citizens' human rights, whether they are deliberate or through failure to protect individuals and groups. Others emphasize the structural foundations of liberty and rights that provide humans with basic opportunities and conditions for well-being; they would brand as criminal the failure of states to provide food, shelter, or medical services.

Using the critical lens of gender violence enables us to better see what happens when state actors carry guns, harass, injure, arrest, shoot, and kill in spaces where schoolchildren, boys and girls, are attempting to go about their daily lives. Investigations of this violence reveal how these abuses intertwine with land theft, evictions, incarceration, and other forms of domination by a state that seems to do its work with impunity. The particular vulnerabilities of female children subjected to the everydayness of this gendered order alert us to the urgent need to address state criminality, acknowledging its violent penetrability, and to adopt a feminist lens that goes beyond normative GBV analyses to accept the inescapability of refusal. Juxtaposing GBV analyses with the settler-colonial one allows us to expose the colonized's agential power and modes of refusal as accounts against an ongoing history of dispossession. Feminist theorization and activism fail when they neglect and turn a blind eye to the voices of invisible victims of GBV or use normative analyses, instead of moving toward refusal of the settler state's GBV. Refusals, native scholar Simpson writes, "tell us something about the way we cradle or embed our representations and notions of sovereignty and nationhood; and they critique and move us away from statist forms of recognition" (2007, 78).

Just as the international feminist community has demanded in other contexts—most successfully around sexual and gender-based violence in war zones, in failed states, and in violence perpetrated by nonstate actors (often "jihadists" as in the case of Boko Haram)—it first should hold the Israeli state accountable for such violations and failures as creating unsafe routes to school, exposing schoolgirls to daily harassment, and inflicting terror through abusive treatment, arrests, and killing. Second, it should challenge GBV as an apparatus inhabiting power, a mode of global governance, and call out the active collusion between settler colonialism, state crime, and sexualized violence against unseen, invisible, or hyper-visibilized "dangerous" entities. Schoolgirls' voices and state criminality against girls' spaces of education suggest that feminist incorporation of GBV is not about its exclusion or inclusion in the working of power politics, but rather about comprehending the assemblages of violence that are integral to it. The feminist agenda's refusal of the gendered regime of control is beyond crucial—it is an ethical commitment, otherwise we fail the subject about which we care. Failing to attend to the voices of schoolgirls and women silenced by intense securitization, policing, and sacralized politics creates a GBV regime of carcerality, a carceral entrapment that not only hides, but allows, advances, and broadens the harmful effect of gender violence, creating a feminist regime of foreclosure.

NOTES

1. The voices offered here are based on ongoing research that started in 1996, but, more specifically, my work with schoolchildren in the past ten years. See, for example, Shalhoub-Kevorkian 2015b, 2015c, 2019, 2020, 2021; Shalhoub-Kevorkian and Marshi 2021.
2. The intensified securitization of Jerusalem and its invasive surveillance, punitive law enforcement, and state violence include the encouragement of Jewish Israeli individuals to carry weapons and use them at the first feeling of suspicion. It is a privatized mode of carrying arms, as Shir Hever (2015) explains. See also Graham (2010, 98) and Human Rights Watch (2017). It should be stressed that in Israel, individuals eighteen years and older are automatically drafted into the army, and therefore can walk in public spaces with guns. Carrying guns is not limited to the police and formal security personnel. Young and old soldiers, private security companies, and individuals, including settlers, may also bear arms. For example, in a period of tension in Jerusalem, senior Israeli politicians called on Israelis to carry arms and defend themselves rather than rely on formal security forces (Hasson 2015). Furthermore, in 2018, Israel eased restrictions on carrying guns to "improve" the response to terrorist attacks (Bachner 2018).
3. Indeed, the 2011 OCHA report, "Israeli Settler Violence in the West Bank," indicates a 165 percent increase between 2009 and 2011 in the number of weekly settler attacks resulting in Palestinian casualties, Palestinian property damage, and the harming of Palestinians' livelihoods (as cited in Shalhoub-Kevorkian and David 2015). In addition, in their 2018 article, Eiran and Krause state that "fifty-one percent of price-tag attacks target personal property, generally that of Palestinians in the West Bank." The violence of settlers is clearly gendered and sexualized, as explained by David (2021).
4. For background on Mohammed Abu-Khdeir, see Silver (2017).
5. For example, on January 23, 2016, a thirteen-year-old schoolgirl was shot and killed. Al Jazeera notes, "Luba al-Samri, spokeswoman for the Israeli police, told local media that Abu Eid had been in an argument with her parents before leaving home with the intention of carrying out a stabbing attack" (Strickland 2016). See also Kershner (2016). On September 21, 2016, a thirteen-year-old schoolgirl was shot and killed (Dearden 2016). On Monday, October 25, another schoolgirl was shot and killed (Silver 2015).
6. Numbers, names, and details can be found on the website, "Israel-Palestine Timeline: The Human Cost of Conflict" (https://israelpalestinetimeline.org/women/). In 2014, four Palestinians under the age of eighteen were killed in the first half of the year as were two Israelis (Remember These Children 2014).
7. Some prominent works in this field include Green and Ward 2000; Chambliss 1989; Cohen 1993; Kauzlarich 1995; and Ward and Green 2000 and 2016.

REFERENCES

Al Jazeera. 2015. "Palestinian Baby Burned to Death in Settler Attack." July 31. https://www.aljazeera.com/news/2015/7/31/palestinian-baby-burned-to-death-in-settler-attack.

Alexander, Jacqui. 1994. "Not Just (Any) Body Can Be a Citizen: The Politics of Law, Sexuality and Postcoloniality in Trinidad and Tobago and the Bahamas." *Feminist Review* 48: 5–23. https://doi.org/10.2307/1395166.

Aretxaga, Begoña. 2001. "The Sexual Games of the Body Politic: Fantasy and State Violence in Northern Ireland." *Culture, Medicine and Psychiatry* 25, no. 1: 1–27. https://doi.org/10.1023/A:1005630716511.

Association for Civil Rights in Israel (ACRI). 2008. "Background Information on East Jerusalem Education." September 4, 2008. https://law.acri.org.il/en/2008/09/04/background-information-on-east-jerusalem-education/.

ACRI. 2015. "East Jerusalem: Facts and Figures 2015." https://law.acri.org.il/en/wp-content/uploads/2015/05/EJ-Facts-and-Figures-2015.pdf.

ACRI. 2017. "East Jerusalem: Facts and Figures 2017." http://www.acri.org.il/en/wp-content/uploads/2017/05/Facts-and-Figures-2017.pdf.

Bachner, Michael. 2018. "Hundreds of Thousands of Israelis Okayed to Carry Guns under New Rules." *Times of Israel*, August 20. https://www.timesofisrael.com/hundreds-of-thousands-more-israelis-okayed-to-carry-guns-under-new-rules/.

Battell Lowman, Emma, and Adam J. Barker. 2016. *Settler: Identity and Colonialism in 21st Century Canada*. Halifax, NS: Fernwood Publishing.

Benvenisti, Meron. 1996. *City of Stone: The Hidden History of Jerusalem*. Berkeley: University of California Press.

Chambliss, William J. 1989. "State Organized Crime: The American Society of Criminology, 1988 Presidential Address." *Criminology* 27, no. 2: 183–208. https://doi.org/10.1111/j.1745-9125.1989.tb01028.x.

Chiodelli, Francesco. 2018. *Shaping Jerusalem: Spatial Planning, Politics and the Conflict*. Abingdon, UK: Routledge Research in Planning and Urban Design.

Churchill, Ward. 2004. *Kill the Indian, Save the Man: The Genocidal Impact of American Indian Residential Schools*. San Francisco: City Lights Publishers.

Cohen, Stanley. 1993. "Human Rights and Crimes of the State: The Culture of Denial." *Australian and New Zealand Journal of Criminology* 26, no. 2: 97–115. https://doi.org/10.1177/000486589302600201.

David, Yossi. 2021. "Gendering Political Conflict: The Racialized and Dehumanized Use of Gender on Facebook." *Feminist Media Studies*. https://doi.org/10.1080/14680777.2021.1905020.

Dearden, Lizzie. 2016. "Israeli Soldier Shoots Unarmed Palestinian Girl, 13, at West Bank Checkpoint." *Independent*, September 22. https://www.independent.co.uk/news/world/middle-east/israeli-soldier-shoots-unarmed-palestinian-girl-13-west-bank-checkpoint-eliyahu-alfei-menashe-baraa-ramadan-eweisa-a7322456.html.

De Leeuw, Sarah. 2009. "'If Anything Is to Be Done with the Indian, We Must Catch Him Very Young': Colonial Constructions of Aboriginal Children and the Geographies of Indian Residential Schooling in British Columbia, Canada." *Children's Geographies* 7, no. 2: 123–40. https://doi.org/10.1080/14733280902798837.

Eiran, Ehud, and Peter Krause. 2018. "Old (Molotov) Cocktails in New Bottles? 'Price-tag' and Settler Violence in Israel and the West Bank." *Terrorism and Political Violence* 30, no. 4: 637–57. https://doi.org/10.1080/09546553.2016.1194271.

Graham, Stephen. 2010. *Cities under Siege: The New Military Urbanism*. London: Verso.

Green, Penny, Thomas MacManus, and Alicia de la Cour Venning. 2015. *Countdown to Annihilation: Genocide in Myanmar*. London: International State Crime Initiative.

Green, Penny, and Tony Ward. 2000. "State Crime, Human Rights, and the Limits of Criminology." *Social Justice* 27, no. 1: 101–15. https://www.jstor.org/stable/29767193.

Hammami, Rema. 2004. "On the Importance of Thugs: The Moral Economy of a Checkpoint." *Middle East Research and Information Project*, INC 231 (Summer): 26–34. https://doi.org/10.2307/1559433.

Hammami, Rema. 2019. "Destabilizing Mastery and the Machine Palestinian Agency and Gendered Embodiment at Israeli Military Checkpoints." *Current Anthropology* 60, no. S19: 87–97. https://doi.org/10.1086/699906.

Hasson, Nir. 2015. "Jerusalem Mayor Calls on Civilians to Carry Weapons in Wake of Terror Attacks." *Haaretz*, October 8. https://www.haaretz.com/.premium-jerusalem-mayor-calls-on-civilians-to-carry-weapons-in-wake-of-terror-attacks-1.5406662.

Hasson, Nir. 2016. "Arab Students in Jerusalem Get Less Than Half the Funding of Jewish Counterparts." *Haaretz*, August 23. https://www.haaretz.com/israel-news/.premium-arab-students-in-jerusalem-get-less-than-half-the-funding-of-jews-1.5427909.

Hever, Shir. 2015. "Unleashing Mob Violence in Jerusalem: An Act of Desperation." *Middle East Eye*, October 14. https://www.middleeasteye.net/opinion/unleashing-mob-violence-jerusalem-act-desperation.

Hinton, Alexander Laban, Andrew Woolford, and Jeff Benvenuto, eds. 2014. *Colonial Genocide in Indigenous North America*. Durham, NC: Duke University Press.

Human Rights Watch. 2017. "Israel/Palestine: Some Officials Backing 'Shoot-to-Kill.'" January 2, 2017. https://www.hrw.org/news/2017/01/02/israel/palestine-some-officials-backing-shoot-kill.

Ihmoud, Sarah. 2015. "Mohammed Abu-Khdeir and the Politics of Racial Terror in Occupied Jerusalem." *Borderlands* 14, no. 1: 1–28.

Israeli National Council for the Child. 2016. "The State of Young Children in Israel 2015." https://bernardvanleer.org/publications-reports/state-young-children-israel/.

Jabareen, Yosef Rafeq. 2010. "The Politics of State Planning to Achieve Geopolitical

Ends: The Case of the Recent Master Plan for Jerusalem." *International Development Planning Review* 32, no. 1: 27–43. https://doi.org/10.3828/idpr.2009.11.

Jabareen, Yosef Rafeq. 2017. "The Right to Space Production and the Right to Necessity: Insurgent versus Legal Rights of Palestinians in Jerusalem." *Planning Theory* 16, no. 1: 6–31. https://doi.org/10.1177/1473095215591675.

Jacobs, Margaret D. 2005. "Maternal Colonialism: White Women and Indigenous Child Removal in the American West and Australia, 1880–1940." *Western Historical Quarterly* 36, no. 4: 453–76. https://doi.org/10.2307/25443236.

Jacobs, Margaret D. 2009. *White Mother to a Dark Race: Settler Colonialism, Maternalism, and the Removal of Indigenous Children in the American West and Australia, 1880–1940*. Lincoln: University of Nebraska Press.

Kauzlarich, David. 1995. "A Criminology of the Nuclear State." *Humanity and Society* 19, no. 3: 37–57. https://doi.org/10.1177/016059769501900304.

Kauzlarich, David, Rick A. Matthews, and William J. Miller. 2001. "Toward a Victimology of State Crime." *Critical Criminology* 10: 173–94. https://doi.org/10.1023/A:1015744304749.

Kershner, Isabel. 2016. "Palestinian Girl with Knife Killed by Israeli Guard, Police Say." *New York Times*, January 23. https://www.nytimes.com/2016/01/24/world/middleeast/palestinian-girl-13-shot-dead-in-west-bank.html.

King, Richard C. 2007. "Arming Desire: The Sexual Force of Guns in the United States." In *Open Fire: Understanding Global Gun Cultures*, edited by Charles Fruehling Springwood, 87–97. New York: Berg Publishers.

Mazali, Rela, Smadar Ben Natan, Niv Hachilli, and Galit Lubetzky. 2017. *Loose Guns: Israeli Controlled Small Arms in the Civil Sphere: How Many Guns and How Much Control?* Tel Aviv: Gun Free Kitchen Tables Project and Isha L'Isha Feminist Center.

Moses, Dirk. 2004. *Genocide and Settler Society: Frontier Violence and Stolen Indigenous Children in Australian History*. New York: Berghahn Books.

Nasrallah, Rami. 2008. "Jerusalem and Its Suburbs: The Decline of a Palestinian City." In *Jerusalem and Its Hinterlands*, edited by Omar Yousef, Rassem Khamaisi, Abdallah Owais, and Rami Nasrallah, 47–52. Jerusalem: The International Peace and Cooperation Center.

Nitzan-Shiftan, Alona. 2006. "The Israeli 'Place' in East Jerusalem: How Israeli Architects Appropriated the Palestinian Aesthetic after the '67 War." *Jerusalem Quarterly* 27: 15–27.

Office of the High Commissioner for Human Rights (OHCHR). 2011. "Optional Protocol to the Convention on the Rights of the Child on Communication Procedure," New York, December 19. *United Nations Treaty Collection*. https://treaties.un.org/pages/ViewDetails.aspx?src=TREATY&mtdsg_no=IV-11-d&chapter=4&lang=en.

Pullan, Wendy. 2013. "Conflict's Tools: Borders, Boundaries and Mobility in Jerusalem's Spatial Structures." *Mobilities* 8, no. 1: 125–47. https://doi.org/10.1080/17450101.2012.750040.

Razack, Sharene H. 2015. *Dying from Improvement: Inquests and Inquiries into Indigenous Deaths in Custody*. Toronto: University of Toronto Press.

Remember These Children. 2014. "Children Remembered." https://www.remember thesechildren.org/remember2000.html.

Shalhoub-Kevorkian, Nadera. 2006. "Negotiating the Present, Historicizing the Future—Palestinian Children Speak about the Israeli Separation Wall." *American Behavioral Scientist* 49, no. 8: 1101–24. https://doi.org/10.1177 /0002764205284721.

Shalhoub-Kevorkian, Nadera. 2014. "Criminality in Spaces of Death: The Palestinian Case Study." *British Journal of Criminology* 54, no. 1: 38–52. https://www.jstor .org/stable/23640287.

Shalhoub-Kevorkian, Nadera. 2015a. "Israel in the Bedroom: Citizenship and Entry Law." In *Security Theology, Surveillance and the Politics of Fear*, edited by Nadera Shalhoub-Kevorkian. Cambridge: Cambridge University Press.

Shalhoub-Kevorkian, Nadera. 2015b. "Childhood: A Universalist Perspective for How Israel Is Using Child Arrest and Detention to Further Its Colonial Settler Project." *International Journal of Applied Psychoanalytic Studies* 12, no. 3: 223–44. https://doi.org/10.1002/aps.1456.

Shalhoub-Kevorkian, Nadera. 2015c. "Stolen Childhood: Palestinian Children and the Structure of Genocidal Dispossession." *Settler Colonial Studies* 6, no. 2: 142–52.

Shalhoub-Kevorkian, Nadera. 2019. *Incarcerated Childhood and the Politics of Unchilding*. Cambridge: Cambridge University Press.

Shalhoub-Kevorkian, Nadera. 2020. "Unchilding and the Killing Boxes." *Journal of Genocide Research* 23, no. 3: 490–500. https://doi.org/10.1080/14623528.2020 .1829840.

Shalhoub-Kevorkian, Nadera. 2021. "Children Speaking against Home Arrest: Decolonising Racial Penologies." *British Journal of Social Work* 51, no. 4: 1374–91. https://doi.org/10.1093/bjsw/bcab042.

Shalhoub-Kevorkian, Nadera, and Yossi David. 2015. "Is the Violence of Tag Mehir a State Crime?" *British Journal of Criminology* 56, no. 5: 835–56. https://doi .org/10.1093/bjc/azv101.

Shalhoub-Kevorkian, Nadera, and Sarah Ihmoud. 2016. *In the Absence of Justice: Embodiment and the Politics of Militarized Dismemberment of Occupied Jerusalem*. UN Women.

Shalhoub-Kevorkian, Nadera, and Amir Marshi. 2021. "Iron Caging the Palestinian Home: Child Home Arrest in Occupied East Jerusalem as Lawfare." *Jerusalem Quarterly* 85 (Spring): 106–24.

Silver, Charlotte. 2015. "Schoolgirl Executed by Israeli Soliders." *Electronic Intifada*, October 26, 2015. https://electronicintifada.net/blogs/charlotte-silver/school girl-executed-israeli-soldiers.

Silver, Charlotte. 2017. "Jewish Terrorists Get Special Treatment." *Electronic Intifada*, July 6. https://electronicintifada.net/blogs/charlotte-silver/jewish-terrorists -get-special-treatment-israel.

Silver, Jake. 2020. "Familiar Pixels: Imag(in)ing the Dead and the Political in Israel/Palestine." *American Anthropologist* 123, no. 1: 1–17.

Simpson, Audra. 2007. "On Ethnographic Refusal: Indigeneity, 'Voice' and Colonial Citizenship." *Junctures* 9: 67–80.

Smith, Andrea. 2003. "Not an Indian Tradition: The Sexual Colonization of Native Peoples." *Hypatia* 18, no. 2: 70–85. https://doi.org/10.1111/j.1527-2001.2003.tb00802.x.

Springwood, Charles Fruehling. 2014. "Gun Concealment, Display, and Other Magical Habits of the Body." *Critique of Anthropology* 34, no. 4: 450–71. https://doi.org/10.1177/0308275X14543394.

Strickland, Patrick. 2016. "Israeli Guard Shoots Dead 13-Year-Old Palestinian Girl." Al Jazeera, January 23. https://www.aljazeera.com/news/2016/1/23/israeli-guard-shoots-dead-13-year-old-palestinian-girl.

Tawil-Souri, Helga. 2011a. "Colored Identity: The Politics and Materiality of ID Cards in Palestine/Israel." *Social Text* 107, 29, no. 2: 67–97.

Tawil-Souri, Helga. 2011b. "Qalandia Checkpoint as Space and Nonplace." *Space and Culture* 14, no. 1: 4–26. https://doi.org/10.1177/1206331210389260.

Usher, Graham. 2006. "The Wall and the Dismemberment of Palestine." *Race and Class* 47, no. 3: 9–30. https://doi.org/10.1177/0306396806061084.

Ward, Tony, and Penny Green. 2000. "Legitimacy, Civil Society, and State Crime." *Social Justice* 27, 3, no. 82: 76–93. https://www.jstor.org/stable/29768037.

Ward, Tony, and Penny Green. 2016. "Law, the State, and the Dialectics of State Crime." *Critical Criminology* 24: 217–30. https://doi.org/10.1007/s10612-015-9304-5.

Wilson, Nigel. 2017. "Fatima Hjeiji: Seventh Child Killed by Israel in 2017." *Al Jazeera*, May 9. https://www.aljazeera.com/news/2017/5/9/fatima-hjeiji-seventh-child-killed-by-israel-in-2017.

Wolfe, Patrick. 2006. "Settler Colonialism and the Elimination of the Native." *Journal of Genocide Research* 8, no. 4: 387–409. https://doi.org/10.1080/14623520601056240.

EIGHT · *Shahla Talebi*

Power, Subjectivity, and Sexuality in Iranian Political Prisons

Relating her experience of torture and rape in prison, Azar Al-Kannan, an Iranian Kurdish woman and a former political activist, confesses in a videotaped interview many years later, "I know rape is a form of torture, most people would say it is... but for me rape is not just torture. I do not remember the pain of lashes the same way I feel the pain of rape." Azar elaborates: "And I feel it every day, all the time. I still feel [the interrogator's] dirty hands on my body." Tears wash down her face as she repeats: "It is true that torture too is a violation, but for me rape is different; it feels different" (Farid 2009a).

Azar is aware that many critics of violence consider rape in prison as yet another form of torture. Regardless, she seems to at once confirm and question this perspective that she finds insufficient for capturing the visceral feelings and embodied memories she still carries. For Azar, in this equivalence—collapsing sexual and other forms of violence together—something of the materiality of her somatic experience is left obscured, disembodied, uncooked. Even if she agrees that sexual violence is a means of asserting power over her political subjectivity, she does not find this discursive construction sufficient to contain all the sensations of her experience. Bodily experience is of course not separable from discourses that define and delineate the perimeters of the body and experience. Azar's confession thus begs the question for those who seek to understand and condemn sexual violence, including rape in war and prison: what is behind her notion of sexuality that allows it to become so inexorably entwined with her subjectivity and hence so destructive to it when violated?

In exploring this question, I refuse two common approaches. First, the culturalist approach is often deployed to explain, or rather explain away, violence against women when it comes to a case like this, of an Iranian woman born in a Muslim family. In this view, either Middle Eastern or Muslim cultures are inherently sexually violent, making rape simply an extension of Muslim male degradation of women. Culturalists would interpret Azar's differentiation of rape from torture as an indication of sexuality in these cultures invoking greater anxiety than elsewhere. They would find this as an evidence of an obsessive concern with honor and modesty, whether expressed in veiling, virginity, or violent punishment of women for sexual infractions. However, these reductive Orientalist arguments fail to illuminate the real experiences of political prisoners like Azar and the two other women, Fatemeh and Zohreh, whose stories and views I will also share in this essay. Conversely, the second common approach assumes that rape is experienced as a universally traumatic violence, no matter where and under what circumstances, as if class, religion, race, nationality, ethnic background, and so forth, have no role in the way its impact is experienced. Universalist reactions like Azar's are therefore normal and require no specific explanation. However, my lived experience with women with whom I shared years of imprisonment and my ethnographic research with many others I came to know later through the networks forged by Iranian ex-prisoners within Iran and in exile suggest otherwise.

In telling the stories of these three women who were political prisoners under two different regimes, I hope to open up a discussion of sexuality, sexual violence, and subjectivity that takes into account the particularity of the modern historical moment and the specific conditions within which these experiences are lived, discerned, remembered and relived. My attempt is to avoid succumbing either to culturalist assumptions about the special attitudes of Muslims or to universalist explanations about the trauma of sexual violation, both of which reinforce the implicit binaries of male domination and women's vulnerability.

WOMEN AND VIOLENCE

Violence against women has received ample attention from scholars and policy makers, as this volume explores. In the last few decades regulation and criminalization have played central roles in feminist efforts to combat GBVAW. In both media and policy discourses, debates around sexual violence have become central in various fields such as the religious, political, legal, and medico-psychological. Women's bodies have been made sites of power and conflict. Rape, of women and sometimes even men, has come to be understood as a weapon of war, an emblem of ethnoreligious conflict, and a form of torture in political persecution. In various circumstances when women are kidnapped during national or ethnic conflicts, the return of the "women of the nation" (Najmabadi 1998) has been pursued as a "matter of national honor" (Das 2006, 24). Under the pretense of saving Muslim women, warmongers have deployed the trope of "honor killings" as a manifestation of "the shackles of their tradition" (Abu-Lughod 2013; Volpp, this volume). States have often leveraged sexual violence as a means to other ends, whether to assert national sovereignty or to undermine the sovereignty of other states, usually by vilifying "barbaric" others in order to claim innocence and superiority over them or to justify military intervention as a humanitarian endeavor.

Against these tropes, I am inviting us to contemplate "a radical refashioning of the normative problem space" (Scott 2004) that may allow us to pose different sets of questions. This entails traversing more jagged and exploratory paths than those paved by the standard discourses about sexual violence. This means to embark on a journey toward a more nuanced discussion of power, subjectivity, and sexuality in relation to violence, without emptying them of their historical, socioeconomic, and political contexts and their fluid interconnections. Yet acknowledging their constantly transforming and transformative characteristics and relations should not obscure the rigidifying affects that constructed categories and historical discourses produce or so often sustain. Rather than considering categories like "religion" or "culture" as separate from other social categories and constructs, I aim to explore how they interweave in the lived experiences of individuals. I begin with Azar, a Kurdish-Iranian woman and former political prisoner, now living in Europe. I will contemplate why, for Azar, experiencing rape in prison is so different from all the other forms of torture.

Indeed, this is the main question of this chapter. How do we explain why subjection to rape is often assumed to crush its victims' souls more drastically than other forms of violence? Is it due to this significance that we, as subjects of modernity, have attributed to sexuality, as Foucault (1978) has suggested that sexual violence is more likely to be utilized as an instrument of power? Has the delineation of sexuality as a universal natural phenomenon, bereft of history, culture, or relations of power, been so pervasively effective that it has acquired an internalized meaning, capable of crossing all boundaries? Is that why sexual violence is often experienced with such an affective viscerality? Could the cultivation of this widespread universalizing discourse of femininity and masculinity, especially in relation to the gendered character of most, if not all, modern nation-states be a factor in fostering sexual violence and its assumed power to shatter the souls of many of its victims? What is behind this hegemonic meaning, and meaning making, that renders it capable of producing such acts and their potential "imaginary" and "real" affects?

I meditate on these questions in narrating the experiences of three former Iranian political prisoners, one imprisoned under the Shah's regime, and two under the Islamic Republic. To say that their subjectivity is ingrained in and informed by modern universalizing discourses on gender and sexuality alongside the Shi'i ethos is necessary yet still reductive. I thus approach their experiences in the singularity and situatedness of their "happenings" and the subsequent affective reactions to them. Cognizant of the fact that their lived realities are not reducible to discourse, I hope to allow their stories to tell themselves in their multilayered and unfixed nuances, in ever-excessive, unarrestable lives of their own. I urge us to listen to and hear them in a way that makes it possible to engage culture, religion, gender, sexuality, and violence from a stance that allows for individuals to be at once the product of their habitus and its shaper (Bourdieu 1977), but not in a neat dialectical mold. Rather, in their constant becoming, reckoning that individuals and their world are formed and reformed in a messier and more complex constellation of conditions and factors, where memories and embodied histories intermingle in the way we come to live in the modern world. This means that modernity itself, no matter how radically unique, is not a total rupture from preceding traditions. Nightmare or not, as Marx (1898, 4) suggests, the "tradition of all dead generations weighs" on us and our way of being in the world.

While these women's experiences are multifaceted, my aspirations are modest. I try to understand the implications of the way our modern notions of subjectivity, including our sense of ourselves as political subjects, have been linked to, if not defined in relation to, our sense of gender and sexuality (Foucault 1978; Butler 2011). I also ponder how the illusion of the autonomous subject is interlaced with the modern dualistic view of the body and the mind, with imagined frontiers drawn between the self and the other, the individual and the collective body. As these stories illustrate, our subjectivity is inherently entangled with, and inseparable from, other subjectivities, with power breathing in and out of all our relations, within and without.

Always already intersubjective becomings, subjects are neither fixed nor confined to humans. Rather than merely being an "existing subject" that internalizes power, as Butler (1997) argues, "the subject is spawned as an ambivalent effect of power." Challenging these Cartesian binaries and dominant discourses allows for a different reading of "Muslim subjects" that breaks the "shackles" of these ahistorical, universalizing hegemonic sentiments. A more nuanced rendition of the relationships among power, self, and subject in their socioeconomic, religiocultural, political, and historical contingencies could generate more complex insights into questions of violence, rape, and trauma.

POLITICAL SUBJECTIVITY AND GENDERED SEXUALITY

Angela Davis and Cassandra Shaylor's assertion that "violence in prison is directed at the psyche as well as the body" (2001, 7) speaks for the experiences of Fatemeh, Zohreh, and Azar, the three Iranian women political prisoners whose stories I will be narrating. Yet we must not read their statements in dualistic terms, perpetuating such binaries as the psyche and the body or the body and the mind. Nor should we lose sight of the fact that violent conditions may lead to extremely different outcomes for survivors; for instance, the survivor may reemerge as a radically transformed or a less flexible person. Moreover, these stories show both the limits of survival and the potential for ongoing transformation of the survivor.

In attempting to decipher lived experiences within a web of entwined factors—from culture, religion, class, ideology, to language and hegemonic discourses—one comes face to face with a paradox: while lived experience reveals the superficiality of these, it also forces us to recognize their effective and affective power. That these categories are constructed or that none stand on its own does not undermine their significance in producing and/or informing ideas, sentiments, desires, fantasies, and embodied discourses. Born to and shaped by these categories, we are constantly internalizing, negotiating, confirming, resisting, and in the process reshaping them. I remain mindful of these realities as I strive to elucidate the relationship between our modern notions of gender, sexuality, and subjectivity in relation to sexual violence.

Since questions of sexual violence and subjectivity have been the concern of scholars of various academic disciplines, engaging with the questions compels us to converse with diverse theoretical approaches while acknowledging that none of them may capture their slippery and excessive reality. Regardless of their limitations, these discourses and theoretical framings are the lexicons and syntaxes that render our contemplation and conversation possible. Obviously, the three women whose views and experiences I recount are not representative of all Iranian political prisoners. Despite the singularity of each lived experience, teasing out some common threads may provide rich commentaries on the conditions of subject formation in connection to different modalities and meanings of violence. It may also reveal a great deal about the relations between political subjectivities, gender, and sexuality in modern Iran, and perhaps beyond.

Imprisoned during the 1970s and 1980s while in their late teens or early twenties, all three activists were born to and raised in Muslim families with firm beliefs in modesty and gender propriety. Regardless of their own religio-political views, their background could not but have had a significant impact on their senses of themselves as women. This background was also interwoven with their sense of themselves as political subjects which, like many urban educated Iranians at the time, was colored by a frantic anxiety to be and act as modern autonomous subjects. As with all Iranian activists of the period, their political subjectivity was deeply influenced by anticolonial, Latin American, and Marxist sentiments, as well as by Shi'i ethos and cultures of the time in Iran. In pointing out these commonalities in the context within which the three women grew up, I seek to demonstrate how an array of factors, including their adherence to and embodiment of modern discourses about self, body, mind, soul, and subjectivity played a profound role in the ways they experienced sexual violence in prison. Their ideas and attitudes and their way of performing their assumed roles were inexorably linked to the prevailing meanings assigned to gender and sexuality, also rooted in a dominant sense of thinking of humans as "political animals." Thus, rather than retreating to a universal or homogenized religio-cultural explanation, the constellation of all these parameters shows their historicity, and the singularity of their experiences without self-parochializing (Keane 2018).

FATEMEH: VICTORIOUS HUMILIATION?

One morning in the summer of 1983 Fatemeh returned to the ward, looking pale and exhausted, with bruises covering her arms and shoulders. "Can't show the rest but I am bruised everywhere," she told me, her prison inmate friend. Despite complaining about "a very bad headache" and her "aching body," she smiled, somewhat victoriously. She seemed almost pleased with her injuries as she related the events of the long night she had spent at the interrogation building. Years later, I still vividly remember her account, still feel the anxiety that vibrated as she recounted what had happened.

For hours I waited in the hallway, time passing very slowly. It must have gotten dark outside [she was blindfolded]*, for other prisoners were sent back and it all had gone quiet. It felt spooky. Up to then I expected interrogation and nervously anticipated torture, but now my mind began to flutter. Shiver rushed through my body. Anxiously I wondered: "What's he planning to do with me? Why has he kept me here this late?" I could not tell how long I'd been waiting but I was exhausted. My legs felt tired; my stomach was making embarrassing noises; guess I had been too anxious to feel my hunger. Except for the moans of tortured prisoners from nearby cells, my groaning stomach, and my heartbeat pounding in my ears, all else was silent. But then, I heard my interrogator's footsteps, walking as slowly and as quietly as possible, obviously to startle me with his sudden appearance, though I smelled and sensed his presence even before feeling his heavy shadow as if on my chest. I knew he was standing in front of me, motionless, scrutinizing my reactions. Still I was startled when, in a swift move, he suddenly grabbed my chador and dragged me with him. I heard a heavy metal door open. He pushed me inside and slammed the door. Now alone, I lifted my blindfold. I was in a toilet. A toilet? Why, I wondered.*

About half an hour later when he came into the small toilet, his belly almost touched my body. I felt nauseous. I could hear his breathing, could smell him. In a whisper he told me how I could not refuse to tell him everything and give him what he wanted. He said this in a tone that terrified me. What does he mean by these last words? Why does he whisper? What does he want from me? Even the thought of it mortified me. I wished he had just taken me to the basement for torture. But now with him moving even closer, my heartbeat became erratic. I can't really remember much but recall him saying how he could break any resistance and that I should not even imagine resisting. In between his whispers, his silence made me edgier, for I could not tell what he was about to do; I imagined the worst. He was intentionally playing with my nerves. I simultaneously trembled and felt paralyzed. Frantically I thought: It is happening! How was I to stop him? How was I to fight back?

> *Suddenly his tone shifted. Furiously, through his teeth, he now called me names and hit me, first with an aftabeh[1] and then with a broom. I tried to cover my face while he hit my head and body. I felt infuriated that instead of "regular torture" he beat me in this degrading manner but was relieved that the repulsive act I had imagined had not transpired. The worse he hit, the more assured I became that he wasn't going to rape me. Although demoralized and hurting physically, these faded in comparison with the agony I had felt thinking of rape. Instead of a demand for information, in my overwhelming anxiety I had interpreted his words—"You would give me what I want"—as a sexual threat. Now how thrilled I was that he referred to me as khabis (evil).[2] Throughout the night, he left only to return to beat again. The last time, I guess he left for his morning prayers. A few hours later a guard brought me back to the ward. Despite this awful headache and aching body, I am just so happy that I wasn't raped and that he got really furious with me.*

Born and raised in a southern town to a working-class Muslim family, Fatemeh was a leftist activist whose views had a general affinity with the political culture of her time. To comprehend Fatemeh's anxieties and reactions to the situation she describes, we must examine them not merely in their personal uniqueness but also in relation to their engendering and generative conditions. As a woman of her socioeconomic and religio-cultural background, and as a political activist of that historical moment (early 1980s), a range of interrelated formative discourses and embodied practices, as well as socioeconomic and religio-cultural factors, shaped her "subjective identities" (Scott 1986, 1086). As Joan Scott argues, any analysis of gender must take into account the multirepresentational character of cultural symbols, the normative concepts that come to interpret them, the interplay of power, the role of social and political institutions, and the ways gendered subjective identities are formed in relation to this complex labyrinth of factors (1986, 1068).

The factors Scott mentions should not be seen in isolation from one another or pieced together as mere assemblages of separate entities; nor should we confine ourselves to the normative meanings assigned to them. Anthropologists have observed that anxieties and sentiments about gender and sexuality are not naturally produced but are rather grounded in specific conditions and embedded in hegemonic ethico-moral discourses and embodied practices, which are themselves constructive of, and in turn constructed by, normative ideas, including those of gender and sexuality. "Being a woman" as Denise Riley suggests, "is also inconstant, and can't provide an anthological foundation" (1988, 1–2). Fatemeh's fear of sexual violation is anchored in a complex, constantly shifting power relation—not in her womanhood or cultural/religious background, neither of which are static and monolithic, nor are her relation to and senses of them. In the confinement of prison, her gender and sexuality are even more manifestly knit to power and her "modern" political subjectivity, where both politics and violence carry more fluid meanings.

Fatemeh does not approach her body as if it were a single fixed entity on which a unitary form of violence is inflicted—note that she differentiates between "regular torture," degrading beatings, and sexual violence. Nor is her psyche a mere recipient of "bodily" pain. Rather, the psyche itself may induce pain as well as being a factor that impacts how pain is experienced. While aware of the severity of the pain of "regular torture," Fatemeh agonizes over the possibility of sexual violation, which for her is qualitatively different from the pain of "regular torture." In Fatemeh's rendition, pain, the body that endures it, and the violence that inflicts the pain are not abstractions but are produced and experienced as interactive processes in connection with the ideas and mores that are shaped by, and shape, her sense of herself.

For Fatemeh, like Azar, rape in prison is not just another, even if the worst, form of torture, but a distinctively different phenomenon. She seems to view rape as capable of shattering her political subjectivity. She assumes "regular torture" as "appropriate" for her political persona and thus feels furious when beaten by *aftabeh* and broom; she finds this manner of beating unfitting the elegance and gravity of her political subjectivity. She embodies the reverence she assigns to political activism and activists. Yet this particular sense of indignity is insignificant in comparison to what she imagines would have occurred with rape. From the way she cringes and feels mortified even at the possibility of being raped, she seems to see rape as a drastic refraction of and insult not only to her intellectual and sociopolitical subjectivity but to the core of her humanity.

Fatemeh is not alone in feeling this way. Having been socialized within and breathing the air of gender and sexual norms of the society of that modernist time, most Iranian revolutionaries shared aspects of these ideas and inclinations. Their values and desires were informed by, though not always in conformity with, the modern Iranian religious Shi'i ethos, prevailing secular and liberal discourses, as well as Russian, Chinese, and Latin American Marxism and liberation theology. In the 1970s and the 1980s, like many other revolutionaries around the world, most political activists in Iran assumed that resisting torture was a matter of ideology and the strength of the soul, rather than strength of the body. In this sense, they often presented "physical torture" as capable of breaking the body but not necessarily the soul. Yet even among those who thought of rape as a form of torture, most women activists I have spoken with have suggested that rape still invoked more profound trepidation than nonsexual violence.

If the beatings by a toilet broom injured Fatemeh's political character by mocking the solemnity of her resistance, in my conversation with Fatemeh, she told me how rape would have devastated her in an entirely different way than any "torture." It seems she imagines that rape would have inflicted a fatal assault on the entirety of her ego, dealing a ruinous blow to the most formative aspects of her sense of being in the world. Rape seemed to be able to crush something much more significant than her mere body. Subjectivity, character, identity, dignity, or whatever term we may use for it, would have been plundered by rape, as for many other prisoners. That sexual violence could ravage the "core" of her "true" humanity exposes the way gender and sexuality are interlinked with power, subjectivity, and our modern notion of personhood.

GENDER, SEXUALITY, AND DEATH

Exploring the views of influential Western scholars about the connection between human sexuality and immortality, Beverley Clack (2002) remarks how for Simone de Beauvoir, the "fundamentally tragic" nature of human life "takes a more explicitly gendered shape; if women are to escape the absurdity of human condition, they must escape the immanence of biological experience that subsumes them in the physical world of decay and death." In de Beauvoir's view, she argues, "woman's biological function connects her intimately to death" and so "freedom from the female, while involving a change in social mores, also lies in overcoming the bodily processes that invariably defines her" (2002, 43).[3] Clack asserts that not only de Beauvoir but many other major western thinkers from Socrates to Sartre considered flesh intimately bound to decay, death, and earth. Assuming a more natural connection between flesh and women, they linked women even more strongly to decay, death, and earth. For these thinkers, according to Clack, only the intellectual or spiritual products of the mind or soul are capable of transcending and overcoming death. Such ideas were embraced by most

Iranian intellectuals, including women activists who tried to show themselves as beyond or aloof from sexual desire and femininity. While their male comrades mostly upheld similar views, they often had conflicting attitudes toward women activists: their ideal female counterpart would act "manly" in resistance but remain feminine in responding to the desires of particular male comrades. As women they were to comply with many of the prevailing social norms of femininity, some of which were shared by the revolutionaries.

Returning to Fatemeh, one may wonder whether her anxiety about rape could also, at least in part, be due to her fear of being reduced to the decaying flesh, to a "bare life" that neither she nor her comrades would consider "worth living" (Agamben 1998). Echoing the views of Socrates and/or Plato, Fatemeh and a majority of Iranian dissidents of that period agreed that "an unexamined life is not worth living." In a famous poem, Ahmad Shamloo, a prominent contemporary poet, spoke of those who lived their life without asking questions as worse than the dead. Ali Shariati, arguably the most influential figure in popularizing revolutionary Shi'ism among the educated youth, spoke of "we, the despicable ones" who were not even worthy of mourning the shahids who, he suggested, were the real living ones. The leftist writer Samad Behrangi mocked those who lived in comfort, oblivious to the pain and predicament of others as "chokh bakhtiar" (literally meaning very fortunate but used derogatorily here to refer to someone who is confined in his or her own trivial happiness with no care for others). Being conscious of the sociopolitical maladies of one's surroundings and acting to change them were seen as signs of one's true humanity, hence rendering life worth living. Resistance and even death were necessary against an imposed condition of bare life—that of being reduced to mere biological existence. Given these political convictions about humanity and life, it would not be too far-fetched to imagine Fatemeh's anxiety about sexual violence not as a product of "patriarchal" Islamic cultures, as stereotypes might have it, but related to the way her sexuality was bound to her political subjectivity, which meant her very humanity and her condition of being truly alive in the world. But why does she see her sexuality as being intertwined with her humanity?

Richard Sennett (1981) has argued that while working on different historical periods, he and Foucault, separately, came to realize the significance of sexuality in "people's definition of themselves." Sennett marvels at the way sex has become "the medium through which individuals seek to define their personalities, their tastes" and "the means by which people seek to be conscious of themselves." He describes having arrived at the study of the relationship between subjectivity and sexuality from his initial attempt at understanding subjectivity in terms of solitude, specifically "the conditions of family, work and political life, prompting people to consider themselves to be alone, or to feel 'alone with themselves.'" This lacing of sexuality, subjectivity, and sense of the self, and this notion of "being alone in the world" regarding a sense of responsibility toward others characterized the paradoxes of being an Iranian political activist at least since the 1960s.

Take Fatemeh's case. The condition of feeling alone with herself in facing her interrogator makes her respond to and enact ideas and values that like language are only partially hers (Bakhtin 1982). She simultaneously performs her subjectivity individually as a modern educated woman and an autonomous leftist political subject, a while as a persona she stands for a collective, for the ideals and mores of womanhood and political subjectivity. Becoming a self means recognizing being of and with others and yet singular; alone yet part of an "ecology of selves" (Kohn 2013, 17) of which we often lose sight. While Fatemeh's sense of being alone results in feeling helpless against the interrogator, manifested acutely in her anxiety about her inability to fight against his possible sexual advance, she is interpolated in the worlds of many others. She shares and acts on their values and expectations. The sexual violence and its threat to her humanity does not merely target her as an isolated subject but threatens her intersubjective self, her sense of being in the world of, and with, others. Her fear is also not solely about losing herself but of losing herself in the eyes of those others and about failing to fulfill her assumed role in relation to her responsibilities toward her multiple communities. As a political subject, failing to live responsively toward others would render her existence futile, hollowing her from its "true" meaning. It would reduce her living condition to mere bare life. Her reactions in the face of an imagined sexual violence are not explainable in universal and abstract terms. She is an Iranian, leftist woman, educated by and embodying modern discourses, born to a Muslim family, yet she is not reducible to any of these categories. As a leftist woman she feels compelled to prove, against all the regime's propaganda, that communists are not "unethical" and that leftist women are not sexually loose. That the meanings of unethical and loose are themselves embedded in modern Shi'i ethos and a rendition of Iranian Marxism that was dominant in her era reveals the constellations of factors and contingencies that shape her subjectivity. Yet in facing all the challenges in prison, the illusion of being a sovereign autonomous subject is significant at once as a source of strength and the potential to crush the soul if failed to uphold it.

Sexuality, Freedom, and the Political

Fatemeh, like Azar, seems to believe that physical pain only attacks her body and not her soul. But why does she differentiate rape from other forms of torture, seeing it as something that could damage her soul? Here I want to meditate on whether this could have something to do with inconsistencies between the subject, her desires, and her sense of freedom. One key aspect of Fatemeh's struggle, as well as that of Azar, and of Zohreh whose story I will tell later, is about a desire for and a perception of an impossible sovereignty that is always already porous, both penetrated and penetrable. These three women seem to fear the annihilation and survival of a self that is inexorably intertwined and intermixed with others and embedded in various forms of sociality. To this point I will return, but for now let's turn to Zohreh's story.

At the time of her arrest in the mid-1970s, Zohreh was a young college student. Born and raised in a religious Muslim bazari family in Tehran, until her arrest she considered herself a religious person. Horrendous torture left her with a displaced jaw, deformed feet, broken ribs, and a body marked with scars. Yet Zohreh intimated to me that torture was not what led to her "crumbling" in the Shah's prison, but "that most humiliating experience."

> Under the unbearable pain of torture, I kept calling God for help. I screamed and begged Him to save me from my agony. I called and called. But no help came. God had forsaken me. The interrogators kept teasing: "Where is God here to help you? No one can help you here but you." But I called and called until I finally stopped. What was God good for if he would not help me when I needed him the most? I lost my belief in God in that torture room. With my injured face and dislocated jaw, I could barely eat or drink; even crying was excruciatingly painful. The wounds on my feet were infected; my broken ribs made sneezing, coughing, or lying down a nightmare. Sleep-deprived, with no change of clothes or shower, I was a mess, but not broken. Not until that evening.
>
> That evening, Rasouli (one of the most notorious interrogators of SAVAK [the Shah's secret police]) took me to the prison clinic.[4] With all that pain

I had not even noticed the usual cramps I'd get during my period. I had not even felt that my period had started. Sitting on a bench in the waiting area [blindfolded], I could tell, from the moans and whispers, that men prisoners were there too. When my name was called, I stood up to follow a guard who grabbed my sleeve to guide me. Suddenly I heard Rasouli shouting: "Hey Zohreh, you piece of shit, you garbage, you dirty shit. Look at what you've done you motherfucker. You've messed up everything, bloodied the bench, your pants; you mass of shit, you dirty whore." Imagine he is saying all this in front of our men comrades. How can I ever explain my embarrassment, my melting away, my crumbling inside? Tears were burning my eyes and my face like a hot iron; such an unbearable shame. All of a sudden Rasouli stopped cursing, and in a mockingly intimate tone but loud voice he said: "Zohreh, you poor girl (bichareh),[5] don't you have any other tonokeh [underpants],[6] to change into? Do you want me to pull down my tonokeh and give it to you? Do you want my tonokeh"?

I was ruined. I wished my body could just melt, evaporate, vanish from the face of the earth. But it kept aching; I felt its heaviness, its tremble, its heat. I wished the earth would open its mouth and gulp me down; wished a sudden death; shivered imagining our male comrades thinking of my period and of the mess I had made. Rasouli's words about his tonokeh kept echoing. Why did the earth not swallow me? I was very skinny but at those moments felt very heavy. I felt my knees bend under my heavy weight; wished I could shrink, become invisible but I felt all eyes were on me, piercing through me. Feeling hollowed, dirty, utterly abject, I returned to my cell.

No, I could not live one more minute with this filth inside. I asked for interrogation but had to suffocate through a hellish night till morning when they finally called me. With such urgency I told my interrogator everything I knew, as if my breathing relied on emptying myself of all that I had held in, as if peeling off the filth I felt inside, scrubbing away the memory of that humiliating experience, vacating myself from all that had gotten me to this moment. I wanted to cleanse myself from it all, from activism, from comrades, all that was connected to this past; I wanted to ruin my political character, to wash away my loyalties, values, everything I'd held so dear till then, as if to bury them as a way of forgetting what I assumed to be their consequences, which had dragged me to who I had become, a disgusting abject creature. I told them things even they did not expect to hear. But the more I tried to wash myself of it, to rid myself of all the information I had, the filthier I felt. The dirtier I felt, the more urgently I scratched out all the details of what I knew. Lost, drawn, turned into filth, I had become an utter abject.

LOST IN CORPORALITY?

How should one read Zohreh's experience? Why is she so ashamed of her male political prisoners' "poisonous knowledge" (Das 2006, 54) about her period, her bloody underpants, and of Rasouli's remarks about his "*tonokeh*"? Why are these stranger "comrades" so essential to her sense of being in the world? As an activist, she seeks affirmation in seeing herself as proper through their eyes. As Mary Bosworth argues, we "are always at the same time audience and actor. We view others while they look at us" (2003, 139). Quoting Braidotti (1994, 98) Bosworth notes, "the formation of our subjectivity is continually 'in process' and dependent upon repetitive performativity." In the process of identification with or responding to gazes, not all equal, and through repetitive performativity, the illusion of coherent stable subjectivities takes form.

Zohreh's identification with other political prisoners in the context of the progressive and modernist culture of the time that deemed speaking of female menstruation in front of men inappropriate leads to her sense of filthiness. Rasouli aims to invoke the intense anxiety of the educated urban Iranian of the time about showing that they had broken away from what they considered vulgar and nonmodern. His verbal "vulgarity" is a knife cutting through Zohreh's insides, collapsing the boundaries between his and her "cultural class" (Bourdieu 1977). He pollutes her by breaking apart the difference, opening her to the uncontrolled, uninhabited, uncivil outside. Within the particular dynamic of power in prison, Rasouli's words carry the cultural power that makes Zohreh feel naked, contaminated, and violated in front of her comrades. His words and vernacular throw her out of her consciously lived worlds into an abyss of untamed lust and obscenity. What she imagines her comrades see in and of her, behind their blindfolded eyes, is the mirror of what she now sees herself as—a sexual object, a decaying flesh, a base matter, a vulgar being reduced to the level of "animals." But why this shattering imagery? What does this "verbal" sexual objectification violate in Zohreh and why?

"Sexual objectification," Catharine MacKinnon states, "is the primary process of the subjection of women. It unites act with word, construction with expression, perception with enforcement, myth with reality. Man fucks woman; subject, verb, object" (1989, 124). While MacKinnon admits sexual relations are social, in her analysis, as Joan Scott argues, "there is nothing except the inherent inequality of the sexual relation itself to explain why the system of power operates as it does. The source of unequal relations between the sexes is, in the end, unequal relations between the sexes." MacKinnon does not explain how this "inequality of which sexuality is the source" is embodied in and works in a "whole system of social relationships" (Scott 1999, 34). Studying "women in isolation" says Scott, "perpetuates the fiction that one sphere, the experience of one sex, has little or nothing to do with the other" (1999, 32). Anne McClintock has extended this critique by noting that "one of the most valuable and enabling moves of recent feminist theory has been its insistence on the separation of sexuality and gender and the recognition that gender is as much an issue of masculinity as it is of femininity" (2013, 7).

Sexual objectification must hence be analyzed not as a woman's or man's issue but as the condition under which a mode of power has been engraved in historical spaces and times. A major characteristic of this mode of power has been a deep inequality in various, if not all, aspects of life, demarcating earthly and at times even spiritual relations. Gender and sexual inequalities are part of these general relations of power that, even while shifting, have often been reinforced, leading hence to their endurance and lasting impacts. This inequality results from, and is reproduced through historical, sociopolitical, economic, religiocultural, geographical, even at times biological factors. It is consistently reenacted and reinvigorated in discourses and the practice of everyday life (de Certeau 1984). Our notions of, and relation to, our body and our sense of ourselves are also caught in this labyrinth and entangled in these uneven relations of power. Our subjectivity is thus produced in conscious, and at times unconscious, acts of conforming to or resisting these normativities and their power dynamics. Occasionally, we may find ourselves trapped in the very ethico-moral discourses against which we seem to be fighting. In this coordinate plane the axes of our various desires, worldviews, and ideals originate and come to meet one another. Falling out of it may be experienced as the loss of gravity, the core, the anthological anchor.

It is in this plane that the three interrogators from these different times and spaces share "cultural capital" with one another without knowing each other; and it is partially through utilizing this shared "cultural capital" that they can assert their power over Fatemeh, Zohreh, and Azar. Note that

Zohreh's interrogator is a member of SAVAK, under the so-called secular regime of the Shah. Zohreh enters prison identifying as a Muslim. Fatemeh's interrogator, an ardent supporter of the Islamic Republic, claims to hold a master's degree in political science from India. He claims he is doing what he does to defend the revolution. Fatemeh is a novice leftist, from a working-class and somewhat religious family. Finally, Azar's interrogator seems to be from the same region as hers, Kurdistan, and knows the status of her family in town. Regardless of these various positions, however, the three women seem to express or experience the same anxiety about sexual violence; they seem to feel their bodies have become, or may become, the territory of the enemy to squeeze or rob them of their sense of themselves through abjecting violations of their sovereignty, with the "sexed body" (Rydström 2002; Evans 2008) being at once the frontiers of one's sovereignty and the potential domain of its collapse. Where can one look to avoid such an entrapment in one's "body" or find a release from it without falling back on the dichotomy of body and mind? How does one restore the body in flesh in its living, multifaceted, and variegated modalities, meanings, and conceptualizations, which have become obscured by reductive hegemonic discourses?

In Sara Heinämaa's view, "the phenomenological framework offers a well-grounded and subtle way of distinguishing between different meanings of the body: the body as an object of biosciences, the body as a piece of matter, the body as an instrument of will, and the body as an expression of the soul" (2004, xvi). While Zohreh's interrogator may act as if he is treating her body as a piece of matter, he is quite aware that for Zohreh her body, in relation to him, is the instrument of her will and the expression and vessel of her soul. They both see her body as an interactive sociocultural living terrain subject to language, ideology, and social praxes. It is based on this shared knowledge that he "knows" how to effectively cut through her body and soul by using those particular words in those specific tones in that certain space and time.

What this tells us yet again is that no matter how many discursive distinctions we may make about the gendered and sexed body, in the end the body, in all its modalities, becomes entangled in the intersubjective relations of power. Similarly, the possibility for the person's reemergence in the aftermath of violence does not necessarily lie in the body itself, but in refusing to allow the force of destruction to take over, in seeking a much greater plasticity to one's selfhood and a far more fluid zone from which one may negotiate one's being in the world. One must find a new perception of the self that is constantly in flux, that refuses to lend itself to reifying, totalizing, and atomizing discourses, that recognizes one's profound sociality, one's connection to other selves, one's belonging to the community, to the world at large. For some, this could mean creating a protective spiritual space. Mehdi Memarpour, a male prisoner in the early 1980s, relates how after he feels his soul has been raped in prison, he sits for the most sincere and longest prayer of his life and speaks to God.[7] Taking refuge in this protected space, from then on, he erects a wall between himself and the rest of the world until he finds the strength to speak publicly about his experience many years later.

Solitude in fact helps Memarpour shield himself from the maladies of the self and his surroundings; instead his way of recuperating is to put all his trust in God and in the protective space he creates through this spiritual connection with Him. For Zohreh, who had been shunned by her inmates for her betrayal, having awoken from her recurring nightmare and deciding to tell her story to a naïve young political prisoner (me) was perhaps the beginning of engendering a possibility to bring her feelings to language. In expressing her experience in words, she sees, as if from outside, what she had experienced, and only then she is able to expose what had sunk so deep inside her and made her feel herself as filth. Through words, she is able to put this picture out there not only for this stranger inmate to see but for her own seeing, now outside of herself. The tears, the shivering bodies, the warmth of the other's hands holding hers melted a hole in the iron gate of the abyss where all she could see before was massive filth. After that night, after she gave her story a way to travel beyond herself, something began to emerge, slowly, timidly, reluctantly, but surely. More than a year after that night and just before the revolution, when the women prisoners spent the night saying goodbye to one another and waiting to be released in the morning, she stood there with tearful eyes hoping someone would hug her too or accept her hugs. But even without the hugs, she was there, feeling the connection, feeling connected, to whatever extent that could be possible. When a prisoner to whom we all referred as mother hugged her, the sobs seemed to come from such a deep place in her soul that one could not but imagine the door of the abyss had been cracked open.[8]

Although in the accounts of Fatemeh, Zohreh, and Azar, the intricacies of their subjectivities and their relation to sexuality are presented in truncated form, their stories illuminate both the power of normative discourses and their motility over time. Their stories are of survival. They have lived through and after their experience, not merely discursively and symbolically, but in the flesh. This very fact, being alive in flesh, makes it possible for them to change the renditions of their experiences and to find other ways to make meanings for and of them. Yet as their original tellings make manifest, it is not their mere experience that has the power to push the confining boundaries and revive life again. There is also a need for a different problem space where different questions can be asked from different angles. To this I will return after yet another story.

SEXUAL VIOLENCE, GENDERED SACRIFICE, AND ANTHROPOLOGY

In her interview on rape in prison with Reza Allamehzadeh, an Iranian filmmaker, Azar Al-Kannan, the Iranian Kurdish political activist with whose words I introduced this essay, relates the pain of feeling helpless while hearing her infant daughter's cries as she herself is under torture (Farid 2009a, 2009b). When she was arrested in 1983, at the age of eighteen, Azar was already married and had an eight-month-old child. She admits feeling psychologically devastated following severe torture and emotional abuse yet identifies her experience of rape as the cause of her two suicide attempts. She recognizes rape as a means of asserting power but differentiates its visceral impact in a way that shows the link she assumes between sexuality and subjectivity.

In the interview, Azar describes the respected status of her family, which she attributes to their political activism. She mentions that her husband has had to flee their town, that her brother had been executed, and that her cousin was imprisoned for a long time. She accentuates the way people in their Kurdish town held the family in high esteem because of their dissidence. "My interrogator kept telling me that I walked with my head too high (with pride) and promised to do something to destroy my pride but I could never imagine he meant rape. I just thought of harsher torture." Then one day her interrogator calls her in, handcuffs her, unbuttons her blouse, pulls down her pants and rapes her. With tears streaming down her face, she explains how, handcuffed, she could not fight, nor could she scream for he had forced a silky scarf he used to wear around his neck into her mouth. Afterward he calmly buttons her blouse, pulls up her pants, and sends her back to her cell.

After her second suicide attempt, her father is allowed to visit her in the hospital. In a disappointed tone he asks her why she has tried to kill herself. "I asked him if he really wished to know and he said yes. I told him that I was raped by my interrogator (she actually says "by my officer"). For a moment my father was frozen and remained speechless. Then with tears running down his face he told me to do whatever I felt I needed to do and that I should not worry for my daughter and that he, my sister, and my mother would all look after her."

How should we understand her father's reaction? Assuming she had chosen suicide to escape "regular torture" or imprisonment, the father is disappointed in his daughter, who is supposed to maintain the family's status by following in their activist footsteps. He expects her to show that she too is strong, capable of enduring torture and the hardships of prison to stand up for her ideas. But after learning about the rape, Azar's father seems to "comprehend" and support, even encourage, her decision, for he too interprets the rape as an insult—both to the core of Azar's being and to the way people view her family—not merely a hardship she must endure. Azar's father understands the rape as an attempt to radically undermine the family's dignity and reputations both as political dissidents and as respected members of the community. Azar sympathizes with him, imagining what her rape must mean to him and to her entire family.

It is actually the interviewer's line of questioning that leads Azar to speak of rape. He asks, "What was the most painful experience for you in prison?" [the interview is in English and a woman is translating it into Farsi]. Azar's response is, "All forms of torture and emotional abuse in prison are painful to remember." But this answer does not appear to satisfy the interviewer, or perhaps this is part of the interview plot. He asks the question again, in more specific terms: "What was that particular single experience that was the worst for you?" Azar responds with a question: "You mean rape?" And receiving the affirmative answer, she begins talking about it. After telling her story, she is asked if she had told her family about her experience—Azar lives with her husband and her daughter. She says she has done so only recently, before going public with it. "My daughter asked if I thought of her before attempting suicide. I told her 'Honestly no. I could not have.'"

IN SEARCH OF LIFE

In the context of massive kidnapping and raping of women during the partition of India and Pakistan, Veena Das (1997) offers an analysis of Sadat Hassan Manto's short story titled "Khol Do" (Open It). She recounts how in the story Sakina, a young woman trying to cross the border along with her father, disappears only to be found nearly dead after being gang raped. In the stiflingly hot operating room, the doctor points to the window and tells the nurse to "open it." Das narrates how, while unconscious, Sakina hears these words as "the command of the other" and "her hands move toward the tape of the salwar (trouser) and fumble to loosen it" (Das 2006, 46). In her initial reading of this story Das emphasizes Sakina's traumatic entrapment in the world of her rapists. Having lost language, she hears those words as the command for rape, hence attempts to loosen the tape of her salwar. In her 2006 revisiting of the same text, Das relates how she had originally missed a significant aspect of this story: in seeing Sakina's hands moving to her salwar, the father recognizes a different kind of opening. He sees in the movement of her hands the presence (or the return) of life, hence his joyous cry: "My daughter is alive—my daughter is alive" (2006, 46).

Das compares this "fictive" anecdote with the "archetypal motif" of hundreds of accounts that claim to be based on true experience, in which a girl, "having been subjected to rape and plunder," finds her way back to her parents' home only to hear from them: "Why are you here—it would have been better if you were dead." She highlights the father's joy in recognizing his daughter's survival in Manto's "fiction" in contrast to those "true" accounts that emphasize the privileged position of family or kin's "honor" over the life of the raped woman. The latter's power is manifested in the "widespread belief in such narrative truths" and the belief in the myth of "sacrificing daughters for honor" (Das 1997, 76–77). This underscores the other response as a way to embrace life, cherishing any potential for a different discourse to emerge, one that does not bow down to the normative myths, that does not chain us to our atomized, isolated selves or entrap us with the perpetuating trope of family or community honor.

In her ethnographic research, Das witnesses the overwhelming silence among women and their families about abduction and rape. Referring to this "poisonous knowledge" that women kept hidden, Das observes how "these memories were sometimes compared to poison that makes the inside of the woman dissolve, as solid is dissolved into a powerful liquid" or how in other times women who had lived through those experiences spoke of themselves as "a discarded exercise book" and of their body as a "parchment of losses" (1997, 84). In a later reading of Manto's short story, Das recognizes the conscious decisions by these women to remain silent for their own survival and for that of their family or/and community. Das shows how the stories we tell are transformed by looking at them with different eyes and from different analytical lenses. In opening the stories to divergent theoretical perspectives, and engaging them from various angles, one may arrive at a space that is fertile with greater potentials for recognizing and engendering life and transformation. What this also means is to realize that to speak of "culture" or "religion" as if they are a myth from the past, rather than constantly shifting living and lived realities, leads to expanding the very trap which Das seeks to avoid by reexamining her own blind spots by exploring new ways of seeing, hearing, sensing, imagining, and telling.

Having become privy to the stories of these three women we may now understand that their feelings and reactions about sexual violation cannot be explained by clinging to arguments about their "Islamic Middle Eastern culture." Nor can their subjectivities be reduced to the force of fixed ideas about sexuality and/or gender normativity. If there are similarities, they have as much, if not more, to do with their complex multidimensional subjectivity formed in the modern, postenlightenment capitalist world, with their sense of selfhood embedded in the ideals of free-willed, agentive choice-making individuality. It is in the atmosphere of an atomized individualism, with an assumption of a sovereign subject and her or his free choice, that we may, at least to some extent, discern the meanings these invasive and violent acts come to signify. Despite the profound power of these hegemonic discourses, however, their limit is revealed in the way, for instance, the body/mind or body/soul dichotomy they embraced entirely collapses in the face of their lived experiences.

Zohreh chooses to cleanse herself from the filth by "scribing" information from her mind and relaying it to the interrogators. Scribing, filth, and so on are often attributed to the body. In the process of this "cleansing" Zohreh not only destroys herself as an activist but harms her comrades both by burying them within and by causing their arrest and perhaps even their death in reality. Inversely, in attempting to kill herself Azar in fact tries to destroy the other who she assumes has invaded and polluted her and undermined her political dignity. The paradox of the discourses and realities cannot be better illustrated than in the fact that both she and her interrogator realize she is not an independent individual with free choices; they both rely on the knowledge that the assumed pollution is contagious and will "soil" her family and her community. Her self-destruction is intended to cleanse this pollution so her family and community may maintain their sense of dignity. It is important to also note that neither the modalities of violences nor their impact are identical for Azar, Fatemeh, and Zohreh. The reactions to them do not conform to conventional expectations either. Although the sexual assault to which Zohreh was subjected was mainly verbal, she experienced it as ruinous to the entirety of her being, indicating how the boundaries of discourse, materiality, body, and soul are elastic and permeable, as are the meanings we give them. Zohreh tries to cleanse herself of all her former political loyalties, as if ridding herself of her political subjectivity. In Azar's case where rape, in the conventional sense of the term, has actually happened, she attempts to kill herself to save her political subjectivity and that of those related to her. She is left with a pain that is still fresh not merely in her memory but in her body; nearly three decades later she still feels it vividly and viscerally.

To the extent that Fatemeh, Zohreh, and Azar assume they have a grip on themselves and are able to sustain their will to resist in line with the modern discourses on the body and soul, they seem to feel unbroken. They become dismayed, however, when they attribute to rape the power of violating their very being, contaminating it with the other, reducing them to flesh, and leaving them with an abrogated soul. They seem to see rape, through penetration, either verbal or physical, as something that obliterates the borders of the self and the other, destroying any sense of sovereignty due to invasion by the other within. It is this other, now having conquered and defeated the self through violent penetration, that attempts in killing/suicide seek to eject.

Despite their different experiences, the meanings that Azar, Zohreh, and Fatemeh attach to their sense of self and sexuality belong as much to them as to their society, as with the "internally persuasive word" that, according to Bakhtin (1982, 345), is "half-ours and half-someone else's." The sense of the self that survives and/or outlives them in living through these experiences cannot therefore be construed in isolation from their social intersubjective existence. This is true also of the impact of their experiences on others. As Bruce Fink asserts, "Other people's views and desires flow into us via discourse" and "in so far as desire inhabits language, and in a Lacanian framework, there is no such thing as desire, strictly speaking, without language—we can say that our unconscious is full of such foreign desires" (1997, 9). Let's assume language here stands for all that is social and historical. As such, the desire and the character of the ego depend on the condition of life and the always social and historically contingent meaning assigned to life and death. The desiring ego is not a single, fixed, and insular entity but is constantly shifting and becoming, both responsive to other egos and enmeshed in a world of beings, things, and their histories. Desires are thus generated by a mix of all that is foreign and becomes native and the native rendered foreign, where the sense of inside and outside the self is itself in flux. The body/soul that connects to the ego, or to the self, is subject to all these historical conditions and their affects, reflective of and reflecting the hegemonic discourses that delineate them, though never entirely reducible to or in absolute conformity with them.

Meditating on the historicity of the ego and the desires in relation to two modes of history—one that comes before and outlives the ego (in the form of language, tradition, culture, religion, polity, and so on) and the other as the imminent, contingent—reveals the intricacies of such binaries as self and other, body and soul, discursive and materiality, or resistance and crushing. Let's ponder to what extent it is possible to actually consider the sexual assaults on the three women, either imagined or occurred, separate from the conditions prior to their occurrence. Recall, for instance, Zohreh's situation before the moment she identifies as radically devastating to her sense of herself. Let's envision her state of being at the time. She has been severely tortured and is in excruciating pain, sleep deprived, unable to eat or drink, feverish with infected wounds, and removed from family and friends—her only human contacts being with the interrogators and guards, and having lost her trust in God and with that her sense of identification as a believer and a Muslim. Is it then really unimaginable to postulate how fragile and anxious she must have felt about the possibility of failing to uphold her political loyalties for much longer? The body that is to be the vessel for her being in the world in flesh is now a means of torture, the enemy's tool to exert ravaging pain on her; it has indeed turned into her enemy. It has become the source of embarrassment, beyond her control, a decaying, polluting, and polluted flesh that challenges and undermines her intellectual faculty, her political subjectivity, and her propriety as a modern woman subject. Has the body thus not already become the terrain of the other? While Zohreh attributes her breakdown to Rasouli's vulgar words, one cannot ignore the vulnerable state of her body and psyche as she hears and reacts to those words. Azar too admits that even before being raped she was feeling both physically and psychologically devastated and frail. Could she not already be feeling the assault on her pride for seeing how her body fails her by lending itself to the interrogator to utilize it as a tool of torture and her suffering? But we are still left to ask why for them sexual violence is so radically different from other forms of violations of their body?

Why is it that even though it is forced on them, those who have been subjected to rape often think of it in terms of an abjection that so drastically defiles their dignity, leaving them with a sense of degraded self? We may tell ourselves that sexual violence is particularly sensitive, due to the religio-cultural attributions and the concept of sin, which in a secular context is translated as guilt. One may even venture to explain this by revisiting the primordial notion of the "value" of women as reproducing assets, making their sexuality at once a source of their power and vulnerability, while also binding their personhood to their sexuality. In this case, the argument would be that this notion has had an enduring life, internalized and embodied by the victims for the most part. But does this argument really explain why as political subjects Azar, Fatemeh, and Zohreh could not consider their body as the plane upon which the interrogator exercises his power regardless of the form of violence? Why can't they see sexual violence also affecting their body so that like Epictetus they could also say: "You can chain my leg but not even Zeus can overcome my power of choice" (2014, 6)? Let's recall how Azar's father expected Azar to endure "torture" but found her attempt to kill herself totally understandable after she was raped. What ethoses and/or pathoses lie behind all this? What kind of dark fantasy may render surviving an experience of sexual violence so challenging to so many?

THE UNDESIRED OTHER'S VICIOUS FANTASY?

> Fantasy is integral to the subject's achievement of the sense of being. Fantasy engages the subject's desire, manifested as it is in the relation to the desire of the Other, the Other's lack, to object a. In this way, object a (unspeakable, unrepresentable, unable to be signified) enters into the fantasy as that which can be manipulated and played with in the way that is most pleasing to the subject, that incites the most enjoyment and excitement. (Grace 2009, 46)

But what of those situations when the desire of the other is one's most tormenting fantasy? What figures in Fatemeh, Zohreh, and Azar's imagination, imageries, and fantasies result in their intensely visceral reaction with profound ramifications on their subjectivity? Whose fantasies do they "host" in these maliciously invasive and forced relationships of the other with, and within, them? Sexual humiliation comes to define, and shatter, Zohreh's subjectivity, and her sense of being in the world. It smashes her trust in God and in herself, leading her to betray her political loyalties. The paradox of this story lies in an illusory sense of autonomous subject, on the one hand, and the collective ground in which the meaning making takes place, on the other. The idea that "I am what I am, I am what I want" (Povinelli and DiFruscia 2012) in a reversed logic engenders her self-abjection. Following the (albeit subjective) humiliating experiences, not only Zohreh, but Azar too seem to think, as if in a gesture of a negative fantasy, that to assure the annihilation of the abject, they must destroy the self which has been invaded by and become the object of the abhorrent desire of the other. It has offered the other the fulfillment of its darkest fantasy. How does one, they seem to ask of themselves, be oneself and live with oneself while having become the source of *jouissance* for the enemy's libidinous assertion of power. In the case of Fatemeh who dreads this possibility when she assumes it is coming, this negative fantasy may appear even more puzzling.

Why would anyone entertain, even if unconsciously, such dark fantasies? As profound as this question is, it cannot be reduced to simple psychological explanations or to reductive reading of psychoanalytic theories. To read such brutal, violent situations only in relation to the general desire of the ego for life and death, or as the desire of the ego for self-negating fantasies does not give us much food for thought. It will be highly erroneous to contemplate these individuals' attitudes, desires, and fantasies outside of the conditions of the time and the context in which violence and torture, including sexual violence, had become "normal" means of silencing and crushing political resistance. This context is as much global as it is local, as the revelations about what some members of the US military did to Iraqi prisoners in the Abu-Ghraib prison brought home so forcefully.

Only after reckoning with these realities can we make some sense of the implications of the dreadful fantasies that, in Zohreh's case, manifested themselves in her desire to hold on to her political loyalty which was so detrimental to her sense of the self. Under torture, this desire to retain her political loyalty became so tenuous, so radically fragile, so consistently under threat and on the verge of falling apart, that it perhaps pushed her to incorporate Rasouli's words as the negative fantasy or the fantasy of the other to turn her into merely nonsubject flesh, an abject being. This abjection might not be perceived as entirely her but as a state of fragility in which she feels invaded by and becomes the other, allowing the other/the self to subvert her sense of herself as a whole, as an autonomous subject. With the other having seized and taken over her from within, she inflicts damage on her comrades and feels disgusted by her "filthy" othered self. She [it] is the enemy now acting from within her.

This desperate desire to survive as a sovereign subject, as a political agent whose life must be worth living in the face of the invasion of the other within, begets the urge to resist and, through the ideation of the negative fantasy, to destroy the invaded self. This annihilation of the self is meant to preserve an ideal sense of wholeness, through its negation, holding on to it even if as a negative idea. Self-annihilation may also be a way of asserting some control over the lost self, since one gives in to the other yet renders the power over it undone through disowning or vacating the desired self by becoming the other of the self. Again we come full circle to the same paradox: the desire of the subject for an impossible sovereignty while always already hosting others within, and even speaking in the language and upholding ideas that are never entirely one's own, that one shares at least partially with the enemy. Azar's interrogator deploys rape as a means of dismantling her family's political dignity, and Azar attempts suicide to regain it; both rely on these shared meaning makings. The paradox also lies in a sense of subjectivity that is constantly fluctuating but through its encasement in a single body gives the illusion of a coherent unity, and a deceptive sense of autonomy.

Fatemeh's apprehension about possible rape is not merely because she knows rape actually happens in prison or because exaggerated rumors about the frequency of its happening are used as a technique of intimidation, itself a form of torture. Her trepidation is also because her sense of subjectivity is rooted in an ideal of the political that is intertwined with norms of gendered sexuality. Undermining either aspect appears tantamount to the loss of herself. Sharing these sentiments, she, even if unconsciously, becomes a host to the desires of the other within. I want to emphasize that the angst Fatemeh, Zohreh, and Azar experience is less about sexuality per se and more about imagining their subjectivity in relation to sexuality and the power that threatens their subjectivity as a whole through sexual assault. Their desires and fantasies, we might say, are "caught up in cultural ideologies rather than material sexuality" (Felluga 2015, 302), where "cultural ideologies" refers not to the normative meaning of culture but to those ideologies which highlight the attitude of an epoch—a capitalist modern world in which the desire for, and the fantasy of, individual autonomy are constantly reproduced yet simultaneously rendered illusory.

Fatemeh, Zohreh, and Azar deal with the inside/outside of their connections to their political community; to their comrades, families, society; to their history; and to the interrogators. In being caught up in hegemonic ideas and cultural ideologies which are also those of the torturer, Zohreh symbiotically hosts both the pleasure of the interrogator and the abjection of her comrades. In this sense, she seems to undertake a kind of deathwork— the Freudian framework that outlines the simultaneous drive for survival and death. Assuming themselves to have turned into sexual objects overpowered by the other (the interrogator, the ideological other) Fatemeh,

Zohreh, and Azar feel rape as an absolute loss of sovereignty. Sexual violence becomes utterly destructive of their intellectual sovereignty, which for them lies at the heart of their humanity.

It is in releasing oneself from these ideas of an isolated self, capable of giving a coherent account of the self (Butler 2005) that one may find new meanings to such violent experiences, meanings that do not allow the "enemy" to achieve its goal of crushing one's body/soul or sucking life out. For the subjects of sexual violence, the key to survival is to remain with others, with the community, to outlive the violence and break away from the ideological entrapments that bind one to the horrendous fantasies of the perpetrator other. For the rest of us, the task is to follow the example of Sakina's father in Manta's "Khol Do" who embraces and cherishes his daughter's life, hence undermining the power of her rapists.

CONCLUSION

I have asked, in this essay, why sexual violence so often has a greater impact on its subjects than other forms of violence. In telling the stories of three Iranian women activists who encountered sexual violence—in the forms of imagined, verbal, or physical forced penetration—during interrogation and imprisonment, I have tried to experiment with various means of approaching the question. All along, my intention was to avoid either culturalist or universalizing theories of the relationship of violence to sexuality, the body, or subjectivity.

My main contention is that the modern capitalist world and its dominant discourses have been integrated into the ideas of most educated Iranians. One could speculate that the views and reactions of Azar, Zohreh, and Fatemeh to torture and sexual violence resulted from their religio-cultural upbringing and its accompanying gender and sexual norms. One could also assume that they would "naturally" be traumatized by their experiences. There is a partial truth in these assumptions. Yet their ways of experiencing their bodies might better be understood if we realized that the same wounds mean something different in different places and at different times, depending on the economic or political conditions or events that create the values of one's life or death in the world today.

The translation of the body into discourse has significant implications, at once capable of creating possibilities and encumbrances. Yet as long as life goes on, as long as the body lives on, the potentiality of transformation pulsates even in its most dormant form. Life in flesh outweighs corporeality; power relations shift; ideas change; and the self may come to be visualized differently. This is how Zohreh came to narrate her account to me after a long silence, in the middle of the night in that cell during the Shah's regime. And it is how Azar finds the strength to tell her daughter, her husband, and even the public about her rape after three decades. Although neither woman radically questions their previous sentiments, their emergent selves are pregnant with new possibilities. In this excess rests hope, even in despair—the hope of outliving shattered selves and recreating new ones.

We, too, as anthropologists and feminists, must write about sexual violence, and violence in general, in a way that embraces life. Instead of buying into the dominant logic that torture—and here in particular sexual violence—is totalizing and destructive, hence bestowing enormous power on its perpetrators, we too must pay attention to the father's joy in Manta's story; he sees in the movement of Sakina's hand the presence of life, not a signifier for the dishonoring act of her rapists. In expressing joy because "[his] daughter is alive," he refuses to succumb to the desire of the rapists to crush her or his dignity. We must refuse to speak of sexual violence as a defining factor in our sense of selfhood but recognize the shifting and multidimensional character of myriad influences and power relations and contingencies that make us not who we *are* but who we are constantly *becoming*, always already intersubjectively. We should strive toward queering our normative perceptions and open up broader spaces where neither seeking problems nor asking questions are confined within conventional problem spaces.

As human beings we are always already sociopolitical beings, yet our loyalties are far more diverse and inconsistent to be so simplistically tied to our gender and sexuality. To live and to be alive is to know that all that seems solid can melt into the air (Marx and Engels 1848, 17). Echoing Stephen Dillon, who writes about American women prisoners and the role of drawings and images in their lives in prison, I want to leave us "not with the prisoner's curse, but with the dream."

> Unlike a curse, a dream does not concern itself with the life of the captor. A dream sidesteps the future of a world that is dead and tries to imagine a place and time that can leave the prison behind.... [T]he hope of queerness lies in this illegibility—its attempt to escape what is always tracking it down, always working toward its capture. (Dillon 2015, 181)

NOTES

1. An aftabeh is a kind of ewer many Iranians use to wash their genitalia and bottom during toileting.
2. Interrogators often called a resistant prisoner a "khabis," or malicious person.
3. In *Toward a Phenomenology of Sexual Difference: Husserl, Merleau-Ponty, Beauvoir* (2004, xiii), Sara Heinämaa argues that Beauvoir does not believe "the cause or reason for women's suppression is in their bodies" but considers the "concept of repetition" as the factor behind the endurance of "sexual hierarchy." She explains: "Beauvoir's idea of woman as a *becoming* is different from the idea of *gender* as a sociocultural construct."
4. To prevent prisoners from dying of torture, so that the torture could continue, prisoners' wounds were minimally treated in the prison clinic.
5. The term "bichareh" connotes helplessness, someone left with no means or choice.
6. *Tonokeh* is a word for underwear no longer used by most urban Iranians. It was replaced by *lebas-e-zir*, literally underwear, a more sterilized term. Using tonokeh instead of lebas-e-zir was a sign of uncultured vulgarity, suggestive of nonmodern, uneducated status. Similarly, "pestan band," literally breast fastener or keeper (bra), was replaced by the French words *soutian* and *corset*. Tonokeh was specifically used as a way to wound Zohreh's intellectual character and question her sexual propriety.
7. From his testimony in the Iran-Tribunal hearing in October 2012, discussed in Talebi (2019).
8. This mother was arrested again under the Islamic Republic, and this time she was hugged by other inmates before walking to her execution.

REFERENCES

Abu-Lughod, Lila. 2013. *Do Muslim Women Need Saving?* Cambridge, MA: Harvard University Press.

Agamben, Giorgio. 1998. *Homo Sacer: Sovereign Power and Bare Life*. Stanford, CA: Stanford University Press.

Bakhtin, M. M. 1982. *The Dialogic Imagination: Four Essays*, edited by Michael Holquist. Austin: University of Texas Press.

Bosworth, Mary. 2003. "Gender, Race, and Sexuality in Prison." In *Women in Prison: Gender and Social Control*, edited by Barbara H. Zaitzow and Jim Thomas, 137–54. Boulder, CO: Lynne Rienner Publishers.

Bourdieu, Pierre. 1977. *Outline of a Theory of Practice*. Cambridge: Cambridge University Press.

Braidotti, Rosi. 1994. *Nomadic Subjects: Embodiment and Sexual Difference in Contemporary Feminist Theory*. New York: Columbia University Press.

Butler, Judith. 1997. *The Psychic Life of Power: Theories of Subjection*. Stanford, CA: Stanford University Press.

Butler, Judith. 2005. *Giving an Account of Oneself*. New York: Fordham University Press.

Butler, Judith. 2011. *Bodies That Matter: On the Discursive Limits of Sex*. New York: Routledge.

Clack, Beverley. 2002. *Sex and Death: A Reappraisal of Human Mortality*. Cambridge: Polity Press.

Das, Veena. 1997. "Language and Body: Transaction in the Constitution of Pain." In *Social Suffering*, edited by Arthur Kleinman, Veena Das, and Margaret M. Lock. Berkeley: University of California Press.

Das, Veena. 2006. *Life and Words: Violence and the Descent into the Ordinary*. Berkeley: University of California Press.

Davis, Angela, and Cassandra Shaylor. 2001, "Race, Gender, and the Prison Industrial Complex: California and Beyond." *Meridians* 2, no. 1: 1–25. https://www.jstor.org/stable/40338793.

De Certeau, Michel. 1984. *The Practice of Everyday Life*. Berkeley: University of California Press.

Dillon, Stephen. 2015."The Prisoner's Dream: Queer Visions from Solitary Confinement." *Qui Parle: Critical Humanities and Social Sciences* 23, no. 2: 161–84. https://doi.org/10.5250/quiparle.23.2.0161.

Epictetus. 2014. *Discourses, Fragments, Handbook (Oxford World Classics)*. Translated by Robin Hard. Oxford: Oxford University Press.

Evans, Harriet. 2008. "Sexed Bodies, Sexualized Identities, and the Limits of Gender." *China Information* 22, no. 2: 361–86. https://doi.org/10.1177/0920203X08091550.

Farid, Parvaneh. 2009a. "Rape in Prisons of Iran—Azar Al Kanaan (English—Part 1 of 2)." YouTube video, 7:37. https://www.youtube.com/watch?v=B87IQAtUUNA.

Farid, Parvaneh. 2009b. "Rape in Prisons of Iran—Azar Al Kanaan (English—Part 2 of 2)." YouTube video, 8:58. https://www.youtube.com/watch?v=fSnPP6wtYAM.

Felluga, Dino Franco. 2015. *Critical Theory: The Key Concepts*. London: Routledge.

Fink, Bruce. 1997. *The Lacanian Subject: Between Language and Jouissance*. Princeton, NJ: Princeton University Press.

Foucault, Michel. 1978. *The History of Sexuality, Volume 1*. Translated by Robert Hurley. London: Penguin.

Foucault, Michael, and Richard Sennett. 1981. "Sexuality and Solitude." *London Review of Books* 3, no. 9: 3–7.

Grace, Victoria. 2009. "Gendered Violence and Sacrificial Logics: Psychoanalytic Reflections." In *Theorizing Sexual Violence*, edited by Renée J. Heberle and Victoria Grace, 31–54. New York: Routledge.

Heinämaa, Sara. 2004. *Toward a Phenomenology of Sexual Difference: Husserl, Merleau-Ponty, Beauvoir*. Lanham, MD: Rowman and Littlefield Publishers.

Keane, Webb. 2018. "Saba Mahmood and the Paradox of Self-Parochialization." *Public*

Books, August 3. https://www.publicbooks.org/saba-mahmood-and-the-paradoxes-of-self-parochialization/.

Kohn, Eduardo. 2013. *How Forests Think: Toward an Anthropology Beyond the Human.* Berkeley: University of California Press.

MacKinnon, Catharine A. 1989. *Toward a Feminist Theory of the State.* Cambridge, MA: Harvard University Press.

Marx, Karl. 1898. *The Eighteenth Brumaire of Louis Bonaparte.* Translated by Daniel De Leon. New York: International Publishing Company.

Marx, Karl, and Friedrich Engels. 1848. *The Communist Manifesto.* Translated by Samuel Moore. New York: Bantam Classics.

McClintock, Anne. 2013. *Imperial Leather: Race, Gender, and Sexuality in Colonial Contest.* New York: Routledge.

Najmabadi, Afsaneh. 1998. "Crafting an Educated Housewife in Iran." In *Remaking Women*, edited by Lila Abu-Lughod, 91–125. Princeton, NJ: Princeton University Press.

Povinelli, Elizabeth, and Kim Turcot DiFruscia. 2012. "A Conversation with Elizabeth A. Povinelli." *Trans-Scripts* 2: 76–90.

Riley, Denise. 1988. *"Am I that Name?" Feminism and the Category of Women in History.* Basingstoke, UK: Palgrave Macmillan.

Rydström, Helle. 2002. "Sexed Bodies, Gendered Bodies: Children and the Body in Vietnam." *Women's Studies International Forum* 25, no. 3: 359–72. https://doi.org/10.1016/S0277-5395(02)00261-3.

Scott, David. 2004. *Conscripts of Modernity: The Tragedy of Colonial Enlightenment.* Durham, NC: Duke University Press.

Scott, Joan Wallach. 1986. "Gender: A Useful Category of Historical Analysis." *The American Historical Review* 91, no. 5: 1053–75.

Scott, Joan Wallach. 1999. *Gender and the Politics of History.* New York: Columbia University Press.

Talebi, Shahla. 2019. "Ethnography of Witnessing and Ethnography as Witnessing: Topographies of Two Court Hearings." *Political and Legal Anthropology Review* 42: 226–43. https://doi.org/10.1111/plar.12316.

III

CIVILIZING INTERVENTIONS

Development & Humanitarianism

NINE · *Dina M. Siddiqi*

Child Marriage in the Feminist Imagination

Sometime in 1972, amid heated debates in the Constituent Assembly, Bangladesh Mahila Parishad (BMP) placed a sixteen-point charter before the prime minister of newly independent Bangladesh. A women's platform once affiliated with the communist party, BMP was ideally placed to chart a feminist agenda for a postcolonial state with explicitly socialist leanings. Its vision included free and mandatory education for girls, implementation of existing laws against polygamy, equal work opportunities for women, child care, antidowry legislation, and measures to stop child labor. Point 8 urged the government to realize the equal rights of women in divorce and to put an end to "coerced marriages of *adult* women against their will"(Banu 2014, 310, emphasis added).

Two features of this progressive and forward-thinking document stand out. First, child marriage as cultural practice did not preoccupy feminist imaginations at that particular juncture. Unlike dowry, the marriage of girl children was not identified as an entrenched "tradition" marked for elimination. Second, the broader question of violence against women—in which child marriage debates are nested today—did not merit explicit mention. In retrospect, the charter's silence on violence, sexual or otherwise, appears surprising. After all, women's issues entered the new state's discourse through the figure of the sexually violated woman/girl in the time of the Liberation War (Banu 2014, 71, 93; D'Costa 2011; Mookherjee 2015). Fifty years later, the discourse of violence against women (or VAW) is everywhere, a master category and fundamental aspect of state and nonstate efforts to ensure both gender justice *and* economic development. Since the 1980s, numerous women's groups have mobilized against rape, sexual harassment, and dowry-related violence, along with acid throwing, trafficking, and *fatwa*-driven violence. The addition of child marriage to this list in the last decade might appear to be unremarkable—as yet another patriarchal tradition in need of correction or elimination.

In this chapter, I seek to trouble the taken-for-granted assumptions that render child marriage an *obvious* object of feminist, state, or developmental concern today. It should go without saying that I do not argue "for" child marriage, however it is defined. Nor do I suggest that this is an empirical issue that needs to be set right. Questions of why the issue of child marriage surfaced when it did, especially in light of its apparent insignificance during the founding moments of the nation, and why it has become so tenaciously attached to feminist and developmental anxieties as well as to Bangladesh's global image, constitute the core of this chapter. The analysis that follows unpacks this unanticipated category and traces the sites, ideological assumptions, and differential stakes through which it is given meaning.

My interest in child marriage stems from a broader concern with the ways contemporary gender politics in the South are often tangled in and refracted through northern geopolitical, economic, religious, and feminist discourses (Abu-Lughod 2013; Hammami 2019). This interest has been heightened by multiple encounters in unexpected locations with Bangladesh's child marriage "problem"—from human rights reports on climate change to foreign policy briefs on the world's sex-trafficking problem. What can the study of the global circuits through which Bangladesh's child marriage problem travels tell us about the legibility of gendered forms of violence? How do feminists in a transnational space like Bangladesh—a geopolitically marginal Muslim majority nation with a high density of NGOs—negotiate the complexities of neoliberal donor and corporate agendas, geopolitical securitization frames, and calls to global feminist unity?

In what follows, I track the late twentieth-century marking of child marriage as harmful cultural practice as it coincides with a critical shift in gendered figurations of economic development, in which the girl child increasingly eclipses the Third World woman as key agent of development. I go on to argue that the particular framing this entails—as a violation of a *child*'s rights—enables homogenized and flat readings of otherwise complex social conditions and life courses, and so of possible forms of redress. These flattened readings draw on and reproduce a series of oppositions around the trope of childhood (sexual) innocence, simultaneously marking certain female bodies as transgressive or troublesome. As the innocent female subject of state protection, the girl child also must comply with a normative childhood script. This particular figuration displaces potentially thorny questions around adolescent female sexuality, consent, and agency, producing a double bind for feminists and the postcolonial state.

An especially robust trope, child marriage often serves as a site in and through which cultural anxieties and visions for society are articulated (Khoja-Moolji 2015a, 40; Sweis 2012; Tambe 2019). Like sati and veiling, child marriage in colonial South Asia and the Middle East signaled cultural backwardness and was used to consolidate lines of civilizational difference (Mani 1998; Major 2011; Sinha 2006; Surkis 2019; Tambe 2019). While the girl child and her sexual consent in marriage featured centrally in nationalist debates on social reform in colonial Bengal (part of which became East Pakistan, and is now Bangladesh) in the early twentieth century, that discussion revolved primarily around the identity of upper caste Hindu communities; the stakes for Muslim Bengalis were muted and indirect (Amin 1996; Major 2011; Sarkar 2008). Ironically, in the politically volatile decades of the 1920s and 1930s in British India, Hindu nationalists actively sought to sever any association of child marriage with Brahmanical norms, seeking to recast it as a problem of Muslim backwardness that originated from the Prophet's marriage to Aisha (Pande 2020).

The idea of sexual precocity as an index of civilizational inadequacy was deeply embedded in imperial ideologies of difference, and postcolonial states inherited age standards as a means to establish geopolitical hierarchies among ostensibly equal sovereign nations. Under the umbrella of antitrafficking campaigns undertaken by the League of Nations in the 1920s and 1930s, age of consent debates became a "plank for indexing hierarchy among nations" (Tambe 2019, 20). In its first decade of existence, the United Nations took on questions of early marriage and age of consent, leading to the 1962 Convention on Consent to Marriage, Minimum Age of Marriage, and Registration of Marriage. Ashwini Tambe (2019) suggests that the success of this effort lies in the specific framing used at the time: an expansion of the scope of slavery to include forced marriage and child marriage. Tambe adds that the expanded definition of slavery deflected attention from European states' intimate involvement in the transatlantic slave trade and as well as from Nazi slave labor camps, the most immediate example of slavery at the time (2019, 89–91). The trope of child marriage as slavery reappears in twenty-first century discussions on "third world" girls and their futures (see, for instance, the 2012 Thematic Report on Servile Marriage presented to the UN Human Rights Council in a Report of the Special Rapporteur on Contemporary Forms of Slavery, including its Causes and Consequences [Shahinian 2012]).

What kinds of ideologies and interventions are legitimized and what kinds of analytical and other moves are foreclosed as a result of this historical legacy? Now that it has (re)appeared in the contemporary period as a more expansive and powerful sign linked to state projects under neoliberalism, how do differently positioned Bangladeshi feminists negotiate, recalibrate, or refuse hegemonic neoliberal narratives of progress, and related assumptions of religious or cultural backwardness in which the discourse of eliminating child marriage is embedded?

In Bangladesh today, child marriage arguably serves as an index of civilizational inadequacy, an unseemly obstacle to attaining middle income status, and modernity more generally. It is, simultaneously, a site through which contemporary cultural anxieties over female adolescent sexuality—especially in relation to the development imperative to bring impoverished women and girls "out" into the labor market—are articulated, obscured, or contested. Child marriage narratives rely on "stock" perpetrators, among which patriarchal fathers, cruel husbands, conniving imams, or corrupt government officials (i.e., "bad" Muslim males) figure prominently (see Khoja-Moolji 2015a and 2015b). In the prevailing discursive environment, child marriage works to reference Islam without naming it as such. Overt allusions to religion are unnecessary given certain conditions of epistemic hegemony. Once Bangladesh is imagined as a *Muslim* country, as it is in most external accounts, lines between "culture" and "religion" can be easily collapsed.

In this backdrop, I argue that the "panic" around child marriage does less visible but critical ideological work, helping to reaffirm neoliberal development narratives and smooth over contradictions around discourses of girls' empowerment and poverty reduction. Here we might ask, following Abu-Lughod, what Bangladeshi girls are being saved *to*, once they are saved *from* child marriage. Quite likely, their aspirations center on employment in one of the four million apparel-export factories that dot the urban landscape of Dhaka and Chittagong. Therein lies the cunning of this form of global governmentality: once the category of child marriage is deployed and understood as a barbaric practice and a violent cultural norm that stands in the way of girls' empowerment *and* national development—it works to obscure the actual capitalist violence awaiting those who labor in factories. Images of girls at risk from tradition and predatory men (implicitly racialized as Muslim) also invisibilize the structural causes of poverty and inequality (Wilson 2015). In short, shifting the source and site of scandal from the neoliberal state and the hyper-extractive, financialized global order in which it is nested, to the realm of culture and norms, forecloses critical lines of interrogation.

A flourishing field of "girl studies" has emerged in the last two decades. Reflecting systemic global asymmetries, the rich scholarship in this area tends to foreground the viewing or consuming ethical subject situated in the global north and her will to civilize. It lays bare the lure of investing in the rescue of that most "authentic" of victims—the girl child in the South for Euro-American women or girls whose agency is thereby reaffirmed (e.g., MacDonald 2016; Switzer 2013). Alternately, existing accounts demonstrate—powerfully and persuasively—the ways Western development organizations and local experts authorize particular life trajectories and scripts required to produce ideal neo-liberalized girl citizens, enabling some interventions and foreclosing others (Khoja-Moolji 2018; Moeller 2018). My essay builds on these critical and much needed interventions but also shifts focus to histories of feminism in the global South.

Bangladesh happens to be a particularly dense site of transnational neoliberal governance; it is a favored place for global experimentation and expert knowledge production, especially around population control and reproductive technologies (see Murphy 2017). In some iterations, it is the smiling face of capitalism. Its impressive social indicators, its booming garment industry, and its successful microcredit programs provide material proof of the viability of neoliberal development policy. The bodies of poor rural women and girls are centrally implicated in the creation of this "Aid Lab," as Naomi Hossain (2017) has called the country. With respect to child marriage, Bangladesh is considered to be something of a paradox in the developing world since impressive educational gains for females and significantly lowered fertility rates have occurred "*despite low age at marriage*" (World Bank 2008, 113, emphasis added). That such improvements occurred without an upward shift in age at marriage upends conventional gender and development narratives in which cultural practices such as early marriage are understood to stand in the way of women's empowerment, unsettling the implicit logics of modernization at work. This paradox makes the country an especially productive space through which to explore the questions raised above.

GIRLS MEAN BUSINESS? "SMART ECONOMICS" AND THE CHILD MARRIAGE PROBLEM

Far from being another "overlooked" tradition, child marriage (re)surfaces as an object of state and feminist concern globally and in Bangladesh at a critical political and economic juncture. Its framing—as a violation of the rights of the girl *child* (not adolescent or young woman), and as obstacle to prosperous individual/national/global futures—corresponds to the corporatization or "financialization" of development, in which Grameen Bank–inspired microfinance played a critical role (Roy 2010). With their time-bound, measurable, and financially feasible objectives, the Millennial Development Goals (MDGs) adopted by UN member states in 2000 perfectly encapsulated this global project. Along with a renewed stress on measuring and mapping poverty, "smart economics," or the business case for investing in women/programs for gender equality, featured centrally in what came to be called the New Poverty Agenda (Chant 2016; Cornwall 2018). Manifested in slogans such as "gender empowerment is smart economics," the idea of female empowerment as pathway to economic growth (and profits) appealed to a broad array of actors with very different interests, from multilateral institutions such as UN Women and international NGOs (INGOs) like Plan International, to corporations, investment banks, and philanthro-capitalists. The new reimagined Third World woman was cast not just as a victim to be rescued but as "an icon of indefatigable efficiency and altruism," whose entrepreneurial labor would contribute to fighting global poverty (Roy 2010, 69). In this, she prefigured the twenty-first-century self-responsibilized Third World girl as agent and instrument of development.

By the time Roy's book was published in 2010, the girl child had begun to overshadow, if not replace, her adult counterpart in development discourse. Michelle Murphy traces the roots of this shift to the 1990s, when older notions of human capital were discursively repurposed so that embodiment itself became a site of financial investment, of "an anticipatory, future oriented calculation of value" (2017, 115). Thus, Third World bodies that once possessed negative or low value were potentially improvable and investable—at least when provided with the right conditions. Kalpana Wilson suggests this ascendancy broadly marks the shift from liberal to neoliberal feminism in development thought, with responsibility shifting entirely onto the individual girl, after an initial investment in her human capital (Wilson 2015, 819). The affective associations of the figure of the child within existing transnational humanitarian logics—emblematic of (sexual) innocence, suffering, and futurity—facilitated this transition. Increasingly, unlike her adult counterpart, only the girl is on the "right" side of time.[1]

However, she can have a productive future only if her present can be molded appropriately. In Murphy's words: "The figure of the 'Third World girl'—typically represented as South Asian or African, often Muslim—has become the iconic vessel of human capital. *Thoroughly hetero-sexualized, her rates of return are dependent on her forecasted compliance with expectations to serve family, to adhere to heterosexual propriety,* to study hard, to be optimistic, and hence her ability to be thoroughly 'girled.'" (Murphy 2017, 117, emphasis added). In other words, the girl's potential value—her rate of return—hinges on strict compliance with a set of gendered expectations, a normative script of childhood that produces dutiful daughters who stay strictly within the bounds of heterosexual convention. Those who do not "adhere to (presumably localized norms of) heterosexual propriety" by getting pregnant, having sex outside of marriage, or eloping, are evicted from this system.

Child marriage threatens to undermine speculative future value and its associated normative script of a sexually innocent childhood. In the next section, I take a closer look at the crystallization of child marriage as a category of GBVAW in the first two decades of the millennium, and the meanings it accrues as it circulates through development, philanthropic, and other intersecting sites before it travels back and refracts these other worlds onto rural Bangladesh. To this end, I review a select set of studies and policy measures on child marriage published between 2012 and 2014.

NAMING, FRAMING, AND CLASSIFYING CHILD MARRIAGE

Two discursive shifts are evident in the years that followed the launch of the New Poverty Agenda. One is the trend toward collapsing the categories of early, forced, and child marriage. The second is the classification of child marriage as a form of GBVAW, and/or a harmful cultural practice on par with female genital cutting (FGC). As we will see, shifts in terminology frequently ignore or elide statistical trends and evidence. Practices of naming (e.g., all marriages under eighteen are "child marriages") and classification (e.g., child marriage as a harmful cultural practice in the same category as FGC) enable the active disavowal of adolescent sexuality, among other things.

I begin with a 2013 policy paper issued by the Council on Foreign Relations, an influential US think tank (Vogelstein 2013). Entitled *Ending Child*

Marriage: How Elevating the Status of Girls Advances US Foreign Policy Objectives, the report makes no distinctions between early, child, and forced marriages. Child marriage is described as a threat to prosperity and stability, its effects "harmful not only to girls, but also to families, communities, and economies—*and to U.S. interests*—around the globe" (2, emphasis added). The report recommends that the United States leverage child marriage more prominently in its diplomatic dealings with affected states.

Yemen is one of four countries profiled in the Council's report, even though it does *not* appear in an enclosed table of the ten countries with the highest prevalence of child marriage. Undaunted by the paucity of reliable statistics, the author draws on a Euro-American best seller "penned" by ten-year-old Nujood Ali in conjunction with a French journalist on the young girl's quest for divorce. Postcolonial feminist scholars, especially those who work on the so-called Muslim world, have written at length about the ideological labor performed by the construction and circulation of "memoirs" like Nujood's (Ahmad 2009; Abu Lughod 2013). These stories of escape from Islam belong to a genre of writing that emerged in Europe and North America in the 1990s and took off after 9/11 (Abu-Lughod 2013, 87). Force and bondage are the defining themes of this lurid, exposé style of writing, which trades on the international consensus on the value of "choosing freely" (Abu-Lughod 2013, 87). Forced and child marriages are natural themes for this genre, in which distinctions between Muslim women and girls are frequently blurred, perhaps because Muslim women are always already infantilized in such frames. These books travel and circulate through critical spaces in Euro-American popular culture, accumulating meanings through specific discursive maneuvers. In his review of the book, the *New York Times* journalist Nicholas Kristof remarked that, "little girls like Nujood may prove more effective than missiles at defeating terrorists" (2010). Here Kristof relies on a much-rehearsed strategy of blaming local culture/tradition/religion for any form of "bad behavior" on the part of non–Euro-Americans, allowing him to elide the realm of geopolitics altogether (Volpp 2000). This rhetorical move not only exempts the United States from any culpability for the underlying conditions that drive many Yeminis to "terrorism," but also reprises the broader logic on which the Council on Foreign Relations report draws: saving brown Muslim women is profitable for US national interests. Given the multiple stakes for the United States in the country, the preoccupation with child marriage in Yemen in the Council report makes perfect sense. The cover photo of an older "Middle Eastern" looking man and his young girl bride are identified inside as a Yemeni couple. These visual and rhetorical cues rely for their meanings on Orientalized discourses already in circulation (Khoja-Moolji 2015a, 51). That the evidence inside does not point to Yemen having a child marriage problem appears to be irrelevant.

A 2014 study commissioned by the Ford Foundation—a progressive donor whose grants critically shaped feminist knowledge production in postindependent Bangladesh—illuminates another dimension of the nexus between knowledge and power. Margaret Greene, the author of *Ending Child Marriage in a Generation: What Research Is Needed?* begins with the observation that it is only in the preceding five years or so (that is, around 2009) that the discussion has favored the use of "child marriage" rather than "early" or "forced" marriage. She does not specify whose voices count as contributing to "the discussion" or why the shift took place, other than that girls *often agree* to early marriage. She goes on to note that because there is no universally accepted definition of "child," issues of consent can become murky (Greene 2014, 2, emphasis added). Having acknowledged the complexities involved, in a remarkable illustration of tautological thinking Greene then justifies her use of the term "child marriage" because "it has gained currency among practitioners and applied researchers and is the shorthand the field is currently using for this reason" (2). Greene does not specify why the term gained currency in "the field" or what/who constitutes said field in which the terms of debate are set. She touches on but skims over the key node of discomfort for those who embrace a normative child marriage script—that girls often agree to early marriage and that questions of consent cannot always be easily settled.

What Greene leaves unsaid is that development professionals may well prefer the term "child marriage" as a way to elide the conceptual and practical complexities that adolescent sexuality throws up. The globally accepted definition of the child as anyone under eighteen flattens social complexity but also secures an absolute binary between the knowing agentic adult and the sexually innocent child, who by this definition is incapable of consent (Malkki 2015; Ticktin 2017).

Greene's study was published in 2014, the year that the UN General Assembly passed a resolution asking all member states to pass and enforce laws banning child marriage. The resolution formalized the global governmentalization of child marriage in the twenty-first century. It is worth pausing here to note that, other than the (forgotten) 1962 Convention, until recently, no major UN declarations on women, such as CEDAW (1979), the Declaration on the Elimination of Violence Against Women (1993), the International Conference on Population and Development (ICPD) (1994), and the Beijing Platform for Women (1995), names child marriage either as an issue of violence against women or as an impediment to development. While Article 16 of CEDAW, which calls for equal rights in marriage, is much contested, it does not mention age per se. Equally significant, Section 4.21 of the Platform of Action of the ICPD calls for free and full consent in marriage, enforcement of a minimum legal age of consent, and raising the minimum age where necessary. Section 4.22 urges states to prohibit FGC where it exists, while the next section lists practices (such as infanticide, trafficking, and prenatal sex selection) that states are urged to take measures to prevent. The separate section on the girl child makes no reference to child marriage.[2]

In contrast, today, all UN agencies refer to child marriage either as a "harmful" or "traditional" practice, a human rights abuse, and/or form of GBVAW. In *Marrying Too Young: Ending Child Marriage*, the late Babatunde Osotimehin, executive director of UNFPA, called child marriage a human rights abuse (UNFPA 2012). Even though the report stated that incidents of child marriage had already "drastically changed" or "showed significant decrease" in some countries and across different regions, the language conveyed a sense of urgency, if not panic, in discussions of *projected* numbers of "child brides" ("staggering implications," "no time to lose" in the absence of timely interventions) (UNFPA 2012, 24, 25). The same year, UNICEF issued a "report card" on the state of the world's children, in which child marriage was addressed in some depth (UNICEF 2012, 39). Referred to as a harmful cultural practice, child marriage was classified as distinct from the general category of GBVAW. A separate chapter on violence lists child marriage in passing as a possible source of domestic violence (UNICEF 2012, 32).

The Sustainable Development Goals (SDGs) are more explicit in their naming practices.[3] Target 5.2, for example is: "Eliminate all forms of violence against all women and girls in the public and private spheres, including trafficking and sexual and other types of exploitation." Target 5.3 follows up with: "Eliminate all harmful practices, such as child, early and forced marriage and female genital mutilation." No explanation is proffered as to why child marriage is listed as a harmful practice rather than another form of violence against women and girls, and why it is classified along with FGC. As Sally Engle Merry notes in her ethnography of CEDAW procedures, genital cutting is the "*poster child* and *prototype*" of the category of harmful cultural practice (2006, 27). The placement of child marriage alongside female genital mutilation conjures up the culturalized horror associated with the category of harmful cultural practices itself. Merry observes that even if rarely articulated, notions of what it means to be civilized remain pervasive in UN documents (Merry 2006, 13). Nineteenth-century narratives of progress and racial difference can be smuggled into prevailing theoretical models though the binary of tradition and modernity, and an implicit juxtaposition of civilization defined in opposition to culture. It is this understanding of culture as tradition—timeless, static, and discriminatory—on which the category of harmful traditional practices rests (13).

Critical feminist scholars have also noted the reinscription of colonial and imperial hierarchies in the spatial and ethnic distribution of practices labeled traditional or harmful (Grewal 1999; Ko 2007; Volpp 2000). Representation of adolescent sexuality in prevailing discourses of child marriage offers a stark illustration. The unmarked Euro-American "girl" is generally represented as an agentive sexual subject, in contrast to her counterpart in the South (Wilson 2015, 820). The latter's sexual agency, read as "precocity" and/or "uncontrolled fertility," must be contained before it becomes a threat to her future productivity and so to national and global well-being. Framed as a pathology of backward cultures/religions grafted on to particular geographical spaces and people, "saving" Muslim and other brown girls from their cultures (through the prevention of child marriage) into a future of laboring for the neoliberal economy can proceed apace. This framing also accounts for why, even though until 2018, most US states permitted marriage of legal minors as young as twelve, such knowledge does not elicit the same horror or outrage from Euro-American populations.

It is no surprise then that the US government has taken conscious steps to stop child marriage elsewhere. In 2013, the US Congress approved a bill that identified child marriage as a breach of fundamental human rights. Attached to the Violence Against Women Reauthorization Act of 2013, it mandated all foreign aid programs to incorporate a comprehensive integrated strategy to prevent child marriage in developing countries. The bill also required US embassies to include child marriage rates in their individual country reports on human rights— thereby setting up the conditions to produce metrics for comparison and ranking. It would be easy to dismiss the bill as yet another act of liberal feminist imperialism. But US feminists were not directly responsible for this piece of legislation, which was the result of active lobbying on the part of two members of The Elders—"an independent group of global leaders working together for peace, justice and human rights," according to their website. In a *Washington Post* op-ed the year before, Elders Reverend Desmond Tutu and Graca Machel had urged the Obama administration to make the elimination of child marriage a foreign policy goal. In their words, "Without tackling child marriage, the US government cannot hope to achieve its development ambitions" (The Elders 2013). The rhetorical structure of Machel and Tutu's appeal reproduces the logic of imperial and developmental benevolence. It also draws on the multiple logics of millennial development—the first being the underlying assumption that the "development ambitions" of the United States are beneficial, ethical, and profitable for all concerned.

The passage of the bill was widely considered to be a victory for Girls not Brides (GNB), a global consortium set up in 2011 under the aegis of the Clinton Global Initiative (CGI), with funding from the Ford Foundation, the Nike Foundation, the NoVo Foundation. The high standing of the Elders provided moral legitimacy. Because of the names attached to it, GNB has had considerable influence in shaping child marriage debates globally. GNB makes no distinction between child and early marriage and assumes that forced marriage necessarily includes child marriage (Girls Not Brides USA 2019). The organization actively lobbies Congress to take into consideration "child marriage and related practices" in the formulation of US foreign policy. For instance, on International Girl Child Day in 2017, the co-chairs of GNB USA published a piece entitled "Empower Girls, Change the World" on the congressional foreign policy blog; it characterized child marriage as a "practice *rooted in inequitable gender norms* that place boys' rights, education and economic successes above those of girls" (Patel et al. 2017, emphasis added). This allowed the authors to forge an otherwise tenuous link between child marriage and FGC, by implication interchangeable, context-free, harmful cultural norms.

GNB's London-based secretariat coordinates and supports the work of member organizations globally. According to the CGI website, GNB's mission is to "seed activities to end child marriage in priority countries (Clinton Global Initiative n.d.). Bangladesh is one such priority country, and most significant NGOs, as well as Bangladesh Mahila Parishad, are members of the local chapter. GNB is one node in the broader circuit through which the (re)-governmentalized global imperative to address child marriage travels to and plays out in the national space of Bangladesh.

THE CHILD MARRIAGE "PARADOX": NUMBERS AND TIMELINES

Critical scrutiny of available statistics and the discursive production of child marriage (shifts in language and modes of classification over time) allows us to rethink the so-called Bangladesh paradox—dramatic improvements in girls' education, fertility, and infant mortality rates alongside the persistence of child marriages.[4] Rather than a puzzle, the numbers may simply pose an empirical challenge to reigning wisdom, revealing inconsistencies in the anchoring logic of neoliberal narratives of girls' empowerment.

As a benchmark for changes in language and classification over time, I turn to a landmark study commissioned by the World Bank in 2008. *From Whispers to Voices: Gender and Social Transformation in Bangladesh*, an analytically sophisticated, insightful report authored by two leading feminist academics, mentions child marriage just three times, twice in relation to Bangladesh Mahila Parishad (6 and 27), and once on incidences of "very early child marriage" (World Bank 2008, 121). Throughout, the preferred term is "low age of marriage." The chapter on violence against women makes no mention of child marriage. We learn that the proportion of women marrying very early (by age fifteen) declined by almost half over time from 71 percent (cohort age forty-five-to-forty-nine) to 37 percent among women aged twenty-to-twenty-four and that age at marriage has remained low at about sixteen years. In the chapter on marriage, the authors argue that, "the important development in Bangladesh is not that median age at marriage in Bangladesh has remained low (although there have been some improvements in the last decade) but that education [rose] and fertility dropped *despite low age at marriage*" (113, emphasis added). The tone in this passage is measured: it is not meant to sound an alarm. Rather, policymakers and researchers are perplexed that low age at marriage did not hamper the attainment of development goals such as gender parity in education or lowered fertility rates. Clearly, the empirical data, however measured, poses a critical challenge to development orthodoxy around the relation between backward cultural mores (low age at marriage) and gendered developmental goals (education for girls, fewer children, and by implication greater reproductive control, and access to labor markets). The numbers also undermine the broader truths of girls' empowerment discourse—that child marriage stands in the way of education more generally, without which development (read growth) cannot take place.

In the decade between 2008 and 2018, the discursive ground shifted dramatically, with liberal feminism and "smart economics" conjoined through the resuscitated specter of child marriage. By 2017, the World Bank had commissioned a major multicountry study on the economic impacts of child marriage. In the words of the lead investigator, Quentin Wodon, "Ending this practice is not only the morally right thing to do but also the economically smart thing to do" (World Bank 2017). In the prolific development literature on Bangladesh, references to "early age at marriage" gave way increasingly to "child marriage," which soon came to be "widely perceived as an *intractable* problem that is culturally entrenched and immutable" (Amin et al. 2018, 4, emphasis added). In the intervening years, a veritable cottage industry seems to have grown around the subject, ranging from thoughtful policy briefs by the New York-based Center for Reproductive Rights (2018) to sensationalist coverage in *Foreign Policy* magazine ("Bangladesh's Child Marriage Problem Is the World's Human Trafficking Crisis," from November 8, 2019). Even when the contents are substantive, the title itself can reproduce tired tropes of dependency and powerlessness. This is exactly what the title of a Human Rights Watch (2015) report—"Marry Before Your House Is Swept Away: Child Marriage in Bangladesh"—seemingly aimed at potential funders does.

It is no surprise that the public sphere is saturated with news of efforts to eradicate child marriage. Op-ed pieces ("Early Marriage: A Contributor to 'Modern Slavery' in Bangladesh?" [July 27, 2018]); news stories ("Girls Save Friend from Early Marriage" [Shibli 2018]); and reports of workshops and seminars ("Ending Child Marriage: All Stakeholders Must Work Together, Say Speakers" [*The Daily Star* 2019]) and "Still the Highest in the Region" [Al-Masum Molla 2019]) are ubiquitous. In all these pieces, early and child marriage are often used interchangeably. Framed through the prism of GBVAW, child marriage in Bangladesh is routinely declaimed as one of the worst forms of rights violence.[5] Alternately, it is characterized as a social pandemic (*The Daily Star* 2019).

UN documents on Bangladesh reveal a similar shift in classifying and naming. A visitor to the Bangladesh profile of UN Women's global database on violence against women will find at the top of the page, listed under Prevalence Data on Different Forms of Violence against Women, four sets of statistics. The first three pertain to physical, sexual, and intimate partner violence. The final measure is of child marriage. Similarly, an SDG site lists child or early marriages alongside acid attacks, rape, murder, physical torture, dowry, family conflict, suicide, and *hilla* (intermediate) marriage (Sustainable Development Goals Fund 2017). Enfolded within VAW case studies, such juxtapositions draw on and reproduce assumed equivalency among these otherwise disparate and radically incommensurate practices.

Equally compelling are the numbers themselves. The alarmist tone of most reports goes against UNICEF's own assessment, noted above, that the practice of child marriage is declining globally, including in Bangladesh, especially for girls under the age of fifteen (UNFPA 2012, 24). A quick look at the latest official data reveals "a slow but steady increase over time in the median age at first marriage among women age 20–49, from 14.4 years in 1993–94 to 15.3 years in 2007 and 16.3 years in 2017–18. The proportion of women age 20–24 who were married by age 18 declined from 73% in 1993–94 to 65% in 2011; by 2017–18, it had inched down to 59%" (National Institute of Population Research and Training [NIPORT], and ICF 2020, 42). UNICEF reports that of the over 50 percent of women currently in their mid-twenties who were married before they turned eighteen, nearly 18 percent were below fifteen years (UNICEF n.d.).

According to UN Women (2016), the child marriage prevalence rate in Bangladesh is at 58.6 percent.[6] This figure (listed by UNICEF as 66 percent [2011, 120]) has been extraordinarily generative over the years, reproduced without scrutiny or disaggregation in popular media and policy research (see, for instance, Al-Masum Molla 2019).

But what exactly does the 59 percent stand for? A closer look reveals first that the data are organized by age cohorts, with fifteen and eighteen years as cutoff points. Thus, as of March 2019, less than a quarter (22 percent) of those who were between twenty and twenty-four years old had been married by age fifteen (UNICEF 2021). It follows that the remaining population of girls were married when they were sixteen and seventeen. What is glossed over in classifying all marriages under eighteen as child marriages? What kind of violence is enabled when the distinctions between a twelve-year-old forced into marriage and a seventeen-year-old who may be clear about her desires are obliterated? These are not questions that can be asked within the current framing of the child marriage problem, which produces subjects who are always already victims, terrorized by culture/religion/patriarchy. It also produces new meanings for child marriage—whether as an index of violence or, in the other direction, as a metric or measure of success in struggles against GBVAW.

Discourses of child marriage as either social evil or epidemic become hypervisible as they travel through intersecting "local" and global domains. Indeed, the lines between transnational and local are difficult to disentangle at times. Given the stress on measurable change, it is no surprise that the on-the-ground efforts most likely to receive global recognition, as well as funding, tend toward highly individualized, decontextualized, metrics-oriented activities. The "Wedding Busters," sponsored in part by the Bangladesh chapters of Plan International (2016) and GNB, are a case in point. These community-based child protection committees composed of adolescent boys and girls are trained in surveillance and will directly intervene in child weddings in their locality: in vigilante fashion, whenever they hear of an impending or ongoing child marriage, they rush to the spot in order to dissuade the parents or guardians involved. They also inform law enforcement authorities. The website of GNB Bangladesh frequently features profiles of young girls "saved from being married," in their words. The measure of success is quite literally in the number of girls "saved" at the altar. Newspaper headlines routinely reprise this language of rescue. "Girls Save Friend from Early Marriage" was the headline for a story in the *Daily Star* on July 21, 2018.

In this context, a feminist demographer working with adolescent girls remarked that the public drama of rescue on the spot appealed to those who subscribe to a savior paradigm. She noted that this kind of child marriage narrative needed a villain: the qazi (judge), the parents, or those who provide forged birth certificates. She added that parents who sought to bypass the authorities or these committees would travel to a neighboring locality if they were intent on going through with the marriage of their underage daughter. In the narrative that emerges, parents are the villains, either because they do not know better or because their cultural norms condemn them to care more about saving face than attending to their daughter's welfare. There is no space in this paternalistic pedagogical space to question *why* parents would be desperate enough to travel to a different locality to get daughters married. The structural context that shapes parental "choices" is rendered invisible, even irrelevant, in this frame.

In 2013, eighteen-year-old Keshab Roy, member of *Surjomukhi*, a local affiliate of the Wedding Busters in northern Bangladesh, was one of six young people to receive the first-ever United Nations Youth Courage Award for "demonstrating leadership in the fight to get every child into school." According to one newspaper, Keshab had prevented the "child marriages of 25 teenage girls, and stopped about a hundred children so far from being school dropouts" (Assaduzaman 2013). Media accounts relate the story of a young boy whose life changed when he discovered Surjomukhi. Keshab himself does not appear to have been in danger of being married early without consent. The son of a day laborer, he was forced to leave school and take up work in a scrap metal shop in the seventh grade, following a family medical emergency. Surjomukhi's director apparently convinced Keshab's father to reenroll him in school, though readers are not told whether financial assistance was offered to the father. In this narrative framing, the root problem appears to be one of persuasion, rather than of distribution of scarce resources. The implication is that parents who don't know better must be enlightened. Keshab's tasks at Surjomukhi include promoting sanitation, birth registration, and encouraging women to go to safe delivery centers—standard development work, it would seem (Assaduzaman 2013). The narrative purchase of his story has little to do with his own struggle against poverty.

Despite studies that show access to education to be most strongly tied to economic means or privilege, the active deprivation of education due to culture or religion haunts policy documents, scholarship, and public imaginations. A recent blog authored by a respected Bangladesh scholar of girls' education provides a vivid illustration of the stickiness of this logic. The seemingly bold title, "Gender Equity in Schools in Muslim Countries: It Can Be Done," reaffirms assumptions that "Muslim countries" by virtue of being Muslim majority, have problems achieving gender equity in schooling without external intervention. In case this is not clear to the reader, the blog begins with this sentence: "Muslim countries worldwide have problems with gender equality." As evidence, he draws on the Global Gender Gap Report, noting that none of the ten most successful countries offering equal opportunities for men and women are Muslim. He goes on to report that of the ten countries with the worst child school attendance, seven are Muslim: Nigeria, Pakistan, Cote d'Ivoire, Ethiopia, Burkina Faso, Niger, and Yemen (Asadullah 2014). This is a shockingly misleading list, given that Nigeria, Cote d'Ivoire, and Ethiopia are not "Muslim countries," whatever that might mean. The author elaborates that these countries are often hot spots for violence against women and schoolgirls. As evidence, he offers up the example of Boko Haram and the Taliban, presumably relying on readers' associations of Muslim male violence and female oppression. He neglects to mention that, Muslim or not, most of these are also places wracked by violence and war, invariably colonial, capitalist, and transnational in nature. Islam is made the (not so) implicit culprit. Asadullah's reference to Malala Yousufzai recalls Khoja-Moolji's analysis noted above, especially the ways Malala's suffering is generalized and comes to stand for the collectivity of Muslim girls (Khoja-Moolji 2015b, 544).

METRICS IN THE AID LAB: A BRIEF DETOUR

Bangladesh's child marriage debates intersect at global and national levels in other way as well. As noted earlier, the financialization of development led to a renewed emphasis on metrics. Ever the site of developmentalist experimentation, Bangladesh came into the line of vision of a new global think tank, the Copenhagen Consensus, in 2015 when the latter turned its attention to the SDGs.[7] In a global first, the Copenhagen Consensus partnered with the NGO BRAC with the objective of preparing a "data driven prioritization" map to attaining the SDGs. As part of this process, the Copenhagen Consensus commissioned a cost-benefit analysis of possible strategies to reduce child marriage. Professors from Duke University and researchers from the celebrated Abdul Lateef Jamil Poverty Action Lab (J-PAL, best known for the Nobel Prize two of its associates received for their work on Randomized Control Trials at MIT carried out the child marriage study (Field et al. 2016). Their research found that even modest financial incentives in the form of cooking oil had substantial impact on the marriage age of girls.

The recommendation for conditional cash transfers as a stand-alone intervention received immediate and sustained resistance from scholar-activists who rightly feared money would be reallocated from multidimensional, holistic empowerment programs to decontextualized direct cash transfers (see Amin et al. 2017). A flurry of op-eds on high profile sites such as a London School of Economics blog and in the journal *Economic and Political Weekly* ensued. Ultimately the cooking oil subsidy idea did not find many takers. More recently, Bangladeshi feminists have produced powerful critiques of the place of "data driven prioritization" and RCTs in development programming (Nazneen 2016; Kabeer 2019).

My point in bringing up the above example is not to challenge the effectiveness of conditional cash transfers but to note that the stress on metrics produces a distribution of value in which some programs and interventions come to be valorized more than others. In other words, metrics do critical ideological work, both locally and globally. As Rema Hammami persuasively argues in relation to the globally accepted measurement of domestic violence, seemingly neutral metrics are produced through a complex global power-knowledge nexus, serving to construct the very social problem or category they are meant to target or measure (Hammami 2019). The narrative logic involved in determining any particular metric then shapes the nature of available interventions.

Drawing on Hammami's insights, we can ask what it is that the category of "child marriage" does in the context of Bangladesh. Most obviously, the term glosses over critical differences in experience and subjectivity, producing instead an imagined victim-subject who must be saved before it is "too late." Second, the figuration of the child as helpless victim produces a sense of urgency that privileges certain kinds of interventions over others. In this light, the special emphasis at a roundtable discussion in 2019 making available remedies such as online apps and hotlines appears obvious and necessary (*Daily Star* 2019). Despite the widespread recognition that poverty and insecurity are two core factors underlying early marriage, once child marriage is understood as an intractable *cultural* "norm" in need of ideological correction, measures such as building community awareness and providing individual legal training present themselves as the most obvious and effective interventions. In this discursive environment, the otherwise glaring absence of structural interventions is barely noticeable.

Hammami reminds us that along with its "everyday productivity," categories such as child marriage also accomplish wider geopolitical work (Hammami 2019, 497). In this instance, invocations of the child bride call forth and reauthorize Orientalized imaginaries, reinscribing civilizational difference. The violence of the state or of transnational capital—their role in producing conditions of poverty or insecurity—falls out of the frame. Export-led growth is the only vision of development deemed desirable or feasible (see, for instance, Paprocki 2018).

WHOSE FEMINIST AGENDA?

The structuring role of the SDGs in Bangladeshi political economy ensures that child marriage features prominently in public and development discourse. The Government of Bangladesh (GoB) recently rolled out a much-anticipated National Action Plan to End Child Marriage 2018–2030, with the objective of eliminating the practice by 2030. Earlier budgets showed "an upward trend" in allocations for ending child marriage (UNICEF 2014). A look at these earlier allocations reveals business as usual in some ways; key interventions include social safety net programs, adolescent health, and opportunities for secondary education for girls. With or without an apparent epidemic of child marriages, these programs would be funded. Perhaps the GoB too is allocating funds creatively.

This leaves open the question of why child marriage as a problem would suddenly be taken up by feminists, with such apparent enthusiasm. Why was it an issue everywhere in the women's movement, I asked my activist friends in the summer of 2017. A puzzled look and "no it isn't," was a first response from a respected scholar activist. The feminist group to which she belonged, and had cofounded, worked on issues of sexuality, including adolescent sexuality and VAW, but not child marriage per se. My friend reconsidered her initial response by musing on how there was more than one women's movement in the country. "The MDGs, SDGs drive so much of what goes on," she continued. "That's where you should look." This comment gestured to the blurred borders between NGOs and the women's movement, and national and international agenda setting (Karim 2011; Feldman 1997). "I keep getting calls for proposals for child marriage-related activities, which we're not interested in. I circulate the announcements outside the organization but nobody's picking up the bait," she ended.

Another friend in the field of public health responded more directly, without hesitation. "There's so much money in it, that's why. The Dutch have poured in millions, as part of their sexual and reproductive health and rights (SRHR) programs. The UK has also invested substantial amounts in research and programs on child marriage, as part of a longer term global intervention in the girl/adolescent." Could what appeared to be child marriage hysteria to me be just a symptom of the postrecession world in which activists and researchers were adjusting to a new financial environment? There is some truth to this explanation. After all, bills need to be paid and staff cannot be thrown out on the streets once a project is over. In an environment in which funding is highly competitive and scarce, those already working around issues of adolescent health, fertility, and sexuality have been able to creatively redeploy donor interest in their work.

Still, why had people not talked about it before? A human rights lawyer offered me a pragmatic and persuasive answer. "It was always there, we knew about it. Now that the donors are interested, we have the resources to do something about it. It's just like with the Domestic Violence Act. Donor funding helped us push through *our* agenda."

I remained curious about the terminology. Why call it "child" marriage, if everyone agreed that a twelve-year-old forced into marriage was qualitatively different from a seventeen-year-old who chose to elope? A decade earlier I had been part of a series of animated conversations among activists about the lines between child, early, and forced marriages. The conceptual slippages and difficulties that a series of transnational forced marriage cases as well as several local cases of teenage girls eloping with lovers had precipitated those discussions.

A friend involved with designing and supervising programs for adolescent girls in rural areas had this to say: "I tried to use the more progressive term 'delayed marriage' in the field. But I got push back from the research assistants and local administrators. I was told it wasn't in our culture. *We don't believe in delay*, they said." She added that she found herself using the term "child marriage" for pragmatic reasons. She went on to explain, "It's for communication, primarily. That is, *people know what it means*. I also use it to avoid conceptual complexities in the field. I can refer to anyone marrying under 18 to be involved in a child marriage, because that is the legal age according to UNICEF."

In a cultural environment in which marriage is universal and the pathway to full adulthood, delay implies a disruption in the *right* time to get married. However, the right time to be married is contextual, and open to change if we are to go by official statistics. In an important but curiously neglected study, Streatfield et al. (2015) use demographic surveillance data from Matlab—arguably the global capital of developmental experimentation—to argue there is a hidden rise in marriage age. According to their findings, two-thirds of the sample population misreported age at marriage, with over 50 percent *underreporting* their age. They suggest the misreporting was not random but likely associated with rising dowry practices (Streatfield et al. 2015, 108). One cannot help but wonder why this theory of underreporting age at marriage has not been explored further.

If local understandings of child marriage seem to operate on a different register from UN sanctioned legal language, how then do "people know what [child marriage] means?" Perhaps such knowledge indexes the success of various awareness-raising campaigns, and reflects the disciplinary power of development discourse. The invocation of UNICEF—which here stands for the global or civilizational—signals the governmentalizing work of child marriage discourse.

Clearly, the relationship between the discursive power of the development regime and the women's movement is more complicated and layered than any model of imposition from above, or even of funding constraints, suggests. Feminists learn to navigate interstitial spaces, creatively reworking transnational imperatives in pragmatic and more contextually relevant ways.

THE TROUBLE WITH THE GIRL CHILD

The girl child agenda has intensified a more general double bind in which the GoB finds itself. On the one hand, it is beholden to transnational capital and the demand for a particular mode of girls' empowerment. On the other, the elected government must contend with contradictory urban middle-class sensibilities—the desire to appear modern and anxiety over "unregulated" adolescent sexuality, as well as a largely rural target group with very different investments in child marriage debates. Much-touted success in bringing gender parity in schooling (read "free mixing"), along with the hypervisibility of young female garment workers in urban spaces, produces deep sexual anxiety at moments of crisis (Siddiqi 2003). The generative power of emergent discourses and tropes—of innocent girls exposed to increasingly dangerous situations because of national development—cannot be underestimated. In this backdrop I would like to suggest that the GoB's 2016 amendment of the Child Marriage Restraint Act of 1929, which legalized marriages for girls under eighteen years in "special circumstances," in other words, with parental consent and/or approval from the courts but with no concern for the girl's consent, was neither a move to appease "fundamentalists" nor a desire to fudge statistics. Rather, the amendment offers a way to reconcile this particular double bind (with the added benefit of keeping Islamist allies content).

Heated feminist debates within Bangladesh reanimated Orientalized tropes of (Muslim) girls forced to marry their rapists, as evident in the coverage and framing of the issue in Europe and the United States.[8] Feminist labor rights leader and ruling party Member of Parliament Shirin Akter publicly asked if she would be forced to marry her daughter to a rapist under the law (Prothom Alo 2017). GNB's Bangladesh chapter warned the provision would encourage child marriage and legitimize statutory rape. Opponents launched a global petition that stated that with "the stroke of her pen, Bangladesh's Prime Minister can become a champion for millions of girls—or pass a law that could force girls to marry their rapists."[9] A Reuters story titled "Bangladesh Law Allowing Child Brides May Legitimize Rapes" included the following quote from GNB Bangladesh: "We are concerned that this new act could lead to widespread abuse, legitimize statutory rape, allow parents to force their girls to marry their rapists, and further encourage the practice of child marriage in a country with one of the highest child marriage rates in the world" (Paul and Bhalla 2017). "Child Rape Fears: Fury over new law in Bangladesh that legalises child brides and 'could reduce minimum age of marriage to zero'" declared a headline in the UK tabloid the *Sun* (Charlton 2017). Kofi Annan, chair of The Elders, wrote an open letter to the prime minister, warning her of the dangers of lowering the minimum age of marriage for girls in their communities.

Rumors swirled that the prime minister, having recently learned of age-of-marriage laws in various US states, did not see why Bangladesh should be sanctioned for a practice still legal in the West. Apocryphal or not, the underlying logic reproduced notions of Euro-American civilizational superiority and authority to set normative standards. The prime minister's detractors speculated that lowering the age of marriage was calculated to improve Bangladesh's prospects of meeting SDG 5, working on the flawed assumption that legalized marriages over sixteen would not count as "child" marriages in aggregate national statistics. I came across this "explanation" regularly during my fieldwork—a reminder of how deeply transnational imperatives are entangled with national self-presentation.

Official discourse also reflects the structuring role of a paternalistic, colonial mentality within an asymmetrical development regime, in which "the rural masses" and their urban counterparts are constructed as backward, traditional, and/or irrational. "Our rural society is very cruel," the head of the Parliamentary Committee on Women and Children has said. "They will point their finger at the pregnant girl. She will be an outcaste in school. People will say nasty things to the girl's parents" (Sattar and Barry 2017). The State Minister for Women and Children is on record saying that the provision would help "tackle elopement and unwanted pregnancies" (Asadullah and Wahhaj 2015). She added this would allow parents to manage situations in which daughters had been subjected to sexual harassment and other threats.

The shared assumption at work in these statements is that adolescent girls "exposed" to boys or men will invariably be duped into sex, unless of course they are subjected to sexual assault or rape first. The narrative not only erases adolescent sexual agency but also naturalizes the extraordinary levels of public violence that girls face routinely in contemporary Bangladesh. Following the protectionist logic at work in this discursive universe, whether it is rape or consensual sex, marriage is the solution.

Empirical evidence constantly disrupts the global narrative as exemplified in the SDGs "of sexually innocent children forced to leave school for untimely marriage" in the words of a recent paper from India (Mehra and Nandy 2020; see also John 2021). Mehra and Nandy show how in the face of societal and state neglect, girls exert control and agency through developing romantic relationships, which can lead to marriage. My own research indicates that girls who lack alternatives to socially sanctioned nonmarital sex often elope or claim to be married to their sexual partners (Siddiqi 2005, 2012, 2015). Usually these are girls between the ages of sixteen and eighteen and their budding sexual desires go against the grain of accepted social practice. When they do elope, of their own will, they are "recovered" —forced to return to their families through recourse to colonial-era legal provisions. Consensual sexual activity comes to be criminalized as rape, abduction, or sexual abuse. This contradiction places progressive Bangladeshi feminists in a double bind. The sexually active adolescent disrupts the script of innocence on which activists have come to rely in their struggle against early marriage. The adolescent girl's reduction to an innocent, asexual, unknowing child affirms normative liberal conceptions of the child, "as being bereft of agency at the very moment in which she express[es] agency" (Roy 2017, 877).

(NO) TIME FOR MARRIAGE?

Recourse to a normative child marriage script might seem to be the most practical or strategic measure in the short run, but much is lost and foreclosed in this desire to forge the practical by covering over that which does not fit the story line. Unfortunately, discussion of adolescent sexual subjectivity and desire is precluded by the singular focus on age. At the same time, the will to improve or civilize through the bodies of women is very much part of the project of development; child marriage is just the latest category that draws on and reproduces this older civilizational framework. As a result, certain questions cannot be framed, asked, or heard. Most obviously, a reductive focus on child marriage displaces structural analyses in favor of reforming/remaking/eliminating "backward" kinship and cultural expectations, ones regularly tied in the current global context to religion. Feminist (and other) imaginations are necessarily disciplined when ongoing, interconnected relational histories of impoverishment, climate catastrophe, dispossession, and extraction remain out of the frame (Appel 2017; Paprocki 2021). Certain forms of violence—of the kind regularly faced by young female Bangladesh garment factory workers, for instance—fade into the backdrop, so that laboring itself can be framed as liberatory (Hickel 2014, 1362). Albeit indirectly, the affective power of the child marriage narrative underwrites and naturalizes export-led development as social progress, foreclosing other ways of imagining how and what the good life can be. It is time to take back this narrative, and reframe it in ways that actually serve the girls and adolescents it is meant to protect.

NOTES

I would like to thank the two anonymous reviewers for their comments and suggestions; Laura Charney for her editorial assistance; Rema Hammami for her close and incisive reading of multiple drafts; and Lila Abu-Lughod for her generosity and intellectual comradeship.

1. Nike was one of the earliest corporations to take up this investment strategy. In 2008, the Nike Foundation launched "The Girl Effect" in conjunction with the UN and Novo Foundations. The Girl Effect was branded as a theory of social change that rested on "the unique potential of 250 million adolescent girls to end poverty for themselves and the world" (cited in Moeller 2018, 20).
2. Bangladeshi feminists did raise the question of child marriage at the Fourth World Conference in Beijing.
3. See UN Department of Economic and Social Affairs (2015) for the Sustainable Development Goals.
4. This section has greatly benefited from Rema Hammami's insights.
5. See, for instance, "Child Marriage Most Egregious Human Rights Violation" (Staff Correspondent 2016).
6. Data source: UNICEF global databases, 2018, based on Demographic and Health Surveys (DHS), Multiple Indicator Cluster Surveys (MICS) and other nationally representative surveys.
7. According to its website, its studies are conducted by more than 300 economists from internationally renowned institutions, including seven Nobel Laureates, to advise policy-makers and philanthropists on how to spend their money most effectively.
8. For an analysis of so-called marriages to rapists, see Siddiqi (2015).
9. The petition, called "PM Hasina: Lead the World on Child Marriage," can be found at https://secure.avaaz.org/campaign/en/bangladesh_child_marriage_law_fb1/.

REFERENCES

Abu-Lughod, Lila. 2013. *Do Muslim Women Need Saving?* Cambridge, MA: Harvard University Press.

Ahmad, Dohra. 2009. "Not Yet Beyond the Veil: Muslim Women in American Popular Literature." *Social Text* 27, no. 2: 105–31. https://doi.org/10.1215/01642472-2008-024.

Amin, Sajeda, Niaz Asadullah, Sara Hossain, and Zaki Wahhaj. 2017. "Can Conditional Transfers Eradicate Child Marriage?" *Economic and Political Weekly* 52, no. 6: 1–10.

Amin, Sajeda, Jyotirmoy Saha, Masuma Billah, Nargis Sultana, Eashita Haque, and Surojit Kundu. 2018. *Accelerating Action to End Child Marriage in Bangladesh*. New York: Population Council.

Amin, Sonia. 1996. *The World of Muslim Women in Colonial Bengal, 1876–1939*. Leiden: Brill.

Appel, Hana. 2017. "Toward an Ethnography of the National Economy." *Cultural Anthropology* 32, no. 2: 294–322. https://doi.org/10.14506/ca32.2.09.

Asadullah, Niaz. 2014. "Gender Equity in Schools in Muslim Countries: It Can Be Done," *The CSAE Blog: Centre for the Study of African Economies*, October 20. https://blogs.csae.ox.ac.uk/2014/10/gender-equity-in-schools-in-muslim-countries-it-can-be-done/.

Asadullah, Niaz, and Zaki Wahhaj. 2015. "Child Marriage Law and Freedom of Choice." *The Daily Star*, August 29. https://www.thedailystar.net/op-ed/politics/child-marriage-law-and-freedom-choice-134188.

Assaduzaman, E. A. M. 2013. "Bravo, Keshab! UN Award for His Efforts to Prevent Child Marriage." *The Daily Star*, July 17. https://www.thedailystar.net/news/bravo-keshab.

Banu, Ayesha. 2014. "Feminism in Bangladesh 1971–2000: Voices from Women's Movement." Ph.D diss., University of Dhaka.

Center for Reproductive Rights. 2018. *Ending Impunity for Child Marriage in Bangladesh: Normative and Implementation Gaps*. New York: Center for Reproductive Rights.

Chant, Sylvia. 2016. "Women, Girls and World Poverty: Empowerment, Equality or Essentialism?" *International Development Planning Review* 38, no. 1: 1–24. https://doi.org/ 10.3828/idpr.2016.1.

Charlton, Corey. 2017. "Child Rape Fears: Fury over New Law in Bangladesh that Legalises Child Brides and 'Could Reduce Minimum Age of Marriage to Zero.'" *The Sun*, March 8. https://www.thesun.co.uk/news/3040056/bangladesh-new-law-child-brides-legal/.

Clinton Global Initiative. n.d. "Girls Not Brides: Partnership to End Child Marriage, 2011." Accessed August 2021. https://www.clintonfoundation.org/clinton-global-initiative/girls-not-brides-partnership-end-child-marriage-2011.

Cornwall, Andrea. 2018. "Beyond "Empowerment Lite": Women's Empowerment,

Neoliberal Development and Global Justice." *Cadernos Pagu* 52: n.p. https://doi.org/10.1590/18094449201800520002.

The Daily Star. 2019. "Roundtable Discussion on Child Marriage Restraint Act 2017." May 19. https://www.thedailystar.net/law-our-rights/news/roundtable-discussion-child-marriage-restraint-act-2017-1744420.

The Daily Star. 2019. "Ending Child Marriage: All Stakeholders Must Work Together, Say Speakers." January 10. On file with author.

D'Costa, Bina. 2011. *Nation-Building, Gender and War Crimes in South Asia.* London: Routledge.

The Elders. 2013. "U.S. Legislates to Prevent Child Marriage Worldwide." March 4. https://theelders.org/news/us-legislates-prevent-child-marriage-worldwide/.

Feldman, Shelley. 1997. "NGOs and Civil Society: (Un)stated Contradictions." *The ANNALS of the American Academy of Political and Social Science* 554, no. 1: 46–65. https://doi.org/10.1177/0002716297554001004.

Field, Erica, Rachel Glennerstern, Nina Buchmann, and Kyle Murphy. 2016. "Cost Benefit Analysis of Strategies to Reduce Child Marriage in Bangladesh: Bangladesh Priorities." Copenhagen: Copenhagen Consensus Center.

Girls Not Brides USA. 2019. "Enlisting the Whole Government to Benefit the Whole Girl: Ending Child, Early, and Forced Marriage." https://www.girlsnotbrides.org/wp-content/uploads/2015/07/Enlisting-the-Whole-Government-to-Benefit-the-Whole-Girl_Web-March-2019-Update.pdf.

Greene, Margaret. 2014. *Ending Child Marriage in a Generation: What Research Is Needed?* Ford Foundation and GreeneWorks. https://www.fordfoundation.org/media/1890/endingchildmarriage.pdf.

Grewal, Inderpal. 1999. "Women's Rights as Human Rights: Feminist Practices, Global Feminism, and Human Rights Regimes in Transnationality." *Citizenship Studies* 3, no. 3: 337–54. https://doi.org/10.1080/13621029908420719.

Hammami, Rema. 2019. "Follow the Numbers: Global Governmentality and the Violence Against Women Agenda in Occupied Palestine." In *Governance Feminism: Notes from the Field,* edited by Janet Halley, Prabha Kotiswaran, Rachel Rebouché, and Hila Shamir, 479–504. Minneapolis: University of Minnesota Press.

Hickel, Jason. 2014. "The 'Girl Effect': Liberalism, Empowerment and the Contradictions of Development." *Third World Quarterly* 35, no. 8: 1355–73. https://doi.org/10.1080/01436597.2014.946250.

Hossain, Naomi. 2017. *The Aid Lab: Understanding Bangladesh's Unexpected Success.* Oxford: Oxford University Press.

Human Rights Watch. 2015. "Marry before Your House Is Swept Away: Child Marriage in Bangladesh." June 9. https://www.hrw.org/report/2015/06/09/marry-your-house-swept-away/child-marriage-bangladesh.

John, Mary. 2021. *Child Marriage in an International Frame: A Feminist Review from India.* New Delhi: Routledge India.

Kabeer, Naila. 2019. "Randomized Control Trials and Qualitative Evaluations of a

Multifaceted Programme for Women in Extreme Poverty: Empirical Findings and Methodological Reflections." *Journal of Human Development and Capabilities* 20, no. 2: 197–219. https://doi.org/10.1080/19452829.2018.1536696.

Karim, Lamia. 2011. *Microfinance and Its Discontents: Women in Debt in Bangladesh.* Minneapolis: University of Minnesota Press.

Khoja-Moolji, Shenila. 2015a. "Girls, Education, and Narratives of Progress: Deconstructing the Discourse on Child Marriage." In *Educating Adolescent Girls Around the Globe: Challenges and Opportunities*, edited by Sandra L. Stacki and Supriya Baily, 40–57. New York: Routledge.

Khoja-Moolji, Shenila. 2015b. "Reading Malala: (De)(Re)Territorialization of Muslim Collectivities." *Comparative Studies of South Asia, Africa, and the Middle East.* 35, no. 3: 539–56. https://doi.org/10.1215/1089201X-3426397.

Khoja-Moolji, Shenila. 2018. *Forging the Ideal Educated Girl: The Production of Desirable Subjects in Muslim South Asia.* Berkeley: University of California Press.

Ko, Dorothy. 2007. *Cinderella's Sisters: A Revisionist History of Footbinding.* Berkeley: University of California Press.

Kristof, Nicholas. 2010. "Divorced Before Puberty." *New York Times*, March 3. https://www.nytimes.com/2010/03/04/opinion/04kristof.html.

MacDonald, Katie. 2016. "Calls for Educating Girls in the Third World: Futurity, Girls, and the 'Third World Woman.'" *Gender, Place and Culture.* 23, no. 1: 1–7. https://doi.org/10.1080/0966369X.2014.991699.

Major, Andrea. 2011. "Mediating Modernity: Colonial State, Indian Nationalism and the Renegotiation of the 'Civilizing Mission' in the Indian Child Marriage Debate of 1927–32." In *Civilizing Missions in Colonial and Postcolonial South Asia: From Improvement to Development*, edited by Michael Mann and Carey Anthony Watt, 165–190. London: Anthem Press.

Malkki, Liisa. 2015. *The Need to Help: The Domestic Arts of International Humanitarianism.* Durham, NC: Duke University Press.

Mani, Lata. 1998. *Contentious Traditions: The Debate on Sati in Colonial India.* Berkeley: University of California Press.

Al-Masum Molla, Mohammad. 2019. "Still the Highest in the Region: In 2006–17, 59pc Marriages in Bangladesh Involved Girls Below 18, UN Study Finds." *The Daily Star*, April 17. https://www.thedailystar.net/backpage/news/still-the-highest-the-region-1730674.

Mehra, Madhu, and Amrita Nandy. 2020. *Why Girls Run Away to Marry: Adolescent Realities and Socio-Legal Responses in India.* New Delhi: Partners in Law and Development India. https://ssrn.com/abstract=3560854.

Merry, Sally Engle. 2006. *Human Rights and Gender Violence: Translating International Law into Local Justice.* Chicago: University of Chicago Press.

Moeller, Kathryn. 2018. *The Gender Effect: Capitalism, Feminism and the Corporate Politics of Development.* Berkeley: University of California Press.

Mookherjee, Nayanika. 2015. *The Spectral Wound: Sexual Violence, Public Memories, and the Bangladesh War of 1971.* Durham, NC: Duke University Press.

Murphy, Michelle. 2017. *The Economization of Life*. Durham, NC: Duke University Press.

National Institute of Population Research and Training (NIPORT), and ICF. 2020. *Bangladesh Demographic and Health Survey 2017–18*. Dhaka, Bangladesh: NIPORT and ICF.

Nazneen, Sohela. 2016. "Subversively Complicit? Negotiating Gender Knowledge." In *Feminist Subversion and Complicity: Governmentalities and Gender Knowledge in South Asia*, edited by Maitrayee Mukhopadhyay. New Delhi: Zubaan, 15882.

Pande, Ishita. 2020. *Sex, Law, and the Politics of Age: Child Marriage in India, 1891–1937*. Cambridge: Cambridge University Press.

Paprocki, Kasia. 2018. "We Need to Change the Way We Talk about Climate Change." *Al Jazeera*, February 23. https://www.aljazeera.com/opinions/2018/2/23/we-need-to-change-the-way-we-talk-about-climate-change.

Paprocki, Kasia. 2021. *Threatening Dystopias: The Global Politics of Climate Change Adaptation in Bangladesh*. Ithaca, NY: Cornell University Press.

Patel, Gayatri, Helena Minchew, Lyric Thompson, and Rachel Clement. 2017. "Empower Girls, Change the World." *Thehill.com*, October 11. https://thehill.com/blogs/congress-blog/foreign-policy/355014-empower-girls-change-the-world/.

Paul, Ruma, and Nita Bhalla. 2017. "Bangladesh Law Allowing Child Brides May Legitimize Rape: Charities." *Reuters*, March 1. https://www.reuters.com/article/us-bangladesh-child-marriage/bangladesh-law-allowing-child-brides-may-legitimize-rape-charities-idUSKBN16855I.

Plan International. 2016. "Wedding Busters: Child Marriage-Free Zones in Bangladesh," November 1. https://plan-international.org/video/wedding-busters-child-marriage-free-zones-bangladesh.

Prothom Alo. 2017. "Amar Konnya Ki Tobe Dhorshorker Kachhe Biye Dite Hobe" ("Will I Have to Marry My Daughter to a Rapist?"). March 2. On file with author.

Roy, Ananya. 2010. *Poverty Capital: Microfinance and the Making of Development*. London: Routledge.

Roy, Srila. 2017. "Enacting/Disrupting the Will to Empower: Feminist Governance of 'Child Marriage' in Eastern India." *Signs: Journal of Women in Culture and Society*. 42. no. 4: 868–91.

Sarkar, Mahua. 2008. *Visible Histories, Disappearing Women: Producing Muslim Womanhood in Late Colonial Bengal*. Durham, NC: Duke University Press.

Sattar, Maher, and Ellen Barry. 2017. "Bangladesh Weakens Long-standing Law against Underage Marriage." *New York Times*, February 27. https://www.nytimes.com/2017/02/27/world/asia/bangladesh-underage-marriage-law.html.

Shahinian, Gulnara. 2012. "Report of the Special Rapporteur on Contemporary Forms of Slavery, Including Its Causes and Consequences (Thematic Report on Servile Marriage)." *United Nations General Assembly*, July 10. https://digitallibrary.un.org/record/731967?ln=en.

Shibli, Abdullah. 2018. "Early Marriage: A Contributor to 'Modern Slavery' in Bangladesh?" *The Daily Star*, July 27. https://www.thedailystar.net/opinion/open-dialogue/early-marriage-contributor-modern-slavery-bangladesh-1611511.

Siddiqi, Dina M. 2003. "Beyond the Doomsday Scenario: After the MFA." *Himal Southasian*, July 1: n.p. https://www.himalmag.com/beyond-the-doomsday-scenario/.

Siddiqi, Dina M. 2005. "Of Consent and Contradiction: Forced Marriages in Bangladesh." In *'Honour': Crimes, Paradigms and Violence against Women*, edited by Sara Hossain and Lynn Welchman, 282–307. London: Zed Press.

Siddiqi, Dina M. 2012. "Blurred Boundaries: Sexuality and Seduction Narratives in 'Forced Marriage' Cases from Bangladesh." In *"Honour'" and Women's Rights: South Asian Perspectives*, edited by Manishe Gupte, Ramesh Awasthi, and Shraddha Chickerur, 155–83. Pune: MASUM Press.

Siddiqi, Dina M. 2015. "Scandals of Seduction and the Seductions of Scandal." *Comparative Studies of South Asia, Africa and the Middle East* 35, no. 3: 508–24. https://doi.org/10.1215/1089201X-3426373.

Sinha, Mrinalini. 2006. *Specters of Mother India: The Global Restructuring of an Empire*. Durham, NC: Duke University Press.

Staff Correspondent. 2016. "Child Marriage Most Egregious Human Rights Violation." *The Daily Star*, November 30. https://www.thedailystar.net/city/child-marriage-most-egregious-human-rights-violation-1322770.

Streatfield, Peter Kim, Nahid Kamal, Karar Zunaid Ahsan, and Quamrun Nahar. 2015. "Early Marriage in Bangladesh: Not as Early as It Appears." *Asian Population Studies* 11, no. 1: 94–110. https://doi.org/10.1080/17441730.2015.1012785.

Surkis, Judith. 2019. *Sex, Law and Sovereignty in French Algeria, 1830–1930*. Ithaca, NY: Cornell University Press.

Sustainable Development Goals Fund. 2017. "Case Study: Addressing Violence against Women in Bangladesh." https://www.sdgfund.org/sites/default/files/case_study_-_bangladesh_-_en.pdf.

Sweis, Rania Kassab. 2012. "Saving Egypt's Village Girls: Humanity, Rights, and Gendered Vulnerability in a Global Youth Initiative." *Journal of Middle East Women's Studies* 8, no. 2: 26–50. https://doi.org/10.2979/jmiddeastwomstud.8.2.26.

Switzer, Heather. 2013. "(Post) Feminist Development Fables: The Girl Effect and the Production of Sexual Subjects." *Feminist Theory* 14, no. 3: 345–60. https://doi.org/10.1177/1464700113499855.

Tambe, Ashwini. 2019. *Defining Girlhood in India: A Transnational History of Sexual Maturity Laws*. Chicago: University of Illinois Press.

Ticktin, Miriam. 2017. "A World without Innocence." *American Ethnologist* 44, no. 4: 577–90. https://doi.org/10.1111/amet.12558.

UNFPA. 2012. *Marrying Too Young: Ending Child Marriage*. New York: United Nations Population Fund. https://www.unfpa.org/sites/default/files/pub-pdf/MarryingTooYoung.pdf.

UNICEF. n.d. "Ending Child Marriage: Towards Evolution of Social Behaviour." https://www.unicef.org/bangladesh/en/ending-child-marriage. Accessed October 10, 2022.

UNICEF. 2011. "The State of the World's Children 2011." New York: United Nations

Children's Fund. https://www.unicef.org/sowc2011/pdfs/SOWC-2011-Main-Report_EN_02092011.pdf.

UNICEF. 2012. "Progress for Children: A Report Card on Adolescents, Number 10 (April 2012)." New York: United Nations Children's Fund. https://www.unicef.org/publications/files/Progress_for_Children_-_No._10_EN_04232012.pdf.

UNICEF. 2014. "Ending Child Marriage: Progress and Prospects." New York: United Nations Children's Fund. http://www.unicef.org/media/files/Child_Marriage_Report_7_17_LR.pdf.

UNICEF. 2021. "Child Marriage." *UNICEFData*, October 2021. https://data.unicef.org/topic/child-protection/child-marriage/.

UN Department of Economic and Social Affairs. 2015. "The 2030 Agenda for Sustainable Development." UN General Assembly. https://sdgs.un.org/goals.

UN Women. 2016. "Global Database on Violence against Women: Bangladesh." *UN Women*. https://evaw-global-database.unwomen.org/en/countries/asia/bangladesh#4.

Vogelstein, Rachel. 2013. *Ending Child Marriage: How Elevating the Status of Girls Advances US Foreign Policy Objectives*. New York: Council on Foreign Relations Press.

Volpp, Leti. 2000. "Blaming Culture for Bad Behavior." *Yale Journal of Law and the Humanities*. 12, no. 1: 89–116. https://digitalcommons.law.yale.edu/yjlh/vol12/iss1/3.

Wilson, Kalpana. 2015. "Towards a Radical Re-appropriation: Gender, Development, and Neoliberal Feminism." *Development and Change* 46, no. 4: 803–32. https://doi.org/10.1111/dech.12176.

World Bank. 2008. *Whispers to Voice: Gender and Social Transformation in Bangladesh*. Bangladesh Development Series (22). Dhaka, Bangladesh: World Bank. http://hdl.handle.net/10986/26334.

World Bank. 2017. "Child Marriage Will Cost Developing Countries Trillions of Dollars by 2030, Says World Bank/ICRW Report." *The World Bank*, June 27. https://www.worldbank.org/en/news/press-release/2017/06/26/child-marriage-will-cost-developing-countries-trillions-of-dollars-by-2030-says-world-bankicrw-report.

TEN · *Rema Hammami*

Catastrophic Aid

GBV Humanitarianism
in Gaza

In 2010, in the aftermath of Israel's first comprehensive military bombardment of Gaza (Operation Cast Lead) I was approached by United Nations Development Fund for Women (UNIFEM) representatives urgently seeking a social scientist to analyze the findings of a household survey they had done about the war's impacts on Gazans. Called a "gender needs assessment," the survey had been designed by the "UN humanitarian interagency gender team" under the supervision of a "gender in humanitarian response" consultant whose prior experience was in the 2004 South Pacific tsunami. Given that the myriad UN and EU assessments I'd read seemed to be written by socially blind civil engineers, I accepted what I saw as an opportunity to highlight the actual social impact of Israel's war on Gazans. But the survey themes, the framing of questions, and the overall methodology were problematic. I tried to imagine respondents' puzzled responses when asked if they knew of "sex trafficking" during the war. Whole sections used the language of displacement, as if Gazans had the possibility to flee beyond a few kilometers in any direction. Questions on access to justice assumed injustice was highly gendered but only internal to Gazan society. The same went for questions about protection and security. Survey questions referenced various types of GBV (gender-based violence) and their possible connections to the war; but like most questions about the war's gender impacts, they asked for respondents' general *perceptions* rather than their actual experiences.[1]

I recovered what I could from the survey data and tried to show that the priority issues for Gazans were destroyed livelihoods, lack of work, lack of potable water and cooking fuel, lack or inappropriateness of food aid, as well as the traumatic effects of the war on everyone, but especially children. However, even before its publication, a UN media outlet was already disseminating what would become the report's single and enduring "finding": "An unpublished UNIFEM survey of male and female heads of 1,100 Gaza households conducted between 28 February and 3 March indicates there was an increase in violence against women during and after the 23-day war which ended on 18 January" (*The New Humanitarian* 2009).

Post publication, "the finding" was reiterated by the top UN Humanitarian official in Palestine, despite that in both the report and presentations, I had emphasized that this "finding" was based on respondents' general *perceptions, not* on their actual experiences or witnessing acts gender violence.[2] Gazans' responses to questions regarding other forms of violence was the same; all forms of violence had increased during and after the war. For instance, they responded that "killings by Israel had risen *after* the war" as had "imprisonment by Palestinians"—neither phenomena indicated by the army of human rights organizations whose eyes were so fully trained on Gaza during these periods. Gazans' responses might better be understood as traumatic expressions of the continuing effects of living through three weeks of relentless bombardment by the most powerful army in the Middle East without any possibility of escape or shelter. It was how the anguish about the military violence they had just experienced could be voiced through the rigid set of survey questions that had been posed to them. These were not empirical observations, let alone objective facts.

Yet the "finding" about a rise in domestic violence seamlessly entered into humanitarian common sense—endlessly restated in subsequent agency reports and funding proposals aimed at addressing Gaza's "GBV problem." Only in retrospect did I realize that the alleged finding was a significant node in a larger process underway—the entry of the global GBV humanitarian apparatus into Gaza. At a strategic moment when international donor conferences were being held about Gaza's reconstruction after the first of what would become four full-scale Israeli military aggressions, UNIFEM's "evidence" was able first to overcome the unhelpful and contrary findings four years earlier (of the first Palestinian domestic violence survey by the Palestinian Bureau of Statistics in 2005) that the prevalence of domestic violence was actually lower in Gaza than in the West Bank. Moreover, it provided "evidence" of the specific causal linkage between war and gender violence that lies at the crux of humanitarian GBV. Since then, humanitarians have funded a slew of other surveys using UN global "best practice" frameworks for measuring violence against women (VAW) in the Global South, frameworks that are designed to produce the very "pandemic" that justifies their preordained interventions (Hammami 2019). These surveys serve to reiterate the core connection between Gaza's humanitarian crisis and its domestic violence problem and to fuel the urgency for ever more humanitarian GBV interventions.

CATASTROPHIZING GAZA

Gazans' contemporary situation goes beyond its dire history as a territory founded on and ruled by Israeli state violence and its logics of displacement and dispossession. Often described as the world's largest internment camp or open-air prison, Darryl Li (2008) has perhaps more aptly described contemporary Gaza as an animal pen. Until 2005 Israeli modalities of control over Gaza were harsher but similar to those used in the West Bank: spatial containment and territorial segregation; a crushing mobility regime; and economic coercion through controlling the main levers of the economy. These were always interspersed with periods of outright military violence, when the mechanisms were resisted or proved insufficient. But once Israel pulled its military and settlers out of Gaza in 2005 and with the subsequent takeover of governance by Hamas in 2007, the existing modalities were stepped up and augmented by new more destructive ones: the demolition of Gaza's main agricultural areas to create military buffer zones and the imposition of a suffocating economic blockade that didn't just punish Gaza's economy but dispensed with it altogether. Following Israel's declaration of the Gaza Strip as a "Hostile Territory" in 2008, the nature of direct violence used against the population entered an unprecedented lethal era. Since 2009 Israel has undertaken four devastating comprehensive military assaults on the population, with ever more permissive rules of engagement. The death toll of more than 3,000 Gazans (the vast majority noncombatants) from the first three major operations suggests that rather than just an animal pen, Gaza might be considered an abattoir.

Adi Ophir (2010) has named these lethal recalibrations of Israeli modalities of control over Gaza "catastrophization". He describes it as a mode of governance whose aim is to increase the volume and degree of evils inflicted on the population while minimizing their means of protection against them. Through controlling the living conditions of the target population (including their environment, access to food, medicines and medical care, water, electricity, and building materials) catastrophization is a more subtle form of killing. Rather than an event, it is a set of carefully modulated policies for necropolitical rule legitimized through keeping the process from passing a final (and undetermined) catastrophic threshold. As such, catastrophization attempts to theorize the fusing of biopolitical and necropolitical techniques through which Israel has delivered Gazans into a stasis of permanent immiseration. Through keeping these techniques within limits that avert the so-called catastrophic threshold, Israel is able to simultaneously evade responsibility for the effects of its practices, divert attention from itself as their root cause, and keep global focus on the urgency of averting the "ultimate" catastrophe. This is enabled by a seeming opposite that is fused into this particular strategy of necropolitical rule: a humanitarian apparatus that alleviates its effects and operates to keep the catastrophic threshold at bay.

The various stages of 2005–2008 through which Israel moved to dispense with its identity as a belligerent military occupation over Gaza is paralleled by the ever-increasing entry of global humanitarianism into the scene and ultimately, Gaza's reframing as both a "Humanitarian Crisis" and space of humanitarian operation. As many analysts have shown (e.g., Feldman 2009; Li 2008; Ophir 2010; Weizman 2011; Winter 2016), this global humanitarian apparatus that now attends to the Gaza "crisis" never counters the logics of Israeli rule nor simply counters its effects; but rather is constitutive of its ongoing operation[3]. It divests Israel of any practical responsibility for the population wholly under its control. It frames Gazans' politically induced suffering as a "humanitarian crisis," precluding recognition of Israeli culpability in its production. And ultimately through these maneuvers, it instantiates Israel as a humanitarian partner (along with the international community) in alleviating Gazans' suffering. Humanitarian GBV in Gaza is never out of step with these rationales.

ENTER GAZA'S GBV PROBLEM

It was in the context of this shift from a space of "belligerent occupation" to one of "humanitarian crisis" that Gaza's population became subject to a powerful assemblage of humanitarian actors and aid flows that succeeded in instantiating the prevention or treatment of GBV into the urgent and near exclusive gender concern in Gazan society. How was this accomplished? Producing evidence of Gaza's GBV problem through "global best practice" techniques of measurement laid the initial groundwork (Hammami 2019). That "evidence" was indisputable given it could rely on long-held truths about the congenital violence of Palestinian/Islamic masculinity, now amplified by the society being under an "Islamic terrorist" government.

Gender violence, though in the language of "family or domestic violence" and grounded in intimate understandings of local gender and social dynamics, has been a homegrown issue and locus of activism by the Palestinian women's movement since at least the mid-1990s. But by the end of the first decade of the millennium, those local discourses and forms of activism had been supplanted by the power and resources of humanitarian GBV operating in the context of Gaza's ongoing catastrophization. Due to the international boycott of the Hamas authorities, humanitarian GBV has been forced to operate through local Palestinian NGOs (including those with long-standing records in human rights, along with the community of historic women's rights organizations), as well as creating some new ones focused purely on gender violence. GBV has almost completely recoded previous activisms of these existing organizations. Gender legal reform, women's economic empowerment, and gender mainstreaming into political structures have all been buried under the power of GBV awareness raising and advocacy, or legal aid to GBV survivors. In this context, older agendas only persist if they are recalibrated to serve the needs of GBV prevention or meet the needs of GBV victims.

Analyzing its evolution over the subsequent decade suggests that to understand the core rationales underlying humanitarian GBV in Gaza, it may be more productive to focus on the "what"—the content of GBV humanitarian care—than the usual critical focus on the "whom" of care (Fassin 2012). Focusing on the substance of GBV interventions in Gaza, based on a 2017 in-depth interview-based field study, leads us away from the familiar framings of humanitarianism as a politics of care (Ticktin 2011) or even as "triage" (Redfield 2008) toward recognizing it as a technology of rule within contemporary projects of global securitization (Hammami and Adwan 2017). The modalities of humanitarian GBV in Gaza overwhelmingly focus on treating Gazans' "cultural pathology" through civilizational pedagogies. These proceed through a limited menu of standardized practices that respond only to their own global referents and inner logic, virtually impervious to local realities and local actors capable of creating interventions more relevant to local contexts. Extremely dependent on its resources, Gaza's precaritized NGO women activists and frontline antiviolence workers, as well as the destitute women seeking their services, have few choices but to work within its modalities, constantly subverting its everyday logics in attempting to meet actual needs and priorities.

HUMANITARIAN GBV VERSUS GLOBAL VAW

Though emerging from the global VAW agenda, humanitarian GBV is a particular transmutation of it. Given the ascendance of humanitarianism over development in contemporary imperial geopolitics, humanitarian GBV (as the most highly resourced and visible gender-focused response in any humanitarian emergency) may be more visible and powerful than its VAW precursor. The codification of the VAW agenda over the 1990s into UN conventions, norms, and practices has been well documented by both critics and supporters. Despite its evolution and migration through the halls of global power, it remains wedded to a radical or dominance feminist position about the causes of VAW (patriarchy) as well as appropriate responses to it (criminalization), while offering a liberal feminist prescription for its ultimate eradication: gender equality. This is why it continues to use the older feminist language of "women" rather than "gender" when naming the particular type of violence it seeks to address (as well as the gender of the victims vulnerable to it).

Translated as normative global practice in Third World contexts, the VAW agenda is completely state-centric. It puts the onus of change on national governments and makes them responsible for combatting violence against women. Local women's organizations (NGOs) are positioned as critical but secondary agents in this process. With donor support and the backing of UN conventions and mechanisms, they are to raise public awareness and lobby their governments to address their particular national version of the global VAW "pandemic." The global agenda provides a comprehensive template for how the state should address VAW, offering women's advocacy NGOs a clear road map of policy and legal reforms toward which to work.[4] In sum, the global focus of the VAW agenda has been on governmentalizing the prevention and treatment of violence against women, including domestic violence.

Humanitarian GBV began to emerge as a recalibration of global VAW at the end of the Balkan civil wars, becoming consolidated as its own agenda following the Rwandan genocide. These were conflicts that propelled sexual violence to become the foundational issue of VAW's entry into neohumanitarianism. Both critical and celebratory literature on the rise of the "sexual violence in war" agenda focuses on feminist legal activists' achievement of its criminalization in international law, as evidenced by the seven UN security council resolutions passed on it since 2000 (Engle 2020).[5] As Sara Meger notes, "Conflict related sexual violence now rivals nuclear and biological weapons, terrorism and arms proliferation for receiving the most attention among security actors" (2016, 150).

This highly visible thread of legal activism has been paralleled by a less visible codification of VAW as GBV into humanitarian protocols and procedures on the ground. The main emphasis remains on sexual violence, both during war and in "emergencies," as well as in the context of humanitarian spaces set up in their aftermath.

By 2005, the supreme policy-making body of humanitarianism within the UN system, the Inter-Agency Standing Committee (IASC) produced guidelines that codified GBV as a normative component of humanitarian intervention.[6] Their publication triggered a deluge of practitioner literature dense with definitions and modalities for integrating GBV concerns within the complex infrastructure and coordination mechanisms that attend to humanitarian action.[7] The current humanitarian GBV bible (cited in any international agency report in Gaza) is the second IASC *Handbook for Coordinating Gender-based Violence Intervention in Humanitarian Settings*, released in 2015.

In contrast to global VAW, there is a strong presentism in humanitarian GBV. The goals are limited to prevention and mitigation versus long-term political transformation. Interventions are degovernmentalized and kept in the hands of temporary international sovereigns on the ground whose local agents (NGOs and local staff) are mobilized not as agents of national change (as were local NGOs directing their efforts at their own states), but simply as deliverers of what Peter Redfield (2008) has called "humanitarian kits": short-term modular forms of aid.

In the IASC protocols, the main agents of treatment and preventing recurrence of sexual violence in postconflict settings are humanitarians themselves; it is they who organize local staff and if they exist, local NGOs to administer the actual mitigation and treatment activities. The role of national governments is virtually irrelevant; their acquiescence to humanitarian agents implementing the guidelines is preferable but not necessary for them to go forward (IASC 2015, 19).

The main content of interventions is mainstreaming GBV prevention activities into normative humanitarian sectoral activities (in setting up camps/shelter, education, health, water and sanitation, etc.), again, with the international humanitarians being responsible for their implementation. Beyond the parameters of mainstreaming, only GBV education/sensitization appears everywhere in the guidelines; it is to be given to humanitarian actors, local staff, and communities. Finally, victim-specific treatment is narrowed down to a few practical interventions: medical and immediate prophylactic care; psychosocial counseling; and the creation of "safe spaces" for victims.

Law, justice, and policing (components prioritized by global VAW) are completely deemphasized.[8]

The constant shifting of the adjective attached to violence in humanitarian GBV suggests that from its beginning as an agenda focused on sexual violence against women in war, it has now come to encompass a wider range of violations of women's human rights as these had been framed by global VAW. The first UNHCR 1995 guidelines used only "sexual" violence in its title, while the second (2001) used "sexual and gender based violence (or SGBV)." The 2005 IASCI handbook dropped "sexual" and from then on, GBV becomes the hegemonic term in humanitarianism.[9] The main author of the 2015 IASC guidelines describes some of the practical conceptual considerations by UN agencies that led to this terminological outcome (Ward and UN Women 2013, 19). But a broader view might consider the ultimate triumph of "GBV" as reflecting a process of negotiation and final codification in which the already powerful VAW agenda (now braced with UN-wide mandates of gender mainstreaming and gender equality) reshaped the final humanitarian outcome. Thus, although "women" was lost to gender, gender within humanitarianism stands for a wide array of practices of harm against women simply because they are women. And as the IASC guidelines underscore, although the gender in GBV includes men as possible victims, global experience shows that it is overwhelmingly women and girls who are victimized. Finally, while "sexual" was no longer highlighted in the name — in practice its detection and mitigation continue to take priority in humanitarian modalities.

It is when translated into concrete settings that the seemingly expansive global definitions show their inherently exclusionary racial gendered logics. In the practical application of the definitions in Gaza, humanitarian GBV assumes that gender violence is overwhelmingly kin-based (family, marriage); enacted by Gazan males against Gazan females; and its source (regardless of Israeli economic and military violence) is rooted in the bedrock of local patriarchal Islamic culture.

What Does Humanitarian GBV Look Like in Gaza?

In 2013, the United Nations Family Planning Association (UNFPA) Palestine office undertook its first survey of how donors had distributed resources to GBV interventions in Gaza over the previous years.[10] As is often the case in development and humanitarianism, almost a third of resources had gone into upper-level research, administrative, and coordination activities that didn't directly benefit Gazan NGOs, frontline workers, or their constituencies (Hammami and Adwan 2017). Second to these was an almost even split of 25 percent each going to prevention-focused interventions and treatment-focused activities. Funding to prevention-focused activities, in turn were equally divided between "awareness" and "advocacy" interventions. Among treatment-focused activities there was a clear hierarchy: psychosocial interventions garnered 10 percent; legal aid 7 percent; and health and economic empowerment only 4 percent (Hammami and Adwan 2017).[11] The immediate local beneficiaries of these resources are fifteen Gazan NGOs, two of which work only on GBV and were founded after humanitarian GBV had arrived on the scene. Under these NGOs are more than forty local charitable or community associations, termed by humanitarians "community-based organizations" (CBOs) that have been an important conduit for humanitarian aid and play a critical role in transmitting NGO GBV programming (especially in awareness/advocacy) to local communities.

POLITICAL ECONOMIES OF "AWARENESS"

GBV awareness and advocacy activities have garnered as many resources as all of the treatment services for victims taken together. Almost any day of the week a GBV awareness session is being held somewhere in Gaza. Nur, the head of a community association in Rafah, explained that local NGOs had delivered more than 150 awareness sessions at their premises the previous year. She added, "In the courses about GBV, we teach the definitions of violence, its reasons, how to avoid violence and its effects. . . . Sometimes, donors fund the same project and the same target group but they just change the name of the project. For example, we have a project called 'helping damaged women' and another one called 'helping women who survived from war!' Technically they are the same but just the name is changed."

NGOs involved in delivering these sessions were openly critical of what had become an industry they referred to as "counting numbers." Given that there were so many donor resources available for awareness sessions (and few resources for anything else) and few qualifications necessary to deliver them, everyone had gotten into the awareness "business" that was predicated on showing donors how many participants (or "targets") they had reached. A blurb from UNRWA's Gaza Gender Initiative is exemplary: "The 38 women who were selected . . . participated in awareness raising discussion groups on the prevention of GBV and attended eight sessions on topics including the types of GBV, its causes and consequences, women's rights and the Convention on the Elimination of Discrimination against Women (CEDAW), [and] Personal Status Law in Palestine.... This session is one of 21 sessions conducted by the Women's Programme Centres targeting over 800 women and men across the Gaza strip" (UNRWA 2016). The capaciousness of GBV awareness training also allows it to be used for dual humanitarian purposes. Donor-supported job creation schemes enable local NGOs to hire young women university graduates, left jobless in Gaza's destroyed labor markets, as GBV trainers on short-term contracts. Ahmad, head of a Legal Aid NGO criticized this use of GBV trainings:

> The least effective [GBV activity] is awareness stuff—it's a crowded field [with] so many organizations and the same people are targeted over and over again.... Trainers get one or two courses and then they repeat what they heard or read. They deliver awareness as a repeat performance.... there are organizations that do a TOT [training of trainers course] with a new [university] graduate. Give her 8 hours of TOT when she's just graduated and then some information and tell her to go do awareness... all she has is technical information and definitions.

The content of these sessions tends to follow a set format laid out by a few GBV awareness training manuals that have been produced with donor support in Arabic and that prioritize international frameworks.[12] The recurring topics include: (1) data on the extent of VAW/GBV in Palestine; (2) terms and definitions (Gender versus Sex, Violence, UN definitions of VAW, GBV, differences between Gender Equality versus Gender Equity, all based on the Universal Declaration on the Elimination of Violence Against Women, and CEDAW); (3) the five types of gender-based violence according to UN definitions, broken down into the various types within each category (sexual, physical, psychological/moral, harmful traditional practices, and social/economic violence); (4) the WHO's ecological model of GBV and the Duluth, "Cycle of Violence Wheel" (in advanced courses); and (5) the harmful effects of GBV on the individual, family, society, and state. The thematic sessions are also standardized. They include exercises, including role-playing and other participatory activities, and presentations of victim case studies, sometimes as short film clips and at other times as written narratives.

While these are core components of local Arabic manuals that, as explained above, are based on materials produced by international agencies and INGOs and reflect their normative frameworks and priorities, they are never pure mimics. Local manuals tend to downplay the United Nations as the authoritative source of the definitions. More specialized ones integrate a focus on women's legal rights within Gaza's system of family law. All of them add localized meanings, situations, and cases, in what Sally Engle Merry (2006) would call a process of vernacularization. For instance, in explaining economic GBV, one local manual provides examples based on familiar situations such as "preventing her from working or forcing her to work, and also control over her property and her right to inherit and control over her possession of money (taking her monthly salary) . . . or depriving her of money to spend on her needs." In the same manual, we find a similarly localized definition of social GBV: "Society gives men privileges to deal with decisions concerning women and the home and children, excluding them and treating them as inferior. Other types of social violence include views toward divorced women and preventing them from leaving the house, imposing guardians on women in issues of self-determination such as marriage, divorce, travel and education. Also within social violence is the imposition of customs and traditions practiced by society on women to ensure obedience and submission to the culture of masculinity."

What participants might get in terms of changed ideas or consciousness from these sessions is unknown, as suggested by the critical comments of some interviewees. Nahla, now in prison for murdering a husband she had been forced to marry, described having been sent to one of these awareness sessions, "Once the Social Affairs sent me to attend a workshop. It was about violence against women and then we [role] played for a bit."

However, the open secret is why women (and sometimes men) show up to these sessions and what they hope to gain from them. As Aitemad Muhanna's (2013) study of changing gender relations in a Gaza under siege has shown, a main effect of enforced male joblessness has been to thrust formerly dependent housewives into the public arena in an endless search for humanitarian aid. The first stop for these women, most of whom have never been in the labor market or had much experience with public authorities, is their local CBO. These local associations have become pivotal mediums for humanitarians to transmit aid to both refugee and nonrefugee communities. As one intimate partner violence (IPV) victim, Maysun, confessed, "I'd go to any seminar the Handicapped Society in the Nada Towers have. I needed aid coupons, assistance. My sister's daughter is handicapped and I'd go with her whenever there was a seminar."

Attendance at a GBV awareness-raising seminar held by an NGO trainer at your local association does not end with receiving the coveted food aid coupon. The transactional nature of the relationship is more indirect. By being a loyal local constituent of your CBO and attending these sessions (for which the association will receive room rental and other costs from the sponsoring NGO), a woman will be remembered when the CBO receives aid to distribute. In the meantime, all CBOs and NGOs know that refreshments are a critical dimension of awareness sessions (whether a hot meat sandwich or something cold and cheaper). And they, along with the NGOs who pay for the refreshments, regularly face the dilemma of whether to turn away the many destitute women who have brought their children along for a free lunch. Firyal and Tahani, from local NGOs with long track records in GBV services, summed up the well-known consensus: "Most of the women [beneficiaries] are dealing with [awareness sessions] as a business" and "the ladies are so smart; some of them move around from institution to institution, abusing it [GBV awareness]. And then when a woman needs some information on GBV, she goes and asks her neighbor! The same faces repeat among target groups, though not all."

Rather than the ideological content and/or the great strides in raising popular awareness touted in donor reports, for those engaged with them, these activities operate as conduits of material aid to various constituents differentially placed in Gaza's internal hierarchy of need and suffering. Within the larger humanitarian economy in Gaza, GBV awareness is part of the humanitarian trickle-down economy, operating similar to what Douma and Hilhorst (2012) have described as a "political economy of SGBV programming" in the Congo. The large and almost singular resource flows provided by humanitarian GBV create not only immense dependencies but reinforcing loops in what Heaton has called "perverse incentive structures" (2014, 626). Here local NGOs are at the top of the hierarchy, funding their own staff while providing short-term work to unemployed young women. Next in line are the local associations and charities who live hand-to-mouth from random donations and what NGOs pass on to them. As Firyal went on to explain, "The CBOs have a problem. I mean if you have money to pay for room rental and hospitality, then they will welcome you, whatever the topic, violence or any other topic. But if you can't pay the room rent and hospitality for their target groups even if they need the topic, they won't host you. The priority is for the one who pays."

And finally, at the bottom of the hierarchy, are the near-destitute women and their children who receive a free lunch and the hope of accessing future material forms of humanitarian aid.

At the same time the flows create a set of interlinked dependencies in the other direction: to survive, destitute women need to show up to their local association. In turn, to survive, the CBO needs to deliver these "targets" to NGOs, who in turn need to deliver them to donors. When looked at from this vantage point—the "counting of numbers" mentioned above (of beneficiaries and awareness sessions) shows how the power of humanitarian calculability not only depends on hierarchies of material desperation but actively reproduces them.

Awareness sessions always end with a self-justifying list of how to prevent GBV: through public awareness and advocacy activities; through collection and unification of data on its prevalence; through delivery of services for its treatment (as well as protection systems for victims); through empowerment of women to be economically independent; and finally, through repealing laws that facilitate "honor killings." All are precisely the activities that Gazan NGOs undertake within the frame of humanitarian GBV.

ADVOCATING GBV: FORECLOSED PERFORMANCES

If awareness training is the everyday workhorse of humanitarian GBV, advocacy is its public star. But as Nariman, a legal rights activist explained, content-wise there was little difference between the two: "Not only around GBV but on other issues the whole efforts of advocacy around changing laws and legislation has really dried up. Advocacy is still done but it's all awareness and consciousness raising." Advocacy as a buzzword has been around from the period of the Oslo Peace Process in the 1990s, but then it was always attached to lobbying. In the Oslo period these concepts taken together had represented the NGO-style political activism of the Palestinian women's movement in campaigns focused on changing specific policies or legislation through lobbying members of the Palestinian Legislative Council. Humanitarian GBV advocacy projects in Gaza bear no resemblance to this past meaning. In current GBV discourse in Gaza, advocacy appears alone, and always in English. The political context (stalemated division between the West Bank PA and Gaza Hamas authorities) does present a dilemma for anyone seeking to conjoin lobbying and advocacy. But it is donors' "no-contact" policy with the Hamas authorities (who have been under international sanctions since 2008), along with the power of donor resources, that has reshaped the meaning and content of advocacy under the hegemony of humanitarian GBV.

Donor-supported GBV advocacy has no specific transformative goal or local address. In Gaza, it is a free-floating series of public and semipublic performances about the ills of GBV and advertisements of the ability, will, and successes of Gaza's humanitarians to address it. As Buthaina, a women's rights activist explained, "All of the advocacy is squeezed into the period of the 16 Days Campaign Against Violence but then the rest of the year advocacy activities are scattered—and there's no accumulation. It's no good. Because it's an international campaign everyone wants to put their mark on it and get highlighted in the media, but after that they go quiet and there's no follow-up."

Great publicity surrounds these events, as an UNRWA News report from December 9, 2011 makes clear:

> A thousand-strong audience gathered in Gaza City yesterday for a festival to combat violence against women. The event marked the end of the global campaign, 16 Days of Activism Against Gender Violence. The festival was a unique opportunity to bring together a range of Gazan voices to take a stand for women's human rights. The festival featured traditional Palestinian dance dabkeh, theatre performance and film screenings . . . All performances increased the audience's awareness, understanding and recognition of the problem of violence against women as a public issue and a violation of human rights. (UNRWA 2011)

Since this advocacy is executed under the rubric of the global "16 Days of Activism Against Gender Violence Campaign" it serves to credentialize Gaza's humanitarian GBV assemblage within the global circuits of anti-VAW activism. Since 2010, humanitarian GBV has orchestrated the annual event, providing funds through which local NGOs and their constituents produce a dizzying array of posters, brochures, radio and TV spots, films, plays, art competitions, and even an opera about the ills of GBV. It has brought in the talents of local male superstars to combat GBV (Muhammad Assaf, the Gazan winner of Arab Idol, as well as the popular '48 Palestinian rap group DAM) while at the same time providing an annual surge of resources for the everyday work of awareness-raising sessions. The 16 Days always includes at least one festival, usually staged at Gaza's best public auditorium, the Rashad al Shawwa Cultural Center, and always involves a sit-in (usually staged at the Square of the Unknown Soldier) in front of the Legislative Council's generally empty premises. The theater and festival audience is overwhelmingly the humanitarian assemblage itself and its local NGO constituents, family, and friends. While the heads of GBV-focused NGOs and CBOs always appear at the annual sit-in, their numbers are swelled by busing in the poor and destitute women who are their humanitarian beneficiaries.

Gaza's integration into the global 16 Days Against Violence framework might be considered just one of the many humanitarian schemes that have used global cultural formats in attempts to make the plight of Gazans visible to global publics. UNRWA, for example, staged three Guinness Book of World Records events, with Gazan children attempting to fly the largest number of kites; hold the biggest parachute; or dribble the largest number of soccer balls simultaneously. These initiatives are guided by a liberal politics of recognition: through performing global cultural scripts, the hope is that Gazans might appear as recognizably human to mainstream media and global liberal publics. That these logics motivate the staging of the 16 Days campaign by humanitarian GBV is clear from the amount of messaging about it that is in English and the regular use of the 16 Days global brand of orange T-shirts and caps and the slogan "Unite to End Violence."

Rather than simply depoliticizing the remnants of whatever politics remained in women's NGO lobbying/advocacy, these events suggest that humanitarian GBV has fundamentally transformed it into a simulated activism aimed at a vague and amorphous global audience, that is likely not watching. And while aimed at making Gazan women appear human to global publics through staging performances of activism that mimic those of liberal subjects elsewhere, it more likely reconfirms them within the perceptual grid they are already captured in; as ontological others, Muslim women victims of a local patriarchal violence. Rather than instantiating them as agents in an amorphous global sisterhood, the framing of this "activism" more likely holds them firmly in the grip of contemporary imperial rescue narratives. This is suggested by following English language promotional coverage of the 2016 sit-in put out by the Palestinian NGO Network (PNGO): "Hundreds of women and representatives of the Palestinian NGOs and the civil society participated in a solidarity sit-in organized by the women sector of the Palestinian NGO's Network (PNGO) in Gaza as part of the 16 Days campaign against gender violence within the project of Enhance Civil Society Capacity to Work for Democratic Independence in Palestine Project in Partnership with Norwegian People's Aid (NPA). The participants raised unified posters and banners with the hashtag #ProtectUs_thanks" (PNGO Portal 2016a).

The representation above (and in similar coverage by donors of 16 Days events over the years) suggests that the Gazan women activists are completely captured within global frames, which raises the question of how to account for their seeming acquiescence; either as naïveté (they are dupes) or as cynical instrumentalality (participating in a parody of activism in order to please donor paymasters). But there are more complex dynamics at play. We first need to think about the politics of representation; who are the agents of representation and to what intended audience?

Local (Arabic) media coverage of the chants at the same 2016 sit-in show how the women activists attempted to widen the political and perceptual limits of the 16 Days global template: "A thousand greetings to the Palestinian woman; unity, unity national unity; A thousand greetings to the steadfast women of the nation; A thousand greetings to the women prisoners; A woman's voice is not evil, a woman's voice is a revolution; Openly, Openly, let's speak openly: We don't want to see discrimination; we want to live in dignity; no to violence against women; violence against women is a violation of human rights; united to end violence against women" (PNGO Portal 2016b). Here they asserted women's nationalist political agency, paid tribute to women political prisoners and women's steadfastness, and called for national unity and the end of the political division between Hamas and Fateh. These chants are interspersed with the usual global messages about women's human rights and the need to end discrimination and violence against women. In local messaging, every one of the 16 Days campaigns in Gaza has highlighted the centrality of Israeli violence along with the normative women's human rights/GBV discourse. The slogan for the 2015 campaign was End the Occupation/End Violence (*inha al ihtilaal/inha al 'unf*). Above, in 2016, the actual slogan—"The Right of Return and Dignity for Palestinian women (*haq al 'awda w al-karama lil-mar'a a- falastiniyya*)"—was hard won by local women's organizations against the protests of donors who considered the right of return (by Palestinian refugees) too politically charged.

Although folding these nationalist messages into the global feminist frame might speak to some local publics, it is unlikely that they can shift the wider perceptual field that Gazan women are already captured in. This is especially the case, given that International Humanitarians always excise this nationalist messaging in their representations of the Gazan 16 Days, emphasizing the conformity of its content with normative global anti-GBVAW discourse.

CLAIMS OF PROTECTION

But the "#ProtectUs_thanks" hashtag used at the 2016 sit-in suggests that the ambiguities (and therefore potentialities and confusions) inherent in the term gender-based violence (and the discursive formation of humanitarianism they are part of) facilitate Gazan women activists' engagement with these deeply limiting frames. Protection is a powerful but multivalent concept, with a particular legacy of meaning among Palestinians that is not apparent to outside audiences. Going back to the beginning of the Israeli occupation in 1967, Palestinian leaders and political movements have recurrently called for an international protection force to be deployed in the West Bank and Gaza, as prescribed in International Humanitarian Law (IHL) including the Geneva conventions that relate to Palestinians under occupation. The geopolitical futility that has always marked calls for Palestinians' protection through the normative mechanisms of the UN is summed up by the last formal attempt made in 2000. A draft resolution for a weaker "international observer force" for Palestinians (put forth by the nonaligned movement and France) was met with the response by the then Secretary General Kofi Annan and the United States that such a move could not be taken without the consent of Israel. As Dove (2009, 80) notes, "R2P [the UN's 2005 Responsibility to Protect doctrine] will never be applied to the P-5 [permanent members of the security council] states themselves nor to any territories in which the perpetrators of atrocities are their allies.... This is why we won't hear about R2P in relation to Colombia, Israel or Saudi Arabia."

Since 2005, when the extremely problematic Responsibility to Protect doctrine was passed at the UN World Summit, "Protection" has become a major component of what global humanitarians claim they do. In humanitarianism its normative meaning is limited to the need to attend to universal rights frameworks when undertaking any aspect of humanitarian action. Or, as defined by the United Nations Office for the Coordination of Humanitarian Affairs (OCHA), humanitarian protection encompasses all activities "aimed at ensuring full respect for the rights of the individual in accordance with human rights law, international humanitarian law and refugee law." Elizabeth Ferris observes that "Protection is now very much in vogue in the humanitarian world. Everyone's talking about it, everyone's 'doing' it: developing policies on protection, assessing protection needs, incorporating protection into mainstream practice, developing protection indicators" (2011, xii).

The actual protection of civilians in war is not the responsibility of humanitarians but of "duty bearers" (which in IHL refers to state and, increasingly, nonstate actors). The protection role of humanitarians is to ensure that they themselves do not cause rights violations in their programming, as well as to monitor rights violations by others and to advocate (that word again!) for duty bearers to address them. Within Palestine's humanitarian industry, the occupation in all its effects is described as a "protracted protection crisis with humanitarian consequences."[13] Job listings abound for UN agency "protection officers," OCHA's weekly update on Israeli human rights violations is called "Protection of Civilians Weekly," and GBV is regularly described as "a key protection concern in the occupied territories." More concretely, in the labyrinthine governing structure of the humanitarian assemblage (the Cluster system), the "GBV, working group" operates in Palestine (as elsewhere) under the "Protection Cluster." Given the absence of any "gender" working group among the other six clusters, this means that only gender attached to violence has any operational identity within the system.[14]

Thus, in practice the humanitarian version of protection only deals with mitigating the effects of "rights violations" particularly when "duty bearers" perpetrate them. In Gaza, humanitarian protection translates into feeding the population made destitute by Israel's blockade and economic warfare; providing them with tents or rebuilding their homes when Israel destroys them; and treating the effects of Israeli violence on their psyches with psychosocial first aid and counselling. UNRWA, for instance, simply lists most of its routine operations in Gaza as constituting "protection activities" (UNRWA 2016).[15] For a slew of agencies, monitoring and reporting of rights violations is the core protection activity they undertake, potentially critical when bringing "rights violators" to justice.[16] And similar to the framing of politics in humanitarian GBV, protection's one political activity is advocacy. However, advocacy is always counterposed to the exigencies of "access" for humanitarians. Public criticism of human rights violations by the main duty bearer is likely to deny them access to the humanitarian space.

What becomes clear is that "protection" is not at all about physically or politically protecting civilians against state violence. Rather it is the means through which rights language can be attached to the low horizon of humanitarian mitigation. The logic is guileful: on the one hand, it asserts that civilians have rights to live in dignity and freedom from violence and that these rights should be protected even in times of war. On the other, it asserts that humanitarians do not have the responsibility to protect either these rights nor the civilians who are bearers of them.

Within this logic, GBV positioned as a "protection concern" (and in Gaza, "a key protection concern") plays a number of useful functions. It provides a semblance of exceeding the miserly limits of protection (not simply mitigating a particular violation of rights but also preventing it) at the same time that it allows for advocacy without raising the ever-present danger of losing "access." Israel is not going to ban (more likely it will applaud) humanitarians for raising GBV as a wholly Gazan "rights violation" that reflects the pathologies of the victim community.[17] The outcome is that through discursive slippage, it implies that a key activity of humanitarians is the protection of Palestinian women from their own society's violence.

If we return to the "#ProtectUs_thanks" twitter hashtag placards that women NGO leaders carried at the 2016 sit-in, we see the multiple meanings of protection at work. The reading of the sign by the local media (and as advanced in one of the women's speeches) is a Palestinian plea for international protection against Israeli aggression. Local reporting makes this clear: "[They]raised unified posters and banners of hashtag (#ProtectUs_thanks). They called upon the international community to work to end all forms of violence against women, particularly the Israeli occupation's violations and aggression, and they called to end the internal division and achieve national unity" (PNGO Portal 2016b). The speeches also included demands on the Palestinian authorities to provide the necessary protections to women from domestic violence, but they also centrally linked violence and lack of protection with Israeli aggression and the nonresponse of the international community.[18] For humanitarians, who paid for the signage, the message of the hashtag fits seamlessly into their messaging, as a demand by Gazan women for their government to step up and protect them from domestic violence. And with the slippage surrounding protection (added to the "_thanks" ending of the hashtag) it can also appear as a plea to humanitarians and the world to keep protecting them from Palestinian violence.

MISSING WOMEN'S SHELTERS

Along with eliding or erasing meanings counter to its normative discourse, humanitarian GBV also evicts from its frame a parallel world of local interventions that challenge its singular status. Donors and international NGOs supporting GBV prevention and treatment interventions in Gaza constantly invoke the IASC 2015 handbook and claim that their programming has been informed by its guidelines. In this way, they place themselves and their GBV programming in Gaza within humanitarian modalities. In the West Bank, ironically, the very same donors invoke the Palestinian Authority's 2011 "National Strategy to Combat Violence Against Women"[19] explicitly using the acronym VAW rather than GBV in all its work there. Thus, in the West

Bank the global VAW agenda operates under the auspices of donor-led "state building" and works to governmentalize VAW prevention and treatment, while in Gaza, humanitarian GBV operates to actively *de*-governmentalize its prevention and treatment. The Hamas government authorities are explicitly excluded and instead humanitarian GBV empowers INGOs and local NGOs as the addressees and agents of GBV mitigation. This geopolitical division of labor between VAW and GBV requires the erasure from the humanitarian frame of Hamas services to battered women in Gaza. A Palestine Facts and Figures report on VAW by UN women declares: "There are currently 4 anti-violence centers/shelters in Palestine: Mehwar Centre in Bethlehem, functioning under the umbrella of the Ministry of Social Affairs, the Family Defense Society shelter in Nablus, the Women's Centre for Legal Aid and Counselling emergency shelter in Jericho and Al-Hayat Centre in Gaza" (UN Women n.d.).

Despite GBV being touted as one of their major protection concerns in Gaza, the humanitarian assemblage does not even offer the most rudimentary services of a battered women's shelter. Al Hayat Center, the sole one in Gaza mentioned in the report above, is run by an NGO but doesn't meet the most basic criteria of a women's shelter: providing overnight accommodation. Rather, Al Hayat more squarely fits into what the humanitarian literature calls "women and girl safe spaces" that are explicitly distinguished from shelters (UNFPA 2015). However, there is one dedicated battered women's shelter operating in Gaza, called Beit al Aman. The problem is that Beit al Aman was founded and is run by the Hamas government authorities. While the NGO is materially supported and heavily promoted by the humanitarian GBV assemblage (even though its services do not go beyond those of other NGO service providers) there is no mention of the government shelter in any humanitarian publications on GBV services in Gaza—and in Palestine more broadly. Simultaneously, through massaging the wording, the NGO made it onto the short list of Palestinian shelters—the only one to be called an "anti-violence center" rather than a shelter.

While there has been a conflict between humanitarian GBV and the Hamas-run Beit al Aman, the total excision of the shelter from their representation of GBV services in Gaza speaks to geopolitical rationales and the power of humanitarians to enact them. The NGO, Al Hayat Center, began as a donor-supported project to create a women's shelter based on the experience of the Mehwar Center in the West Bank. However, the founding of Al Hayat coincided with the political conflict between Hamas and Fateh, which led to the former coming to governmental power within Gaza. As is the case for NGOs under the West Bank PA, the Hamas authorities would not let the NGO shelter operate until it applied for a permit from the Interior Ministry. Due to international sanctions on the Hamas government (called the "no contact policy"), the humanitarian assemblage refused to ask for a permit and the NGO shelter was never opened.

Beit al Aman, the Hamas shelter, initially got lurid international press coverage, with some local women NGO leaders deriding its "Islamist" approach to the women under its care. The problem, according to its current director Hanadi Skeik, was that the Hamas authorities had initially opened it as a dumping ground for "women and girls thrown in the streets or that they couldn't send to the prison." The mix of cases (teenage runaways, delinquents, and sex workers, as well as battered women) led to it being run like a security facility. Skeik has radically changed this. Originally a volunteer social worker in the "Young Muslim Women's Unit" at the Ministry of Social Affairs, she accepted the director position only on the condition that the Hamas minister in charge would allow her to run the center specifically for battered women, using an all-female professional staff.

Since she took over in 2012, Skeik runs Beit al Aman not much differently than any of the shelters run by secular women's NGOs in the West Bank. Located in an attractive building with a courtyard garden and a volleyball pitch, it can house fifty women and their children in private rooms and suites. It offers a lounge, library, and theater/TV room (with no restrictions on what channels can be watched). The staff includes nine counselor/social workers, two psychiatrists, a nurse, two occupational trainers, and a policewoman. Beit al Aman uses the services of the Palestinian Center for Human Rights, a secular human rights NGO, to represent women in their legal cases. And it clearly follows what is called in the professional practitioner literature "a victim-centered approach," basing the case management strategy on the preferences and priorities of the women themselves. The only religious content in its programming comes in the completely optional religious study sessions offered to women at the shelter in the evenings.

Many local NGO GBV service providers surreptitiously work with the shelter and have excellent working relations with its director and staff. However, it is the NGO pseudoshelter that receives humanitarian resources and visibility, and its director continues to actively perpetuate the negative Islamist image of its rival, denigrating Beit al Aman as lacking essential services and treating the women staying there as if they were criminals.[20] Women at the Hamas shelter who have employment and don't want to lose it, or young women in university who don't want to miss classes, are in fact free to sign themselves out ("on their own responsibility") in order to do so. In cases where there's a clear and present danger to a woman's life, the director has them accompanied by a policewoman. Beit al Aman has actively worked to overcome the social stigma (in Gaza and Palestinian society at large) attached to battered women's shelters, first by offering regular day services like those of other NGO service providers (i.e., legal, psychological, and social counseling) so that a wider sector of women will come to use and know the facility. They have opened the doors of the shelter to secondary-school girls and women at Hamas-sponsored summer camps so that they can learn about its services; they also hold entertainment and sports activities in the courtyard and theater. These strategies are intended to decriminalize the space in the popular imagination, while also being a means to spread the word to women about the shelter. As Skeik says, "We don't have the resources to make brochures and distribute them."

The way the shelter deals with the usual cases of battered women is indistinguishable from the way that most professional NGO service providers do. For the initial three days, clients are told to simply rest and make no decisions. Then they meet with social, psychological, and legal counselors. The details of the case are thus clarified and the woman is given information on her options. Three paths are laid out: to pursue a case in the Shari'a courts; to pursue reconciliation through a reconciliation committee; or to have the police and prosecutors "scare" the perpetrator. The decision is shared with a "case conference," and depending on the path the woman chooses to take, either a representative from the Ministry of Interior's Public Relations Departments (if she wants the police and public prosecutors involved), a specialist from the Reconciliation Committee of the Legal Scholars Association (if she chooses reconciliation/informal justice), or a lawyer and social worker from the Palestinian Center for Human Rights (if she wants to pursue a court case) will be brought in. Except for using police pressure, these are the same options (along with social and psychological counselling) that NGO providers offer.

The director does not use rights language or the discourse of empowerment. Nor does she use the words gender or gender-based violence. Her discourse is about women victims of violence and when she mentions rights it is in the context of legal rights in Shari'a. She locates causes of VAW (like many of the NGO providers) in the economic crisis of male breadwinners in Gaza under the blockade and wars, as well as in "norms and traditions" that she insists are *not* Islamic. She is critical of "tribal reconciliation" solutions (what the humanitarians and some NGOs call the "informal justice system") and says it's a case of "letting the oppressor pile more injustice on the oppressed." At the same time, she sees the practical limitations of prevailing family law and constantly works with the current high judge of the Shari'a courts to find loopholes and solutions. She also works with the two Fatwa Committees in Gaza (at Islamic and al-Aqsa Universities) when addressing sensitive legal decisions (such as on abortions for rape and incest victims beyond the first trimester).

Rather than working according to a set ideological frame, both her discourse and strategies are completely pragmatic: how to find the least unjust and best workable solution available within the multilayered complex of constraints (social, economic political, legal and geopolitical) that confronts these cases in Gaza.[21] Finding the means to reintegrate women back into society (in Gaza this means reintegrating them into their family or reuniting them with their husband) is a priority because otherwise women would be, as the director says, stuck in "a prison within a prison." Rather than representing a conservative stance on saving the family at any cost, hers is a position built on the practical implications of divorce for most women in Gaza. Although most women face formidable obstacles in pursuing a divorce, it is the gendered material structure of women's lifeworlds that makes almost anything preferable to actually getting one. Most women have never been in the labor force and do not have the minimum requirements to find employment in Gaza's already destroyed labor markets, so divorce would plunge them into abject poverty. Levels of social welfare and court-ordered maintenance payments barely sustain basic food needs. In addition, due to the prevailing legal codes, they do not have access to independent housing and thus have to return to their natal family as a burden. And finally, there is the issue of legal custody in family law: women have to hand physical custody of daughters over to their fathers at eleven and sons at nine years of age (Shehada 2018). It is not surprising that out of twelve cases of married women IPV victims being treated by NGO providers who were interviewed for the UN Women report on which this chapter is based, only two pursued a divorce themselves. In the case of the Beit al Aman, if women return to their husbands, the shelter insists that they first draw up a series of conditions, signed by the husband and witnessed by the staff. Rather than it having a legal standing, the director admits it is a means of intimidation, to let perpetrators know there are authorities watching them. The shelter actively follows up with the cases for six months.

The erasure of Beit al Aman from the humanitarians' representation of GBV services in Gaza might be understood as simply a case of the instrumental politics of humanitarian neutrality. Caught between the contending demands of western donors' "no contact policy" but needing to avoid conflict with the Hamas authorities (to ensure continued "access"), perhaps the safest position for them was to ignore the shelter's existence. But why not simply mention the shelter, without any value judgment attached to it, rather than completely expunging it from the scene? Obviously, the larger political rationales at work here could not be sustained if other agents of rescue were allowed to exist in Gaza. In the imaginative theater of humanitarianism, actors belong to only three possible categories: humanitarian rescuers, exemplary victims (Malkki 1996), or perpetrators (Belloni 2005). That the perpetrators (here Hamas, as well as Muslim patriarchs) could be agents of rescue and in ways that might be legible within normative scripts of humanitarian GBV is epistemologically untenable. This erasure is especially necessary given that the Hamas shelter does not diverge much from their own practical prescriptions, and actually fulfils the promises of protection that remain unfulfilled by humanitarian GBV.

WAR VIOLENCE/GENDER VIOLENCE:
SHELTERS IN THE 2014 WAR

Like protection, "shelter" is an emotive but polyvalent signifier in the context of Gaza. Since 1948, shelter has been the master signifier for refugee dwellings and thus the common technical term for most homes in Gaza. Shelter took on an additional humanitarian meaning in the context of Israel's major military aggressions on Gaza: it came to signify "emergency shelters," given the total absence of bomb shelters. With Israel preventing Gazans' escape from the theater of war, in the first three wars families seeking refuge from bombing and ground troops only had the option of seeking shelter in institutions that Israel was less likely to bomb indiscriminately. Under the assumption that the privileges and immunities of UN installations would be respected, families preferred to flee to UNWRA buildings. In the first major war (2008/2009) fifty UNRWA schools were used as emergency shelters for 50,000 civilians fleeing their homes. In the 2014 war, the sheer scale of those forced to seek refuge (half a million, almost 30 percent of the population) meant that eighty-one UNRWA schools became designated emergency shelters, hosting 300,000 men, women, and children seeking refuge (while 200,000 others ended up in government schools, mosques, and churches). Nevertheless, in 2014 Israel bombed seven UNRWA schools that were serving as "emergency shelters," killing forty-four civilians seeking refuge inside them.

By 2014, the humanitarian apparatus had already passed through two major wars in Gaza through which to learn how to prepare for another. However, when it came to the specific issue of "emergency shelter," the evolution of "emergency preparedness" never went beyond superficial recalibrations. It certainly did not involve investments in building bomb shelters for the population it was to protect. Nor did it involve better equipping schools by addressing their limited sanitation infrastructure (few toilets/no showers), already identified in 2009 as creating a public health risk while exacerbating Gazans' already extreme sense of vulnerability and insecurity.[22] The only perceptible change humanitarians made was to segregate men from women and children within the internal space of the schools. By 2014 women and children were sheltered in the classrooms while men stayed in the school courtyards and balconies.[23]

Gender segregation of school shelters was the only "gender response" to humanitarian gender analysis of emergency shelters that emerged from the 2009 war, responding to distress voiced by young women about the 2009 assault in quotes like this: "My whole extended family and I went to a school shelter where 60 people were crammed into a classroom. The first night we almost died from the cold. So we asked the people who were already there for blankets. There was nothing: no water, no food, no covers. My whole life I'll never forget sleeping on the bare floor tiles, sleeping in a room with 60 people, most of them young men. In my whole life I've never slept near anyone. We'd cover our heads in our sleep and wake covered up" (UNIFEM 2009, 60).

This was a common gendered narrative and its anguished emotional register was shared by women and men who'd spent that war in UNRWA school shelters. At the same moment Israeli bombing had destroyed women's sense of psychic and bodily security, the corporeal boundaries that attended to their sense of ethical personhood were compromised in the crammed and chaotic space of the shelter. Yet here was a humanitarian gender "finding" that translated easily. First, it was easily comprehensible to Orientalist imaginaries. Humanitarian discourse articulated it as an issue related to Gazans' "strict social codes of segregation between men and women . . . [wherein] women and girls are confined to the private sphere of their homes" (UN Women and OCHA 2015). Second, it fit into a highly favored mode of humanitarian intervention in Gaza (as elsewhere) as a treatable "psychosocial need."[24] And finally, segregating men and women did not involve any costly infrastructural investment. Just a spatial re-sorting of Gazan bodies by gender. That women expressed similar distress in 2009 over the shelter bathrooms was never addressed. Humanitarian response was selective and built on the lowest horizons of minimum standards.

But what is most apparent in the difference in humanitarian discourse on "shelter" between the 2009 and 2014 wars is that in the first, humanitarian GBV was totally absent while by 2014 it had succeeded in colonizing most areas of "gender in emergency response." Even while Israeli bombardment was at its height, myriad projects for the inevitably needed GBV treatment services in its aftermath were already being listed in UN OCHA's "flash appeals" (some shamelessly inserting the words "life-saving" next to the words "GBV services"). But it was once the bombing stopped that humanitarian GBV really got to work. With the apparatus now fully in place, the initial aim was to uncover the ways the war contributed to Gaza's now already-established "GBV problem" through an archetypical humanitarian research method called "a rapid assessment tool." Of particular focus was the specific community under the humanitarians' direct care during the war: the "IDPs," women who had ended up in UNRWA shelters.

Less than two months after the war, the United Nations' GBV "sub cluster working group" published the findings of the rapid assessment it had commissioned from a Gazan woman journalist, under the obtuse title "Protection in the Windward" that had a clearer subtitle: "Conditions and Rights of Internally Displaced Girls and Women During the Latest Israeli Military Operation on the Gaza Strip" (UNFPA 2014). The stated goal of the assessment was to understand women's and girls' gender-specific experience of the war in emergency shelters and whether emergency response had appropriately attended to their "specific protection needs." The focus of the report was on women's and girls' experiences of gender-based violence while in the UNRWA school shelters.

From the outset, the study locates women within Gaza's already well-established high GBV levels that, according to expert knowledge and experience of war and armed crisis, are inevitably going to rise both during the war and in its aftermath. The report goes on to try and excavate the forms of GBV that women and girls (and as an afterthought, men) experienced in the midst of Israeli bombardment while in the unsafe haven of Gaza schools. Restrictions on girls' movement within the shelters was cited as the most commonly reported form of GBV. Other forms include "verbal violence and maltreatment by the shelters' administrators who made [girls] feel humiliated whenever they asked for things they needed" (UNFPA 2014, 11). Verbal harassment by young men was labeled "sexual violence" and the insufficient lighting and lack of locks on bathroom doors was treated as a threat of sexual abuse (UNFPA 2014, 16). The report repeatedly notes that women were subjected to psychological, physical, and sexual violence while in the shelters, but the examples offered are not dramatic. One interviewed woman reported that violence against women often involved husbands "using bad and humiliating words in front of everyone, as well as shouting and angry looks" (UNFPA 2014, 11). Others cited the refusals of shelter administrators to give them what they needed as cases of violence (UNFPA 2014, 11). Other types of reported GBV included being pushed when lining up for food aid or verbal harassment by strangers. While a few cases of husbands hitting wives, and many cases of mothers hitting daughters, were reported, the main forms and meanings of physical violence that emerge is women's experience of physical stress and discomfort due to chaos and crowding. The report does finally admit that "psychological violence" was the predominant type of GBV women experienced.

But it is the report's findings on sexual violence experienced by women (and men) in the shelters that lays bare the absurdity of forcing the physical and mental suffering and extreme military violence that Gazans endured during the war into the straitjacket of humanitarian GBV discourse. The report cites a few men who considered the forced separation from their wives a form of sexual violence (UNFPA 2014, 30). Similarly, some women when asked whether they experienced any sexual violence responded with the issue of sexual deprivation because "spouses could not approach each other due to a lack of places allocated for spouses in the shelter" (UNFPA 2014, 19).

At face value, the study's "findings" might suggest failure in terms of humanitarian GBV's ability to produce standard forms of evidence about women's greater vulnerability to specifically gendered forms of violence in the context of war. Instead it captures varieties of interpersonal conflict and aggression that would surely occur among any population living in intense fear, insecurity, overcrowding, and chaos, without protection or reprieve from deadly bombing for fifty-one days. But the tone of the report does not betray any sense of failure to produce the proper evidence. The material is presented with total self-confidence, the content of evidence and the specific details of what is being called GBV here all made secondary to the technical definitions and procedures of measurement that create the report's truth value.

The accomplishment of the report is its performance of humanitarian GBV's technical competence and its commitment to the humanitarian norms specific to it. Just producing the report meets the goal of humanitarianism's rationale for being. As such, a year later, in the annual report to the UN Secretary General (on the situation of Palestinian women in the Occupied Palestinian Territories), the report simply lays claim to the particular truth on which it is built: "A rapid assessment by UNFPA conducted after the 2014 conflict revealed that the protracted crisis and related displacement, lack of privacy and lack of basic services had exacerbated people's sense of vulnerability, leading to violence against women" (United Nations Economic and Social Council 2016). That the GBV evidence might not have been "good enough" is simply an impossibility within the operations of power and regime of truth through which the humanitarian apparatus reproduces itself.

THE DESPERATE SEARCH FOR SEXUAL VIOLENCE

In Gaza, humanitarian GBV has always been bereft of its iconic and most productive victim: the victim of sexual violence in war. Despite the fact that the "rapid assessment" of GBV experiences in UNRWA shelters during the 2014 war found instead expressions of sexual deprivation, a year later, rumor and "local experts" helped fill in the gap, enabling sexual deprivation to be re-inscribed as "rape in war." A year after the rapid appraisal, a study by two international humanitarian NGOs set out once again to establish a relationship between the war and a rise in GBV, but this time through producing statistical evidence (Müller and Barhoum 2015). Using the normative global statistical frame (the Conflict Tactics Scale), the researchers compared PCBS prevalence data (from 2010) with data they generated by asking women about their experiences of various acts of domestic violence during and after the war.

The findings were disappointing, contradicting the global common sense. During the war IPV levels had dramatically declined compared to 2010, and postwar they barely returned to their prewar levels. But humanitarian GBV commonly frames their research in "expert interviews and focus groups" to avoid relying solely only narratives of the general populace – whose responses might run counter to the desired conclusions. Local GBV experts provided "witness evidence" to the fact that rapes had indeed occurred in the shelters. According to the report, "some of the focus group discussions did indicate that they believed that violence levels against women decreased during that time [in the midst of the 2014 Gaza war], with the exception of shelters where much violence, particularly rapes, were witnessed" (Müller and Barhoum 2015, 50).

One wonders what witnesses did as this was occurring, especially if they were gender experts, but this puzzling finding about rape requires interpretation. When I asked two Gaza colleagues about the "rape in shelters" finding, they explained that it was some local NGO GBV specialists' misinterpretation of the issue of sexual deprivation and how some shelter administrators had attempted to resolve it. It is important to note that for fifty-one days under hellish bombing, families and intimate partners were completely physically divided from each other in the gender-segregated shelters. And it is also important to consider that sexual deprivation is a narrow physiological term for more complex dimensions of physical and emotional intimacy and closeness that would be especially vital in times of extreme insecurity and fear. Recognizing these circumstances, one month into the war some shelter directors opened administrative offices of the school/shelter to be used for short periods as intimate conjugal space. One can imagine that for some women, embarrassment at being publicly seen going into the space with their spouse might have outweighed desire or willingness. Did some wives feel coerced? This was obviously not always the case, as the women had so openly stated their own sexual needs to researchers of the "rapid appraisal." That the complex and contradictory experiences of Gazan men's and women's need for sexual and other intimacy during the war could be reduced to "rape in war" speaks to the dehumanizing logics at work here.

CONCLUSION

In terms of the operations of humanitarian GBV, it would seem that Gazan women and girls are marked out as exemplary victims deserving to be saved from Gazan men, who have been marked off by imperial geopolitics as the bearers of the pathological violence of Islamic patriarchy that Gazan women, Israelis, and the liberal west all suffer from. Rather than focusing on who is excluded from care, here I have focused on the "what" and "how" of care. Humanitarian GBV attends only to a specific condition that Gazan women and girls are said to suffer from—violence at the hands of Gazan men, even when the evidence contradicts this claim. Their suffering at the hands of Israel's all engulfing sovereign violence or from its catastrophization of their lives is not part of the urgent humanitarian work of arresting Gaza's GBV problem. In this frame, Gazan women and girls, rather than bearing the range of needs and capacities of a full human, are reduced to the specific ill that GBV humanitarians have marked out as their mission to treat. But even the specific forms of care through which humanitarian GBV attends to its object in Gaza are highly selective, raising the more fundamental question of what the "care" in this context actually accomplishes. Similar to findings of ethnographic studies on humanitarian SGBV programming in Congo (Autesserre 2012; D'Errico et al. 2013; Heaton 2014), women survivors of family violence and local NGO workers in Gaza constantly voiced needs and priorities completely at odds with the GBV "care" that was on offer, such as secure housing, schooling for children, and access to stable work and income (including for abusive husbands). And as the (misrepresented) calls of Gazan women NGOs during the 16 Days campaigns attest, they also consistently emphasize the priority of fundamental *political* intervention to end the state of punishment that Gazans have been forced to inhabit. None of this is unknown to most international humanitarians on the ground. But as has been shown elsewhere (Dunn 2012; Redfield and Bornstein 2010; Veit and Tschörner 2019) the priority is on the fundamental need for the humanitarian apparatus to reproduce itself within the logic of global aid flows whose technical frames are completely foreclosed. In the case of humanitarian GBV, providing only forms of care that performatively contribute to its own perpetuation simultaneously perpetuates the civilizational paradigms on which the catastrophization of Gazan lives depend.

NOTES

The research on which this chapter is based was undertaken for UN Women in Gaza in late 2016/early 2017 as an assessment of international donors' GBV programming. Because of Israel's mobility restrictions, I was not allowed to enter Gaza myself and instead relied on my co-researcher, Andaleeb Adwan, and a small team of field researchers to undertake the interviews and ethnographic observation. As such, while Adwan is not the coauthor of this paper (as she was for the UN Women report), she is its critical cocreator. Although Adwan is not responsible for its errors or judgments, this chapter is built on her knowledge and insight. Despite having written my dissertation on Gaza, living and working there for six years, I was unable to physically be present there for many years because of the Israeli blockade, which explains the absence of first-person ethnographic depth. See Hammami and Adwan (2017).

1   It was only later that I learned that the survey themes and approach had attempted to meet the 2006 guidelines on "the post crisis needs assessment for

recovery and gender equality" laid out by The Inter-Agency Standing Committee (IASC), the governance mechanism within the UN that codifies humanitarian norms and practices (IASC 2006).

2 As Lazzarini (2009) writes in an OCHA report, "The Gaza population's distress is compounded by the lack of civilian protection. Israel's Cast Lead military operation of 27 December 2008–18 January 2009 provides a devastating example.... Women and children in particular are paying a high price, as shown by a recent UN survey revealing an increase in the prevalence of domestic and gender-based violence."

3 See Terry (2002) for a similar reading of the political logics of Humanitarianism in other contexts.

4 These included national legislation to criminalize VAW; police- and justice-sector reform and sensitization for dealing with victims; the provision of shelter and rehabilitation; and VAW-sensitive policies and services within the health and social services sectors

5 Of the ten security council resolutions on Women, Peace and Security since 2000, seven resolutions address sexual violence in conflict specifically (SCR 1820 (2008), 1888 (2009), 1960 (2010) and 2106 (2013), 2122 (2013), 2242 (2015), and 2467 (2019). See Women's International League for Peace and Freedom (n.d.).

6 The initial framing of Humanitarian GBV was shaped by the priorities of the two UN agencies first tasked with elaborating protocols to treat it. The United Nations High Commission for Refugees (UNHCR) emphasized protecting women from further sexual violence through safety procedures in the refugee camps while the United Nations Population Fund (UNFPA), with its emphasis on reproductive health, medicalized the protocols to treat victims. These concerns were both integrated into and displaced by the IASC guidelines.

7 See the 2015 IASC "Guidelines for Integrating Gender-Based Violence Interventions in Humanitarian Action." For a sense of the subsequent massive literature see the IASC GBV guidelines website: https://gbvguidelines.org/en/.

8 The guidelines suggest victims should be supported to access whatever local formal or informal justice systems exist, and in the long term, policies put in place during the emergency should always think to the poststabilization phase—with the hope that they can be "scaled-up" to the national level.

9 One UN report, in explaining these ongoing changes in acronyms, states that GBV was first added to sexual violence in order to reflect the "commitment to address types of violence other than sexual that were evident in the setting, particularly domestic violence and harmful traditional practices" (Ward and UN Women 2013, 18). But the continuing insistence on using SGBV was in order to "emphasize the urgency of protection interventions that address the criminal character and disruptive consequences of sexual violence for victims/survivors and their families" (Ward and UN Women 2013, 18). Where "women" was used in a humanitarian frame, it was VAWG (violence against women and girls, the

preferred language of UN Women—the agency most associated with the global VAW agenda).

10 The findings used here are from the original UNFPA data set disaggregated for Gaza; the UNFPA 2016 published report of their findings merged the data on the occupied territories making an analysis of the Gaza distribution impossible. See the more detailed discussion of the Gaza in data in Hammami and Adwan (2017).

11 The final 15 percent of funds cover unnamed child and family protection, as well as "service delivery" activities.

12 For a good example see UNRWA's Arabic Training Manual, "Working with Gender-based Violence Survivors," https://www.unrwa.org/userfiles/2012061163026.pdf.

13 See its continued use as the main characterization of the "occupied Palestinian territory" in OCHA 2021.

14 The five other thematic clusters are food security, shelter, education, health/nutrition, and water/sanitation/hygiene.

15 The list of their protection actions in Gaza includes mitigating the consequences of the blockade through service delivery (predominantly food aid) and undertaking "public and private advocacy" to have the blockade lifted, providing shelter (including home reconstruction) for families with inadequate homes or "displaced by the conflict," promoting "safe and violence free schools" along with equipping teachers to support children traumatized by the conflict, and finally, providing specific interventions to treat the problems of "widespread violence, including Gender-Based Violence and poverty."

16 Humanitarian monitoring also has a more instrumental purpose. During Israel's three major wars on Gazans, humanitarian monitoring counted the dead and wounded, counted the number of buildings and amount of infrastructure destroyed, calculated the number of people made food insecure, and the number of children in need of psychosocial interventions (and women in need of GBV interventions)—and immediately translated them into budget items in the ensuing spate of "Flash Appeals" for emergency humanitarian funding.

17 Charli Carpenter (2006) has shown the real-world effects of humanitarians invoking gender essentialisms in order to gain access in the case of Srebrenica. Consistently conflating women and children with innocent civilians in that context served to confirm Bosnian men as legitimate targets of genocide by Serbian forces.

18 For how consistently Gazan women's organizations focus on international protection from Israeli violence during the 16 Days campaigns, see the Palestinian Centre for Human Rights' (2018) statement for it two years later that almost desperately reiterates the same message.

19 That was passed by the then ministerial committee of the Abu Mazen Government following the strategies elaborated by the National Committee to Combat VAW in 2008.

20   For an example of vilification of Beit al Aman see Gisha (2016).
21   For similar readings of the Islamic family law courts in Gaza and how women pragmatically negotiate their constraints (often with the flexibility and support of male judges) see Shehada (2018).
22   While not dealing with fundamental issues of access to water and sanitation, ironically many donors (including UNFPA, UNRWA, and World Vision) highlighted that they distributed "dignity kits" to women IDPs in emergency shelters. The "dignity kits" include, along with sanitary napkins, soap, shampoo, toothbrush/toothpaste—all unusable due to the inadequate water infrastructure in the schools. Women and their children were forced to beg for access to bathrooms in private homes during cease-fires in order to address basic hygiene needs.
23   The analysis I wrote for the problematic UN survey on Gaza in 2009 (mentioned at the outset of this chapter) emphasized this issue of women's experiences of bodily vulnerability in UNRWA schools during Israel's first major war in 2008–2009. It emerged in qualitative interviews undertaken to overcome the problematic survey data. I never imagined the miserly way that humanitarians would translate it into their operations. See UNIFEM (2009).
24   For critical analyses of the humanitarian psychosocial industry in Gaza, see Abu Hamad et al. (2015), Hart (2010), and Hart and La Forte (2013).

REFERENCES

Abu Hamad, Bassam, Nicola Jones, Nadia Al Bayoumi, and Fiona Samuels. 2015. "Mental Health and Psychosocial Service Provision for Adolescent Girls in Post-Conflict Settings: The Case of the Gaza Strip." Rebuild Consortium Country Report. https://www.alnap.org/help-library/mental-health-and-psychosocial-service-provision-for-adolescent-girls-in-post-conflict.

Auteserre, Severine. 2012. *The Trouble with the Congo*. Cambridge: Cambridge University Press.

Belloni, Roberto. 2005. "Is Humanitarianism Part of the Problem? Nine Theses." Belfer Center for Science and International Affairs, Harvard Kennedy School. https://www.belfercenter.org/publication/humanitarianism-part-problem-nine-theses.

Carpenter, Charli. 2006. "*Innocent Women and Children': Gender, Norms and the Protection of Civilians*." Burlington VT: Ashgate Press.

D'Errico, Nicole, Tshibangu Kalala, Louise Nzigire, Felicien Maisha, and Luc Kalisya. 2013. "'You Say Rape, I Say Hospitals. But Whose Voice Is Louder?' Health, Aid and Decision-Making in the Democratic Republic of Congo." *Review of African Political Economy* 40, no. 135: 51–66. https://doi.org/10.1080/03056244.2012.761962.

Douma, Nynke, and Dorothea Hilhorst. 2012. "Fond De Commerce? Sexual Violence Assistance in the Democratic Republic of Congo." Occasional Paper 2. *Disaster Studies*. Wageningen, NL: Wageningen University.

Dove, Fiona. 2009. "The Responsibility to Protect." *Development Dialogue* 53: 77–82.

Engle, Karen. 2020. *In the Grip of Sexual Violence in Conflict: Feminist Interventions in International Law*. Stanford, CA: Stanford University Press.

Fassin, Didier. 2012. *Humanitarian Reason: A Moral History of the Present*. Berkeley: University of California Press.

Feldman, Ilana. 2009. "Gaza's Humanitarianism Problem." *Journal of Palestine Studies* 38, no. 3: 22–37.

Ferris, Elizabeth. 2011. *The Politics of Protection: The Limits of Humanitarian Action*. Washington, DC: Brookings Institution.

Gisha. 2016. "Restrictions on Freedom of Movement Take a Toll on Women in the Gaza Strip." *Gisha.org*, March 8, 2016. http://gisha.org/en/restrictions-on-freedom-of-movement-take-a-toll-on-women-in-the-gaza-strip/.

Hammami, Rema. 2019. "Follow the Numbers: Global Governmentality and the Violence against Women Agenda in Occupied Palestine." In *Governance Feminism: Notes from the Field*, edited by Janet Halley, Prabha Kotiswaran, Rachel Rebouche, and Hila Shamir, 479–504. Minneapolis: University of Minnesota Press.

Hammami, Rema, and Andaleeb Adwan. 2017. "Navigating through Shattered Paths: NGO Service Providers and Women Survivors of Gender-Based Violence: An Assessment of GBV Services in Gaza." UN Women, September 2017. https://www.humanitarianresponse.info/en/operations/occupied-palestinian-territory/document/navigating-through-shattered-paths-ngo-service.

Hart, Jason. 2010. "Protecting Palestinian Children from Political Violence: The Role of the International Community." *Forced Migration Policy Briefing #5, Oxford Department of International Development*. Oxford: University of Oxford. https://www.refworld.org/pdfid/4e5f3b722.pdf.

Hart, Jason, and Claudia La Forte. 2013. "Mandated to Fail? Humanitarian Agencies and the Protection of Palestinian Children." *Disasters* 37, no. 4: 627–45.

Heaton, Laura. 2014. "The Risks of Instrumentalizing the Narrative on Sexual Violence in the DRC: Neglected Needs and Unintended Consequences." *International Review of the Red Cross* 96, no. 894: 625–39.

Inter-Agency Standing Committee (IASC). 2006. "Women, Girls, Boys & Men. Different Needs—Equal Opportunities. IASC Gender Handbook for Humanitarian Action." December 21, 2006. https://interagencystandingcommittee.org/gender-and-humanitarian-action-0/documents-public/women-girls-boys-men-different-needs-equal-5.

Inter-Agency Standing Committee (IASC). 2015. "Guidelines for Integrating Gender-Based Violence Interventions in Humanitarian Action." https://gbvguidelines.org/en/.

Lazzarini, Philippe. 2009. "Putting Dignity at the Heart of the Humanitarian Crisis in the Occupied Palestinian Territory." *Humanitarian Exchange*, September 1.

https://unispal.un.org/DPA/DPR/unispal.nsf/0/94AAC7CC45B5C8A285257649004E4024.

Li, Darryl. 2008. "Disengagement and the Frontiers of Zionism." *Middle East Report*, February 16. http://www.merip.org/mero/mero021608.

Malkki, Liisa. 1996. "Speechless Emissaries: Refugees, Humanitarianism, and Dehistoricization." *Cultural Anthropology* 11, no. 3: 377–404. https://doi.org/10.1525/can.1996.11.3.02a00050.

Meger, Sara. 2016. "The Fetishization of Sexual Violence in International Security." *International Studies Quarterly* 60, no. 1: 149–59.

Merry, Sally Engle. 2006. *Human Rights and Gender Violence: Translating International Law into Local Justice*. Chicago: University of Chicago Press.

Muhanna, Aitemad. 2013. *Agency and Gender in Gaza: Masculinity, Femininity and Family during the Second Intifada*. London: Ashgate.

Müller, Catherine and Laila Barhoum. 2015. "Violence Against Women in the Gaza Strip after the Israeli Military Operation Protective Edge 2014." Alianza por la Solidaridad and Action Aid. https://www.alianzaporlasolidaridad.org/axs2020/wp-content/uploads/STUDY-VAW-GAZA-Final-Version.pdf.

The New Humanitarian. 2009. "UN Tracks Rising Violence against Women in Gaza." *The New Humanitarian*, March 24. https://www.thenewhumanitarian.org/feature/2009/03/24/un-tracks-rising-violence-against-women-gaza.

Ophir, Adi. 2010. "The Politics of Catastrophization: Emergency and Exception." In *Contemporary States of Emergency: The Politics of Military and Humanitarian Interventions*, edited by Didier Fassin and Mariella Pandolfi, 59–88. New York: Zone Books.

Palestinian Centre for Human Rights. 2018. "On the International Day for the Elimination of Violence against Women, an Open Call for the International Community to Provide Protection for Palestinian Women" (translated from Arabic). November 25, 2018. https://www.pchrgaza.org/ar/?p=16309.

PNGO Portal. 2016a. "PNGO Women Sector Organized Sit-In in Gaza within 16 Days of Activism against Gender Violence Campaign" *PNGO Portal*, November 26. https://en.pngoportal.org/post/528/PNGO-women-sector-organized-sit-in-in-Gaza-within-16-Days-of-Activism-Against-Gender-Violence-Campaign.

PNGO Portal. 2016b. "With the Participation of Hundreds of Women, the Network's Women Sector Organizes a Sit-In in Gaza as Part of the Activities of the 16-Day Campaign to Combat Violence against Women" (translated from Arabic). November 24. Accessed February 2022.

Redfield, Peter. 2008. "Vital Mobility and the Humanitarian Kit." In *Biosecurity Interventions: Global Health and Security in Question*, edited by Andrew Lakoff and Stephen Collier, 147–71. New York: Columbia University Press.

Redfield, Peter, and Erica Bornstein. 2010. "An Introduction to the Anthropology of Humanitarianism." In *Forces of Compassion: Humanitarianism between Ethics and Politics*, edited by Erica Bornstein and Peter Redfield, 3–30. Santa Fe, NM: School for Advanced Research Press.

Shehada, Nahda. 2018. *Applied Family Law in Islamic Courts: Shari'a Courts in Gaza*. Abington, UK: Routledge.

Terry, Fiona. 2002. *Condemned to Repeat: The Paradox of Humanitarian Action*. Ithaca, NY: Cornell University Press.

Ticktin, Miriam. 2011. *Casualties of Care Immigration and the Politics of Humanitarianism in France*. Berkeley: University of California Press.

United Nations Development Fund for Women. 2009. "Towards Gender Equality in Humanitarian Response: Addressing the Needs of Women and Men in Gaza." https://www.unwomen.org/en/digital-library/publications/2009/1/towards-gender-equality-in-humanitarian-response-addressing-the-needs-of-women-and-men-in-gaza-a-guidebook-for-the-humanitarian-sector.

United Nations Economic and Social Council. 2016. "Commission on the Status of Women, Sixtieth Session." March 14–24, 2016. https://unispal.un.org/DPA/DPR/unispal.nsf/0/AEDB553BDA3E949985257F42005E0D8E.

United Nations Office for the Coordination of Humanitarian Affairs (OCHA). 2013. "Occupied Palestinian Territory Consolidated Appeal 2013." https://reliefweb.int/sites/reliefweb.int/files/resources/CAP%202013%20OPt.pdf.

OCHA. 2021. "Occupied Palestinian Territory," *Global Humanitarian Overview*. https://gho.unocha.org/occupied-palestinian-territory.

United Nations Population Fund (UNFPA). 2014. "Protection in the Windward: Conditions and Rights of Internally Displaced Girls and Women during the Latest Israeli Military Operation on the Gaza Strip." United Nations Population Fund, State of Palestine. https://reliefweb.int/report/occupied-palestinian-territory/protection-windward-conditions-and-rights-internally-displaced.

UNFPA. 2015. "Women and Girls Safe Spaces: A guidance note based on lessons learned from the Syrian crisis." UNFPA Regional Syria Response Hub, March 2015. https://www.unfpa.org/sites/default/files/resource-pdf/UNFPA%20UNFPA%20Women%20and%20Girls%20Safe%20Spaces%20Guidance%20%5B1%5D.pdf.

United Nations Relief and Works Agency (UNRWA). 2011. "Gazans join forces to combat violence against women." UNRWA Press release, December 9, 2011. https://reliefweb.int/report/occupied-palestinian-territory/gazans-join-forces-combat-violence-against-women.

UNRWA. 2016. "Gaza Situation Report 176." UNISPAL Newsroom, December 11, 2016. https://unispal.un.org/DPA/DPR/unispal.nsf/0/7EDC9EB20D9FECE58525808700509E93.

UNRWA. n.d. "Outline of Protection Initiatives." https://www.unrwa.org/userfiles/file/publications/UNRWA-Protection.pdf.

UN Women. n.d. "Facts and Figures: Ending Violence against Women." http://palestine.unwomen.org/en/what-we-do/ending-violence-against-women/facts-and-figures.

UN Women and UN Office for the Coordination of Humanitarian Affairs (OCHA). 2015. "Needs of women and girls in humanitarian action in Gaza: Gender Alert for the 2016 Response Plan." http://www.unrwa.es/EBDHsevilla2015/wp-content/uploads/2015/11/UNW-OCHA-Gender-Alert-Gaza.pdf

Veit, Alex, and Lisa Tschörner. 2019. "Creative Appropriation: Academic Knowledge and Interventions against Sexual Violence in the Democratic Republic of Congo." *Journal of Intervention and Statebuilding* 13, no. 4: 459–79. https://doi.org/10.1080/17502977.2019.1627041.

Ward, Jeanne, and UN Women. 2013. "Violence against Women in Conflict, Postconflict and Emergency Settings." *United Nations Entity for Gender Equality and the Empowerment of Women.* https://www.endvawnow.org/uploads/modules/pdf/1405612658.pdf.

Weizman, Eyal. 2011. *Lesser Evils: Scenes of Humanitarian Violence from Arendt to Gaza.* London: Verso.

Winter, Yves. 2016. "The Siege of Gaza: Spatial Violence, Humanitarian Strategies, and the Biopolitics of Punishment." *Constellations* 23, no. 2: 308–17. https://doi.org/10.1111/1467-8675.12185.

Women's International League for Peace and Freedom. n.d. "About Women, Peace and Security in the Security Council." *PeaceWomen* (blog). https://www.peacewomen.org/security-council/WPS-in-SC-Council.

ELEVEN · *Sima Shakhsari*

What Counts as Violence?

Transgender Refugees, Torture, and Sanctions

> A refugee is someone who has been forced to flee his or her country because of persecution, war or violence. A refugee has a well-founded fear of persecution for reasons of race, religion, nationality, political opinion or membership in a particular social group. Most likely, they cannot return home or are afraid to do so. War and ethnic, tribal and religious violence are leading causes of refugees fleeing their countries. Two-thirds of all refugees worldwide come from just five countries: Syria, Afghanistan, South Sudan, Myanmar and Somalia.
> —UNITED NATIONS HIGH COMMISSIONER FOR REFUGEES (UNHCR).[1]

Even if sexual orientation has not been explicitly codified in the definition of the "refugee" in the international refugee regimes, the United Nations High Commissioner for Refugees (UNHCR) includes some queer and trans people in the refugee recognition and resettlement processes, based on meeting the criterion of "belonging to a particular social group." Membership in a particular social group is interpreted by the UNHCR as either sharing a characteristic that "is immutable or so fundamental to human dignity that [one] should not be compelled to forsake it," or "a characteristic which makes a group cognizable or sets it apart from society at large. The characteristic will often be one which is innate, unchangeable, or which is otherwise fundamental to identity, conscience, or the exercise of one's human rights" (Organization for Refuge, Asylum and Migration [ORAM] 2011, 6–7). The Organization for Refuge, Asylum and Migration (ORAM), one of the non-profit organizations with a close working relationship with the UNHCR, explains that "gay men have the immutable characteristic of being sexually or emotionally attracted to men, and lesbians to women. Transsexuals' gender identity, rather than their sexual orientation," ORAM explains, is viewed as "immutable and fundamental to the person's identity" (ORAM 2011, 7).

The assumptions of a refugee's "immutability" in the essentialist juridical discourses of asylum produce the refugee as one with a fixed, timeless, and universally homogenous identity. It is inevitable that queer refugee applicants repeat essentialist notions of identity to fit the "immutability of character," the criterion that qualifies gays, lesbians, and trans people as refugees (Shakhsari 2014). Applicants' narratives, their material conditions, and their multiple and complex subjectivities are reduced to rational and linear definitions in order to match the acceptable "immutable" identity, defined and sanctioned by the refugee law, and reified by some diasporic queer organizations that coach queer refugees in homonormativity. However, the regulatory practices of the human rights regimes conceal the process of the construction of normative refugee subjects, by portraying them as prior to discourse. In other words, the persecution and protection duo, necessary to the upholding of refugee regimes, relies on fixed and universal constructions of sexual and gender identity (LGBTI) as *the* defining factor to grant queer and trans people the ticket to belonging to deserving "particular social groups." Rather than succumbing to these essentialist definitions that authorize queer and trans asylum, we may ask instead, or in addition, what forms of violence are simultaneously enacted and erased when the qualifying criteria for refugee recognition fixes iconic identities, relies on accounts of identity-based gender violence, and excludes conditions that produce refugees in the first place? In particular, in the case of Iranian queer and trans refugees, I am interested in the trivialization of the violence of economic sanctions by the refugee regimes (which include multiple states, UNHCR, NGOs, and diasporas) that are invested in the naturalization and deployment of fixed sexual identities in uneven geopolitical terrains. What is at stake when, under the deadly economic sanctions that have been imposed by the United States, the material conditions of Iranian queer and trans refugees are reduced to one aspect of their existence (their gender identity) within hegemonic narratives of queer and trans refuge? (Shakhsari 2014; Allouche 2017).

By drawing attention to the kinds of epistemic and material violence that refugee regimes engender through the trivialization of the sanctions that have devastated Iranians for decades, I hope to show how the hegemonic language of "forced surgeries" and "torture" that has come to define the Iranian trans refugee experience in the international media and refugee regimes normalizes economic violence in a time when sanctions are subjecting the most vulnerable segments of the Iranian population (including working-class and rural trans people) to death. Sanctions have produced refugees by forcing many Afghans and working-class queer and trans Iranians to leave Iran for Turkey, where the UNHCR has an office. Despite the refugee regimes' claims of protection of refugee rights, the dire conditions of refugee life in Turkey and immigration restriction of "third countries of asylum" in North America and Europe continue to make refugee lives expendable.[2] In this chapter, I show how geopolitics, biopolitics, and necropolitics come together to produce the myth of refugee protection, while subjecting those who are seen as threats to the "international community" to death.

I base my argument on my ethnographic research among queer and trans asylum seekers in Turkey, where refugees wait for their cases to be processed by the UNHCR. In the past decade, Turkey has seen a significant surge in the number of non-Syrian asylum seekers. This includes Iranian queer and trans refugee applicants and Afghan refugees who have left Iran (and not Afghanistan) after the tightening of the economic sanctions. Yet the dominant refugee discourse emphasizes state persecution of LGBTI people and the medical torture of trans Iranians as reasons for granting asylum, completely ignoring the role of the sanctions in the lives of the marginalized Iranians—many of whom have fled Iran exactly because of the sanctions in the last decade. The exceptionalization of violence against queer and trans people in Iran is not inconsistent with the refugee rights narratives in cases such as honor killing or female genital operations, where gender violence is ethnicized.[3] Much like other gender violence narratives in refugee regimes, the Middle East is represented as exceptionally transphobic or homophobic, while the United States, Israel, and Europe appear as safe havens for queer and trans people.[4] Reproducing American exceptionalism and European superiority, such narratives label gender affirming surgeries in Iran as torture, while conveniently ignoring the past and present realities of sterilization and lack of healthcare for queer and trans people in the United States and Europe. Medical malpractice in cases of gender affirming surgeries is dismissed as individual wrongdoing in North America and Europe whereas they become human rights violations in Iran. This selective condemnation of human rights violations is evident in the fact that the US trans women of color are never included in the UNHCR's category of "belonging to a particular social group," even as trans women of color are subjected to rampant violence in the United States and elsewhere. In the same vein, it is unimaginable that the UNHCR would consider Black and Muslim men in the United States as belonging to a particular social group that is targeted by gender violence, in a time when the "dangerous masculinity" of Black and Muslim men has become the alibi for state racism and police brutality. The living condition of queer and trans asylum seekers in Turkey, where refugees live temporarily under the protection of the UNHCR until they are resettled in the United States, Canada, and Europe, is one example of the discrepancies of human rights claims of refugee regimes.[5]

TURKEY AS TEMPORARY REFUGE

Even though narratives of south to north movement dominate the mainstream refugee discourse, most refugees live and stay in the "Global South." In fact, according to the Canadian Council of Refugees, only three percent of world's refugees live in North America. Turkey currently hosts the largest number of refugees worldwide. As of 2020, out of 4.1 million refugees in Turkey, 3.7 million are Syrians. The remaining 400,000 asylum-seekers and refugees are mainly from Afghanistan, Iraq, and Iran (UNHCR 2019).

Turkey extends protection under the 1951 United Nations Convention Relating to the Status of Refugees only to persons originating in Europe. However, the Turkish government allows non-European asylum seekers to remain in Turkey temporarily while their refugee recognition and resettlement cases are pending with the UNHCR. Upon registration with the UNHCR office in Ankara, asylum seekers are assigned to small satellite cities where they are registered by the Turkish police and are required to stay while they are interviewed multiple times and evaluated through medical and sometimes psychological examination over the span of several years by the UNHCR, the Turkish government, and the embassy of the country of asylum. If recognized as refugees by the UNHCR, refugees are assigned to a third country of asylum for permanent resettlement and are interviewed and medically examined by the embassy of the country of asylum.

The UNHCR assesses LGBTI claims based on the "truth" of applicants' sexual identity. To test the truthfulness of refugee applicants' claims, the UNHCR assesses the consistency of the applicant's story, the alignment with the "country profile" (the accumulated knowledge about human rights violations in the applicant's home country), and the authenticity of their sexual identity. Before the UNHCR improved its guidelines and produced literature to educate its staff, many trans asylum seekers were asked invasive questions about their preferred sexual position, the number of sexual partners they have had, or whether they had been to a "gay bar" in Turkey. These questions are meant to verify that the applicants are "true refugees," which often translated into the authenticity of their identities as "true gays and lesbians," or "true transgender" individuals. While the UNHCR officers are no longer supposed to ask intrusive questions, the "right questions" are about the applicant's personal life history and childhood, when they started to "feel different," the applicant's family reaction, and their experiences with the police and authorities in Iran. The assumptions of inherent homosexuality or trans-ness underlie the questions about childhood memories. What further authenticates what are assumed to be immutable sexual and gender identities is "verification"—through letters from LGBTI organizations or performances of acceptable and "believable" (read white and middle class) sexual identity by refugees. Some of the diasporic queer organizations that support gay and trans applicants repeat essentialist notions of sexual identities that define authentic LGBTI individuals. These organizations often consider sexuality in Iran to be backward, repressed, and in need of liberation. They police queer refugees' sexuality through reproducing Eurocentric class-based and racially specific norms of sexual identity. As such, particular forms of modern sexual identity that are recognized and deemed legitimate by the refugee rights regimes are produced and regulated according to normative notions of race, class, and gender, in a nexus that includes the UNHCR, queer NGOs, queer refugees, and states (Shakhsari 2014).

Normative notions of authentic gender and sexuality are not the only conventions that queer refugee applicants must repeat convincingly in multiple interviews. The UNHCR officers also test the credibility of an applicant's claim for a "well-founded fear of persecution." In order to present a successful and legitimate claim to asylum officers, applicants are expected to repeat stories that demonize the "home country," thus reproducing the narratives of Third World backwardness and barbarism versus First World freedom (Abu-Lughod 2013; Anker 2005; Grewal 2005; Luibhéid 2008; Razack 1998; Volpp 2006). In the process of normalization, linear progression from the past to future is integral to refugee stories. The linear logic of human rights renders refugees as those who move from the temporally lagging and spatially backward "homeland" toward the future of progress (Fortier 2001), where they are handed the "gift of freedom" (Nguyen 2012). Paradoxically, the temporal logic of refugee rights discourse erases difference by universalizing sexual identities while emphasizing the difference of a "Third World" temporal lag.

For most non-Syrian refugee applicants in Turkey, the third country of asylum is Canada, the United States, Australia, or one of a few European countries. The registration process with the UNHCR or its partner organizations, registration and assignment to small satellite towns in Turkey, interviews with the UNHCR for refugee status determination, and interviews with the third country of asylum, take several years. During this time, asylum seekers are required to pay for their own basic expenses, including housing, food, transportation, and health care. While many refugees live a precarious life in Turkey, most queer refugees have added hardship because they receive limited or no financial support from their families, often face harassment in small Turkish satellite cities, experience work and housing discrimination, and have limited access to health care, hormones (in case of trans people), and queer and trans-friendly mental health services. When filing complaints with the Turkish police, they are encouraged to "dress like real men or women" to avoid being harassed. Sometimes, police interpreters who are refugees themselves "out" queers and ridicule them publicly, and some UNHCR officers are homophobic and transphobic. Perhaps because some sympathetic staff at the UNHCR are aware of the vulnerability of queer and trans refugees in small Turkish towns, they started to process LGBTI cases more quickly (second only to Baha'i refugee cases) and with a low rejection rate. The faster processing of queer and trans applicants has given them the reputation of being "golden cases." This reputation has also made queer and trans refugee cases prone to allegations of fraud. Although the UNHCR staff I interviewed acknowledged that "fake cases" were rare, queer and trans refugees feel that some interviewers cross-examine refugee applicants and insinuate that they are lying about their sexuality, a subject to which I will return later.

KILLING SOFTLY WITH SANCTIONS

The "golden case" reputation of queer and trans refugees (which as I will argue shortly is no longer the case) was partially owed to the UNHCR's "known fact" that Iran is not safe for queer and trans people and that Iranian trans people are survivors of torture. This "fact" overshadows other reasons for which many Iranian queer and trans refugee applicants have been leaving Iran in search of a better life. Interestingly, most trans Iranians I interviewed in Turkey said they had left Iran because of lack of economic opportunities. The phrase that I heard over and over was, "I left because I had no future in Iran." If we put this insight together with the UNHCR's report that the number of Iranian queer and trans refugee applicants in Turkey increased drastically after 2010, the question becomes what might have compelled Iranian queer and trans refugees to leave Iran in significantly higher numbers after 2010? To add to the complexity of the situation, 2010 also saw an overwhelming increase in the total number of refugee applicants in Turkey, culminating in a backlog in the refugee registration processes. What might have led to the increased number of refugee applicants in Turkey after 2010?

The Syrian refugee crisis might seem like the most obvious reason for the increased number of refugees in Turkey and the UNHCR's backlog. However, I was told by an UNHCR officer that Syrian refugees in Turkey constituted a separate administrative category, and that Syrians were admitted to Turkey through a different emergency program administered by the Turkish government. In other words, the backlog in the UNHCR cases in Turkish satellite cities was not because of the Syrian crisis. This officer told me that the number of non-Syrian refugees had increased from 5000 in 2009 to 50,000 in 2013. According to this officer, the backlog in the non-Syrian cases was mainly due to the increase in the number of Afghan refugees who had left Iran (home to three million Afghans) after the Obama administration tightened the sanctions on Iran. While millions of Afghan refugees left Afghanistan for Pakistan and Iran (as well as India, the United States, and Europe) during the rise of Taliban and the US occupation of Afghanistan from the 1980s into the first decade of the new millennium, the significant number of Afghan asylum seekers that came to Turkey after 2010 were those who left Iran (and not Afghanistan), because of the deteriorating economic situation in Iran. The "second migration" of Afghan refugees, some of whom had lived in Iran for decades, was due to the harsh economic conditions, cuts in state subsidies, and rising xenophobia in Iran. Under the pressure of the economic sanctions, when many Iranians have had to take more than one job to make the ends meet, scarcity and competition for jobs and resources has led to scapegoating Afghan refugees in Iran.[6]

The tightening of what Obama (proudly) called the "crippling economic sanctions" during his presidency led to harsh economic conditions that affected the most vulnerable Iranians. While the United States has consistently imposed sanctions on Iran since the Iranian revolution in 1979, those the Obama administration imposed were the harshest in the history of the US sanctions on Iran (Colvin 2010). On July 1, 2010, President Obama signed the Comprehensive Iran Sanctions, Accountability, and Divestment Act of 2010 (CISADA) to amend the Iran Sanctions Act of 1996 (ISA).[7]

CISADA added new types of restrictions that devastated the Iranian economy.[8] The new sanctions imposed excruciating economic pressure on the Iranian population—especially the working class—and jeopardized Iranian lives by making life-saving medicine unaffordable (Erdbrink 2012). The imposition of the CISADA in 2010 and the bullying by the United States and Europe pressured the Iranian state to sign the JCPOA (The Joint Comprehensive Plan of Action in 2012, which lifted some of the sanctions). The Trump administration's reversal of the JCPOA and the imposition of "maximum pressure," which continue under Biden administration, have devastated the Iranian economy, and exacerbated the longstanding effects of the sanctions.

Among the less obvious but deadly effects of the sanctions are its environmental effects. After Obama imposed penalties for selling petrol to Iran, resulting in a 75 percent decrease in imports, Iran started to refine its own oil. The Iranian state's hasty decisions in implementing "independent development" to remedy the crippling sanctions have resulted in home-grown technologies and production of petrol and diesel that contains 10–800 times more contaminants than the international standard (Soroush and Madani 2014). The increasing rate of cancer (especially breast cancer) in Iran, along with the lack of access to life-saving cancer treatment (because of the sanctions) has subjected the Iranian population to a "soft death."[9]

Even as the US Treasury Department's Office of Foreign Assets Control (OFAC) issued guidance that humanitarian items (such as medicine) would not face US sanctions, the sanctions on Iranian oil and Iran's Central Bank have reduced the Iranian state's ability to afford medicine and medical supplies. Though on paper a limited amount of medicine is exempt from the sanctions, because of the sanctions on the Central Bank, financial transactions are subjected to penalties, or capped at a level that render exemptions meaningless, so suppliers refrain from selling medical supplies and life-saving medicine to Iran.[10]

The sanctions mostly affect those at the margins of the Iranian society, including working-class women, working-class queer and trans people, and Afghan refugees. The economic situation has made queer and trans working-class people, especially those who have visible markers of queerness, more vulnerable to job loss and violence. With the tightening of sanctions, Iranian queer and trans refugee applicants, along with other marginalized segments of the Iranian population such as Afghan refugees, bore the brunt of the sanctions and they left Iran for Turkey in hopes of resettlement in a third country of asylum. For trans people, the Iranian state's austerity measures meant major cuts in subsidies for gender affirming surgeries. Even as queer and trans Iranian asylum seekers and Afghan refugees who left Iran for Turkey do not fall under the same category according to the UNHCR's criteria, they have something in common: they are economic refugees. Yet the UNHCR does not recognize economic marginalization as grounds for granting asylum. If it did, a large number of people in the world (including in the United States) who are affected by global capitalism's economic violence (such as lack of access to universal health care in the United States) would be eligible for asylum.

As many Afghans started to leave Iran after the sanctions devastated the Iranian economy, the number of refugee applications in the UNHCR offices in Turkey grew exponentially. Unable to handle the overwhelmingly high number of refugee applications, the UNHCR in Turkey stopped processing Afghan cases altogether. The suspension of Afghan refugee cases by the UNHCR highlights the fact that the temporality of rights is contingent on geopolitical interests of the "liberating states" that govern the human rights regimes. In other words, freezing Afghan cases after the influx of Afghan refugees from Iran to Turkey in the aftermath of Obama's crippling sanctions is a clear example of how the refugee recognition is contingent on the relationship between the United States (as the top funder of the UNHCR) and the "country of origin" from where refugees emerge. As I have argued elsewhere (Shakhsari 2014), during the rise of the Taliban, Afghan refugees were recognized by the UNHCR as those "deserving" the "protection" of rights regimes. Millions of Afghan people became refugees in neighboring countries such as Iran. In the 1990s, Iran hosted the largest number of refugees in the world (mostly from Afghanistan and Iraq). As a result, the UNHCR maintained a good relationship with Iran—the UNHCR Commissioner in Ankara told me and a colleague in the mid-1990s that the UNHCR could only recognize a limited number of refugees from Iran so as not to upset the Iranian government (Shakhsari 2014). After the occupation of Afghanistan by US forces, the UNHCR ceased to prioritize Afghan refugee applicants. In fact, with the influx of Afghan refugees to Turkey after the tightening of the sanctions on Iran, the UNHCR officer told me that since the "liberation" of Afghanistan, Afghan refugees were encouraged to return to Afghanistan, as the Taliban rule had ended.[11]

The discrepancies and inconsistencies of the refugee recognition process also show that the designation of an act as the "violation of human rights" committed by states, and the prioritization of refugees' lives are temporally and spatially contingent. This is apparent in the way that the priority of "refugee rights" may change before and after "liberation," even if "liberation" has reduced the living conditions for many Afghan people. The universal claims of rights are contradictory in the way that lives of Afghan refugees are worthy of saving at one point, and expendable at another. Just as the recognition of a refugee as one who deserves rights is contingent on time, the location of the violation is a determinant in refugee recognition decisions. Unlike the abstract definition of a refugee, there is a vast difference between Afghan, Iranian, Iraqi, or Syrian refugees and asylum seekers in Turkey. This difference is not due just to nationality, but also to the temporal and spatial constitution of refugee categories in the international human rights regimes. As I mentioned before, because the United States is a major contributor to the UNHCR's programs, it is not surprising that the decisions on refugee recognition are contingent on the relationship between the "country of origin" and the United States at different times (i.e., prioritization of refugees changes accordingly). Lastly, the recognition of a violation as grounds for refugee admission is contingent on geopolitics. According to indices that divide states into violators and protectors of rights, the same violation in the territory of a "liberating state" may be dismissed as a "crime" committed by one individual against another (for example, transgender murders in the United States), and not as an indicator of the "violation of human rights" or the failure of the state to protect "particular social groups." As I will discuss below, medical malpractice in gender affirmation surgeries is one such example.

TORTURE

In 2013, with the help of a group of Iranian queer and trans asylum seekers in Turkey, I started a network called *Sayeh*. Our goal was to support queer and trans asylum seekers in Turkey through crowdsourcing to help refugees pay for their *kimlik*, an identity card that all asylum seekers need to have as a part of their refugee application process.[12] We also helped pay for emergency medical expenses and gas bills during an unusually cold winter in Kayseri. As an academic who had interviewed many queer and trans asylum seekers, and the only member of *Sayeh* who was not an asylum seeker, I also advocated on behalf of queer and trans refugees with the UNHCR when possible. I asked UNHCR officers to expedite the processing of cases of those who had been waiting for a long time with no interviews, or who had medical emergencies and/or were living under dire conditions in Turkey.[13] In one of my meetings, a UNHCR officer asked me to give him the names of transgender applicants whom I had met during my research. He said he wanted to expedite the cases of Iranian transgender applicants for two reasons: because they were at higher risk of experiencing violence and because they were survivors of torture.

This UNHCR officer's concern about trans applicants in Turkey was legitimate. As is the case in many parts of the world, including Europe and North America, non-passing trans people face violence for threatening the norms of sex and gender.[14] Because refugee applicants are not legally allowed to work in Turkey, if trans and queer refugees do manage to find illicit jobs, they may be subjected to labor abuse at the workplace. Many trans refugee applicants I interviewed talked about sexual assault and harassment at work and on the streets. Many could not even find illegal work because they did not pass as cis men and women; or if they did pass, they were often "outed" by others to their employers and fired as a result.[15] The Turkish state's immigration policies and random raids and deportations of refugees who have no choice but to work illegally have exacerbated the harshness of living conditions of refugees in Turkey. Many Iranian refugees, particularly queer and trans people with fewer work opportunities, can barely afford to pay for their expenses. Those without jobs can barely live on their savings because of the depreciation of the Iranian currency as a result of the sanctions.[16]

While I gave the UNHCR officer a list of names and was thrilled to know that he acknowledged the vulnerability of trans refugees, I was surprised to hear him characterize Iranian trans asylum seekers as "survivors of torture." In a well-meaning and confident tone, he explained to me that the UNHCR knew about medical malpractice in trans surgery procedures in Iran. The "fact" the UNHCR employee relayed to me has emerged from a hegemonic narrative that has been produced and circulated by some Iranian opposition NGOs outside of Iran. Even as these NGOs claim to advocate for queer and trans rights, by circulating this narrative they are constructing trans people as either victimized gays and lesbians who are forced to undergo surgery, or misguided individuals who chose surgeries due to ignorance, false consciousness, or lack of education about their bodies and "true selves." Characterizing all gender affirming surgeries that take place in Iran as torture, these organizations and individuals are denying trans people agency in their decision to have medical procedures. These organizations insist that the Iranian state's subsidies for gender affirming surgeries are in fact the Iranian state's policy of sterilizing queers. According to this narrative, people who are "authentically gay or lesbian" are forced to have "sex change" surgeries by the homophobic Iranian state. These outside groups maintain that the

Iranian state's antisodomy laws are the reason the state not only encourages, but forces, "true homosexuals" to be sterilized and to change their biological sex. In this discourse, trans people who go through the medical procedure in Iran are believed to do so under pressure and without informed consent. Take for example, this excerpt from the *Washington Blade*, a newspaper that represents itself as "America's LGBT News Source." Quoting Arsham Parsi, the poster child of what we might call gay imperialism and the LGBTI refugee rescue industries, the newspaper reports,

> Parsi also noted to the *Blade* and during the briefing that the Iranian government encourages transgender people to undergo sex-reassignment surgery—offering them financial assistance and other incentives to do so. He said nearly half of those who underwent the procedure were not trans, but gay. (Lavers 2014)

The gay torture discourse is not just produced by mainstream gay and lesbian news outlets in North America and Europe. Several opposition groups that include Justice for Iran (JFI), 6Rang, Iranian Queer Railroad, and Human Rights Watch, among others, are adamant that gender reaffirming surgeries (or "sex reassignment surgeries" as JFI calls these procedures) are torture.[17] According to these groups, the Iranian state's subsidies of the surgeries are part of a conspiracy to eradicate gays and lesbians in Iran. By citing the Sharia Law in the Iranian constitution, these organizations argue that because homosexual acts are against Islamic law in Iran, Iranian gays and lesbians succumb to surgery, fearing the death penalty.

While some of these organizations (such as IRQR) grossly exaggerate the accounts of state prosecution of Iranian queer and trans people, others (such as JFI and 6Rang) have tried to move beyond such exaggerations by basing their analysis on the definition of torture in international law; a (very literal) reading of the Iranian constitution; and interviews with a select group of (mostly) lesbian refugees. Yet, these organizations' accounts, such as a report by JFI and 6Rang called *Diagnosing Identities, Wounding-Bodies: Medical Abuses and Other Human Rights Violations against Lesbian, Gay and Transgender People in Iran*, also undermine the agency of trans people and dismiss the history of trans activism. During a focus group discussion that I organized for trans refugees in Kayseri, many participants expressed their anger at queer organizations such as 6Rang for excluding them from meetings that they held in their visits to Turkey from Europe and Canada. Many trans men critiqued 6Rang's lesbian representative's assumption that trans men are "really lesbians" who are duped by the state into having surgery or hormone therapy. Several trans women were offended by this organization's exclusion of trans women on the grounds that trans women are "in fact men who are forced to have surgeries," or that they have male privilege. After being criticized by trans people, 6Rang and its sister organization, JFI, have included some trans testimonies in their reports. Yet the scant number of trans testimonies about malpractice or the low quality of surgeries by some doctors in Iran are twisted to prove JFI's point about the transphobia of the Iranian medical and psychological establishments and the Iranian state. While there is no question about the transphobia of many practitioners in Iran, like elsewhere, the JFI report exceptionalizes Iran as a transphobic torture hub. JFI and 6Rang's attempts to appear trans-friendly are undermined by the biological essentialism they promote and the multiple slippages by authors who misgender trans men.[18] The narratives of trans regret in this report uncannily resemble discourses perpetuated by ultraconservative evangelists in the United States.[19]

The JFI report cites Article 1 of the Committee Against Torture's definition as:

> [a]ny act by which severe pain or suffering, whether physical or mental, is intentionally inflicted on a person for such purposes as obtaining from him or a third person information or a confession, punishing him for an act he or a third person has committed or is suspected of having committed, or intimidating or coercing him or a third person, or for any reason based on discrimination of any kind, when such pain or suffering is inflicted by or at the instigation of or with the consent or acquiescence of a public official or other person acting in an official capacity.

Based on this definition, JFI alleges that "sex reassignment surgeries may in some instances cross the threshold of ill-treatment that is tantamount to torture" (Justice for Iran and 6Rang 2014, 41). In a leap from "some instances" to arguing that surgeries in Iran are substandard, the JFI report then concludes that the Iranian state is guilty of torture because "[t]he application of the criterion of severe pain or suffering is relatively straightforward, particularly in national contexts where sterilization and sex reassignment surgeries are of poor quality and performed in wanton disregard of international standards, rendering transgender persons seriously scarred, injured and disfigured" (41).

It is true that the Iranian state, like many other modern biopolitical states, uses its medical, psychological, and legal apparatus to produce an optimal form of "normal" life while excluding or disposing of its ethnicized or queer others. As Najmabadi (2013) has argued, despite its subsidies for gender affirming surgeries, many elements in the Iranian state's medical, legal, religious, and psychological apparatus remain invested in the binary of gender and wish to exclude trans people from full citizenship. However, the Iranian state's normalization of trans people wherein passing as cis becomes the measure of "success" is hardly exceptional. Neither is the Iranian state—from its medical and psychological establishments to its legal and religious apparatus—uniformly or exceptionally either transphobic or trans-friendly. To demonize Iran as a "torture hub" erases the complexity of Iranian society and state, working with a top-down theory of power wherein trans activists and individuals can only appear as victims of a monolithic and repressive Islamic state. As Najmabadi has rightly argued (2013), trans activists have had a significant and active role in negotiating and contesting legal, religious, and medical discourses and practices regarding transgender people in Iran. To reduce the multiplicity of positions, behaviors, and attitudes to a single narrative of repression and torture is not only inaccurate, but an erasure of the long history of Iranian trans activism.

The report produced by JFI and 6Rang marks Iran as a "highly gendered society," while presenting Germany and other European countries as egalitarian. The authors of the report seem to forget the binary constructions of sex and gender that are foundational to colonial modernity and still persist in everyday lives of North Americans and Europeans, from legal and medical documents to advertising, standards of beauty, and organization of space, just to mention a few examples. While neoliberal multiculturalism and homonationalism as the modus operandi in North America and Europe may produce the myth of a gender-blind or race-blind West, the fact remains that the binary construct of gender and sex remain deeply rooted in these locations that the JFI lauds as models of gender equality. As many scholars have argued (Abu-Lughod 2013; Kauanui 2018; Morgensen 2011; Massad 2008; Moallem 2005; Somerville 2000; among others), the naturalization of sex/gender/desire binary constructs, heteronormativity, and nuclear family are all part and parcel of racial capitalism, colonial modernity, and settler colonial sexuality. The United States and European countries have a long history of biopolitical practices to enforce gender norms, including the forced sterilization of nonwhite populations, intersex people, disabled people, and the poor. While JFI contrasts the backwardness and transphobia of the Iranian state to the progressive policies in Europe, there is no mention of the forced sterilization of trans people or rampant malpractice in gender affirmation surgeries in Europe and the United States, even in their recent histories.[20]

This exceptionalization of violence against trans people in Iran is in line with the geopolitical logics that underlie many human rights organizations' frameworks. While medical malpractice or transphobic violence in North America and Europe get dismissed as mistakes or crimes committed by one individual against another, they are represented as systematic forms of torture and a violation of human rights for those states not recognized as enlightened protectors of rights. In fact, the 1951 Refugee Convention and the UNHCR definition of a refugee as someone who "owing to a well-founded fear of being persecuted for reasons of race, religion, nationality, membership of a particular social group or political opinion, is outside the country of his nationality, and is unable to, or owing to such fear, is unwilling to avail himself of the protection of that country" does not seem to apply to queer and transgender refugees (or citizens) who are subjected to police violence, economic violence, and racism in North America and Europe. My point is not to simply compare; if we are to move beyond an international comparative approach that reifies the sovereignty of nation-states and erases inequalities of power in the so-called family of nations, we need to pay attention to uneven geopolitical relations and forms of transnational governmentality that include not only the state, but nonstate, parastate, and supranational entities that may encompass (or traverse) privatized security regimes, universities, NGOs, diasporas, multinational corporations, and the UN. Such an approach would require that we pay attention to diasporic political formations and NGOs as parts of a wider geopolitical assemblage that operates through the rhetoric of human rights.

Knowledge produced by NGOs and diasporic LGBTI organizations often becomes a source for testimonials which are then cited as expert knowledge in refugee rights regimes. As I noted earlier, to strengthen their cases, some trans asylum seekers repeat the narrative that surgery is torture. Refugee applicants understand that tapping into the language of the UNHCR and the NGOs increases their chances of being recognized as "true refugees." As I mentioned earlier, to prove the "truth" of their claims, refugee applicants have no choice but to demonize their "home country" and repeat stories about how oppressive and violent their "culture" is. They have learned to present accounts of torture and violence that will make their cases persuasive to UNHCR officers. It is understandable that many queer and trans refugee applicants who are desperate to "pass" the refugee tests repeat the stories that they have rehearsed over and over to organizations, media, and academics, in hopes that the interviewers can do something for them. The discourse of torture has become the naturalized narrative about medical surgeries in Iran because of this circulation between human rights organizations, LGBTI-advocacy NGOs, refugees, and the UNHCR.

WHAT COUNTS AS VIOLENCE?

While the diasporic advocacy NGOs and humanitarian refugee regimes are fixated on gender affirming surgeries as torture, it is the geopolitical logic of refugee regimes, articulated through the racial and sexual order of refugee rights, that we need to study for the ways it subjects many trans refugees to violence in the name of protection. This form of violence (that is never recognized as such in standard refugee rescue narratives) can be seen in the experiences of Sohrab and Minoo, a couple that I came to know in a Turkish satellite city. Sohrab, a passing trans man who had managed to acquire top surgery as well as phalloplasty in Iran, fell in love with his co-worker, Minoo, a teacher and single mother who was going through a divorce from her previous husband in Iran. Minoo, who had not suspected that Sohrab was trans before they started dating, was also in love with Sohrab. The couple decided to get married after a couple of years of getting to know each other. Minoo's ex-husband found out that Sohrab was trans and threatened to "out" him to Minoo's family. Fearing losing custody of their child and their jobs in Iran, and not being able to make the ends meet under the harsh economic conditions there, Sohrab, Minoo, and their—then tween—son left for Turkey, hoping to find a better future in a third country of asylum.

While the UNHCR gave them their first interview relatively fast, the rest of their process was extremely slow and difficult. They were registered immediately but had to wait for eight years in Turkey before they were resettled in Canada through private sponsorship.[21] During their eight years in Turkey, Sohrab, his wife, and their son were subjected to several interviews in which the UNHCR officers cross-examined them and compared their stories. Sohrab and Minoo, who had kept Sohrab's trans identity from their son, had let the UNHCR know that they wanted to wait for their son to get older before they talked to him about Sohrab's gender. They were upset that the UNHCR officers had asked their son about his relationship to Sohrab, whether he knew why his parents were applying for asylum, and whether he was exposed to indecency or abuse. Paradoxically, Sohrab and many other transgender refugees who are compelled to provide medical documents (often issued by the Iranian state) to the UNHCR to prove the authenticity of their gender identity, are also susceptible to charges of fraud because of what is perceived to be the "concealed truth" of their gender. As Toby Beauchamp (2009) has argued, the surveillance of trans bodies is not as much about transgender identification as it is about the assumed deception underlying transgressive or nonnormative gender presentation. The assumption of deception is naturalized in UNHCR's model of cross-examining refugees in general. But precisely because trans bodies are already suspect (as bodies that conceal the "truth" of gender), the Iranian trans refugee applicants are doubly scrutinized. They face multiple obstacles in overcoming suspicion, even if the UNHCR deems them vulnerable victims of torture because of the surgery. This suspicion affected Sohrab, Minoo, and their son in devastating ways.[22]

Sohrab's phalloplasty surgery (which he had in Iran) developed complications, causing him physical discomfort in his groin area. He needed to have another surgical procedure to treat the pain. Like many asylum applicants, Sohrab preferred not to seek medical and mental health services through UNHCR referral, because the UN-referred professionals report the results of refugees' health condition back to the agency. The UNHCR, in turn, relays this information to the "third country of asylum." This often prolongs refugees' resettlement processes, as the third countries of asylum expect the refugees with health issues to receive a "reasonable" number of treatment sessions before they are allowed to enter its territory so that they do not become a "public charge."[23] Because of his pain, however, Sohrab decided he had to see a UNHCR-referred doctor. He was told by the doctor that considering what his refugee healthcare affords him in Turkey, and because Iran has better medical procedures for the particular surgery that Sohrab needed, he would have better quality medical care if he were to have the surgery in Iran. Sohrab decided to wait. Meanwhile, he was unable to get a well-paid job because most available jobs for refugee men involve heavy lifting, which Sohrab was unable to perform because of his medical condition. Minoo too had to stop working after being sexually harassed by her employers in her under-the-table jobs in the food and service industry. An employer who made an advance on her told her that she needed a "real man."

By the time the UNHCR recognized Sohrab and his family as "true refugees" and assigned them for resettlement in Canada, the Canadian government had closed its borders temporarily to non-Syrian refugees. Even as the Canadian president, Justin Trudeau posed with Syrian refugees to show Canada's benevolence toward refugees, thousands of non-Syrian refugees who were assigned for resettlement in Canada were stuck in Turkey with no answers from the UNHCR. Having waited for a long time for an interview from the Canadian embassy and desperate to leave Turkey, Sohrab and Minoo applied to change their country of asylum to the United States. Unfortunately, a few months later, Donald Trump became president. By the time the bureaucratic process of changing their resettlement country was approved, the "Muslim ban" that excluded Iranian refugees from entering the United States went into effect. Sohrab and Minoo were not able to resettle either in Canada or in the United States. The UNHCR did not respond to their requests for resettlement and marked their file as "refused to be resettled."

The story of Sohrab, Minoo, and their son encapsulates the multiple contradictions in the racial and sexual logics of the global refugee regime. While the assumptions of trans deception and the normalization of the binary of gender in refugee regimes have practically wrecked the life of Sohrab and his family, it is not just the perceived deception of the trans bodies and the suspicion of presenting a "false case" that contributed to the delay in their refugee process. Sohrab and Minoo believed that their son, a teenage Iranian boy, was treated like a criminal in UNHCR interviews. As he grew up during their long wait in Turkey, Sohrab and Minoo's son represented the dangerous masculinity of a young cis Iranian man, unworthy of asylum. Even as Sohrab's transness made him a victim of torture and worth saving for his gender and Iranian-ness, his son's gender and Iranian-ness made him into a suspect of terrorism by default. This discrepancy reveals the underlying gendered racism of refugee regimes that seem to exempt trans men from the suspicions of terrorism while attaching criminality and the fear of terrorism to cis Iranian men. As a trans man, Sohrab's victimhood is also suspect, because his transness carries with it the threat of deception. While terror and fear stick to Iranian cis men's bodies, pity, deception, and weakness are affective registers through which the bodies of trans Iranian men traverse refugee regimes. This masculinist discourse constructs trans men as neither "man enough" to be terrorists, nor "normal enough" to be good fathers. The suspicions about Sohrab's transness, assumptions about his sexual perversion and child abuse, combined with the threat that his son represented as an Iranian cis man, prolonged their interview processes, subjecting Sohrab, Minoo, and their son to a precarious life in Turkey for eight years.

The saga of Sohrab, Minoo, and their son highlights the tacit violence of the refugee regime, where sexual identities and discourses of gender-based violence and torture are mobilized to reproduce the civilizational missions of rescue that themselves rely on the neoliberal logic of private sponsorship and fluctuating geopolitical considerations.[24] Abandoned by the UNHCR and unable to resettle in Canada or the United States, Sohrab and Minoo tried to find private sponsors in Australia or Canada. Finally, they succeeded in finding a group of volunteers to sponsor them through Canada's private sponsorship program. It took almost a year of fundraising for the private sponsors to raise the required $23,000 Canadian dollars to help Sohrab, Minoo, and their son to move to Canada in 2021—only a few months before their son was legally an adult and therefore disqualified from being included in their refugee case.

SANCTIONED TORTURE

Sohrab, Minoo, and their son are among a handful of lucky refugees who are able to find private sponsorship. Many queer and trans refugees who do not receive the sympathy that a nuclear family such as Sohrab, Minoo, and their son garners continue to wait with slim prospects of finding sponsors in the highly competitive demand for private sponsorship. In fact, the situation of queer and trans refugees has worsened in recent years. In 2018, without an explanation, the UNHCR transferred the responsibility of registering and processing non-Syrian refugees to Turkey's Directorate General of Migration Management. This sudden administrative transfer of responsibility has caused many problems for all non-Syrian refugees, particularly queer and trans applicants who are discriminated against by many local offices that privilege heterosexual families.[25] In addition, the US "Muslim Ban" and the temporary suspension of non-Syrian refugee admissions in Canada meant that many refugees who had been officially recognized by the UNHCR (i.e., they "passed the test") are still waiting in Turkey for resettlement.[26] Even for Iranian queer and trans refugees, "the golden cases" who had higher acceptance rates and relatively shorter waiting periods than most refugee applicants (because they were considered to be at risk of persecution in Iran and homophobic and transphobic attacks in Turkey), the process has become increasingly long. Up until 2009, the refugee recognition and resettlement process for most Iranian queer and trans asylum seekers took anywhere from one and a half to three years. At the time of writing of this piece, some Iranian queer and trans applicants have been waiting for as long as nine years because of the UNHCR's backlog, administrative changes, and the immigration restrictions in the third countries of asylum.

The abstract category of "LGBTI REFUGEE" recuperates homogenous and prediscursive sexual identities while it reifies civilizational binaries that separate the homophobic "Third World" from the free and gay and trans-friendly "first world." This categorization does not begin to capture the living situations of queer and trans people in satellite cities in Turkey, such as the ones I met, where those marked as refugee applicants are stripped of rights in the name of rights. The geopolitical order that designates queer and trans Iranians as belonging to "a particular social group" and highlights narratives of "forced surgeries" as torture ends up effectively erasing forms of violence that subject Iranian queer and trans refugees to slow death (Berlant 2007), even as they are supposedly fast-tracked for protection by human rights regimes. The economic, environmental, and everyday violence of sanctions that subjects the Iranian population at large to death, forcing the most vulnerable segments of the Iranian population to become refugees, is effectively erased in dominant refugee accounts that divorce gender violence from its geopolitical context. As part of a geopolitical assemblage that manages life and death, the international refugee regime justifies its own violence through authorizing the definition of violence or violation of rights, assigning violation and protection roles according to the colonial logic, and by reducing the purview of violence to the state, thus exonerating "nongovernmental" entities by assuming the violating/violent state to have monopoly over violence. To reduce transgender Iranians to survivors of torture is not just a violent masquerade that attempts to hide the slow death of millions of Iranians under the deadly sanctions (especially during the COVID-19 pandemic). It is a disservice to working-class Iranian trans refugees in Turkey whose everyday struggles for survival under the "protection" of refugee regimes is overshadowed by a single narrative of torture. Considering that many refugees characterize waiting indefinitely in the sluggish tempo of refugee processing zones as torture, and knowing that many Iranians describe living under the deadly sanctions as torture, is it not accurate to say that both sanctions and indefinite waiting in refugee processing zones are sanctioned torture, the survivors of which will never be recognized as such by the refugee regimes?

NOTES

1   From the UNHCR web page, "Who Is a Refugee?" https://www.unrefugees.org/refugee-facts/what-is-a-refugee/.

2   For disposability of queer life in relationship to geopolitics, see *Queer Necropolitics* (Haritaworn, Kuntsman, and Posocco 2014).

3   For example, as Lila Abu-Lughod (2011) has asked, why is intimate violence labeled as "honor killing"—and only discussed through reductive cultural explanations—when it is comes to the Middle East, but considered domestic violence" when it happens in Europe and North America? Christine Walley (1997) asks a similar question in discussing exceptionalism in relation to female genital operations.

4   For literature on Israeli pinkwashing see works by Karma Chávez and Ghadir Shafie (2019), Maya Mikdashi (2011), and Jasbir Puar (2007), among others.

5   The emerging scholarship on gender and refugee regimes is challenging the dominant refugee discourses and the neoliberal humanitarianism frameworks. This includes works by, among others, Emina Buzinkic (2020), Nithya Rajan (2019), and Laura Charney (2021).

6   According to the UNHCR, in 2010, Afghan and Iraqi refugees accounted for almost half of all refugees under UNHCR's responsibility worldwide, while "three out of ten refugees in the world were from Afghanistan" (UNHCR 2010).

7   Even though P5+1 (The UN Security Council's five permanent members—China, France, Russia, the United Kingdom, and the United States—plus Germany) signed the "Iran Deal" in 2015, a slew of US sanctions remained in place. In 2018, Trump signed an executive order that reversed Obama's nuclear agreement with Iran. Trump's order required that the harsh sanctions be reimposed within 90–180 days.

8   For a detailed list of the restrictions, see the U.S. Department of State web page, "Iran Sanctions": https://www.state.gov/iran-sanctions/.

9   See *Politics of Rightful Killing* (Shakhsari 2020b) on how sanctions kill "softly" in the name of rights (as opposed to the manner described as "shock and awe").

10 As Human Rights Watch reported in April 2020, "the definition of drugs under US export regulations—which includes prescription and over-the-counter medicines and medical devices—excludes certain vaccines, biological and chemical products, and medical devices—including medical supplies, instruments, equipment, equipped ambulances, institutional washing machines for sterilization, and vehicles carrying medical testing equipment. This means that some of the equipment crucial to fighting the virus, such as decontamination equipment, and full-mask respirators, require a special license."

11 It would be interesting to see how the United States and the UNHCR will change their policy toward Afghan refugees after the resurgence of the Taliban in what is now called the Islamic Emirate of Afghanistan.

12 *Kimlik* cards used to cost almost US $200. In 2015, the laws changed, and asylum seekers did not have to pay out of pocket for their *kimlik*. Yet many queer and trans refugees have not been able to access healthcare or affordable medicine, despite having *kimlik*.

13 While I was able to establish a working relationship with an officer (a gay man

who, unlike many officers, was sympathetic to queer and trans cases), the UNHCR stopped responding to my advocacy emails when the numbers of refugee cases increased exponentially.

14   While the UNHCR's attention to trans people resulted in faster interviews with some trans applicants by the UNHCR, many trans people have waited in Turkey for as long as nine years. There seems to be no accountable organization that advocates for the refugees. KAOS GL, one of the few NGOs that has a working relationship with the UNHCR, claims that once the file is sent to the embassy of the "third country of asylum," it can no longer advocate for refugees.

15   Asylum seekers are not legally allowed to work in Turkey. However, because they have to pay for their own expenses, most people work illegally in the food industry, sweatshops, textile factories, beauty salons, and construction, among other industries. Much like other states, the Turkish state turns a blind eye to undocumented workers because they provide cheap labor. Many people I interviewed complained about their employers (either Turkish or Iranian middlemen who ran sweatshops) withholding their wages or sexually harassing them.

16   The harsh living conditions for many queer and trans refugees and the long and uncertain waiting period without access to affordable healthcare, the right to work, and affordable housing, have resulted in increasing numbers of suicides and health-related deaths among queer and trans refugees in Turkey. These deaths often go unnoticed and do not make it into official records or the news (Shakhsari 2014).

17   For example, see the Human Rights Watch (2010) report: "We Are a Buried Generation: Discrimination and Violence against Sexual Minorities in Iran."

18   See page 26 of the JFI report, for example.

19   For examples of the "regret" narratives see Rod Dreher's 2018 article in *The American Conservative*, "The Coming Trans Medical Backlash" and Walt Heyer's 2016 article in *The Federalist*, "Pushing Kids into Transgenderism Is Medical Malpractice."

20   Examples of malpractice, denial of medical service to trans individuals, and forced sterilizations of intersex people in North America and Europe abound. For a few examples see Worriedmom (2019); Dobner (2017); Fowler (2017); Anarte (2019); Kang (2016); and Human Rights Watch (2017).

21   When I wrote the first draft of this chapter, Sohrab, Minoo, and their son were still not sure when and where they would be resettled. After eight years of waiting in Turkey, and with the help of a group of private sponsors, they finally raised enough money to move to Canada in 2021.

22   Sohrab is not the only trans man who has had to prove the truth of his gender to the UNHCR officers and the third country of asylum. As I have written elsewhere (Shakhsari 2014), the Iranian state has significantly reduced the subsidy for gender affirming surgeries since the sanctions devastated Iran's economy. Showing me his notarized Iranian medical and psychological evaluation re-

cords that identifies him by the Iranian state as a person with "gender identity disorder," Sahand, a trans man living in Denizli who could not afford surgery in Iran, told me, "They only gave me a 2.5 [million] Toman loan which was barely enough for my hysterectomy and ovariectomy." Sahand, who used expired testosterone that he had brought from Iran and had a full beard, would bind his chest tightly to pass at the construction site where he worked. He was suspected of not being a genuine trans person by the UNHCR officer who interviewed him in his first interview. Being constantly subjected to suspicion as both refugee and trans makes passing an ironic reality of queer and trans refugee applicants in Turkey. The term used when one is recognized as a refugee by the UNHCR is "ghabool shodam" ("I was accepted" or "I passed the exam"). Passing the test of being transgender according to the UNHCR standards and passing as straight and cisgender at work or in public in Turkey are both forms of survival for trans refugees who are subjected to policing and surveillance on a daily basis. Many transgender women who cannot pass as cisgender face hostility and violence from Turkish society while seemingly under the protection of UNHCR. Because most employers discriminate against trans women, sex work is a common viable option. Because of the criminalization of sex work, many trans women who are subjected to rape and domestic violence do not report the violence they experience either to the Turkish police or to the UNHCR, as they fear being deported or rejected for engaging in prostitution.

23 The UNHCR randomly orders medical and psychological evaluation by "experts" for some queer and trans refugee applicants. A UNHCR staff member told me that many Iranian queer and trans refugees suffer from mental health issues and depression because of the trauma that they have suffered in Iran. Trauma, explained through the juxtaposition of an abusive past against a future of freedom, becomes the impetus for psychological evaluations. These evaluations become another barrier to resettlement of queer and trans refugees, who when diagnosed with trauma-related mental illness, are barred from entering the borders of the third country of asylum until they are "corrected" and ready for a trauma-free life (Shakhsari 2014).

24 I have argued elsewhere (Shakhsari 2020a) that deployments of "queer kinship" in private refugee sponsorship programs, wherein white, middle-class citizens of the United States, Canada, or Europe adopt queer and trans refugees as their "own," inevitably rely on colonial relations of dependency and rescue and neoliberal notions of freedom. Private refugee sponsorships programs are perhaps where the right-seeking benevolence of queer liberals and the restrictive measures of the state in the form of immigration laws come to a comfortable coexistence through the colonial legacies of rescue that depend on narrations of misery. At the same time, these forms of sponsorship are the only way out for queer and trans refugees who are left with no choice but to find their own private sponsors.

25 For the obstacles that Afghan refugees face after the 2018 changes see Leghtas and Thea (2018).

26 For an excellent account of queer and trans refugees "waiting" in Turkey, see Elif Sari's (2020) dissertation, "Waiting in Transit: The Sexuality of (Im)Mobility and Iranian LGBTQ Refugees in Turkey."

REFERENCES

Abu-Lughod, Lila. 2011. "Seductions of the 'Honor Crime.'" *differences* 22, no. 1: 17–63. https://doi.org/10.1215/10407391-1218238.

Abu-Lughod, Lila. 2013. *Do Muslim Women Need Saving?* Cambridge, MA: Harvard University Press.

Allouche, Sabiha. 2017. "(Dis)-Intersecting Intersectionality in the Time of Queer Syrian-Refugee-ness in Lebanon." *Kohl: A Journal for Body and Gender Research* 3, no. 1: 59–77. https://kohljournal.press/dis-intersecting-intersectionality.

Anarte, Enrique. 2019. "Transgender Germans Demand Compensation for Sterilization." *Reuters*, December 31. https://www.reuters.com/article/us-germany-lgbt-rights-feature-trfn/transgender-germans-demand-compensation-for-sterilization-idUSKBN1YZ0YF.

Anker, Deborah E. 2005. "Refugee Law, Gender and the Human Rights Paradigm." In *Passing Lines: Sexuality and Immigration*, edited by Brad Epps. Cambridge, MA: Harvard University Press.

Beauchamp, Toby. 2009. "Artful Concealment and Strategic Visibility: Transgender Bodies and U.S. State Surveillance After 9/11." *Surveillance and Society* 6, no. 4: 356–66. https://doi.org/10.24908/ss.v6i4.3267.

Berlant, Lauren. 2007. "Slow Death (Sovereignty, Obesity, Lateral Agency)." *Critical Inquiry* 33, no. 4: 754–80. https://doi.org/10.1086/521568.

Buzinkic, Emina. 2020. "Pushback as a Technology of Crimmigration." In *Causes and Consequences of Migrant Criminalization*, edited by Neža Kogovšek Šalamon, 157–70. New York: Springer.

Canadian Council for Refugees. n.d. "Most refugees are in the Global South." https://ccrweb.ca/en/most-refugees-are-global-south.

Charney, Laura. 2021. "Mapping Gender Violence along the Balkan Route: Humanitarian Assemblages, Securitization Policies, and the Experiences of Women Refugees and Migrants." Rapoport Center Human Rights Working Paper Series: The Bernard and Audre Rapoport Center for Human Rights and Justice at The University of Texas School of Law. https://law.utexas.edu/humanrights/projects/mapping-gender-violence-along-the-balkan-route-humanitarian-assemblages-securitization-policies-and-the-experiences-of-women-refugees-and-migrants/.

Chávez, Karma, and Ghadir Shafie. 2019. "Pinkwashing and the Boycott, Divestment, and Sanctions Campaign." *Journal of Civil and Human Rights* 5, no. 5: 32–48. Special issue: Palestine on the Air. https://doi.org/10.5406/jcivihumarigh.2019.0032.

Colvin, Ross. 2010. "Obama Says New U.S. Sanctions on Iran Toughest Ever." *Reuters*,

July 1. https://www.reuters.com/article/us-obama-iran/obama-says-new-u-s-sanctions-on-iran-toughest-ever-idUSTRE66001Z20100702.

Dobner, Jennifer. 2017. "Transgender Patient Files Malpractice Suit against Utah Physician Who Removed Their Ovaries." *The Salt Lake Tribune*, August 1. https://www.sltrib.com/news/politics/2017/07/30/transgender-patient-files-malpractice-suit-against-utah-physician-who-removed-their-ovaries/.

Dreher, Rod. 2018. "The Coming Trans Medical Backlash." *The American Conservative*, March 28. https://www.theamericanconservative.com/the-coming-trans-medical-backlash/.

Erdbrink, Thomas. 2012. "Iran Sanctions Take Unexpected Toll on Medical Imports." *New York Times*, November 2. http://www.nytimes.com/2012/11/03/world/middleeast/iran-sanctions-take-toll-on-medical-imports.html?pagewanted=all&_r=0.

Fortier, Anne-Marie. 2001. "'Coming Home': Queer Migrations and Multiple Evocations of Home." *European Journal of Cultural Studies* 4, no. 4: 405–24. https://doi.org/10.1177/136754940100400403.

Fowler, Lilly. 2017. "New Lawsuit: Local Hospital Denied Surgery to Trans Patient." *Crosscut*, December 21. https://crosscut.com/2017/12/providence-hospital-catholic-denies-transgender-patient-surgery-aclu-lawsuit.

Grewal, Inderpal. 2005. *Transnational America: Feminisms, Diasporas, Neoliberalisms*. Durham, NC: Duke University Press.

Haritaworn, Jin, Adi Kuntsman, and Silvia Posocco, eds. 2014. *Queer Necropolitics*. Abingdon, UK: Routledge.

Heyer, Walt. 2016. "Pushing Kids into Transgenderism Is Medical Malpractice." *Federalist*, September 21. https://thefederalist.com/2016/09/21/pushing-kids-transgenderism-medical-malpractice/.

Human Rights Watch. 2010. "We Are a Buried Generation: Discrimination and Violence Against Sexual Minorities in Iran." New York: Human Rights Watch. https://www.hrw.org/sites/default/files/reports/iran1210webwcover_1.pdf.

Human Rights Watch. 2017. "I Want to Be Like Nature Made Me: Medically Unnecessary Surgeries on Intersex Children in the US." New York: Human Rights Watch. https://www.hrw.org/report/2017/07/25/i-want-be-nature-made-me/medically-unnecessary-surgeries-intersex-children-us.

Human Rights Watch. 2020. "US: Ease Sanctions on Iran in COVID-19 Crisis." hrw.org, April 6. https://www.hrw.org/news/2020/04/06/us-ease-sanctions-iran-covid-19-crisis.

Justice for Iran and 6Rang. 2014. *Diagnosing Identities, Wounding-Bodies: Medical Abuses and Other Human Rights Violations against Lesbian, Gay and Transgender People in Iran*. Germany: Justice for Iran (JFI) and Iranian Lesbian and Transgender Network (6Rang). https://justice4iran.org/wp-content/uploads/2014/06/Pathologizing-Identities-Paralyzing-Bodies.pdf.

Kang, Akhil. 2016. "Sustaining Trans Individuals' Claims to Medical Negligence."

Jurist Legal News and Commentary, March 8. https://www.jurist.org/commentary/2016/03/akhil-kang-transgender-rights/.

Kauanui, J. Kēhaulani. 2018. *Paradoxes of Hawaiian Sovereignty: Land, Sex, and the Colonial Politics of State Nationalism*. Durham, NC: Duke University Press.

Lavers, Michael K. 2014. "Iran a 'Paradox' for LGBTs." *Washington Blade,* June 19. https://www.washingtonblade.com/2014/06/19/iran-paradox-lgbts/.

Leghtas, Izza, and Jessica Thea. 2018. "You Cannot Exist in This Place: Lack of Registration Denies Afghan Refugees Protection in Turkey." *Refugees International*, December 13. https://www.refugeesinternational.org/reports/2018/12/13/you-cannot-exist-in-this-place-lack-of-registration-denies-afghan-refugees-protection-in-turkey.

Luibhéid, Eithne. 2008. "Queer/Migration: An Unruly Body of Scholarship." *GLQ: A Journal of Lesbian and Gay Studies* 14, nos. 2–3: 169–90. https://doi.org/10.1215/10642684-2007-029.

Massad, Joseph A. 2008. *Desiring Arabs*. Chicago: University of Chicago Press.

Mikdashi, Maya. 2011. "Gay Rights as Human Rights: Pinkwashing Homonationalism. *Jadaliyya*, December 16. https://www.jadaliyya.com/Details/24855.

Moallem, Minoo. 2005. *Between Warrior Brother and Veiled Sister: Islamic Fundamentalism and the Politics of Patriarchy in Iran*. Berkeley: University of California Press.

Morgensen, Scott. 2011. *Spaces between Us: Queer Settler Colonialism and Indigenous Decolonization*. Minneapolis: University of Minnesota Press.

Najmabadi, Afsaneh. 2013. *Professing Selves: Transsexuality and Same-Sex Desire in Contemporary Iran*. Durham, NC: Duke University Press.

Organization for Refuge, Asylum and Migration (ORAM). 2011. *Unsafe Haven: The Security Challenges Facing Lesbian, Gay, Bisexual and Transgender Asylum Seekers in Turkey (Updated edition)*. Istanbul: Helsinki Citizens' Assembly—Turkey and San Francisco: ORAM—Organization for Refugee, Asylum and Migration. https://www.refworld.org/docid/524c114f4.html.

Nguyen, Mimi Thi. 2012. *The Gift of Freedom: War, Debt, and Other Refugee Passages*. Durham, NC: Duke University Press.

Puar, Jasbir K. 2007. *Terrorist Assemblages: Homonationalism in Queer Times*. Durham, NC: Duke University Press.

Rajan, Nithya. 2019. "What Do Refugees Want? Reading Refugee Lip-Sewing Protests through a Critical Lens." *International Feminist Journal of Politics* 21, no. 4: 527–43. https://doi.org/10.1080/14616742.2019.1638811.

Razack, Sherene. 1998. *Looking White People in the Eye: Gender, Race, and Culture in Courtrooms and Classrooms*. Toronto: University of Toronto Press.

Sari, Elif. 2020. "Waiting in Transit: The Sexuality of (Im)Mobility and Iranian LGBTQ Refugees in Turkey." PhD diss., Cornell University.

Shakhsari, Sima. 2014. "The Queer Time of Death: Temporality, Geopolitics, and Refugee Rights." *Sexualities* 17, no. 8: 998–1015.

Shakhsari, Sima. 2020a. "Displacing Queer Refugee Epistemologies: Dreams of Trespass, Queer Kinship, and Politics of Miseration." *Arab Studies Journal* 28, no. 2: 108–33.

Shakhsari, Sima. 2020b. *Politics of Rightful Killing: Civil Society, Gender, and Sexuality in Weblogistan*. Durham, NC: Duke University Press.

Somerville, Siobhan B. 2000. *Queering the Color Line: Race and the Invention of Homosexuality in American Culture*. Durham, NC: Duke University Press.

Soroush, Nazanin, and Kaveh Madani. 2014. "Every Breath You Take: The Environmental Consequences of Iran Sanctions." *The Guardian*, November 21. https://www.theguardian.com/world/iran-blog/2014/nov/21/iran-environmental-consequences-of-sanctions.

UNHCR. 2010. "Global Trends, 2010." https://www.unhcr.org/4dfa11499.pdf.

UNHCR. 2019. "UNHCR Operations Worldwide: Turkey." http://reporting.unhcr.org/node/2544?y=2020#year.

UNHCR. n.d. "Islamic Republic of Iran." Accessed January 15, 2022. https://www.unhcr.org/en-us/islamic-republic-of-iran.html.

US Department of State. n.d. "Iran Sanctions." Accessed August 23, 2021. https://www.state.gov/iran-sanctions/.

Volpp, Leti. 2006. "Disappearing Acts: On Gendered Violence, Pathological Cultures, and Civil Society," *PMLA: Publication of the Modern Language Association of America* 121, no. 5: 1631–38. https://www.jstor.org/stable/25501636.

Walley, Christine. 1997. "Searching for 'Voices': Feminism, Anthropology, and the Global Debate over Female Genital Operations." *Cultural Anthropology* 12, no. 3: 405–38. https://www.jstor.org/stable/656558.

Worriedmom. 2019. "Catching Up with Renowned Phalloplasty Surgeon, Dr. Curtis Crane." *4thwavenow*, August 26. https://4thwavenow.com/tag/transgender-malpractice/.

IV MEDIA FRAMES

TWELVE · *Rafia Zakaria*

Weaponized Bodies

Female Genital Cutting and
Immigrant Exclusion

When it comes to female genital cutting (FGC), there is just one kind of story that is deemed permissible for publication. That story follows a clear moral arc: there are the perpetrators, puppets whose actions are dictated by arcane religious and cultural mores; there is the victim, generally helpless; and finally there are the heroes—the activists, state officials, and whoever else steps in to stop the practice. Over the years, as more and more campaigns against FGC have emerged, this narrative has remained the same, never complicated or questioned or even critically assessed. I have chosen to use the term *female genital cutting* intentionally because I believe that it is more descriptive and accurate than *female genital mutilation*, given the range of cuts or excisions that are performed.

It's a status quo that I have tried to disrupt with little success. The subject is a delicate one. The indictment of certain cultural practices like FGC, coupled with the efforts of gender rights groups and even governments to quash them, makes for a powder keg that editors shy away from. I know this, because I have tried. One common reaction to my efforts is a skepticism about my own allegiances. I am, after all, a brown woman and even though I come from a cultural context that does not prescribe FGC, my very inclination to question how policing against this form of gender violence can become a means of racial and cultural profiling renders me somewhat suspect in the eyes of some of the gatekeepers of US journalism. It is almost as if they have decided that there is a whiff of complicity about me, one that is too disruptive to the existing narrative about FGC.

It is a pity, this refusal. The moral arrangement of the various characters involved in FGC, while pleasing Western readers and editors in suggesting that "something *is* being done," also creates a cover of sorts for bad actors, states, militias, or whoever else uses the cover of fighting FGC for other kinds of surveillance and profiling. The existing arrangement of moral actors in the FGC narrative, from the bad perpetrators driven by a barbaric culture and the good activists ensuring that young bodies are not mutilated, is thus extracted and kept separate from the larger issue of the treatment of Black and brown female bodies by the very state forces that claim to be fighting FGC. The zealotry of anti-FGC programs in this sense stands in contrast to the acquiescence to exclusion of the same Black and brown bodies caged and refused entry into European states and the United States. Nor can the issue be juxtaposed against other mutilations, one example being the forced hysterectomies alleged by fifty-seven women in US Immigration and Customs Enforcement (ICE) facilities (Chapin 2020). Similarly, no connection can be drawn to the policing of Black girls' bodies in American schools where they are six times more likely to be given a school suspension for minor dress code violations (Rhor 2019) or in everyday life where Black girls as young as five are subjected to humiliations by police officers (Ritchie 2017).

I was almost able to tell this story and to put these violations of Black and brown bodies that get little attention—perpetrated as they are by white and Western men and women—up against the enthusiasm to police these bodies to ensure that their labias remained intact. The editor who almost permitted me to tell it was female and white and around my own age. We had a long conversation in a Washington, DC, coffee shop (prior to COVID-19) on the topic. In the discussion I emphasized the need to connect FGC to other forms of violence enacted upon the bodies of Black and brown women.

I walked away that day with a commission to write a piece. In the essay, as we had agreed, I would talk about the use of anti-FGC policing as a means of racial profiling and intimidation of migrants who feared a forced examination of their genitalia. I finished the draft two or three days after I left DC. Triumphant that I had finally found an editor who would trust me to write this piece, I sent the draft to her with an email laden with gushing gratitude.

Then there was nothing. One, then two, then three days passed, then a week and then ten days. Finally, I decided I should send an email asking her whether she had had the chance to read the piece. I spent two hours on this email, making sure that it hit just the right notes. Then on the eleventh day I sent it. Within twenty-four hours my fear was confirmed. She had read the piece and she liked it, but she had shown it to a senior editor, an older white woman. This woman, with whom I had never worked, had a visceral reaction to the piece. She did not want the magazine to be used as a platform for questioning the brutality of FGC and suggesting, through what she read as a thinly disguised argument, that it was just not that bad. They would not be publishing the piece, but they would pay me a kill-fee to compensate for the time that I had spent on it. I was told that I should feel free to take the piece to another publication.

I have tried many other publications to no avail. In each case I have been confronted with some version of the events that I recounted above. FGC, I was being told in so many words and rejections, was an untouchable topic. Its tricky parameters were off limits. There was just no point in running an essay that sought to raise questions, complicate, or assess critically, this particular form of gender violence.

This chapter has grown out of my frustration with the gatekeepers of the American media establishment. It attempts to place FGC procedures and policing within the larger context of the policing of Black and brown women by state authorities and also by the transnational feminist organizations allied with those states. I hope that the story I tell here reveals the problems with insulating the question of FGC from the processes of discussion and critique and the complicity of American mainstream media in silencing those who would broaden the frame.

CRIMINALIZING FGC, DENATURALIZING CITIZENS

I was surprised when I first saw Dr. Jumana Nagarwala's picture in the *New York Times* in the spring of 2017. It is an image from the website of her workplace, a Detroit hospital. In it, she smiles at the camera, and the pastel blue of her special Bohra head covering is visible, tied securely under her chin. I recognized it from my childhood in Karachi when I had neighbors who wore Dawoodi Bohras. I had come know, and in many ways envy, the Bohri girls I went to school with. They were encouraged to work outside the home — their mothers and aunts and sisters all did. And there were other, even more coveted freedoms. While I was cloistered and forbidden to even talk to boys, they faced few such restrictions. Male and female contact did not ruffle feathers; it seemed, instead, a matter of course. Compared to the rest of Pakistan, Muslims belonging to the Bohra community, a small Shiite sect, were considered liberal and progressive.

The headline in the *New York Times* read, "Michigan Doctor is Accused of Genital Cutting of 2 Girls."[1] Most of the information in the article was derived from a complaint filed against Nagarwala by the federal government. Nagarwala, an emergency room physician in Detroit, had allegedly performed a "genital cutting" procedure on two seven-year-old girls. The ritual is said to have originated in the teachings of the Bohra community, whose current leader, Syedna Muffadal Saifuddin, has endorsed the practice (though has also urged diaspora Bohras to abide by the law of the land) (Chandran 2016). Beyond the community, the practice is not prevalent in South Asia. Indeed, I had never heard of it until I migrated to the West.

The details in Nagarwala's indictment are chilling.[2] In February 2017, the two girls were spirited away by their parents from their homes in Minnesota to a hotel in Michigan. There, an evening trip to the doctor was explained to the girls as a way to ease a tummy ache. And then, the dark crime itself—FGC, carried out by a female doctor while the girls lay on an examination table. The evidence of the crime is on their bodies. The news caused an uproar. In an America with whetted appetites for hating Muslims, here were more reasons. Representatives of Muslim organizations, when they did get a chance to appear on cable television, underscored the truth that FGC has nothing to do with Islam, and is not supported by any religious directive. It was a cultural and not a religious practice, they emphasized earnestly.

Hardly anyone seemed to notice the difference. Here was a doctor entrusted with health and healing now committing a criminal act on minors, subjecting them to a human rights violation. Nagarwala was charged, taken into custody, jailed, and denied bail. She posed a flight risk, the judge said; prosecutors agreed, calling her "a danger to the public." It took five months, after members of her community posted a $4.5 million bond (assembled from real estate holdings), before she was released and confined to home detention.

When I read about the incident, I was perplexed. It seemed unfathomable that this kindly looking doctor had carried out a procedure that is known to be cruel and torturous. At the same time, I wondered about Nagarwala and her motivations: could a woman from a progressive community be the enforcer of such a practice? My hesitation did not center on the practice itself, but on the furor around it. Was the dread and revulsion that feminists—myself included—feel against FGC being deployed to justify Islamophobia? In an America where Muslims have an entrenched position as the devils within, and in a broader Western world where veils are banned and burkinis are forcibly removed, do anti-FGC campaigns provide cover for yet another invasion of the bodies of Muslim women?

Two months after Nagarwala was released on bail, Donald J. Trump was elected president. Before long, he enacted what was first called the *Muslim ban* (see Volpp, this volume) but has since become known as the *travel ban*. It did not apply to India and Pakistan, where most of the Bohra community lives, but it did apply to African countries such as Somalia and Sudan, countries where FGC is practiced.

The ban was an early prognostication of a transformation that would be largely invisible. Rule by rule, the Trump administration, under the aegis of self-appointed immigration czar Stephen Miller, began to meticulously throttle the country's immigration system in ways that ensured that Black and brown immigrants in particular could be excluded or banished. Theirs was a diabolical recipe, one that made use of swift and subtle rule changes and executive orders that required neither debate nor legislative action.

According to a report issued by the Migration Policy Institute, the last three months of 2017 saw 39,000 arrests by ICE (a 43 percent increase over the same period in the prior year) (Capps et al. 2018). The administration cut refugee admissions by half from the already dire 110,000 limit the Obama administration had implemented. Then there were the little changes that meant big reductions in the number of legal visa applicants, such as an executive order expanding in-person interview requirements, a process that would be sure to slow things down. Consular visa officials were ordered (via a rule change) to demand increasing amounts of evidence—including extensive travel history and usernames to social media accounts—from visa applicants as part of something called "extreme vetting." Additionally, in February 2018, the administration inaugurated the National Vetting Center, whose essence was to come up with even more onerous requirements. Through an executive order titled "Buy American and Hire American," the president also made it harder for employers to hire legal immigrants, choking the processes through which highly technical workers could obtain visas.

Perhaps more pernicious, however, were a number of "operations" whose exclusionary potential was obvious. Among them was Operation Second Look that revitalized the notion of "denaturalization," a political tool last utilized during the McCarthy era (American Immigration Law Association 2021). It grants the power to reexamine any and all applications of naturalized citizens, even from decades ago. The American citizens themselves would have no idea that they were being scrutinized until actual court proceedings were opened against them. Since these would be civil proceedings (even though their ultimate consequence would be deportation), the burden of proof required to file a complaint would be an almost woeful nothing. Even if the claim was ultimately dismissed, a naturalized citizen looking to protect his or her right to keep citizenship would have to endure the investigation and the inevitable legal costs incurred. Because these were civil and not criminal proceedings, there was no Sixth Amendment right to counsel and the level of proof required of the state was merely a preponderance of the evidence.

"We finally have a process in place to get to the bottom of all these bad cases and start denaturalizing people who should not have been naturalized in the first place," then-US Citizenship and Immigration Services (USCIS) director L. Francis Cissna said in an interview regarding the planned opening of the Los Angeles office to house Operation Second Look (Lind 2018). In addition to the people already hired, ICE later applied for additional funding of $207.6 million and permission to hire 300 more agents.

They got to work initiating denaturalization proceedings. Unsurprisingly, they chose to go after child sexual abusers, a class of people for which the general American public would have little sympathy. In late 2017, the government initiated proceedings against five sexual offenders from Mexico, Colombia, and Nigeria. The complaint alleged that the five had "concealed" their crimes on their naturalization applications because they had not confessed to crimes that had been committed before naturalization. The government, in its complaint, ignored the fact that the convictions took place *after* the naturalizations proceedings were complete.

The consequences of this last bit are particularly frightening. Any naturalized citizen convicted of a crime with any connection to something that took place prior to naturalization is under this precept vulnerable to losing citizenship. In effect, a different standard is created between naturalized and native-born citizens, where the latter can accept guilty plea deals for alleged crimes, while naturalized citizens would risk losing citizenship if they did the same thing.

That the denaturalization program insidiously expands the breadth of legal exclusion of brown and Black people is evident, but in Trump's America, it did not stop there. In a political milieu that bartered in Islamophobia, FGC was harnessed as another pretext to justify further intrusions.

INTRUSIVE SURVEILLANCE

Operation Limelight, launched by ICE in the summer of 2018, was one of these. Designed by the Homeland Security Investigation's (HSI) Human Rights Violators and War Crimes Center, Operation Limelight seeks to "bring awareness to FGC and deter its practice by educating the public about the risks and penalties associated with it."[3] "What has been and continues to be a traumatic ritual for some, is in fact a codified human rights violation," said one male agent from the HSI program at Washington Dulles airport. "Enforcement is a key piece here," said another male agent who was a part of the program's initiation at JFK and Newark airports.

Other than these bits, scant information is available about Operation Limelight. The USCIS provides meager information regarding the public health dimensions of FGC or any plans to develop (as has been done in the UK) an accompanying public health initiative. According to the ICE press release, agents who have received FGC-related training were (and likely will be again if Republicans gain control of the House and Senate in 2022) stationed at large airports, where they select individuals from "high risk" countries to accost and then provide with "informational brochures" about FGC, with the intention of deterring them from carrying out "vacation cutting" (taking girls to receive the procedure in countries where it is legal). In another press release, the modus operandi seemed a bit clearer: "Agents engaged approximately 700 individuals in the international terminal destined for Dubai, Addis Ababa, Ethiopia, Cairo, and San Salvador. Approximately 40% of passengers were traveling with children. Flight crew and airline employees in the international areas were also provided materials for additional outreach."

Taken alone, these efforts seem well-intentioned and even valiant. However, considered under a regime where immigrants from certain countries are increasingly being shut out, they are another possible weapon of exclusion. The unclear nature of who is targeted to receive information about FGC serves to conceal what information is being gathered prior to targeting passengers and whether crude racial profiling is in operation. Nor is there any consideration of the fact that being accosted by an ICE officer at an airport creates the very rational impression that the exchange is part of some interrogatory effort rather than related to public health and safety. Even though the Trump administration has ended, the Biden administration has not (in the case of Operation Limelight) made any announcement regarding the program's present or future. The impact of COVID-19 and the implementation of disease-related controls may also have had an impact on the program's status.

This convenient lack of clarity around whether the people who were accosted under the banner of Operational Limelight are being educated or surveilled is replicated in the way the number of women and girls at risk of FGC in the United States was tabulated. The statistics, which were referenced in the press statements about the initiation of Operation Limelight, all originate in a 2016 paper by Goldberg et al. titled "Female Genital Mutilation/Cutting in the United States: Updated Estimates of Women and Girls at Risk, 2012." The paper takes the number of female immigrants from various African and Middle Eastern countries and multiplies it with the rates of FGC prevalent in those countries to conclude that the risk of FGC in the United States had increased threefold since 1990, with over half a million women and girls at risk.

The paper, popularized by the Trump administration but compiled by the CDC under President Obama's administration, presents FGC as a kind of impervious issue. Undoubtedly, underscoring the egregiousness of the crime has led to a moral impunity attached to those who campaign and advocate against it. A stark moral binary is created and FGC is branded a "cultural" crime. The effect is that whole cultures are rendered suspect, possible supporters of barbaric practices, unless they loudly declare their allegiance to programs and efforts to eliminate it from their communities. Their signing on to these campaigns in turn legitimizes the premise that their culture is indeed barbaric, and that they need external and international assistance to make it less so. Enter the good actors, the saviors.

The fact that these programs are not community generated or directed means that the level of intrusion that is considered acceptable in policing against FGC is never passed through any sort of community consensus, let alone consent. Anyone who is Muslim or Black or brown or Somali, who may critique this sort of airport thuggery by ICE officials allegedly "protecting" the genitalia of brown and Black girls, is automatically tossed into the pile of secret supporters of the practice. Since the culture that permits FGC is itself considered bad and community members automatically complicit unless they insist otherwise, it is only ICE agents of an increasingly white nationalist state who can do the job.

That these operations were being implemented by an administration that had otherwise shown no regard for human rights violations or the lives of Black and brown people should raise some red flags. What will young Muslim girls with parents accused of enacting FGC during a vacation to Nairobi have to do to satisfy ICE agents? Will they have to disrobe and expose their genitalia? What are the consequences for parents if they do not? What about women over the age of eighteen who choose to get the procedure? Will their naturalized fathers and mothers be prosecuted when the women see a doctor for medical treatment? Beneath these questions lie the mechanics of advocacy around FGC. If the complexities or differences in belief between various communities are not highlighted in anti-FGC campaigns, it is because nuance is the enemy of action. In order to urge action from people who belong to communities where FGC does not occur, the campaign against the practice has to be presented in black-and-white terms.

This is not itself a problem. The problems lie in the misuse of this moral binary as a smokescreen for other issues that are not in fact black-and-white. In this particular case, that means attaching FGC to unrelated intrusions into the lives and bodies of Muslim women in particular. Should the fact that some communities engage in this practice even in the United States become a vehicle for demonizing those entire communities, even made the basis for losing citizenship? It is this last point that represents a clever strategic move, a deft utilization of the cover of anti-FGC campaigns to achieve the goals of a white nationalist immigration agenda.

As the first missions of Operation Limelight were being initiated at America's airports in the summer and fall of 2018, Dr. Jumana Nagarwala's case was heading to trial. The mothers of the girls were also among the accused. In the run up to trial, federal investigators said they were considering whether Nagarwala's act could be part of a national FGC conspiracy that spanned New York, Chicago, and Los Angeles, and so they expanded their probe into those cities as well.

The hearing began in November 2018. The government accused Nagarwala of having violated a 1996 law that states that someone who "knowingly circumcises, excises, or infibulates the whole or any part of the labia majora or labia minora or clitoris of another person who has not attained the age of 18 years" is subject to a fine and/or five years in prison.[4] In addition, Nagarwala stood accused of a conspiracy to travel to other states to commit FGC over a period of twelve years.

No one was ready for the outcome. Judge Bernard Friedman of the United States District Court for the Eastern District of Michigan, presiding over the first FGC trial in the United States, ruled that the FGC law passed by Congress (coming up for scrutiny by the judicial branch for the very first time) was unconstitutional. The judge evaluated whether the Commerce Clause of the US Constitution permitted Congress to pass an anti-FGC law.

Judge Friedman determined that no, the federal government did not have the power to legislate against FGC and dismissed most of the charges against Nagarwala and the other defendants. It was up to individual states, Friedman concluded, to take up the issue as a criminal matter.

They have done just that. As of September 2019, there are seven bills pending in various state legislatures that seek to criminalize FGC (thirty-five states already have some legislation pertaining to the issue). One of the states that initiated the proceedings following the verdict in the Nagarwala case was Minnesota, home to the largest Somali population outside of Somalia. Somalia is one of the countries subject to the travel ban; it is also a country where FGC is known to have been practiced. In January 2019, the Minnesota legislature pushed forward a bill that would impose even tougher penalties on parents who inflict the procedure on their children. Mary Franson, the Republican legislator who sponsored the bill, argued that FGC is equivalent to "child endangerment such as criminal sexual conduct and assault with a deadly weapon" (McKay 2019).

Whether the passage of the Minnesota law will reduce FGC is unknown, but it will likely be successful in heaping further suspicion on the Somali-American community, justifying the constant surveillance of young Somali mothers and their children as possible perpetrators/victims of FGC. Once again, since the culture itself is considered the sole culprit, external intrusions into community health centers and other intimate places to find out which children or women may have had the procedure will likely increase, as will reporting requirements for doctors and nurses. Instead of encouraging victims to seek help, this could have a chilling effect, deterring the use of all government services. If what may have happened to daughters decades ago can lead to new prosecutions of mothers or fathers, even denaturalization and deportation, better to stay quiet and stay at home. A number of US states—Illinois to Idaho to Iowa and Kansas—have all since passed these laws.

For the Trump administration, the passage of state laws helped create a wide net that could become the pretext for thousands of exclusions. Fathers and mothers of thousands of Somali girls could be investigated, and even if they were absolved of suspicion of FGC, other tiny mistakes might emerge as grounds for denaturalization. The absolution of Somali parents then would depend on making the genitalia of young Somali girls available for inspection by federal agents. The Biden administration for its part has not pursued any prosecutions but neither has it challenged the convoluted web of immigration restrictions and anti-FGC laws that can coalesce to become the basis for excluding a vast swathe of naturalized citizens.

WHOSE VOICES?

In 1980, the Egyptian feminist, anti-FGC activist, and author Nawal El Saadawi was invited to the United Nations conference on Women in Copenhagen. Saadawi had just published the English edition of her book, *The Hidden Face of Eve: Women in the Arab World* (incorrectly translated from its Arabic title, *The Naked Face of Arab Women*), which begins with an account of her own clitoridectomy. As the scholar Amal Amireh (2000, 220–21) points out, the media coverage of the 1980 UN conference distorts Saadawi's position on the issue, portraying it as an indictment of her own culture that permits such barbarity. The coverage overlooks what Saadawi herself had written in the introduction: that she disagreed with Western feminists who insisted on focusing only on female circumcision as proof of "the unusual and barbaric oppression to which women are exposed only in African or Arab countries," leading to "a feeling of superior humanity."

It is this paradigm of superior humanity that seems to be at play forty years later in the discussion around the Nagarwala case, and it is just as detrimental to the elimination of the practice as the doctors secretly performing it. The crowds of journalists eager to cover the case and the politicians eager to capitalize on its Muslim perpetrators appear to be motivated not by the singular horror of the act but rather by the potential for celebrity that it offers, the ways in which it can be molded to fit the Islamophobic mood of the moment, justifying intervention for the greater good of improving the lesser morals of swathes of humanity. These grotesque underpinnings, and the colonial paradigm of superior humanity against "other" inhumanity that they substantiate, are another sort of mutilation, less visible but still brutal, a forced and rough seizure of humanity that appears entirely acceptable and that bears no criminal penalty.

Consider what happened to Somali-American congresswoman Ilhan Omar when she was asked to issue a condemnation of FGC. Frustrated by a question that would never be asked of other female representatives, Omar replied, "How often? Should I make a schedule? Does this have to be on repeat every five minutes?" Her response indicates how Muslim women are required to constantly talk about aspects of their culture that underscore their otherness and reify Orientalist views. Unsurprisingly, however, it was framed by many in the media as closeted support for FGC, even though Omar voted in favor of the bill to ban FGC in her own state of Minnesota (Goba 2019).

There are many anti-FGC activists within the Somali-American and Dawoodi Bohra communities who are questioning the practice and campaigning hard for an end to it. Dawoodi Bohra anti-FGC activists have formed two groups, WeSpeakOut and Sahiyo, to offer women who have undergone the procedure safe spaces to share their experiences. These organizing efforts have polarized the community and led to protests and petitions by outsiders demanding that the Indian government ban the practice. While there are Dawoodi Bohra women who accept, like many in the rest of the community, that circumcision is a religious duty incumbent on men and women, the debate within the community is reducing the secrecy around the practice. This discourse, though, has mostly only received attention in Indian and local papers, with transnational advocacy efforts reluctant to cede space to local campaigns.

Ignoring the voices of the women who are actually invested in bringing meaningful change within their community is nothing new. In the realm of international advocacy, FGC has become a panacea that justifies brutish comparisons between civilized and barbaric cultures and then relies on the contrast to render some women's bodies terrain for politics. The women advocating for change within the Dawoodi Bohra community, women who have the power to make the most impact, are drowned out by the Hollywood actresses, declared anti-Muslim celebrities like Ayaan Hirsi Ali, and ICE agents who have installed themselves as protectors-in-chief of the bodies of Black and brown women. The genitalia of Muslim women had become, in Trump's America, another battleground. The questions that remain are whether this can change with the Biden administration and if the media is willing to publish stories that raise complex questions about weaponizing women's bodies. It would also be valuable to further expose how this current formulation of the FGC issue internationally constrains feminists in developing nations to cultivate strategies that counter the violence in transformative ways.

NOTES

This chapter is adapted with permission from Rafia Zakaria, "Weaponized Bodies: Female Genital Mutilation as a Pretext for Exclusion." 2019. *Adi Magazine: Rehumanizing Policy*, Fall 2019. https://adimagazine.com/articles/weaponized-bodies/.

1   The article, written by Jacey Fortin, was published in the *New York Times* on April 13, 2017 and can be found at https://www.nytimes.com/2017/04/13/us/michigan-doctor-fgm-cutting.html.

2   Details of the case, *United States of America v. Jumana Nagarwala*, filed at the United States District Court for the Eastern District of Michigan, can be found at: https://www.justice.gov/opa/press-release/file/957381/download.

3   The ICE press release, "Special Agents Renew Efforts against Female Genital Mutilation at Dulles airport," from June 14, 2019, can be found at https://www.ice.gov/news/releases/special-agents-renew-efforts-against-female-genital-mutilation-dulles-airport.

4   The Female Genital Mutilation Act, 18 United States Code 116, is available at https://www.law.cornell.edu/uscode/text/18/116.

REFERENCES

American Immigration Law Association. 2021. "Denaturalization Efforts by USCIS." AILA Doc. No. 18072705. https://www.aila.org/advo-media/issues/all/featured-issue-denaturalization-efforts-by-uscis.

Amireh, Amal. 2000. "Framing Nawal Al Saadawi; Arab Feminism in a Transnational World." *Signs: Journal of Women in Culture and Society* 26 (1): 215–49.

Capps, Randy, Musharraf Chishti, Julia Gelatt, and Angel Ruiz Soto. 2018. "Revving Up the Deportation Machinery: Enforcement under Trump and the Pushback." *Migration Policy Institute*, May 2018. https://www.migrationpolicy.org/research/revving-deportation-machinery-under-trump-and-pushback.

Chandran, Rina. 2016. "Muslim Leader in India under Fire from Activists for Supporting FGC." *Reuters*, April 26. https://www.reuters.com/article/india-FGC-bohra-speech-idINKCN0XQ1FE.

Chapin, Angelina. 2020. "57 Migrant Women Say They Were Victims of ICE Gynaecologist." *The Cut*, October 28. https://www.thecut.com/2020/10/migrant-women-detail-medical-abuse-forced-hysterectomies.html.

Goba, Kadia. 2019. "Rep Ilhan Omar Was Asked to Condemn FGC—Again. She Was Not Happy." *Buzzfeed News*, July 23. https://www.buzzfeednews.com/article/kadiagoba/ilhan-omar-questions-muslim-american-politicians-FGC.

Goldberg, Howard, Paul Stupp, Ekwutosi Okoroh. Ghenet Becera, David Goodman, and Isabella Danel. 2016. "Female Genital Mutilation/Cutting in the United States Updated Estimates of Women and Girls at Risk 2012." *Public Health Report* 13 (2): 340–47.

Lind, Dara. 2018. "Denaturalization Explained: How the Trump Administration Can Strip Immigrants of Their Citizenship." *Vox Media*, July 18. https://www.vox.com/2018/7/18/17561538/denaturalization-citizenship-task-force-janus.

McKay, Hollie. 2019. "Minnesota Lawmaker's Push for Tougher FGC Laws Faces Opposition." *FOX News*, February 19. https://www.foxnews.com/politics/the-push-to-prosecute-parents-for-FGC-in-minnesota-proves-a-struggle-for-republican-lawmaker?fbclid=IwAR1PfOZS0-GD73_Z5ZXDU1r5xRME9dGeKy8ZIcyLjaJvo4ciKCrr8UsgXoA.

Rhor, Monica. 2019. "What Can Be Done to Stop the Criminalization of Black Girls: Rebuild the System." *USA Today*, May 14. https://www.usatoday.com/in-depth/news/2019/05/14/black-girls-school-discipline-racism-disparities-pushout-solutions/1121061001/.

Ritchie, Andrea. 2017. "How Black Women's Bodies Are Violated as Soon as They Enter School." *The Guardian*, August 17. https://www.theguardian.com/us-news/2017/aug/16/black-women-violated-us-policing-racial-profiling.

THIRTEEN · *Samira Shackle*

Breaking the Frame

The Power of Media Narratives
and the Question of Agency

In 2010, I was working as a staff writer at the *New Statesman*, a London-based political and cultural magazine. The editor liked to run "special issues" which featured articles grouped around a particular theme. I proposed an issue looking at Pakistan, and was given the opportunity to edit the package, my first major editing project. This was an issue close to my heart; I have Pakistani origins and felt strongly that the media coverage of Pakistan only ever hit a single note. Whether the article was about a fashion show or a literary festival, it was always framed by terrorism. Pakistani friends and family joked about the formula: "In a country where there are bombs, there is also fashion."

This time, my editor agreed that there was scope to look beyond the blood-and-guts coverage of terrorist violence and the overspill from the conflict in Afghanistan. I commissioned a wide range of articles—a long essay examining the geopolitics and, yes, terrorism, but also a reported piece on the Kashmiri border conflict, a short story by a prominent Pakistani writer, and a profile of the country's founder Muhammad Ali Jinnah. It was a nuanced package intended to engage thoughtfully with Pakistan's many challenges, while also dispelling stereotypes. But when it came to the presentation, things were out of my hands: after all, I was still a junior member of staff. The issue went to print with an editorial describing Pakistan as "the laboratory for world destruction" (New Statesman 2010) and a front cover featuring a cartoonish time bomb daubed with the Pakistani flag.

This was a harsh demonstration, early in my career, of the importance of framing—and the difficulty of challenging established media narratives, particularly when reporting on non-Western countries or people. In 2010, when I produced this issue, Pakistan was a big story in the British media—but it was on very clear grounds. Those grounds were that Pakistan was a nuclear power beset by terrorism and that it was an unstable ally to the West. It seemed everything had to be seen through this lens.

Around two years later, I quit my job and moved to Pakistan to work as a freelance journalist, interested in engaging more with my heritage and exploring some of these issues directly. I recall a conversation, soon after I moved, with a male British journalist who worked for an international news agency, about the incident with the *New Statesman* special issue on Pakistan. From his perspective, there was no problem with the framing my editor had chosen. He also saw no problem with writing, for instance, about a fashion show in Lahore in the context of terrorism—even though it had nothing to do with that specific fashion show—because terrorism was the thing that made Pakistan interesting. Therefore, if it wasn't for the "peg" of terrorism, the fashion show wouldn't be written about in the international media at all, and nor would a special issue of a magazine be needed.

These limiting frameworks that define the way we discuss a particular country or topic are prevalent across the media. In most countries around the world, there are huge problems with the way that the media discusses gendered violence—from the shame attached to attacks on bodily integrity, to victim-blaming language, to a lack of proper critical consideration of economic or structural contributing factors. To varying extents and of course, with some notable exceptions, this is the case domestically in countries from Pakistan to Egypt, America to the UK. When it comes to western discussions of gendered violence in the global south, these two problematic frameworks collide, compounding the issue of limited and unhelpful coverage. Patriarchal assumptions and framing devices are accompanied by a whole other set of stereotypes and frameworks about the "other," which dictate not just how we see female victims of violence, but also the male perpetrators. These might include Orientalized binaries: civilized versus barbaric, free versus oppressed, rational versus irrational. Through these lenses, Muslim women appear as a homogenous oppressed group, and Muslim men as an equally homogenous group of savages. This removes women's agency, essentializes the issue of gendered violence, and obscures proper examination of the problem and potential solutions.

The terms "violence against women" (VAW) and "gender-based violence" (GBV) are expansive, describing a whole host of behaviors that ranges from assaults on bodily integrity to economic, structural, and political violence.

These terms are employed in a broad range of settings, embedded within local, national, and global governance. As we question the uses of the terms within these frameworks and how they might enforce crude binaries or one particular way of seeing the world, another problem arises: as journalists and researchers, how can we avoid propagating patriarchal or Orientalizing frameworks in the course of carrying out research? Why does this framing matter? Is it ever useful? How can reporters working in an international context for predominantly western audiences think critically about these frameworks? And how can this critical thought then be applied practically, particularly given commercial and editorial pressures from the outlets we work for?

The way that news stories are framed and contextualized has an impact on how readers consume the information and what they judge important. A simple way of understanding basic framing devices is as "episodic" or "thematic" (Iyengar and Simon 1993). Episodic frames focus on an immediate event or incident, giving little or no information about underlying issues or context. Thematic frames focus on the bigger picture, perhaps providing statistics, expert analysis, or other information to help the reader view the story in a broader context.

When it comes to reporting stories of GBV, all over the world, the framing tends to be episodic: focusing on one particular incident of violence without explaining the context. This can end up misrepresenting the facts and glossing over the broader social issues connected to these cases. One US study examined newspaper coverage of domestic violence fatalities in 1998 in the state of Washington (Bullock and Cubert 2002). Researchers found that 70 percent of the articles omitted the nature of the relationship between victim and perpetrator, and consequently left out contextual information on patterns of abuse that occurred before the homicide. A startling 90 percent presented the cases as isolated incidents, rather than placing domestic violence in a broader context as a major, pervasive societal problem.

These frameworks around GBV collide with those that govern discussion of the Islamic world, best summed up by Edward Said's much-cited idea that the West creates and re-creates the East through binaries that imply the superiority of the West and inferiority of the East. In many media representations, Islam, Islamic practice, or Islamic culture is not diffuse, varied, and changeable, but monolithic and static. The essentialism of these representations allows an easy stereotyping—Islam is "other" in a fundamental way that allows people to be discussed in a way that non-Muslim subjects might not be. There are very clear ways that this manifests in the context of gender. A striking example was the discourse used during the "War on Terror." Take this comment from George W. Bush's farewell statement in 2009: "Afghanistan has gone from a nation where the Taliban harbored Al Qaeda and stoned women in the streets to a young democracy that is fighting terror and encouraging girls to go to school" (Bush 2009). The position of women is used as a marker of cultural progress, and sets up the world in two distinct categories: good versus evil, civilized versus barbaric.

As Lila Abu-Lughod has argued, this was not the first time that the oppression of women was used as a marker of barbarity as opposed to Western civility. In her 2002 article "Do Muslim Women Really Need Saving?," she pointed out parallels between this War on Terror narrative of "saving Afghan women" and arguments made during the British colonization of India, when stereotyped Indian men were portrayed as the cause of women's suffering and, consequently, a reason for the British to stay in India (Abu-Lughod 2002). Of course, it is highly debatable whether either the British colonization of India or the US-led invasion of Afghanistan made a positive difference to all women's lives overall. What is certain is that there is a dominant narrative that othered women—Muslim, Arab, or South Asian—are weak and in need of rescue, while othered men are barbaric and threatening.

When it comes to journalists covering GBV in the Global South or a context that is somehow other to an intended western audience, further questions about where we should place our focus come into play—primarily, the overriding international frameworks around GBV. There is an assumption that for women, GBV is always the priority violence that needs to be highlighted and treated. But in fact, in a context of war, civil unrest, or economic destitution, experiences of GBV might not be the top priority on a hierarchy of violence, as far as these individual women are concerned. There is value in considering the specifically gendered ways that conflict or economic hardship might affect women, but in a context of war or destitution, GBV is not always the lens through which women view their own experiences. By filtering their experiences exclusively through this lens, we risk creating and enforcing yet another limiting framework, along with those that dictate how journalists often talk about particular countries, or about men and women who the readership might consider to be "other."

As a journalist frequently writing about gender-related stories both in Muslim-majority countries and the UK, as well as covering issues affecting Muslim communities within the UK, I am aware that it is all too easy for the reporter to become part of the problem, and I try to be well-attuned to these deeply entrenched media narratives. Many journalists who cover the kinds of stories I do—focusing largely on the human impact of major events—talk about the motivating purpose of giving a platform to people who might not otherwise have an outlet to tell their stories, or shining a light on an underreported issue with the hope of effecting change. Yet too often reporting relies on well-established racist tropes—civilized versus barbaric, free versus oppressed—to fill in the gaps that should be filled by diligent reporting.

Perhaps inevitably, individual journalists who are concerned with these issues tend to look for individual solutions; that is, focusing on their own work and trying to make sure that their interviews are carried out in a trauma-informed and sensitive way, and that the work they produce does not perpetuate damaging stereotypes or racialized language. These efforts are worthwhile, but they do nothing to address bigger, systemic issues: difficult questions such as the choice of stories which are covered in the first place, and the broader media narratives that are established when a particular type of story is repeatedly reiterated. Journalists operate within a wider media ecosystem, with pressure from editorial desks to get particular case studies or stories; if you have been commissioned to report and write a story on VAW in a particular context, then that is what you will do, and that will be the organizing principle you apply to your research. Clearly, even for those striving to make their own work ethical and considered, there are no easy fixes.

That said, language does matter. Emphasizing that these cases involve individuals is one way of avoiding a lazy Orientalizing shorthand. This can offset the way in which the ownership of sexual crimes can become a political game, with crimes by men of certain backgrounds taken as indicative of problems with their whole community. But when it comes to focusing on individual men to offset the risk of generalizing about race or religion, one must remain aware of equally damaging frameworks that justify or normalize male violence. The research cited earlier, which studied reporting of domestic violence related fatalities in Washington State in 1998, also noted that those stories that involved a perpetrator with a high social status had a skewed focus on the perpetrator, emphasizing for instance, a doctor suddenly breaking and murdering his wife, rather than the woman he murdered (Bullock and Cubert 2002).

The study came out in 2002, but this pattern is still evident across the media, and it is particularly noticeable when it comes to violence perpetrated by white men. In July 2018 in the UK, a former councilor with the nativist right-wing political party UKIP was found guilty of murdering his wife. Most newspaper headlines led with "Ex-UKIP councilor Stephen Searle." Many also included a quote from the presiding judge, who said that Searle's wife's discovery of Searle's "act of infidelity in one way or another led to this." Another quote was widely cited from Searle's friend and former UKIP colleague Bill Mountford: "I still regard Steve as fundamentally a decent man who has found himself in circumstances beyond his control. I'm not condoning it in any way but I was very, very sad to hear of Steve's conviction. I'm well aware domestic disputes can get out of hand but I feel equally sorry for both Steve and his now deceased wife" (BBC News 2018). None of the reports made mention of a history of domestic violence, or of the fact that in the UK two women are killed every week by a current or former partner.

Connected to the need to provide context to avoid a lazy and stigmatizing othering is the question of the role of culture. A notoriously nebulous and difficult-to-define entity, "culture" is all-too-often deployed to stigmatizing effect in media coverage of gendered violence. When GBV cases involve white or Western victims and perpetrators, it tends to be posited as a problem of individuals. When it involves people of color or people from the global south, it tends to be presented as a congenital problem of their culture.

In the UK, this has been evident in some of the reporting on the story of sexual grooming gangs in cities and towns around the country. The most prominent case took place in Rotherham, where there is a large Pakistani Muslim population. The abuse was ongoing for many years, but the first convictions—and the accompanying national scandal—were in 2010. Another set of convictions took place in August 2017 in Newcastle. In both cases (and in numerous others in between), the victims were mostly white girls and the perpetrators were mostly South Asian men. A substantial proportion of the coverage has focused primarily on this fact, and on the idea that South Asian men think that white girls are sexually available and therefore treat them with contempt. Repeatedly, these harrowing stories of child abuse have been presented as a culture clash. "British Pakistani men ARE raping and exploiting white girls . . . and it's time we faced up to it," read the headline for a tabloid newspaper column written by the Labour MP for Rotherham in the aftermath of the Newcastle convictions (Champion 2017). It is likely that some South Asian men hold that view. It is also likely that some men of all races and religions are contemptuous of women and view them as sexually available. Indeed, the vast majority of convictions for child abuse in the UK are of white men, yet no generalities are drawn from this fact.

Coverage of the 2017 case in Newcastle throws these issues into stark relief. One case involved a group of Muslim men, primarily of Pakistani origin. A typical headline from the *Daily Telegraph* in December 2017 read: "Grooming gangs of Muslim men failed to integrate into British society." You wouldn't have known from the coverage, but a year earlier, a group of white men elsewhere in England had been convicted of the same crime. A typical headline from the BBC in December 2016 read: "'Evil' men raped and trafficked girls in Coventry." One set of men's actions was framed as a perfectly predictable result of their failure to integrate into society; the others—indisputably part of that society—were cast as "evil" and "sick" aberrations.

This idea has been examined in an academic context, notably in Leti Volpp's essay "Blaming Culture for Bad Behavior." Exploring how wildly depictions of early marriage vary, she writes: "When the actors involved are immigrants of color, we label behavior that we consider problematic as 'cultural,' and understand this term to mark racial or ethnic identity. Thus, we consider early marriage by a Mexican immigrant to reflect 'Mexican culture.' In contrast, when a white person commits a similar act, we view it as an isolated instance of aberrant behavior, and not as reflective of a racialized culture. Under this schema, white people are individual actors; people of color are members of groups" (Volpp 2000, 90).

This has a serious impact. In the reporting of the grooming cases, the emphasis on the clash of civilizations and of British Muslims as an enemy within obscured some of the other—hugely important—factors that led to the abuse of these girls. Most of the victims were highly vulnerable. The majority were either in the care system or in very unstable homes; the people who were supposed to be responsible for their safeguarding neglected them consistently over the course of years. Many had repeatedly reported the abuse to police and social workers, and had been disbelieved, a harsh illustration that it was not only the perpetrators who held these vulnerable, working-class girls in contempt. Very serious structural issues about how children in the care system are safeguarded (or not), and how victims of sexual violence are treated by the police, went underscrutinized as a result of the emphasis on racial politics. It would be entirely possible to acknowledge that British Asian men are disproportionately involved in this model of abuse (if indeed this is the case; as Ella Cockbain has shown [Cockbain and Tufail 2020], and as a recent Home Office report acknowledged, the data are far from conclusive), while still examining the particulars of each case and what allowed it to happen and to continue. Instead, the public has been presented with a repetitive story that relies on stereotyping and lets multiple state agencies off the hook.

Looking internationally, the same patterns can be observed. Amid the chaos of the wars in Syria and Iraq, sexual violence has been one prevalent form of violence. Much of the media coverage, particularly in 2014–2015, focused obsessively on the horrendous violence perpetrated against Yazidi women and girls who had escaped from ISIS captivity. Details sometimes bordered on the uncomfortably salacious: slave markets, forced marriages, and multiple rapes. In September 2014, a group of four academics wrote a piece for the *Washington Post* arguing that this coverage risked being counterproductive: "To scholars of sexual violence, these media narratives look typical in three related ways: They are selective and sensationalist; they obscure deeper understandings about patterns of wartime sexual violence; and they are laden with false assumptions about the causes of conflict rape" (Crawford, Hoover Green, and Parkinson 2014).

The violence against Yazidi women is an exceptionally extreme example of sexual violence. But it is not the whole story. As these scholars point out in their piece, as in any war, the "rape crisis" is complicated and is not perpetrated by any one group. In Syria, regime forces have been responsible for thousands of rapes since the conflict began in 2011. Islamist groups and rebels have also been responsible for violations. Further to this, women displaced by conflict, often left widowed or without a male guardian, face exploitation and abuse in refugee camps or host countries. The stories about ISIS sexual violence fit neatly into the box about barbarism versus civility. There is clear journalistic and moral value in covering the worst atrocities in any conflict or repressive state—but as the scholars argue in the *Washington Post*, "reports of Islamic State imprisonment and rape of Yazidi women have effectively erased more common and complex patterns." These patterns include the exploitation of Syrian refugees in Lebanon and Jordan by landlords and employers, and the trafficking of women from official refugee camps. There is a full range of issues, from abuse by regime forces, to the rape of men, to the extreme poverty of refugee populations, that are common to many conflicts around the world.

The emphasis on sexual violence against Yazidi women—in both the media and in the international community—did little to address the needs or recognize the agency of victims. Academic fieldwork with Yazidi refugees in Iraqi camps for internally displaced people suggests that western media stories sensationalized and systematically misrepresented the views of these victims of violence. A study of English-language media coverage of the Sinjar genocide concluded that one effect of the extraordinary emphasis on the physical suffering of Yazidi women was to efface and silence Yazidi men. Veronica Buffon and Christine Allison (2016, 191) note, based on interviews: "By contrast the discourse of the Yezidis themselves foregrounds the collective nature of the genocide and sets it within a historical framework of persecution and marginalisation."

Abuse might be part of an established social problem, armed conflict, or part of a community history, and reporters should seek to understand and explain that. Sometimes media identify a specific incident and focus on the tragic aspects of that particular incident—for example, the horrific case of Jyoti Singh, the young woman who died after being gang raped in Delhi in 2012. The story hit the international headlines and was recounted in graphic detail across the world's media. But the best coverage of the Delhi rape case did not just state that India is the rape capital of the world, but highlighted complex contributing factors such as skewed gender ratios in Indian cities due to decades of infant femicide, and economic conditions that have led to large populations of men becoming migrant laborers. The best coverage also emphasized the long-standing work of Indian feminists. Finding out how individuals and communities have coped with the trauma of sexual violence in the longer term, or steps that communities have taken themselves, usually adds helpful insight. This is precisely the kind of context that is often lacking in popular media coverage. Where journalists and editors do make the effort to look at broader issues and go beyond established narratives—such as the sensationalist story of "Yazidi sex slaves" as an isolated phenomenon—it can improve the quality of reporting and of information that reaches the public. But this still doesn't answer the question of which stories get covered in the first place, and whose interests they serve. How, then, can journalists who are stuck within media paradigms, carry out their work ethically, and avoid perpetuating harm? And how much difference can their efforts realistically make?

All too often, women's voices are removed from their own stories. Research by the Australian National Research Organization for Women's Safety found that less than 8 percent of stories in the Australian media about violence against women included any comment at all from survivors. A person does not cease to be an individual because they have endured something terrible: they retain their individuality and agency, and stories that do not reflect this do their subjects a disservice. When it comes to women who are Muslim or perceived as "other" in some way, this issue of the stripping away of agency, individuality, and voice is often even more noticeable.

Back in 2015, I interviewed Mandana Hendessi, the regional director for the Middle East for the NGO Women for Women International. She objected to the way that women have often been portrayed as victims. "With the Yazidi women, to some degree, I felt that their experiences were sensationalized. In none of those articles have I read anything about how they resisted. There's no mention of women trying to take things in their control. The very fact they ran away the moment they had the opportunity—that shows incredible resilience. Some self-harmed with corrosive substances on their faces to protect themselves from the men, and some shaved their eyebrows and eyelashes. But the way it has been portrayed in the media, it looks like these women had no power. Stripping them of agency removes their dignity" (Shackle 2015).

The question of agency is intimately linked to the question of the frameworks imposed on stories. Researcher Anna Salden has argued that the media focus on the spectacle of "the hurt female body" presents an "incomplete image of the actual victimhood experienced by Yazidi women." This forms a framing which distracts from the "structural and epistemic violence that was done to the community long before the current genocide, which still plays a role in the limited effort taken to restore the lives of the Yazidis" (2017, 11). The women with whom Salden spoke were concerned with getting back missing family members, including girls, but they viewed their victimhood as primarily collective, involving genocide of their community. And like refugees around the world, they highlighted the "human deprivation" they were suffering in the refugee camps themselves: inadequate food, shelter, safety, and access to healthcare. While Western media has a tendency to emphasize the atrocities committed by ISIS, these women also blamed Arab governments, their neighbors, and the "international community" that was not doing enough for them (Salden 2017, 50–59). This comes back to the question of agency: the "hurt female body" narrative erased the resilience, activism, and resistance of the Yazidi women Salden encountered in the camps.

When we, as journalists, are considering how to think critically about the media frameworks we are forced to work within and how to turn that critical thought into something productive within our own work, this question of agency is absolutely essential. In her book *Gender, Orientalism, and the "War on Terror,"* Maryam Khalid describes the mechanisms by which

Muslim women are portrayed as a homogenous oppressed group—often by journalists, scholars, or policy makers ignoring women's current and historical involvement in feminism and broader political struggles. This reinforces the assumption that people in these countries haven't evolved to the extent the West has, and places women as subjugated objects (Khalid 2017).

For decades, feminist scholars have written about women and anger, conceptualizing it as both a painful response to conditions of injustice, and as a potentially potent political force. Back in 1981, Audre Lorde wrote: "Focused with precision, it can become a powerful source of energy serving progress and change . . . useful against those oppressions, personal and institutional, which brought that anger into being" (Lorde 1981, 280). In the course of reporting on stories related to VAW, I have often heard women talk powerfully about their rage. During a trip to Iraq in 2017, I interviewed a mother and daughter from Mosul. The daughter, Aya, who was twenty, had been sold off by male family members to an ISIS official who raped her. Her mother, Shukria, had desperately sought to find her. The two women were reunited and living in a Kurdish refugee camp. Although they were in a profoundly disempowered position, I felt it was important to show their anger and the steps they had taken to obtain justice, and to that end, included this (Shackle 2018): "The uncle who sold Aya off has since been killed in an airstrike. She doesn't know what happened to the man who held her captive, but thinks he met the same fate. The mother and daughter are clear on one thing: they want justice. 'I reported the names of everyone involved—my uncles, my cousins—to the security forces,' Aya said. Shukria added, 'if I saw them again, I would not wait for the soldiers to come. I would rip their limbs off myself.'" It should be obvious that women might feel visceral rage after injustice, but this type of rage often doesn't make it through to the printed page. I think it's important to include it, but of course a single report on a single issue can only go so far in tackling deep, systemic issues.

The question of women's anger points to a broader issue about allowing women to tell their stories on their own terms. And this is not restricted to the way these stories are told in the media. Given that aid is frequently tied to GBV—with support available to GBV survivors only, for instance—some women learn that in order to access humanitarian aid or meet requirements for asylum in Western countries, they must highlight their GBV experiences in ways that are aligned with the dominant rhetoric from the international media and NGOs. There is substantial scholarship on the problematic issue of women being forced to present themselves within these dominant frames in order to access international rights or protections. Forcing women to fit their stories into these frameworks and viewing or presenting them solely as victims of GBV is another way in which their agency is undermined. Even the best media coverage, which makes efforts to emphasize women's agency and allow them to tell their stories on their own terms, can play into this and reinforce the idea that GBV is all that matters, and that it somehow exists separately from other forms of violence or hardship. The problem can begin with the way in which journalists secure access to survivors—in a conflict situation, this often happens through NGOs, who might have a particular interest in or focus on certain forms of violence—and continues through to the way in which a story is edited, headlined, and promoted to readers. From the perspective of an editorial desk or social media team, familiar narratives offer an easy way of organizing and presenting complex material. Yet this creates—or enforces—a feedback loop between media coverage, NGO work, and political priorities.

"Anyone Here Been Raped and Speaks English?" was the title of a memoir by war correspondent Edward Behr. The title referred to a question he heard another journalist shout at a group of Belgian nuns in war-ravaged Congo in the 1960s. Although today's reporters might not be so crass in their phrasing, stories of specific-types of suffering are still what many are after. In an article for the *Daily Beast* in 2015, Erbil-based lawyer and researcher Sherizaan Minwalla lambasted Western journalists for their insensitive treatment of Yazidi women and search for salacious details of sexual violence with no regard for how this affected their subjects. "Does the public's interest in knowing explicit details of sexual violence outweigh these victims' urgent need for safety and privacy? I don't think so and there are indications that victims would agree," she wrote (Minwalla 2015).

It goes without saying that journalists operate under high levels of editorial pressure to get not just a good story, but often a very particular story. However, I would argue that it is not just this, but also the othering impulse outlined above that allows western journalists who are otherwise sensitive and considerate people to throw that basic sensitivity out of the window in certain contexts. There are clear journalistic guidelines for the reporting of sexual or other gender-based violence—or, indeed, for reporting on any kind of trauma. Organizations such as the Dart Center at Columbia University produce detailed guidance on trauma-aware journalism, which is freely available for freelancers and for use in newsrooms, while many major news outlets have their own codes of practice. Reporting on any traumatic event requires special care, sensitivity, ethical consideration, and an awareness of the psychological impact of trauma. This is particularly true of sexual violence and intimate partner violence. Sexual violence is a deeply traumatic experience, and the retelling of an event can trigger a resurgence of the emotions the survivor felt during an attack. In cases where sexual violence has been used systematically during conflict, it can prompt trauma among a whole community, or trigger changes in how communities relate to themselves and others. But an inherent and sometimes overt racism is often present in mainstream foreign reporting, with subjects dehumanized by the Western reporter in pursuit of a story. During a research trip I took to Iraq in 2017, the Yazidi translator I worked with told me that she had at points refused to proceed with interviews after Western journalists abruptly asked questions such as: "How many times were you raped?" or "How did it feel when you miscarried your baby?"

When I have discussed these issues with other journalists, many agree. But some have expressed the view that it is better to cover these stories insensitively than not at all. There is also a dominant view that to question the frameworks and narratives that surround certain regions, certain communities, certain topics, is to seek to censor negative stories. After all, is it not important to cover the brutal treatment of women under ISIS? In response to criticism of coverage about sexual grooming in the United Kingdom, columnists and reporters have responded by asking: are we supposed to ignore the uncomfortable aspects of these cases? "The BBC has enraged license fee-payers by allegedly downplaying the role of Pakistani gangs in Rotherham's sex abuse scandal," read one tabloid article in 2014 (De Graff 2014).

I've heard similar arguments made about gender-based oppression in the international context. Journalists sometimes feel that they are stuck between a rock and a hard place: cover stories about gender-based violence and risk being accused of sensationalizing or using racist tropes. Don't cover them and you are potentially censoring yourself, failing to shed light on an important issue, and doing a disservice to those suffering the oppression.

This argument boils down to the idea that it is important that GBV is reported on and that such issues are widely discussed in order to try to effect the kind of practical changes that could protect women. But, as has been documented, this is not what has happened in practice; the emphasis on saving women in Afghanistan in 2001 has not necessarily resulted in long-term, sustainable improvements for women. This pattern risks being repeated with Yazidi women; as researchers Johanna E. Foster and Sherizaan Minwalla found when they interviewed Yazidi women about western media practices, "most women ultimately shared strong feelings that journalists and the world had betrayed them when they gave their harrowing stories, but did not receive help in return" (Foster and Minwalla 2018, 56). In this instance, and more broadly, when it comes to rape in the refugee context, the steps that need to be taken to protect women are not particularly headline-grabbing initiatives: the proper policing of refugee camps, extensive psychosocial support for women who have been victims of sexual violence, and economic empowerment for women displaced by conflict to reduce their vulnerability to exploitation. But only by understanding the complicated nature of the problem might effective long- and short-term solutions be put in place. A singular focus on GBV and the bodies of female survivors obscures rather than illuminates these issues.

This is why it is crucial to consider the political, structural, and economic factors that might contribute to these events. For example, a discussion of GBV in Afghanistan would be incomplete without some consideration of the impact of decades of civil war, foreign occupation, state and international violence, and the related chronic economic problems. An examination of VAW in the Syrian refugee context would be incomplete without consideration of the economic disadvantage and precarious immigration status of this group. Individual journalists seeking to improve the quality of their own work can strive to emphasize the particulars of a case while not being blind to the political realities that sit behind it. But this can only go so far, given that we are bound by the political and market imperatives of the media organizations we work for. Even the most sensitive, considered reporting on a particular issue might inadvertently contribute to the wider media frameworks that tell us that there is only one issue of concern in a particular place, be it terrorism or conflict related sexual violence.

There are no simple solutions. An individual journalist cannot change all the narratives that dominate our profession: it is the buildup of many different articles employing the same frameworks, over a period of time, that gives these frameworks their power—in Said's words, a "well organized sense that these people over there [are] not like 'us' and [don't] appreciate 'our' values—the very core of traditional orientalist dogma" (Said 2003). But each individual can think critically about how these frameworks function within their own work. For example, language is integral to our understanding of GBV—words reflect subtle assumptions about responsibility, blame, and agency as well as the very nature of the violence itself. The language we use can often make male perpetrators of violence invisible—we say, for instance "the woman was raped" rather than, "a man raped the woman." Those of us trying to break out of the misogynistic or patriarchal frameworks that dominate so much mainstream media coverage can make efforts to be clear in our language choices, think about who is active, who is present, and who is being obscured; in short, make intentional choices to use neutral language to accurately communicate the nature of this violence (Murphy 2011).

There is a limit to what individual journalists can do to counter the media frameworks within which we work. Even if we are the ones actually doing the field reporting, we still have to go through several tiers of editors and typically have no input in the headlines or photographs that accompany the finished story. But an awareness of the frameworks we must work within is essential, and can only strengthen the quality of coverage. It is an oft-repeated truism that journalism is all about reporting the facts and finding the "truth." But facts are, by necessity, selected, curated, and chosen in order to produce a certain effect. Which facts? What does it mean to cover one story, such as the sexual harassment of refugee women, without reference to another, such as the socioeconomic deprivation that exacerbates their vulnerability? Who does it serve to place the focus in this way? Who are we positing as perpetrators, and who as victims? Who are we allowing the privilege of direct quotations that let them speak for themselves, and who is being denied? These are questions worth asking on every assignment. Blindly adhering to the dominant frameworks that bind most media coverage places women, particularly othered women, as passive victims, dehumanizes anyone who is "other," and obscures structural inequality and state injustice. And that is not an accurate reflection of the facts that are supposed to be our guiding principle.

REFERENCES

Abu-Lughod, Lila. 2002. "Do Muslim Women Really Need Saving? Anthropological Reflections on Cultural Relativism and Its Others." *American Anthropologist* 104, no. 3: 783–90.

BBC News. 2018. "Ex-UKIP Councillor Stephen Searle Guilty of Murdering Wife," July 17. https://www.bbc.co.uk/news/uk-england-suffolk-44861508.

Buffon, Veronica, and Christine Allison. 2016. "The Gendering of Victimhood: Western Media and the Sinjar Genocide." *Kurdish Studies* 4, no. 2: 176–96. https://doi.org/10.33182/ks.v4i2.427.

Bullock, Cathy Ferdinand, and Jason Cubert. 2002. "Coverage of Domestic Violence Fatalities by Newspapers in Washington State." *Journal of Interpersonal Violence* 17, no. 5: 475–497. https://doi.org/10.1177/0886260502017005001.

Bush, George W. 2009. "Full Text of George W. Bush's Farewell Address." *U.S. News*, January 9. https://www.usnews.com/news/national-news/articles/2017-01-09/president-george-w-bushs-farewell-address-jan-19-2009.

Champion, Sarah. 2017. "British Pakistani Men ARE Raping and Exploiting White Girls . . . and It's Time We Faced Up to It." *The Sun*, August 10. https://www.thesun.co.uk/news/4218648/british-pakistani-men-raping-exploiting-white-girls/.

Cockbain, Ella, and Waqas Tufail. 2020. "A New Home Office Report Admits Grooming Gangs Are Not a 'Muslim Problem.'" *The Guardian*, December 19. https://www.theguardian.com/commentisfree/2020/dec/19/home-office-report-grooming-gangs-not-muslim.

Crawford, Kerry F., Amelia Hoover Green, and Sarah E. Parkinson. 2014. "Wartime Sexual Violence Is Not Just a 'Weapon of War.'" *Washington Post*, September 24. https://www.washingtonpost.com/news/monkey-cage/wp/2014/09/24/wartime-sexual-violence-is-not-just-a-weapon-of-war/?utm_term=.6edc40d74f77.

De Graff, Mia. 2014. "Don't Use the A-Word: BBC Accused of Censorship over Rotherham Child Abuse by Failing to Mention That Gangs Were Asian." *Daily Mail*, August 27. http://www.dailymail.co.uk/news/article-2735465/BBC-accused-sanitising-news-coverage-Rotherham-child-abuse-Asian-gangs-failing-refer-perpetrators-ethnicity.html.

Foster, Johanna E., and Minwalla, Sherizaan. 2018. "Voices of Yazidi Women: Perceptions of Journalistic Practices in the Reporting on ISIS Sexual Violence." *Women Studies International Forum* 67: 53–64. https://doi.org/10.1016/j.wsif.2018.01.007.

Iyengar, Shanto, and Adam Simon. 1993. "News Coverage of the Gulf Crisis and Public Opinion: A Study of Agenda-Setting, Priming, and Framing." *Communication Research* 20: 365–83. https://doi.org/10.1177/009365093020003002.

Khalid, Maryam. 2017. *Gender, Orientalism and the "War on Terror."* London: Routledge.

Lorde, Audre. 1981. "The Uses of Anger." *Women's Studies Quarterly* 25, nos. 1 and 2: 278–85.

Minwalla, Sherizaan. 2015. "Has Anyone Here Been Raped by ISIS?" *The Daily Beast*, May 18. http://www.thedailybeast.com/has-anyone-here-been-raped-by-isis?source=facebook&via=mobile.

Murphy, Wendy J. 2011. "The Need for Accurate Language in Penn State Coverage." *The Crime Report*, November 23. https://thecrimereport.org/2011/11/23/2011-11-murphy-blog-on-sex-terms/.

New Statesman. 2010. "Leader: Pakistan—the Laboratory for World Destruction." *The New Statesman* (print), August 19, 2010.

Said, Edward. 2003. "A Window on the World." *The Guardian*, August 2. https://www.theguardian.com/books/2003/aug/02/alqaida.highereducation.

Salden, Anna. 2017. "The Inversion of Victimhood: New Social Agency for IDP Yazidi Women?" MA thesis, University of Utrecht.

Shackle, Samira. 2015. "Is the Way the Media Reports Islamic State's Treatment of Women Making Things Worse?" *New Statesman*, June 29. http://www.newstatesman.com/politics/2015/06/way-media-reports-islamic-state-s-treatment-women-making-things-worse.

Shackle, Samira. 2018. "The Bureaucracy of ISIS." *Prospect Magazine*, January 19. https://www.prospectmagazine.co.uk/politics/the-bureaucracy-of-isis.

Volpp, Leti. 2000. "Blaming Culture for Bad Behavior." *Yale Journal of Law and the Humanities* 12: 89–116. https://digitalcommons.law.yale.edu/yjlh/vol12/iss1/3.

FOURTEEN · *Nina Berman*

Dressed Up, Stripped Down

Media Depictions of Conflict Rape

A young Black woman stands erect and seminaked, her back straight in profile view. Her pregnant belly is fully outstretched. Her hands rest on her breasts covering her nipples, which are not permitted to be seen. She is wearing a short ponytail, which highlights the shape of her head and the line of her jaw. Her mouth is closed. She is neither smiling, nor sad. Her expression is neutral, alert, at attention. She is staring off camera as if waiting instructions.

This is the opening picture in a *Time* magazine article from March 2016 reporting on conflict rape and survivor programs in sub-Sahara Africa.[1] In the online version, there is no name or caption identifying the photo, only the headline, provocative and promising: "The Secret War Crime"—each word its own line in large black type with "Crime" positioned right next to the woman's belly. Below in smaller white letters, "'The most shameful consequence of conflict comes out in the open.' By Aryn Baker | Photographs by Lynsey Addario for TIME."

The background of the image is gray and bland without spatial or temporal context. The young woman could be standing in a medical office in New York or an apartment in Kampala. In lighting and composition, the image aesthetically recalls depictions of colonized and enslaved men and women photographed naked as specimen studies to support theories of white racial superiority, such as Louis Agassiz's 1850 daguerreotypes from South Carolina (Wallis 1995). Unlike the daguerreotypes, this woman's body fills a modern computer screen. Embedded at the top are five blue and red social media tabs on which viewers can click and register their approval or disapproval on Facebook, Twitter, Pinterest, and so on.

The story begins: "First they shot her husband. Then the soldiers killed her two sons, ages 5 and 7. When the uniformed men yanked her daughter from her hands next, Mary didn't think it could get any worse."

The opening lines might lead the reader to believe that the pregnant woman in the main photo is Mary, the woman whose story starts the piece. But she's not. Nowhere in the online feature story (unless one clicks to a separate page with reporters' notes) is the woman in this shocking photograph ever identified. Image and text are disconnected. Rather, her naked body, presented to the viewer for inspection, is an aesthetic lure, a generic illustration, a stand-in for every Black African woman raped and forcibly impregnated in war.

As we continue through the story we learn Mary (no last name) is from South Sudan. She was raped, lost her family, and is now in Uganda at a safe house run by an American Christian organization based in Alabama called Make Way Partners. The story then moves to the Democratic Republic of the Congo (DRC) with reporting about programs for survivors. Near the end, we return to Uganda and Make Way Partners to learn that "Not all women see their children conceived in rape as burdens."

Enter Ayak.

> I want a family, I want a husband. But the doctors say there is no cure for my disease. No one will ever marry me." She cradles her pregnant belly with both hands and smiles sadly as she envisions a lonely future. "This baby will be my friend. He will keep me company."

Ayak is the near-naked woman posing at the beginning of the story, although again that connection is never made for the reader unless one clicks to the reporters' notes or has a print version of the piece. We learn that Ayak lost her family to a rebel attack in Bentiu, South Sudan. While on the run, she was raped, and then raped again at a United Nations camp, impregnated and infected with AIDS. We don't learn anything more about her prospects for care or the conditions of the camp or who actually raped her and who might be held accountable. Context is erased, creating a depoliticized narrative, where the perpetrators can only be imagined as nefarious dark-skinned others.

Ayak's age and last name are left out without any reason given. Normally, if a subject is only partially identified, the reader is told why, perhaps to protect a person's identity or to shield a minor. Ayak's single first name, without annotation, reinforces the generic utility of her image and simultaneously infantilizes and exoticizes her.

Despite the thrust of the article being about recovery and treatment programs for survivors, the opening photograph and several others show women or girls alone without any supportive community. While the text purports to be a kind of upbeat survey on new innovative programs in the DRC dealing with trauma and recovery, the story's main image focuses on a woman without visible care or comfort. We the reader, the predominantly white Western audience, become stand-ins for the subject's own community of caring which is a popular visual approach when documenting pain and suffering. Picturing victims alone, absent of caregivers or support, can emphasize qualities of trauma and fragility. The lone figure allows the viewer to scrutinize the pained survivor without distraction.

Now for the reporters' notes.

Clicking to a new page, "The Secret War Crime: How Do You Ask Women to Relive Their Worst Nightmares," we learn that the idea for the naked belly portrait came to photographer Lynsey Addario in her sleep. When she woke up, she discussed the idea with the NGO director Kimberly Smith, who we learn is also a rape survivor. In fact, Smith has carefully cultivated her own rape story by "Islamic Darfuri refugees" into a media commodity, writing a book and granting interviews which highlight her survivor status (Brekke 2014). "How a Courageous Christian Woman Who Survived Rape at the Hands of Slave Raiders in Sudan Keeps Braving Bombs and Violence to Save Orphans" was the headline in right-wing American commentator Glenn Beck's the *Blaze*.[2]

Smith supported Addario's idea for Ayak to pose undressed and the two approached Ayak together with the offer. Addario says Ayak "didn't hesitate at all." The experience is then reported as a moment of sisterhood among survivors, whereby the journalists helped create for the subject an empowering transformation. The reporting and picture taking by the white Western women become a vehicle for Ayak's emotional healing and resolution. The photographer wrote:

> *Over time Ayak's body language changed: she stood proudly, more confidently, at peace. It seemed that the very act of photographing Ayak and her unborn child gave her the opportunity to celebrate the very thing her perpetrators had tried to rob from her—her beauty and her dignity.*

> For two days, we all shared deeply personal experiences, which often culminated in tears, and sometimes, oddly, in laughter. Photographing Ayak and listening to her story was a privilege—and an extremely positive, intimate moment amongst three women who had all, in fact, experienced some form of rape or sexual assault as a weapon of war in our lives.

I'm not questioning the emotion of the picture taking moment, or the intensity of the experience for the reporting team. What I do question is the equivalency suggested by mentioning that the three women are somehow intimately linked because they all experienced some form of sexual violence. Ayak was violently displaced from home, country, and family. She was raped multiple times, at age seventeen. She became pregnant with no access to abortion. She has HIV and is apparently without medicine. She is living in a state of poverty, in a safe house in a foreign country, run by an American Christian woman she only recently met. She is about to have her first baby with no clear means of support or family structure and no path back to her home country. But none of that is terribly important. The main attraction here is that Ayak, with the help of her American enablers, is worthy of our gaze because despite her rape, she embraces her unborn child, and in doing so becomes beautiful.

Time brands itself through its individual photographers and has more than once emphasized a photographer's state of mind, compassion, dedication, and sacrifice to the story. Informing readers that the photographer and writer also experienced some form of sexual assault serves one purpose: it's designed to put the readers at ease and assuage any feelings of discomfort around the ethics of the picture. The knowledge validates the image production and grants the *Time* reporters what Nicholas Kristof refers to as "bridge character" status (2012). They become white portals into the consumption of the Black other. It also conjures a parallel idea in the reader's mind that *Time* is a similarly compassionate and noble corporate entity. In this construction, *Time* is doing Ayak a favor. The "very act of photographing" gave Ayak a unique, once in a lifetime opportunity for her as a pregnant rape survivor to disrobe and proudly pose for all the world to see, as though she was Demi Moore, naked on the cover of *Vanity Fair*, showing off her full pregnant belly.

I interviewed the former *Time* international photo editor who commissioned and edited the Ayak piece. To her, the Ayak image was "poignant" and "what I thought worked best to tell the story." In hindsight, she said she regrets that the picture had so much prominence, including as *Time*'s international cover. "It overwhelmed the real issue," she says. "People weren't talking about rape or the situation in Sudan, they were talking about the ethics of the photograph. The larger conversation/debate was entirely around the picture, not Ayak's story, or the situation in Sudan or Congo. Greater understanding about how rape is used as a weapon in modern warfare both in Sudan or in Congo was ultimately the point for me. Both Ayak and Mary's stories are heartbreaking, and I wanted people to know their stories. I believe to be a responsible global citizen we need to be informed about issues affecting our world."

Yet the image is not constructed to inform; rather like so much of modern aestheticized photojournalism, it serves to shock and awe. "There are so many other ways to show our shared humanity than to focus on the blood or bodies of victims," said former NPR photo editor Laura Beltrán Villa who founded the Native Agency which represents photojournalists and documentary photographers from the majority world. "If I said to you I lost my mother, I don't need to show you my dead mother."

Smith, the NGO director who brokered the Ayak photo session, while satisfied with the visual presentation, was ultimately somewhat disappointed, the *Time* photo editor recalled, because the story, despite its provocative cover, didn't generate the desired impact. I tried to follow up with Smith to ask her how the photograph had impacted Ayak, and learn more about the conversations around consent. She didn't respond and appears to have shut down Make Way Partners after earning an annual salary of over $165,000. Some members of the Make Way Partners team have since rebranded their efforts as Lift Up the Vulnerable but without Smith's participation.

Allowing a client, a refugee, who has been raped and traumatized to appear nearly naked in the international press is quite an ask. Does Ayak, or for that matter any other rape survivor in a similar situation where their food, shelter, and well-being is dependent on one person or organization, really feel free in that moment to say no? Alternatively, just because a subject says yes, or provides consent, doesn't mean the journalist needs to proceed. Given the intense social stigma surrounding rape and the often fluid security situations in conflict areas, surely best practices would require photographing with caution and not for provocation.

American editors have on many occasions refused to commission or publish pictures deemed too disturbing or sensitive for American audiences. In the Iraq War, we rarely saw images of dead US soldiers or even coffins returning to Dover Air Force Base since such visuals undermine American projections of power and dominance. Moreover, military families might take offense, or readers might see the pictures as unpatriotic, or the Pentagon might get angry and deny journalists continued embed access (Kamber 2010).

But no such similar sensitivity appears to exist around images that call to mind the long, sordid, violent colonial history of racist visual representations of dark-skinned African women in Western media. Beltrán Villa said photographers at Native Agency so often feel "slapped in the face," by pictures they see published and "the lack of knowledge of the historical context of how photography was used and is still being used."

Time's decisions around anonymity and baring, identification and representation, raise serious questions around the depiction of pain and suffering of Black and brown women for predominantly white Western consumption (Cole 2012). Do different ethical standards exist when white reporters venture abroad to document "foreign," nonwhite rape survivors for the benefit of primarily white American and European audiences, as opposed to documenting domestic stories of rape where understatement and/or anonymity are respected over shock and provocation (Jayawardane 2017)? Women journalists from white Christian-dominated countries are given the special privilege of seeing, while Black and brown women are put in a role of existing to be seen. When the narrative flips and it is Western white women who have been raped by Western white men, their identities must then be protected (Eriksson Baaz and Stern 2013). An example of this is the May 24, 2014 *Time* cover story about rape focusing on the sexual assault crisis at American college campuses. The cover shows no image of a near-naked woman or a pregnant rape survivor, or any survivor at all, only a red and white athletic banner with the word RAPE.[3]

A GORGEOUS FREEDOM

The *Time* piece on conflict rape is worth considering alongside a story in the *New York Times* from 2018 about women who were kidnapped by Boko Haram and since released.[4] Like the *Time* story, the image of victimhood is reframed as female empowerment with the reporters and photographers cast as conduits and cheerleaders for this transformation. Being seen, coming out, unveiling, and entering the spotlight of the world stage in a kind of journalistic striptease become central elements of both stories.

In the *Time* piece, the rape survivor disrobes to show her newly found confidence. In the *New York Times* piece, the survivors are prettied up, directed to stand before studio lights, head turned and tilted just so—like dolls—to show their newly won dignity enabled through the largesse of the *New York Times*.

Like the *Time* Ayak picture, the *New York Times* piece situates the Boko Haram women in decontextualized, abstracted spaces, which highlight the body but eliminate the politics. In the process, the voices and statements of the women themselves, and perhaps more importantly the broader circumstances that led to the sexual violence, become secondary to the aestheticized representation of the female figure.

In April 2014, Boko Haram kidnapped at gunpoint 276 girls from a Nigerian government boarding school in Chibok, prompting a local and international outcry and spawning the popular hashtag #BringBackOurGirls. The group published a propaganda video soon after saying that they had liberated the girls by converting them to Islam. The video, inserted into the *New York Times* story, shows dozens of girls dressed in gray and black coverings sitting on the ground.

Intense interest followed the Chibok girls and other Boko Haram kidnap victims, with reports of beatings, rapes, and forced marriages. The story, like so many tales of female abduction, struck an attractive chord with Western editors who published multiple features about the girls and the efforts to find them.

The *New York Times* also devoted significant resources to the topic with several articles reported by West Africa bureau chief Dionne Searcey, often with images by Australian photographer Adam Ferguson, a frequent *Times* contributor and noted war photographer. An October 2017 online interactive feature about teenage girl suicide bombers who managed to escape Boko Haram won the reporting duo industry awards with Ferguson's pictures praised for their dramatic aesthetic which referenced cinema and fashion photographic language (Searcey 2017).

The team re-created aesthetic elements of the suicide bomber feature in the April 2018 interactive "Kidnapped as Schoolgirls by Boko Haram: Here They Are Now." Once again, each character is pictured alone, under studio lighting with rich, saturated colors. Ferguson added an additional visual reference to his lighting scheme from Ben Enwonwu's famous painting of Nigerian princess Adetutu "Tutu" Ademiluyi which had recently sold at auction for $1 million.

The interactive opens with an ominous text appearing on black background, next to the Boko Haram propaganda video. "Boko Haram dressed them in dark gowns and head coverings." Scroll down, fade in, the glimmer of a woman emerges from the black background. She's wearing bright red. "Four years later, more than a hundred have been freed." Liberation as seen through wardrobe change.

The teenage girls have thrown off their oppressive gray robes, put on jewelry and makeup, and fixed their hair, and are now gorgeous. Scrolling down, woman after woman, eighty-three photographed in one day against different-colored backdrops, appear in a seemingly random array of rectangle blocks which float across the screen like catalog models without smiles. The viewer naturally goes to click on a picture, for added text, or maybe audio. But there is nothing. The women are mute, only to be gazed upon, like perfect princesses. Each figure is fully named, but beyond that there is little contextual information connected to their portrait. As the feature progresses, something strange happens. A select few subjects briefly come to life, eyes move in slow motion, a head ever so lightly turns toward the camera. The head movement is in sync with their eyes blinking, the movement akin to a puppet on a string. Certain pictures explicitly telegraph eroticism. One woman, head turned away from the camera, poses in a skin tight, off the shoulder, shimmering back zipped, stunning, magenta pink dress. She is seen from behind, the photographic angle accentuating the curve of her hips. Freed Boko Haram girl reimagined as a Roland Mouret dress model. The reporters notes on the story follow:

> *We wanted to photograph the young women whose images the world knew mostly when they were teenagers, in dark robes with sad faces, from a video Boko Haram released about a month after they were kidnapped. Our hope was to portray them through a series of portraits in a dignified manner, as the young women they had become.*

> *For days, we visited every office and called every authority figure we could think of in Nigeria. No one would budge. In hopes of getting a meeting to plead our case, we even tried wooing a minister's secretary with a piece of cake. No luck. Adam set up a studio in a friend's apartment and photographed our driver, just for practice.*

> *To pass the time, we cycled through our favorite playlists. We must have listened to "Jolene" by Dolly Parton a dozen times, finally turning to every John Denver song ever recorded. We were going stir crazy. No one would grant us permission to photograph the ex-captives.*

At this point, one might wonder why the journalists didn't just give up and scrap the project since no one except the reporting team and their editors were invested in a story which had dubious news value. In addition, the reporters were cautioned that the women were traumatized and needed time away from the public spotlight. They were also informed that the women were high-profile targets for militants still at large and so ongoing security was an issue. Yet when they eventually photographed the women they used their full names to identify them. For two years the team had covered the Boko Haram story but had never been able to meet any of the Chibok girls, the ones who launched the #BringBackOurGirls hashtag. As though on a mission, they needed to show that the girls in "dark robes with sad faces," were now free—from their Islamic captors and safely situated on a "pristine" campus where their days are filled "with math and English classes, karaoke and selfies, and movie nights with popcorn." A former US Navy ROTC (Reserve Officer Training Corps.) administrator oversees their reeducation which includes messages reminding them of proper civilized behavior. "Remember to flush the toilet and wash your hands," a poster reads. The girls joyfully attend church services. A scant few of the former captives are Muslim, but we are never told if they too find joy or comfort in prayer.

Just as *Time* framed its photograph of Ayak as an opportunity for her to erase the shame of rape, the *New York Times* team wasn't going to give up until they allowed the Chibok girls their moment in the light, their "portraits of dignity." In this case, achieving dignity also means a successful integration into Western culture courtesy of the American University in Nigeria and Christian prayer.

Dignity in journalism is not just about lighting and wardrobe. It's also about giving characters a full space to speak. In this treatment, the women are turned into aesthetic objects, disconnected from their individual stories, grouped together as an array of colors and mute block shapes, scrolling down, fading in and out, with a disturbing come-hither animation. If not for the headline and the occasional caption, the presentation could pass as an online shopping page.

The *Time* and *New York Times* pieces show how current industry practices in visualizing conflict rape emphasize the savior role played by Western feminist journalists in bringing healing to Black and brown rape victims through the photographic encounter. The aesthetics of this encounter are influenced by the commercial demands of the new digital media economy and the nonstop race for eyeballs, clicks, likes, and shares. In this landscape, spectacular images rule. As the former *Time* editor told me, it's harder every day to get people to "pay attention."

MEDIA, FEMINISM, AND SEXUAL VIOLENCE IN WAR

Stories about violence against women and conflict rape were always a hard sell. The war-reporting industry has historically been the domain of male journalists and editors more interested in battles, weapons, and the courage or sacrifice of combatants, as opposed to the consequences of military campaigns on women and children. Stories of white Western armies committing rape are especially rare, and almost nonexistent in the American media context. Western journalists, with some notable exceptions, have tended to reinforce, wittingly or not, the foreign policy aims of their own governments, by either mythologizing the goodness of their own armies and denying both the gender violence inherent in imperialist and colonial campaigns or as seen in so much post-9/11 "War on Terror" coverage, by presenting the US military as a force for the liberation of Muslim women from Muslim men.[5]

There is perhaps no better an example of selective media denial of Western rape atrocities than the American war in Vietnam. One is hard pressed to find any stories of rape or of American sexual atrocities in contemporaneous media accounts or in the subsequent 30,000 plus books on the subject until 2010 with Gina Marie Weaver's *Ideologies of Forgetting: Rape in the Vietnam War*. Weaver documented with horrific detail large-scale rape perpetrated by US troops against both Vietnamese women and American female GIs. Military veterans told her rape was "pretty SOP"—meaning Standard Operating Procedure. Another called it a "mass military policy." It was so prevalent, that there was a special term coined for soldiers who raped and then murdered Vietnamese women. They were known as "double veterans" (Weaver 2010, 35).

Tens of thousands of Vietnamese children were born from US soldiers. Reporting on the story, journalists wrote critically about the communist Vietnamese government's mistreatment of these children without mentioning rape. Denied in the popular telling were both the vast commercial sex industry constructed to serve American troops and the rape of Vietnamese civilians during patrols, where GIs would routinely turn weapon searches into rapes, conflating both acts into one and the same (Weaver 2010, 55). Raping as searching.

As late as 2013, three years after Weaver's book, and the same year that Nick Turse published his shattering account *Kill Anything That Moves*, which documents extensive atrocities by US troops in Vietnam including widespread sexual violence, the *New York Times* ran a story reporting on a heartfelt reunion between an aging US veteran and his long-lost Vietnamese offspring (Dao 2013). The story positions the veteran in a falsified social construct which imagines a kind of romantic love fest between local Vietnamese women and their American military suitors engaged in frolicking "one-night stands." The account stands in complete denial of the revised historical record and the pervasiveness of gender violence. As Weaver writes, "to admit these violences, would demand that the militarized American exceptionalism from which such behavior sprang was problematic at its very core" (Weaver 2010, 7). And ignoring them gives the impression that rape is not something white Western armies do.

So, while the historical record of that war is slowly being rewritten to include sexual violence by US troops against Vietnamese women and girls, and within the US military itself, there is no corresponding visual record which would help solidify a broader popular understanding about sexual violence by American military members during the Vietnam War or what happened to survivors. The pictures simply don't exist and this absence ends up giving Western armies a pass. It prevents a sense of shared humanity and the formation of a virtual community and understanding around images of distant events (Sliwinski 2011).

The first post–Vietnam War where conflict rape became front-page news was in Bosnia-Herzegovina in the early 1990s. By this time, more women served as writers, editors, and photographers, transforming Western media companies. Empowered by a shifting social and political context, these reporters saw domestic violence and rape culture as newsworthy and vital issues.

Prominent Western journalists including Alexandra Stiglmayer, Roy Guttman, and John Burns wrote early detailed accounts documenting mass organized rape by Serb nationalists against Bosnian Muslim girls and women as part of an ethnic-cleansing campaign. Some photographers, myself included, reported the story with images of survivors, witnesses, and confessed perpetrators, but these visuals were rare; most photographers focused on more visible evidence of ethnic cleansing such as the concentration camps, the siege of Sarajevo, and the massacre at Srebrenica.

Widespread rape in Bosnia and then in Rwanda led to the creation in 1998 of a permanent International Criminal Court (ICC), and the subsequent designation of rape as a war crime. This coincided with aforementioned changes in the journalism profession which helped popularize conflict rape reporting. The simultaneous digital revolution meant rape stories would require more dynamic visual approaches to satisfy web-based image-oriented platforms. At the same time, the growing human rights and NGO industries embraced photojournalism language as part of their visual communications strategies, producing material virtually indistinguishable from journalism entities. The result was a symbiotic network of survivors, media subjects, aid workers, and journalism publications which made reporting on conflict rape not just easily accomplishable but profitable. For photographers, stories of conflict rape and gender violence became a much easier sell and even career makers.

PHOTOJOURNALISM AND HUMANITARIANISM

In 2006 Jonathan Torgovnik, an Israeli-born photographer living in New York, traveled to Rwanda to work on an AIDS story for *Newsweek* magazine. He learned that many Tutsi women with HIV had contracted the disease as a result of rape during the genocide and subsequently given birth to children who were shunned. He returned to Rwanda on his own to more fully document the issue and for the next three years, working with a Rwandan translator and fixer connected to a local NGO, he traveled the country interviewing and photographing rape survivors and their children. They were families, he told me, "created from the enemy, so to speak."

He used medium format color film, an external flash, and a Hasselblad camera to make portraits of the mother and child together. Situated in and around the family homes, the photographs are expertly framed and highly detailed, with rich vibrant colors and a hint of artificial light which adds to the constructed nature of the photograph. "I didn't have an agenda except to try through the faces of the mothers to translate the heaviness of what happened, and I found it interesting, that whole interaction or lack of interaction (between mother and child) during the photographic process." He photographed the women after first interviewing them, and the words and testimonies "were as important if not more important than the pictures themselves," he said.

In the photographs, the women and children look squarely at the camera, their expressions serious or strained, blank or neutral. No one is smiling. Knowing the context, the viewer looks to discern the relationship between mother and child, is there love, or rejection, is she embracing the child's hand or pushing it away? It's an uncomfortable viewing experience and when looking at the pictures I can't help feeling privy to a secret which I don't deserve to know (Crawley 2012).

The series *Intended Consequences* was an industry sensation. Published in both the United States and Europe, it generated a huge reader response with more than $250,000 donated following the first publications in *Stern* and the *Telegraph*. Other magazines soon followed. *Aperture* published a book; Mediastorm produced a duPont-winning film; a fine art photography exhibition traveled internationally and Torgovnik was honored with multiple photographic prizes. He used the donations as the seed money for Foundation Rwanda, an NGO he established to educate children born of rape in Rwanda, including those children in his initial photographs.

"We're in the middle of this time when we're skeptical of whether our work is making a difference. But I do think that it is making a difference. And this is a small example. As of today, Foundation Rwanda has supported 860 families. To take all these 860 children through secondary school education and the mothers through therapy and through vocational training and through forming cooperatives to learn English and to learn skills to sustain themselves financially all came from people responding to the media publication. It started from the photograph. It started from a word. It started from people being exposed to the images and being drawn in. It's a testament that people aren't completely numb."

Critics of Torgovnik's work maintain that his visual approach is antithetical to structural change because rather than assigning agency to the subjects, he perpetuates the language of victimhood which allows the privileged viewer to voyeuristically regard the pain of another. In the end, it's the observer who, by feeling sad, can then feel good by digging into their pocket and affirming their own moral worthiness (Crawley 2012, 1).

Intended Consequences has never been screened in Rwanda. The Foundation Rwanda website cannot be accessed within the country. These measures are necessary to protect the rape survivors from further stigmatization. This divorce also serves to depoliticize the work by locating it in a new media terrain where the aims of journalism and humanitarian efforts are inextricably linked. One of the goals of journalism is to hold power accountable, but for this to happen the journalism must also exist in a political space where subject and audience are engaged in an ongoing discourse around issues central to achieving justice and equity. In the new formulation of photojournalist as humanitarian, impact is measured not by policy change or accountability but by the response of viewers and whether or not the pictures carry enough punch to monetize page views into charitable donations.

Torgovnik recently returned to Rwanda to report on how the children, now young adults, had processed the information about their origins. This new project, *Disclosure*, re-creates the *Intended Consequences* series ten years later. I asked him about consent especially given that the subjects were now indebted to him in some fashion through the foundation's work.

Prior to making his new set of pictures, he sent a social worker to identify those families who wanted to participate in the project update. The consent form was thoroughly explained beforehand, but in one case, something happened. He was visiting with a family with whom he had remained especially close. "It was all positive and everything was okay and I'm taking the picture, and then I actually do have them sign a release form not only to cover myself, but really for them to understand what this is going to be used for. And the daughter, suddenly freaked out. She's really intelligent and we had actually sent her to a really good school and she speaks English fluently and she's like, I don't want this stuff up. I want to go study in Europe and I don't want this to be online anywhere and for people, for my classmates, to suddenly see I was born from rape." The irony was not lost on him; the education the woman achieved through his foundation helped her understand the pitfalls of being pictured as a child of rape for Western consumption.

CONCLUSION

We live in a visual culture and journalists cannot ignore the importance of image making in the investigation and documentation of conflict rape and gender violence. Those who might argue that it is never ethical to photograph or publish an image of a rape survivor run the risk of erasing the truth about the prevalence of gender violence in war and conflict. Not to photograph is to deny a vital language by which individuals and communities construct understanding and imagine a path forward. While feminism has helped bring stories of conflict rape to the forefront, the digital attention-seeking economy and the dependence on journalism for clicks and likes runs the risk of cheapening survivors' stories by turning them into aesthetic vehicles whereby the picture, rather than the story, takes prominence. The reliance on NGOs, Christian aid organizations, and the human rights industry for access to conflict rape survivors encourages depoliticization of narratives thus reducing conflict rape to individual accounts of terror and ultra-violence committed by non-Western men, against marginalized non-Western women, or feel-good stories about resilience over pain accomplished through the photographic encounter. Moreover, the selective focus by which the dominant Western media decides what rape story is worth seeing, is inextricably linked to the politics and commercial priorities of the commissioning entities which rarely turn the lens on their own militaries and instead promote a white Western exceptionalism through the cover of feminism.

NOTES

1. As defined by the United Nations in "Report of the Secretary-General on Conflict-Related Sexual Violence" (2017), "the term 'conflict-related sexual violence,' as used in the present report, refers to rape, sexual slavery, forced prostitution, forced pregnancy, forced abortion, enforced sterilization, forced marriage, and any other form of sexual violence of comparable gravity perpetrated against women, men, girls or boys that is directly or indirectly linked to a conflict. This link may be evident in the profile of the perpetrator (often affiliated with a State or non-State armed group, including a terrorist entity or network), the profile of the victim (who is frequently an actual or perceived member of a persecuted political, ethnic or religious minority, or is targeted on the basis of actual or perceived sexual orientation and gender identity), the climate of impunity (which is generally associated with State collapse), cross-border consequences (such as displacement or trafficking in persons) and/or violations of the provisions of a ceasefire agreement. The term also encompasses trafficking in persons when committed in situations of conflict for the purpose of sexual violence/exploitation."

    The *Time* story was published in various formats, including the international magazine, the print domestic issue, and an online feature. For the purposes of this chapter, we will focus on the online version, published on March 10, 2016; it can be found at https://time.com/war-and-rape/. The international cover, published on March 21, 2016, can be found within the reporter's notes at http://web.archive.org/web/20160311024954/http://time.com/4211877/secret-war-crime-rape/.

2. The article, written by Billy Hallowell in 2014, can be found at https://www.theblaze.com/news/2014/11/19/how-a-courageous-christian-woman-who-survived-rape-at-the-hands-of-slave-raiders-in-sudan-keeps-braving-bombs-and-violence-to-save-orphans.

3. Praise for this approach includes Peter Jacobs's (2014) *Business Insider* article, "New Time Magazine Cover Is a Powerful Statement about Sexual Assault

on College Campuses," at https://www.businessinsider.com/new-time-magazine-rape-cover-2014-5.

4   The article, by Dionne Searcey and Adam Ferguson, titled "Kidnapped as Schoolgirls by Boko Haram, Here They Are Now," was published by the *New York Times* on April 11, 2018 and can be accessed at https://www.nytimes.com/interactive/2018/04/11/world/africa/nigeria-boko-haram-girls.html.

5   For an example of this coverage, see Aryn Baker's (2010) article in *Time*, "What Happens If We Leave Afghanistan" at http://content.time.com/time/covers/0,16641,20100809,00.html.

REFERENCES

Brekke, Kira. 2014. "Philanthropist Kimberly Smith Shares the Harrowing Tale of Being Raped by Darfuri Refugees." *Huffington Post*, July 22. https://www.huffpost.com/entry/kimberly-smith-raped-in-darfur_n_5607041.

Cole, Teju. 2012. "The White Savior Industrial Complex." *Atlantic*, March 21. http://www.theatlantic.com/international/archive/2012/03/the-white-savior-industrial-complex/254843/.

Crawley, Karen. 2012. "Unintended Consequences: Representations of Rwandan Women and Their Children Born from Rape." *The Australian Feminist Law Journal* 36, no. 1: 87–106. https://doi.org/10.1080/13200968.2012.10854469.

Dao, James. 2013. "Vietnam Legacy: Finding G.I. Fathers, and Children Left Behind." *New York Times*, September 15. https://www.nytimes.com/2013/09/16/us/vietnam-legacy-finding-gi-fathers-and-children-left-behind.html.

Eriksson Baaz, Maria, and Maria Stern. 2013. *Sexual Violence as a Weapon of War?: Perceptions, Prescriptions, Problems in the Congo and Beyond (Africa Now)*. London: Zed Books.

Jayawardane, M Neelika. 2017. "The Problem with Photojournalism and Africa." *Al Jazeera*, January 18. https://www.aljazeera.com/opinions/2017/1/18/the-problem-with-photojournalism-and-africa.

Kamber, Mike. 2010. "Military Censorship." *BagNewsnotes*, October 17. https://www.readingthepictures.org/2010/10/mike-kamber-military-censorship/.

Kristof, Nicholas. 2012. "Q3: NYTimes Columnist Nicholas D. Kristof Answers Questions." *The New York Times* (Facebook), July 9. http://www.facebook.com/video/video.php?v=424427794200.

Searcey, Dionne. 2017. "Boko Haram Strapped Suicide Bombs to Them. Somehow These Teenage Girls Survived." *New York Times*, October 25. https://www.nytimes.com/interactive/2017/10/25/world/africa/nigeria-boko-haram-suicide-bomb.html.

Sliwinski, Sharon. 2011. *Human Rights in Camera*. Chicago: University of Chicago Press.

Turse, Nick. 2013. *Kill Anything That Moves: The Real American War in Vietnam*. New York: Metropolitan Books.

United Nations. 2017. Report of the Secretary-General on Conflict-Related Sexual Violence. S/2017/249, April 15. https://www.un.org/en/events/elimination-of-sexual-violence-in-conflict/pdf/1494280398.pdf.

Wallis, Brian. 1995. "Black Bodies, White Science: Louis Agassiz's Slave Daguerreotype." *American Art* 9, no. 2: 38–61. https://www.jstor.org/stable/i356275.

Weaver, Gina Marie. 2010. *Ideologies of Forgetting: Rape in the Vietnam War*. Albany: State University of New York Press.

CONTRIBUTORS

LILA ABU-LUGHOD is the Joseph L. Buttenwieser Professor of Social Science at Columbia University where she teaches anthropology and gender studies. Her scholarship, strongly ethnographic and mostly based on long-term research in Egypt, has focused on the relationship between cultural forms and power; the politics and ethics of knowledge and representation of the Arab and Muslim worlds; and the dynamics of gender politics and the international circulation of women's rights talk. Her books and articles have been translated into fourteen languages and include *Veiled Sentiments: Honor and Poetry in a Bedouin Society* (1986/2006/2016); *Writing Women's Worlds: Bedouin Stories* (1993/2008); *Remaking Women: Feminism and Modernity in the Middle East* (1998); *Dramas of Nationhood: The Politics of Television in Egypt* (2005); *Nakba: Palestine, 1948, and the Claims of Memory* (2007, with A. H. Sa'di) and *Do Muslim Women Need Saving?* (2013). Her current work focuses on Palestinian memory, museums, settler-colonial politics, and acknowledgments. The recipient of numerous awards and fellowships, she has taken special pleasure in directing or cofounding a number of collaborative institutes at Columbia University that foster critical research and thought, most notably the Center for the Study of Social Difference, out of which this collaborative book emerged.

NINA BERMAN is Professor of Journalism, Columbia University, with an expertise in documentary photography and photojournalism. Her work focuses on war, trauma, militarization, and political resistance. As a freelance photojournalist, in the 1990s she reported for *Time* and *Newsweek* on gender violence in Bosnia and Afghanistan. Since 2001, she has focused her work mainly on the United States. Monographs include *Purple Hearts—Back from Iraq* (2004), *Homeland* (2008), and *An Autobiography of Miss Wish* (2017). Awards and fellowships include the Center for Documentary Studies at Duke University, the Open Society Institute

Documentary Fund, the World Press Photo Foundation, and the MIT-Knight Foundation. Her work is represented in the permanent collections of the Smithsonian National Museum of American History; the Library of Congress; the Museum of Fine Arts, Houston; Harvard Art Museums; and the Bibliothèque national de France. She has participated in workshops around the world for young photographers and writes frequently on photojournalism ethics and practice for the *Columbia Journalism Review*.

INDERPAL GREWAL is Professor Emeritus of Women's, Gender, and Sexuality Studies at Yale University where she was also Professor in American Studies, in the Ethnicity, Race and Migration Studies Program, and the South Asian Studies Council. She is the author of *Home and Harem: Nation, Gender, Empire and the Cultures of Travel* (1996), *Transnational America: Feminisms, Diasporas, Neoliberalisms* (2005), and *Saving the Security State: Exceptional Citizens and Twenty-first century America* (2017). With Caren Kaplan, she has written and edited *Gender in a Transnational World: Introduction to Women's Studies* (2001, 2005) and *Scattered Hegemonies: Postmodernity and Transnational: Feminist Practices* (1994). With Victoria Bernal, she has edited *Theorizing NGOs: States, Feminism and Neoliberalism* (2014). She is one of the editors of a *Social Text* special issue (40:3) entitled "Security from the South." Her ongoing projects include feminist research on practices of "security," a book on visuality and violence in India, and a project on masculinity and bureaucracy in postcolonial India.

REMA HAMMAMI is Associate Professor of Anthropology at Birzeit University, where she directs the PhD Program in Interdisciplinary Social Sciences. A founder and faculty member of the Institute of Women's Studies at Birzeit University, she directed its graduate program in Gender and Development and has chaired Birzeit University's Right to Education Campaign. She cofounded and directed the Women's Affairs Centre in Gaza and is currently Vice President of Insaniyyat, the Society of Palestinian Anthropologists. Her current work focuses on the geopolitics of gender, development, and humanitarianism in the contexts of the interlinked forces of international trusteeship and Israeli colonialism. Recent publications in *Current Anthropology* and *Settler Colonial Studies* as well as edited volumes by Duke University Press and the University of Minnesota Press focus on the everyday politics of gender, women's activism, embodiment, and survival within Israel's spatial apparatus of colonial control and dispossession. She has undertaken studies for UN agencies various aspects of gender, development, and humanitarianism in Palestine. Recipient of the Prince Claus Chair in Equity and Development at the Institute of Social Studies in The Hague, she has also been a Carnegie Centennial Scholar at Columbia University and a Mahmoud Darwish Visiting Fellow in Palestinian Studies at Brown University.

JANET R. JAKOBSEN is Claire Tow Professor of Women's Gender and Sexuality Studies at Barnard College, Columbia University, where she served as Director of the Barnard Center for Research on Women (BCRW) for fifteen years and as Dean for Faculty Diversity and Development. She studies ethics and public policy with a particular focus on social movements related to religion, gender, and sexuality, including activist responses to violence. Her most recent book is *The Sex Obsession: Perversity and Possibility in American Politics* (2020), which was a 2021 Lambda Literary Award finalist. With Ann Pellegrini she cowrote *Love the Sin: Sexual Regulation and the Limits of Religious Tolerance* (2003) and coedited *Secularisms* (2008), and with Elizabeth Castelli she coedited *Interventions: Academics and Activists Respond to Violence* (2004). She has held fellowships from the American Association of University Women, the Center for the Humanities at Wesleyan University, and the Center for the Study of Values in Public Life at Harvard Divinity School.

SHENILA KHOJA-MOOLJI is the Hamad bin Khalifa al-Thani Associate Professor of Muslim Societies at Georgetown University. An interdisciplinary scholar working at the intersections of gender, Islam, and South Asian studies, her research interests include Muslim girlhood(s), masculinities and sovereignty, and Ismaili Muslim women's history. She investigates these topics empirically in relation to Muslims in South Asia and in the North American diaspora. Khoja-Moolji is the author of two award-winning books: *Forging the Ideal Educated Girl: The Production of Desirable Subjects in Muslim South Asia* (2018) and *Sovereign Attachments: Masculinity, Muslimness, and Affective Politics in Pakistan* (2021). Her forthcoming book traces the transnational lives of displaced Shia Ismaili Muslim women. Her articles have appeared in *Signs: Journal of Women in Culture and Society, Feminist Theory, Comparative Studies of South Asia, Africa and the Middle East, Journal of South Asian Studies, Discourse: Studies in the Cultural Politics of Education*, and *Feminist Teacher*, among others. She also pursues an active public scholarship agenda, with opinion pieces and essays appearing in the *New York Times*, the *Washington Post*, and the *Huffington Post*.

VASUKI NESIAH is Professor of Human Rights and International Law at the Gallatin School at New York University. She teaches human rights, international law and racial capitalism, alternative internationalism, and critical race theory. Nesiah has published on the history and politics of human rights, humanitarianism, international criminal law, reparations, global feminisms, and decolonization. Her current book projects include *International Conflict Feminism* and *Reading the Ruins: Slavery, Colonialism and International Law*. A founding member of Third World Approaches to International Law (TWAIL), she is also coediting *TWAIL: A Handbook*. Her previous TWAIL book was the coedited *Bandung, Global History and International Law: Critical Pasts and Pending Futures* (2017). A selection of recently published book chapters and articles include: "'A Mad and Melancholy Record': The Crisis of International Law Histories" (2021), "An UnAmerican Story of American Empire" (2021), "Critical Legal Studies: A Curious Case of Hegemony Without Dominance" (2021), "A Double Take on Debt: Reparations Claims and Regimes of Visibility in a Politics of Refusal" (2022), and "Feminist Approaches to International Law" with Karen Engle and Diane Otto (2022). She is originally from Sri Lanka.

SAMIRA SHACKLE is a multi-award-winning freelance writer and reporter based in London. She is a regular contributor to the *Guardian Long Read*. From 2020–23 she was editor-in-chief of the *New Humanist* magazine. Her first book, *Karachi Vice*, was published in 2021. It tells the story of five ordinary citizens of Pakistan's largest city.

SIMA SHAKHSARI is an Associate Professor and the Chair of the Department of Gender, Women and Sexualities at the University of Minnesota. They earned their PhD in Cultural and Social Anthropology at Stanford University and have held postdoctoral positions at the University of Pennsylvania's Wolf Humanities Center and the Women's and Gender Studies Department at the University of Houston. Their book, *Politics of Rightful Killing: Civil Society, Gender, and Sexuality in Weblogistan* (2020), received the Fatima Mernissi Honorable Mention at the Middle East Studies Association in 2021. Shakhsari has published several articles and book chapters on queerness, cyberspace, geopolitics, refugees, and necropolitics in journals and books including *Feminist Studies*; *Sexualities*; *International Journal of Middle East Studies*; *Comparative Studies of South Asia, Africa, and the Middle East*; *Queer Necropolitics*; and *Transgender Studies Reader II*.

NADERA SHALHOUB-KEVORKIAN is a Palestinian feminist who holds the Lawrence D. Biele Chair in Law at the Faculty of Law-Institute of Criminology and the School of Social Work and Public Welfare at the Hebrew University of Jerusalem and the Global Chair in Law at Queen Mary University of London. Her research focuses on trauma, state crimes and criminology, surveillance, gender violence, law and society, and genocide studies. She is the author of numerous academic articles in journals in multiple fields. Her books include *Militarization and Violence against Women in Conflict Zones in the Middle East: The Palestinian Case Study* (2010), *Security Theology, Surveillance and the Politics of Fear* (2015), and *Incarcerated Childhood and the Politics of Unchilding* (2019). She has also coedited two books, the latest of which is entitled *When Politics are Sacralized: Comparative Perspectives on Religious Claims and Nationalism* (2021).

DINA M. SIDDIQI is Clinical Associate Professor, Global Liberal Studies, New York University. A cultural anthropologist by training, her research, grounded in the study of Bangladesh, joins development studies, transnational feminist theory, and the anthropology of labor and Islam. She has published extensively on the global garment industry, nonstate gender justice systems, sexuality and rights, and the cultural politics of Islam and nationalism. Some of her most recent publications include "Scandalising the Supply Chain: Looking Back at 40 years of Bangladesh's Garment Industry" (2022) and "Weaponizing Paperwork—Rohingya Belonging and Statelessness" (2020). Professor Siddiqi is currently engaged in a project on economic development, discourses of empowerment, and the travels of civilizational feminisms. She sits on the editorial boards of *Contemporary South Asia*, *Dialectical Anthropology*, and the *Journal of Bangladesh Studies*. She frequently collaborates with feminist colleagues at various Bangladeshi human rights organizations—including Ain o Salish Kendra, Nagorik Uddyog, and Bangladesh Legal Aid and Services Trust (BLAST).

SHAHLA TALEBI is an Associate Professor at Arizona State University, where she is on the faculty of religious studies and the anthropology of religion of the School of Historical, Philosophical and Religious Studies. Her book, *Ghosts of Revolution: Rekindled Memories of Imprisonment in Iran* (2011), won the 2011 Outstanding Academic Title Award given by *Choice Magazine*, and was the co-winner (Gold Medal) of the 2012 Independent Publisher Book Awards. Dr. Talebi's work has also appeared in various academic journals, including *Comparative Studies of South Asia, Africa, and the Middle East* and

Journal of Middle East Women's Studies, and edited book volumes. Her article on revolutions in recent Iranian history was published in the Oxford Handbook series in July 2018. She was the 2017–2018 Anthony E. Kaye Fellow at the National Humanities Center where she worked on her book about contested memories of martyrdom in postrevolutionary Iran.

LETI VOLPP is the Robert D. and Leslie Kay Raven Professor of Law and the Director of the Center for Race and Gender at the University of California, Berkeley. She researches and writes about citizenship theory, immigration law, culture, and identity. Her most recent publications include "Migrant Justice Now" (*Colorado Law Review*, 2021); "Pushing Out and Bleeding In: On the Mobility of Borders," in Peter Niesen, ed., *The Shifting Border: Ayelet Shachar in Dialogue* (2020); "Refugees Welcome?" (*Berkeley La Raza Law Journal*, 2018); and "Passports in the Time of Trump" (*Symplokē*, 2018). She is the coeditor of the volumes *Looking for Law in All the Wrong Places: Justice Beyond and Between* (with Marianne Constable and Bryan Wagner, 2019) and *Legal Borderlands: Law and the Construction of American Borders* (with Mary Dudziak, 2006).

RAFIA ZAKARIA is an author, editor, and attorney. She is a fellow at the African American Policy Institute, and is a weekly columnist at *The Baffler* in the United States as well as for DAWN, Pakistan's largest and oldest English language daily, since 2009. Her column is syndicated in newspapers all over the world and is regularly republished in the *Deccan Chronicle*, *The Wire India*, *Kathmandu Post*, *Sri Lanka Guardian*, and *New Straits Times*, among others. Her latest book *Against White Feminism* (2021) was one of NPR's "Most Favorite Books of 2021." She also writes regularly for Guardian Books and is a CNN Opinion contributor. From 2009 through 2015 Rafia served on the Board of Directors of Amnesty International USA; she was the first Pakistani-American woman to do so. In Fall 2016 she was part of the "How Should Journalism Cover Terrorism" Project at the Tow Center for Digital Journalism at Columbia University. In the fall of 2017 she, along with political scientists Kate Cronin-Furman and Nimmi Gowrinathan, published the "Emissaries of Empowerment" report for the Colin Powell Center for Civic and Public Leadership. Rafia is also the author of *The Upstairs Wife: An Intimate History of Pakistan* (2015) and *Veil* (2017).

INDEX

Abdul Lateef Jamil Poverty Action Lab (J-PAL), 310–11
abortion, religion and, 167n9
Abu-Khdeir, Muhammed, 243
Abu-Lughod, Lila, 11–12; on child marriage, 296; declaration on Muslim Ban, 130–32; on honor killings, 218, 381n3; honor killings and, 123; on Muslim women, 408; on securofeminism, 88–112
activism: child marriage and, 312–13; Gaza gender-based violence and, 332–39; humanitarian GBV simulation of, 338–39; Pakistani honor killings and, 209, 213–28; religion and, 155, 161, 163–65; status linked to, 278
Addario, Lynsey, 422, 424
Ademiluyi, Adetutu "Tutu," 428
Adivasi, 187, 190
advocacy. *See* activism
Afghanistan: drone use in, 69, 158; imperial intervention masked as protection for women of, 2, 38n1; media coverage of, 418; military policy and religion in, 156–57; refugees from, 363–64, 366–68, 381n6; Rule of Law Field Force in, 67–68; US occupation of, 369–70, 408
Africa: colonial view of religion in, 152; gender-based persecution in, 58; ICC bias toward, 58, 79n10. *See also* specific African countries
African Union, withdrawal from ICC and, 58
Afridi, Shahid, 220
Agassiz, Louis, 422
agency of women: media erasure of, 413–19; securofeminism and, 104–12

age of consent: child marriage and, 295–97; cultural differences in, 301
age-of-marriage laws, in US, 295, 315
Ahmad, Muneer, 182, 184
Ahmed, Saifuddin, 185
Akter, Shirin, 314
Al Hassan Mahmoud, ICC case against, 55–59, 64, 68–77
Al Hayat Center, 343, 402
Ali, Ayaan Hirsi, 124, 139–40, 402
Ali, Nujood, 300
Al Jazeera, 213
Al-Kannnan, Azar, 259–61, 277–78
Allamehzadeh, Reza, 277
Alliumuddin, Mohammed, 197
Al Mahdi, 79n11
Almaleki, Noor, 136
American Bar Association (ABA), 66, 70
amicus briefs in Muslim Ban rulings, 130–31, 145n15
Amireh, Amal, 401
Amnesty International, 188; Mali human rights crisis and, 64
Anderlini, Sanam Naraghi, 92–93, 105, 108, 114n11
Annan, Kofi, 315, 340
Ansar Dine paramilitary group: counterrorism interventions and, 63–64; criminalization of forced marriage and, 73–74; gender persecution and, 55–59; lawfare and, 68; securitization politics and, 11
Ansari, Qutubuddin, 186–89
Anti-Honor Killings Laws (Pakistan), 210, 217
antitrafficking campaigns, age of consent debates and, 295

Antrobus, Peggy, 33
"Anyone Here Been Raped and Speaks English?" (Behr), 416–17
AQIM (Al-Qaeda in the Islamic Maghreb), 56, 68, 73
Arab Americans: conflation of Islam with, 158; student activist as, 164–66
Arab nationalism, humanitarian GBV in Gaza and, 338–39
Aretxaga, Begoña, 246
armed conflict, violence against women and, 7–8. *See also* war
armed occupation, as sexual violence, 245–48
Aroussi, Sahla, 108
Assaf, Muhammad, 337
Assam, anti-Muslim violence in, 183
asylum seekers: economic conditions as motivation for, 366–70; queer/trans essentialist definitions for, 362–64; refugees compared to, 370, 382n15; third country asylum for, 364, 366, 368–69, 376–77
The Atlantic magazine, 160
Aurat Foundation, 214
Australia: forced separation of Indigenous children in, 249; refugees to, 366
Australian National Research Organization for Women's Safety, 413
awareness activities, Gaza gender-based violence and, 332–36
Ayaan Hirsi Ali Foundation, 28, 124, 139–40, 144n6
Azam, Sultan, 213
Azar, Alex, 166n5
Aziz, Sahar, 114n13

Ba, Oumar, 58, 79nn10–11
Babri Masjid violence, 183
backwardness/civilization dualism, GBVAW in context of, 21
Baker, Aryn, 422
Bakhtin, Mikhail, 281
Bakker, Alexandrah, 56
Balkan civil wars, humanitarian gender-based violence and, 329. *See also* Bosnian genocide; Srebrenica massacre
Baloch, Qandeel, 18–20, 209–15, 217–28
Baloch, Waseem, 209
Bangladesh: child marriage in, 295–97, 304–9, 311–13; Ford Foundation support for feminism in, 301; GBVAW and development imperatives in, 22–23; girl child agenda and, 314–16; metrics and financialization of development in, 310–11; paradox of improvement and persistence of child marriage in, 305–9; transnational neoliberalism in, 297
Bangladesh Mahila Parishad (BMP), women's rights charter by, 293–94
Bannon, Steve, 124
Bano, Asifa, 198
ban Sharia law movement, 155
Barnett, Michael, 63–64
Basu, Amrita, 198
BBC, India coverage of, 181
Beauchamp, Toby, 377
Beauvoir, Simone de, 268, 288n3
"Because Religion" (Jakobsen), 13
Beck, Glenn, 424
Becoming Mulan? Female Western Migrants to Isis (Hoyle, Bradford, and Frenett 2015), 99–100
Bedouin, Awlad 'Ali, 218
Behr, Edward, 416
Behrangi, Samad, 269
Beijing Platform for Women, 302
Beijing UN Fourth World Conference on Women (1995), 7–8, 32–33
Beit al Aman women's shelter (Gaza), 343–47
Beltrán Villa, Laura, 426–27
Bensouda, Fatou, 68, 71, 73
Berman, Nina, 29, 422–36
Biden, Joseph, 126; domestic terrorism policy, 158; Iranian policy of, 368; Operation Limelight and, 397–98, 400; renunciation of Islamophobia by, 158
biopolitics: binary constructs of sex and

gender and, 374–76; feminist genealogy and, 6–10; governance and, 36; Israeli gendered violence and, 251–52; state power and GBVAW and, 16–20
Biswas, Soutik, 187
BJP party (India), 19, 177–78, 180–82, 185, 191, 198–202, 202n5
Black Americans, policing of girls' bodies and, 392
"Blaming Culture for Bad Behavior" (Volpp), 411
The Blaze (Beck), 424
body: gendered weaponization of, 240–45, 391–402; subjectivity of women prisoners, 274–77; translation into discourse of, 286–87
body searches of schoolgirls, by Israeli police and military, 246–48
Boko Haram, 309; kidnapping of Chibok girls by, 57–58; media coverage of kidnappings by, 427–31
Bosnian genocide, 355n17, 432–33
Bosworth, Mary, 273
Bourke-White, Margaret, 184
Brah, Avtar, 218
Brass, Paul, 183–84
Braude, Ann, 163–66
#BringBackOurGirls, 428, 430
Brown, Wendy, 56, 70
Burns, John, 432
Burundi, withdrawal from ICC by, 58
Bush, George W., 13, 61, 408; Islamic rhetoric of, 159–60, 167n18, 168n19; war on terror under, 157–58, 164–65
Bush, Jeb, 168n19
Bush, Laura, 62, 158
Butler, Judith, 263
"Buy American and Hire American" executive order, 395

"Caliphettes" (Rafiq & Malik), 12, 102
Canada: forced removal of Indigenous children in, 249; refugee policies in, 366, 377–78
Canadian Council of Refugees, 364

capitalism: child marriage and violence of, 296–97, 311; feminism and, 2; neoliberal economic violence and, 369; race and, 374; transnational governance and, 297–98
Caplan-Bricker, Nora, 127
Carpenter, R. Charli, 199, 355n17
caste-based violence (India), 177–78, 184, 187, 203n7
catastrophization of Gaza, Israeli state violence and, 326–27
Catholicism, immigration policy and, 154–55
Cavanaugh, William T., 151
Center for Reproductive Rights, 306
Center for Security Policy, 155
Center for Security Studies (CSS), 59–60
Chad, inclusion in US Muslim Ban, 125–27
CHANNEL deradicalization program, 99
checkpoint crossings, Palestinian school children and, 239–40
Cheney, Dick, 69
Chertoff, Emily, 76
Chibok girls: Boko Haram kidnapping of, 428–31; media focus on, 29–30
Chidester, David, 152–53, 164
child abuse, media coverage of, 410–13
child labor, child marriage and, 296, 314, 316–17
child marriage: declines in, 305, 307; development imperatives and outlawing of, 22–23; in feminist imagination, 293–317; financial incentives for reducing, 310–11; naming, framing and classification of, 299–304; politics and economics and, 298–99; statistics and data on, 305–9; as threat to future value of women, 299
Child Marriage Restraint Act (1929), 314
children: cultural differences in definition of, 301; feminist scholarship on, 235–36; Israeli gendered violence against, 241–52
Christian Broadcasting Network, 13, 125

Christianity: Islamic similarities to, 156; as normative religious model, 152, 157–58; refugees, alleged religious persecution of, 127–28, 168n19; secularism and, 159–61; terrorism and, 158; violence and, 159

Chuang, Theodore, 130, 145n12

Cissna, L. Francis, 396

citizenship, Indian law on, 179

Citizenship Amendment Act (CAA) (India), 177–79

civilizational: backwardness/civilizational dualism, 21; sexual precocity as, 295–97

civil society organizations (CSs), CVE and, 95

Clack, Beverley, 268–69

Clarke, Kamari, 14

class: child marriage and, 314; feminism and, 36–37; honor crimes and, 211–15, 225–26; impact of sanctions and, 363, 368; Indian hierarchies and inequalities and, 186, 199; Muslim misleadership class, 80n19; political prisoners in context of, 273–77; sexual identity and, 365, 383n24; sexual violence against women prisoners and, 260, 266, 273, 275; state structures and, 16–17

Clinton, Hillary, 38n5

Clinton Global Initiative (CGI), 304

Clooney, Amal, 4

Cockbain, Ella, 411–12

Cocks, Joan, 225

Code of Criminal Procedure (Pakistan), 214

Cohen, Aviv, 69, 107

Cohn, Carol, 107

colonialism: binary constructions of sex and gender and, 374–76; child marriage and, 295, 303–4, 315–16; gender-based violence and, 235–36; Indian violence and, 184–89, 198–202; Pakistan legal codes and, 214; photography and, 422, 427; religion and, 151–53, 161–62; *terra nullius* principle and, 68–69; women's position in, 408

Commerce Clause (US Constitution), 399–400

common sense, Gramscian concept of: child marriage and, 23; developmental agenda and, 23–24; Gaza violence and humanitarianism and, 325–26; GBVAW and, 3, 9, 13, 28; global governance and, 59; humanitarianism and, 31–32; International Conflict Feminism and, 90; Islamophobia and, 124; media framing of GBVAW and, 9, 28; Muslim ban and, 128, 144; religion and violence and, 151; secular *vs.* religious perspectives and, 13; women, peace and security agenda and, 31

communal violence (India), 184–90

community-based organizations (CBOs), in Gaza, 332, 334–35

community-based programs, child marriage campaigns and, 307–8

"A Comparative Approach to Estimating the Annual Number of Honor Killings in the United States Among People from North African, Middle Eastern, and Southeast Asian (MENASA) Countries," 141–42

Comprehensive Iran Sanctions, Accountability and Divestment Act (2010) (CISADA), 367–68

"Conditions and Rights of Internally Displaced Girls and Women During the Latest Israeli Military Operation on the Gaza Strip" (UNFPA 2014), 349–51

conflict feminism. *See* international conflict feminism

conflict rape, 29, 422–35, 436n1

Conflict Tactics Scale, 351

Congress Party (India), 182–83, 191, 197

consensual sex, child marriage and, 315–16

conservative gender ideologies, women, peace and security initiatives and, 92–93

Convention on Consent to Marriage, Minimum Age of Marriage, and Registration of Marriage (1962) (UN), 295

Convention on the Elimination of Dis-

crimination against Women (CEDAW), 70, 103, 301–3
Cook, Joanna, 104, 114n9
cooking oil subsidy, as child marriage reduction strategy, 310–11
Coomaraswamy, Radhika, 97, 102, 106
Copelon, Rhonda, 56
Copenhagen Consensus, 310
Corbett, Rosemary, 156
corporations, CVE and, 95, 113n5
corporeality, subjectivity and, 273–77
"Costs of War" project, 38n8, 110
Council of Europe, 73–74
Council on Foreign Relations, 299–301
Countering Violent Extremism (CVE): architecture of fear and, 93–97; feminist engagement with, 93–97; gender-based persecution and, 58–59; generalization of Muslim threat and, 102–5; global governance projects and, 59; inclusivity imperative for, 90–93; International Conflict Feminism and, 71–76; interventions and, 59–64; language of, 108–12; lawfare and, 66–70; securofeminism and, 11–12, 106–12; soft security and, 88–91l; women as violent extremists and, 97–102
Counterinsurgency (COIN) Guide (US), 65–67
counterterrorism: Ansar Dine and, 63–64; Countering Violent Extremism initiatives and, 59–64, 71–72, 90–93; feminist engagement with, 11, 88–89; global governance projects and, 59; securofeminism and, 106–12; women recruits and, 105
Counter-Terrorism Committee (CTE), 71–72
Counter-Terrorism Committee Executive Directorate (CTED), 71–72
Counter-Terrorism Implementation Task Force (CTITF), 71–72
"A Course Correction for the UN Women, Peace and Security Agenda" (International Crisis Group), 31–32

cow-protection (India), lynching of Muslim men and, 189–91
Creative Associates International, 95
crimes against humanity, religious-based gender persecution and, 55–59
Criminal Law Amendment (2016) (Pakistan), 218
criminal reporting methods, Muslim Ban and, 132–33
critical feminism, 303
Cruel Intentions (George Washington University Program in Extremism), 99
cultural capital, inequality as, 274–75
culture: child marriage and, 293–97, 299–304, 311, 313; developmental goals and, 305; education access and, 309; honor killings and, 123–24, 212–13; International Conflict Feminism and, 71–76; media coverage of gender violence and, 410–13; narratives of forced and child marriage in, 300; political prisoners in context of, 273–77; sexual violence and, 260, 280–83
Cunning of Recognition (Povinelli), 2
Curtis, Ric, 142–43

Daesh. *See* Islamic State (ISIS)
Daily Beast, 416
Dalits, caste, 177–78, 187, 190, 191; sexual violence and, 198–99
Dart Center (Columbia University), 416–19
Das, Veena, 278–80
data collection, Muslim Ban language on, 128–34
Davis, Angela, 263
Dawoodi Bohra culture, female genital cutting and, 393, 401–2
death, sexuality and, 268–73
Declaration on the Elimination of Violence Against Women, 301
degovernmentalized intervention, Gaza GBV humanitarianism and, 330–32, 343

Democratic Republic of Congo (DRC), 423–24; conflict and gender violence in, 8, 423–24
democratic transition, GBVAW in context of, 22–23
denaturalization, US policy of, 395–96
dependency trope, child marriage issue and, 25, 306
de-radicalization programs: preventive focus in, 60, 62; side effects of, 96–97. *See also* radicalization
development framework: child marriage and, 298–99, 301–2, 304–9, 313; culture and, 305; feminist genealogy and, 6–10; GBVAW and, 20–27; *vs.* humanitarianism ascendancy in Gaza, 329–30; metrics and financialization of, 310–11
Diagnosing Identities, Wounding-Bodies: Medical Abuses and Other Human Rights Violations against Lesbian, Gay and Transgender People in Iran (JFI & 6Rang), 372
dignity, in journalism, 430–32
dignity kits, distribution to Gaza women of, 356n22
Dillon, Stephen, 287
Disclosure (Torgovnik), 435
ditto theory of Indian violence, 184
dog attacks, Palestinian students' experience of, 240–41
dog whistle, honor killings invocation as, 124, 144n5
domestic violence: child marriage and, 23, 302; development and humanitarianism and, 21; fatalities, media coverage of, 407, 409–10; in Gaza, 26, 325–26, 328–29, 342, 351; honor killings distinguished from, 123, 381n3; measurements of, 310–11; Muslim Ban linked to, 131, 140; responses to, 165; in Turkey, 383n22; violent extremism and, 113n4
Do Muslim Women Need Saving? (Abu-Lughod), 111, 408, 439
"Do Muslim Women Really Need Saving?" (Abu-Lughod), 408

Douglass, Frederick, 18–19
Douma, Nynke, 335
Dove, Fiona, 340
Dressler, Markus, 154
Dunlap, Charles, 65
Duqqah, Walid, 15
Dutta, Arko, 186–88
duty bearers, in international humanitarian law, 340–41

Eastern bloc countries, democratic transition and GBVAW in, 22–23
Economic and Political Weekly, 310
economic conditions: child marriage and, 299–300, 305–9; Gaza GBV humanitarianism and, 334–35; in Iran, 366–70; as refugee motivation, 366. *See also* smart economics
economic growth, education access and, 309
education: gender equity in, 309, 314; increased access in Bangladesh to, 305, 308–9; in Occupied East Jerusalem, 238–40
Ejaz, Sheikh, 223
The Elders, 303–4, 315
empire. *See* imperialism
empire, humanitarian empire, 199
Empire Lite interventionism, 67–69
"Empower Girls, Change the World" (GNB), 304
Ending Child Marriage: How Elevating the Status of Girls Advances US Foreign Policy Objectives (Council on Foreign Relations), 299–301
Ending Child Marriage in a Generation: What Research Is Needed? (Greene), 301
Engle, Karen, 3, 14, 20, 33–34, 89
Enhance Civil Society Capacity to Work for Democratic Independence in Palestine Project in Partnership with Norwegian People's Aid (NPA), 338–39
"Enhancing Public Safety in the Interior of the United States" (US Presidential Exec. Order No. 13768), 132

Enlightenment thought, reason vs. religion in, 152
environment, GBVAW linked to control of, 17
Enwonwu, Ben, 428
Epictetus, 283
episodic framing, in media coverage, 407–13
Epure, Georgina, 56
equal rights, human rights vs., 153
European Center for Law and Justice, 73; queer and trans healthcare barriers in, 363
European Court of Human Rights, 63
European Union, 93
exclusion: honor killings as proxy for, 124; security as grounds for, 143–44; of terrorists, 127; xenophobia and Islamophobia as basis for, 138
Executive Orders on "Protecting the Nation from Foreign Terrorist Entry into the United States." See Muslim Ban

facial illegitimacy, Supreme Court Muslim Ban rulings, 134, 145n14
failed states, gender violence in, 5–6, 18
family law in Gaza, 334, 346–47
fantasy, of undesired Other, sexual violence and, 283–86
Fassin, Didier, 25, 39n13
Fateh, Hamas conflict with, 343–44
fear, architecture of, securofeminism, 93–97
Federal Shariat Court (Pakistan), 214
female genital cutting (mutilation): child marriage linked to, 293–97, 299–304; criminalization of, 393–96, 399–400; immigration exclusion and, 391–402; media framing of, 28; Muslim women's opposition to, 401–2; Operation Limelight and, 397–400; weaponization of body and, 391–402
"Female Genital Mutilation/Cutting in the United States: Updated Estimates of Women and Girls at Risk, 2012" (Goldberg), 398
feminism: Al Hassan case and, 57; in Bangladesh, 310–11, 316; child marriage and, 293–317; demonization in patriotic rhetoric of, 135–36; development discourse and, 298–99; female genital cutting and, 394–95, 401–2; GBVAW and, 1–6; genealogy of, 6–10; geopolitics and, 37; girl studies scholarship and, 297–99, 314–16; humanitarian law and, 24–27, 329–31, 339; imperialist co-optation of, 3–6; in India, 181, 198–202, 413; Indian gender violence and, 198–202; International Criminal Court and, 57–59, 70; in Iran, 162, 260–61; journalism and, 430–31, 435–36; limitations and conflicts within, 30–38; on masculinity and weapons, 245–46; Muslim women and, 164, 166, 415; Pakistani honor killings and, 211–12, 218, 226–28; postcolonial state and, 293, 300–303; religion and, 164, 166; scholarship on children, 235–36; secular state and, 165–66; securitization politics and, 10–13; separation of sexuality and gender in, 274; sexual violence in war and, 431–32; smart economics and, 305; state criminality and militarization and, 14–20, 252; xenophobic deployment of, 124–27. See also governance feminism; international conflict feminism; second wave feminism; securofeminism; transnational feminism
Ferguson, Adam, 428–29
Ferris, Elizabeth, 340
fertility, Bangladesh decline in, 305
Final Solution (documentary film), 186
Fink, Bruce, 281
Flynn, Michael, 153
forced marriage: criminal charges for, 73–74; narratives of, 300
forced surgeries, for Iranian queer and trans persons, 362–64. See also gender-affirming surgeries; sex-reassignment surgeries

Ford Foundation, 301
foreign-born nationals, detection and exclusion of, 127
foreign policy: child marriage linked to, 299–300, 304; religion and gender violence and, 160–61
Foreign Policy magazine, 106, 306
Forestier, Marie, 57
Fortuyn, Pim, 128
Foster, Johanna E., 417
Foucault, Michel, 261
Foundation Rwanda, 434–35
Fourth Circuit Court of Appeals, Muslim Ban rulings by, 130, 132
Fourth Geneva Convention, 234
France: Burka ban in, 63; Libyan bombing by, 63–64, 80n17; Mali air strikes by, 59, 61–62, 64, 69, 80n13; Middle East intervention by, 63–64
Franson, Mary, 400
Fraser, Nancy, 2, 30
Frenett, Ross, 95, 113n5
Friedman, Bernard (Judge), 399–400
"The Future She Deserves" initiative (US Mission to UN), 96

G4S security firm, 136
Gaddafi, Muammar, 64
Gaddafi, Seif, 64
Gandhi, Indira, 183
gay rights discourse: Muslim Ban incorporation of, 128; torture framing of Iranian transgender medicine in, 371–76; transgender and gay refugees and, 361–64. *See also* LGBTI recognition; queer identity
Gaza: advocacy activities in, 336–39; catastrophization of, 326–27; changing gender relations in, 334; economic conditions in, 326–27, 334; family law in, 334; Fatwa Committees in, 346; GBV awareness and advocacy in, 332–36; gender-based violence and humanitarianism in, 324–25, 331–32; humanitarian crisis framework in, 327–28; increased violence in, 325; Israeli bombing of emergency shelters in, 347–51; lack of women's shelters in, 343–47; local humanitarian interventions in, 342–47; Palestinian humanitarian services in, 336–39, 343–45; political economy of awareness in, 332–36; politics of humanitarianism in, 329, 340–43; protectionist policies in, 339–42; women's shelters in, 343–51
Gaza Gender Initiative (UNRWA), 332–33
gender: death and, 268–73; religion and, 154–55, 158
Gender, Orientalism and the "War on Terror" (Khalid), 414–15
gender-affirming surgery, in Iran, torture framework for, 371–76. *See also* sex-reassignment surgeries
gender-based persecution, 57–58, 70, 72–76; verification of LGBTI claims for, 365–66
gender-based violence (GBV): anti-Muslim mobilization based on, 12–13; awareness and advocacy activities and, 332–36; cultural specificity of honor killings and, 123; in Gaza, 327–28; government support for, 1–6; humanitarian intervention and, 324–53; IASC codification of, 330; in India, 177–202; Indian lynchings as, 195–97; Israeli state criminality and, 233–52; in media narratives, 406–19; religion and, 151–66; religious persecution and, 56–59; state and political institutions and, 13–20; women's participation in, 97–102
gender-based violence/violence against women (GBVAW): child marriage and, 299–304; development and humanitarianism as interventions in, 20–27; emergence of, 1–6; feminist genealogy and, 6–10; mainstreaming of, 30–38; state and political institutions and, 13–20
gender equality, Muslim immigrants linked to, 135

"Gender Equity in Schools in Muslim Countries: It Can Be Done," 309
gender violence: armed occupation as, 245–48; ethnicization of, 362–64; geopolitical framing of, 376–79; Indian women's protest against, 179; war violence and, 347–51
geopolitics: child marriage and, 294–95, 300, 311; colonialism and, 235–36; feminism and, 37; Gaza GBV humanitarianism and, 329, 340–47; GBVAW and, 6–10, 20–22, 35; homophobia and, 27; Indian state and imperialist policies in, 187; Islamophobia and, 60; Israeli violence and, 26; Palestinian protection and, 340–42; power structure of, 34; state criminality and, 235; temporality of rights and, 369–70; transgender refugees and, 362–63, 375–80
Georgetown Institute for Women, Peace and Security, 94
German Institute on Radicalization and De-radicalization Studies, 96
Germany, homicide statistics in, 141–42
Ghassem-Fachandi, Parvis, 184–86
Gill, Aisha, 218
A Girl in the River: The Price of Forgiveness (documentary film), 216–17
girl child agenda, 297; child marriage and, 314–16; economic value of girls and, 298–99
Girl Effect program (Nike), 317n1
Girls not Brides (GNB), 304, 308, 311, 314
Global Center for Countering Violent Extremist Ideologies, 88, 108
Global Community Engagement and Resilience Fund (GGERF), 93
Global Counter Terrorism Forum (GCTF) (2015), 91–93
global gag rule, 167n9
Global Gender Gap Report, 309
global governance, international criminal law and, 56–59
global humanitarian apparatus, Gaza crisis and, 327

Global Justice Center, 57
global security: development and humanitarianism, 20–21; gender violence and, 6–10; securofeminism and, 106–7; state apparatuses, 9–10, 13–20; violence and, 1–6. *See also* securofeminism
Global Terrorism Forum, 30
Goldberg, Howard, 398
Goldsmith, Jack, 67–68
Gordon, Neve, 65
governance feminism: limits of, 30–31; securofeminism and, 89, 106; state and political institutions and, 12, 14–20
Governance Feminism (Nesiah), 79n12
Gowrinathan, Nimmi, 101
Grameen Bank, 298
Greene, Margaret, 301
Greenwald, Glenn, 61
Grenfell, Laura, 56, 70
Grewal, Inderpal, 18–19, 28, 34, 177–202, 211, 243; "media-ted" concept of, 123
Grey, Rosemary, 74–76
Guest House for Young Widows (Moaveni), 103
Gujarat, postcolonial violence in, 182–89
Guru, Gopal, 187
Guterres, António, 94
Gutting, Gary, 168n20
Guttman, Roy, 432

Haaretz, 238
Haider, Iqbal, 216
Hall, Stuart, 181–82, 210
Halley, Janet, 30, 34–35, 89
Hamas: Gaza takeover by, 326–27; Gaza women's shelters run by, 343; humanitarian services to women in Gaza, 336–39, 343–47
Hammami, Rema, 23–26, 29, 310–11, 324–53
Handbook for Coordinating Gender-based Violence Intervention in Humanitarian Settings (IASC), 330–31
Harrington, Carol, 8

Hartman, Saidiya V., 18–19
Hawai'i v. Trump, 130–31
Hayes, Ben, 114n13
Heaton, Laura, 24, 334–35
Hedaya counterterrorism center, 91, 93
Heinämaa, Sara, 275, 288n3
Hendessi, Mandana, 414
Henshaw, Simon, 138–39
Hever, Shir, 253n2
The Hidden Face of Eve: Women in the Arab World (Saadawi), 401
hierarchies of humanity, SGBVAW research and, 25
Hilhorst, Dorothea, 335
Hillary Doctrine, 38n5
Hindu Right activists, 180
Hindutva (Indian nationalism), 177–78, 180–82; anti-Muslim violence and, 183–89; lynchings and, 189–97
Hirsi Ali. *See* Ali, Ayaan Hirsi and Ayaan Hirsi Ali Foundation
Holland, François, 59, 61
Holland, honor killings in, 142
Homeland Security, Department of, 63, 94, 124, 126–31, 143, 397
Homeland Security Investigation (HSI) Human Rights Violators and War Crimes Center, 397
homonationalism, 128
honor crimes/honor killings: anti-honor killings laws (Pakistan) and, 210, 217; cultural specificity of, 123, 144n4; data in US on, 138–42; defined, 123; disappearance in Muslim Ban of, 133–34; feminist scholarship and, 12, 15, 18–20; as justification for war, 261; Muslim Ban and, 122–44; national security linked to, 126–28; in Pakistan, 209–28; transparency and data collection in Muslim Ban concerning, 128–34; Trump's invocation of, 136–38, 153
Honor Diaries, 140
hooks, bell, 38
Hossain, Naomi, 297
humanitarian gender-based violence: advocacy and awareness programs and, 332–36; emergency response framework for, 347–51; initial framing of, 329–32, 354n6; local interventions and, 342–47; media coverage of, 337–39; sexual humanitarianism and, 361–64; sexual violence victims and, 351–53; terminology changes in, 354n9
humanitarianism: feminist genealogy and, 6–10; GBVAW and, 20, 24–27; gender-based violence in Gaza and, 324–53; monitoring component of, 355n16; paternalism and, 25; photojournalism and, 433–35; SGBV interventions and, 40n14; whole-of-society paradigm and, 63–64
humanitarian reason, 39n13
human rights: child marriage and, 298–99, 303–4, 306–9; Iranian queer and transgender health care framed as violation of, 363–64; Pakistani honor killing and, 210–28; Palestinian gender-based violence and, 234–35; refugee recognition process and, 361, 364–70; religion and, 153; securitization politics and, 11–13, 111–12; Third World backwardness frame in, 365–66; violence against women and, 331–32
Human Rights and Gender Justice Clinic (HRGJ), 72–73
Human Rights Watch (HRW), 306; Indian violence and, 197; torture framing of Iranian transgender medicine in, 372
Huntington, Samuel, 154–55

Ideologies of Forging: Rape in the Vietnam War (Weaver), 431
Ignatieff, Michael, 67
immigrant communities: bad acts by, 123–24; criminal stereotyping of, 133–34
Immigration and Nationality Act, 125–26
immigration policy: Huntington's critique of, 154–55; Muslim Ban as, 122–44
immutability principle, transgender and gay refugees and, 362
imperialism: in Afghanistan, 2, 38n1; co-

optation of feminism and, 3–6; feminism and, 3–6; humanitarianism and, 199; in India, 187; postcolonial criticism and, 14; protection of women linked to, 2, 381n1. *See also* colonialism
imperial state projects, GBVAW entanglement in, 3
incentive structures, sexual violence in war and, 24–25
inclusivity, securofeminism and, 90–93
Inder, Brigid, 72
India: gender-based violence in, 14–15, 19, 177–202; kidnapping and raping of women in, 278–79, 413; lynching of men in, 5; media framing in, 28; pogroms in, 19, 177, 180–88, 198–99, 201–2; postcolonial violence in, 182–89
Indian Age newspaper, 184
Indigenous Australians, politics of recognition and, 2
inequality: concerns over GBVAW *vs.* focus on, 18, 25; securofeminist omission of, 107–12
"Initial Section 11 Report" (Dept. of Justice and Dept. of Homeland Security), 143–44
Intended Consequences (Togovnik), 433–35
Inter-Agency Standing Committee (IASC), 330–31, 342
International Centre for the Study of Radicalisation, 104
International Civil Society Action Network for Women's Rights, Peace and Security (ICAN), 92, 105
International Conference on Population and Development (ICPD), 301–2
international conflict feminism (ICF): agendas of, 79n12; culture wars and, 71–76; emergence of, 11, 14, 90; gender-based violence and, 59, 62–64; global governance projects and, 59
International Criminal Court (ICC), 432–33; African bias in, 58, 79n10; Al Hassan Mahmoud case, 55–59, 64, 70; counterterrorism campaigns and, 69–70; Executive Orders, 37; Gaddafi indictments and, 64; gender violence jurisprudence in, 5–6, 38n3; International Conflict Feminism and, 71–76; Lawfare and, 65–70; war crimes jurisprudence and, 11
international criminal law: African engagement in, 79n11; gender-based persecution and, 56–59; WPS and CVE agendas and, 72–76
International Criminal Tribunal for the Former Yugoslavia, 29, 38n3
International Crisis Group, 31, 95
international humanitarian law: duty bearers in, 340–41; protection forces in, 340; war and, 65. *See also* humanitarianism
international human rights law, gender-based persecution and, 70
international law, humanitarian GBV in Gaza *vs.*, 329–32
International Law Commission (ILC), 57
International Law Girls, 57, 74–75
international non-government organizations INGOs), GBV awareness in Gaza and, 333–34
International Refugee Law, gender-based persecution and, 56
international refugee regime, persecution-protection framework for, 362–64
intersectionality, culture and international conflict feminism and, 75–76
intersubjectivity, of power, corporeality and, 274–77
interventions: Countering Violent Extremism and, 59–64; incentive structures for, 24–25; lawfare and, 66–70; responsibility to protect and, 63–64. *See also* military intervention
Int'l Refugee Assistance Project v. Trump, 130, 132–33
Invisible Women (UNDP/ ICAN), 105
Iran: Afghan refugees in, 366; economic conditions in, 366–70; GBVAW and sexual humanitarianism in, 26–27; Muslim Ban and, 125; oil production in, 368;

INDEX 455

Iran (*continued*)
  political prisoners in, 262; queer and trans refugees from, 362–64, 366–70, 382n22; rape and sexual violence in, 14–15, 20; refugees in Turkey from, 364; subjectivity and gendered sexuality of women prisoners in, 263–64; transgender healthcare conditions and policies in, 368, 370–76, 382n22; Trump's regime change agenda in, 162; US military policy and religion in, 156; US sanctions in, 362–64, 366–70, 382n7; women in political prisons of, 259
Iranian Queer Railroad, 372
Iran Sanctions Act of 1966 (ISA), 367–68
Iraq: feminist scholarship on, 110–12; GBVAW entanglement in, 3–4; Muslim Ban and, 125, 144n7; photographic images of war in, 426–27; refugees in Turkey from, 364, 381n6; US empowerment of Imams in, 156; women activists involved in, 34
Ireland, body searches in, 246
Isa, Tina, 141, 145n21
Islam: Baloch's challenges to, 222–28; barriers to education linked to, 309; child marriage linked to, 295–97; Christianity's similarities to, 156; Countering Violent Extremism rhetoric and, 59–64, 81n27; gender-based persecution under, 57–64; media coverage and framing of, 407–13; Orientalist framing of, 21; Pakistan legal codes and, 214; pious women in, 103–5; US view of, 153. *See also* Muslim
Islamic law, marriage in, 74
Islamic Police, 68
Islamic Republic. *See* Iran
Islamic State (ISIS, ISL): gender-based persecution charges against, 57–58; ICC and, 69–70; kidnap and rape of Yazidi women by, 10–13, 25, 29, 76, 412–15; moderate Muslim mobilization against, 96; women recruits to, 12, 97–105
Islamophobia: criminalization of forced marriage and, 75–76; gender violence, 12–13; homophobia and racism linked to, 136; honor killings and, 123–24; in India, 179–82; institutionalization of, 155; securofeminism and, 102–5, 111–12
Islamophobia and the Politics of Empire: 20 Years after 9/11 (Kumar), 27–28
Israel: armed occupation as sexual violence in, 245–48; bombing of Gaza emergency shelters by, 347–51; Gaza bombardment by, 324–26; Palestinian occupation by, 236–37; settlers violence against Palestinians in, 242, 253n2; shoot-to-kill policy in, 249–50; state criminality and gender-based violence in, 233–52; state violence in Gaza and, 326–27

Jafri, Ehsan, 186–87
Jakobsen, Janet R., 12–13, 151–66
Jamal, Amina, 223–24
Jamal, Asad, 214
Jamieson, Ruth, 17–18
Janah, Sunil, 184
Japanese Americans, Muslim Ban compared to treatment of, 146n25
Jihad Against Violence campaign, 113n4
jihadi radicalization, securofeminist perspectives on, 96, 98–99, 102
Jilani, Hina, 215
Jinnah, Muhammad Ali, 405
John, Mary, 315
Joint Comprehensive Plan of Action (2012) (JCPOA), 368, 381n7
Justice for Iran (JFI), 372–76

KOAS GL (NGO), 382n14
Kapur, Ratna, 18
Kashmir lockdown, 180–81
Kazi, Nazia, 80n19
Kennedy, David, 32
Kenny, Cóman, 69
Khalid, Lubna, 209
Khalid, Maryam, 414–15
Khan, Ghulam Ishaq, 214

Khan, Junaid, 192–95, 197
Khan, Nabiya, 178–79
Khan, Syed Sarifuddin, 195–96
Khattak, Ajmal, 216
Khoja-Moolji, Shenila, 19–20, 209–28, 309
Khol Do (Open It) (Manto), 278–80
"Kidnapped as Schoolgirls by Boko Haram: Here They Are Now" (interactive presentation), 428–29
Kill Anything That Moves (Turse), 432
kimlik (Turkish identity card), 370, 381n12
Koğacıoğlu, Dicle, 218–19
Koh, Harold, 69, 78n7
Kony, Joseph, 57
Korematsu v. United States, 146n25
Kosmatopoulos, Nikolas, 109
Kristof, Nicholas, 300, 425
Kumar, Deepa, 27–28
Kundnani, Arun, 114n13

land use and occupation, GBVAW linked to control of, 17
language: gender violence and, 276, 281–83; media framing of gender violence and, 409–13, 418–19
Latinx community, Pulse massacre victims from, 135
lawfare, 81n24; International Criminal Court and, 65–70
Lawfare: gender-based violence and, 59; global governance projects and, 59
League of Nations, 295
legal activism, gender-based violence and, 330–32
LGBTI recognition: knowledge production and, 375–76; sexual humanitarianism and, 27–28; Third World framing of, 380; UNHCR criteria for, 364–66. *See also* gay rights discourse
Li, Darryl, 326
Liberation War (Bangladesh), 293–94
Libya: American and French bombing in, 63–64, 80n17; bombing of, 69; Muslim Ban and, 125
Life magazine, 184

Lift Up the Vulnerable, 426
local governments and institutions: child marriage in context of, 307–8; humanitarian GBV in Gaza and, 341–47
Loken, Meredith, 103–4
London School of Economics, 310
Lorde, Audre, 11, 415
Lord's Resistance Army, 57, 78n7
lynchings, Hindutva sovereignty and, 189–97

Machel, Graca, 303–4
MacKinnon, Catharine, 273–74
MADRE, 72–73
Mahmood, Saba, 156
Mahmoud, Al-Hassan, 11, 68
Make Way Partners, 423, 426
male desire, Baloch's focus on, 224–28
Mali: Ansar Dine operations in, 63–64; criminalization of forced marriage in, 73–76; French bombing of, 59, 61–62, 64, 69, 80n13; gender violence in, 55–56, 62–64; ICC role in, 55–59; ICF framing of women in, 62–64
A Man's World: Exploring the Roles of Women in Countering Terrorism and Violent Extremism (Fink, Zeiger & Bhulai), 91, 95
Mandair, Arvind-Pal S., 154
Manto, Sadat Hassan, 278–80
Maputo Protocol on the Rights of Women in Africa, 70
"Marry Before Your House Is Swept Away: Child Marriage in Bangladesh" (Human Rights Watch), 306
Marrying Too Young: Ending Child Marriage (Osotimehin), 302
Marx, Karl, 262
Mateen, Omar, 134–36
material productivity, sexual violence in war (SGBV) and, 24–27
Matlab, child marriage data, 313
Matlub, Raja, 212, 224
Mbarushimana, Callixte, 72
McEvoy, Kieran, 17–18

meaning, culture and struggle over, 181–82
media coverage: of Arab women, 401–2; Boko Haram kidnappings, 427–31; bridge characterization of victims in, 425; child marriage in, 306–9; of conflict rape, 29, 422–36; of female genital cutting, 391–402; feminist journalism, 430–31, 435–36; of Gaza GBV humanitarianism, 337–39; GBVAW and, 27–30; of Indian Shaheen Bagh protest, 178–80; of India violence, 184–88, 201–2; of Iranian queer and trans refugees, 363–64; journalistic guidelines for, 416–19; Kashmir lockdown in India and, 180–82; lynchings of Indian Muslims in, 191–93; narrative power of, 405–19; Pakistani honor killings in, 209–28; Qandeel Baloch coverage in, 217–28; religion in, 159; women's voices removed in, 413–16; of Yazidi women's kidnapping and rape by ISIS, 25, 29, 76, 412–19
Meger, Sara, 329
Mehra, Madhu, 315–16
Mehta, Nalin, 185–86
Memarpour, Mehdi, 276
Mercy Corps (Jordan), 102
Merry, Sally Engle, 11, 107, 302–3, 335
Mesa-Bains, Amalia, 38
microfinancing, child marriage and, 298
Middle East: child marriage in, 295; transphobic/homophobic media representations of, 363
migrant women, securofeminist perspectives concerning, 102–5
Migration Policy Institute, 395
Mikdashi, Maya, 135
militarism: gendered weaponization of life, body and space and, 240–45; in India, 178; lawfare and, 65–70; secular state and, 164–66; violence against women and, 7–8; voyeurism in Palestine of, 241–42
military intervention: in Afghanistan, 3; counterterrorism and, 68–69; CVE initiatives, 61, 66; feminist agenda and, 3; humanitarianism as justification for, 261; Islamophobia and, 30; in Libya, 64, 70; in Mali, 62–63, 70; NGO support of, 67; Responsibility to Protect doctrine and, 8, 81n22
Millennial Development Goals (MDGs), 298
Miller, Stephen, 124, 395
Minwalla, Sherizaan, 416, 417
Mlambo-Ngcuka, Phumzile, 106
moderation, extremism and, 88–89
Modi, Narendra, 180–83, 185, 191, 196–97
Mohanty, Chandra, 40n21
Moonshot CVE, 95
MotherSchools initiative, 95–96, 101–2
Mothers for Life, 96
Mountford, Bill, 410
MS-13 gang (Los Angeles), 133–34
Muhanna, Aitemad, 334
Mukwege, Denis (Dr.), 3
Murad, Nadia, 3, 10–13
Murphy, Michelle, 298–99
Musawah (Islamic feminist group), 103
Muslim Ban: data used as basis for, 138–43; honor crimes and, 28, 122–44; impact on trans and queer refugees of, 378–80; legal background for, 125–26; legal challenges to, 12–13; religion as focus in, 162; securitization politics and, 126–27; transparency and data collection provisions in, 128–34; Trump's imposition of, 122–23; Trump's speeches about, 134–38
Muslim men: criminalization of, 11; Indian violence against, 18–180, 182, 187–98; media narrative concerning, 410–13
Muslim Personal Laws (India), 179
Muslim rights organizations, amicus briefs in Muslim Ban cases by, 130–31
Muslims: barriers to education linked to, 309; child marriage linked to, 295–97, 300; CVE initiatives and networks with, 94–96; female genital cutting linked to, 394–96; Indian violence against,

183–89; misleadership class of, 80n19; mobilization against and criminalization of, 12–13, 17, 27–28; securofeminist perspectives on, 91–93, 102–5; side effects of de-radicalization programs on, 96–97

"The Muslim Women (Protection of Rights on Marriage) Bill" (India), 179–80

Muslim women: anti-FGC activism among, 401–2; feminist organizations, 113n4; Indian Shaheen Bagh protest by, 178–80; India violence against, 177–80, 200; media victimization framing of, 408, 413–19; protests by, 19; securofeminist perspectives on, 102–5; US profit in saving of, 300–301; as violent extremists, 97–105

Mustehan, Momina, 212

Myanmar, Rohingya genocide in, 57, 79n8

Naber, Nadine, 164
Naeem, Mufti, 221–22
Nagar, Richa, 40n19
Nagarwala, Jumana (Dr.), 393–96, 399, 401
Najmabadi, Afsaneh, 374
Nandy, Amrita, 315–16
narrative, media framing of gender violence in, 405–19
narratives, of child marriage, 300, 303
National Action Plan to End Child Marriage 2018–2030 (Bangladesh), 311–13
National Centre of Expertise on Honour Violence, 142
nationalism: Christianity and, 158, 162; GBVAW and, 17; in India, 177–78; Muslim Ban and invocation of, 128
National Register of Citizens and National Population Register, 179
National Security Council, neighborhood partnerships and, 161
"National Strategy to Combat Violence Against Women" (Palestinian Authority), 342–43

National Ulema and Mushaikh Council (Pakistan), 223
Native Agency, 426
NATO Rule of Law Field Support Mission (NROLFSM), 67–68
necropolitics: governance and, 36; Israeli state violence in Gaza as, 326–27
Nehru, Jawaharlal, 183
Nellie massacre (Assam), 183
neoliberalism: child marriage and, 296; feminism and, 11; GBVAW and development imperatives and, 22–23; homonationalism and multiculturalism and, 374; impact in India of, 184–85
Neo News, 222
Nesiah, Vasuki, 5–6, 11–12, 14, 20, 55–77, 90
Neuman, Gerald, 134, 145n14
neutralization, state terror as, 249
New Poverty Agenda, 298
news media. *See* media
New Statesman magazine, 405–6
Newsweek magazine, 29–30, 433
New Yorker magazine, 213
New York Times, 29, 212–13, 394, 427–31
New York Times Magazine, 139, 159, 300
Ní Aoláin, Fionnuala, 31, 106–7, 113nn7–8
Nike Foundation, 317n1
Ninth Circuit Court of Appeals, Muslim Ban rulings by, 129–31
Nobel Prize, feminist achievement and, 3–4, 11
nongovernmental organizations (NGOs): child marriage and, 312; GBVAW and development imperatives and, 23, 34–35; GBV awareness and advocacy in Gaza and, 332–36, 343–47; humanitarian GBV in Gaza and, 331–32; lawfare and, 67–70; trans refugees and, 375–76, 382n14; violence against women agenda and, 329–32
nonstate actors: lawfare and, 69–70; state-sponsored violence and use of, 17–18
North Korea, Muslim Ban and, 125–27

Obaid-Chinoy, Sharmeen, 213, 216–17
Obama, Barack, 60–61, 69, 80n14, 93; Afghanistan surge under, 159; immigration policy under, 395; Iran sanctions under, 366–68; on Islam, 159–61, 165, 169n20; Syrian refugee policy, 138, 367–68; war on terrorism under, 158, 167n10
objectification, of women's sexuality, 273–77
Occupied East Jerusalem (OEJ): education in, 238–40; gender-based violence against Palestinian schoolgirls in, 233–36; Israeli surveillance regime in, 236–37
Office of Faith-Based and Neighborhood Partnerships, 160, 168n20
Office of Foreign Assets Control (OFAC) (US Treasury Department), 368
Omar, Ilhan, 401
One2One, 100
Oosterveld, Valerie, 56
Open Society Justice Institute, 56
Operation Barkhane, 63
Operation Cast Lead, 324
Operation Limelight, 397–400
Operation Second Look, 395–96
Operation Serval, 51, 59, 61
Ophir, Adi, 326–27
Organization for Refuge and Migration (ORAM), 361–62
Organization for Security and Cooperation in Europe (OSCE), 98
Organization of Women's Freedom in Iraq (OWFI), 72–73
Orientalism: child marriage framed by, 301, 311, 314–15; gender violence research and, 21, 27; Iranian political prisoners and, 260; media framing of gender violence and, 407–18
Oslo Peace Process, 336
Osotimehin, Babatunde, 302
Otto, Dianne, 14, 20, 32, 107
Oudraat, Chantal de Jonge, 98

Pakistan: Afghan refugees in, 366; GBVAW in, 19–20; honor killings in, 15, 209–28; kidnapping and raping of women in, 278–79; media narrative about, 405–19; terrorism framework in coverage of, 406
Pakistan Muslim League-Nawaz, 223
Pakistan Penal Code, 209, 214, 216
Pakistan Tehrik-e-Insaaf, 222
Palestinian Authority, 342
Palestinian Center for Human Rights, 344–45
Palestinian Legislative Council, 336
Palestinian NGO network (PNGO), 338
Palestinians: awareness agenda and, 333–36; GBV humanitarianism in Gaza and, 324–53; history of Israeli occupation, 236–37; humanitarian focus on, 25–26; Israeli state criminality and gender-based violence for, 233–52, 235n3; Israeli violence against women and girls, 5, 14–15, 20, 233–52; protectionist logic in humanitarian programs for, 339–42; resistance of women and girls, 19
Parishad, Mahila, 304–5
Parliamentarians for Global Action (PGA), 69–70
Parliamentary Assembly of the Council of Europe (PACE), 73
Parliamentary Committee on Women and Children (Bangladesh), 315
Parsi, Arsham, 372
Partition of India, violence during, 184–85, 196, 198–202
patriarchy, state and political institutions and, 13–20
patriotism, docility linked to, 135–36
Pellegrini, Ann, 153–54
Personal Status Law (Palestine), 333
Perugini, Nicola, 65
Pervez Butt, Hina, 223
photography: GBVAW and, 29–30; of Indian lynchings, 192–95; photojournalism, 186–87, 195, 422–35
Plan International, 308
Playing with Fire collective project, 40n19

pogroms: in India, 19, 177, 180–88, 198–99, 201–2; media accounts of, 182
police violence, dangerous masculinity trope for Black and Muslim men and, 364
political anthropology, sexual violence and gendered sacrifice and, 277–78
political institutions: religion and, 157–62; violence and, 13–20
political prisons (Iran), 259–87; corporeality and, 273–77; women's personal account, 264–68
political subjectivity: sexuality and, 269–71; of victims of sexual violence, 280–83
politics of care, humanitarian GBV and, 328–29
Pompeo, Mike, 153
postcolonialism: child marriage and, 295–97, 300; feminist genealogy and, 7; Indian Muslims and, 182; Indian state violence and, 182–89, 195–97; state and political institutions and, 14
poverty, early marriage and, 311
Povinelli, Elizabeth, 2
Powell, Colin, 67
power: child marriage issue and, 306; gender-based violence/violence against women (GBVAW) and systems of, 1–6, 32–38; knowledge and, 301; media frames and, 28; sexual objectification and, 274–77; women's bodies as sites of, 261
Pratt, Nicola, 33
Presidential Proclamation (EO-3), 125–26
Press Trust of India, 185
PREVENT (British GBV program), 96–97, 99
Preventing Violent Extremism (PVE), feminist involvement in, 7–8, 92–93
private sector, CVE capitalization by, 95
professional organizations, amicus briefs in Muslim Ban cases by, 130–31
"Prosecuting Crimes of International Concern: Islamic State at the ICC?" (Kenny), 69
"Prosecuting Terrorists at the International Criminal Court: Reevaluating an Unused Legal Tool to Combat Terrorism" (Cohen), 69
Prosecutor v. Issa Sesay, Morris Kallon and Augustine Gbao, 74
protected space: Gaza's lack of for women, 343–47; as refuge from violence, 276
"Protecting the Nation from Foreign Terrorist Entry into the United States" (EO-1 and EO-2), 122–23, 126–28. See also Muslim Ban
protectionist logic: child marriage and, 315–16; Gaza GBV humanitarianism and, 339–42
"Protection of Civilians Weekly" (OCHOA), 340–41
"#ProtectUs_thanks" hashtag, 339–42
Protestantism, immigration policy and, 155
Puar, Jasbir, 128, 135–36
public health organizations: amicus briefs in Muslim Ban cases by, 130–31; child marriage and, 312
public health policies, policing and surveillance of women's bodies and, 27–28
Public International Law and Policy Group, 56
Pulse massacre, 134–35
push-pull factors, women as violent extremists and, 99–103

Qaiser, Saba, 216–17
Qavi, Mufti Abdul, 222–23, 226
Qisas and Diyat Ordinance (Pakistan), 214–15
queer refugees: private refugee sponsorship programs, 383n24; refugee regimes and, 361–80; sanctions in Iran, impact on, 366–70; torture allegations against Iran for, 370–76; Turkey as refuge for, 364–66; war on terror and, 135–37
Qureshi, Qasim, 197

race: dangerous masculinity trope for Black and Muslim men and, 364; female genital cutting and, 391–93, 398–400; GBVAW and, 14–15, 17, 33–34; Israeli gendered violence and, 248–52; Jim Crow violence and, 191–92, 196; lynchings in India and, 192–97; photojournalism and, 423–35; religion and, 158; war on terror and, 135–37

radicalization: approaches to countering, 60; counterterrorism efforts and, 106, 109; indicators of, 62, 75, 97; push factors, 100–101; securofeminism and, 89, 96, 98–99, 102, 110; violent extremism and, 109; of women, 89. *See also* deradicalization programs

Radio Deutchevelle, 181

Raees, Farid, 220–21

Rai, Amit, 135–36

Rajagopal, Arvind, 187

rape: child marriage linked to, 314–15; conflict rape, 29, 422–35, 436n1; humanitarian gender-based violence and, 351–53; in India, 278–79; in Iranian political prisons, 259–60, 268–69; media narrative framing of, 412–19; in Pakistan, 278–79; political subjectivity of, 266–68; sexuality and subjectivity of, 277–78; as war crime, 432–33; as weapon of war, 3–4, 8, 261

Rapid Action Force (India), 187

Rashtriya Swayamsevak Sangh (RSS), 177–78

Rasool, Bilquis Yakub, 188–89

Razack, Sherene, 133, 144n8, 181–82

Reagan, Ronald, 167n9

reason, religion *vs.*, 152, 166n3

Redfield, Peter, 330

refugees: Christian refugees, political focus on, 125, 127–28; defined, 361; gender-based persecution and, 56; Muslim Ban on, 122–44; UNHCR recognition process for, 361, 364–70

refusal, of GBVAW, 19

Rehman, Habibur, 215

religion: child marriage and, 316–17; colonialism and, 151–53; communal violence and, 184–90; defined, 152; dialogue model for, 168n21; education access and, 309; GBVAW and, 17; gender and, 158; gender-based persecution and, 13, 55–59, 71–77; gender-based violence and, 151–66; honor killings and, 123–24; Indian communal violence and, 184–89; Iranian political prisons and Shi'i ethos, 266–68; media of, 159; narrative of gender violence in, 157–62; race and, 158; secularism and, 152–55, 157–62; sexual conservatism and, 154–57, 162–66; US view of Islam and, 153; violence and, 151, 164–66; women, peace and security initiatives and, 92–93, 108. *See also* specific religions

religious persecution, honor killings coupled with, 127–28

repressive state projects: feminism and, 22; GBVAW entanglement in, 3; Islamic State, 374

resistance: of GBVAW, 19; to gender violence, 269

RESOLVE network, 93

Responsibility to Protect (R2P) doctrine, 8, 63–64, 81n22, 340–42

Rohingya genocide, 57, 79n8

Rome Statute, 56, 69–70, 72–73, 78n3

Roy, Ananya, 199

Roy, Keshab, 308–9

Ruhat-e-hillal (Pakistani government committee), 222

rule of law, lawfare and, 66–70

Rule of Law Approaches to Countering Violent Extremism (ABA), 66

Rule of Law Field Force (ROLFF) (Afghanistan), 67

Rumsfeld, Donald, 69

RUSI think tank, 60, 80n15

Rwanda, genocide and rape in, 29–30, 329, 432–35

Saadawi, Nawal El, 401–2
Sachar Committee (India), 191
sacrifice, rape as, 278–83
Shahabuddin, Sardar, 223
Said, Amina, 141, 145n17, 145n21
Said, Edward, 407, 418
Said, Sarah, 141, 145n17, 145n21
Saifuddin, Syedna Muffadal, 394
Salden, Anna, 414
sanctuary jurisdictions, Trump's threat to, 132
Sangtin Writers Collective, 40n19
Sartre, Jean-Paul, 268
Sarwar, Samia, 215
SAVAK (Iranian state police), 275
savior paradigm: child marriage campaigns and, 308; female genital cutting and, 398; Hindutva agenda and invocation of, 180; media coverage of rape and, 430
Sawab Center (UAE), 93
Sayeh network, 370
Scenes of Subjection (Hartman), 18–19
Scheduled Castes and Tribes (India), 183
Schlaffer, Edith, 101–2
Scott, Joan, 274
Searcey, Dionne, 428
Searle, Stephen, 410
second wave feminism, capitalism and, 2
secularism: Christianity and, 159–61; Indian postcolonial violence and, 184–89; religion and, 152–55, 157–62; sexuality and, 163–66
Secularism and Religion-Making (Mandair & Dressler), 154
Secularisms (Pellegrini & Jakobsen), 153–54
securitization politics: evolution of, 10–13; media frames and, 28; Muslim Ban and, 126–28; state and political GBVAW discourse and, 13–20; violence against women and, 7–8; women's rights vs., 97
Security Council (UN): international gender violence resolutions and, 63; interventionism and, 63–64; recognition of GBVAW by, 3–5, 30, 38n4; Resolution 1325, 71, 90, 93, 107; Resolution 1373, 63; Resolution 1820, 63; Resolution 1973, 64; Resolution 2242, 63
Security Council Resolution 1325, 8, 40n19
securofeminism, 11–12, 88–112; architecture of fear and, 93–97; generalization of Muslim threat and, 102–5; inclusivity in, 90–93; limitations of, 106–12; women recruits to violent extremism and, 97–102
self, sense of, sexual violence and loss of, 281–83
self-annihilation, sexual violence and, 284–86
Sennet, Richard, 269–70
Senussi, Abdulla, 64
September 11, 2001, Muslim Ban and invocation of, 127
Sessions, Jeff, 124, 138–39
settler colonialism. *See* colonialism
Sewall, Sarah, 71–72, 90–93
sex-reassignment surgeries, 372–73. *See also* gender-affirming surgeries
sexual conservatism, religion and, 154–57, 162–66
sexual deviation, hyperracialization and, 136
sexual freedom, Muslim immigrants linked to, 135
sexual grooming gangs, media coverage of, 410–13, 417
sexual humanitarianism, nonnormative sexuality and identity and, 26–27
sexuality: child marriage and, 315–16; death and, 268–73; freedom and, 271–73; modernity and, 261; objectification of, 273–77; Pakistan honor killings and role of, 210–11; political subjectivity and, 269–71; religion and, 154–55
sexual precocity, as civilizational index, 295–97
sexual slavery, feminist campaigns against, 111, 114n15

sexual violence, 259; anthropology of, 277–78; in Bangladesh, 293–94; humanitarian GBV discourse and, 349–51; humanitarian gender-based violence and, 351–53; in India, 179, 198–202; Indian women's protest about, 179; media coverage of, 416–19; undesired Other and, 283–86; as weapon of war, 3–4. *See also* gender violence

sexual violence in war (SGBW): agenda for, 329–32; feminist research on, 3, 39n13; humanitarian scholarship and, 24–27; media coverage of, 412–13, 431–32; monopolization of aid for victims of, 40n14; prosecutory zeal concerning, 18

Shackle, Samira, 25, 28–29, 405–19

Shaheen Bagh protests, 177–82, 201–2

Shakhsari, Sima, 23–24, 26–27, 361–80

Shalhoub-Kevorkian, Nadera, 20, 108–9, 233–52

Sharia law: Ansar Dine's interpretation of, 56, 74–76; Gaza GBV humanitarianism and, 345–47; ICC and, 70, 73–76; US anti-Sharia movement, 155

Shariati, Ali, 269

Sharif, Nawaz, 215, 217–18, 226

Shaylor, Cassandra, 263

Sheikh, Zaheera, 188–90

Shi'i ethos, Iranian political prisons and, 266–69

Shipley, Heather, 154, 157

Shirkat Gah (Pakistani women's rights organization), 213–14

shock doctrine politics, democratic transition and GBVAW and, 22–23

Siddiqi, Dina, 22–23, 293–317

Sikh pogrom (India), 183–86, 197

Simon, Jonathan, 136

Simpson, Audra, 252

Singal, Jesse, 139

Singh, Jyoti, 413

Singh, Manmohan, 191

6Rang, 372–74

16 Days of Activism Against Gender-Based Violence, 30, 337–39

Skeik, Hanadi, 344–47

Slaughter, Anne-Marie, 69

slavery: child marriage and, 295; sexual slavery, 111, 114n15

smart economics, child marriage and, 298–99, 305–9

Smith, Andrea, 245

Smith, Kimberly, 424, 426

social media: honor killings and, 211–28; lynchings in India on, 192–95; Qandeel Baloch on, 219–28; Shaheen Bagh protest on, 181–82

Socrates, 268–69

soft counterterrorism: CVE and, 62–64; emergence of, 11–12; responsibility to protect (R2P) as, 63–64; securofeminism and, 88–89

Somalia, Muslim Ban and, 125

Sotomayor, Sonia, 126, 146n25, 162, 165

South Africa, withdrawal from ICC by, 58

South Asia, child marriage in, 295

spatial violence: access to education and, 238–40; militarism and, 240–45; in Occupied East Jerusalem, 238–40

Spillers, Hortense, 200

Srebrenica massacre, 355n17, 432

state: accountability for terror by, 248–52; child marriage and violence of, 311; criminality and, 39n9, 248–52; gender violence of, 13–20, 243–45; humanitarian GBV and, 329–32; Israeli gender-based violence and criminality of, 233–52; lynching and presence of, 197; Pakistani honor killings and, 214–15; Pakistani women's autonomy and, 223–24; religion and, 153–54, 164–66; securofeminism and, 108–9; violence and, 13–20, 181–82, 202n1

State Minister for Women and Children (Bangladesh), 314

Stiglmayer, Alexandra, 432

Streatfield, Peter Kim, 313

Strong Cities Network, 93

subjectivity: gender violence and, 260–63;

political subjectivity and gendered sexuality, 263–71
Sudan, Muslim Ban and, 125
suicide, rape victims' attempts at, 277–78, 280
Sullivan, Andrew, 164
Sullivan, Winnifred, 159–61
"The Sultanate of Women" (Patel), 12, 102
Supreme Court, Muslim Ban rulings by, 123–26, 132–34, 145n14, 162
Surjomukhi program, 308–9
surveillance: hyper-surveillance, of Palestinians, 235–36
surveillance regime: female genital cutting and, 377, 397–400; Israeli-occupied Palestinians, 236–37
Sustainable Development Goals (SDGs), in Bangladesh, 302, 311–13, 315
Syria: GBVAW entanglement in conflict of, 3–4; Muslim Ban and, 125; refugees in Turkey from, 364, 366

Talebi, Shahla, 19–20, 259–87
Taliban, 309, 369; gender-based persecution charges against, 57–58, 70; justice apparatus of, 67–68
Tambe, Ashwini, 295
Tamil Tigers, 101
Teltumbde, Anand, 190
terra nullis principle, 68
terrorism: Countering Violent Extremism as response to, 59–64; erasure of victims' race or ethnicity in, 136; gender-based violence linked to, 153; honor killings linked to, 136–37; ICC role in terms of, 58; media narrative about, 406; Muslim Ban justification linked to, 124–26, 132, 135; religion linked to, 156; state terror, 248–52; women recruits to, 102–5
third country asylum, refugee resettlement in, 364, 366, 368–69, 376–77
Third World context: in feminism, 36; girlhood in frame of, 23, 294–95, 298–99; international law and, 14, 18; sexual identity and, 364–65; violence against women and, 329
"This *Is* a Religious War" (Sullivan), 159–60
Thought for Action Kit (U.S. Institute for Peace), 101
Ticktin, Miriam, 27, 38, 301, 328
"Till Martyrdom Do Us Part: Gender and the ISIS Phenomenon (Saltman & Smith), 99–100
Time magazine, 181, 422, 425–27, 430–31
Tod, Pinjra, 178
Torgovnik, Jonathan, 433–35
torture: of Iranian queer and trans persons, allegations of, 362–64, 371–76; Israeli state engagement in, 19, 249; rape and, 16, 259–61, 267–68, 271–73; state perpetration of, 15–16, 26
transgender refugees: masculinist discourse about, 377–80; private refugee sponsorship programs, 383n24; refugee regimes and, 361–80; sanctions in Iran, impact on, 366–70; torture allegations involving Iranian transgender persons, 370–76; Turkey as refuge for, 364–66; violence against, 376–79
transnational feminism, 40n21; child marriage in context of, 307–8
transparency, Muslim Ban invocation of, 128–34
triple talaq (Muslim instant divorce, India), 179
Trudeau, Justin, 377–78
True, Jacqui, 40n16
Trump, Donald, 12–13, 88, 93; denaturalization proceedings under, 395–96; drone warfare and, 158; Islamophobia of, 158, 162, 165; Muslim Ban and, 122–44, 378, 395, 400; on religion and violence, 162; religion in, 153; reversal of JCPOA by, 368, 381n7
Trump v. Hawaii, 123, 146n25
Trump v. Int'l Refugee Assistance Project, 125
Tschörner, Lisa, 25

Turkey: honor crimes in, 218; Iranian refugees in, 362–64; queer and trans refugees in, 370–80; refugee population in, 364–67; surge of asylum seekers in, 363–64
Turse, Nick, 432
Tutu, Desmond, 303–4

Uncomfortable Truths; Unconventional Wisdom (WASL), 108
UN Commission on Human Rights (UNHCR), GBVAW and, 37, 93
UN Conference on Women (Copenhagen), 401
undesired Other, sexual violence and, 283–86
undocumented immigrants: criminal stereotyping of, 133–34; in Pulse massacre, 135
UNESCO, 93
UN General Assembly, 301
UN High Commissioner for Refugees (UNHCR), 331; Afghan refugees and, 366–70, 381n11; queer and trans refugees, 366–80, 382n22, 382nn14–16, 383n23; refugee recognition and resettlement process of, 361, 364–70, 375; sexual violence guidelines, 331, 354n6, 361–64; Syrian refugees, 379–80; Turkish office of, 362–66
UNICEF, 302, 307, 313
unipolarity, GBVAW and, 8
United Arab Emirates, 94
United Kingdom: child marriage research and programs in, 312; honor killings in, 142; media framing of gender violence in, 408–13; Muslim racialization and stereotyping in, 28–29
United Nations: child marriage and, 295; GBVAW entanglement in, 32–38; US collaboration on CVE with, 93–97. *See also* Security Council (UN)
United Nations Development Fund for Women (UNIFEM), 324–26

United Nations Development Programme (UNDP), 93, 105
United Nations Family Planning Association (UNFPA), 331–32, 349–51
United Nations Office for the Coordination of Humanitarian Affairs (OCHA), 340–41
United Nations Relief and Works Agency (UNRWA), Gaza GBV humanitarianism and, 332–33, 337–39, 341–42, 347–51
United Nations Youth Courage Award, 308
United States: ban Sharia law movement in, 155; dangerous masculinity trope for Black and Muslim men in, 364; forced removal of Indigenous children in, 249; homicide statistics in, 141–42; immigration system in, 395–96; queer and trans healthcare barriers in, 363, 382n20; refugees to, 366; religious freedom claims in, 159; sanctions on Iran by, 362–64, 381n10; UNHCR support from, 370; vigilante actions against Muslims in, 102
UN Women, global database of, 306–7
UN Women and International Crisis Group, 12, 93, 105–6
US Agency for International Development (USAID), feminists and CVE and, 93
US Citizenship and Immigration Services (USCIS), 396–97
US Civil Society Working Group on Women, Peace and Security, 92
US Constitution, Muslim Ban and, 125
US Immigration and Customs Enforcement (ICE): denaturalization proceedings, 395–96; forced sterilization by, 392; Muslim Ban and, 132; Operation Limelight and, 397–400, 402
US Institute for Peace, 98, 101
US State Department, 1–5; feminists and CVE and, 93
"U.S. Strategy to Support Women and Girls at Risk from Violent Extremism and Conflict" (Pompeo 2019), 105
US War Department, 146n25
Utas, Mats, 25

Vale, Gina, 104, 114n9
Veit, Alex, 25
Venezuela, Muslim Ban and, 125–27
vernacularization, of Gaza GBV, 334
victimcy, 25, 27
Vietnam War, American soldier's sexual violence in, 29, 431–32
violence against women (VAW): in Bangladesh, 293–94; child marriage in case studies of, 306–7; codification of agenda for, 329; Gaza humanitarianism and, 342–43; government support for, 1–6; in media narratives, 406–19; Muslim Ban invocation of, 127–28; regulation and criminalization efforts for, 260–61
Violence Against Women Reauthorization Act (2013), 303
violent extremism (VE): containment toolkits used for, 109; Islam linked to, 59–64; securofeminist perspective on, 107–12; women's vulnerability and resistance to, 71–76. *See also* specific forms of violence, CVE
visas, detection and exclusion of terrorists through, 127
Volpp, Leti, 12–13, 122–44, 153, 411

Wall Street Journal, 212
war: costs of, 109–11; Israeli bombing of Gaza shelters in, 347–51; lawfare and, 65
war crimes: Al Hassan case and, 55–59; sexual violence and, 24–27
war on terror: Indian Islamophobia and, 182; racial-sexual hierarchies and, 33–34; religion and, 157–62, 164–66; securitization politics and, 10–11; violence against women and, 7–8, 431
War on Terror, media coverage and framing of, 408
Washington Blade newspaper, 372
Washington consensus, 67
Washington Post, 412
Washington v. Trump, 129

weaponization of gender, 11; Israeli armed occupation and, 245, 253n2
Weaver, Gina Marie, 431
"Wedding Busters" campaign, 308
Westat report on honor killings in US, 139–40
West Bank: GBV advocacy in, 325, 336; international protection force in, 340; Israeli controls in, 326; VAW humanitarianism in, 342–43; women's shelters in, 343–44
Western bias: child marriage research and, 297; feminism and, 91–93
Whispers to Voices: Gender and Social Transformation in Bangladesh (World Bank), 305
Who Are We? (Huntington), 154–55
whole-of society strategy: CVE and, 63–64, 95–97; lawfare and, 66–70
Wilders, Geert, 128
Wild Religion (Chidester), 164
Wilson, Kalpana, 298
WISE. *See* Women's Initiative for Spirituality and Equality
Wodon, Quentin, 306
Wolf, Frank, 139
Wolfe, Patrick, 235–36
women: erasure in media coverage of, 413–16. *See also* violence against women (VAW)
Women, Peace and Security agendas (WPS) (UN): establishment of, 8; feminist engagement with, 11, 89–90, 92–93; power systems and, 32–38; securofeminism and, 107–11. *See also* Security Council (UN), Resolution 1325
Women, Peace and Security (WPS) Index, 62–63, 80n20
"Women and Countering Violent Extremism" (Idris with Abdelaziz), 94
Women and Extremism program (Institute for Strategic Dialogue), 99
Women Deliver (NGO), 33

Women for Women International (NGO), 414
Women in International Security (WIIS), 98
Women's Alliance for Security Leadership (WASL), 92, 102, 108
women's autonomy, Pakistan's pathologization of, 223–24
Women's Initiative for Gender Justice, 57, 72
Women's Initiative for Spirituality and Equality (WISE), 112n1, 113n4
Women's International League for Peace and Freedom (WILPF), 71–72, 107
women's labor, investment value of, 23
Women's Marches (Aurat March Karachi) (Pakistan), 227
women's peace and security (WPS), CVE approach to, 71–76

Women's Programme Centres (Gaza), 333
women's shelters (West Bank), 343–44
Women Without Borders/Sisters Against Violent Extremism, 95–96, 101–2
World Bank, 93, 305–6

Yazidi women, ISIS kidnapping and sexual violence involving, 10–13, 25, 29, 76, 412–19
Yemen: Muslim Ban and, 125; US foreign policy in, 300
Yousafzai, Malala, 11, 309
YouTube, 186–87

Zahid, Maria, 212
Zakaria, Rafia, 28, 391–402
Zelenz, Anna, 103–4
Zia, Maliha, 214
Zia ul-Haq, 214, 223–24